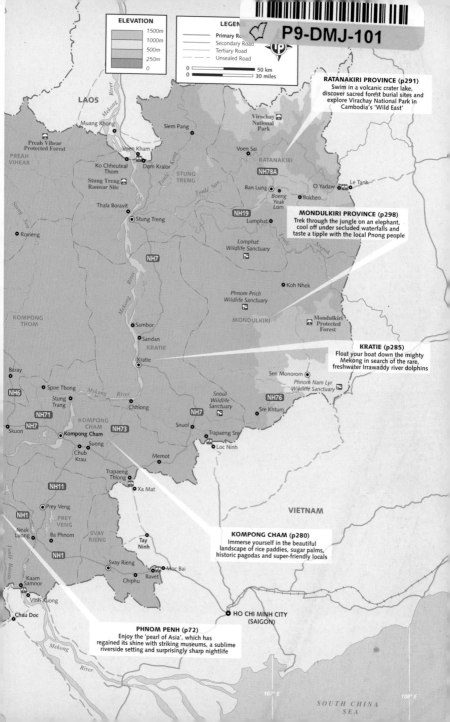

P9-DMJ-101

ELEVATION
1500m
1000m
500m
250m
0

LEGEND
Primary Road
Secondary Road
Tertiary Road
Unsealed Road

0   50 km
0   30 miles

LAOS

Mekong River

Muang Khong

Siem Pang

Virachay National Park

Preah Vihear Protected Forest

Voen Kham

Voen Sai

RATANAKIRI

RATANAKIRI PROVINCE (p291)
Swim in a volcanic crater lake, discover sacred forest burial sites and explore Virachay National Park in Cambodia's 'Wild East'

PREAH VIHEAR

Ko Chheuteal Thom

Dom Kralor

Stung Treng Ramsar Site

STUNG TRENG

Tonlé San

NH78A

Ban Lung

Boeng Yeak Lom

O Yadaw

Le Tanh

Bokheo

Thala Boravit

Stung Treng

NH19

Lumphat

MONDULKIRI PROVINCE (p298)
Trek through the jungle on an elephant, cool off under secluded waterfalls and taste a tipple with the local Pnong people

Rovieng

Lomphat Wildlife Sanctuary

Tonlé Srepok

Koh Nhek

NH7

KOMPONG THOM

Sambor

Sandan

Phnom Prich Wildlife Sanctuary

MONDULKIRI

Mondulkiri Protected Forest

KRATIE

Kratie

KRATIE (p285)
Float your boat down the mighty Mekong in search of the rare, freshwater Irrawaddy river dolphins

Sen Monorom

Phnom Nam Lyr Wildlife Sanctuary

Baray

NH6

Spoe Tbong

Mekong River

Stung Trang

Chhlong

Snoul Wildlife Sanctuary

Sre Khtum

NH76

NH71

KOMPONG CHAM

NH73

NH7

Snuol

Skuon

NH7

Kompong Cham

Suong

Chub Krau

Memot

Trapaeng Sre

Loc Ninh

KOMPONG CHAM (p280)
Immerse yourself in the beautiful landscape of rice paddies, sugar palms, historic pagodas and super-friendly locals

NH11

Trapaeng Thlong

Xa Mat

Prey Veng

PREY VENG

Ba Phnom

SVAY RIENG

Tay Ninh

VIETNAM

NH1

Neak Luong

Svay Rieng

Moc Bai

Kaam Samnor

Chiphu

Bavet

Vinh Xuong

Chau Doc

HO CHI MINH CITY (SAIGON)

PHNOM PENH (p72)
Enjoy the 'pearl of Asia', which has regained its shine with striking museums, a sublime riverside setting and surprisingly sharp nightlife

Mekong River

Mekong River

107° E

108° E

SOUTH CHINA SEA

On The Road

NICK RAY Coordinating Author
This photo was taken at Prasat Preah Vihear
(p268), the king of the mountain temples, and has
to be one of my favourite views in Cambodia –
the extensive plains of lowland Cambodia melting
into the infinite horizon. It's possible to approach
the temple via a motorway from the Thai side of
the border, but much more of a challenge is a
motorcycle adventure from the Cambodian side.
This was where the Khmer Rouge made their
last stand, so you still need to be careful of land
mines, but equally dangerous are the ferocious
winds that whip across the ridge. Make sure those
tent pegs are firmly secured!

DANIEL ROBINSON On Battambang's 'bamboo train' (see p247), you click and clack through the countryside on warped rails – until two cars meet on the single track. The car with more passengers (or carrying
a motorbike like the one behind me in this photo) is given priority; the other car has to be disassembled
to allow it through.

For full author biographies see p360.

Cambodia Highlights

Travellers and Lonely Planet staff share their top experiences in Cambodia. Do you agree with their choices, or have we missed out your favourites? Go to lonelyplanet.com/cambodia and tell us your highlights.

JOHN BANAGAN

1 BAYON, ANGKOR WAT

Ever get the feeling you're being watched? More than 200 carved stone faces, thought to be portraits of the Khmer King Jayavarman VII, gaze down from the lofty towers of Bayon (p161), giving visitors a distinct inferiority complex.

Laurakb, traveller

JULIET COOMB

2 THE PEOPLE OF CAMBODIA

Cycling around Cambodia gave us the opportunity to visit the main attractions as well as smaller towns and villages. Wherever we went, one thing remained constant: the Cambodian people love to chat! We were greeted with smiles and a chorus of hellos wherever we went, and the high standard of English among the young enabled more in-depth discussions. Although some were shy at first, we found that stumbling through a sentence in Khmer (p351) soon broke the ice, and before long the conversation was flowing.

Claire Dann and Tabitha Langford, travellers

ANDERS BLOMQVIS

3 TA PROHM

The temple of Ta Phrom (p166), in the middle of the jungle at Angkor, is one of the most awe-inspiring places I have ever been. Walk through the ruined temples, half devoured by the giant roots of the trees, and pull a Lara Croft if you can!

Crisonthemove, traveller

ROYAL PALACE & SILVER PAGODA

Angkor Wat is impressive, but head to the Royal Palace (p83) in the nation's capital for a truly rich experience! The Silver Pagoda's temple floor, covered with gleaming silver tiles, seems out of place in the weathered Cambodian landscape. The Royal Palace grounds are equally remarkable. Cambodia is a land of extremes, and this is the lush, royal end of it.

moontorch, traveller

CAROL WILEY

4

BATTAMBANG

I had an awesome day exploring the country-side around Battambang (p240) on the back of a motorbike. We hired moto drivers for the day who took us to visit local villages – we saw the muscle-straining way that rice noodles are made, watched chillies drying in the sun and smelled the unforgettable stench of giant vats of maturing fish paste. Caked in dust by the end of the day, we then climbed aboard the ingenuous bamboo train for the ride back to Battambang.

Sasha Baskett, Lonely Planet staff

DANIEL BOAG

5

DANIEL ROBINSON

6 BOKOR HILL STATION

Walk among the ruins of the ghostly Bokor Hill Station (p221), an old colonial retreat built by the French in the 1920s and later occupied by Khmer Rouge and Vietnamese forces in the war. The eery hotel has been likened to the one in *The Shining*, but this one has bullet holes in the walls.

cheryn, traveller

BAMBOO TRAIN

Take one engine and an axle, place on railway tracks and balance fence panel on top – welcome to Cambodia's bamboo train (p247). Take your seat and hold on tight, relying on your ten-year-old driver to suss whether there's a train coming in the opposite direction. Short prayer, optional.

providores, traveller

7

MASSAGE IN SIEM REAP

After sweltering among the temples, we opted for a soothing massage with Siem Reap's blind masseurs (p125). Have you ever conversed with someone where neither of you spoke the same language and they couldn't interpret your visual clues? Despite comic misunderstandings, we finally donned loose pyjamas and lay down. An elderly woman, with an astonishing amount of strength in her small hands, began pummelling me. It may not have been the soothing experience I was looking for (although my companion thoroughly enjoyed his massage), but I was inspired on so many levels – ability despite disability; determination in spite of circumstance.

Jennifer Garrett, Lonely Planet staff

8

9

CRAB IN KEP

The seaside town of Kep (p224) is slowly waking up from its post-war slumber and is fast becoming a fresh-seafood mecca. Picking our own sea creatures and having them prepared before our eyes while kicking back at a no-frills beachfront café made this a real highlight. We joined the banter and bought crab from the women keeping the crustaceans fresh in floating baskets – the competition is fierce and it's a lot of fun. We were spoilt for choice, but the omnipresent crab with Kampot pepper is surely not to be missed. We left Kep licking our lips.

Annelies Mertens, Lonely Planet staff

Contents

Regional Map Contents

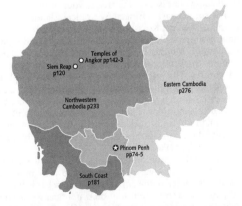

Temples of
Angkor pp142-3
Siem Reap
p120
Eastern Cambodia
p276
Northwestern
Cambodia p233
Phnom Penh
pp74-5
South Coast
p181

Destination Cambodia

There's a magic about Cambodia that casts a spell on many who visit this charming yet confounding kingdom. Ascend to the realm of the gods at the mother of all temples, Angkor Wat, a spectacular fusion of symbolism, symmetry and spirituality. Descend into the hell of Tuol Sleng and come face to face with the Khmer Rouge and its killing machine. Welcome to the conundrum that is Cambodia: a country with a history both inspiring and depressing, an intoxicating place where the future is waiting to be shaped.

The years of fear and loathing are finally over and Angkor is once more the symbol of the nation, drawing pilgrims from across the globe. Peace has come to this beautiful yet blighted land after three decades of war, and the Cambodian people have opened their arms to the world. Tourism has well and truly taken off, yet a journey here remains an adventure as much as a holiday.

Contemporary Cambodia is the successor state to the mighty Khmer empire, which, during the Angkor period, ruled much of what is now Laos, Thailand and Vietnam. The remains of this empire can be seen at the fabled temples of Angkor, monuments unrivalled in scale and grandeur in Southeast Asia. The traveller's first glimpse of Angkor Wat, the ultimate expression of Khmer genius, is simply staggering and is matched by only a few select spots on earth, such as Machu Picchu or Petra.

Just as Angkor is more than its wat, so too is Cambodia more than its temples. The chaotic yet charismatic capital of Phnom Penh is a hub of political intrigue, economic vitality and intellectual debate. All too often overlooked by hit-and-run tourists ticking off Angkor on a regional tour, the revitalised city is finally earning plaudits in its own right thanks to a gorgeous riverside location, a cultural renaissance, and a dining and drinking scene to rival the best in the region.

Siem Reap and Phnom Penh may be the heavyweights, but to some extent they are a bubble, a world away from the Cambodia of the countryside. This is the place to experience the rhythm of rural life and timeless landscapes of dazzling rice paddies and swaying sugar palms. Spend some time in the *srok* (provinces), as Cambodians call them, enjoying a *dar leng* (walkabout) to discover the true flavour of the country.

The south coast is fringed by tropical islands, with barely a beach hut in sight. The next Ko Samui or Gili Trawangan awaits discovery and, for now, visitors can play Robinson Crusoe. Inland from the coast lie the Cardamom Mountains, part of a vast tropical wilderness that provides a home to elusive wildlife and is the gateway to emerging ecotourism adventures. The mighty Mekong River cuts through the country and is home to some of the region's last remaining freshwater dolphins; cyclists or dirt bikers can follow the river's length as it meanders through traditional communities. The northeast is a world unto itself, its wild and mountainous landscapes a home for Cambodia's ethnic minorities and an abundance of natural attractions, including thundering waterfalls and pristine crater lakes.

Despite this beautiful backdrop, life is no picnic for the average Cambodian. It remains one of the poorest countries in Asia and it's a tough existence for much of the population, as they battle it out against the whims of nature and, sometimes, of their politicians. According to the United Nations Development Programme (UNDP; www.undp.org), Cambodia

FAST FACTS

Population:
About 15 million

Life expectancy: 58 years

Infant mortality:
95 per 1000 births

GDP: US$8.3 billion (2007)

Adult literacy rate: 73.6%

Number of tourists per year: 2 million and rising

Number of monks in Cambodia: 60,000

Annual freshwater fish catch: 290,000–430,000 tonnes per year

Bombs dropped on Cambodia: 539,000 tonnes

Number of psychiatrists in Cambodia: 20

remains poorer than Mongolia and El Salvador, just scraping in ahead of Mauritania, while Transparency International (www.transparency .org), the anticorruption watchdog, rates the country a lowly 151 out of the 163 countries ranked. Income remains desperately low for many Khmers, with annual salaries in the hundreds of dollars, not thousands, and public servants such as teachers unable to eke out a living on their meagre wages.

Cambodia's pristine environment may be a big draw, but much of it is currently under threat. Ancient forests are being razed to make way for plantations, rivers are being sized up for major hydroelectric power plants and the south coast is being explored by leading oil companies. All this helps add up to an ever-stronger economy, which is growing at an incredible 10% a year, but it's unlikely to encourage the ecotourism that is just starting to develop.

Cambodia is like the teen starlet who has just been discovered by an adoring public: everyone wants something from her but not everyone wants what is best for her. The government, long shunned by international big business, is keen to benefit from all these newfound opportunities. Contracts are being signed off like autographs and there are concerns for the long-term interests of the country.

Tourism has brought many benefits to Cambodia: it provides opportunity and employment for a new generation of Khmers, has helped to spark a rebirth of the traditional arts, and has given the country a renewed sense of pride and optimism as it recovers from the dark decades of war and genocide. However, not all tourism has been good for the country and there is the dark side of sex tourism, human exploitation and a casino culture. Cambodia is in a great position to benefit from the mistakes of other countries in the region and follow a sustainable road to tourism development. However, it may be that the government is more focused on the short-term gain that megabucks investments can provide. Can Cambodia be all things to all visitors? So far, so good, but a new era is about to begin and the beaches are the next battleground.

There are two faces to Cambodia: one shiny and happy, the other dark and complex. For every illegal eviction of city dwellers or land grab by a general, there will be a new NGO school offering better education, or a new clean-water initiative to improve the lives of the average villager. Such is the yin and yang of Cambodia, a country that inspires and confounds. Like an onion, the more layers you unravel, the more it makes you want to cry, but these are spontaneous tears, sometimes of sorrow, sometimes of joy.

Despite having the eighth wonder of the world in its backyard, Cambodia's greatest treasure is its people. The Khmers have been to hell and back, struggling through years of bloodshed, poverty and political instability. Thanks to an unbreakable spirit and infectious optimism, they have prevailed with their smiles intact; no visitor comes away from Cambodia without a measure of admiration and affection for the inhabitants of this enigmatic kingdom.

Cambodia: beaches as beautiful as Thailand but without the tourist tide; wilds as remote as Laos but even less explored; cuisine as subtle as Vietnam but yet to be discovered; and temples that leave Burma and Indonesia in the shade. This is the heart of Southeast Asia, with everything the region has to offer packed into one bite-sized country. If you were only planning to spend a week in Cambodia, it's time to think again.

Cambodia is still a predominantly rural society and as much as 80% of the population still lives in the countryside, working in agriculture and fishing.

Getting Started

A journey to Cambodia offers a window on the soul of Southeast Asia. The magnificent temples of Angkor are unrivalled, and beyond the rich legacy of the ancient Khmer empire lie the buzzing capital of Phnom Penh, hundreds of kilometres of unspoilt tropical beaches, the mighty Mekong River, a vibrant culture and some of the friendliest people in the region. It's not the most sophisticated destination in the world (though for many this makes it all the more charming), so be sure to pack some patience and humour. Cambodia is full of surprises, and is a place for adventure as much as a vacation.

See Climate Charts (p308) for more information.

WHEN TO GO

Cambodia can be visited at any time of year. The ideal months are December and January, when humidity levels are relatively low, there is little rainfall and a cooling breeze whips across the land, but this is also peak season when the majority of visitors descend on the country.

From early February temperatures keep rising until the killer month, April, when the mercury often exceeds 40°C. Some time in May or June, the southwestern monsoon brings rain and high humidity, cooking up a sweat for all but the hardiest of visitors. The wet season, which lasts until October, isn't such a bad time to visit, as the rain tends to come in short, sharp downpours. Angkor is surrounded by lush foliage and the moats are full of water at this time of year. If you are planning to visit isolated areas, however, the wet season makes for tough travel.

Some visitors like to coordinate their trip with one of the annual festivals, such as Bon Om Tuk or Khmer New Year (see p19).

COSTS & MONEY

The cost of travelling in Cambodia covers the whole spectrum, from almost free to outrageously expensive, depending on taste and comfort. Penny-pinchers can survive on as little as US$10 per day, while budget travellers with an eye on enjoyment can live it up on US$25 a day. Midrange travellers can turn on the style with US$75 to US$100 a day, staying in smart places, dining well and travelling in comfort. At the top end, flash US$200 a day or more to live a life of luxury.

Accommodation starts from as little as US$2 to US$5 in popular destinations. Spending US$10 to US$20 will add to the amenities, such as air conditioning, satellite TV, fridge and hot water. Stepping up to US$50, you enter

---

DON'T LEAVE HOME WITHOUT...

Bring as little as possible. Cambodia has everything you find at home and it's usually available at lower prices. All the soaps and smellies are plentiful, and clothing, shoes and backpacks are available at a fraction of the price in the West. Tampons are available in all major towns and cities, but not in more remote areas.

A Swiss Army knife or equivalent comes in handy, but you don't need 27 separate functions, just one blade and an opener. A torch (flashlight) and compass are also useful.

Other handy items: earplugs to block the ever-present noise, a universal plug adaptor, a rain cover for your backpack and insect repellent to keep the bugs at bay. Finally, the secret of successful packing: plastic bags – not only do they keep things separate and clean, but also dry. That means a lot at the end of a long, wet day.

THE PRICE OF INFLATION

After several years of stability, inflation in Cambodia is once again on the rise. The figure for 2007 was around 10%, but already in the first quarter of 2008 it was above the 20% mark. Rice has trebled in price and cooking gas has doubled. Petrol prices continue to soar and this is having a knock-on effect on electricity costs. The long and short of it is that as we go to press, some costs may be higher than quoted in this book. It may be prudent to round up moto and remorque fares by 25% or more. Hotels and restaurants are also starting to raise prices to cover rising electricity bills and food overheads. Cambodia is still cheaper than home, but it is no longer the bargain it once was.

---

the world of three-star standards and charming boutique resorts. Forking out US$100 or more brings a five-star fling. Don't be afraid to negotiate for a discount if it is low season or traffic is down.

While Cambodian cuisine may not be as well known as that of its neighbours Thailand and Vietnam, it can certainly compete with the best of them. Snack on the street or chow down in the market, with meals starting at just 1000r or so, or indulge in a banquet for a couple of bucks. Khmer restaurants are a step up in comfort, and a local meal will cost US$1 to US$2. Next are the sophisticated Khmer, Asian and international restaurants. Meals start from about US$3 at the cheaper places, rising to more like US$10 at the smarter ones, and US$50 or more is possible if you go wild with the wine list.

Domestic flights link Phnom Penh to Siem Reap. Fast boats link several popular destinations in Cambodia and the journey can be more scenic than by road. There is now a healthy selection of bus companies connecting towns and cities throughout Cambodia and prices are rock bottom. On the rougher roads, share taxis and pick-ups take the strain. Train travel is no longer possible, as passenger services have been suspended, but that could be seen as a blessing in disguise given that trains crawl along at an average speed of 20km/h. For ultimate flexibility, rent a car or 4WD and travel with a guide.

Visitors to Angkor (which is surely everybody coming to Cambodia) will have to factor in the cost of entrance fees, which are US$20 for one day, US$40 for three days and US$60 for one week. An additional expense is transport to get to, from and around the ruins; from US$2 for a bicycle, US$6 to US$8 for a *moto* (small motorcycle with driver), US$10 to US$15 for a *remorque* (trailer pulled by a bicycle or motorcycle) and US$25 to US$35 for a car.

Small budget, big budget, it doesn't really matter; Cambodia is the place to be. Soak it up in the style that suits.

HOW MUCH?

Hotel room with air-con US$10-20

Restaurant meal US$3-10

Internet access per minute US$0.40-1.50

Cambodia Daily newspaper 1200r

Krama (checked scarf) 3000r

TRAVELLING RESPONSIBLY

Since our inception in 1973, Lonely Planet has encouraged readers to tread lightly, travel responsibly and experience the magic of independent travel. International travel is growing at a jaw-dropping rate and we still firmly believe in the benefits it can bring but, as always, we encourage you to consider the impact your visit will have on both the global environment and the local economies, cultures and ecosystems.

Cambodia has been to hell and back and there are many ways that you can put a little back into the country. Staying a bit longer, travelling further and spreading the wealth around is obvious advice, but even for those on a short stay, it is possible to engage with locals in markets and spend money in restaurants and outlets that assist disadvantaged Cambodians. See the boxed text, p67, in the Food & Drink chapter, as well as the Eating

TOP 10

CAMBODIA
Phnom Penh
Myanmar (Burma)   Vietnam

ANCIENT TEMPLES

Cambodia is the temple capital of Asia. The kingdom is littered with the lavish legacy of the god-kings. Choose from majestic mountain-top temples, forbidding and forgotten jungle fortresses, incredible carved riverbeds and pre-Angkorian brick cities.

1 Angkor Wat (p154), the mother of all temples

2 Banteay Chhmar (p255), the forgotten fortress of the northwest

3 Banteay Srei (p175), the jewel in the crown of Angkorian art

4 Bayon (p161), with its 216 enigmatic faces

5 Beng Mealea (p178), Angkor-sized but swallowed by jungle

6 Kbal Spean (p176), the River of a Thousand Lingas

7 Koh Ker (p264), a usurper capital of huge proportions

8 Prasat Preah Vihear (p268), king of the mountain temples

9 Sambor Prei Kuk (p272), the first temple city in the region.

10 Ta Prohm (p166), left as explorers first saw it – nature run riot

TRAGEDIES IN WORDS

In stark contrast to the glories of the Angkor empire is the dark void into which Cambodia plunged in the 1970s. A brutal civil war raged for five years, delivering the Khmer Rouge to power. This regime turned the clocks to Year Zero in what was to become one of the world's most radical and bloody revolutions. Read your way into these tumultuous events to understand how it all happened.

1 *Sideshow: Kissinger, Nixon and the Destruction of Cambodia* by William Shawcross (1979)

2 *Brother Enemy* by Nayan Chanda (1985)

3 *History of Cambodia* by David Chandler (1994)

4 *Prince of Light, Prince of Darkness* by Milton Osbourne (1994)

5 *The Pol Pot Regime* by Ben Kiernan (1996)

6 *Voices from S-21* by David Chandler (1999)

7 *First They Killed My Father* by Luong Ung (2001)

8 *The Gate* by Francois Bizot (2003)

9 *Pol Pot: The History of a Nightmare* by Phillip Short (2004)

10 *The Lost Executioner* by Nic Dunlop (2005)

ADVENTURES

If you are looking for adventure in Asia, then you have come to the right place. The roads may be rough, but the stories will be smooth and stay with you forever. One thing is for sure, an adventure is never far away in Cambodia.

1 Make the overland pilgrimage to Prasat Preah Vihear (p268)

2 Beachcomb on the beautiful island of Koh Kong (p188)

3 Learn to ride like a mahout at the Elephant Valley Project (p302) in the remote northeast

4 Paddle a dugout through the flooded forest of Kompong Phhluk (p139)

5 Go underground at Kampot's cave pagodas (p218)

6 Ride the bamboo train in Battambang (p247)

7 Camp out in the jungle at the temple of Preah Khan (p262)

8 Catch a fast boat from Siem Reap to Battambang (p245)

9 Pan for gold in the Wild East town of Mimong (p303)

10 Trek across the remote Cardamoms from Thmar Bang to Aural (p189)

and Shopping sections in the Phnom Penh and Siem Reap chapters for more ideas.

The following websites have more information on sustainable tourism and tips on responsible travel:

Cambodia Community-Based Ecotourism Network (www.ccben.org) The official website promoting community-based ecotourism in Cambodia. Browse here for more on projects and initiatives across the country.

ChildSafe (www.childsafe-cambodia.org) Learn about the ChildSafe campaign, which aims to stop child-sex tourism and raise awareness of the problem.

Heritage Watch (www.heritagewatch.org) The home of the heritage-friendly tourism campaign to raise interest in remote heritage sites and their protection.

Responsible Travel (www.responsible-travel.org) A no-nonsense website with common-sense advice on how to travel with a conscience.

Stay Another Day (www.stay-another-day.org) A great website dedicated to tempting tourists into staying another day in Cambodia, packed with ideas on day trips, project visits and alternative things to see and do.

TRAVEL LITERATURE

The classic Cambodian read is Norman Lewis' *A Dragon Apparent: Travels in Cambodia, Laos & Vietnam* (1951), an account of his 1950 foray into an Indochina that would soon disappear. In the course of his travels, Lewis circumnavigated Tonlé Sap Lake, with a pause at Angkor. The book has been reissued as part of *The Norman Lewis Omnibus* (1995).

Written by writers who know and love their countries, *To Asia with Love: A Connoisseur's Guide to Cambodia, Laos, Thailand and Vietnam* (2004), an anthology edited by Kim Fay, is a delightful introduction to Cambodia and the Mekong region for those looking for some inspiration and adventure. A new *To Cambodia with Love* is on the cards and should be out some time during the lifetime of this book.

Travels in Siam, Cambodia, Laos and Annam (1864) by Henri Mouhot has been reprinted in English by White Lotus and gives the inside story of the man credited with 'rediscovering' Angkor.

Jon Swain's *River of Time* (1995) takes the reader back to an old Indochina, partly lost to the madness of war, and includes first-hand accounts of the French embassy stand-off in the first days of the Khmer Rouge takeover.

Tim Page's *Derailed in Uncle Ho's Victory Garden* (1995) covers this legendary photographer's quest for the truth behind the disappearance of photojournalist Sean Flynn (son of Errol) in Cambodia in 1970, and his mission to secure a monument to fallen correspondents on all sides of the Indochina conflict.

An excellent account of life on the Mother River is *The River's Tale: A Year on the Mekong* (2001) by Edward Gargan. A war-protester-turned-foreign-correspondent, Gargan sees for himself how Cambodia and its neighbours have brought themselves back from the brink.

The Indochina Chronicles (2005) by Phil Karber is a lively travelogue taking in adventures and misadventures in Cambodia, Laos and Vietnam.

Amit Gilboa's *Off the Rails in Phnom Penh – Guns, Girls and Ganja* (1998) deals with such murky subjects as prostitution and drugs. It feels like he got too close to his subject at times and it's not really a side of Cambodia of which Khmers are proud.

The ultimate spoof guidebook, *Phaic Tăn: Sunstroke on a Shoestring* (2004) is a pastiche of Southeast Asian countries that pokes fun at all of us. No-one is spared, not the locals, not the travellers – not even hallowed guidebook authors.

'includes first-hand accounts of the French embassy stand-off in the first days of the Khmer Rouge takeover'

INTERNET RESOURCES

Andy Brouwer's Cambodia Tales (www.andybrouwer.co.uk) Gateway to all things Cambodian, this site includes comprehensive links to other sites and regular travel articles from veteran Cambodia adventurers. Includes a daily blog from his new home in Cambodia.

Angkor Wat Portal (www.angkor.com) When it comes to links, this site has them, spreading its cyber-tentacles into all sorts of interesting areas.

Biking Southeast Asia with Mr Pumpy (www.mrpumpy.net) The definitive but dated website for cyclists passing through Cambodia is written with candour and humour by Mr Pumpy's best friend Felix Hude.

Expat Advisory (www.expat-advisory.com) News and events site aimed at expats in Asia, with up-to-date information on happenings in Phnom Penh.

Lonely Planet (www.lonelyplanet.com) Information on travelling to and within Cambodia, the Thorn Tree Travel Forum and up-to-date travel news.

Ministry of Tourism (www.mot.gov.kh) The official Cambodian tourism website is a touch dated but there are some useful links for hotels, restaurants and travel agents.

Oriental Tales (www.orientaltales.com) Short stories, articles and inspiring photos of travel throughout Southeast Asia.

Tales of Asia (www.talesofasia.com) This popular website has up-to-the-minute information on overland travel in Cambodia, including webmaster Gordon Sharpless' personal obsession, the Bangkok–Siem Reap run.

Things Asian (www.thingsasian.com) Bubbling with information on the culture of the Mekong region, this site has everything including architecture, literature and fashion.

Events Calendar

Why not plan your trip to coincide with one of Cambodia's major festivals? Holidays and festivals take place according to the lunar calendar, so dates vary from year to year. Check the internet (www .mot.gov.kh) for this year's exact dates.

JANUARY–APRIL

CHAUL CHNAM CHEN
(CHINESE NEW YEAR)   late Jan–mid-Feb
The Chinese inhabitants of Cambodia celebrate their New Year somewhere between late January and mid-February – for the Vietnamese, this is Tet. As many of Phnom Penh's businesses are run by Chinese, commerce grinds to a halt around this time and there are dragon dances all over town.

CHAUL CHNAM KHMER
(KHMER NEW YEAR)   mid-Apr
This is a three-day celebration of the Khmer New Year, and is like Christmas, New Year and birthdays all rolled into one. Cambodians make offerings at wats, clean out their homes and exchange gifts. It is a lively time to visit the country as the Khmers go wild with water and talcum powder, leaving a lot of bemused tourists looking like plaster-cast figures. Large crowds congregate at Wat Phnom in the capital, but females should watch out for the over-eager attention of young gangs of males. Throngs of Khmers flock to Angkor, and it's absolute madness at most temples, so avoid the celebration if you want a quiet, reflective Angkor experience.

MAY–AUGUST

CHAT PREAH NENGKAL
(ROYAL PLOUGHING CEREMONY)   early May
Led by the royal family, the Royal Ploughing Ceremony is a ritual agricultural festival held to mark the traditional beginning of the rice-growing season. It takes place in front of the National Museum, near the Royal Palace in Phnom Penh, and the royal oxen are said to have a nose for whether it will be a good harvest or a bad one.

VISAKHA PUJA
(BUDDHA DAY)   May/Jun
Celebrating Buddha's birth, enlightenment and *parinibbana* (passing away), activities are centred on wats. The festival falls on the eighth day of the fourth moon and is best observed at Angkor Wat, where you can see candlelit processions of monks.

SEPTEMBER–DECEMBER

P'CHUM BEN
(FESTIVAL OF THE DEAD)   Sep/Oct
This festival is a kind of All Souls' Day, when respects are paid to the dead through offerings made at wats. This includes paper money as well as food and drink, all passed through the medium of the monks.

BON OM TUK
(WATER FESTIVAL)   Oct/Nov
Celebrating the epic victory of Jayavarman VII over the Chams who occupied Angkor in 1177, this festival also marks the natural phenomenon of the reversal of the current of the Tonlé Sap River. It is one of the most important festivals in the Khmer calendar and is a wonderful, if hectic, time to be in Phnom Penh or Siem Reap. Boat races are held on the Tonlé Sap and Siem Reap Rivers, with each boat colourfully decorated and holding 40 rowers. As many as two million people flood the capital for the fun and frolics, so be sure to book ahead for accommodation.

Itineraries
CLASSIC ROUTES

CAMBODIA SNAPSHOT   Two Weeks

Whether you start in Siem Reap and travel south, or head north to Angkor, this is the ultimate journey, via temples, beaches and the capital.

Hit **Phnom Penh** (p72) for sights such as the impressive **National Museum** (p84), with its excellent Angkorian sculpture collection, and the stunning **Silver Pagoda** (p83). There is superb shopping at the **Psar Tuol Tom Pong** (p109), and a **night shift** (p106) that never sleeps.

Take a fast boat to **Phnom Da** (p230), then go south to the colonial-era town of **Kampot** (p215). From here, visit **Bokor Hill Station** (p221), the seaside town of **Kep** (p224) and the cave pagodas at **Phnom Chhnork** and **Phnom Sorsia** (p218).

Go west to **Sihanoukville** (p193), Cambodia's beach capital, to sample the seafood, dive the nearby waters or just soak up the sun. Backtrack via Phnom Penh to **Kompong Thom** (p270) to get a foretaste of what's to come by visiting the pre-Angkorian brick temples of **Sambor Prei Kuk** (p272).

Finish the trip at Angkor, a mind-blowing experience with which few sights compare. See **Angkor Wat** (p154), perfection in stone; **Bayon** (p161), weirdness in stone; and **Ta Prohm** (p166), nature triumphing over stone – before venturing further afield to **Kbal Spean** (p176) or the jungle-clad **Beng Mealea** (p178).

This trip can take two weeks at a steady pace or three weeks at a slow pace. Public transport serves most of this route. Rent a motorbike for side trips to Kep and Sambor Prei Kuk, and try out a *remorque-moto* (trailer pulled by a motorcycle) at Angkor. More money, less time? Rent a car and set the pace.

THE BIG ONE   One Month

Cambodia is a small country and even though the roads are often bad and travel slow, most of the big hitters can be visited in a month.

Setting out from **Phnom Penh** (p72), take in the beauty of the northeast, following the Run to the Hills itinerary (p23). Choose between **Ratanakiri Province** (p291) and **Mondulkiri Province** (p298) to ensure maximum time elsewhere. The gentle hills of Mondulkiri are better for budget travellers as traversing overland is easy, while Ratanakiri makes sense for those planning an overland journey between Cambodia and Laos. Tough choice…can't decide? Flip a coin, if you can find one in this coinless country.

Head to the south coast, taking the route outlined in Cambodia Snapshot (opposite). Take your time and consider a few nights in comeback **Kep** (p224) or one of the nearby islands, and a boat trip from **Sihanoukville** (p193) to explore the up-and-coming islands off the coast. On your way back to the capital, check out **Kirirom National Park** (p116), home to pine trees, black bears and some spectacular views of the Cardamom Mountains.

Then it's time to turn northwest and head to charming **Battambang** (p240), one of Cambodia's best preserved colonial-era towns and a base from which to discover rural life and ride the bamboo train. Leave in style by fast boat to **Siem Reap** (p118), passing through stunning scenery along the snaking Sangker River, and turn your attention to the **temples of Angkor** (p140).

Visit all the greatest hits in and around Angkor, but use the extra time to venture further to the rival capital of **Koh Ker** (p264), which is cloaked in thick jungle, or **Prasat Preah Vihear** (p268), where it is all about location, location, location – a mountain temple perched precariously atop a cliff-face on the Thai border.

Overlanders can run this route in reverse, setting out from Siem Reap and exiting Cambodia by river into Vietnam or Laos. Entering from Laos, divert east to Ratanakiri before heading south. Getting about is generally easy, as there are buses on the big roads, taxis on the small roads and buzzing boats on the rivers.

ROADS LESS TRAVELLED

THE LOST TEMPLES OF THE NORTHWEST

The magnificent temples of Angkor are renowned for their splendour, but these represent no more than the capital of what was an unrivalled empire spanning Southeast Asia. In the steaming jungles of Cambodia, forgotten to the world for centuries, lie several stunning religious monuments that make the perfect excuse to extend your adventure.

The beauty of this tough trip on rough roads is that it is the alternative way to link Cambodia's vibrant capital, Phnom Penh, with Siem Reap, gateway to Angkor. Starting in **Phnom Penh** (p72), head north through **Kompong Thom** (p270) and on to the pre-Angkorian capital of **Sambor Prei Kuk** (p272), Asia's first temple city. Bid farewell to civilisation from here and make the tough journey northwest to the vast jungle temple of **Preah Khan** (p262), one of the largest structures from the Angkorian era.

Continue on to **Koh Ker** (p264), a usurper capital from the 10th century, with a wealth of monuments spread throughout the forest.

Last of the temples is **Prasat Preah Vihear** (p268). The height of Angkorian architectural audacity, its foundation stones stretch to the edge of a precipitous cliff. Breathe in the views as they are simply enormous. From here, it is a long run to **Siem Reap** (p118) via the former Khmer Rouge stronghold of **Anlong Veng** (p258), where you can visit Pol Pot's cremation site. In Siem Reap, finish with the compulsory **temples of Angkor** (p140) or continue to the beautiful **Banteay Chhmar** (p255) if you still have the energy reserves.

This is a tough trip with little in the way of public transport. It takes at least a week and should not be attempted in the wet season. Seasoned motorbike riders can do it on a dirt bike. For less pain, a 4WD is the way to go. The trip is possible using a combination of pick-up truck and *moto* (small motorcycle with driver), but you'll need massage therapy afterwards.

RUN TO THE HILLS

Northeast Cambodia is a world unto itself, a landscape of rolling hills and secret waterfalls, and home to a patchwork of ethnic minorities, many of whom still use elephants to get around. It's not only the sights and sounds that are different up here, the temperature is notably cooler, as both Mondulkiri and Ratanakiri Provinces lie at almost 1000m.

Leaving the capital **Phnom Penh** (p72), pass through the bustling Mekong town of **Kompong Cham** (p280) before heading east to **Sen Monorom** (p299), the charming capital of Mondulkiri Province. Spend a few days here to bathe at **Bou Sraa Waterfall** (p303), one of Cambodia's biggest waterfalls; learn to ride an **elephant** (p302) and explore Pnong villages before heading back to the Mekong at **Kratie** (p285). This attractive little town is the base for an encounter with one of the rarest mammals on earth, the elusive Irrawaddy river dolphin, which lives in ever-dwindling numbers upstream from here.

Push north up the Mekong to **Stung Treng** (p289). To the east lies **Ban Lung** (p292), provincial capital of Ratanakiri Province and base for an adventure to remember. From here plunge into Cambodia's most beautiful natural swimming pool at **Boeng Yeak Lom** (p296), ride an elephant through the rubber plantations to the stunning waterfall of **Ka Tieng** (p296) or visit the medieval **gem mines** (p296) where much of Cambodia's zircon comes from.

Adventurers and motorbikers can link Mondulkiri and Ratanakiri Provinces directly via the village of **Koh Nhek** (p304). Sen Monorom to Koh Nhek is a breeze, but the roads all but disappear from there and a *moto* driver as a guide is almost essential.

On main roads, this trip is easy to manage using share taxis or pick-ups, but until the roads are finished it's a frightening prospect in the wet season. Motorbikers can link Mondulkiri and Ratanakiri Provinces on one of Cambodia's more devilish roads – not for amateurs. Finishing up in Ratanakiri, overlanders can carry on into Laos.

TAILORED TRIP

UNTAMED CARDAMOMS & UNEXPLORED COAST

Visitors can get a sense of the diverse ecosystems of the Cardamom Mountains – from the rainforested highlands down to the mangrove-fringed shoreline and pristine beaches – along the **Koh Kong Conservation Corridor** (p186), in Cambodia's far southwestern corner. Based in the one-time smugglers' port of **Krong Koh Kong** (p182), travel by *moto* or boat to the **Tatai River** (p187), where you can stay in ecologically sustainable accommodation. Drive inland to the **Thma Bang ranger station** (p189), in

the Central Cardamoms Protected Forest, to explore the Areng River habitats of the endangered dragonfish (Asian arowana) and Siamese crocodile (p190). Krong Koh Kong is also a good base for an excursion by open skiff through the pristine mangrove forests of **Peam Krasaop Wildlife Sanctuary** (p187) and on to **Koh Kong Island** (p188), whose western side has seven unspoiled beaches, some with lagoons. The northwest coast of **Botum Sakor National Park** (p190) is just across the channel from the island, but the superb beaches further south are easier to get to from **Koh Sdach** (p191), a stop on the **Sihanoukville–Krong Koh Kong ferry** (p185) that's not far from some excellent snorkelling grounds. To visit the park's mangrove-lined east coast – including **Ta Op stream** (p190) and its monkeys – hire a boat in **Andoung Tuek** (p191), where you can also take an early morning ride upriver to the village of **Chi Phat** (p191). Once notorious for its poachers, it is now the site of a pioneering community-based ecotourism project.

History

The good, the bad and the ugly is a simple way to sum up Cambodian history. Things were good in the early years, culminating in the vast Angkor empire, unrivalled in the region during four centuries of dominance. Then the bad set in, from the 13th century, as ascendant neighbours steadily chipped away at Cambodian territory. In the 20th century it turned downright ugly, as a brutal civil war culminated in the genocidal rule of the Khmer Rouge (1975–79), from which Cambodia is still recovering.

THE ORIGIN OF THE KHMERS

Cambodia came into being, so the legend says, through the union of a princess and a foreigner. The foreigner was an Indian Brahman named Kaundinya and the princess was the daughter of a dragon king who ruled over a watery land. One day, as Kaundinya sailed by, the princess paddled out in a boat to greet him. Kaundinya shot an arrow from his magic bow into her boat, causing the fearful princess to agree to marriage. In need of a dowry, her father drank up the waters of his land and presented them to Kaundinya to rule over. The new kingdom was named Kambuja.

Like many legends, this one is historically opaque, but it does say something about the cultural forces that brought Cambodia into existence, in particular its relationship with its great subcontinental neighbour, India. Cambodia's religious, royal and written traditions stemmed from India and began to coalesce as a cultural entity in their own right between the 1st and 5th centuries.

Very little is known about prehistoric Cambodia. Much of the southeast was a vast, shallow gulf that was progressively silted up by the mouths of the Mekong, leaving pancake-flat, mineral-rich land ideal for farming. Evidence of cave-dwellers has been found in the northwest of Cambodia. Carbon dating on ceramic pots found in the area shows that they were made around 4200 BC, but it is hard to say whether there is a direct relationship between these cave-dwelling pot makers and contemporary Khmers. Examinations of bones dating back to around 1500 BC, however, suggest that the people living in Cambodia at that time resembled the Cambodians of today. Early Chinese records report that the Cambodians were 'ugly' and 'dark' and went about naked. However, a healthy dose of scepticism is always required when reading the culturally chauvinistic reports of imperial China concerning its 'barbarian' neighbours.

For the full flavour of Cambodian history, from the humble beginnings in the prehistoric period through the glories of Angkor and right up to the present day, grab a copy of *The History of Cambodia* by David Chandler (1994).

TIMELINE

4200 BC	AD 100	245
Cave dwellers capable of making pots inhabit caves around Laang Spean; archaeological evidence suggests the vessels these people were making were similar to those still made in Cambodia today.	The process of Indianisation begins with the arrival of Indian traders and holy men: the religions, language and sculpture of India start to take root in Cambodia.	The Chinese Wei emperor sends a mission to the countries of the Mekong region and is told that a barbarous but rich country called Funan exists in the Delta region.

THE EARLY CAMBODIAN KINGDOMS

Cambodian might didn't begin and end with Angkor. There were a number of powerful kingdoms present in this area before the 9th century.

From the 1st century, the Indianisation of Cambodia occurred through trading settlements that sprang up on the coastline of what is now southern Vietnam, but was then inhabited by the Khmers. These settlements were important ports of call for boats following the trading route from the Bay of Bengal to the southern provinces of China. The largest of these nascent kingdoms was known as Funan by the Chinese, and may have existed across an area between Ba Phnom (p279) in Prey Veng Province, a site only worth visiting for the archaeologically obsessed today, and Oc-Eo in Kien Giang Province in southern Vietnam. Funan would have been a contemporary of Champasak in southern Laos (then known as Kuruksetra) and other lesser fiefdoms in the region.

Funan is a Chinese name, and it may be a transliteration of the ancient Khmer word *bnam* (mountain). Although very little is known about Funan, much has been made of its importance as an early Southeast Asian centre of power.

It is most likely that between the 1st and 8th centuries, Cambodia was a collection of small states, each with its own elites that often strategically intermarried and often went to war with one another. Funan was no doubt one of these states, and as a major sea port would have been pivotal in the transmission of Indian culture into the interior of Cambodia.

The little that historians do know about Funan has mostly been gleaned from Chinese sources. These report that Funan-period Cambodia (1st to 6th centuries AD) embraced the worship of the Hindu deities Shiva and Vishnu and, at the same time, Buddhism. The *linga* (phallic totem) appears to have been the focus of ritual and an emblem of kingly might, a feature that was to evolve further in the Angkorian cult of the god-king. The people practised primitive irrigation, which enabled successful cultivation of rice, and traded raw commodities such as spices with China and India.

From the 6th century, Cambodia's population gradually concentrated along the Mekong and Tonlé Sap Rivers, where the majority remains today. The move may have been related to the development of wet-rice agriculture. From the 6th to 8th centuries it was likely that Cambodia was a collection of competing kingdoms, ruled by autocratic kings who legitimised their absolute rule through hierarchical caste concepts borrowed from India.

This era is generally referred to as the Chenla period. Again, like Funan, it is a Chinese term and there is little to support the idea that Chenla was a unified kingdom that held sway over all of Cambodia. Indeed, the Chinese themselves referred to 'water Chenla' and 'land Chenla'. Water Chenla was located around Angkor Borei and the temple mount of Phnom Da (p230), near the present-day provincial capital of Takeo, and land Chenla in the

---

Cambodia's Funan-period trading port of Oc-Eo, now located in Vietnam's Mekong Delta, was a major commercial crossroads between east and west, and archaeologists here have unearthed Roman coins and Chinese ceramics.

Founded by King Isanavarman I in the early 7th century, Sambor Prei Kuk was originally known as Isanapura and was the first major temple city to be constructed in Southeast Asia.

600	802	889
The first inscriptions are committed to stone in Cambodia in ancient Khmer, offering historians the first contemporary accounts of the pre-Angkorian period other than Chinese sources.	Jayavarman II proclaims independence from Java in a ceremony to anoint himself a devaraja (god-king) on the holy mountain of Phnom Kulen, marking the birth of the Khmer Empire of Angkor.	Yasovarman I moves the capital from the ancient city of Harihara (Roluos today) to the Angkor area, 16km to the northwest, and marks the location with three temple mountains.

upper reaches of the Mekong River and east of Tonlé Sap Lake, around Sambor Prei Kuk (p272), an essential stop on a chronological jaunt through Cambodia's history.

THE RISE OF THE ANGKOR EMPIRE

Gradually the Cambodian region was becoming more cohesive. Before long the fractured kingdoms of Cambodia would merge to become the greatest empire in Southeast Asia.

A popular place of pilgrimage for Khmers today, the sacred mountain of Phnom Kulen (p177), to the northeast of Angkor, is home to an inscription that tells of Jayavarman II (r 802–50) proclaiming himself a 'universal monarch', or *devaraja* (god-king) in 802. It is believed that he may have resided in the Buddhist Shailendras' court in Java as a young man. Upon his return to Cambodia he instigated an uprising against Javanese control over the southern lands of Cambodia. Jayavarman II then set out to bring the country under his control through alliances and conquests, the first monarch to rule most of what we call Cambodia today.

Jayavarman II was the first of a long succession of kings who presided over the rise and fall of the greatest empire mainland Southeast Asia has ever seen, one that was to bequeath the stunning legacy of Angkor. The key to the meteoric rise of Angkor was a mastery of water and an elaborate hydraulic system that allowed the ancient Khmers to tame the elements. The first records of the massive irrigation works that supported the population of Angkor date to the reign of Indravarman I (r 877–89) who built the *baray* (reservoir) of Indratataka. His rule also marks the flourishing of Angkorian art, with the building of temples in the Roluos area, notably Bakong (p174).

By the turn of the 11th century the kingdom of Angkor was losing control of its territories. Suryavarman I (r 1002–49), a usurper, moved into the power vacuum and, like Jayavarman II two centuries before, reunified the kingdom through war and alliances, stretching the frontiers of the empire. A pattern was beginning to emerge, and is repeated throughout the Angkorian period: dislocation and turmoil, followed by reunification and further expansion under a powerful king. Architecturally, the most productive periods occurred after times of turmoil, indicating that newly incumbent monarchs felt the need to celebrate, even legitimise their rule with massive building projects.

By 1066 Angkor was again riven by conflict, becoming the focus of rival bids for power. It was not until the accession of Suryavarman II (r 1112–52) that the kingdom was again unified. Suryavarman II embarked on another phase of expansion, waging costly wars in Vietnam and the region of central Vietnam known as Champa. Suryavarman II is immortalised as the king who, in his devotion to the Hindu deity Vishnu, commissioned the majestic temple of Angkor Wat (p154). For an insight

India wasn't the only power to have a major cultural impact on Cambodia. The island of Java was also influential, colonising part of water Chenla in the 8th century.

The ancient Khmers were like the Romans of Southeast Asia, building a network of long highways across the region to connect their regional cities.

924	**1002**	**1112**
Usurper king Jayavarman IV transfers the capital to Koh Ker and begins a mammoth building spree, but the lack of water sees the capital move back to Angkor just 20 years later.	Suryavarman I comes to power and expands the extent of the kingdom by annexing the Buddhist kingdom of Louvo, known as Lopburi in modern-day Thailand, and increases trade links with the outside world.	Suryavarman II commences the construction of Angkor Wat, the mother of all temples, dedicated to Vishnu and designed as his funerary temple.

into events in this epoch, see the bas-reliefs on the southwest corridor of Angkor Wat, which depict the reign of Suryavarman II.

Suryavarman II had brought Champa to heel and reduced it to vassal status, but the Chams struck back in 1177 with a naval expedition up the Mekong and into Tonlé Sap Lake. They took the city of Angkor by surprise and put King Dharanindravarman II to death. The following year a cousin of Suryavarman II rallied the Khmer troops and defeated the Chams in another naval battle. The new leader was crowned Jayavarman VII in 1181.

A devout follower of Mahayana Buddhism, Jayavarman VII (r 1181–1219) built the city of Angkor Thom (p159) and many other massive monuments. Indeed, many of the temples visited around Angkor today were constructed during Jayavarman VII's reign. However, Jayavarman VII is a figure of many contradictions. The bas-reliefs of the Bayon (p161) depict him presiding over battles of terrible ferocity, while statues of the king depict a meditative, otherworldly aspect. His programme of temple construction and other public works was carried out in great haste, no doubt bringing enormous hardship to the labourers who provided the muscle, and thus accelerating the decline of the empire. He was partly driven by a desire to legitimise his rule, as there may have been other contenders closer to the royal bloodline, and partly by the need to introduce a new religion to a population predominantly Hindu in faith. However, in many ways he was also Cambodia's first socialist leader, proclaiming the population equal, abolishing castes and embarking on a programme of school, hospital and road building.

For more on the Angkorian period, see p140.

DECLINE & FALL OF ANGKOR

Angkor was the epicentre of an incredible empire that held sway over much of the Mekong region, but like all empires, the sun was to eventually set.

A number of scholars have argued that decline was already on the horizon at the time Angkor Wat was built, when the Angkorian empire was at the height of its remarkable productivity. There are indications that the irrigation network was overworked and slowly starting to silt up due to the massive deforestation that had taken place in the heavily populated areas to the north and east of Angkor. Massive construction projects such as Angkor Wat and Angkor Thom no doubt put an enormous strain on the royal coffers and on thousands of slaves and common people who subsidised them in hard labour and taxes. Following the reign of Jayavarman VII, temple construction effectively ground to a halt, in large part because Jayavarman VII's public works quarried local sandstone into oblivion and had left the population exhausted.

Another challenge for the later kings was religious conflict and internecine rivalries. The state religion changed back and forth several times during the twilight years of the empire, and kings spent more time engaged

One of the definitive guides to Angkor is *A Guide to the Angkor Monuments* by Maurice Glaize, first published in the 1940s and now out of print. Download it free at www.theangkorguide .com.

Chinese emissary Chou Ta Kuan lived in Angkor for a year in 1296, and his observations have been republished as *The Customs of Cambodia* (2000), a fascinating insight into life during the height of the empire.

1152

Suryavarman II is killed in a disastrous campaign against the Dai Viet (Vietnamese), provoking this rising northern neighbour and sparking centuries of conflict between the two countries.

1177

The Chams launch a surprise attack on Angkor by sailing up the Tonlé Sap, defeat the powerful Khmers and occupy the capital for four years.

1181

The Chams are vanquished as Jayavarman VII, the greatest king of Angkor and builder of Angkor Thom, takes the throne, changing the state religion to Mahayana Buddhism.

in iconoclasm, defacing the temples of their predecessors, than building monuments to their own achievements. From time to time this boiled over into civil war.

Angkor was losing control over the peripheries of its empire. At the same time, the Thais were ascendant, having migrated south from Yunnan to escape Kublai Khan and his Mongol hordes. The Thais, first from Sukothai, later Ayuthaya, grew in strength and made repeated incursions into Angkor before finally sacking the city in 1431 and making off with thousands of intellectuals, artisans and dancers from the royal court. During this period, perhaps drawn by the opportunities for sea trade with China and fearful of the increasingly bellicose Thais, the Khmer elite began to migrate to the Phnom Penh area. The capital shifted several times over the centuries but eventually settled in present day Phnom Penh.

From 1600 until the arrival of the French in 1863, Cambodia was ruled by a series of weak kings beset by dynastic rivalries. In the face of such intrigue, they sought the protection – granted, of course, at a price – of either Thailand or Vietnam. In the 17th century, the Nguyen lords of southern Vietnam came to the rescue of the Cambodian king in return for settlement rights in the Mekong Delta region. The Khmers still refer to this region as Kampuchea Krom (Lower Cambodia), even though it is well and truly populated by the Vietnamese today.

In the west, the Thais controlled the provinces of Battambang and Siem Reap from 1794 and held much influence over the Cambodian royal family. Indeed, one king was crowned in Bangkok and placed on the throne at Udong (p113) with the help of the Thai army. That Cambodia survived through the 18th century as a distinct entity is due to the preoccupations of its neighbours: while the Thais were expending their energy and resources in fighting the Burmese, the Vietnamese were wholly absorbed by internal strife. The pattern continued for more than two centuries, the carcass of Cambodia pulled back and forth between two powerful tigers.

> The commercial metropolis that is now Ho Chi Minh City (Saigon) in Vietnam was, in 1600, a small Cambodian village called Prey Nokor.

THE FRENCH IN CAMBODIA

The era of yo-yoing between Thai and Vietnamese masters came to a close in 1864, when French gunboats intimidated King Norodom I (r 1860–1904) into signing a treaty of protectorate. Ironically, it really was a protectorate, as Cambodia was in danger of going the way of Champa and vanishing from the map. French control of Cambodia developed as a sideshow to their interests in Vietnam, uncannily similar to the American experience a century later, and initially involved little direct interference in Cambodia's affairs. The French presence also helped keep Norodom on the throne despite the ambitions of his rebellious half-brothers.

By the 1870s French officials in Cambodia began pressing for greater control over internal affairs. In 1884 Norodom was forced into signing a treaty

1219	**1253**	**1296**
Jayavarman VII dies in his 90s and the empire of Angkor slowly declines due to a choking irrigation network, religious conflict and the rise of powerful neighbours.	The Mongols of Kublai Khan sack the Thai kingdom of Nanchao in Yunnan, sparking an exodus southwards which brought them into direct conflict with the weakening Khmer empire.	Chinese emissary Chou Ta-kuan spends one year living at Angkor and publishes the Memorials on the Customs of Cambodia, the only contemporary account of life at the great Khmer capital.

that turned his country into a virtual colony, sparking a two-year rebellion that constituted the only major uprising in Cambodia until WWII. The rebellion only ended when the king was persuaded to call upon the rebel fighters to lay down their weapons in exchange for a return to the status quo.

During the following decades senior Cambodian officials opened the door to direct French control over the day-to-day administration of the country, as they saw certain advantages in acquiescing to French power. The French maintained Norodom's court in a splendour unseen since the heyday of Angkor, helping to enhance the symbolic position of the monarchy. In 1907 the French were able to pressure Thailand into returning the northwest provinces of Battambang, Siem Reap and Sisophon in return for concessions of Lao territory to the Thais. This meant Angkor came under Cambodian control for the first time in more than a century.

> The French did very little to encourage education in Cambodia, and by the end of WWII, after 70 years of colonial rule, there were no universities and only one high school in the whole country.

King Norodom I was succeeded by King Sisowath (r 1904–27), who was succeeded by King Monivong (r 1927–41). Upon King Monivong's death, the French governor general of Japanese-occupied Indochina, Admiral Jean Decoux, placed 19-year-old Prince Norodom Sihanouk on the Cambodian throne. The French authorities assumed young Sihanouk would prove pliable, but this proved to be a major miscalculation (see the boxed text, opposite).

During WWII, Japanese forces occupied much of Asia, and Cambodia was no exception. However, with many in France collaborating with the occupying Germans, the Japanese were happy to let their new French allies control affairs in Cambodia. The price was conceding to Thailand (a Japanese ally of sorts) much of Battambang and Siem Reap Provinces once again, areas that weren't returned until 1947. However, with the fall of Paris in 1944 and French policy in disarray, the Japanese were forced to take direct control of the territory by early 1945. After WWII, the French returned, making Cambodia an autonomous state within the French Union, but retaining de facto control. The immediate postwar years were marked by strife among the country's various political factions, a situation made more unstable by the Franco-Viet Minh War then raging in Vietnam and Laos, which spilled over into Cambodia. The Vietnamese, as they were also to do 20 years later in the war against Lon Nol and the Americans, trained and fought with bands of Khmer Issarak (Free Khmer) against the French authorities.

> Cambodia's turbulent past is uncovered in a series of articles, oral histories and photos in an excellent website called 'Beauty and Darkness: Cambodia, the Odyssey of the Khmer People'. Find it at www.mekong .net/Cambodia.

THE SIHANOUK YEARS

The post-independence period was one of peace and great prosperity, Cambodia's golden years, a time of creativity and optimism. Phnom Penh grew in size and stature, the temples of Angkor were the leading tourist destination in Southeast Asia and Sihanouk played host to a succession of influential leaders from across the globe. However, dark clouds were circling, as the American war in Vietnam became a black hole, sucking in neighbouring countries.

1353	1431	1594
Lao prince Chao Fa Ngum ends his exile at Angkor and is sponsored by his Khmer father-in-law on an expedition to conquer the new Thai kingdoms, declaring himself leader of Lan Xang (land of a million elephants).	The expansionist Thais sack Angkor definitively, carting off most of the royal court to Ayuthaya, including nobles, priests, dancers and artisans.	The temporary Cambodian capital of Lovek falls when, according to legend, the Siamese fire a cannon of silver coins into the capital's bamboo defences. The soldiers cut down the protective bamboo to retrieve the silver, los_ing the city expos_

SIHANOUK: THE LAST OF THE GOD-KINGS

Norodom Sihanouk has been a towering presence in the topsy-turvy world of Cambodian politics. A larger-than-life character of many enthusiasms and shifting political positions, his amatory exploits dominated his early life. Later he became the prince who stage-managed the close of French colonialism, led Cambodia during its golden years, was imprisoned by the Khmer Rouge and, from privileged exile, finally returned triumphant as king. He is many things to many people, a political chameleon, but whatever else he may be, he has proved himself a survivor.

Sihanouk, born in 1922, was not an obvious contender for the throne, as he was from the Norodom branch of the royal family. He was crowned in 1941, at just 19, with his education incomplete. In 1955 Sihanouk abdicated and turned his attention to politics, his party winning every seat in parliament that year. By the mid-1960s Sihanouk had been calling the shots in Cambodia for a decade. During this period, after innumerable love affairs, he finally settled on Monique Izzi, the daughter of a Franco-Italian father and a Cambodian mother, as his consort.

The conventional wisdom was that 'Sihanouk is Cambodia', his leadership the key to national success. However, as the country was inexorably drawn into the American War in Vietnam and government troops battled with a leftist insurgency in the countryside, Sihanouk increasingly was seen as a liability. With the economy in tatters, his obsessive involvement in the Cambodian film industry (p55) and his public announcements proclaiming Cambodia 'an oasis of peace' suggested a man who had not only abdicated from the throne but also from reality.

On 18 March 1970 the National Assembly voted to remove Sihanouk from office. Sihanouk went into exile in Beijing and joined the communists. Following the Khmer Rouge victory on 17 April 1975, Sihanouk returned to Cambodia as head of the new state of Democratic Kampuchea. He resigned after less than a year and was confined to the Royal Palace as a prisoner of the Khmer Rouge. He remained there until early 1979 when, on the eve of the Vietnamese invasion, he was flown back to Beijing. It was to be more than a decade before Sihanouk finally returned to Cambodia.

Sihanouk never quite gave up wanting to be everything for Cambodia: international statesman, general, president, film director, man of the people. On 24 September 1993, after 38 years in politics, he settled once more for the role of king. His second stint as king was a frustrating time; reigning rather than ruling, he had to take a back seat to the politicians. He pulled Cambodia through a political impasse on several occasions, but eventually enough was enough and he abdicated on 7 October 2004. Many reasons for his abdication were cited (old age, failing health), but most observers agree it was a calculated political decision to ensure the future of the monarchy, as the politicians were stalling on choosing a successor. His son King Sihamoni ascended the throne and Cambodia came through another crisis. However, Sihanouk's place in history is assured, the last in a long line of Angkor's god-kings.

In late 1952 King Sihanouk dissolved the fledgling parliament, declared martial law and embarked on his 'royal crusade': his travelling campaign to drum up international support for his country's independence. Independence was proclaimed on 9 November 1953 and recognised by the

1618	**1772**	**1834**
The Cambodian capital moves to Udong for prolonged periods, a pair of strategic hills located about 40km west of Phnom Penh.	Cambodia is caught between the powerful Vietnamese and Siamese, and the latter burn Phnom Penh to the ground, another chapter in the story of inflamed tensions that persists today.	The Vietnamese take control of much of Cambodia during the reign of Emperor Minh Mang and begin a slow revolution to 'teach the barbarians their customs'.

Geneva Conference of May 1954, which ended French control of Indochina. In 1955, Sihanouk abdicated, afraid of being marginalised amid the pomp of royal ceremony. The 'royal crusader' became 'citizen Sihanouk'. He vowed never again to return to the throne. Meanwhile his father became king. It was a masterstroke that offered Sihanouk both royal authority and supreme political power. His newly established party, Sangkum Reastr Niyum (People's Socialist Community), won every seat in parliament in the September 1955 elections and Sihanouk was to dominate Cambodian politics for the next 15 years.

Although he feared the Vietnamese communists, Sihanouk considered South Vietnam and Thailand, both allies of the mistrusted USA, the greatest threats to Cambodia's security, even survival. In an attempt to fend off these many dangers, he declared Cambodia neutral and refused to accept further US aid, which had accounted for a substantial chunk of the country's military budget. He also nationalised many industries, including the rice trade. In 1965 Sihanouk, convinced that the USA had been plotting against him and his family, broke diplomatic relations with Washington and veered towards the North Vietnamese and China. In addition, he agreed to let the communists use Cambodian territory in their battle against South Vietnam and the USA. Sihanouk was taking sides, a dangerous position in a volatile region.

During the 1960s Cambodia was an oasis of peace while wars raged in neighbouring Vietnam and Laos. By 1970, that had all changed. For the full story, read *Sideshow: Kissinger, Nixon and the Destruction of Cambodia* by William Shawcross (1979).

These moves and his socialist economic policies alienated conservative elements in Cambodian society, including the army brass and the urban elite. At the same time, left-wing Cambodians, many of them educated abroad, deeply resented his domestic policies, which stifled political debate. Compounding Sihanouk's problems was the fact that all classes were fed up with the pervasive corruption in government ranks, some of it uncomfortably close to the royal family. Although most peasants revered Sihanouk as a semidivine figure, in 1967 a rural-based rebellion broke out in Samlot, Battambang, leading him to conclude that the greatest threat to his regime came from the left. Bowing to pressure from the army, he implemented a policy of harsh repression against left-wingers.

By 1969 the conflict between the army and leftist rebels had become more serious, as the Vietnamese sought sanctuary deeper in Cambodia. Sihanouk's political position had also decidedly deteriorated – due in no small part to his obsession with film-making, which was leading him to neglect affairs of state. In March 1970, while Sihanouk was on a trip to France, General Lon Nol and Prince Sisowath Sirik Matak, Sihanouk's cousin, deposed him as chief of state, apparently with tacit US consent. Sihanouk took up residence in Beijing, where he set up a government-in-exile in alliance with an indigenous Cambodian revolutionary movement that Sihanouk had nicknamed the Khmer Rouge. This was a definitive moment in contemporary Cambodian history, as the Khmer Rouge exploited its partnership with Sihanouk to draw new recruits into their small organisation. Talk to many

1864	**1885**	**1907**
The French force King Norodom I into signing a treaty of protectorate, which prevents Cambodia being wiped off the map and thus begins 90 years of French rule.	Rebellion against French rule in Cambodia breaks out in response to a new treaty giving the French administrators wide-ranging powers. The treaty is signed under the watch of French gunboats in the Mekong River.	French authorities successfully negotiate the return of the northwest provinces of Siem Reap, Battambang and Preah Vihear, which have been under Thai control since 1794.

former Khmer Rouge fighters and they all say that they 'went to the hills' (a euphemism for joining the Khmer Rouge) to fight for their king and knew nothing of Mao or Marxism.

DESCENT INTO CIVIL WAR

The lines were drawn for a bloody era of civil war. Sihanouk was condemned to death *in absentia*, an excessive move on the part of the new government that effectively ruled out any hint of compromise for the next five years. Lon Nol gave communist Vietnamese forces an ultimatum to withdraw their forces within one week, which amounted to a virtual declaration of war, as no Vietnamese fighters wanted to return to the homeland to face the Americans.

On 30 April 1970, US and South Vietnamese forces invaded Cambodia in an effort to flush out thousands of Viet Cong and North Vietnamese troops who were using Cambodian bases in their war to overthrow the South Vietnamese government. As a result of the invasion, the Vietnamese communists withdrew deeper into Cambodia, further destabilising the Lon Nol government. Cambodia's tiny army never stood a chance and within the space of a few months, Vietnamese forces and their Khmer Rouge allies overran almost half the country. The ultimate humiliation came in July 1970 when the Vietnamese occupied the temples of Angkor.

In 1969 the USA had begun a secret programme of bombing suspected communist base camps in Cambodia. For the next four years, until bombing was halted by the US Congress in August 1973, huge areas of the eastern half of the country were carpet-bombed by US B-52s, killing what is believed to be many thousands of civilians and turning hundreds of thousands more into refugees. Undoubtedly, the bombing campaign helped the Khmer Rouge in their recruitment drive, as more and more peasants were losing family members to the aerial assaults. While the final, heaviest bombing in the first half of 1973 may have saved Phnom Penh from a premature fall, its ferocity also helped to harden the attitude of many Khmer Rouge cadres and may have contributed to the later brutality that characterised their rule.

Savage fighting engulfed the country, bringing misery to millions of Cambodians; many fled rural areas for the relative safety of Phnom Penh and provincial capitals. Between 1970 and 1975 several hundred thousand people died in the fighting. During these years the Khmer Rouge came to play a dominant role in trying to overthrow the Lon Nol regime, strengthened by the support of the Vietnamese, although the Khmer Rouge leadership would vehemently deny this from 1975 onwards.

The leadership of the Khmer Rouge, including Paris-educated Pol Pot and Ieng Sary, had fled into the countryside in the 1960s to escape the summary justice then being meted out to suspected leftists by Sihanouk's security forces. They consolidated control over the movement and began to move

In Francis Ford Coppola's *Apocalypse Now* a renegade colonel, played by Marlon Brando, goes AWOL in Cambodia. Martin Sheen plays a young soldier sent to bring him back, and the ensuing encounter makes for one of the most powerful indictments of war ever made.

Lon Nol's military press attaché was known for his colourful, even imaginative media briefings that painted a rosy picture of the increasingly desperate situation on the ground. With a name like Major Am Rong, few could take him seriously.

Pol Pot travelled up the Ho Chi Minh Trail to visit Beijing in 1966 at the height of the Cultural Revolution there. He was obviously inspired by what he saw, as the Khmer Rouge went even further than the Red Guards in severing links with the past.

1942	1947	1953
Japanese forces occupy Cambodia, leaving the administration in the hands of Vichy France officials, but fan the flames of independence as the war draws to a close.	The provinces of Battambang, Siem Reap and Sisophon, seized by the Thais during the Japanese occupation, are returned to Cambodia.	Sihanouk's royal crusade for independence succeeds and Cambodia goes it alone without the French on 9 November, ushering in a new era of optimism.

against opponents before they took Phnom Penh. Many of the Vietnamese-trained Cambodian communists who had been based in Hanoi since the 1954 Geneva Accords returned down the Ho Chi Minh Trail to join their 'allies' in the Khmer Rouge in 1973. Many were dead by 1975, executed on orders of the anti-Vietnamese Pol Pot faction. Likewise, many moderate Sihanouk supporters who had joined the Khmer Rouge as a show of loyalty to their fallen leader rather than a show of ideology to the radicals were victims of purges before the regime took power. This set a precedent for internal purges and mass executions that were to eventually bring the downfall of the Khmer Rouge.

It didn't take long for the Lon Nol government to become very unpopular as a result of unprecedented greed and corruption in its ranks. As the USA bankrolled the war, government and military personnel found lucrative means to make a fortune, such as inventing 'phantom soldiers' and pocketing their pay, or selling weapons to the enemy. Lon Nol was widely perceived as an ineffectual leader, obsessed by superstition, fortune tellers and mystical crusades. This perception increased with his stroke in March 1971 and for the next four years his grip on reality seemed to weaken as his brother Lon Non's power grew.

Despite massive US military and economic aid, Lon Nol never succeeded in gaining the initiative against the Khmer Rouge. Large parts of the countryside fell to the rebels and many provincial capitals were cut off from Phnom Penh. Lon Nol fled the country in early April 1975, leaving Sirik Matak in charge, who refused evacuation to the end. 'I cannot alas leave in such a cowardly fashion…I have committed only one mistake, that of believing in you, the Americans' were the words Sirik Matak poignantly penned to US ambassador John Gunther Dean. On 17 April 1975 – two weeks before the fall of Saigon (now Ho Chi Minh City) – Phnom Penh surrendered to the Khmer Rouge.

THE KHMER ROUGE REVOLUTION

Upon taking Phnom Penh, the Khmer Rouge implemented one of the most radical and brutal restructurings of a society ever attempted; its goal was a pure revolution, untainted by those that had gone before, to transform Cambodia into a peasant-dominated agrarian cooperative. Within days of coming to power the entire population of Phnom Penh and provincial towns, including the sick, elderly and infirm, was forced to march into the countryside and work as slaves for 12 to 15 hours a day. Disobedience of any sort often brought immediate execution. The advent of Khmer Rouge rule was proclaimed Year Zero. Currency was abolished and postal services were halted. The country cut itself off from the outside world.

In the eyes of Pol Pot, the Khmer Rouge was not a unified movement, but a series of factions that needed to be cleansed. This process had already begun with attacks on Vietnamese-trained Khmer Rouge and Sihanouk's supporters, but Pol Pot's initial fury upon seizing power was directed against

1955	1962	1963
King Sihanouk abdicates from the throne to enter a career in politics; he founds the Sangkum Reastr Niyum (People's Socialist Community) party and wins the election with ease.	The International Court rules in favour of Cambodia in the long-running dispute over the dramatic mountain temple of Preah Vihear, perched on the Dangkrek Mountains.	Pol Pot and Ieng Sary flee from Phnom Penh to the jungles of Ratanakiri to launch a guerrilla war against Sihanouk's government with training from the Vietnamese.

BLOOD BROTHER NO 1

Pol Pot, Brother No 1 in the Khmer Rouge regime, is a name that sends shivers down the spines of Cambodians and foreigners alike. It is Pol Pot who is most associated with the bloody madness of the regime he led between 1975 and 1979, and his policies heaped misery, suffering and death on millions of Cambodians.

Pol Pot was born Saloth Sar in a small village near Kompong Thom in 1925. As a young man he won a scholarship to study in Paris, and it is here that he is believed to have developed his radical Marxist thought, later to transform into the politics of extreme Maoism.

In 1963 Sihanouk's repressive policies sent Saloth Sar and comrades fleeing to the jungles of Ratanakiri. It was from this moment that he began to call himself Pol Pot. Once the Khmer Rouge was allied with Sihanouk, following his overthrow by Lon Nol in 1970 and subsequent exile in Beijing, its support soared and the faces of the leadership became familiar. However, Pol Pot remained a shadowy figure, leaving public duties to Khieu Samphan and Ieng Sary.

When the Khmer Rouge marched into Phnom Penh on 17 April 1975, few people could have anticipated the hell that was to follow. Pol Pot and his clique were the architects of one of the most radical and brutal revolutions in the history of mankind. 1975 was Year Zero and Cambodia was on a self-destructive course to sever all ties with the past.

Pol Pot was not to emerge as the public face of the revolution until the end of 1976, after returning from a trip to his mentors in Beijing. He granted almost no interviews to foreign media and was seen only on propaganda movies produced by government TV. Such was his aura and reputation that by the last year of the regime a cult of personality was developing around him and stone busts were produced.

When the Vietnamese invaded Cambodia on 25 December 1978, Pol Pot and his supporters fled into the jungle near the Thai border, from where they spent the next decade launching attacks on government positions in Cambodia.

Pol Pot spent much of the 1980s living in Thailand and was able to rebuild his shattered forces and once again threaten Cambodia. His enigma increased as the international media speculated as to the real fate of Pol Pot. His demise was reported so often that when he finally passed away, many Cambodians refused to believe it until they had seen his body on TV or in newspapers. Even then, many were sceptical and rumours continue to circulate about exactly how he met his end. He died on 15 April 1998.

For more on the life and times of Pol Pot, pick up one of the excellent biographies written about him: *Brother Number One* by David Chandler or *Pol Pot: The History of a Nightmare* by Phillip Short.

the former regime. All of the senior government and military figures who had been associated with Lon Nol were executed within days of the takeover. Then the centre shifted its attention to the outer regions, which had been separated into geographic zones. The loyalist Southwestern Zone forces under the control of one-legged general Ta Mok were sent into region after region to purify the population, and thousands perished.

1964	**1969**	**1970**
Following the US-sponsored coup against President Diem in South Vietnam in 1963, Sihanouk veers to the left, breaking diplomatic ties with the USA and nationalising the rice trade, antagonising the ethnic Chinese business community.	US President Nixon authorises the secret bombing of Cambodia, which starts with the carpet bombing of border zones, but eventually spreads to the whole country, continuing until 1973 and killing as many as 250,000 Cambodians.	Sihanouk throws in his lot with the Khmer Rouge after being overthrown by military commander Lon Nol and his cousin Prince Sirik Matak, and sentenced to death *in absentia*, marking the start of a five-year civil war.

For a fuller understanding of the methodical machine that was the Khmer Rouge's interrogation and torture centre of S-21, read the classic but chilling *Voices from S-21* by David Chandler (1999).

The cleansing reached grotesque heights in the final and bloodiest purge against the powerful and independent Eastern Zone. Generally considered more moderate than other Khmer Rouge factions, the Eastern Zone was ideologically, as well as geographically, closer to Vietnam. The Pol Pot faction consolidated the rest of the country before moving against the east from 1977 onwards. Hundreds of leaders were executed before open rebellion broke out, sparking a civil war in the east. Many Eastern Zone leaders fled to Vietnam, forming the nucleus of the government installed by the Vietnamese in January 1979. The people were defenceless and distrusted – 'Cambodian bodies with Vietnamese minds' or 'duck's arses with chicken's heads' – and were deported to the northwest with new, blue *krama* (scarves). Had it not been for the Vietnamese invasion, all would have perished, as the blue *krama* was a secret party sign indicating an eastern enemy of the revolution.

It is still not known exactly how many Cambodians died at the hands of the Khmer Rouge during the three years, eight months and 20 days of their rule. The Vietnamese claimed three million deaths, while foreign experts long considered the number closer to one million. Yale University researchers undertaking ongoing investigations estimated that the figure was close to two million.

To the End of Hell: One Woman's Struggle to Survive Cambodia's Khmer Rouge is the incredible memoir of Denise Affonco, one of the only foreigners to live through the Khmer Rouge revolution due to her marriage to a senior intellectual in the movement.

Hundreds of thousands of people were executed by the Khmer Rouge leadership, while hundreds of thousands more died of famine and disease. Meals consisted of little more than watery rice porridge twice a day, meant to sustain men, women and children through a back-breaking day in the fields. Disease stalked the work camps, malaria and dysentery striking down whole families; death was a relief for many from the horrors of life. Some zones were better than others, some leaders fairer than others, but life for the majority was one of unending misery and suffering in this 'prison without walls'.

As the centre eliminated more and more moderates, Angkar (the organisation) became the only family people needed and those who did not agree were sought out and destroyed. The Khmer Rouge detached the Cambodian people from all they held dear: their families, their food, their fields and their faith. Even the peasants who had supported the revolution could no longer blindly follow such madness. Nobody cared for the Khmer Rouge by 1978, but nobody had an ounce of strength to do anything about it…except the Vietnamese.

Only a handful of foreigners were allowed to visit Cambodia during the Khmer Rouge period of Democratic Kampuchea. US journalist Elizabeth Becker was one who travelled there in late 1978; her book *When the War Was Over* (1986) tells her story.

ENTER THE VIETNAMESE

Relations between Cambodia and Vietnam have historically been tense, as the Vietnamese have slowly but steadily expanded southwards, encroaching on Cambodian territory. Despite the fact the two communist parties had fought together as brothers-in-arms, old tensions soon came to the fore.

From 1976 to 1978, the Khmer Rouge instigated a series of border clashes with Vietnam, and claimed the Mekong Delta, once part of the Khmer empire.

1971	1973	1975
Lon Nol, leader of the Khmer Republic, launches the Chenla offensive against Vietnamese communists and their Khmer Rouge allies in Cambodia, but it turns out to be a disaster. He also suffers a stroke, but struggles on as leader until 1975.	Sihanouk and his wife Monique travel down the Ho Chi Minh Trail to visit his Khmer Rouge allies at the holy mountain of Phnom Kulen near Angkor, a propaganda victory for Pol Pot.	The Khmer Rouge march into Phnom Penh on 17 April and turn the clocks back to Year Zero, evacuating the capital and turning the whole nation into a prison without walls.

THE POLITICS OF DISASTER RELIEF

The Cambodian famine became a new front in the Cold War, as Washington and Moscow jostled for influence from afar. As hundreds of thousands of Cambodians fled to Thailand, a massive international famine relief effort, sponsored by the UN, was launched. The international community wanted to deliver aid across a land bridge at Poipet, while the new Vietnamese-backed Phnom Penh government wanted all supplies to come through the capital via Kompong Som (Sihanoukville) or the Mekong River. Both sides had their reasons – the new government did not want aid to fall into the hands of its Khmer Rouge enemies, while the international community didn't believe the new government had the infrastructure to distribute the aid – and both were right.

Some agencies distributed aid the slow way through Phnom Penh, and others set up camps in Thailand. The camps became a magnet for half of Cambodia, as many Khmers still feared the return of the Khmer Rouge or were seeking a new life overseas. The Thai military convinced the international community to distribute all aid through their channels and used this as a cloak to rebuild the shattered Khmer Rouge forces as an effective resistance against the Vietnamese. Thailand demanded that, as a condition for allowing international food aid for Cambodia to pass through its territory, food had to be supplied to the Khmer Rouge forces encamped in the Thai border region as well. Along with weaponry supplied by China, this international assistance was essential in enabling the Khmer Rouge to rebuild its military strength and fight on for another two decades.

Incursions into Vietnamese border provinces left hundreds of Vietnamese civilians dead. On 25 December 1978 Vietnam launched a full-scale invasion of Cambodia, toppling the Pol Pot government two weeks later. As Vietnamese tanks neared Phnom Penh, the Khmer Rouge fled westward with as many civilians as it could seize, taking refuge in the jungles and mountains along the Thai border. The Vietnamese installed a new government led by several former Khmer Rouge officers, including current Prime Minister Hun Sen, who had defected to Vietnam in 1977. The Khmer Rouge's patrons, the Chinese communists, launched a massive reprisal raid across Vietnam's northernmost border in early 1979 in an attempt to buy their allies time. It failed, and after 17 days the Chinese withdrew, their fingers badly burnt by their Vietnamese enemies. The Vietnamese then staged a show trial in which Pol Pot and Ieng Sary were condemned to death for their genocidal acts.

A traumatised population took to the road in search of surviving family members. Millions had been uprooted and had to walk hundreds of kilometres across the country. Rice stocks were destroyed, the harvest left to wither and little rice planted, sowing the seeds for a widespread famine in 1979 and 1980.

As the conflict in Cambodia raged, Sihanouk agreed, under pressure from China, to head a military and political front opposed to the Phnom Penh

During much of the 1980s, the second-largest concentration of Cambodians outside of Phnom Penh was in the Khao I Dang refugee camp on the Thai border.

1977

The Pol Pot faction of the Khmer Rouge launch their bloodiest purge against the Eastern Zone of the country, sparking a civil war along the banks of the Mekong and drawing the Vietnamese into the battle.

1979

Vietnamese forces liberate Cambodia from Khmer Rouge rule on 7 January 1979, just two weeks after launching the invasion, and install a friendly regime in Phnom Penh.

1980

Cambodia is gripped by a terrible famine, as the dislocation of the previous few years means that no rice has been planted or harvested, and worldwide Save Kampuchea appeals are launched.

government. The Sihanouk-led resistance coalition brought together – on paper, at least – Funcinpec (the French acronym for the National United Front for an Independent, Neutral, Peaceful and Cooperative Cambodia), which comprised a royalist group loyal to Sihanouk; the Khmer People's National Liberation Front, a noncommunist grouping formed by former prime minister Son Sann; and the Khmer Rouge, officially known as the Party of Democratic Kampuchea and by far the most powerful of the three. The heinous crimes of the Khmer Rouge were swept aside to ensure a compromise that suited the great powers.

During the mid-1980s the British government dispatched the Special Air Service (SAS) to a Malaysian jungle camp to train guerrilla fighters in land mine–laying techniques. Although officially assisting the smaller factions, it is certain the Khmer Rouge benefited from this experience. It then used these new-found skills to intimidate and terrorise the Cambodian people. The USA gave more than US$15 million a year in aid to the noncommunist factions of the Khmer Rouge-dominated coalition.

For much of the 1980s Cambodia remained closed to the Western world, save for the presence of some humanitarian aid groups. Government policy was effectively under the control of the Vietnamese, so Cambodia found itself very much in the Eastern-bloc camp. The economy was in tatters for much of this period, as Cambodia, like Vietnam, suffered from the effects of a US-sponsored embargo.

In 1984 the Vietnamese overran all the major rebel camps inside Cambodia, forcing the Khmer Rouge and its allies to retreat into Thailand. From this time the Khmer Rouge and its allies engaged in guerrilla warfare aimed at demoralising their opponents. Tactics used by the Khmer Rouge included shelling government-controlled garrison towns, planting thousands of mines in rural areas, attacking road transport, blowing up bridges, kidnapping village chiefs and targeting civilians. The Khmer Rouge also forced thousands of men, women and children living in the refugee camps it controlled to work as porters, ferrying ammunition and other supplies into Cambodia across heavily mined sections of the border. The Vietnamese for their part laid the world's longest minefield, known as K-5 and stretching from the Gulf of Thailand to the Lao border, in an attempt to seal off the guerrillas. They also sent Cambodians into the forests to cut down trees on remote sections of road to prevent ambushes. Thousands died of disease and from injuries sustained from land mines. The Khmer Rouge was no longer in power, but for many the 1980s was almost as tough as the 1970s, one long struggle to survive.

THE UN COMES TO TOWN

As the Cold War came to a close, peace began to break out all over the globe, and Cambodia was not immune to the new spirit of reconciliation. In September 1989 Vietnam, its economy in tatters and eager to end its

Between four and six million land mines dot the Cambodian countryside. Lifetime rehabilitation of the country's estimated 40,000 victims costs US$120 million.

Journalist Henry Kamm spent many years filing reports from Cambodia and his book *Cambodia: Report from a Stricken Land* is a fascinating insight into recent events.

Learn more about politics and life in Cambodia during the 1980s; pick up *Cambodia After the Khmer Rouge* by Evan Gottesman, which sheds new light on a little-known period.

1982	1984	1985
Sihanouk is pressured to join forces with the Khmer Rouge as head of the Coalition Government of Democratic Kampuchea (CGDK), a new military front against the Vietnamese-backed government in Phnom Penh.	The Vietnamese embark on a major offensive in the west of Cambodia and the Khmer Rouge and its allies are forced to retreat to refugee camps and bases inside Thailand.	There is a changing of the guard at the top and Hun Sen becomes Prime Minister of Cambodia, a title he still holds today with the Cambodian People's Party.

THE NAME GAME

Cambodia has changed its name so many times over the last few decades that there are understandable grounds for confusion. To the Cambodians, their country is Kampuchea. The name is derived from the word Kambuja, meaning 'those born of Kambu', the mythical founder of the country. It dates back as far as the 10th century. The Portuguese 'Camboxa' and the French 'Cambodge', from which the English name 'Cambodia' is derived, are adaptations of 'Kambuja'.

Since gaining independence in 1953, the country has been known in English by various names before coming full circle:

- The Kingdom of Cambodia
- The Khmer Republic (under Lon Nol, who reigned from 1970 to 1975)
- Democratic Kampuchea (under the Khmer Rouge, which controlled the country from 1975 to 1979)
- The People's Republic of Kampuchea (under the Vietnamese-backed government from 1979 to 1989)
- The State of Cambodia (from mid-1989)
- The Kingdom of Cambodia (from May 1993)

It was the Khmer Rouge that insisted the outside world use the name Kampuchea. Changing the country's official English name back to Cambodia was intended as a symbolic move to distance the present government in Phnom Penh from the bitter connotations of the name Kampuchea, which Westerners associate with the murderous Khmer Rouge regime.

international isolation, announced the withdrawal of all of its troops from Cambodia. With the Vietnamese gone, the opposition coalition, still dominated by the Khmer Rouge, launched a series of offensives, forcing the now-vulnerable government to the negotiating table.

Diplomatic efforts to end the civil war began to bear fruit in September 1990, when a peace plan was accepted by both the Phnom Penh government and the three factions of the resistance coalition. According to the plan, the Supreme National Council (SNC), a coalition of all factions, would be formed under the presidency of Sihanouk. Meanwhile the UN Transitional Authority in Cambodia (Untac) would supervise the administration of the country for two years with the goal of free and fair elections.

Untac undoubtedly achieved some successes, but for all of these, it is the failures that were to cost Cambodia dearly in the 'democratic' era. Untac was successful in pushing through many international human-rights covenants; it opened the door to a significant number of nongovernmental organisations (NGOs) who have helped build civil society; and, most importantly, on 25 May 1993, elections were held with an 89.6% turnout.

Western powers, including the US and UK, ensured the Khmer Rouge retained its seat at the UN general assembly in New York until 1991, a scenario that saw those responsible for the genocide representing their victims on the international stage.

1989	1991	1993
As the effects of President Gorbachev's perestroika (restructuring) begin to impact on communist allies, Vietnam feels the pinch and announces the withdrawal of its forces from Cambodia.	The Paris Peace Accords are signed, in which all parties, including the Khmer Rouge, agree to participate in free and fair elections supervised by the UN.	The pro-Sihanouk Royalist party Funcinpec under the leadership of Prince Ranariddh wins the popular vote, but the CPP threaten secession in the east to muscle their way into government.

However, the results were far from decisive. Funcinpec, led by Prince Norodom Ranariddh, took 58 seats in the National Assembly, while the Cambodian People's Party (CPP), which represented the previous communist government, took 51 seats. The CPP had lost the election, but senior leaders threatened a secession of the eastern provinces of the country. As a result, Cambodia ended up with two prime ministers: Norodom Ranariddh as first prime minister, and Hun Sen as second prime minister.

Some critics contend that the UN presence kick-started Cambodia's HIV/Aids epidemic, with well-paid overseas soldiers boosting the prostitution industry.

Even today, Untac is heralded as one of the UN's success stories. The other perspective is that it was an ill-conceived and poorly executed peace because so many of the powers involved in brokering the deal had their own agendas to advance. To many Cambodians, it must have seemed a cruel joke that the Khmer Rouge was allowed to play a part in the process.

The UN's disarmament programme took weapons away from rural militias who for so long provided the backbone of the government's provincial defence network against the Khmer Rouge. This left communities throughout the country vulnerable to attack, while the Khmer Rouge used the veil of legitimacy conferred upon it by the peace process to re-establish a guerrilla network throughout Cambodia. By 1994, when it was finally outlawed by the government, the Khmer Rouge was probably a greater threat to the stability of Cambodia than at any time since 1979.

Untac's main goals had been to 'restore and maintain peace' and 'promote national reconciliation' and in the short term it achieved neither. It did oversee free and fair elections, but these were later annulled by the actions of Cambodia's politicians. Little was done during the UN period to try to dismantle the communist apparatus of state set up by the CPP, a well-oiled machine that continues to ensure that former communists control the civil service, judiciary, army and police today.

The Documentation Center of Cambodia is an organisation established to document the crimes of the Khmer Rouge as a record for future generations. Its excellent website is a mine of information about Cambodia's darkest hour. Take your time to visit www.dccam.org.

THE SLOW BIRTH OF PEACE

When the Vietnamese toppled the Pol Pot government in 1979, the Khmer Rouge disappeared into the jungle. The guerrillas eventually boycotted the 1993 elections and later rejected peace talks aimed at creating a ceasefire. The defection of some 2000 troops from the Khmer Rouge army in the months after the elections offered some hope that the long-running insurrection would fizzle out. However, government-sponsored amnesty programmes initially turned out to be ill-conceived: the policy of reconscripting Khmer Rouge troops and forcing them to fight their former comrades provided little incentive to desert.

In 1994 the Khmer Rouge resorted to a new tactic of targeting tourists, with horrendous results for a number of foreigners in Cambodia. During 1994 three people were taken from a taxi on the road to Sihanoukville and subsequently shot. A few months later another three foreigners were

1994	**1995**	**1997**
The Khmer Rouge target foreign tourists in Cambodia, kidnapping and killing groups travelling by taxi and train to the south coast, reinforcing Cambodia' overseas image as a dangerous country.	Prince Norodom Sirivudh is arrested and exiled for allegedly plotting to kill Prime Minister Hun Sen, removing another potential rival from the scene.	Second Prime Minister Hun Sen overthrows First Prime Minister Norodom Ranariddh in a military coup, referred to as 'the events of 1997' in Cambodia.

seized from a train bound for Sihanoukville and in the ransom drama that followed they were executed as the army closed in.

The government changed course during the mid-1990s, opting for more carrot and less stick in a bid to end the war. The breakthrough came in 1996 when Ieng Sary, Brother No 3 in the Khmer Rouge hierarchy and foreign minister during its rule, was denounced by Pol Pot for corruption. He subsequently led a mass defection of fighters and their dependants from the Pailin area, and this effectively sealed the fate of the remaining Khmer Rouge. Pailin, rich in gems and timber, had long been the economic crutch which kept the Khmer Rouge hobbling along. The severing of this income, coupled with the fact that government forces now had only one front on which to concentrate their resources, suggested the days of civil war were numbered.

By 1997 cracks were appearing in the coalition and the fledgling democracy once again found itself under siege. But it was the Khmer Rouge that again grabbed the headlines. Pol Pot ordered the execution of Son Sen, defence minister during the Khmer Rouge regime, and many of his family members. This provoked a putsch within the Khmer Rouge leadership, and the one-legged hardline general Ta Mok seized control, putting Pol Pot on 'trial'. Rumours flew about Phnom Penh that Pol Pot would be brought there to face international justice, but events dramatically shifted back to the capital.

A lengthy courting period ensued in which both Funcinpec and the CPP attempted to win the trust of the remaining Khmer Rouge hard-liners in northern Cambodia. Ranariddh was close to forging a deal with the jungle fighters and was keen to get it sewn up before Cambodia's accession to Asean, as nothing would provide a better entry fanfare than the ending of Cambodia's long civil war. He was outflanked and subsequently outgunned by Second Prime Minister Hun Sen. On 5 July 1997 fighting again erupted on the streets of Phnom Penh as troops loyal to the CPP clashed with those loyal to Funcinpec. The heaviest exchanges were around the airport and key government buildings, but before long the dust had settled and the CPP once again controlled Cambodia. The strongman had finally flexed his muscles and there was no doubt as to which party was running the show.

Following the coup, the remnants of Funcinpec forces on the Thai border around O Smach formed an alliance with the last of the Khmer Rouge under Ta Mok's control. The fighting may have ended, but the deaths did not stop there: several prominent Funcinpec politicians and military leaders were victims of extrajudicial executions, and even today no-one has been brought to justice for these crimes. Many of Funcinpec's leading politicians fled abroad, while the senior generals led the resistance struggle on the ground.

As 1998 began, the CPP announced an all-out offensive against its enemies in the north. By April it was closing in on the Khmer Rouge strongholds of Anlong Veng and Preah Vihear, and amid this heavy fighting Pol Pot evaded justice by dying a sorry death on 15 April in the Khmer Rouge's captivity. The

On 31 March 1997 a grenade was thrown into a group of Sam Rainsy supporters demonstrating outside the National Assembly. Sam Rainsy blamed Hun Sen and the CPP for the attack and even the FBI got involved in the investigation.

To stay on top of recent events in Cambodia, including all the highs and lows of the last decade, check out the Phnom Penh Post website at www.phnompenhpost .com or consider investing in its archived CD-ROM.

For the latest on political gossip in Cambodia, visit http://ki-media.blogspot .com.

1998	**1999**	**2002**
Pol Pot passes away on 15 April 1998 as Anlong Veng falls to government forces, and many observers ponder whether the timing is coincidental.	Cambodia finally joins Asean after a two-year delay, taking its place among the family of Southeast Asian nations, welcoming the country back to the world stage.	Cambodia holds its first ever local elections at commune level, a tentative step in dismantling the old communist system of control and bringing grass-roots democracy to the country.

fall of Anlong Veng in April was followed by the fall of Preah Vihear in May, and the big three, Ta Mok, Khieu Samphan and Nuon Chea, were forced to flee into the jungle near the Thai border with their remaining troops.

The 1998 election result reinforced the reality that the CPP was now the dominant force in the Cambodian political system and on 25 December Hun Sen received the Christmas present he had been waiting for: Khieu Samphan and Nuon Chea were defecting to the government side. The international community began to pile on the pressure for the establishment of some sort of war-crimes tribunal to try the remaining Khmer Rouge leadership. After lengthy negotiations, agreement was finally reached on the composition of a court to try the surviving leaders of the Khmer Rouge. The CPP was suspicious of a UN-administered trial as the UN had sided with the Khmer Rouge–dominated coalition against the government in Phnom Penh and the ruling party wanted a major say in who was to be tried for what. The UN for its part doubted that the judiciary in Cambodia was sophisticated or impartial enough to fairly oversee such a major trial. A compromise solution – a mixed tribunal of three international and four Cambodian judges requiring a super majority of five plus three for a verdict – was eventually agreed upon.

Early 2002 saw Cambodia's first ever local elections to select village and commune level representatives, an important step in bringing grassroots democracy to the country. Despite national elections since 1993, the CPP continued to monopolise political power at local and regional levels and only with commune elections would this grip be loosened. The national elections of July 2003 saw a shift in the balance of power, as the CPP consolidated their grip on Cambodia and the Sam Rainsy Party overhauled Funcinpec as the second party. After nearly a year of negotiating, Funcinpec ditched the Sam Rainsy Party once again and put their heads in the trough with the CPP for another term.

CONTEMPORARY CAMBODIA

Cambodia is at a crossroads in its road to recovery from the brutal years of Khmer Rouge rule. Compare Cambodia today with the dark abyss into which it plunged under the Khmer Rouge and the picture looks pretty healthy, but look to its more successful neighbours and it's easy to be pessimistic. Cambodia must choose its path: pluralism, progress and prosperity or intimidation, impunity and injustice. The jury is still very much out on which way things will go.

Another jury still out is that of the Khmer Rouge trial, sidelined by the politics of the Cold War for two decades, and then delayed by bureaucratic bickering at home and abroad. The trial is finally underway after many a dispute between the Cambodian authorities and the international community, but it is by no means certain that the wheels of justice will turn fast enough to keep up with the rapid ageing of the surviving Khmer Rouge leaders. Military commander Ta Mok died in custody in 2006 and both

When Pol Pot passed away on 15 April 1998, his body was hastily cremated on a pyre of burning tyres without an autopsy, leading many Cambodians to speculate that he was actually murdered.

The Khmer Rouge period is politically sensitive in Cambodia, due in part to the connections the current leadership have with the communist movement, so much so that the genocide is not currently taught in schools.

Evictions and land grabs have resulted in several communities being kicked out of Phnom Penh and moved to arid (or flooded) fields, miles from the city.

2003	2004	2005
The CPP wins the election, but political infighting prevents the formation of the new government for almost a year until the old coalition with Funcinpec is revived.	In a move that catches observers by surprise, King Sihanouk abdicates from the throne and is succeeded by his son King Sihamoni, a popular choice as he has steered clear of politics.	Cambodia joins the WTO, opening its markets to free trade, but many commentators feel it could be counterproductive as the economy is so small and there is no more protection for domestic producers.

Ieng Sary and Nuon Chea are suffering from health complications. In the meantime, the budget for the trial just keeps on rising, reaching the US$150 million mark, amid allegations of corruption and political interference on the Cambodia side. The Khmer people deserve justice after so much suffering, but it could be argued that the nation would have been better served by a truth and reconciliation commission to get to the bottom of the who, how and whys, to cleanse the nation's soul without seeking revenge. Knowing the truth could prove more cathartic to the average Cambodian than seeing a gang of septuagenarian revolutionaries on trial, 25 years too late.

Keep up to date with the latest developments in the Khmer Rouge trial by visiting the official website of the Cambodian Tribunal Monitor at www.cambodiatribunal-monitor.org.

The royal family has been a constant in contemporary Cambodian history and no-one more so than the mercurial monarch King Sihanouk, who once again surprised the world with his abdication in 2004. His relatively unknown son King Sihamoni assumed the throne and has brought renewed credibility to the monarchy, untainted as he is by the partisan politics of the past. Meanwhile, the political arm of the royal family, Funcinpec, has continued to haemorrhage. Prince Ranariddh was ousted as leader of the party he founded, launching his own Norodom Ranariddh Party. Some democrats jumped ship to join Sam Rainsy, while others defected to join the CPP. Meanwhile Ranariddh was forced into exile on charges of 'breach of trust' for adultery and selling the Funcinpec party headquarters. The end result of all the machinations is two parties claiming the royalist mantle, their cause weaker and more divided than ever before.

For a no-holds-barred look at contemporary Cambodia through the eyes of its diverse population, look out for a copy of *Cambodia Now* by Karen Coates.

But there's a new royal family in town, the CPP, and they are making plans for the future with dynastic alliances between their offspring. Just look at the roll call of marriages in the past decade and it soon seems apparent that senior leaders have their eyes firmly on the future and a handover of power to the children of the CPP. At the head of this elite is Prime Minister Hun Sen, who has proved himself a survivor, personally as well as politically, for he lost an eye during the battle for Phnom Penh in 1975.

As the 2008 elections unfold, the CPP and the royalist party remain unlikely bedfellows in government. Sam Rainsy continues to berate the country's rulers for their lack of leadership and is making real inroads in urban areas, setting the stage for some spicy showdowns with the CPP in the coming years. Sometimes they get a little too spicy and in 2005 Sam Rainsy and two of his fellow parliamentarians were stripped of their immunity from prosecution and charged with defamation. The more Cambodia integrates into the regional economy and the more investment continues to flow, the harder it will be for politicians to go back to old ways. One way or the other, it looks like Funcinpec are on a one-way ticket out of the political scene and future contests will be between the entrenched CPP and the upwardly mobile Sam Rainsy Party.

Several of the current crop of Cambodian leaders were previously members of the Khmer Rouge, including Prime Minister Hun Sen and Head of the Senate Chea Sim, although there is no evidence to implicate them in mass killings.

2006	2007	2008
Lawsuits and counter lawsuits see political leaders swapping lead for lawyers in the new Cambodia and the revolving door ends with opposition leader Sam Rainsy back in the country and Prince Ranariddh out.	Royalist party Funcinpec continues to implode in the face of conflict, intrigue and defections, democrats joining Sam Rainsy, loyalists joining the new Norodom Ranariddh Party and others joining the CPP.	It is election time again. Will the CPP triumph again or will Sam Rainsy surge ahead?

The Culture

THE NATIONAL PSYCHE

Since the glory days of the Angkor empire of old, the Cambodian people have been on the losing side of many a historical battle, their country all too often a minnow amid the circling sharks. Popular attitudes have been shaped by this history, and the relationship between Cambodia and its neighbours Thailand and Vietnam is marked by a cocktail of fear, admiration and animosity.

Cambodian attitudes towards the Thais and Vietnamese are complex. The Thais aren't always popular, as some Cambodians feel the Thais fail to acknowledge their cultural debt to Cambodia, still teach that Angkor belongs to Thailand in schools and generally look down on their poorer neighbour. Cambodian attitudes towards the Vietnamese are more ambivalent. There is a certain level of mistrust, as many feel the Vietnamese are out to colonise their country. (Many Khmers still call the lost Mekong Delta 'Kampuchea Krom' or 'Lower Cambodia'.) However, it is balanced with a grudging respect for their 'liberation' from the Khmer Rouge in 1979 (see p36). But when liberation became occupation in the 1980s, the relationship soon soured once more.

The Cambodian and Lao people share a close bond, as Fa Ngum, the founder of the original Lao kingdom of Lan Xang (Land of a Million Elephants), was sponsored by the kings of Angkor.

At first glance, Cambodia appears to be a nation of shiny, happy people, but look deeper and it is a country of contradictions. Light and dark, rich and poor, love and hate, life and death – all are visible on a journey through the kingdom. Most telling of all is the nation's glorious past set against its tragic present.

Angkor is everywhere: on the flag, the national beer, hotels and guesthouses, cigarettes – anything and everything. It's a symbol of nationhood and of fierce pride; Cambodians built Angkor Wat and it doesn't come bigger than that.

Jayavarman VII, Angkor's greatest king, is nearly as omnipresent as his temples. The man that vanquished the occupying Chams and took the empire to its greatest glories is a national hero.

Jayavarman VII was a Mahayana Buddhist and directed his faith towards improving the lot of his people, with the construction of hospitals, universities, roads and shelters.

Contrast this with the abyss into which the nation was sucked during the years of the Khmer Rouge. Pol Pot is a dirty word in Cambodia due to the death and suffering he inflicted on the country. Whenever you hear his name, it will be connected with stories of endless personal tragedy, of dead brothers, mothers and babies, from which most Cambodians have never had the chance to recover. No-one has yet tasted justice, the whys and hows remain unanswered and the older generation must live with the shadow of this trauma.

If Jayavarman VII and Angkor are loved and Pol Pot and the Khmer Rouge despised, then the mercurial Sihanouk, the last of the god-kings who has ultimately shown his human side, is somewhere inbetween. Many Cambodians love him as the 'father of the nation', but to others he is the man who failed the nation by his association with the Khmer Rouge. In many ways, his contradictions match those of contemporary Cambodia. Understand Sihanouk and what he has had to survive and you will understand much of Cambodia.

LIFESTYLE

For many older Cambodians, life is centred on family, faith and food, a timeless existence that has stayed the same for centuries. Family is more than the nuclear family we now know in the West; it's the extended family of third cousins and obscure aunts – as long as there is a bloodline, there is a bond. Families stick together, solve problems collectively, listen to the wisdom of the elders and pool resources. The extended family comes together during times of trouble or times of joy, celebrating festivals and successes, mourning deaths and disappointments. Whether the Cambodian house is big or small, there will be a lot of people living inside.

For more on the incredible life and times of Norodom Sihanouk, read the biography by Milton Osborne, *Prince of Light, Prince of Darkness* (1994).

For the majority of the population still living in the countryside, these constants carry on as they have: several generations sharing the same roof, the same rice and the same religion. But during the dark decades of the 1970s and 1980s, this routine was ripped apart by war and ideology, as the peasants were dragged from all they held dear to fight a bloody civil war and later forced into slavery. Angkar, the Khmer Rouge organisation, took over as the moral and social beacon in the lives of the people. Families were forced apart, children turned against parents, brother against sister. The bond of trust was broken and is only slowly being rebuilt today.

Faith is another rock in the lives of many older Cambodians, and Buddhism has helped them to rebuild their lives after the Khmer Rouge. Most Cambodian houses contain a small shrine to pray for luck, and come Buddha Day the wats are thronging with the faithful.

Food is more important to Cambodians than to most, as they have tasted what it is like to be without. Famine stalked the country in the late 1970s and, even today, malnutrition and food shortages are common during times of drought. For country folk (still the majority of the Cambodian population), their life is their fields. Farmers are attached to their land, their very survival dependent on it, and the harvest cycle dictates the rhythm of rural life.

For the young generation, brought up in a postconflict, postcommunist period of relative freedom, it's a different story – arguably thanks to their steady diet of MTV and steamy soaps. Cambodia is experiencing its very own '60s swing, as the younger generation stands up for a different lifestyle than the one their parents had to swallow. This creates plenty of feisty friction in the cities, as rebellious teens dress as they like, date who they want and hit the town until all hours. But few actually live on their own; they still come home to ma and pa at the end of the day (and the arguments start again).

Cambodia is a country undergoing rapid change, but for now the traditionalists are just about holding their own, although the onslaught of karaoke is proving hard to resist. Cambodia is set for major demographic changes in the next couple of decades. Currently, just 20% of the population lives in urban areas, which contrasts starkly with the country's more-developed neighbours, such as Malaysia and Thailand. Increasing numbers of young people are likely to migrate to the cities in search of opportunity, changing forever the face of contemporary Cambodian society. However, for now, Cambodian society remains much more traditional than in Thailand and Vietnam, and visitors need to keep this in mind.

> Some 80% of the Cambodian population still live in the countryside, a huge number compared with its more-developed Asian neighbours. Expect urban migration to take off in the next decade.

> Even the destructive Khmer Rouge paid homage to the mighty Angkor Wat on its flag, with three towers of the temple in yellow, set against a blood-red background.

Greetings

Cambodians traditionally greet each other with the *sompiah,* which involves pressing the hands together in prayer and bowing, similar to the *wai* in Thailand. The higher the hands and the lower the bow the more respect is conveyed – important to remember when meeting officials or the elderly. In recent times this custom has been partially replaced by the handshake but, although men tend to shake hands with each other, women usually use the traditional greeting with both men and women. It is considered acceptable (or perhaps excusable) for foreigners to shake hands with Cambodians of both sexes.

Dress

Both men and women often wear cotton or silk sarongs, especially at home. Most urban Khmer men dress in trousers and these days many urban women dress in Western-style clothing.

On formal occasions, such as religious festivals and family celebrations, women often wear a *hol* (a type of shirt) during the day. At night they change into single-colour silk dresses called *phamuong,* which are decorated along the hems. If the celebration is a wedding, the colours of such garments are dictated by the day of the week on which the wedding falls. The women of Cambodia are generally modest in their dress, although this is fast changing in the bigger towns and cities.

Travellers crossing the border from liberal Thai islands such as Ko Pha Ngan or Ko Chang should remember they have crossed back in time as far as traditions are concerned, and that wandering around the temples of Angkor bare-chested (men) or scantily clad (women) will not be appreciated.

ECONOMY

Badly traumatised by decades of conflict, Cambodia's economy was long a gecko amid the neighbouring dragons. This finally looks set to change, as the economy has been liberalised and investors are circling to take advantage of the new opportunities. Asian investors are flocking to Phnom Penh, led by the South Koreans who are inking deals for skyscrapers all over the low-rise city. Westerners are starting to realise that they are on to something and investment funds and venture capitalists are sniffing around. It's a far cry from the days of civil war, genocide and famine. However, it's a fairly exclusive boom limited to foreign investors, wealthy Cambodians and a small number of city dwellers. To ensure a stable future, the government needs to expand the opportunities to the people of the countryside.

Before the civil war, rubber was the leading industry and it's bouncing back with new plantations. Other plantation industries taking off include palm oil and paper pulp. Virgin forest is being cut down on the pretext of replanting, but the ecosystem never recovers.

The garment sector is important to the economy, with factories ringing the Cambodian capital. Cambodia is trying to carve a niche for itself as an ethical producer, with good labour relations and air-conditioned factories. It's no picnic in the factories, but the alternative is often the rice fields or the shadowy fringes of the entertainment industry, which is often a one-way ticket into prostitution. When it comes to the garment industry's future, it remains to be seen if profit or purpose will triumph in the international marketplace.

Tourism is a big deal in Cambodia with more than two million visitors arriving in 2007, a doubling of numbers in just three years. Thousands of jobs are being created every year and this is proving a great way to integrate the huge number of young people into the economy. Wages are low by regional standards, but tips can add up to a princely sum that might support an extended family.

Foreign aid was long the mainstay of the Cambodian economy, supporting half the government's budget, and NGOs have done a lot to force important sociopolitical issues onto the agenda. However, with multibillion dollar investments stacking up, it looks like their days in the sun could be numbered, and the government may no longer be influenced by their lobbying.

For many Cambodians, economy is too grand a word, for their life is about subsistence survival. Subject to the vagaries of burning sun and drowning rains, the best they can hope for is a stable crop and the chance to sell a little at the end of the season.

Corruption remains a way of life in Cambodia. It is a major element of the Cambodian economy and exists to some extent at all levels of government. Sometimes it is overt, but increasingly it is covert, with private companies often securing very favourable business deals on the basis of their connections. It seems everything can be bought, including ancient temples, national parks and even genocide sites.

Cambodia's economy is now among the fastest growing in the world, recently hitting the magic 10%-a-year target.

TOP 10 TIPS TO EARN THE RESPECT OF THE LOCALS

Take your time to learn a little about the local culture in Cambodia. Not only will this ensure that you don't inadvertently cause offence or, worse, spark an international incident, but it will also ingratiate you to your hosts. Here are a few top tips to help you go native.

Dress Code

Respect local dress standards, particularly at religious sites. Covering the upper arms and upper legs is appropriate, although some monks will be too polite to enforce this. Always remove your shoes before entering a temple, as well as any hat or head covering. Nude sunbathing is considered *totally* inappropriate, even on beaches.

Making a Contribution

Since most temples are maintained from the donations received, remember to make a contribution when visiting a temple. When visiting a Khmer home, a small token of gratitude in the form of a gift is always appreciated.

Meet & Greet

Learn the Cambodian greeting, the *sompiah* (see p45), and use it when introducing yourself to new friends. When beckoning someone over, always wave towards yourself with the palm down, as palm up with fingers raised can be suggestive, even offensive.

A Woman's Touch

Monks are not supposed to touch or be touched by women. If a woman wants to hand something to a monk, the object should be placed within reach of the monk or on the monk's 'receiving cloth'.

Keep your Cool

No matter how high your blood pressure rises, do not raise your voice or show signs of aggression. This will lead to a 'loss of face' and cause embarrassment to the locals, ensuring the situation gets worse rather than better.

It's on the Cards

Exchanging business cards is an important part of even the smallest transaction or business contact in Cambodia. Get some printed before you arrive and hand them out like confetti. Always present them with two hands.

Deadly Chopsticks

Leaving a pair of chopsticks sitting vertically in a rice bowl looks very much like the incense sticks that are burned for the dead. This is a powerful sign and is not appreciated anywhere in Asia.

Mean Feet

Cambodians like to keep a clean house and it's usual to remove shoes when entering somebody's home. It's rude to point the bottom of your feet towards other people. Never, ever point your feet towards anything sacred, such as an image of Buddha.

Hats Off to Them

As a form of respect to elderly or other esteemed people, such as monks, take off your hat and bow your head politely when addressing them. Never pat or touch an adult on the head – in Asia, the head is the symbolic highest point.

Toothpicks

While digging out those stubborn morsels from between your teeth, it is polite to use one hand to perform the extraction and the other hand to cover your mouth so others can't see you do it.

POPULATION

Cambodia's first census in decades, carried out in 1998, put the country's population at nearly 11.5 million. With a rapid growth rate of 2.4% a year, the population now stands at more than 15 million and is predicted to reach 20 million before 2020.

Phnom Penh is the largest city, with a population of almost two million. Other major population centres include the boom towns of Siem Reap, Sihanoukville, Battambang and Poipet. The most populous province is Kompong Cham, where more than 10% of Cambodians live.

The much-discussed imbalance of men to women due to years of conflict is not as serious as it was in 1980, but it is still significant: there are about 94 males to every 100 females, up from 86.1 to 100 in 1980. There is, however, a marked imbalance in age groups: around 50% of the population is under the age of 16.

> Among Cambodia's 24 provinces, Kandal has the densest population with more than 300 people per square kilometre; Mondulkiri has the sparsest population with just two people per square kilometre.

MULTICULTURALISM
Ethnic Khmers

According to official statistics, around 96% of the people who live in Cambodia are ethnic Khmers, making the country the most homogeneous in Southeast Asia. In reality, anywhere between 10% and 20% of the population is of Cham, Chinese or Vietnamese origin.

The Khmers have inhabited Cambodia since the beginning of recorded history (around the 2nd century), many centuries before Thais and Vietnamese migrated to the region. Over the centuries, the Khmers have mixed with other groups residing in Cambodia, including Javanese and Malays (8th century), Thais (10th to 15th centuries), Vietnamese (from the early 17th century) and Chinese (since the 18th century).

Ethnic Vietnamese

Vietnamese are one of the largest non-Khmer ethnic groups in Cambodia. According to government figures, Cambodia is host to around 100,000 Vietnamese. Unofficial observers claim that the real figure may be somewhere between half a million and two million. They play a big part in the fishing

---

KHMER KROM

The Khmer Krom people of southern Vietnam are ethnic Khmers separated from Cambodia by historical deals and Vietnamese encroachment on what was once Cambodian territory. Nobody is sure just how many of them there are and estimates vary from one million to seven million, depending on who is doing the counting.

The history of Vietnamese expansion into Khmer territory has long been a staple of Khmer textbooks. King Chey Chetha II of Cambodia, in keeping with the wishes of his Vietnamese queen, first allowed Vietnamese to settle in the Cambodian town of Prey Nokor in 1620. It was obviously the thin edge of the wedge – Prey Nokor is now better known as Ho Chi Minh City (Saigon).

Representatives of the Khmer Krom claim that although they dress as Vietnamese and carry Vietnamese identity cards, they remain culturally Khmer. Vietnamese attempts to quash the Khmer Krom language have, for the most part, failed. Even assimilation through intermarriage has failed to take place on a large scale.

Many Khmer Krom would like to see Cambodia act as a mediator in the quest for greater autonomy and ethnic representation in Vietnam. The Cambodian government, for its part, needs to look at the vast numbers of illegal Vietnamese inside its borders, as well as reports of Vietnamese encroachments on the eastern borders of Cambodia. However, the Cambodian government takes a very softly softly approach towards its more powerful neighbour, perhaps borne of the historic ties between the two political dynasties.

and construction industries in Cambodia. However, there is still a great deal of distrust between the Cambodians and the Vietnamese, even among those who have been living in Cambodia for generations.

Ethnic Chinese

The government claims that there are around 50,000 ethnic Chinese in Cambodia. Informed observers say there are more likely to be as many as half a million to one million in urban areas. Many Chinese Cambodians have lived in Cambodia for generations and have adopted the Khmer culture, language and identity. Until 1975, ethnic Chinese controlled the economic life of Cambodia. In recent years the group has re-emerged as a powerful economic force, mainly due to increased investment by overseas Chinese.

Ethnic Cham

Cambodia's Cham Muslims (known locally as the Khmer Islam) officially number around 200,000. Unofficial counts put the figure higher at around 400,000. The Chams live in villages on the banks of the Mekong and Tonlé Sap Rivers, mostly in Kompong Cham, Kompong Speu and Kompong Chhnang Provinces. They suffered vicious persecution between 1975 and 1979, when a large part of their community was exterminated. Many Cham mosques that were destroyed under the Khmer Rouge have been rebuilt.

Ethno-Linguistic Minorities

Cambodia's diverse Khmer Leu (Upper Khmer) or *chunchiet* (minorities), who live in the country's mountainous regions, probably number between 60,000 and 70,000.

The majority of these groups live in the northeast of Cambodia, in the provinces of Ratanakiri, Mondulkiri, Stung Treng and Kratie. The largest group is the Tompuon (many other spellings are used), who number around 15,000. Other groups include the Pnong, Kreung, Kavet, Brau and Jarai.

The hill tribes of Cambodia have long been isolated from mainstream Khmer society, and there is little in the way of mutual understanding. They practise shifting cultivation, rarely staying in one place for long. Finding a new location for a village requires a village elder to mediate with the spirit world. Very few of the minorities wear the sort of colourful traditional costumes found in Thailand, Laos and Vietnam.

Lowland Khmers are being encouraged to migrate to Cambodia's northeast where there is plenty of available land. But this is home to the country's minority peoples who have no concept of property rights or land ownership; this may see their culture marginalised in coming years.

MEDIA

Cambodia's media scene looks to be in good shape on paper, with freedom of the press enshrined in the constitution, but the everyday reality is a different story. Opposition parties have far less access to the media than the dominant Cambodian People's Party (CPP), with many more pro-government newspapers and radio and TV stations. Corruption exists in the local journalism ranks, and it's not unheard of for money to change hands in return for stories benefiting businessmen and politicians. Journalists working for pro-opposition media have to exercise a certain amount of self-censorship in the interests of self-preservation, as there have been several cases of politically motivated or revenge killings.

Khmer TV is mostly in the hands of the CPP, including state-run TVK and private channels like Bayon, but even the 'independent' channels like CTN aren't that independent when you look into who is behind them.

Most urban Cambodians look to cable TV news channels like the BBC and CNN for their news, or tune their radios in to BBC World Service or Voice of America.

RELIGION

Hinduism

Hinduism flourished alongside Buddhism from the 1st century AD until the 14th century. During the pre-Angkorian period, Hinduism was represented by the worship of Harihara (Shiva and Vishnu embodied in a single deity). During the time of Angkor, Shiva was the deity most in favour with the royal family, although in the 12th century he was superseded by Vishnu. Today some elements of Hinduism are still incorporated into important ceremonies involving birth, marriage and death.

Buddhism

Buddhism came to Cambodia with Hinduism, but only became the official religion from the 13th and 14th centuries. Most Cambodians today practise Theravada Buddhism. Between 1975 and 1979 the majority of Cambodia's Buddhist monks were murdered by the Khmer Rouge and nearly all of the country's wats (more than 3000) were damaged or destroyed. In the late 1980s, Buddhism once again became the state religion and today young monks are a common sight throughout the country. Many wats have been rebuilt or rehabilitated in the past decade and money-raising drives for this work can be seen on roadsides across the country.

The ultimate goal of Theravada Buddhism is nirvana – 'extinction' of all desire and suffering to reach the final stage of reincarnation. By feeding monks, giving donations to temples and performing regular worship at the local wat, Buddhists hope to improve their lot, acquiring enough merit to reduce their number of rebirths.

Every Buddhist male is expected to become a monk for a short period in his life, optimally between the time he finishes school and starts a career or marries. Men or boys under 20 years of age may enter the Sangha as novices. Nowadays men may spend as little as one week or 15 days to accrue merit as monks.

> Buddhism in Cambodia draws heavily on its predecessors, incorporating many cultural traditions from Hinduism for ceremonies such as birth, marriage and death; as well as genies and spirits, such as Neak Ta, which link back to a pre-Indian animist past.

Animism

Both Hinduism and Buddhism were gradually absorbed from beyond the borders of Cambodia, fusing with the animist beliefs already present among the Khmers before Indianisation. Local beliefs didn't disappear, but were incorporated into the new religions to form something uniquely Cambodian. The concept of Neak Ta has its foundations in animist beliefs regarding sacred soil and the sacred spirit around us. Neak Ta can be viewed as a Mother Earth concept, an energy force uniting a community with its earth and water. It can be represented in many forms, from stone or wood to termite hills – anything that symbolises both a link between the people and the fertility of their land.

The purest form of animism is practised among the Khmer Leu (see p49). Some have converted to Buddhism, but the majority continue to worship spirits of the earth and skies and the spirits of their forefathers.

Islam

Cambodia's Muslims are descendants of Chams who migrated from what is now central Vietnam after the final defeat of the kingdom of Champa by the Vietnamese in 1471. Like their Buddhist neighbours, the Cham Muslims call the faithful to prayer by banging a drum, rather than with the call of the muezzin, as in most Muslim lands.

Christianity

Christianity made limited headway into Cambodia compared with neighbouring Vietnam. There were a number of churches in Cambodia before the war, but many of these were systematically destroyed by the Khmer Rouge, including Notre Dame Cathedral in Phnom Penh. Christianity made a comeback of sorts throughout the refugee camps on the Thai border in the 1980s, as a number of food-for-faith–type charities set up shop dispensing Jesus with every meal. Many Cambodians changed their public faith for survival, before converting back to Buddhism on their departure from the camps.

WOMEN IN CAMBODIA

The position of women in Cambodia is in a state of transition, as the old generation yields to the new generation, the conservative to the challenging. Traditionally the woman's role has been in the home. While this trend continues among the older generation, there are signs that women of the younger generation won't be limited in the same way.

While something like 20% of women head the household, and in many families women are the sole breadwinners, men have a monopoly on the most important positions of power at a governmental level and have a dominant social role at a domestic level.

Cambodian political and religious policies do not directly discriminate against women, but females are rarely afforded the same opportunities as males. In the 1990s, laws were passed on abortion, domestic violence and human trafficking; these have improved the legal position of women but have had little effect on the bigger picture.

As young children, females are treated fairly equally, but as they get older their access to education has traditionally become more restricted. This is particularly so in rural areas, where girls are not allowed to live and study in wats.

Many women set up simple businesses in their towns or villages, but it is not an easy path should they want to progress further. Women currently make up just 10.9% of legislators in parliament, even though they make up 56% of the voters. Only 15% of administrative and management positions and 35% of professional positions are held by women nationally. It remains a man's world in the sociopolitical jungle that is Cambodia.

Other issues of concern for women in Cambodia are domestic violence, prostitution and the spread of sexually transmitted infections (STIs). Domestic violence is quite widespread but, because of fear and shame, it's not known exactly how serious a problem it is. There is a high incidence of child prostitution and illegal trafficking of prostitutes in Cambodia. See the boxed text, p82, for more on the scourge of child prostitution in Cambodia.

Cambodia has the highest rate of HIV infection in the whole of Southeast Asia. Many families in Cambodia have ended up infected due to the actions of an errant husband. However, infection rates are starting to come under control thanks to the impact of powerful public awareness programmes.

Friends of Khmer Culture is dedicated to supporting Khmer arts and cultural organisations. Its website is www.khmer culture.net.

ARTS

The Khmer Rouge assault on the arts was a terrible blow to Cambodian culture. Indeed, for a number of years the common consensus among Khmers was that their culture had been irrevocably lost. The Khmer Rouge not only did away with living bearers of Khmer culture, it also destroyed cultural artefacts, statues, musical instruments, books and anything else that served as a reminder of a past it was trying to efface. The temples of Angkor were spared as a symbol of Khmer glory and empire, but little else survived. Despite this, Cambodia is witnessing a resurgence of traditional arts and a growing interest in experimentation in modern arts and cross-cultural fusion.

Dance

More than any of the other traditional arts, Cambodia's royal ballet is a tangible link with the glory of Angkor. Its traditions stretch long into the past, when the art of the *apsara* (nymph) resounded to the glory of the divine king. Early in his reign, King Sihanouk released the traditional harem of royal *apsara* that went with the crown.

Dance fared particularly badly during the Pol Pot years. Very few dancers and teachers survived. In 1981, with a handful of teachers, the University of Fine Arts was reopened and the training of dance students resumed.

Much of Cambodian royal dance resembles that of India and Thailand (the same stylised hand movements, the same sequined, lamé costumes and the same opulent stupalike headwear), as the Thais learnt their techniques from the Khmers after sacking Angkor in the 15th century. Where royal dance was traditionally an all-female affair (with the exception of the role of the monkey), there are now more male dancers featured.

Music

The bas-reliefs on some of the monuments in the Angkor region depict musicians and *apsara* holding instruments similar to the traditional Khmer instruments of today, demonstrating that Cambodia has a long musical tradition all its own.

Customarily, music was an accompaniment to a ritual or performance that had religious significance. Musicologists have identified six types of Cambodian musical ensemble, each used in different settings. The most traditional of these is the *areak ka,* an ensemble that performs at weddings. The instruments of the *areak ka* include a *tro khmae* (three-stringed fiddle), a *khsae muoy* (singled-stringed bowed instrument) and *skor areak* (drums), among others.

Much of Cambodia's golden-era music from the pre-war period was lost during the Pol Pot period. The Khmer Rouge targeted famous singers and the great Sin Sisamuth and female diva Ros Sereysothea, Cambodia's most famous songwriters and performers, both disappeared in the early days of the regime.

After the war, many Khmers settled in the USA, where a lively Khmer pop industry developed. Influenced by US music and later exported back to Cambodia, it has been enormously popular.

A new generation of overseas Khmers growing up with influences from the West is producing its own sound. Cambodian Americans are now returning to the homeland, raised on a diet of rap, and lots of new artists are breaking through such as the ClapYaHandz collective started by Sok 'Cream' Visal.

There's also a burgeoning pop industry, many of whose famous stars perform at the huge restaurants located across the Japanese Bridge in Phnom Penh. It is easy to join in the fun by visiting one of the innumerable karaoke bars around the country. Preap Sovath is the Robbie Williams of Cambodia and if you flick through the Cambodian channels for more than five minutes, chances are he will be performing. Soun Chantha is one of the more popular young female singers with a big voice, but it's a changeling industry and new stars are waiting in the wings.

Dengue Fever is the ultimate fusion band, rapidly gaining a name for itself beyond the USA and Cambodia. Cambodian singer Chhom Nimol fronts five American prog-rockers who dabble in psychedelic sounds.

The famous Hindu epic the *Ramayana* is known as the *Reamker* in Cambodia; Reyum Publishing has issued a beautifully illustrated book telling the story: *The Reamker* (1999).

Cambodia's great musical tradition was almost lost during the Khmer Rouge years, but the Cambodian Master Performers Program is dedicated to reviving the country's musical tradition. Visit its website at www .cambodianmasters.org.

One of the greatest '70s legends to seek out is Nuon Sarath, the Jimi Hendrix of Cambodia with his screaming vocals and wah-wah pedals. His most famous song, *Chi Cyclo,* is an absolute classic.

One form of music unique to Cambodia is *chapaye,* a sort of Cambodian blues sung to the accompaniment of a two-stringed wooden instrument similar in sound to a bass guitar without the amplifier. There are few old masters such as Prak Chouen left alive, but *chapaye* is still often shown on late-night Cambodian TV before transmission ends.

Literature

Cambodia's literary tradition is limited and very much tied in with Buddhism or myth and legend. Sanskrit, and later Pali, came to Cambodia with Hinduism and Buddhism and much of Cambodia's religious scripture exists only in these ancient languages. Legend has been used to expound the core Cambodian values of family and faith, as well as obedience to authority.

Architecture

Khmer architecture reached its peak during the Angkorian era (9th to 14th centuries). Some of the finest examples of architecture from this period are Angkor Wat and the structures of Angkor Thom. See p148 for more information on the architectural styles of the Angkorian era.

Today, most rural Cambodian houses are built on high wood pilings (if the family can afford it) and have thatch roofs, walls made of palm mats and floors of woven bamboo strips resting on bamboo joists. The shady space underneath is used for storage and for people to relax at midday. Wealthier families have houses with wooden walls and tiled roofs, but the basic design remains the same.

The French left their mark in Cambodia in the form of some handsome villas and government buildings built in neoclassical style – Romanesque pillars and all. Some of the best architectural examples are in Phnom Penh, but most of the provincial capitals have at least one or two examples of architecture from the colonial period.

Sculpture

Even in the pre-Angkorian era, the periods generally referred to as Funan and Chenla, the people of Cambodia were producing masterfully sensuous sculpture that was more than a mere copy of the Indian forms on which it was modelled. Some scholars maintain that the Cambodian forms are unrivalled even in India itself.

The earliest surviving Cambodian sculpture dates from the 6th century AD. Most of it depicts Vishnu with four or eight arms. A large eight-armed Vishnu from this period is displayed at the National Museum (p84) in Phnom Penh.

Also on display at the National Museum is a statue of Harihara from the end of the 7th century, a divinity who combines aspects of both Vishnu and Shiva, but looks more than a little Egyptian – a reminder that Indian sculpture drew from the Greeks who in turn learnt from the Pharaohs.

Innovations of the early Angkorian era include freestanding sculpture that dispenses with the stone aureole that in earlier works supported the multiple arms of Hindu deities. The faces assume an air of tranquillity, and the overall effect is less animated.

The Banteay Srei style of the late 10th century is commonly regarded as a high point in the evolution of Southeast Asian art. The National Museum has a splendid piece from this period: a sandstone statue of Shiva holding Uma, his wife, on his knee. The Baphuon style of the 11th century was inspired to a certain extent by the sculpture of Banteay Srei, producing some of the finest works to have survived today.

Cambodian architect Vann Molyvann helped shape modern Phnom Penh; some of his best-known buildings include the Olympic Stadium and the Chatomuk Theatre.

For details on the religious, cultural and social context of Angkorian-era sculpture, seek out a copy of *Sculpture of Angkor and Ancient Cambodia: Millennium of Glory* by Helen Jessup (1997).

Look for a copy of *ArtVenues,* a foldout publication promoting contemporary art galleries in Siem Reap, which includes a couple of suggested walking tours.

The statuary of the Angkor Wat period is felt to be conservative and stilted, lacking the grace of earlier work. The genius of this period manifests itself more clearly in the immense architecture and incredible bas-reliefs of Angkor Wat itself.

The final high point in Angkorian sculpture is the Bayon period from the end of the 12th century to the beginning of the 13th century. In the National Museum, look for the superb representation of Jayavarman VII, an image that simultaneously projects great power and sublime tranquillity.

Cambodian sculptors are rediscovering their skills now that there is a ready market among visitors for reproduction stone carvings of famous statues and busts from the time of Angkor.

Reyum is an exhibition space in Phnom Penh established to promote Khmer arts and culture and has given support and encouragement to young artists and writers. Its website is at www .reyum.org.

Painting

There is a new contemporary art scene emerging in Cambodia, which is pushing the boundaries of traditional culture and form. Young artists are emerging unshackled by the baggage of the past to define a new future for Khmer painting. This has been given extra momentum by new galleries and art venues in Phnom Penh and Siem Reap that are promoting these artists to the wider world. Check out places like the Art Café, Java Café and Meta House (p108) in Phnom Penh or Damnak Alliance Café and the Arts Lounge in Hotel de la Paix (p130) in Siem Reap.

Leading lights on the art scene include Tuol Sleng survivor Vann Nath, spiritually inspired artist Chhim Sothy and challenging young Battambang artist Oeur Sokuntevy.

Handicrafts

Rithy Panh's 1996 film *Bophana* tells the true story of Hout Bophana, a beautiful young woman, and Ly Sitha, a regional Khmer Rouge leader, who fall in love and are executed for their 'crime'.

With a tradition of craftsmanship that produced the temples of Angkor, it is hardly surprising to find that even today Khmers produce exquisitely carved silver, wood and stone. Many of the designs hark back to those of the Angkorian period and are tasteful objects of art. Pottery is also an industry with a long history in Cambodia, and there are many ancient kiln sites scattered throughout the country. Designs range from the extremely simple to much more intricate: drinking cups carved in the image of elephants, teapots carved in the image of birds, and jars carved in the image of gods.

Cinema

The film industry in Cambodia was given a new lease of life in 2000 with the release of *Pos Keng Kong* (The Giant Snake). A remake of a 1950s Cambodian classic, it tells the story of a powerful young girl born from a rural relationship between a woman and a snake king. It is an interesting love story, albeit with dodgy special effects, and achieved massive box-office success around the region.

The success of *Pos Keng Kong* has heralded a revival in the Cambodian film industry and local directors are now turning out up to a dozen films a year. However, most of these new films are vampire or ghost films and of dubious artistic value.

Check out the rockumentary on Cambodia's lost rock'n'roll from the 1960s at www.dontthinkivefor gotten.com

At least one overseas Cambodian director has had huge success in recent years: Rithy Panh's *People of the Rice Fields* was nominated for the Palme d'Or at the Cannes Film Festival in 1995. The film touches only fleetingly on the Khmer Rouge, depicting the lives of a family eking out an arduous existence in the rice fields. His other films include *One Night after the War* (1997), the story of a young Khmer kick boxer falling for a bar girl in Phnom Penh, and the award-winning *S-21: The Khmer Rouge Killing Machine* (2003), a powerful documentary in which survivors from Tuol Sleng are brought back to confront their guards.

SIHANOUK & THE SILVER SCREEN

Between 1965 and 1969 Sihanouk wrote, directed and produced nine feature films, a figure that would put the average workaholic Hollywood director to shame. Sihanouk took the business of making films very seriously, and family and officials were called upon to do their bit: the minister of foreign affairs played the male lead in Sihanouk's first feature, *Apsara* (Heavenly Nymph; 1965), and his daughter Princess Bopha Devi the female lead. When, in the same movie, a show of military hardware was required, the air force was brought into action, as was the army's fleet of helicopters.

Sihanouk often took on the leading role himself. Notable performances saw him as a spirit of the forest and as a victorious general. Perhaps it was no surprise, given the king's apparent addiction to the world of celluloid dreams, that Cambodia should challenge Cannes with its Phnom Penh International Film Festival. The festival was held twice, in 1968 and 1969. Sihanouk won the grand prize on both occasions. He continued to make movies in later life and it is believed he has made around 30 films during his remarkable career. For more on the films of Sihanouk, visit the website www.norodomsihanouk.org.

The definitive film about Cambodia is *The Killing Fields* (1985), which tells the story of American journalist Sydney Schanberg and his Cambodian assistant Dith Pran. Most of the footage was actually shot in Thailand: it was filmed in 1984 when Cambodia was effectively closed to the West.

Quite a number of films have been shot in Cambodia in recent years, including *Tomb Raider* (2001), *City of Ghosts* (2002) and *Two Brothers* (2004), all worth seeking out for their beautiful Cambodian backdrops.

The first major international feature film to be shot in Cambodia was *Lord Jim* (1964), starring Peter O'Toole.

SPORT

The national sport of Cambodia is *pradal serey* or Cambodian kick boxing. It's similar to kick boxing in Thailand (don't make the mistake of calling it Thai boxing over here) and there are regular weekend bouts on TV5 and CTN. It is also possible to go to the TV arenas and watch the fights live.

Football is another national obsession, although the Cambodian team is a real minnow, even by Asian standards. Many Cambodians follow the Premier League in England religiously and regularly bet on games.

Pétanque, or *boules*, the French game, is also very popular here and the Cambodian team has won several medals in regional games.

Cambodia is one of the leading lights in disabled volleyball and came third in the world championships, held in Phnom Penh in 2007.

Environment

THE LAND

Cambodia, as we know it today, is the result of a classic historical squeeze. As the Vietnamese moved south into the Mekong Delta and the Thais pushed west towards Angkor, Cambodia's territory – which, in Angkorian times, stretched from southern Burma to Saigon and north into Laos – shrank. Only the arrival of the French prevented Cambodia from going the way of the Chams, who became a people without a state. In that sense, French rule *was* a protectorate that protected.

Modern-day Cambodia covers 181,035 sq km, making it a little more than half the size of Vietnam (about the same size as the US state of Washington, or England and Wales combined). The country is a bit wider (about 580km east–west) than it is tall (about 450km north–south). To the west and northwest it borders Thailand, to the northeast Laos, to the east and southeast Vietnam, and to its south is the Gulf of Thailand.

Cambodia's two dominant geographical features are the mighty Mekong River and the vast lake, Tonlé Sap – see opposite for more on this natural miracle. The Mekong, an incredible 5km wide in places, rises in Tibet and flows for almost 500km through Cambodia before continuing, via southern Vietnam, to the South China Sea.

At Phnom Penh the Mekong splits into three channels: Tonlé Sap River, which connects with Tonlé Sap Lake; the Upper River (called simply the Mekong or, in Vietnamese, Tien Giang) and the Lower River (Tonlé Bassac, or Hau Giang in Vietnamese). The rich sediment deposited during the Mekong's annual wet-season flooding has made central Cambodia incredibly fertile. This low-lying alluvial plain is where the vast majority of Cambodians live, fishing and farming in time with the rhythms of the monsoon.

In Cambodia's southwest quadrant, much of the landmass is covered by forested mountains up to 1764m high. These are the Cardamom Mountains (Chuor Phnom Kravanh), which cover parts of Koh Kong, Battambang, Pursat and Krong Pailin Provinces and include the wildlife sanctuaries of Peam Krasaop (p187) and Phnom Samkos (p239), the Central Cardamoms Protected Forest (p189 and p238), the Southern Cardamoms Protected Forest (p189) and Botum Sakor National Park (p190). Southeast of the Cardamoms, the Elephant Mountains (Chuor Phnom Damrei) cover parts of the provinces of Kompong Speu, Koh Kong and Kampot – where you'll find Kirirom National Park (p116) and Bokor National Park (p219).

The mountains end just north of Cambodia's 435km coastline, a big draw for visitors on the lookout for isolated tropical beaches. There are islands aplenty off the coast of Sihanoukville (p193), Kep (p224) and the Koh Kong Conservation Corridor (p186).

Along Cambodia's northern border with Thailand, the plains collide with a striking sandstone escarpment more than 300km long and up to 550m high: the Dangkrek Mountains (Chuor Phnom Dangkrek). One of the best places to get a sense of this area is Prasat Preah Vihear (p268).

In the northeastern corner of the country, the plains give way to the Eastern Highlands, a remote region of densely forested mountains and high plateaus that extends east into Vietnam's Central Highlands and north into Laos. The wild provinces of Ratanakiri (p291) and Mondulkiri (p298) provide a home to many minority peoples and are taking off as traveller hot-spots.

Cambodia's highest mountain is Phnom Aural in Pursat Province. At just 1764m it isn't one of the world's great climbs but for those ticking off peaks across the planet it can be climbed in two days. Sadly, much of the surrounding area is being logged into oblivion.

Tonlé Sap expands to five times its size and 70 times its volume each year during the wet season and provides a huge percentage of Cambodians' protein intake, 70% of which comes from fish.

In the mid-1960s Cambodia was reckoned to have around 90% of its original forest cover intact. Estimates today vary but it's likely that only about 30% remains.

TONLÉ SAP: THE HEARTBEAT OF CAMBODIA

Tonlé Sap, the largest freshwater lake in Southeast Asia, is an incredible natural phenomenon that provides fish and irrigation water for half the population of Cambodia.

The lake is linked to the Mekong at Phnom Penh by a 100km-long channel that's also known as Tonlé Sap (*tonlé* meaning 'river'). From mid-May to early October (the wet season), the level of the Mekong rises rapidly, backing up Tonlé Sap River and causing it to flow northwest into Tonlé Sap Lake. During this period, the lake swells from 2500 sq km to 13,000 sq km or more, its maximum depth increasing from about 2.2m to more than 10m. Around the start of October, as the water level of the Mekong begins to fall, the Tonlé Sap River reverses its flow, draining the waters of the lake back into the Mekong.

This extraordinary process makes Tonlé Sap one of the world's richest sources of freshwater fish, as flooded forest makes for fertile spawning grounds. Experts believe that fish migrations from the lake help to restock fisheries as far north as China. The fishing industry supports about one million people in Cambodia and an individual fisher's catch on the great lake can average 100kg to 200kg per day in the dry season.

This unique ecosystem has helped to earn Tonlé Sap protected biosphere status – but this may not be enough to protect it from the twin threats of upstream dams and rampant deforestation. The dams – including Sambor Dam near Kratie and Si Phan Done in southern Laos – hold uncertain consequences for the flow patterns of the Mekong and the migratory patterns of fish. Illegal logging loosens topsoil in upland Cambodia and silt is carried down the country's rivers into the lake. The shallowest areas may in time begin to silt up, bringing disastrous consequences not only for Cambodia but also neighbouring Vietnam. Hopefully, action will be taken to protect this unique natural wonder from further harm, but with the Cambodian population growing by 300,000 a year, the task is not going to be easy.

For more information about Tonlé Sap and its unique ecosystem, visit the exhibition about the lake (p124) and the Gecko Environment Centre (p139), both in Siem Reap.

WILDLIFE

Despite Cambodia's tragic history, its forest ecosystems were in excellent shape until the 1990s and, compared with its neighbours, are still relatively intact. The years of war and suffering took their toll on some species, but others thrived in the remote jungles of the southwest and northeast. Ironically, peace brought increased threats, with the logging industry flattening habitat and the illicit trade in wildlife discovering Cambodia's abundance of exotic meats, skins, tusks and bones. Years of inaccessibility mean scientists are only just beginning to research and catalogue the country's plant and animal life. When it comes to the distribution of large mammals, Cambodia has four well-defined biodiversity regions:

- Southwest – the Cardamom Mountains and Koh Kong Province
- Northern plains – centred on Preah Vihear Province
- Northeast – Ratanakiri Province and Virachay National Park
- Eastern plains – centred on Mondulkiri Province

Animals

Cambodia has a weird and wonderful selection of animals. It's estimated that 212 species of mammal live in the country, but most are extremely hard to get a look at in the wild. The easiest way to see a healthy selection is to visit the Phnom Tamao Wildlife Sanctuary (p115) near Phnom Penh, which provides a home for rescued animals and includes all the major species.

Cambodia's larger animals include tigers, elephants, bears, leopards and wild cows. Some of the biggest characters, however, are the smaller creatures, including the binturong (nicknamed the bear cat), the pileated gibbon (the world's largest population lives in the Cardamoms) and the lazy

The *khting vor* (spiral-horned ox), so rare that no-one had ever seen a live specimen, was considered critically endangered until DNA analysis of its distinctive horns showed that the creature had never existed – the 'horns' belonged to ordinary cows and buffalos!

loris, which hangs out in trees all day. The country also has a great variety of butterflies.

The lion, although a familiar sight in statue form around Angkor, has never been seen here.

A whopping 720 bird species find Cambodia a congenial home, thanks in large part to its year-round water resources, first and foremost the marshes around the Tonlé Sap. Relatively common birds include ducks, rails, cranes, herons, egrets, cormorants, pelicans, storks and parakeets, with migratory shorebirds such as waders, plovers and terns around the south coast estuaries. Serious twitchers should consider a visit to Prek Toal Bird Sanctuary (p138); Ang Trapeng Thmor Reserve (p139), home to the extremely rare Sarus crane, depicted on the bas-reliefs at Angkor; the Tmatboey Ibis Project (p267), where the critically endangered giant ibis, Cambodia's national bird, can be seen; and – for the truly adventurous – the Chhep Vulture Feeding Station (p267). For details on bird-watching in Cambodia, check out the Siem Reap–based Sam Veasna Center for Wildlife Conservation (www.samveasna.org).

Cambodia is home to about 240 species of reptile. Four types of snake are especially dangerous: the cobra, king cobra, banded krait and Russell's viper.

ENDANGERED SPECIES

Tragically it's getting mighty close to checkout time for a number of species in Cambodia.

The kouprey (wild ox), declared Cambodia's national animal by King Sihanouk back in the 1960s, and the Wroughton's free-tailed bat, previously thought to exist in only one part of India but recently discovered in Preah Vihear Province, are the only Cambodian mammals on the Globally Threatened: Critical list, the last stop before extinction.

Other animals under serious threat in Cambodia include the Asian elephant, tiger, banteng (wild ox), gaur, Asian golden cat, Asiatic wild dog, black gibbon, clouded leopard, fishing cat, marbled cat, sun bear, wild water buffalo, pangolin (p189), giant ibis and, in the wild, the dragonfish (Asian arowana) and Siamese crocodile (p190).

Cambodia has some of the last remaining freshwater Irrawaddy dolphins (*trey pisaut* in Khmer), instantly identifiable thanks to their bulging forehead and short beak. There may be as few as 75 left, inhabiting stretches of the Mekong between Kratie and the Lao border, and viewing them at Kampi (p288) is a popular activity. More Irrawaddy dolphins inhabit the saline estuaries and mangrove swamps of Koh Kong Province and can be viewed around Peam Krasaop Wildlife Sanctuary (p187) and Ream National Park (p213).

Researchers estimate that about 50 to 100 elephants live in Mondulkiri Province and a similar number live in the Cardamom Mountains, including Botum Sakor National Park.

Snake bites may well be responsible for more amputations in Cambodia than land mines. Many villagers go to the medicine man for treatment and end up with infection or gangrene.

For a close encounter with tigers at the temples of Angkor, watch Jean-Jacques Annaud's 2004 film Two Brothers, the story of two orphan tiger cubs during the colonial period in Cambodia.

NGOS ON THE ENVIRONMENTAL FRONT LINE

The following environmental groups – staffed in Cambodia mainly by Khmers – are playing leading roles in protecting Cambodia's wildlife:

- Conservation International (www.conservation.org)
- Flora & Fauna International (www.fauna-flora.org)
- Maddox Jolie-Pitt Foundation (www.mjpasia.org)
- Wildlife Alliance (formerly WildAid; www.wildlifealliance.org)
- Wildlife Conservation Society (www.wcs.org)
- WWF (www.worldwildlife.org)

TIGER, TIGER, BURNING OUT?

In the mid-1990s, somewhere between 100 and 200 Cambodian tigers were being killed every year, their carcasses bringing huge sums around Asia (especially China) because of their supposed powers of potency (mainly sexual). By 1998 annual incidents of tiger poaching had dropped to 85 and in 2005 just two tigers were killed. Sadly, it's more likely that these estimates reflect a crash in tiger numbers rather than increased community awareness or more effective law enforcement.

Experts fear there may be only 50 of the big cats left in the wild in Cambodia. Numbers are so low that, despite repeated efforts, camera traps set by researchers in recent years have failed to photograph a single tiger, though footprints and other signs of the felines' presence have been recorded. As far as anyone can tell, the surviving tigers live in very low densities in very remote areas, making it difficult for both poachers and scientists to find them – and hard for environmentalists to protect them.

A significant poaching threat comes from police and military units stationed in remote jungle locations. Often, unit commanders supply weapons and ammunitions to poaching gangs in return for a cut of the profits. On the brighter side, some hunters are now being employed as rangers, making it easier to educate other hunters about the terrible ecological impact of 'wildlife crimes'.

At present, tigers are known to inhabit two areas: the central part of the Cardamom Mountains and Mondulkiri Province. In addition, they are thought to be present in small numbers in Virachay National Park (p297), Kulen Promtep Wildlife Sanctuary (p267), Preah Vihear Protected Forest (p268), western Oddar Meanchey Province and perhaps even in Bokor National Park (p219).

For insights, stories and links about tigers in Cambodia and what's being done to protect them, visit the website of the Cat Action Treasury at www.felidae.org.

The Mekong giant catfish, which can weigh up to 300kg, is critically endangered due to habitat loss and overfishing.

For more information on endangered species, check out the website of the World Conservation Union, www.iucnredlist.org.

Plants

No-one knows how many plant species live in Cambodia because no comprehensive survey has ever been conducted but it's estimated that the country is home to 15,000 species (including 2300 vascular plants), at least a third of them endemic.

In the southwest, rainforests grow to heights of 50m or more on the rainy southern slopes of the mountains, with montane (pine) forests in cooler climes above 800m and mangrove forests fringing the coast. In the northern mountains there are broadleaf evergreen forests with trees soaring 30m above the thick undergrowth of vines, bamboos, palms and assorted woody and herbaceous ground plants. The northern plains support dry dipterocarp forests while around the Tonlé Sap there are flooded forests (seasonally inundated). The Eastern Highlands are covered with grassland and deciduous forests. Forested upland areas support many varieties of orchid.

The symbol of Cambodia is the sugar palm tree, whose fronds are used to make roofs and walls for houses and whose fruit is used to produce medicine, wine and vinegar. Sugar palms grow taller over the years but the barkless trunk doesn't get any thicker – thereby retaining shrapnel marks from every battle that has ever raged around them. Sugar palms have been known to survive for many years after being shot clean through the trunk.

Cambodia became the first Southeast Asian country to establish a national park when it created a protected area in 1925 to preserve the forests around the temples of Angkor.

NATIONAL PARKS

In the late 1960s Cambodia had six national parks, together covering 22,000 sq km (around 12% of the country). The long civil war effectively

CAMBODIA'S MOST IMPORTANT NATIONAL PARKS

Park	Size	Features	Activities	Best Time to Visit
Bokor (p219)	1581 sq km	ghost town, views, waterfalls, orange lichen	trekking, biking, wildlife-watching, hopefully not golf	Dec-May
Botum Sakor National Park (p190)	1834 sq km	mangroves, beaches, monkeys, dolphins, elephants	boat rides, swimming, hiking	Dec-May
Kirirom (p116)	350 sq km	waterfalls, vistas, pine forests	hiking, wildlife-watching	Nov-Jun
Ream (p213)	150 sq km	beaches, islands, mangroves, dolphins, monkeys	boating, swimming, hiking, wildlife-watching	Dec-May
Virachay (p297)	3325 sq km	unexplored jungle, waterfalls	trekking, adventure wildlife-watching	Dec-Apr

destroyed this system and it wasn't reintroduced until 1993, when a royal decree designated 23 areas as national parks, wildlife sanctuaries, protected landscapes and multiple-use areas. Several more protected forests were recently added to the list, bringing the area of protected land in Cambodia to over 43,000 sq km, or around 25% of the country.

This is fantastic news in principle, but in practice the authorities don't have the resources, or sometimes the will, to actually protect these areas in any way other than drawing a line on a map. The government has enough trouble finding funds to pay the rangers who patrol the most popular parks, let alone to recruit staff for the remote sanctuaries, though in recent years a number of international NGOs have been helping to train and fund teams of enforcement rangers (see p58).

Among the new protected areas, the Mondulkiri Protected Forest (p303), at 4294 sq km, is now the largest protected area in Cambodia and is contiguous with Yok Don National Park in Vietnam. The Central Cardamoms Protected Forest (see p189 and p238), at 4013 sq km, borders the Phnom Samkos Wildlife Sanctuary (p239) to the west and the Phnom Aural Wildlife Sanctuary to the east, creating almost 10,000 sq km of theoretically protected land. The noncontiguous Southern Cardamoms Protected Forest (1443 sq km; p189) is along the Koh Kong Conservation Corridor (p186), whose ecotourism potential is as vast as its jungles are impenetrable.

ENVIRONMENTAL ISSUES
Logging

The biggest threat to Cambodia's globally important ecosystems is logging, both for timber and to clear land for plantations. During the Vietnamese occupation, troops stripped away swaths of forest to prevent Khmer Rouge ambushes along highways. The devastation increased in the 1990s, when the shift to a capitalist market economy led to an asset-stripping bonanza by well-connected businessmen working hand-in-glove with corrupt members of government.

International demand for timber is huge, and as neighbouring countries such as Thailand and Vietnam began to enforce much tougher logging regulations, foreign logging companies flocked to Cambodia. At the height of the country's logging epidemic (at the end of 1997), just under 70,000 sq km of the country's land area – about 35% of its total surface area – had been allocated as concessions, amounting to almost

Banned in Cambodia, the damning report *Cambodia's Family Trees* (www.globalwitness .org/pages/en/cambodia .html), by the UK-based environmental watchdog Global Witness, lays out all the details about illegal logging in Cambodia.

all of Cambodia's forest land except national parks and protected areas. However, even in these supposed havens, illegal logging continued.

The Royal Cambodian Armed Forces (RCAF) has been the driving force behind much of the recent logging in Cambodia; the RCAF has assisted in legal logging concessions, but it has also logged illegally elsewhere. The proceeds from these operations go into the army's grey (undeclared) budget, although its nominal budget already takes up a huge chunk of the government's cash.

In the short term, deforestation is contributing to worsening floods along the Mekong, but the long-term implications of logging are mind-boggling. Without trees to cloak the hills, the rains will inevitably carry away large amounts of topsoil during future monsoons and in time this will have a serious effect on Tonlé Sap. Will the shallow waters recede as a result of slow siltation, creating a situation similar to that marking the fall of the Angkorian empire? Combined with overfishing and pollution, these problems may lead to the eventual destruction of the lake – a catastrophe of apocalyptic proportions for future generations.

Since about 2002 things have been looking up (there was no further to look down). Under pressure from donors and international institutions – and the kick-ass environmental watchdog Global Witness (www .globalwitness.org) – all logging contracts were effectively frozen pending further negotiations with the government. Industrial-scale logging ceased and the huge trucks thundering up and down the country's dirt highways disappeared. However, small-scale illegal logging continued, including cutting for charcoal production and burning off for settlement, all of which continue to reduce Cambodia's forest cover.

The latest threat to Cambodia's forests comes from 'economic concessions' granted to establish plantations of cash crops such as rubber, mango, cashew and jackfruit, or agro-forestry groves of acacia and eucalyptus to supply wood chips for the paper industry. There are legal limits – land grants for plantations cannot be larger than 100 sq km (yes, that's 10km by 10km!) – but even this generous limit is often flouted. Worse still, there have been cases where concessionaires chop down all the trees to prepare the ground – and then fail to plant anything at all, the 'plantation' being merely a convenient fiction to facilitate clear-cutting.

According to the 'Conservation of Tropical Forests and Biological Diversity in Cambodia', *US Foreign Assistance Act 118/119 Analysis* (April 2005): 'Management of [Cambodia's] rich natural resources, especially forests and the Tonlé Sap Lake, is hampered by corruption, extreme inequality of access rights, insufficient or nonexistent right of tenure, a weak civil society, ethnic divisions and growing population pressures.'

> Back in the early 1990s, Cambodia had such extensive forest cover compared with its neighbours that some environmentalists were calling for the whole country to be made a protected area.

> In September 2005, three enforcement rangers working to prevent illegal hunting and logging in the Cardamom Mountains were murdered in two separate incidents, apparently by poachers.

Pollution

Cambodia has a pollution problem, but it is not of the same nature as the carbon monoxide crises in neighbouring capitals such as Bangkok and Jakarta. In fact, Phnom Penh is the only city in Cambodia that suffers from air pollution. The country does, however, suffer the ill-effects of an extremely primitive sanitation system in urban areas, and nonexistent sanitary facilities in rural areas – only a tiny percentage of the population have access to proper facilities. These conditions breed and spread disease; epidemics of diarrhoea are not uncommon and it is the number-one killer of young children in Cambodia.

Detritus of all sorts, especially plastic bags and bottles, can be seen in distressing quantities on beaches, around waterfalls, along roads and carpeting towns, villages and hamlets all over the country.

DOING YOUR BIT!

Every visitor to Cambodia can make at least a small contribution to the country's ecological sustainability.

- Cambodia's wild animals are under considerable threat from domestic 'bush meat' consumption and the illegal international trade in animal products. It may be 'exotic' to try wild meat such as bat, deer and shark fin – or to buy products made from endangered plants and animals – but doing so will indicate that you condone such practices and, more importantly, add to demand and encourage more hunting.

- Forest products such as rattan, orchids and medicinal herbs are under threat as the majority are collected from the country's dwindling forests. However, some of these products can be harvested sustainably or cultivated, so if you buy them from reputable sources (such as an ecotourism project), local people have the opportunity to earn additional income while protecting natural areas from exploitation and degradation.

- When snorkelling, diving or simply boating, be careful not to touch live coral or to anchor boats on it as this hinders its growth. And don't buy coral souvenirs.

- Many Cambodians remain unaware of the implications of littering. Recently, though, pilot clean-up projects have been launched in places such as Koh Ker and Kirirom National Park. Raise awareness of this issue by setting an example: dispose of all your litter responsibly.

Mekong Be Dammed

With a meandering length of around 4200km, the Mekong is the longest river in Southeast Asia. In terms of fish biodiversity it is second only to the Amazon. Some 50 million people depend on the Mekong for their livelihoods but with regional energy needs spiralling ever upwards, it is very tempting for a poor country like Cambodia – and its none-too-wealthy neighbours – to dam rivers to generate hydroelectric power.

Overseeing development plans for the river is the Mekong River Commission (MRC; www.mrcmekong.org), formed by the UNDP and comprising Cambodia, Thailand, Laos and Vietnam, an organisation that, ostensibly, is committed to sustainable development. But the greatest threat may come from dams being built in China.

Scientists worry about how dams will affect fish migration – some environmentalists claim that they might halve the fish population of the Mekong and perhaps even Tonlé Sap. But perhaps of most concern is the potential impact of dams on the annual monsoon flooding of the Mekong, which deposits nutrient-rich silt across vast tracts of land used for agriculture. Even a drop of just 1m in wet-season water levels would result in around 2000 sq km less flood area around Tonlé Sap, with potentially disastrous consequences for Cambodia's farmers.

Food & Drink

It's no secret that the dining tables of Thailand and Vietnam are home to some of the finest food in the world, so it should come as no surprise to discover that Cambodian cuisine is also rather special. Unlike the culinary colossuses that are its neighbours, the cuisine of Cambodia is not that well known in international circles, but all that looks set to change. Just as Angkor has put Cambodia on the tourist map, so too *amoc* (baked fish with coconut, lemon grass and chilli in banana leaf) could put the country on the culinary map of the world.

Cambodia has a great variety of national dishes, some similar to the cuisine of neighbouring Thailand and Laos, others closer to Chinese and Vietnamese cooking, but all come with that unique Cambodian twist, be it the odd herb here or the odd spice there. The overall impression is that Khmer cooking is similar to Thai cooking but with fewer spices.

Freshwater fish forms a huge part of the Cambodian diet thanks to the natural phenomenon that is Tonlé Sap Lake, and they come in every shape and size from the giant Mekong catfish to teeny, tiny whitebait, which are great beer snacks when deep-fried. The French left their mark too, with baguettes becoming the national bread and Cambodian cooks showing a healthy reverence for tender meats.

Cambodia is a crossroads in Asia, the meeting point of the great civilisations of India and China, and just as its culture has drawn on both, so too has its cuisine. Whether it's spring rolls or curry that take your fancy, you will find them both in Cambodian cooking. Add to this a world of dips and sauces to complement the cooking and a culinary journey through Cambodia becomes as rich a feast as any in Asia.

For the scoop on countryside cooking in Cambodia, pick up *From Spiders to Waterlilies,* a cookbook produced by Romdeng restaurant (p102) in Phnom Penh.

STAPLES & SPECIALITIES

Cambodia's lush fields provide the rice and its abundant waterways the fish that is fermented into *prahoc* (fermented fish paste), which together form the backbone of Khmer cuisine. Built around these are the flavours that give the cuisine its kick: the secret roots, the welcome herbs and the aromatic tubers. Together they give the salads, snacks, soups and stews a unique aroma and taste that smacks of Cambodia. Whatever they are preparing, a Khmer cook will demand freshness and a healthy balance of flavours and textures.

Rice is the principal staple, enshrined in the Khmer word for eating or to eat, *nam bai* – literally 'eat rice'. Many a Cambodian, particularly drivers, will run out of steam if they run out of rice. It doesn't matter that the same carbohydrates are available in other foods, it is rice and rice alone that counts. Battambang Province (p240) is Cambodia's rice bowl and produces the country's finest yield.

Longteine De Monteiro runs several Cambodian restaurants on the east coast of the USA and she has put together her favourite traditional Khmer recipes at www .elephantwalk.com.

For the taste of Cambodia in a bowl, try the local *kyteow,* a rice-noodle soup that will keep you going all day. This full and balanced meal will cost you just 2000r in markets and about US$1 in local restaurants. No noodles? Then try the *bobor* (rice porridge), a national institution, for breakfast, lunch and dinner, and best sampled with some fresh fish and a splash of ginger.

A Cambodian meal almost always includes a *samlor* (traditional soup), which will appear at the same time as the other courses. *Samlor machou banle* (hot and sour fish soup with pineapple and a splash of spices) is popular. Other popular soups include *samlor chapek* (ginger-flavoured pork soup), *samlor machou bawng kawng* (prawn soup similar to the popular Thai tom yam) and *samlor ktis* (fish soup with coconut and pineapple).

Friends (p102) is one of the best-known restaurants in Phnom Penh, turning out a fine array of tapas, shakes and specials to help street children in the capital. Its cookbook *The Best of Friends* is a visual feast showcasing its best recipes.

TRAVEL YOUR TASTEBUDS

No matter what part of the world you come from, if you travel much in Cambodia, you are going to encounter food that is unusual, strange, maybe even immoral, or just plain weird. The fiercely omnivorous Cambodians find nothing strange in eating insects, algae, offal or fish bladders. They will dine on a duck foetus, brew up some brains or snack on some spiders. They will peel live frogs to grill on a barbecue or down the wine infused with cobra to increase their virility.

To the Khmers there is nothing 'strange' about anything that will sustain the body. To them a food is either wholesome or it isn't; it's nutritious or it isn't; it tastes good or it doesn't. And that's all they worry about. They'll try anything once, even a burger.

Much of the fish eaten in Cambodia is freshwater, from the Tonlé Sap lake or the Mekong River. *Trey ahng* (grilled fish) is a Cambodian speciality (*ahng* means 'grilled' and can be applied to many dishes). Traditionally, the fish is eaten as pieces wrapped in lettuce or spinach leaves and then dipped into *teuk trey*, a fish sauce that is a close relative of Vietnam's *nuoc mam*, but with the addition of ground peanuts.

Cambodian salad dishes are also popular and delicious, although quite different from the Western idea of a cold salad. *Phlea sait kow* is a beef and vegetable salad, flavoured with coriander, mint and lemon grass. These three herbs find their way into many Cambodian dishes.

Desserts can be sampled cheaply at night markets around the country. One sweet snack to look out for is the ice-cream sandwich. No kidding – it's popular with the kids and involves putting a slab of homemade ice cream in a piece of sponge or bread. It actually doesn't taste too bad.

Cambodia is blessed with many tropical fruits and sampling these is an integral part of a visit to the country. All the common fruits can be found in abundance, including *chek* (bananas), *menoa* (pineapples) and *duong* (coconuts). Among the larger fruit, *khnau* (jackfruit) is very common, often weighing more than 20kg. Beneath the green skin are bright yellow segments with a distinctive taste and rubbery texture. The *tourain* (durian) usually needs no introduction, as you can smell it from a mile off. The exterior is green with sharp spines while inside is a milky, soft interior regarded by the Chinese as an aphrodisiac. It stinks, although some maintain it is an acquired taste – best acquired with a nose peg.

The fruits most popular with visitors include the *mongkut* (mangosteen) and *sao mao* (rambutan). The small mangosteen has a purple skin that contains white segments with a divine flavour. Queen Victoria is said to have offered a reward to anyone able to transport an edible mangosteen back to England. Similarly popular is the rambutan, the interior like a lychee, but the exterior covered in soft red and green spines.

Best of all, although common throughout the world, are the *svay* (mangoes). The Cambodian mango season is from March to May. Other varieties of mango are available year round, but it's the hot-season ones that are a taste sensation.

DRINKS

Cambodia has a lively local drinking culture, and the heat and humidity will ensure that you hunt out anything on offer to quench your thirst. Coffee, tea, beer, wine, soft drinks, fresh fruit juices or some of the more exotic 'firewaters' are all widely available. Tea is the national drink, but these days it is just as likely to be beer in the glass.

The closest thing Cambodia has to a national dish is *amoc* (baked fish wrapped in banana leaf with coconut, lemon grass and chilli). Sometimes it arrives more like a soup, served in the shell of a young coconut.

Teuk trey (fish sauce), one of the most popular condiments in Cambodian cooking, cannot be taken on international flights in line with regulations on carrying strong-smelling or corrosive substances.

For the inside story on Cambodian cooking, including the secrets of the royal recipes, seek out a copy of *The Cuisine of Cambodia* by Nusara Thaitawat (2000), which includes stunning photography throughout.

Beer

It's never a challenge to find a beer in Cambodia and even the most remote village usually has a stall selling a few cans. Angkor is the national beer, produced in vast quantities in a big brewery down in Sihanoukville. It is a decent brew and costs around US$1.50 to US$3 for a 660ml bottle in most restaurants and bars. Draft Angkor is available for US$1 or less in Phnom Penh and Sihanoukville.

A beer brand from neighbouring Laos, Beer Lao, is very drinkable and is also one of the cheapest ales you can get. Tiger Beer is produced locally and is a popular draft in the capital. Most Khmer restaurants have a bevy of 'beer girls', each promoting a particular beer brand. They are always friendly and will leave you alone if you prefer not to drink. Brands represented include Angkor, Heineken, Tiger, San Miguel, Stella Artois, Carlsberg, Fosters and Becks. Cans of beer sell for around US$1 in local restaurants.

A word of caution for beer seekers in Cambodia. While the country is awash with good brews, there is a shortage of refrigeration in the countryside. Go native. Learn how to say '*Som teuk koh*' ('Ice, please'). That's right, drink your beer on the rocks!

When Cambodian men propose a toast, they usually stipulate what percentage of the glass must be downed. If they are feeling generous, it might be just *ha-sip pea-roi* (50%), but more often than not it is *moi roi pea-roi* (100%).

Wine & Spirits

Local wine in Cambodia generally means rice wine; it is popular with the minority peoples of the northeast. Some rice wines are fermented for months and are super strong, while other brews are fresher and taste more like a demented cocktail. Either way, if you are invited to join a session in a minority village, it's rude to decline. Other local wines include light sugar palm wine and ginger wine.

In Phnom Penh and Siem Reap, foreign wines and spirits are sold in supermarkets at bargain prices, given how far they have to travel. Wines from Europe and Australia start at about US$4, while the famous names of the spirit world cost between US$4 and US$10! Yes, a bottle of Stoly vodka is just US$4.

Most of the locally produced spirits are best avoided, although some expats contend that Sra Special, a local whisky-like concoction, is not bad. At around US$1 a bottle, it's a cheap route to oblivion. There has also been a surge in the popularity of 'muscle wines' (something like Red Bull meets absinthe) with enticing pictures of strongmen on the labels and names like Hercules, Commando Bear and Brace of Loma. They contain enough unknown substances to contravene the Geneva Chemical Weapons Convention and should only be approached with caution.

The local brew for country folk is sugar palm wine, distilled daily direct from the trees and fairly potent after it has settled. Sold in bamboo containers off the back of bicycles, it's tasty and cheap, although only for those with a cast-iron stomach.

Tea & Coffee

Chinese-style *tai* (tea) is a bit of a national institution, and in most Khmer and Chinese restaurants a pot will automatically appear for no extra charge as soon as you sit down. *Kaa fey* (coffee) is sold in most restaurants. It is either black or *café au lait* – served with dollops of condensed milk, which makes it very sweet.

Water & Soft Drinks

Drinking tap water *must* be avoided, especially in the provinces, as it is rarely purified and may lead to stomach complications (p350). Locally produced mineral water starts at 500r per bottle at shops and stalls, though some locals and expats alike doubt the purity of the cheapest stuff. Those with a weak constitution might want to opt for one of the better brands, such as Evian.

Although tap water should be avoided, it is generally OK to have ice in your drinks. Throughout Cambodia, *teuk koh* (ice) is produced with treated water at local ice factories, a legacy of the French.

All the well-known soft drinks are available in Cambodia. Bottled drinks are about 1000r, while canned drinks cost about 2000r and more again in restaurants or bars.

Fruit Shakes

Teuk kalohk are popular throughout Cambodia. They are a little like fruit smoothies and are a great way to wash down a meal. Stalls are set up around local night markets some time before dark and the drinks cost around 2000r. Watch out for how much sugar goes in if you don't like sweet drinks, and pass on the offer of an egg if you don't want it super frothy.

> Traditionally, Cambodians used to eat with their hands like many in India, but in more recent years this has given way to the fork and spoon like in Thailand or Laos, and the chopsticks, an import that came with the large Chinese population in Phnom Penh.

CELEBRATIONS

Cambodians enjoy celebrating, be it a wedding, a festival or a football match. For a festival, the family coffers are broken open and no matter how much they hold, it is deemed insufficient. The money is splurged on those treats that the family may not be able to afford at other times, such as duck, shrimp or crab. Guests are welcomed and will be seated at large round tables, then the food is paraded out course after course. Everyone eats until they can eat no more and drinks beyond their limit. Glasses are raised and toasts are led, everyone downs-in-one. The secret of standing straight come the end of the night is making sure you have plenty of ice in your beer.

WHERE TO EAT & DRINK

Whatever your taste, some eatery in Cambodia is sure to help out, be it the humble peddler with her yoke, a market stall, a local diner or a slick restaurant.

It is easy to sample inexpensive Khmer cuisine throughout the country, mostly at local markets and cheap restaurants. For more refined Khmer dining, the best restaurants are in Phnom Penh (p96) and Siem Reap (p131), where there is also the choice of excellent Thai, Vietnamese, Chinese, Indian, French and Mediterranean cooking. Chinese, and to a lesser extent Vietnamese, food is available in towns across the country due to the large urban populations of both of these ethnic groups.

> The best food blog on Cambodia can be found at www.phnomenon .com, which covers Khmer food, surfing the streets and the up-and-coming dining scene. Originally authored by Phil Lees, it remains to be seen if someone will take up the gauntlet in his absence.

There are few Western fast-food chains in Phnom Penh as yet, but there are a few local copycats. The most successful has been Lucky Burger, with lots of branches in the capital.

There are often no set hours for places to eat but, as a general rule of thumb, street stalls are open from very early in the morning till early evening, while some stalls specialise in the night shift. Most restaurants are open all day, while some of the fancier places are only open for lunch (usually 11am to 2.30pm) and dinner (usually 5pm to 10pm).

Quick Eats

Because so much of life is lived outside the home, street food is an important part of everyday Cambodian life. Like many Southeast Asian people, Cambodians are inveterate snackers. They can be found at impromptu stalls at any time of the day or night, delving into a range of unidentified frying objects. Drop into the markets for an even greater range of dishes and the chance of a comfortable seat. It's cheap, cheerful and a cool way to get up close and personal with Khmer cuisine. Some of the new shopping malls, such as Sorya Shopping Centre (p97) in Phnom Penh, have food courts where it is possible to sample the street food in hygienic air-conditioned comfort.

TOP 10 RESTAURANTS HELPING CAMBODIA

There are lots of NGOs attempting to assist Cambodia as it walks the road to recovery. Some of these have established restaurants and eateries to raise funds and give young disadvantaged Cambodians some experience in the hospitality sector.

- **Epic Arts Café** (p217) – a lively little café assisting the deaf community and promoting arts for the disabled
- **Friends** (p102) – a superb tapas restaurant with delicious shakes and sharp cocktails, helping street children into the restaurant industry
- **French Eats Café** (p244) – a cosy place that helps children from families affected by HIV/AIDS
- **Gelato Italiano** (p211) – a modern, Italian-style gelataria staffed by students from Sihanoukville's Don Bosco Hotel School
- **Les Jardins des Delice** (p131) – part of the Paul Dubrule Hotel School, offering Sofitel-standard cuisine at affordable prices
- **Joe-to-Go** (p131) – offering coffee with a kick before sunrise at Angkor to help fight child trafficking and sex tourism
- **Le Lotus Blanc** (p102) – an excellent French restaurant that helps raise funds and provide training for children from the Stung Meanchey dump area
- **Mekong Blue** (p291) – a relaxing café that is part of a silk cooperative seeking to assist disadvantaged and vulnerable women
- **Romdeng** (p102) – the place for traditional Khmer country cooking, including deep-fried tarantula; part of the Friends family
- **Starfish Bakery & Café** (p210) – a homely café in town offering delectable cakes and shakes, with all proceeds going to community projects

VEGETARIANS & VEGANS

Few Cambodians understand the concept of strict vegetarianism and many will say something is vegetarian to please the customer when in fact it is not. If you are not a strict vegetarian and can deal with fish sauces and the like, you should have few problems ordering meals, and those who eat fish can sample Khmer cooking at its best. In the major tourist centres, many of the international restaurants feature vegetarian meals, although these are not budget options. Cheaper vegetarian meals are usually available at guesthouses. In Khmer and Chinese restaurants, stir-fried vegetable dishes are readily available, as are vegetarian fried rice dishes, but it is unlikely these 'vegetarian' dishes have been cooked in separate woks from other fish- and meat-based dishes. Indian restaurants in the popular tourist centres can cook up genuine vegetarian food, as they usually understand the vegetarian principle better than the *prahoc*-loving Khmers.

EATING WITH KIDS

Family is at the heart of life in Cambodia, so it is hardly surprising to find family-oriented restaurants throughout the country. Most local restaurants will welcome children with open arms, particularly foreign kiddies, as staff don't get a chance to see them up close that often. Sometimes the welcome will be too much, with pinches and pats coming left, right and centre, but such is the way in Cambodia.

Ironically, it is often the upmarket Western restaurants where the reception may be terse if the children are playing up, as some stiff expats seem to have forgotten that they started out life that small. That said, there are plenty of excellent, child-friendly cafés and restaurants in Phnom Penh and Siem Reap

Before becoming a member of the WTO, copyright protection was almost unknown in Cambodia and that spawned a host of copycat fast-food restaurants including KFC (Khmer Fried Chicken?), Pizza Hot and Burger Queen, all now sadly closed.

serving dishes from home. There are rarely children's menus in any places, but with food so affordable, there is little room to quibble.

Most of the snacks children are accustomed to back home are available in Cambodia…and so much more. It is a great country for fruit, and the sweetness of mangosteens or the weirdness of dragon fruit or rambutan is a sure way to get them interested. Playing 'rambutan eyes' with the empty peels is a guaranteed laugh.

There is sometimes monosodium glutamate (MSG) in local Cambodian food. If your child has problems digesting it or you prefer to avoid it, it is better to stick to restaurants with an English-language menu that are used to dealing with tourists.

For more information on travelling with children in Cambodia, see p308.

HABITS & CUSTOMS

Enter the Cambodian kitchen and you will learn that fine food comes from simplicity. Essentials consist of a strong flame, clean water, basic cutting utensils, a mortar and pestle, and a well-blackened pot or two.

Cambodians eat three meals a day. Breakfast is either *kyteow* or *bobor*. Baguettes are available at any time of day or night, and go down well with a cup of coffee.

Lunch starts early, around 11am. Traditionally lunch is taken with the family, but in towns and cities many workers now eat at local restaurants or markets.

Dinner is the time for family bonding. Dishes are arranged around the central rice bowl and diners each have a small eating bowl. The procedure is uncomplicated: spoon some rice into your bowl, and lay 'something else' on top of it.

When ordering multiple courses from a restaurant menu don't worry – don't even think – about the proper succession of courses. All dishes are placed in the centre of the table as soon as they are ready. Diners then help themselves to whatever appeals to them, regardless of who ordered what.

Table Etiquette

Sit at the table with your bowl on a small plate, chopsticks or fork and spoon at the ready. Some Cambodians prefer chopsticks, some prefer fork and spoon, but both are usually available. Each place setting will include a small bowl usually located at the top right-hand side for the dipping sauces.

When serving yourself from the central bowls, use the communal serving spoon so as not to dip your chopsticks or spoon into the food. To begin eat-

Both Phnom Penh and Siem Reap have child-friendly eateries. Check out Le Jardin (p103) or The Living Room (p104) in Phnom Penh or The Singing Tree (p131) in Siem Reap and sit back and relax. Some of the fast-food places in the capital also have children's adventure playgrounds.

DOS & DON'TS

- *Do* wait for your host to sit first
- *Don't* turn down food placed in your bowl by your host
- *Do* learn to use chopsticks
- *Don't* leave chopsticks in a V-shape in the bowl, a symbol of death
- *Do* tip about 5% to 10% in restaurants, as wages are low
- *Don't* tip if there is already a service charge on the bill
- *Do* drink every time someone offers a toast
- *Don't* pass out face down on the table if the toasting goes on all night

ing, just pick up your bowl with the left hand, bring it close to your mouth, and spoon in the rice and food.

It is polite for the host to offer more food than the guests can eat, and it is polite for the guests not to eat everything in sight.

COOKING COURSES

If you are really taken with Cambodian cuisine, it is possible to learn some tricks of the trade by signing up for a cooking course. It's a great way to introduce your Cambodia experience to your friends; no-one wants to sit through the slideshow of photos, but offer them a mouthwatering meal and they will all come running!

Most Cambodian meals are cooked in a large wok, known locally as *chhnang khteak*.

There are courses available in Phnom Penh, Siem Reap, Battambang and Sihanoukville, and more are popping up all the time. In Phnom Penh, Frizz Restaurant offers courses (p88), as do some of the hotels. In Siem Reap, Le Tigre de Papier (p125) offers daily courses in conjunction with the Sala Bai Training School, plus more and more hotels are getting into the game. In Battambang, the Smokin' Pot (p241) is a cracking little kitchen restaurant offering a cheap introduction to the secrets of Cambodian cooking.

EAT YOUR WORDS
Useful Phrases
Where is a ...?

... neuv ai naa? ...នៅឯណា?

restaurant

resturawn, phowjaniyahtnaan រេស្តូរង់, ភោជនីយដ្ឋាន

cheap restaurant

haang baay, resturawn thaok ហាងបាយ, រេស្តូរង់ថោក

food stall

kuhnlaing loak m'howp កន្លែងលក់ម្ហូប

market

psar ផ្សារ

Do you have a menu in English?

mien menui jea piasaa awnglay te? មានម៉ឺនុយជាភាសាខ្មែរទេ?

I'm vegetarian. (I can't eat meat.)

kh'nyohm tawm sait ខ្ញុំតមសាច់

Can I get this without the meat?

sohm kohm dak sait សូមកុំដាក់សាច់

I'm allergic to (peanuts).

kohm dak (sandaik dei) កុំដាក់(សណ្ដែកដី)

What's the speciality here?

tii nih mien m'howp ei piseh te? ទីនេះមានម្ហូបអ្វីពិសេសទេ?

Not too spicy, please.

sohm kohm twœ huhl pek សូមកុំធ្វើហឹរពេក

This is delicious.

nih ch'ngain nah អានេះឆ្ងាញ់ណាស់

The bill, please.

sohm kuht lui សូមគិតលុយ

Can you please bring me ...?

sohm yohk ... mao សូមយក...មក

a fork

sawm សម

a knife

kambuht កាំបិត

a plate
jaan   ចាន
a spoon
slaapria   ស្លាបព្រា

Food Glossary
BREAKFAST

bread	*nohm paang*	នំប៉័ង
butter	*bœ*	ប៊ើរ
fried eggs	*pohng moan jien*	ពងមាន់ចៀន
rice porridge	*bobor*	បបរ
vegetable noodle soup	*kyteow dak buhn lai*	គុយទាវដាក់បន្លែ

LUNCH & DINNER

beef	*sait kow*	សាច់គោ
chicken	*sait moan*	សាច់មាន់
crab	*k'daam*	ក្តាម
curry	*karii*	ការី
eel	*ahntohng*	អន្ទង់
fish	*trey*	ត្រី
fried	*jien, chaa*	ចៀន, ឆា
frog	*kawng kaip*	កង្កែប
grilled	*ahng*	អាំង
lobster	*bawng kawng*	បង្កង
noodles	*mii* (egg), *kyteow* (rice)	មី, គុយទាវ
pork	*sait j'ruuk*	សាច់ជ្រូក
rice	*bai*	បាយ
shrimp	*bawngkia*	បង្គា
snail	*kh'jawng*	ខ្យង
soup	*sup*	ស៊ុប
spring rolls	*naim* (fresh), *chaa yaw* (fried)	ណែម, ឆាយ៉
squid	*meuk*	មឹក
steamed	*jamhoi*	ចំហុយ
vegetables	*buhn lai*	បន្លែ

FRUITS

apple	*phla i powm*	ផ្លែប៉ោម
banana	*chek*	ចេក
coconut	*duong*	ដូង
custard apple	*tiep*	ទៀប
dragon fruit	*phlai srakaa neak*	ផ្លែស្រកានាគ
durian	*tourain*	ធូរេន
grapes	*tompeang baai juu*	ទំពាំងបាយជូរ
guava	*trawbaik*	ត្របែក
jackfruit	*khnau*	ខ្នុរ
lemon	*krow-it ch'maa*	ក្រូចឆ្មារ
longan	*mien*	មៀន
lychee	*phlai kuulain*	ផ្លែគូលេន
mandarin	*krow-it khwait*	ក្រូចខ្វិច
mango	*svay*	ស្វាយ
mangosteen	*mongkut*	មង្ឃុត

orange	*krow-it pow saat*	ក្រូចពោធិសាត់
papaya	*l'howng*	ល្ហុង
pineapple	*menoa*	ម្នាស់
pomelo	*krow-it th'lohng*	ក្រូចថ្លុង
rambutan	*sao mao*	សាវម៉ាវ
starfruit	*speu*	ស្ពឺ
watermelon	*euv luhk*	ឪឡឹក

CONDIMENTS

chilli	*m'teh*	ម្ទេស
fish sauce	*teuk trey*	ទឹកត្រី
garlic	*kh'tuhm saw*	ខ្ទឹមស
ginger	*kh'nyei*	ខ្ញី
ice	*teuk koh*	ទឹកកក
lemon grass	*sluhk kray*	ស្លឹកគ្រៃ
pepper	*m'rait*	ម្រេច
salt	*uhmbuhl*	អំបិល
soy sauce	*teuk sii iw*	ទឹកសុីអុីវ
sugar	*skaw*	ស្ករ

DRINKS

banana shake	*teuk kralohk*	ទឹកក្រឡុកចេក
beer	*bii-yœ*	បៀរ
black coffee	*kaa fey kh'mav*	កាហ្វេខ្មៅ
coffee	*kaa fey*	កាហ្វេ
iced coffee	*kaa fey teuk koh*	កាហ្វេទឹកកក
lemon juice	*teuk krow-it ch'maa*	ទឹកក្រូចឆ្មារ
mixed fruit shake	*teuk kralohk chek*	ទឹកក្រឡុកផ្លែឈើ
orange juice	*teuk krow-it pow sat*	ទឹកក្រូចពោធិសាត់
tea	*tai*	តែ
tea with milk	*tai teuk dawh kow*	តែទឹកដោះគោ
white coffee	*kaa fey ohlay* (ie *café au lait*)	កាហ្វេអូឡេ

Phnom Penh
ភ្នំពេញ

Phnom Penh: the name can't help but conjure up an image of the exotic. The glimmering spires of the royal palace, the fluttering saffron of the monks' robes, and the luscious location on the banks of the mighty Mekong; this is one of Asia's undiscovered gems. But it's also a city on the move, as a new wave of investors move in, perhaps forever changing the character, and skyline, of this classic city. Phnom Penh is a crossroads of Asia's past and present, a city of extremes of poverty and excess, of charm and chaos, but one that never fails to captivate.

Phnom Penh can be an assault on the senses. Motorbikes whiz through the backstreets without a thought for pedestrians; pungent scents float up from stalls and markets; and all the while the sound of life, of commerce, of survival, reverberates all around. But this is all part of the attraction. It's not just another metropolis, the identikit image of a modern capital; it is an older Asia that many dreamed of when first planning their adventures overseas.

Once the 'Pearl of Asia', Phnom Penh's shine was tarnished by the impact of war and revolution. But that's history, and Phnom Penh has risen from the ashes to take its place among the cool capitals of the region. Delve into the ancient past at the National Museum or struggle to make sense of the recent trauma at Tuol Sleng Museum. Browse the city's markets for a bargain or linger in the beautiful boutiques that are putting Phnom Penh on the style map. Street-surf through the local stalls for a snack or enjoy the refined surrounds of a designer restaurant. Whatever your flavour, no matter your taste, it's all here in Phnom Penh.

HIGHLIGHTS

- Be dazzled by the 5000 silver floor tiles of the **Silver Pagoda** (p83), part of the Royal Palace

- Discover the world's finest collection of Khmer sculpture at the stunning **National Museum** (p84)

- Check out the huge dome of **Psar Thmei** (p109), the Art Deco masterpiece that is Phnom Penh's central market

- Delve into the dark side of Cambodian history with a visit to **Tuol Sleng Museum** (p85), essential to understanding the pain of the past

- Experience Phnom Penh's legendary nightlife with a happy-hour cocktail, a local meal and a crawl through the city's **lively bars** (p104)

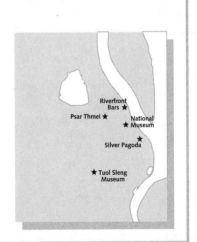

Riverfront Bars ★

Psar Thmei ★

★ National Museum

★ Silver Pagoda

★ Tuol Sleng Museum

| ■ TELEPHONE CODE: 023 | ■ POPULATION: 2 MILLION | ■ AREA: 290 SQ KM |

HISTORY

Legend has it that the city of Phnom Penh was founded when an old woman named Penh found four Buddha images that had come to rest on the banks of the Mekong River. She housed them on a nearby hill, and the town that grew up here came to be known as Phnom Penh (Hill of Penh).

The story gives no hint as to why, in the 1430s, Angkor was abandoned and Phnom Penh chosen as the site of the new Cambodian capital. The move has been much lamented as evidence of cultural decline and the fall of an empire, but it made a good deal of practical sense. Angkor was poorly situated for trade and subject to attacks from the Siamese (Thai) kingdom of Ayuthaya. Phnom Penh commanded a more central position in the Khmer territories and was perfectly located for riverine trade with Laos and China, via the Mekong Delta. The Tonlé Sap River provided access to the rich fishing grounds of Tonlé Sap Lake.

By the mid-16th century, trade had turned Phnom Penh into a regional power. Indonesian and Chinese traders were drawn to the city in large numbers. A century later, however, Vietnamese incursions into Khmer territory had robbed the city of access to sea lanes, and Chinese merchants driven south by the Manchu (Qing) dynasty began to monopolise trade. The landlocked and increasingly isolated kingdom became a buffer between ascendant Thais and Vietnamese. In 1772 the Thais burnt Phnom Penh to the ground. Although the city was rebuilt, Phnom Penh was buffeted by the rival intrigues of the Thai and Vietnamese courts, until the French took over in 1863. Its population is thought not to have risen much above 25,000 during this period.

The French protectorate in Cambodia gave Phnom Penh the layout we know today. The city was divided into districts or *quartiers:* the French administrators and European traders inhabited the area north of Wat Phnom between Monivong Blvd and the Tonlé Sap River; the Chinese merchants occupied the riverfront area south of Wat Phnom to the Royal Palace and west as far as Norodom Blvd; and the Cambodians and Vietnamese lived around and to the south of the palace. By the time the French departed in 1953, they had left many important landmarks, including the Royal Palace, National Museum, Psar Thmei (Central Market) and many impressive government ministries.

The city grew fast in the post-independence peacetime years of Sihanouk's rule. By the time he was overthrown in 1970, the population of Phnom Penh was approximately 500,000. As the Vietnam War spread into Cambodian territory, the city's population swelled with refugees and reached more than two million in early 1975. The Khmer Rouge took the city on 17 April 1975 and, as part of its radical social programme, immediately forced the entire population into the countryside. Different factions of the Khmer Rouge were responsible for evacuating different zones of the city; civilians to the east of Norodom Blvd were sent east, those south of the palace to the south, and so on. Whole families were split up on those first fateful days of 'liberation' and, for many thousands of Cambodians, their experience of the dark days of Khmer Rouge rule depended on which area of the city they had been in that day.

During the time of Democratic Kampuchea, many tens of thousands of former Phnom Penhois – including the vast majority of the capital's educated residents – were killed. The population of Phnom Penh during the Khmer Rouge regime was never more than about 50,000, a figure made up of senior party members, factory workers and trusted military leaders.

Repopulation of the city began when the Vietnamese arrived in 1979, although at first it was strictly controlled by the new government. During much of the 1980s, cows were more common than cars on the streets of the capital, and it was not until the government dispensed with its communist baggage at the end of the decade that Phnom Penh began to develop. The 1990s were boom years for some: along with the arrival of the UN Transitional Authority in Cambodia (Untac) came two billion US dollars, much of it in salaries for expats. Well-connected residents were only too happy to help foreigners part with their money through high rents and hefty price-hikes. Businesses followed hot on the heels of Untac and commercial buildings began to spring up.

Phnom Penh has really begun to change in the last decade, with roads being repaired, sewage pipes laid, parks inaugurated and riverbanks reclaimed. Business is booming in many parts of the city with skyscrapers under development, investors rubbing their

PHNOM PENH

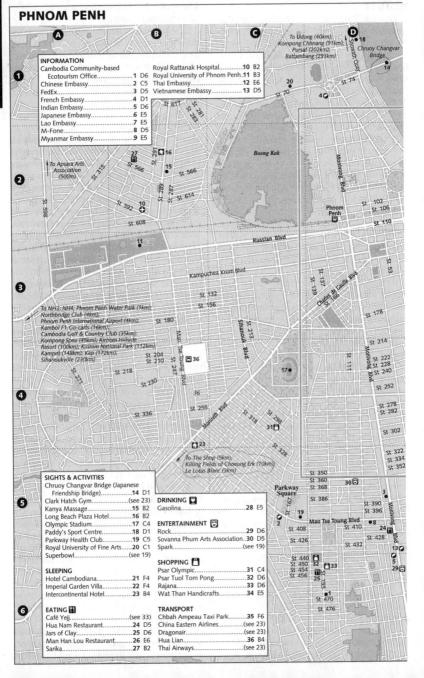

INFORMATION

Cambodia Community-based Ecotourism Office	**1** D6
Chinese Embassy	**2** C5
FedEx	**3** D5
French Embassy	**4** D1
Indian Embassy	**5** D6
Japanese Embassy	**6** E5
Lao Embassy	**7** E5
M-Fone	**8** D5
Myanmar Embassy	**9** E5
Royal Rattanak Hospital	**10** B2
Royal University of Phnom Penh	**11** B3
Thai Embassy	**12** E6
Vietnamese Embassy	**13** D5

SIGHTS & ACTIVITIES

Chruoy Changvar Bridge (Japanese Friendship Bridge)	**14** D1
Clark Hatch Gym	(see 23)
Kanya Massage	**15** B2
Long Beach Plaza Hotel	**16** B2
Olympic Stadium	**17** C4
Paddy's Sport Centre	**18** D1
Parkway Health Club	**19** C5
Royal University of Fine Arts	**20** C1
Superbowl	(see 19)

SLEEPING

Hotel Cambodiana	**21** F4
Imperial Garden Villa	**22** F4
Intercontinental Hotel	**23** B4

EATING

Café Yeji	(see 33)
Hua Nam Restaurant	**24** D5
Jars of Clay	**25** D6
Man Han Lou Restaurant	**26** E6
Sarika	**27** B2

DRINKING

Gasolina	**28** E5

ENTERTAINMENT

Rock	**29** D6
Sovanna Phum Arts Association	**30** D5
Spark	(see 19)

SHOPPING

Psar Olympic	**31** C4
Psar Tuol Tom Pong	**32** D6
Rajana	**33** D6
Wat Than Handicrafts	**34** E5

TRANSPORT

Chbah Ampeau Taxi Park	**35** F6
China Eastern Airlines	(see 23)
Dragonair	(see 23)
Hua Lian	**36** B4
Thai Airways	(see 23)

To Udong (40km);
Kompong Chhnang (91km);
Pursat (202km);
Battambang (293km)

Chruoy Changvar Bridge

Boeng Kak

Phnom Penh

Russian Blvd

Kampuchea Krom Blvd

To Apsara Arts Association (500m)

To NH3; NH4; Phnom Penh Water Park (1km);
Northbridge Club (4km);
Phnom Penh International Airport (4km);
Kambol F1-Go-carts (16km);
Cambodia Golf & Country Club (35km);
Kompong Speu (45km); Kirirom Hillside
Resort (100km); Kirirom National Park (112km);
Kampot (148km); Kep (172km);
Sihanoukville (230km)

To The Shop (5km);
Killing Fields of Choeung Ek (10km);
Le Lotus Blanc (3km)

Parkway Square

Mao Tse Toung Blvd

Sihanouk Blvd

Monivong Blvd

Charles de Gaulle Blvd

Norodom Blvd

hands with the sort of glee once reserved for Bangkok or Hanoi and swanky new restaurants opening up. Phnom Penh is finally on the move as a new middle class emerges to replace the thousands eliminated by the Khmer Rouge, and the elite invest their dollars at home rather than taking the risk of hiding them abroad. Phnom Penh is back, and bigger changes are set to come.

ORIENTATION

Phnom Penh is a fairly easy city in which to navigate as it is laid out in a numbered grid, a little like New York City. The major boulevards of Phnom Penh run north–south, parallel to the banks of the Tonlé Sap and Tonlé Bassac Rivers. Monivong Blvd cuts north–south through the centre of town, passing just west of Psar Thmei. Its northern sector is a busy shopping strip and home to some of the oldest hotels and travel agents in town. Norodom Blvd runs north–south from Wat Phnom, and is largely lined with administrative buildings; the northern end contains banks, while further south are government ministries and embassies. Samdech Sotharos Blvd runs north–south near the riverfront, past the Royal Palace and Silver Pagoda. Sisowath Quay hugs the river and is where many of the city's most popular restaurants and bars are located. The major east–west boulevards are Russian Blvd in the north of town, Sihanouk Blvd, which passes the Independence Monument and ends near the Hotel Cambodiana, and Mao Tse Toung Blvd, a ring road of sorts that also runs north–south in the west of the city.

Intersecting the main boulevards is a network of hundreds of numbered smaller streets. As a rule of thumb, streets running east–west have even numbers that increase as you head south from the Chruoy Changvar Bridge, while streets that run north–south have odd numbers that increase as you head west away from the river.

Most buildings around town have signs with both their building number and street (*phlauv*, abbreviated to Ph) number. Finding a building purely by its address, however, is not always easy, as numbers are rarely sequential. See the boxed text, p76, and pity the postman.

Most buses, taxis and pick-ups arrive in the centre of town around Psar Thmei and it is just a short *moto* (small motorcycle with driver),

KNOWING WHEN YOUR NUMBER'S UP

Navigating the streets of Phnom Penh should be pretty straightforward thanks to the grid system put in place by the French. The total and utter lack of an effective house-numbering system, however, makes some guesthouses, restaurants and offices that bit harder to track down. The long years of war, abandonment and reoccupation destroyed the old system and as residents began to repopulate the city, they seem to have picked numbers out of the air. It is not uncommon to drive past a row of houses numbered 13A, 34, 7, 26. Make sense of that and you might get a job as a code cracker. Worse still, several different houses might use the same number on the same street. The long and the short of it is that when you get to a guesthouse or restaurant recommended in this chapter only to discover it appears to have turned into a *prahoc* (fermented fish paste) shop, don't curse us for the bad smell. Just down the road will be another place with the same number – the guesthouse or restaurant you were looking for...unless, of course, it really has gone into the *prahoc* business.

When getting directions, ask for a cross-reference for an address, such as 'close to the intersection of St 110 and Norodom Blvd'. The letters 'EO' after a street address stand for *étage zéro* (ground floor).

remorque-moto (trailer pulled by motorbike) or taxi ride to most guesthouses and hotels. Some buses arrive at the north end of the riverfront near St 104 and there are persistent rumours the government will eventually develop out-of-town bus stations to ease traffic congestion. The train station is a couple of blocks northwest of Psar Thmei, but there are currently no passenger services. Boats from Siem Reap and Chau Doc (Vietnam) arrive at the tourist boat dock on the Tonlé Sap River at the eastern end of St 108. Hundreds of *motos* await in ambush. Phnom Penh International Airport is 7km west of central Phnom Penh.

Maps

For a handy pocket-size map, look out for a free copy of the *Phnom Penh 3-D Map*, which is distributed at the airport and selected bars and restaurants around the city. Both the *Phnom Penh Visitors' Guide* and the *Phnom Penh Pocket Guides*, freely available in the capital, have up-to-date maps.

INFORMATION

For up-to-date contact information on businesses in Phnom Penh, check out the **Yellow Pages** (www.yellowpages.com.kh). Check out *Phnom Penh Drinking and Dining* (www.cambodiapocketguide.com) for the lowdown on bars and restaurants. The *Phnom Penh Visitors' Guide* (www.canbypublications.com) is brimming with useful information on the capital and beyond, while *AsiaLife Phnom Penh* (www.asialifecambodia.com) is a reliable read.

Bookshops

Bohr's Books (Map p79; 5 Sothearos Blvd) A reliable, locally-owned secondhand bookshop near the riverfront.
Carnets d'Asie (Map p79; 218 St 182) A French-language bookshop in the French Cultural Centre.
D's Books (Map p79; www.ds-books.com; 79 St 240 & 7 St 178) The largest chain of secondhand bookshops in the capital, with a good range of titles, plus a third branch in the Boeng Kak backpacker area.
Monument Books (Map p79; ☎ 217617; 111 Norodom Blvd) The best-stocked bookshop in town, with almost every Cambodia-related book currently in print available. Toys upstairs and a small café downstairs. Operates branches at both international airports.

Emergency

Ambulance (☎ 119)
Fire (☎ 118)
Police (☎ 117)

There are also 24-hour emergency numbers for the English-speaking **tourist police** (☎ 012 942484) or the Khmer-speaking **police** (☎ 012 999999) in Phnom Penh. There is also an emergency number with English-speaking operators for Phnom Penh's **ambulance service** (☎ 724891).

In the event of a medical emergency it may be necessary to be flown to Bangkok. See opposite for details of medical services in Phnom Penh.

Internet Access

Phnom Penh is now well and truly wired, with prices dropping to less than US$0.50 per hour. There are internet cafés across the city. The most convenient are those along the riverfront, but cheaper rates are available in the smaller internet cafés dotted throughout the city and savings can be significant if you are making internet telephone calls.

Many budget guesthouses also offer some sort of internet access, and in the main backpacker areas there are several internet cafés. Anyone staying in more expensive hotels should venture out to find an online fix, as in-house business centres are overpriced.

Several of the midrange and top-end hotels now offer wi-fi access at a price, while many of the more popular cafés, restaurants and bars offer a free service.

Laundry

Most guesthouses around town offer reasonably priced laundry services and there are cheap local laundries scattered across the city. Tourists staying in high-end hotels can save a small fortune by using a local laundry while in town.

Libraries

The National Library (p88) has a pretty limited selection of reading material for foreign visitors, but is set in a lovely building. French speakers should call into the **French Cultural Centre** (Map p79; St 184), which has a good range of reading material.

The **Bophana Centre** (Map p79; ☎ 992174; 64 St 200), established by Cambodian-French filmmaker Rithy Panh, is an audiovisual resource for filmmakers and researchers, and visitors can explore its archive of old photographs and films.

Medical Services

It is important to be aware of the difference between a clinic and a hospital in Phnom

---

PHNOM PENH IN...

One Day

With just a day in town, start early with a riverfront stroll to see the mass tai chi and aerobics sessions taking place in front of the **Royal Palace** (p83), although it seems to be mainly aerobics these days. Grab breakfast at one of the riverfront cafés before venturing into the Royal Palace compound to see the dazzling treasures of the **Silver Pagoda** (p83). Next is the **National Museum** (p84) and the world's most wondrous collection of Khmer sculpture. Take lunch at nearby **Friends** (p102) restaurant, giving street children a helping hand into tourism. After lunch, check out the funky architecture of **Psar Thmei** (p109), but save the shopping for the treasure trove that is **Psar Tuol Tom Pong** (p109), more commonly known as the Russian Market. Take a deep breath and continue to **Tuol Sleng Museum** (p85), a savage reminder of Cambodia's tragic past. Sobering indeed – it may be time for a happy-hour drink to reflect on the highs and lows of the day. Enjoy dinner in one of the many good **Khmer restaurants** (p96) in town, before joining the nightshift at some of the **rockin' bars** (p104).

Two Days

With two days, it is easy to get to grips with Cambodia's capital. Start the day as in the one-day itinerary with a visit to the cultural splendours that are the **National Museum** (p84) and **Royal Palace** (p83). In the afternoon, visit the harrowing **Tuol Sleng Museum** (p85) before continuing on to the **Killing Fields of Choeung Ek** (p86), where prisoners from Security Prison 21 were taken for execution. It is a grim afternoon, but essential for understanding just how far Cambodia has come in the intervening years. Wind up with a sunset cruise on the **Mekong River** (p88) with a beautiful view over the Royal Palace.

On the second day, it is time to get serious about shopping. Browse through Art Deco **Psar Thmei** (p109) and then **Psar Tuol Tom Pong** (p109), a maze of stalls selling everything from textiles and handicrafts to DVDs and cut-price clothing. Keep some cash for the excellent **shops** (p108) that support good causes, all of which stock a solid selection of silk.

In the afternoon, take a look at the **Independence Monument** (p87), modelled on Angkor Wat's central tower, and wander up the riverfront to **Wat Phnom** (p86), where the Khmers prefer to pray for luck. From here it is a short stroll to catch the happy-hour cocktails at the **Elephant Bar** (p104) at Hotel Le Royal, the perfect warm-up for a final fling in Phnom Penh.

Penh. Clinics are good for most situations, but in a genuine emergency it is best to make for one of the hospitals.

Calmette Hospital (Map p79; ☎ 426948; 3 Monivong Blvd; ☽ 24hr) French-administered and the best of the local hospitals.

European Dental Clinic (Map p79; ☎ 211363; 160A Norodom Blvd; ☽ 7.30am-12.30pm & 1.30-7.30pm Mon-Sat) With international dental services and a good reputation.

International SOS Medical Centre (Map p79; ☎ 216911; www.internationalsos.com; 161 St 51; ☽ 8am-5.30pm Mon-Fri, 8am-noon Sat) One of the best medical services around town, but with prices to match. Also has a resident foreign dentist.

Naga Clinic (Map p79; ☎ 211300; www.nagaclinic .com; 11 St 254; ☽ 24hr) A French-run clinic for reliable consultations.

Pharmacie de la Gare (Map p79; ☎ 430205; 81 Monivong Blvd; ☽ 7am-7pm Mon-Sat, 8am-noon Sun) A pharmacy with English- and French-speaking consultants.

Royal Rattanak Hospital (Map pp74-5; ☎ 365555; www.royalrattanakhospital.com; 11 St 592; ☽ 24hr) New international hospital affiliated to Bangkok Hospital and boasting top facilities.

U-Care Pharmacy (Map p79; ☎ 222399; 26 Samdech Sothearos Blvd; ☽ 8am-9pm) International-style pharmacy with a convenient location near the river.

Money

Those looking to change cash into riel need look no further than jewellery stalls around the markets of Phnom Penh. Psar Thmei (p109) and Psar Tuol Tom Pong (p109) are the most convenient.

A number of upmarket hotels offer money-changing services, although this is usually reserved for their guests. Many travel agents can also change travellers cheques and offer credit-card advances for a 5% commission or higher. Most banks in Phnom Penh are open from roughly 8.30am to 3.30pm weekdays, plus Saturday mornings.

ANZ Royal Bank (Map p79; ☎ 726900; 265 Sisowath Quay) ATMs galore all over town, including at supermarkets and petrol stations.

Canadia Bank Head Office (Map p79; ☎ 215286; 265 St 110) Changes travellers cheques of several currencies for a 2% commission, plus free cash advances on MasterCard and Visa. Has an ATM.

Foreign Trade Bank (Map p79; ☎ 723466; 3 St 114; ☽ 7am-3.45pm Mon-Fri) Lowest commission in town on US dollar travellers cheques at 1%.

SBC Bank (Map p79; ☎ 990688; 315 Sisowath Quay; ☽ 8am-8pm) Convenient hours and location, plus represents Western Union.

Those needing to organise an international money transfer can use the Foreign Trade Bank. It may be quicker (and more expensive) to use an international company such as MoneyGram or Western Union. MoneyGram is represented by Canadia Bank, while Western Union can be found at SBC or **Acleda Bank** (Map p79; ☎ 998777; 61 Monivong Blvd).

Post

The main **post office** (Map p79; St 13; ☽ 7am-7pm) is in a charming building just east of Wat Phnom. It offers postal services as well as telephone and fax links. There is another post office on Monivong Blvd, near the corner of Sihanouk Blvd. For average postal rates see p317.

If you need to get valuables or belongings home in a hurry, there are several international courier companies (p317) represented in Phnom Penh.

Telephone & Fax

The cheapest local and domestic calls in Phnom Penh are available from private booths found throughout the city. Whatever the number you are dialling, private booths will have a selection of telephones to make sure you get the best rate. Local calls start at 300r a minute.

Many internet cafés in Phnom Penh offer telephone services at reasonable prices, including internet phone calls, which are much

---

BAG SNATCHING

Bag snatching has become a real problem in Phnom Penh and foreigners are often targeted. Hot spots include the riverfront and busy areas around popular markets, but there is no real pattern and the speeding motorbike thieves can strike any time, any place. More recently, this ended in tragedy for a young French woman who was dragged from a speeding *moto* into the path of a vehicle. Try to wear close-fitting bags such as backpacks that don't dangle from the body temptingly. Don't hang expensive cameras around the neck and keep things close to the body and out of sight, particularly when walking in the road, crossing the road or travelling by *moto, remorque-moto* or *cyclo*. These guys are real pros and only need one chance.

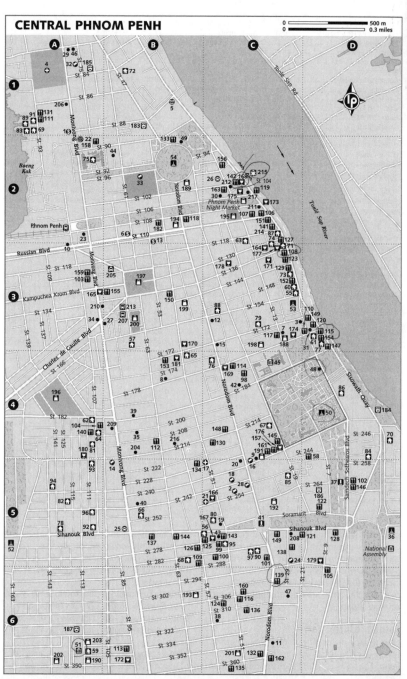

CENTRAL PHNOM PENH

0 — 500 m
0 — 0.3 miles

cheaper than normal international calls, but can involve an irritating delay that turns half the conversation into 'hello?' and 'pardon?'. Most places have Skype services or similar available for those with an account.

For further information on phone and fax services, see p319.

Tourist Information

Due to lack of funding, forget about finding much useful tourist information in Phnom Penh. The tourist office at the airport has details

on certain hotels and can make bookings, but other than this you are effectively on your own. Armed with your guidebook and with tips from your guesthouse or fellow travellers, you should be in good shape.

Cambodia Community-based Ecotourism Network
(CCBEN; Map pp74-5; ☎ 355272; www.ccben.org; 10A St 468; ⏱ 8am-noon, 1.30-5.30pm Mon-Fri) Information on ecotourism and community-based activities all over Cambodia.

ChildSafe (Map p79; www.childsafe-cambodia.org; 186 St 13) Located opposite the popular Friends restaurant, this drop-in office for the ChildSafe campaign aims to raise awareness among visitors about the problems of child begging, sex tourism and more.

Travel Agencies

There are plenty of travel agents around town, including some long-running places near Psar Thmei. Try the following:

Exotissimo (Map p79; ☎ 218948; www.exotissimo.com; 46 Norodom Blvd)

Hanuman Tourism (Map p79; ☎ 218356; www.hanumantourism.com; 12 St 310)

PTM Travel & Tours (Map p79; ☎ 364768; www.ptm-travel.com; 200 Monivong Blvd)

Transpeed Travel (Map p79; ☎ 723999; www.transpeedholiday.com; 19 St 106)

VLK Tourism (Map p79; ☎ 723331; www.vlktravel.com; 195 Monivong Blvd)

DANGERS & ANNOYANCES

Phnom Penh is not as dangerous as people imagine, but it is important to take care. Armed robberies do sometimes occur, but statistically you would be very unlucky to be a victim.

CHILD PROSTITUTION

The sexual abuse of children by foreign paedophiles is a serious problem in Cambodia. Paedophilia is a crime in Cambodia and several foreigners have served or are serving jail sentences. There is no such thing as an isolation unit for sex offenders in Cambodia. Countries such as Australia, France, Germany, the UK and the USA have also introduced much-needed legislation that sees nationals prosecuted in their home country for having under-age sex abroad.

This child abuse is slowly but surely being combated, although in a country as poor as Cambodia, money can tempt people into selling babies for adoption and children for sex. The trafficking of innocent children has many shapes and forms, and the sex trade is just the thin end of the wedge. Poor parents have been known to rent out their children as beggars, labourers or sellers; many child prostitutes in Cambodia are Vietnamese and have been sold into the business by family back in Vietnam. Once in the trade, it is difficult to escape a life of violence and abuse. Drugs are also being used to keep children dependent on their pimps, with bosses giving out *yama* (a dirty meta-amphetamine) or heroin to dull their senses.

Paedophilia is not unique to Western societies and it is a big problem with Asian tourists as well. The problem is that some of the home governments don't treat it as seriously as some of their Western counterparts, although Japan is now catching up with a highly visible billboard campaign around cities. Even more problematic is the domestic industry of virgin-buying in Cambodia, founded on the superstition that taking a virgin will enhance one's power. Even if NGOs succeed in putting off Western paedophiles, confronting local traditions may be a greater challenge.

Visitors can do their bit by keeping an eye out for any suspicious behaviour on the part of foreigners. Don't ignore it – pass on any relevant information such as the name and nationality of the individual to the embassy concerned. There is also a **Cambodian hotline** (☎ 023-720555) and a confidential **ChildSafe Hotline** (☎ 012 296609; www.childsafe-cambodia.org). When booking into a hotel or jumping on transport, look out for the ChildSafe logo, as each establishment or driver who earns this logo supports the end to child sex tourism and has undergone child-protection training. **End Child Prostitution and Trafficking** (Ecpat; www.ecpat.org) is a global network aimed at stopping child prostitution, child pornography and the trafficking of children for sexual purposes, and has affiliates in most Western countries.

Should you become the victim of a robbery, do not panic and do not, under any circumstances, struggle. Calmly raise your hands and let your attacker take what they want. *Do not* reach for your pockets as the assailant may think you are reaching for a gun. You will most likely get any documents back later via your guesthouse or embassy, as the robbers often want only cash and valuables. For the time being, even passports and credit cards seem to be returned. Do not carry a bag at night, as it is more likely to make you a target.

It pays to be cautious in crowded bars or nightclubs that are frequented by the Khmer elite. Many pampered children hang out in popular places, bringing their bodyguards along for good luck. This is fine until a drunk foreigner treads on their toes or they decide they want to hit on a Western girl. Then the problems start and if they have bodyguards with them, it will only end in tears, big tears.

If you ride your own motorbike during the day, some police may try to fleece you for the most trivial of offences, such as turning left in violation of a no-left-turn sign. At their most audacious, they may try to get you for riding with your headlights on during the day although, worryingly, it does not seem to be illegal for Cambodians to travel without their headlights on at night. The police will most likely demand US$5 from you and threaten to take you to the police station for an official US$20 fine if you do not pay. If you are patient with them and smile, you can usually get away with handing over US$1. The trick is not to stop in the first place by not catching their eye.

The riverfront area of Phnom Penh, particularly places with outdoor seating, attracts many beggars, as do Psar Thmei (p109) and Psar Tuol Tom Pong (p109). Generally, however, there is little in the way of push and shove. For more thoughts on how to handle beggar fatigue, see p309.

Flooding is a major problem during heavy downpours in the wet season (June to October). Phnom Penh's drainage system is notoriously unreliable and when the big rains kick off, some streets turn into canals for a few hours. The Japanese government is currently reworking the drains and sewers along the riverfront, which may well ease things. The downside is that much of the riverfront promenade has been fenced off during this work, which is scheduled to continue until 2009.

SIGHTS

Phnom Penh is a relatively small city and most of the major sights are fairly central. The most important cultural sights can be visited on foot and are located near the riverfront in the most beautiful part of the city.

Royal Palace & Silver Pagoda
ព្រះបរមរាជវាំង/និង វត្តព្រះកែវ

With its classic Khmer roofs and ornate gilding, the **Royal Palace** (Map p79; Samdech Sothearos Blvd; admission US$3, camera/video US$2/5; ☺ 7.30-11am & 2.30-5pm) dominates the diminutive skyline of Phnom Penh. It is a striking structure near the riverfront, bearing a remarkable likeness to its counterpart in Bangkok. Hidden away behind protective walls and beneath shadows of striking ceremonial buildings, it's an oasis of calm with lush gardens and leafy havens.

Being the official residence of King Sihamoni, parts of the massive compound are closed to the public. Visitors are only allowed to visit the palace's Silver Pagoda and its surrounding compound. However, photography is not permitted inside the pagoda itself. Visitors need to wear shorts that reach to the knee, and T-shirts or blouses that reach to the elbow; otherwise they will have to rent an appropriate covering. The palace gets very busy on Sundays when countryside Khmers come to pay their respects, but this can be a fun way to experience the place, thronging with locals.

CHAN CHAYA PAVILION
Performances of classical Cambodian dance were once staged in the Chan Chaya Pavilion, through which guests enter the grounds of the Royal Palace. This pavilion is sometimes lit up at night to commemorate festivals or anniversaries.

THRONE HALL
The Throne Hall, topped by a 59m-high tower inspired by the Bayon at Angkor, was inaugurated in 1919 by King Sisowath; the present cement building replaced a vast wooden structure that was built on this site in 1869. The Throne Hall is used for coronations and ceremonies such as the presentation of credentials by diplomats. Many of the items once displayed here were destroyed by the Khmer Rouge. In the courtyard is a curious iron house given to King Norodom by Napoleon III of France, hardly designed with the Cambodian climate in mind.

SILVER PAGODA
The Silver Pagoda is named in honour of the floor, which is covered with over 5000 silver tiles weighing 1kg each, adding up to 5 tonnes of gleaming silver. You can sneak a peek at some of the 5000 tiles near the entrance – most are covered for their protection. It is also known as Wat Preah Keo (Pagoda of the Emerald Buddha). It was originally constructed of wood in 1892 during the rule of King Norodom, who was apparently inspired by Bangkok's Wat Phra Keo, and was rebuilt in 1962.

The Silver Pagoda was preserved by the Khmer Rouge to demonstrate its concern for the conservation of Cambodia's cultural riches to the outside world. Although more than half of the pagoda's contents were destroyed under Pol Pot, what remains is spectacular. This is one of the few places in Cambodia where bejewelled objects embodying some of the brilliance and richness of Khmer civilisation can still be seen.

The staircase leading to the Silver Pagoda is made of Italian marble. Inside, the Emerald Buddha, believed to be made of Baccarat crystal, sits on a gilt pedestal high atop the dais. In front of the dais stands a life-size gold Buddha decorated with 9584 diamonds, the largest of which is a whopping 25 carats. Created in the palace workshops around 1907, the gold Buddha weighs in at 90kg. Directly in front of it is a miniature silver-and-gold stupa containing a relic of Buddha brought from Sri Lanka. To the left is an 80kg bronze Buddha, and to the right a silver Buddha. On the far right, figurines of solid gold tell of the life of the Buddha.

Behind the shrine is a standing marble Buddha from Myanmar (Burma). Nearby is

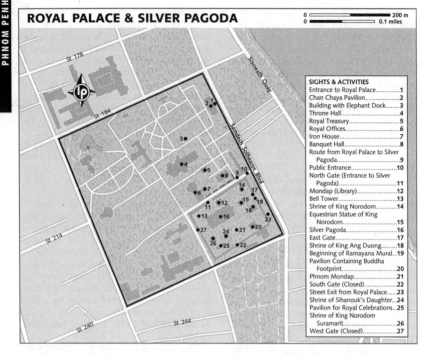

ROYAL PALACE & SILVER PAGODA

a bed once used by the king on his coronation day and designed to be carried by 12 men; the gold-work alone weighs 23kg.

Along the walls of the pagoda are examples of extraordinary Khmer artisanship, including intricate masks used in classical dance and dozens of gold Buddhas. The many precious gifts given to Cambodia's monarchs by foreign heads of state appear rather spiritless when displayed next to such diverse and exuberant Khmer art.

The epic of the *Ramayana* (known as the *Reamker* in Cambodia) is depicted on a beautiful and extensive mural enclosing the pagoda compound, created around 1900; the story begins just south of the east gate and includes vivid images of the battle of Lanka.

Other structures to be found in the complex (listed clockwise from the north gate) include the mondap (library), which housed richly decorated sacred texts that are written on palm leaves; the shrine of King Norodom (r 1860–1904); an equestrian statue of King Norodom; the shrine of King Ang Duong (r 1845–59); a pavilion housing a huge footprint of Buddha; Phnom Mondap, an artificial

hill with a structure containing a bronze footprint of the Buddha from Sri Lanka; a shrine dedicated to one of Prince Sihanouk's daughters; a pavilion for celebrations held by the royal family; the shrine of Prince Sihanouk's father, King Norodom Suramarit (r 1955–60); and a bell tower, whose bell is rung to order the gates to be opened or closed.

National Museum
សារមន្ទីរជាតិ

Located just north of the Royal Palace, the **National Museum of Cambodia** (Map p79; www .cambodiamuseum.info; admission US$3, camera/video US$1/3; ☺ 8am-5pm) is housed in a graceful terracotta structure of traditional design (built 1917–20), with an inviting courtyard garden. The museum is home to the world's finest collection of Khmer sculpture – a millennia's worth and more of masterful Khmer design.

The museum comprises four pavilions, facing the pretty garden. The most significant displays of sculpture are in the courtyards to the left and directly ahead of the entrance, but most visitors approach the collection in a clockwise chronological direction. The pre-Angkorian collection visualises the journey from the human form of Indian sculpture to the more divine form of Khmer sculpture from the 5th to 8th centuries. Highlights include an imposing eight-armed statue of Vishnu from the 6th or 7th century and a staring Harihara, combining the attributes of Shiva and Vishnu. The Angkor collection includes a striking statue of Shiva (c 870 AD), a giant pair of wrestling monkeys, an exquisite frieze from Banteay Srei, and the sublime statue of a seated Jayavarman VII (r 1181–1219), his head bowed slightly in a meditative pose.

The museum also contains displays of pottery and bronzes dating from the pre-Angkorian periods of Funan and Chenla (4th to 9th centuries), the Indravarman period (9th and 10th centuries), the classical Angkorian period (10th to 14th centuries), as well as more-recent works such as a beautiful wooden royal barge. There is a permanent collection of post-Angkorian Buddhas, many of which were rescued from Angkor Wat when the civil war erupted. See p53 for more information.

Unfortunately, it is not possible to photograph the collection, only the courtyard. English- and French-speaking guides (from US$2, depending on group size) are available, and there is also a useful booklet, *The New Guide to the National Museum,* available at the front desk.

Tuol Sleng Museum
សារមន្ទីរទួលស្លែង

In 1975 Tuol Svay Prey High School was taken over by Pol Pot's security forces and turned into a prison known as Security Prison 21 (S-21). This soon became the largest centre of detention and torture in the country. Between 1975 and 1978 more than 17,000 people held at S-21 were taken to the killing fields of Choeung Ek (p86).

S-21 has been turned into the **Tuol Sleng Museum** (Map pp74-5; St 113; admission US$2, video US$5; ⏱ 8am-5.30pm), which serves as a testament to the crimes of the Khmer Rouge. Entry is on the western side of St 113.

Like the Nazis, the Khmer Rouge leaders were meticulous in keeping records of their barbarism. Each prisoner who passed through S-21 was photographed, sometimes before and after torture. The museum displays include room after room of harrowing black-and-white photographs; virtually all of the men, women

and children pictured were later killed. You can tell which year a picture was taken by the style of number-board that appears on the prisoner's chest. Several foreigners from Australia, France and the USA were also held at S-21 before being murdered. Their documents are on display. It is worth paying US$2 to have a guide show you around, as they can tell you the stories behind some of the people in the photographs.

As the Khmer Rouge 'revolution' reached ever greater heights of insanity, it began devouring its own. Generations of torturers and executioners who worked here were in turn killed by those who took their places. During early 1977, when the party purges of Eastern Zone cadres were getting underway, S-21 claimed an average of 100 victims a day.

When the Vietnamese army liberated Phnom Penh in early 1979, there were only seven prisoners alive at S-21, all of whom had used their skills such as painting or photography to stay alive. Fourteen others had been tortured to death as Vietnamese forces were closing in on the city. Photographs of their gruesome deaths are on display in the rooms where their decomposing corpses were found. Their graves are nearby in the courtyard.

Altogether, a visit to Tuol Sleng is a profoundly depressing experience. The sheer ordinariness of the place makes it even more horrific: the suburban setting, the plain school buildings, the grassy playing area where children kick around balls; rusted beds, instruments of torture and wall after wall of disturbing portraits conjure up images of humanity at its worst. It demonstrates the darkest side of the human spirit that lurks within us all. Tuol Sleng is not for the squeamish.

Behind many of the displays at Tuol Sleng is the **Documentation Center of Cambodia** (DC-Cam; www.dccam.org). DC-Cam was established in 1995 through Yale University's **Cambodian Genocide Program** (www.yale.edu/cgp) to research and document the crimes of the Khmer Rouge. It became an independent organisation in 1997 and researchers have spent years translating confessions and paperwork from Tuol Sleng, mapping mass graves and preserving evidence of Khmer Rouge crimes.

French-Cambodian director Rithy Panh's 1996 film *Bophana* tells the true story of Hout Bophana, a beautiful young woman, and Ly Sitha, a regional Khmer Rouge leader, who fall in love but are made to pay for this 'crime' with imprisonment and execution at S-21 prison. It is well worth investing an hour to watch this powerful documentary, which is screened here at 10am and 3pm daily.

Killing Fields of Choeung Ek
វាលពិឃាតជើងឯក

Between 1975 and 1978 about 17,000 men, women, children and infants who had been detained and tortured at S-21 were transported to the extermination camp of **Choeung Ek** (Map pp74-5; admission US$3; ☺ 8-5.30pm). They were often bludgeoned to death to avoid wasting precious bullets.

The remains of 8985 people, many of whom were bound and blindfolded, were exhumed in 1980 from mass graves in this one-time longan orchard; 43 of the 129 communal graves here have been left untouched. Fragments of human bone and bits of cloth are scattered around the disinterred pits. More than 8000 skulls, arranged by sex and age, are visible behind the clear glass panels of the Memorial Stupa, which was erected in 1988. It is a peaceful place today, masking the horrors that unfolded here less than three decades ago.

The Killing Fields of Choeung Ek are 15km from central Phnom Penh and well signposted in English. Most people arrive by bicycle, *moto* or taxi – it's too far to walk. To get here, take Monireth Blvd southwest out of the city. The site is 13km from the bridge near St 271. Take the left fork when the road splits and pretty soon you will find yourself in rural surroundings. Look out for an archway on the left and it's another kilometre or so down this track. A memorial ceremony is held annually at Choeung Ek on 9 May.

The site was recently 'privatised' and is now controlled by a Japanese company, hence the price rise to US$3. Part of the deal involved upgrading the road, which is now surfaced all the way, but many Khmers and foreign observers alike were deeply disturbed that a foreign company was permitted to exploit Cambodia's tragedy.

Wat Phnom
វត្តភ្នំ

Set on top of a 27m-high tree-covered knoll, **Wat Phnom** (Map p79; admission US$1) is on the only hill in town. According to legend, the first pagoda on this site was erected in 1373 to house four statues of Buddha deposited here by the waters of the Mekong River and discov-

ered by Madame Penh. The main entrance to Wat Phnom is via the grand eastern staircase, which is guarded by lions and *naga* (mythical serpent) balustrades.

Today, many people come here to pray for good luck and success in school exams or business affairs. When a wish is granted, the faithful return to deliver on the offering promised, such as a garland of jasmine flowers or a bunch of bananas, of which the spirits are said to be especially fond.

The *vihara* (temple sanctuary) was rebuilt in 1434, 1806, 1894 and 1926. West of the *vihara* is a huge stupa containing the ashes of King Ponhea Yat (r 1405–67). In a pavilion on the southern side of the passage between the *vihara* and the stupa is a statue of a smiling and rather plump Madame Penh.

A bit to the north of and below the *vihara* is an eclectic shrine dedicated to the genie Preah Chau, who is especially revered by the Vietnamese. On either side of the entrance to the chamber containing a statue of Preah Chau are guardian spirits bearing iron bats. On the tiled table in front of the two guardian spirits are drawings of Confucius, as well as two Chinese-style figures of the sages Thang Cheng (on the right) and Thang Thay (on the left). To the left of the central altar is an eight-armed statue of Vishnu.

Down the hill from the shrine is a royal stupa sprouting full-sized trees from its roof. For now, the roots are holding the bricks together in their netlike grip, but when the trees eventually die the tower will slowly crumble, creating the devastation seen at temples around Angkor (p140).

Wat Phnom can be a bit of a circus. Beggars, street urchins, women selling drinks, and children selling birds in cages (you pay to set the bird free, but the birds are trained to return to their cage afterwards) pester everyone who turns up to climb the 27m to the summit. Fortunately it's all high-spirited stuff, and it's difficult to be annoyed by the vendors, who, after all, are only trying to eke out a living. You can also have a short elephant ride around the base of the hill, perfect for those elephant-trekking photos, but without the accompanying sore backside.

Wat Ounalom
វត្តឧណ្ណាលោម

This **wat** (Map p79; Samdech Sothearos Blvd; admission free; ☺ 6am-6pm) is the headquarters of Cambodian

Buddhism. It was founded in 1443 and comprises 44 structures. It received a battering during the Pol Pot era, but today the wat has come back to life. The head of the country's Buddhist brotherhood lives here, along with a large number of monks.

On the 2nd floor of the main building, to the left of the dais, is a statue of Samdech Huot Tat, fourth patriarch of Cambodian Buddhism, who was killed by Pol Pot. The statue, made in 1971 when the patriarch was 80, was thrown in the Mekong by the Khmer Rouge to show that Buddhism was no longer the driving force in Cambodia. It was retrieved after 1979. To the right of the dais is a statue of a former patriarch of the Thummayuth sect, to which the royal family belongs.

On the 3rd floor of the building is a marble Buddha of Burmese origin that was broken into pieces by the Khmer Rouge and later reassembled. On the front right corner of the dais on this floor are the cement remains of a Buddha stripped of its silver covering by the Khmer Rouge. In front of the dais, to either side, are two glass cases containing flags – each 20m long – used during Buddhist celebrations. The walls are decorated with scenes from the life of Buddha and were painted when the building was constructed in 1952.

Behind the main building is a stupa containing an eyebrow hair of Buddha with an inscription in Pali (an ancient Indian language) over the entrance.

Wat Moha Montrei
វត្តមហាមន្ត្រី

Situated close to the Olympic Stadium, **Wat Moha Montrei** (Map pp74-5; Sihanouk Blvd; admission free; ☙ 6am-6pm) was named in honour of one of King Monivong's ministers, Chakrue Ponn, who initiated the founding of the pagoda (*moha montrei* means 'the great minister'). The cement *vihara,* topped with a 35m-high tower, was completed in 1970. Between 1975 and 1979, it was used by the Khmer Rouge to store rice and corn.

Check out the assorted Cambodian touches incorporated into the wall murals of the *vihara,* which tell the story of Buddha. The angels accompanying Buddha to heaven are dressed as classical Khmer dancers and the assembled officials wear the white military uniforms of the Sihanouk period. Along the wall to the left of the dais is a painted wooden lion

from which religious lessons are preached four times a month. The golden wooden throne nearby is used for the same purpose. All the statues of Buddha were made after 1979.

Independence Monument
វិមានឯករាជ្យ

Modelled on the central tower of Angkor Wat, the **Independence Monument** (Map p79; cnr Norodom & Sihanouk Blvds) was built in 1958 to commemorate the country's independence from France in 1953. It also serves as a memorial to Cambodia's war dead (at least those that the current government chooses to remember) and is sometimes referred to as the Victory Monument. Wreaths are laid here on national holidays. Nearby, beside Samdech Sothearos Blvd, is the optimistically named **Cambodia-Vietnam Friendship Monument**, built to a Vietnamese (and rather communist) design in 1979.

Other Sights

The 700m **Chruoy Changvar Bridge** (Map pp74-5), which spans the Tonlé Sap River, is often referred to by visitors as the Japanese Bridge. It was blown up during fighting in 1975. Long a symbol of the devastation visited upon Cambodia, it was repaired in 1993 with US$23.2 million of Japanese funding. Those who have seen the film *The Killing Fields* may be interested to note that it was near here on the afternoon of 17 April 1975 – the day Phnom Penh fell – that Khmer Rouge fighters imprisoned and threatened to kill *New York Times* correspondent Sydney Schanberg and his companions.

Located at the northern end of Monivong Blvd, the **French embassy** (Map pp74-5; ☎ 430020; 1 Monivong Blvd) played a significant role in the dramas that unfolded after the fall of Phnom Penh on 17 April 1975. About 800 foreigners and 600 Cambodians took refuge in the embassy. Within 48 hours, the Khmer Rouge informed the French vice-consul that the new government did not recognise diplomatic privileges and that if all the Cambodians in the compound were not handed over, the lives of the foreigners inside would also be forfeited. Cambodian women married to foreigners could stay; Cambodian men married to foreign women could not. Foreigners wept as servants, colleagues, friends, lovers and husbands were escorted out of the embassy gates. At the end of the month the foreigners were expelled from Cambodia by truck. Many of the Cambodians were never seen again. The building was used for many years as an orphanage and its apparently larcenous residents were blamed by local people for every theft in the neighbourhood. Today a high whitewashed wall surrounds the massive complex and the French have returned to Cambodia in a big way, promoting French language and culture in their former colony.

There is a cluster of private **language schools** (Map p79) teaching English and French on St 184 between Norodom Blvd and the rear of the Royal Palace compound. Between 5pm and 7pm the area is filled with students who see learning English as the key to making it in contemporary Cambodia. This is a good place to meet young locals.

Known collectively as the National Sports Complex, the **Olympic Stadium** (Map pp74-5; near cnr Sihanouk & Monireth Blvds) is a striking example of 1960s Khmer architecture and includes a sports arena and facilities for boxing, gymnastics, volleyball and other sports. Turn up after 5pm to see countless football matches, *pétanque* duels or badminton games.

In order to replace the countless Buddhas and ritual objects smashed by the Khmer Rouge, a whole neighbourhood of private workshops making cement Buddhas, *naga* and small stupas has grown up on the grounds of Wat Prayuvong. While the graceless cement figures painted in gaudy colours are hardly works of art, they are an effort by the Cambodian people to restore Buddhism to a place of honour in their culture. The **Prayuvong Buddha factories** (Map p79; btwn St 308 & St 310) are about 300m south of the Independence Monument.

The **National Library** (Bibliothèque Nationale; Map p79; St 92; ☽ 8-11am & 2-5pm Tue-Sun) is in a graceful old building constructed in 1924, near Wat Phnom. During its rule, the Khmer Rouge turned the building into a stable and destroyed most of the books. Many were thrown out into the streets, where they were picked up by people, some of whom donated them back to the library after 1979; others used them as food wrapping.

ACTIVITIES
Boat Cruises
Boat trips on the Tonlé Sap or Mekong Rivers are very popular with visitors. Sunset cruises are ideal, the burning sun sinking slowly behind the glistening spires of the Royal Palace. It is also possible to charter them further afield for a visit to Koh Sdach or Silk Island, where there is a cottage industry of silk weavers. Local **tourist boats** are available for hire on the riverfront in Phnom Penh and can usually be arranged on the spot for between US$10 and US$20 an hour, depending on negotiations and numbers.

Bowling
There is now just one bowling alley in town, the **Superbowl** (Map pp74-5; Mao Tse Toung Blvd; per hr US$9, shoe hire US$1) at Parkway Square. Hourly rates are per lane, with any number of bowlers.

Cooking Courses
To learn more about the art of Cambodian cooking, sign up for the **Cambodian Cooking Class** (Map p79; ☎ 012 524801; www.cambodian-cooking-class .com; 67 St 240), based at Frizz Restaurant. The cooking class costs US$20/12.50 per full day/ half day, includes a booklet of recipes, and operates daily (except Sundays) at 9am.

Go-carting
Kambol F1 Go-carts (off Map pp74-5; ☎ 210501; per 10min US$7) is a professional circuit located about 12km beyond the airport, and 2km off the road to Sihanoukville. It organises races on Sundays, so if you fancy yourself as the new Michael Schumacher, turn up then. Prices include helmets and racing suits.

Golf
A round of golf is expensive by Cambodian standards, but pretty cheap for the region. Contact **Royal Golf Club** (☎ 366689; NH4; per round Mon-Fri US$35, shoe/club hire US$5/10), on the road to Sihanoukville, or **Cambodia Golf & Country Club** (☎ 363666; NH4; per round US$35, shoe/club hire US$5/10) if you can't survive without a swing.

Gymnasiums
There are plenty of backstreet local gyms in Phnom Penh that charge less than US$1 per hour and have very basic weights. The best all-round gym in town is **Paddy's Sports Centre** (Map pp74-5; ☎ 012 214940; 356 Sisowath Quay), located just north of the Chruoy Changvar Bridge on the right-hand side. Another sophisticated option is the **Clark Hatch Gym** (Map pp74-5; Intercontinental Hotel, cnr Mao Tse Toung & Monireth Blvds; per day US$14).

THE SHOOTING RANGES

Shooting ranges have long been a popular activity for gung-ho travellers visiting Cambodia. Cambodia's lack of law enforcement and culture of impunity allowed visitors to do pretty much anything they wanted in the bad old days. The Cambodian military wasn't blind to the market opportunities this presented, and with a hefty surplus of weapons from 25 years of civil war, it began to offer its own ammunition reduction scheme involving feisty foreigners wanting to do the Rambo thing. A number of military bases near Phnom Penh were transformed into shooting ranges and rapidly became popular with tourists wanting to try their luck with an AK-47, M-60 or B-40 grenade launcher. The government periodically launched crackdowns, but the business continued largely unabated.

And so the show goes on. Visitors can try out a range of weapons, but most of the machine guns work out at about US$1 a bullet. Handguns are available at the lower end, while at the other extreme it is possible to try shooting a B-40 rocket-propelled grenade launcher.

There have been rumours that it is possible to shoot live animals at these places, such as a chicken or cow. Naturally, we in no way endorse such behaviour. Does it ever happen? It is a possibility, as Cambodia is an impoverished country where money talks.

Massage & Spas

There are plenty of massage parlours in Phnom Penh, but quite a few double up as brothels. However, there are also now a lot of legitimate massage centres and a number of superb spas for that pampering palace experience.

Most of the more upmarket hotels offer traditional massage services, but one of the best value options in town is the long-running **Seeing Hands Massage** (Map p79; ☎ 012 680 934; 12 St 13; per hr US$5.50). The blind masseurs here have been in the business for many years and can sort out those niggling aches and pains, offering shiatsu or foot massages. There are several other similar cooperatives around town.

In a similar vein, **Kanya Massage** (Map pp74-5; ☎ 09 683477; 38 St 289; per hr US$5) is run by victims of acid attacks and helps to run a support network for survivors of these horrific crimes.

When it comes to spas, there is now an enticing selection of places. Some of the leading addresses for massage, facials, manicures and the full spa menu:

Amret Spa (Map p79; ☎ 997994; 3 St 57) Smart new spa near the popular 'Golden Mile'.

Bliss Spa (Map p79; ☎ 215754; 29 St 240) One of the most established spas in town, set in a lovely old French house on popular 240.

Champei Spa (Map pp74-5; ☎ 222846; 38 St 57) Khmer, Swedish and other massages, plus beauty care and hairdresser.

In Style (Map p79; ☎ 986747; 63 St 242) Garden spa and wellness centre with massage, facials and spa treatments.

O Spa (Map pp74-5; ☎ 992405; 4B St 75) An oasis of calm with rejuvenating hot-stone massage, plus Balinese and Thai treatments.

Running

A good opportunity to meet local expatriates is via the Hash House Harriers, usually referred to simply as 'the Hash'. A weekly run/walk takes place every Sunday. Participants meet in front of Phnom Penh train station (Map pp74–5) at 2.45pm. The entry fee of US$5 includes refreshments (mainly a lot of beer) at the end.

Swimming

Many of the midrange and top-end hotels have swimming pools in which to cool off on a hot day. Most open their pools to the public for a fee. The Hotel Cambodiana (p95) charges just US$6 during the week, while Hotel Le Royal demands US$20 per day for use of the pool and gym.

The best-value deal in town is currently at Pavilion (p95), which has a leafy swimming pool in its grounds and requires only that swimmers spend US$5 on food and drink in the course of their visit. The bad news for families is that children are not allowed. There is also the tiny swimming pool at popular bar-restaurant Elsewhere (p104); a dip (more than a swim) is free, including children between 4pm and 6pm.

Other options include **Himawari** (Map p79; ☎ 426806; 313 Sisowath Quay), which charges US$10 including access to the gym; **Parkway Health Club** (Map pp74-5; ☎ 982928; 113 Mao Tse Toung; US$6), which has an indoor pool, steam bath, sauna and gym; and **Long Beach Plaza Hotel** (Map pp74-5; ☎ 998007; St 289; US$1), a bargain for a lap-sized pool.

There is also a beautiful swimming pool at L'Elephant Blanc Resort (p95) about 7km out of town on the road to Neak Luong. It costs US$4/2 per adult/child, half again when it is quiet during the week, and there is a decent restaurant-bar here.

WALKING TOUR

What better place to kick off a walking tour of the city (Map p90) than the landmark temple of **Wat Phnom** (**1**; p86), perched atop the only hill in town. Pray for luck like the locals, or at least pray that you won't fall into one of Phnom Penh's open drains on this walking tour. Take a look southwest at the fortress that is the new **US embassy** (**2**; p312) and wonder to yourself how it is that the security-conscious State Department managed to find the only site in Phnom Penh overshadowed by a hill?

Head west along St 92 and pause at the **National Library** (**3**; p88), a classic example of French colonial-era architecture. Just along the road is the striking façade of **Hotel Le Royal** (**4**; p96), now owned by the Raffles group. Bookmark it for a happy-hour cocktail some time between 4pm and 8pm. Turn left on to

Monivong Blvd, the capital's main commercial thoroughfare. Fast approaching on the right is Phnom Penh's **train station (5)**, a grand old building, home to not-so-grand old trains.

Swing southeast towards the dominant dome of **Psar Thmei** (**6**; p109). This is a market to remember, packed to the gunnels with everything and anything you can imagine and some things you can't, such as deep-fried insects and peeled frogs. Browse awhile and take in the natural air-conditioning of this immense centre. Don't get liberal with your wallet, however, as sellers here are known to overcharge. That said, the food stalls are a great place for cheap local bites.

Continue south on St 63 and take a peek at the modern equivalent of the Central Market, aka **Sorya Shopping Centre** (**7**; p107). The food court here is bigger and cleaner than at the market and offers the advantage of air-conditioning.

Snake east on St 154 and then south on to Norodom Blvd, before turning left on to St 178, a lively strip to browse the many **art shops** (**8**; p107). Turn right onto St 19 before swinging west again, along St 240, one of the more

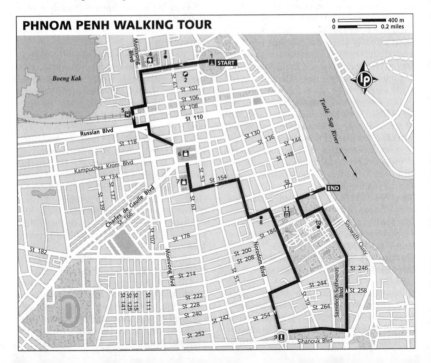

fashionable stretches in the capital. Take your pick from one of the many cafés, restaurants or bars along here to recharge the batteries for the second half of the walk.

Head southwards on to Norodom Blvd again and make for the **Independence Monument** (**9**; p87), which was modelled on the central tower of Angkor Wat and built to commemorate freedom from the French. From here make a loop east and then north.

Take an hour or more to experience the treasures of the **Royal Palace and Silver Pagoda complex** (**10**; p83) before delving into the world's finest collection of Khmer sculpture from the Angkor period at the stunning **National Museum** (**11**; p84). After an hour or so exploring this magnificent old building, wander east towards the riverfront. Stroll riverside along the Tonlé Sap or duck into a bar or restaurant for a well-earned drink.

PHNOM PENH FOR CHILDREN

With its chaotic traffic, lack of public parks and open sewers, at first glance Phnom Penh is not the most child-friendly city in Asia. However, there are a few little gems that help to pass the time in Phnom Penh.

Most sights will be overwhelming for younger children, but the Royal Palace (p83) is an interesting place to explore and Wat Phnom (p86) has the option of an elephant ride around the base.

Many of the leading hotels have swimming pools (p89) that are open to the public for a fee, and the go-cart tracks (p88) might prove popular if you have the next Lewis Hamilton in tow. **Phnom Penh Water Park** (off Map pp74–5; ☎ 881008; Russian Blvd; admission US$5; ☯ 8am-6pm) with its slides and wave pool is a definite hit with the young-uns and a world away from bustling downtown Phnom Penh. There is also a small fairground here. Sorya Shopping Centre (p107) includes a roller-skating rink on the upper floor, while there is ten-pin bowling at Superbowl (p88). There are also lots of children's playgrounds with ball ponds, trampolines and walkways, including one at Pencil Supermarket (p104).

Many of the restaurants and cafés are child-friendly, but there are a few specifically aimed at families, including Le Jardin (p103) and The Living Room (p104), while Fresco (p103) has a cool kiddies corner complete with PlayStation (big kids, hands

off!). Gasolina (p105) is another good option thanks to its huge garden, plus most of the riverfront places draw a breeze.

The most interesting attractions are beyond the city limits and would make good day trips to give the children a break from the hustle and bustle of the city. **Phnom Tamao Wildlife Sanctuary** (p115) is a rescue centre for Cambodia's incredible wildlife and the huge enclosures here include tigers, elephants and bears. Further afield is **Kirirom National Park** (p116), with gentle waterfalls and cooler temperatures, plus the fun **Kirirom Hillside Resort** (p116), which offers fresh air, pine trees, giant dinosaurs and activities such as horse riding and kayaking.

TOURS

Travelling independently, Phnom Penh is a city best enjoyed at your own pace, without the timetable of a tour. If you really want to have an organised city tour, most of the leading guesthouses organise city tours including the sights listed earlier for around US$6 per person. Prices mentioned do not include entrance fees.

Those interested in the new-wave Khmer architecture from the Sangkum era (1953–70) should sign up with **Khmer Architecture Tours** (www.ka-tours.org). These tours take in some of the most prominent buildings in the city and take place on foot or by *cyclo*, usually starting at 8.30am on weekends. The website also includes a DIY map of the most popular walking tour. For more on this landmark architecture, pick up a copy of *Cultures of Independence* (2001) or *Building Cambodia: New Khmer Architecture 1953–70* (2006).

For those wanting to discover another side of Phnom Penh, try **Mango Cambodia** (☎ 998657; www.mangocambodia.com), which offers trips into the surrounding countryside to meet the friendly locals. Supporting sustainable tourism with their country 'detours', Mango Cambodia also operates a small bed-and-breakfast in the capital.

SLEEPING

Phnom Penh now offers a world-class selection of places to stay. There is an excellent range of guesthouses, hotels and luxury palaces to suit all wallets passing through the capital. With the surge in visitors, many new hotels are also under development.

Affordable guesthouses are springing up all over the city. Some places charge as little as US$2 a room; US$5 will guarantee a small room with a fan and there are some smart new pads with air-con rooms from US$10. The best hotel deals in Phnom Penh fall in the midrange category and for around US$25 it is possible to get hooked up with air-con, satellite TV and a smart bathroom. Spend a little more cash and there are places that have a swimming pool for US$50 or under. Top-end travellers will find a selection of properties, including the grand, the bland and the boutique.

Budget

There are two popular backpacker strips, one along the eastern shore of Boeng Kak and the other around the long-running Capitol Guesthouse along St 182 and St 111, just west of Monivong Blvd. The area around Boeng Kak has improved considerably, but the rooms in these guesthouses are pretty basic compared with elsewhere in the city. For those who have seen enough of their fellow travellers to last a lifetime, there are several smaller guesthouses spread across the city.

BOENG KAK AREA

Most of the lakeside guesthouses are built on wooden platforms over Boeng Kak, a seriously polluted body of water that no-one should swim in, however much they have drunk or smoked. The guesthouses used to be rickety shacks with dodgy planking, but are now more solidly built, with great communal areas to while away the day. For some it's like experiencing Ko Pha Ngan in the city, only Boeng Kak isn't quite the Gulf of Thailand.

Unfortunately, this whole area is slated for redevelopment and work has already started on pumping out the lake. This will be a great loss to Phnom Penh, as this area has a unique vibe, so enjoy it while you can. Sunsets over the lake are not to be missed whether you are staying here or not. Valuables should be kept in lockers, as most rooms aren't very secure.

Number 10 Lakeside Guesthouse (Map p79; ☎ 012 725032; 10 St 93; r US$2-8) This stalwart on the lake has some bargain rooms with share bathroom or bigger rooms with hot water and cable TV. The drinking and dining area (smoking and joking for others) is a mellow place to hang out, and there's a boozy boat docked offshore.

Number 9 Guesthouse (Map p79; ☎ 012 766225; 9 St 93; r US$3-8; ✗) The very first lakefront guesthouse is still a popular place thanks to its blooming plants and billowing hammocks. There are more than 50 rooms, but be selective as some are shabby.

Grand View Guesthouse (Map p79; ☎ 430766; St 93; r US$4-10; ✗ ▣) Thailand meets Vietnam, with boxy rooms à la Bangkok housed in a tall, skinny structure à la Saigon. Upper floors involve a real hike, but the views of the lake are unrivalled.

Other places worth a flutter among the many up here:

Same Same But Different (Map p79; ☎ 012 263332; 11 St 93; s/d/tr without bathroom US$2/3/4) More like same same but the same. Comfortable beds and an inviting lounge.

Floating Island (Map p79; ☎ 012 551227; 11 St 93; r US$5-9; ✗) Rooms are much like everywhere else, but there is a great double-decker terrace for a serious view of the sunset.

Simon's II Guesthouse (Map p79; ☎ 012 608892; St 93; r US$10-15; ✗) This big wedding cake of a villa is home to the smartest rooms near the lake, including satellite TV and a bathroom.

PSAR O RUSSEI AREA

Another budget accommodation area starts near Psar O Russei and heads south along a network of backstreets.

Narin Guesthouse (Map p79; ☎ 982554; touch_narin@ hotmail.com; 50 St 125; r US$2-10; ✗) A long-running family place, this still offers some real budget deals, but rooms are quite basic. There is a relaxed terrace for taking some time out.

Dragon Guesthouse (Map p79; ☎ 012 239066; 238 St 107; r US$5-10; ✗) A friendly little guesthouse, all rooms here include cable TV and bathroom. There is also a lively balcony restaurant with an international menu.

Narin 2 Guesthouse (Map p79; ☎ 986131; 20 St 111; r US$3-12; ✗ ▣) More like a hotel, Narin 2 is located just a few blocks away from the Narin.

Spring Guesthouse (Map p79; ☎ 222155; 34 St 111; r US$6-12; ✗) An unfortunate typo on its card says 'bland new building', but it's all about interior comfort and this place has bright, spotless rooms, complete with cable TV. Long-term discounts available.

Sunday Guesthouse (Map p79; ☎ 211623; 97 St 141; r US$5-15; ✗) Rooms have been upgraded here, but not prices, making for a fine deal. The friendly English-speaking staff can help with travel arrangements.

our pick **Sky Park Guesthouse** (Map p79; ☎ 992718; 78 St 111; r US$6-20; ✷) One of a new breed of smart guesthouses in this part of town, the Sky Park is a real bargain for such cleanliness and comfort. Air-con starts at US$10 and all rooms have cable TV and hot water, and there's even a lift.

Good Luck Guesthouse (Map p79; ☎ 012 882936; 74 St 115; r US$6-20; ✷) Almost an identikit of the Sky Park, but maroon rather than orange.

Other good spots in this area:

Tat Guesthouse (Map p79; ☎ 986620; 52 St 125; r US$2-10; ✷) A friendly, family-run place with cheap and cheerful rooms, plus a breezy rooftop restaurant.

Capitol Guesthouse (Map p79; ☎ 724104; capitol@ online.com.kh; 14 St 182; r US$3-16; ✷ 🖳) The original guesthouse in town has several annexes with good-value rooms and a bustling café with travel info.

The King Guesthouse (Map p79; ☎ 220512; www .thekingangkor.com; 74 St 141; r US$3-25; ✷ 🖳) The range of rooms is as wide as the king's girth (that's Elvis, not Sihamoni!) and there is a huge restaurant and travel centre downstairs.

AROUND THE CITY

Other guesthouses are spread evenly across the city.

Okay Guesthouse (Map p79; ☎ 012-920556; St 258; r US$2-15; ✷) Okay is more than OK thanks to a popular restaurant, an appealing garden, great rooms and the best backpacker vibe beyond Boeng Kak. Budget rooms start with share bathroom, and top whack brings air-con, TV and hot water.

Top Banana Guesthouse (Map p79; ☎ 012 885572; www.topbanana.biz; cnr Sts 51 & 278; r US$5-13; ✷) In a great location on a popular corner opposite Wat Langka, this place has a rooftop chill-out area above the dust. Cheap rooms have a share bathroom, while the more expensive include brisk air-con.

our pick **Royal Guesthouse** (Map p79; ☎ 218026; 91 St 154; r US$6-12; ✷) This old-timer has been given a major facelift, with smart rooms, sparkling bathrooms and tasteful decoration. In a good location, there is also a café-restaurant here.

Dara Reang Sey Hotel (Map p79; ☎ 428181; darareangsey@camnet.com.kh; 45 St 13; r US$6-16; ✷) This long-running place has good-value rooms, and the family here really look after the staff.

The Last Home (Map p79; ☎ 012 831702; 21 St 172; r US$6-20; ✷) Recently relocated to a dapper new building behind Wat Ounalom, Last

Home has a loyal following among regular visitors. Added extras include cable TV and newish bathrooms.

Midrange

For those looking to spend between US$15 and US$75 for a room, there are some excellent deals to be had around town. Some of the fancier midrange places with swimming pool are not that far behind the top-range hotels in comfort, but are pleasingly off the pace in price, at just US$40 to US$60. Several places now offer free wi-fi for guests or diners.

As with the budget guesthouses, there is no single midrange hotel area. Probably the best choice, and definitely the best location, is along the riverfront on Sisowath Quay. The area to the southwest of the Independence Monument also has a concentration of midrange deals. The stretch of Monivong Blvd between Russian and Sihanouk Blvds is the old hotel district, but this is hardly the most alluring area of town.

RIVERFRONT AREA

Bright Lotus Guesthouse (Map p79; ☎ 990446; 22 St 178; r US$12-18; ✷) Occupying a strategic corner with top views of the National Museum, Royal Palace and, if you have a neck like Mr Fantastic, the riverfront, this guesthouse is one place where it is worth climbing the stairs.

Hotel Indochine (Map p79; ☎ 724239; indochinehtl @camnet.com.kh; 251 Sisowath Quay; r US$10-20; ✷) One of the oldies on the riverfront, but the price is right. Aim for a balcony river-view, but all rooms include TV, fridge and hot water.

Hotel Indochine 2 (☎ 211525; 28 St 130; US$10-20; ✷) For more comfort but a street view, try its other place around the corner.

our pick **Paragon Hotel** (Map p79; ☎ 222607; 219 Sisowath Quay; r US$15-30; ✷) A 40-room property on a lively stretch of the riverfront, this hotel represents excellent value. All rooms have TV and minibar, plus the pricier options have smart showers.

Mekong Palace Hotel (Map p79; ☎ 998876; 253 Sisowath Quay; r US$15-35; ✷) Formerly the Sunshine Hotel, the new-look Mekong Palace has risen in its place. Top location and comfortable rooms, but the cheaper rooms don't have a window.

River Star Hotel (Map p79; ☎ 990501; www .riverstarhotel.com; 185 Sisowath Quay; r US$25-35; ✷ 🖳) The reliable rooms here include the usual cable TV, fridge and air-con, and are quite spacious. Downstairs is a popular bar-restaurant and there's a lift.

Hope & Anchor (Map p79; ☎ 991190; www.hopeandanchor-cambodia.com; 213 Sisowath Quay; r US$25-50; 🔀) Don't be deceived by the British pub image, as this place is all about continental comfort upstairs, with thoughtfully designed rooms and slick bathrooms. The tempting bar beneath includes a pool table.

Hotel Castle (Map p79; ☎ 211425; www.hotelcastle.com.kh; 4 St 148; s/d from US$50/55; 🔀 💻 🖳) This new hotel is quickly earning a name for itself as one of the better addresses in town. It's not quite on the riverfront, but more than makes up for it with smart business-like rooms, a swimming pool and free wi-fi. Highly recommended.

Bougainvillier Hotel (Map p79; ☎ 220528; www.bougainvillierhotel.com; 277 Sisowath Quay; r US$53-88; 🔀) One of the most impressive midrange options, the rooms are lavishly decorated with Chinese-Khmer furniture and elegant silk. The suites are a worthy investment with acres of space and an unobstructed view of the Tonlé Sap. There is also a highly regarded French restaurant where the complimentary breakfast is served.

Foreign Correspondents' Club (Map p79; ☎ 210142; www.fcccambodia.com; 363 Sisowath Quay; d US$55; 🔀 💻) This landmark location is a fine place to recapture the heady days of the war correspondents. The rooms are delightfully finished in wood and include DVD players. All include a minibar clearly aimed at the journalists who pass through town – the spirits come in 1L bottles rather than miniatures. The restaurant-bar (p101) always draws a crowd.

And there's more:

Renakse Hotel (Map p79; ☎ 215701; 40 Samdech Sothearos Blvd; r US$35-60; 🔀) This grand old dame is a colonial relic tucked away amid lush gardens opposite the Royal Palace. Up for sale, it may well close for a full makeover some time soon.

Khmer Royal Hotel (Map p79; ☎ 223824; www.khmerroyalhotel.com; Sisowath Quay; r US$45-55; 🔀 💻) The brash exterior conceals some smart rooms. Request a river view if available.

CENTRAL PHNOM PENH

One area that is worth seeking out for those wanting good value is the so-called 'Golden Mile', a strip of hotels on St 278 that all feature 'Golden' in their name. There is little to choose between them, as all offer air-con,

cable TV, fridge, hot water and free laundry for around US$15.

Boddhi Tree Umma (Map pp74-5; www.boddhitree.com; 50 St 113; r US$12-32; 🔀 💻) Some might be spooked by the location opposite Tuol Sleng Museum, but for those who don't get nightmares this is a wonderfully atmospheric place to stay. The old wooden house includes aircon options and there is a divine restaurant in the verdant garden.

Golden Tour Eiffel Guesthouse (Map p79; ☎ 225018; 4B St 278; r US$15; 🔀) Rooms here are more like suites, with full kitchens and plenty of extra features, making the rates a real bargain. Monthly discounts available.

Town View Hotel (Map p79; ☎ 992939; 30 St 111; www.townviewhotel.com; r from US$15; 🔀 💻) A smart new hotel in a popular budget district, rooms here are absurdly good value. All include cable TV, minibar and sparkling bathrooms, plus there's a lift.

Kambuja Inn (Map p79; ☎ 223377; 10 St 174; r US$20-35; 🔀) Attractively set in a cluster of old French shophouses near Norodom Blvd, the 10 rooms here offer a degree of charm and comfort. All have a wood and silk trim and the more expensive are almost suites.

Flamingos Hotel (Map p79; ☎ 221640; 30 St 172; r US$25-35; 🔀 💻) A towering hotel for this part of town, the smart rooms include lots of little extras, and bigger bucks bring a bathtub. There's also a lift leading to a relaxed rooftop restaurant and bar.

Hotel Cara (Map pp74-5; ☎ 430066; www.hotelcara.com; 18 St 47; s/d from US$28/33; 🔀) This hotel exudes real style at an affordable price. Rooms are finished in contemporary Khmer materials with original furnishings, and most include a balcony. Downstairs is the Japanese Fusion Restaurant.

Anise Hotel (Map p79; ☎ 222522; www.anisehotel.com.kh; 2C St 278; s US$29-55, d US$35-60; 🔀 💻) A chic hotel in the popular NGO quarter of town, Anise offers flat-screen TVs and internet throughout. Smarter rooms also have DVD players and a safe. There's a great little restaurant, but no lift makes life at the top tough.

Scandinavia Hotel (Map p79; ☎ 214498; www.hotel-scandinavia-cambodia.com; 4 St 282; r US$30-55; 🔀 💻 🖳) Long popular with Phnom Penh aficionados, this place has been renovated and upgraded making for an enticing deal. Rooms include a DVD player and minibar, plus there is a swimming pool in the garden, a restaurant *and* an art gallery.

Manor House (Map p79; ☎ 992566; 21 St 262; s/d from US$33/38; ❄ 🖳 🏊) Set in a small villa in the backstreets, this gay-friendly guesthouse offers artfully decorated rooms and a small swimming pool. Deluxe rooms have a DVD player and wi-fi is available at US$3 per day.

Villa Langka (Map p79; ☎ 726771; www.villalangka .com; 14 St 282; r US$35-100; ❄ 🏊) A new boutique hotel near Wat Langka, the 24 rooms here face a tempting swimming pool and garden café. Cheaper rooms are smaller and the décor gets more expressive with the price, rising to US$100 suites with large balcony and a large flat-screen TV. Add 10% to rates for tax but all include breakfast.

The Billabong (Map p79; ☎ 223703; 5 St 158; r US$36-58; ❄ 🖳 🏊) Near Psar Thmei but an oasis of calm by comparison, this Aussie-run place has 15 rooms set around a large swimming pool. Standard rooms are smallish, so it's better to invest in the pool-view rooms for space and style.

our pick **The Pavilion** (Map p79; ☎ 222280; www .pavilion-cambodia.com; 227 St 19; r US$50-80; ❄ 🖳 🏊) Housed in one of the most elegant French villas in town, this is an atmospheric place to stay. Furnishings show a Chinese-Khmer touch and some have commanding pool views. Recently expanded into a second contemporary building next door, some of the new rooms include a private plunge pool. Free wi-fi and a gorgeous garden to while away the days, but no children allowed.

Kabiki (Map p79; ☎ 222290; www.thekabiki.com; 22 St 264; r from US$50; ❄ 🖳 🏊) The owners of the Pavilion (see above) also have a new family-friendly place, with suite rooms, bunks for kiddies and a lush garden with pool. Both Kabiki and the Pavilion have solar power.

Other places worth a look:

Golden Mekong Hotel (Map p79; ☎ 211721; 205 St 19; r US$25; ❄) Atmospheric hotel behind the royal palace offering a good deal for the standard and comfort.

Frangipani Villa (Map p79; ☎ 012 687717; www .frangipanihotel.com; 20 St 252; r US$25-45; ❄ 🖳) Like a boutique bed-and-breakfast, rooms here have character and include a stylish bathroom. Popular with long-stayers.

Goldiana Hotel (Map p79; ☎ 219558; www.goldiana .com; 10 St 282; s/d US$28/38; ❄ 🖳 🏊) This huge hotel offers a fair deal considering facilities include a pool and gym. Free transfer from the airport.

Boddhi Tree Aram (Map p79; www.boddhitree.com; 70 St 244; r US$64-78; ❄ 🖳) Those on a bigger budget might consider this beautiful and smart new place with stylish rooms.

BEYOND THE CITY

L'Elephant Blanc Resort (off Map pp74-5; ☎ 222988; www.elephantblancresort.com; NH1; r US$25-40; ❄ 🖳 🏊) A lovely little resort beyond the city limits, this is a peaceful retreat for those that have tired of the city life. Rooms are large and comfortable and the pool is a real treat. It tends to be much quieter during the week, as expats descend at the weekend.

Top End

Walk-in rates at many of Phnom Penh's luxury hotels are high by regional standards. Consider booking via the internet or through a travel agent for a better deal, which can be as much as half of the published rates.

Imperial Garden Villa (Map pp74-5; ☎ 219991; www .imperialgarden-hotel.com; 315 Sisowath Quay; s/d US$70/80; ❄ 🖳 🏊) Rooms here are a three-star standard, but a little on the 'business bland' side. However, there are also large residential-style villas available. There's a large pool and a tennis court, plus Mekong views.

The Quay (Map p79; www.thequayhotel.com; Sisowath Quay; ste from US$80; ❄ 🖳 🏊) A new boutique hotel from the FCC group, this riverfront property aims to be carbon neutral in an effort to help the fight against global warming. Sleek and minimalist, this promises to be a stylish venue and includes a fusion restaurant and rooftop swimming pool.

Hotel Cambodiana (Map pp74-5; ☎ 426288; www .hotelcambodiana.com; 313 Sisowath Quay; s/d US$110/115; ❄ 🖳 🏊) A real Phnom Penh landmark, the Cambodiana has recently joined the empire of local tycoon Kith Meng. Rooms and facilities are rapidly being upgraded, ensuring this will once again be one of the smartest places in town. Started in 1967, the unfinished structure and its grounds were used as a military base by the Lon Nol government, and by 1975 thousands of refugees from the countryside sheltered under its concrete roof.

Himawari (Map p79; ☎ 214555; www.himawari hotel.com; 313 Sisowath Quay; apt US$128; ❄ 🖳 🏊) Another residential-style property offering rooms, suites and apartments, Himawari has a great location on the banks of the Mekong. Facilities include a pool and a gym, plus riverside dining. Definitely request a nonsmoking room, as smokers have left their stamp on some rooms.

Intercontinental Hotel (Map pp74-5; ☎ 424888; www.intercontinental.com; cnr Mao Tse Toung & Monireth Blvds; s/d from US$135/145; ❄ 🖳 🏊) The original five-star hotel in town, it was also long the city's tallest building. The location is not ideal, but the comfort is Intercon through and through. Facilities include a Clark Hatch fitness centre, a swimming pool, a business centre, conference facilities, a great breakfast buffet and live music in the lobby bar.

Amanjaya (Map p79; ☎ 219579; www.amanjaya.com; 1 St 154; ste US$155-250; ❉ ⬜) Occupying a superb location near the riverfront, with panoramic views over the Tonlé Sap and Wat Ounalom, the Amanjaya is the leading boutique hotel in Phnom Penh. All rooms are suites, and are spacious and stylish, with elegant Khmer drapes and tropical furnishings. Rates include free wi-fi access. Downstairs is a popular steakhouse and bar, K-West, which draws an expat crowd seeking a slice of home comfort.

ourpick Hotel Le Royal (Map p79; ☎ 981888; www.raffles.com; cnr Monivong Blvd & St 92; r from US$300; ❉ ⬜ ⬛) From the golden age of travel, this is one of Asia's grand old palaces, in the illustrious company of the Oriental in Bangkok and Raffles in Singapore. This classic colonial-era property is Phnom Penh's leading address, with a heritage to match its service and style. Indulgent diversions include two swimming pools, a gym, a spa, and bars and restaurants with lavish food and drink. Between 1970 and 1975 many famous journalists working in Phnom Penh stayed here, and part of the film *The Killing Fields* was set in the hotel (though filmed in Hua Hin, Thailand).

EATING

For foodies, Phnom Penh is a real delight, boasting a superb selection of restaurants that showcase the best in Khmer cooking, as well as the greatest hits from world cuisine such as Chinese, Vietnamese, Thai, Indian, French, Italian, Spanish, Mexican and more. Visitors to Phnom Penh are quite literally spoilt for choice these days. Most local restaurants open around 6.30am and serve food until 9pm or so. International restaurants stay open until about 11pm, but some close between breakfast and lunch or between lunch and dinner.

The best bet for budget dining in Phnom Penh is to head to one of the city's many markets. The dining areas may not be the most sophisticated in the world, but the food is tasty and cheap. If the markets are just too hot or claustrophobic for your taste, then look out for the mobile street sellers carrying

their wares on their shoulders or wheeling it around in small carts.

Local hole-in-the-wall restaurants are slightly more civilised but still very cheap. Many of the international restaurants around town are expensive by local standards, but compared with dining in the West, the prices are very reasonable.

Most of the big hotels have in-house restaurants with multinational menus, but prices tend to be high and tax and service is extra, adding up to a multinational-sized bill.

Some travellers get into the habit of hunkering down on their guesthouse balcony, encouraged by proprietors talking up the dangers of Phnom Penh. Don't do it, as a culinary adventure awaits…

Khmer

After dark, Khmer eateries scattered across town illuminate their beaconlike Angkor Beer signs, hailing locals in for fine fare and generous jugs of draft beer. Don't be shy, and heed the glowing signs – the food is great and the atmosphere lively. A typical meal will cost just 4000r to 8000r and a jug of beer is only 8000r (around US$2). Good hunting grounds include St 184 (Map p79) near the French Cultural Centre and St 108 (Map p79) just to the east of Norodom Blvd.

Soup chhnang dei (cook-your-own soup) restaurants are very popular with Khmers and are great fun if you go in a group. Other diners will often help with protocol, as it is important to cook things in the right order so as not to overcook half the ingredients and eat the rest raw. These places also offer *phnom pleung* (hill of fire), which amounts to cook-your-own beef, shrimp or squid (or anything else that takes your fancy) over a personal barbecue.

The best markets for breakfast and lunch are Psar Thmei (Central Market; Map p79), Psar Tuol Tom Pong (Russian Market; Map pp74–5) and Psar O Russei (Map p79), which is handy given these are also great shopping venues. Most dishes cost a reasonable 2000r to 4000r. There are also several areas around the city with open-air food stalls during the early evening – try **Psar Ta Pang** (Map p79; cnr Sts 51 & 136) for excellent *bobor* (rice porridge) and tasty desserts.

If the market stalls look a little raw, and street-surfing doesn't appeal, then consider the air-conditioned alternative in the shape of

LUU MENG *Nick Ray*

Renowned Cambodian celebrity chef and restaurateur Luu Meng is the face behind a handful of Phnom Penh's best-known restaurants and cafés.

Luu Meng's love of cooking started at a young age, as his Chinese-Cambodian family ran a restaurant on Sothearos Blvd in the late 1960s, not far from his new Thai-Japanese restaurant Bai Thong (p99). 'My family had a typical Chinese restaurant, so I grew up around food and we always ate well,' Luu explains. He joined the Sofitel Cambodiana Hotel (now Hotel Cambodiana) as the country opened its doors to the world once more and soon became one of the country's rising culinary stars. 'I travelled the region, working in Thailand and at the famous Sofitel Metropole in Hanoi,' Meng continues, an experience which brought him into contact with new flavours and regional specialities. Returning to Cambodia, he eventually formed Man Co, the group behind such popular Phnom Penh restaurants as Malis and Topaz.

We discuss Cambodian cuisine and what differentiates it from its neighbours. 'Thai food is hot, spicy and sweet, while Vietnamese is more Chinese influenced,' explains Meng. 'Khmer cuisine is all about fresh spices. There are influences from India, but always with fresh ingredients, not powders. Our cuisine is not as spicy as Thai and we don't use as much fish sauce as Vietnam, although we do love *prahoc* [fish paste].' He pauses to reflect, 'It's all about freshness.'

On the subject of Cambodian tastes and a Cambodian national dish, he is animated, and naturally *amoc* (mild baked fish curry) leads the discussions. '*Amoc* is typically Cambodian and takes advantage of our abundance of fresh fish from the Tonlé Sap,' Meng points out. 'Cambodian cuisine also has some superb salads, which often surprises people. *Sait ko plear* [raw beef salad] can be prepared carpaccio style with fresh, finely grated lemon grass and is a symphony of subtle flavours.'

Travelling widely and cooking for a diverse audience, Meng has taken on many influences, but is quite a traditionalist at heart. 'For me, the most important thing about cooking is quality. Quality of the ingredients, quality of the kitchen, quality of the service,' he continues. 'If a chef knows and understands this, it can be applied to different cuisines.' However, he prefers to concentrate on his strengths and promote local ingredients and traditional dishes. 'If we plan to promote another cuisine, then we bring in a specialist chef from that culinary culture,' he explains. 'That way, we always guarantee the authentic flavour.'

Naturally, we end up discussing the best restaurants in Phnom Penh for traditional Cambodian food. 'For me, you have to go over the bridge [Chruoy Changvar Bridge] for the real taste of Cambodia,' he enthuses. 'Many of the places in town serve a bit of everything from the region, but over the bridge are the real Cambodian restaurants.' A favourite? He laughs. 'It has to be Rum Chang, as they offer very traditional recipes and a peaceful setting.'

Luu Meng is the Managing Director of Man Co (Management Company), which runs several hotels and restaurants in Cambodia.

the **Sorya Shopping Centre Food Court** (Map p79; 4th fl, cnr Sts 63 & 154). Run on the coupon system like in Thailand, there are more than 20 outlets serving Khmer, Chinese, Thai, Vietnamese and more, plus desserts and fruit shakes. It's always full of locals and most dishes are just 4000r to 6000r. A few floors up is **Master Suki Soup** (7th fl; soup from US$5), which may be a Japanese concept but has a very Khmer touch and is a great way to try *soup chhnang dei*, with photos to help choose the ingredients. Superb views over Psar Thmei.

Sa'em Restaurant (Map p79; ☎ 219254; 379 Sisowath Quay; mains US$1-3; ☉ 7am-10pm) Tucked away under a shady terrace, this place has some of the best-value meals on the riverfront. Most of the Khmer and Asian standards are here and even the beer is at giveaway prices.

Khmer Borane Restaurant (Map p79; ☎ 012 290092; 389 Sisowath Quay; mains US$1.50-4; ☉ 11am-11pm) A great little restaurant for traditional Khmer recipes, choose from *trey kor* (steamed fish with sugar palm) or *lok lak* (fried diced beef with a salt, pepper and lemon dip).

Seven Bright Restaurant (Map p79; ☎ 012 833555; St 13; mains US$1.50-5; ☉ 5:30am-10:30pm) This was Gerard Depardieu's hotel lobby in the movie *City of Ghosts*. Good food, likeable location and occasional live music. Early doors make it a great place for breakfast before a boat trip.

Goldfish River Restaurant (Map p79; Sisowath Quay; mains US$2-5; 7am-10pm) Sitting on stilts over the Tonlé Sap, this restaurant may not be designed to impress, but the menu offers authentic Cambodian food. Crab with black pepper, squid with fresh peppercorns; the selection is dizzying with more than 300 dishes available.

K'nyay (Map p79; 225225; 25K Soramarit Blvd; mains US$2-5; noon-9pm Tue-Fri, 7am-9pm Sat, 7am-3pm Sun) A stylish new Cambodian restaurant that is hidden away from the main road in a leafy villa. The menu includes a generous selection of vegetarian and vegan options and original health shakes.

Frizz Restaurant (Map p79; 220953; 67 St 240; mains US$2-5; 7am-10pm) True, the name doesn't sound that Khmer, but the aromatic Cambodian cuisine here is some of the most delicious in town. The restaurant also operates cooking classes (p88) for those wanting to learn some secrets.

Bopha Phnom Penh Restaurant (Map p79; 992800; Sisowath Quay; mains US$2-7; 6am-11pm) Right next door to Goldfish, this place is designed to impress, complete with Angkor-style carvings, heavy furniture and an attractive riverside terrace. The menu includes Khmer, Asian and Western dishes, plus cheaper lunchtime set menus are available. Nightly classical dancing ensures it is popular with tour groups.

Khmer Surin (Map p79; 363050; 9 St 57; mains US$3-6; 11am-10pm) Popular with tour groups thanks to the atmospheric ambience with floor cushions, flowering plants and antique furnishings, this restaurant serves reliable Cambodian and Thai food. Set over three levels, it should be possible to find a quiet corner.

Sugar Palm (Map p79; 220956; 19 St 240; mains US$4-8; 11.30am-late) A homely restaurant-bar on lively St 240, this delivers the traditional taste of Cambodia in cool, contemporary surrounds. Have a cocktail downstairs, then head up to the balcony for dinner.

ourpick Malis (Map p79; 221022; 136 Norodom Blvd; mains US$4-12; 6am-11pm) The leading Khmer restaurant in the Cambodian capital, Malis is a chic place to dine. The garden is the most atmospheric, but air-conditioned dining is available in the warren of a building. The original menu includes beef in bamboo strips, sand goby with ginger and traditional soups and salads. Popular for a

boutique breakfast, as the menu is a good deal at US$1.50 to US$3.

It's Cambodia, of course there are more:

Khmer Kitchen (Map p74-5; 012 712541; 41 St 310; mains US$2-5) Affordably priced food for a local crowd and authentic décor to draw the international crowd.

Dararasmey Restaurant (Map p79; St 63; mains US$2-5) One of the most popular DIY restaurants in Phnom Penh, a lively spot to pass an evening as an amateur chef.

Ponlok Restaurant (Map p79; 212025; 319 Sisowath Quay; mains US$2-6) Great riverfront views from the 3rd floor, but service can be hit and miss.

Amok Café (Map p79; 012 912319; 2 St 278; mains US$3-7; 10am-10pm) Named in honour of one of Cambodia's national dishes, the delicious *amoc* (fish coconut curry in a banana leaf).

Chinese

There are numerous Chinese restaurants around Phnom Penh, many offering an authentic taste of the Middle Kingdom. There are several real-deal Chinese restaurants along St 136, opposite the Phnom Penh Sorya bus station, with names like Peking and Shanghai. These are the perfect place for a budget meal before or after a long bus ride and most also do good dim sum.

Sam Doo Restaurant (Map p79; 218773; 56 Kampuchea Krom Blvd; mains US$2-10; 7am-2pm) Sino-Khmers swear this has the best food in town. Choose from spicy morning glory, signature 'Sam Doo fried rice', *trey chamhoy* (steamed fish with soy sauce and ginger), and fresh seafood. It's open late and has delicious dim sum.

Man Han Lou Restaurant (Map pp74-5; 721966; 456 Monivong Blvd; mains US$5-10; 10am-11pm) Chinese, Khmer, Thai, Vietnamese, this restaurant covers all bases, but the real draw here is the microbrewery turning out beer in golden (lager), red (bitter), black (stout) and 'green' (not sure) shades.

Hua Nam Restaurant (Map pp74-5; 364005; 753 Monivong Blvd; mains US$5-15 and up; 11am-2pm & 5-10pm) One of the original classy Chinese restaurants, this heavyweight dining experience includes such 'delicacies' as goose webs and abalone. Smart, but expensive by local standards.

Thai

ourpick Boat Noodle Restaurant (Map p79; 012 200426; St 294; mains 3000-10,000r; 10am-10pm) This old wooden house, in a leafy garden brimming with water features, offers some of the

DINING OUT 'OVER THE BRIDGE'

The reconstruction of the Chruoy Changvar Bridge (Japanese Friendship Bridge) spanning the Tonlé Sap River created a restaurant boom on the river's east bank. There are dozens of restaurants lining the highway – from the decidedly downmarket to the obviously over-the-top – but most are interesting places for a very Cambodian night out. These are restaurants frequented by well-to-do Khmers, and on the weekend are packed with literally thousands of people on a big night out. Most charge about US$2 to US$5 a dish (with around 300 dishes to choose from). Heading north, the restaurants start to appear about 1km from the bridge on the east bank. Many of the larger places include a resident band and the amps are often cranked up to 11 – remember to sit a fair distance from the stage.

Places come in and out of favour, but following are some of the consistently popular. All are signposted from the main road. A *moto* should cost about US$1 or so each way from the city centre.

- **Boeng Bopha Restaurant** – the food here is similar to elsewhere, but this is a popular place for a younger crowd out drinking.
- **Rum Chang Restaurant** – long one of the best places for authentic Khmer food, there is no band here and the location overlooking the Mekong is very breezy. Recommended by Luu Meng (p97).
- **Ta Oeu Restaurant** – this simple place is popular for its value-for-money food, which has a reputation as being authentic and tasty.
- **Tata Restaurant** – one of the newer breed of smart and sophisticated places, it hosts leading comedians at the weekend and is popular with Cambodians. The food is well-regarded, if relatively expensive.

best-value Thai and Cambodian food in town. With tasty noodle soups for breakfast and special set lunches each day for US$4, it's worth a visit.

Chiang Mai Riverside (Map p79; ☎ 012 832369; 227 Sisowath Quay; mains US$2-5; ⏲ 10am-10pm) One of the original riverfront restaurants, it's still going strong thanks to the taste of Thailand at a reasonable price. The fish cakes are always good, plus there are some authentic curries to spice up your life.

Bai Thong Restaurant (Map p79; ☎ 211054; 100 Samdech Sothearos Blvd; mains US$3-6; ⏲ 11am-2pm & 6-11pm) Smart new eatery dedicated to traditional Thai food with a Japanese twist; the prices are pretty reasonable given the classy ambience.

Vietnamese

Pho Shop (Map p79; Sihanouk Blvd; mains 4000r) For cheap and delicious *pho bo* (Vietnamese beef noodle soup), try this local hole-in-the-wall near Independence Monument. It does genuine *pho* with all the accompaniments and serves cheap beer as the day wears on.

Phò Fortune (Map p79; ☎ 012 871753; 11 St 178; mains from US$1-4; ⏲ 8am-9pm) Great location for good *pho*, the noodle soup that keeps Vietnam on its feet, plus a smattering of dishes from other regions of the world.

Indian & Nepalese

Chi Cha (Map p79; ☎ 366065; 27 St 110; set menus US$2; ⏲ 7.30am-12.30pm) Actually Bangladeshi, this established curry house offers the cheapest subcontinental selection in town. The thalis (set meals) are a bargain, starting from US$2. The menu is 100% halal.

Monsoon (Map p79; 17 St 104; curries US$3-5) Alright, so it's also a sophisticated wine bar and it happens to be in the middle of a 'lively' bar strip, but do not be deceived, for this is home to some of the best Pakistani curries this side of Lahore. Or *lahore na* (very good), as the Cambodians say.

Shiva Shakti (Map p79; 70 Sihanouk Blvd; ⏲ noon-2pm & 6-10pm, closed Mon; mains US$5-15) The leading Indian restaurant in town, the opulent decoration sets the tone for an original menu of Moghul cuisine, but expect to pay US$20 or more for a spread.

More spots for a curry fix:

Curry Pot (Map p79; St 93; mains US$2-4) One of many Indian places in backpackersville, this place turns out some great curries.

FLOWER POWER

Anyone who spends a night or two on the town in Phnom Penh will soon be familiar with young girls and boys hovering around popular bars and restaurants to sell decorative flowers. The kids are incredibly sweet and most people succumb to their charms and buy a flower or two. All these late nights for young children might not be so bad if they were benefiting from their hard-earned cash, but usually they are not. Look down the road and there will be a *moto* driver with an ice bucket full of these flowers waiting to ferry the children to another popular spot. Yet again, the charms of children are exploited for the benefit of adults who should know better but are too poor to worry about it. Think twice before buying from them, as the child probably won't reap the reward.

Mount Everest (Map p79; ☎ 213821; 98 Sihanouk Blvd; curries US$2-5) One of the oldest curry houses in town, the menu includes popular Indian and Nepalese dishes.

Annam (Map p79; ☎ 726661; 1C St 282; mains US$4-7; ⏰ 11.30am-2.30pm & 6-10.30pm) Attractive garden restaurant that offers excellent Indian recipes in refined surrounds.

Italian

our pick Pop Café (Map p79; ☎ 012 562892; 371 Sisowath Quay; ⏰ 11am-3pm & 6-10pm; pizzas US$3-7) Owner Giorgio welcomes diners as if it's his home, making this a popular spot for authentic Italian cooking. Thin-crust pizzas, homemade pastas and tasty gnocchi, it could be Roma.

Happy Herb's Pizza (Map p79; ☎ 362349; 345 Sisowath Quay; pizzas US$4-7; ⏰ 8am-11pm) No, happy doesn't mean it comes with free toppings, it means pizza à la ganja. The nonmarijuana pizzas are also pretty good, but don't involve the free trip.

Luna D'Autumno (Map p79; ☎ 220895; 6C St 29; mains US$5-15; ⏰ 11am-2.30pm & 5.30-10.30pm) This elegant garden restaurant has an open kitchen firing up delicious pizzas from US$6 to US$10. Inside is a sophisticated restaurant with a walk-in wine cellar with bottles from the homeland. The menu includes some delicious seafood and traditional Italian recipes.

Other Italian places:

Nike Pizza (Map p79; 160 St 63; pizzas US$3-7; ⏰ 8am-11pm) Reliable pizzas. Try the 'pineapple porn moan' pizza – silly spelling or pure pleasure?

Le Duo (Map p79; 17 St 228; mains US$5-10; ⏰ lunch & dinner) Popular Italian restaurant set in a garden villa, with fresh pasta and authentic pizzas.

Japanese

Ko Ko Ro (Map p79; ☎ 012 601095; 18 Sihanouk Blvd; dishes US$2-7; ⏰ 11.30am-2pm & 5.30-9pm) This tiny little Japanese restaurant has a big personality

thanks to the friendly and attentive owner who will advise on selection. The walls are plastered with photos of his creations and the fish is very fresh.

our pick Origami (Map p79; ☎ 012 968095; 88 Sothearos Blvd; set menus US$8-15; ⏰ 11.30am-2pm & 5.30-9.30pm) This elegant Japanese eatery takes the art of Japanese food to another level thanks to the charismatic owner. Set menus include beautifully presented sushi, sashimi and tempura sets; affordable business lunches for those in a hurry.

French

Comme a la Maison (Map p79; ☎ 360801; 13 St 57; mains US$3-8; ⏰ 6am-10.30pm) Just like at home, at least if you are lucky enough to live with a first-class French chef, this place offers succulent steaks and a tour of provincial France.

La Marmite (Map p79; ☎ 012 391746; 80 St 108; mains US$5-10; ⏰ 11am-2.30pm & 6-10.30pm) It may not be the most traditional French name, but the menu at La Marmite is a tour de force in the French classics. Choose from daily specials such as scallops or go with the regular menu that includes tender tournedos and herb-infused lamb.

Topaz (Map p79; ☎ 211054; 705 Norodom Blvd; dishes US$5-20; ⏰ 11am-2pm & 6-11pm) One of Phnom Penh's first designer restaurants, Topaz is housed in an elegant villa with reflective pools, a walk-in wine cellar and piano bar. The menu is classic Paris, including delicate Bourgogne snails drizzled in garlic and steak tartare for those with rare tastes.

our pick Van's Restaurant (Map p79; ☎ 722067; 5 St 13; dishes US$5-25; ⏰ 11.30am-2.30pm & 5-10.30pm) Located in one of the grandest buildings in the city, the former Banque Indochine, you can still see the old vault doors as you make your way to the refined dining room upstairs. Dishes are beautifully presented with a decorative flourish, and menu highlights include sea perch carpaccio and tender veal.

La Residence (Map p79; ☎ 224582; 22 St 214; mains US$7-25; ☽ lunch & dinner) Part of Princess Marie's family home has been converted into this classy contemporary restaurant. Pass through the immense wooden doors and enjoy fine French food, including a foie gras speciality menu and superb seafood.

Other places for the Gallic touch:

Le Deauville (Map p79; ☎ 012 843204; St 94; ☽ 11am-10pm; mains US$4-8) French and international cuisine, with a menu of steaks and salads. On Friday, it doubles as a popular bar for well-heeled expats.

Atmosphere (Map p79; ☎ 994224; 141C Norodom Blvd; mains US$5-10) A French bistro near Independence Monument, the menu includes some fine cuts of meat, country salads and tasty desserts.

International

The number of international restaurants in Phnom Penh is ever-expanding and between them they offer a tantalising array of tastes. Heading north along the riverfront from the Royal Palace, the international restaurants come thick and fast.

Cantina (Map p79; 347 Sisowath Quay; mains US$2-4; ☽ 11am-11pm, closed Sat) This is the spot for tostadas, fajitas and other Mexican favourites, all freshly prepared. It's also a lively bar with professional margaritas and tequilas, thanks to local legend and owner Hurley Scroggins.

Kandal House (Map pp74-5; 239 Sisowath Quay; mains US$2-4) A tiny restaurant on the riverfront, the menu includes some delicious homemade pastas, salads and soups, plus a smattering of Asian favourites. Anchor draft available in pints.

Pacharan (Map p79; ☎ 012 556503; 389 Sisowath Quay; dishes US$2-12; ☽ 11am-midnight) A Spanish taverna and tapas restaurant, it grandly occupies one of the finest old buildings in town. Tapas bites include a vegetarian selection and plenty of seafood, plus there is the popular paella. Spanish wines feature strongly.

Riverside Bistro (Map p79; ☎ 213898; 273 Sisowath Quay; mains US$3-9; ☽ 7am-late) This popular corner restaurant has deep wicker chairs that are hard to leave. The menu includes a wide range of meals, including Cambodian favourites like grilled pork on lemon-grass skewers and a strong showing from Central Europe. It doubles as a popular bar later in the night and there are two pool tables here, plus live music.

ourpick Metro Café (Map p79; ☎ 222275; cnr Sisowath Quay & St 148; mains US$3-16) Metro has been turning heads thanks to a striking design, original lighting and an adventurous menu. Small plates are for sampling and include rare-pepper tuna and tequila black-pepper prawns, while large plates include twice-cooked duck with lychee. Linger to enjoy the bar.

Foreign Correspondents' Club (FCC; Map p79; ☎ 724014; 363 Sisowath Quay; mains US$5-15; ☽ 7am-midnight) Famous beyond the borders of Cambodia, almost everyone swings by for a drink during a visit to Phnom Penh. Set in a colonial-era gem with high ceilings, the 'F', as expats call it, has voluptuous views over the Tonlé Sap River and the National Museum. Hit the happy hour between 5pm and 7pm and linger over dinner to soak up the atmosphere, as the menu includes a tempting selection of international dishes.

Riverhouse Restaurant & Lounge (Map p79; ☎ 212302; cnr St 110 & Sisowath Quay; mains US$5-15; ☽ 10am-11pm) One of the most sophisticated riverfront restaurants, the menu includes classic Cambodian cuisine and a strong international selection with a French accent. It gets very busy at the weekend when diners warm up for a night at the upstairs lounge (p105).

It's also worth steering a course away from the river for some more great places.

Boddhi Tree Umma Restaurant (Map pp74-5; 50 St 113; mains US$1.50-5; ☽ 7am-9pm) This is heaven compared to the hell of Tuol Sleng across the road. The lush garden is the perfect place to seek solace and silence after the torture museum. The impressive menu includes fusion flavours, Asian dishes, sandwiches and salads, innovative shakes and tempting desserts.

Del Gusto Café (Map pp74-5; ☎ 012 446710; 43 St 95; mains US$2-4; ☽ 7am-9pm) This beautiful Art Deco–style villa is buried beneath a tumble of tropical plants. The menu here is predominantly Mediterranean, with breads and dips, salads and wraps, all set to a soundtrack of jazz and classical music. Rooms are also available.

Nature & Sea (Map p79; 78 St 51; mains US$2-6; ☽ 8am-10pm) Perched on a rooftop above the lively 278 strip and with views over Wat Langka, this is a place to escape the *moto* madness below. The fruit shakes are excellent and include passionfruit and honey blends. The specialities are savoury whole-wheat pancakes and fresh sea-caught fish.

DINING FOR A CAUSE

There are several restaurants around town that are run by aid organisations to help fund their social programmes in Cambodia. These are worth seeking out, as the proceeds of a hearty meal go towards helping Cambodia's recovery and allow restaurant staff to gain valuable work experience.

Café 151 (Map p79; www.theglobalchild.com; 151 Sisowath Quay; US$1-3; 8am-7pm) A hole-in-the-wall offering coffee with a kick and fresh fruit shakes, with 100% of profits going to help street children.

Café Yejj (Map pp74-5; 170 St 450; mains US$3-5; 7am-5pm Mon-Sat, 9.30am-2pm Sun) An air-con escape from Psar Tuol Tom Pong (aka Russian Market), this bistro-style café specialises in pastas and salads. Or indulge in a frappucino and chocolate brownie. Promoting fair trade and responsible employment.

Ebony Apsara Café (Map p79; 42 St 178; mains US$2-5; 11am-midnight, until 2am weekends) A stylish little café near Norodom Blvd serving health shakes, vegetarian treats, Khmer food and international favourites. A good spot for late-night fixes as 40% of profits go to the Apsara Arts Association (p107).

our pick Friends (Map p79; ☎ 426748; www.friends-international.org; 215 St 13; dishes US$1.50-7; 11am-9pm) One of Phnom Penh's best-loved restaurants, this place offers tasty tapas, heavenly smoothies and creative cocktails. With a prime location near the National Museum, this a must and offers former street children a helping hand into the hospitality industry.

Lazy Gecko Café (Map p79; ☎ 017 912935; 23B St 93; mains US$1.50-4.50; 8am-11pm) Boasting 'homemade hummus just like when mum was dating that chap from Cyprus', this fun place serves international dishes and supports a local orphanage. Thursday is quiz night, while Saturday involves an orphanage visit with dinner and a performance by the children.

Le Café du Centre (Map p79; ☎ 992432; French Cultural Centre, St 184; mains US$1.50-5; 8am-9pm) Another Friends-run restaurant, hidden away in the lush courtyard garden of the French Cultural Centre. Sandwiches and crepes, plus a good selection of ice cream.

Le Lotus Blanc (off Map pp74-5; ☎ 995660; Stung Mean Chey; set menu US$6; noon-2pm Mon-Fri) Fifteen minutes from the city centre, this restaurant acts as a training centre for youths who previously survived by scouring the city dump. Run by French NGO, Pour un Sourire d'Enfant (For the Smile of a Child), it serves classy Western and Khmer cuisine.

Le Rit's (Map p79; ☎ 213160; 14 St 310; breakfast from US$3, set lunch US$5; 7am-5pm Mon-Sat) The three-course lunch and dinners here are a relaxing experience in the well-groomed garden. Set menus include a French flourish, while the main menu is Thai-style. Proceeds assist disadvantaged women to re-enter the workplace.

Romdeng (Map p79; ☎ 092-219565; 74 St 174; mains US$4-6.50; lunch & dinner Mon-Sat) Also part of the Friends' extended family, the elegant Romdeng specialises in Cambodian country fare and offers a staggering choice of traditional Khmer recipes, including the legendary deep-fried spiders.

Tamarind Bar (Map p79; ☎ 012 727197; 31 St 240; mains US$3-9; 10am-midnight) Maghreb meets Moorish with some classic Moroccan tajines and a small selection of tapas, plus some French influence. Downstairs is an inviting bar with high ceilings, while the rooftop is a great open-air dining area for the dry season.

Open Wine (Map p79; ☎ 223527; 219 St 19; mains US$4-15; 9am-11pm) This one-stop shop for dining and drinking includes a large garden restaurant with a bistro menu, a sophisticated French restaurant inside, a boutique wine wholesaler and an ice-cream parlour.

Tell Restaurant (Map p79; ☎ 430650; 13 St 90; mains US$5-15; 11.30am-2pm & 5-11pm) With fondues and *raclettes* (melted chees with vegetables), this restaurant brings a Swiss touch to the Wat Phnom area. Portions are generous and dishes include a selection of tenderised meats. There are also some Asian selections.

More international bites:

Khmer Restaurant (Map p79; ☎ 216336; St 278; mains US$2-4) International? Yes, this small place has great salads and sandwiches, pub-style grub and desserts such as brownies and crumbles.

Alley Cat Café (Map p79; near cnr Sts 178 & 19; mains US$2-5; 11am-11pm) Likeable little restaurant-bar turning out tasty tacos, burritos and enchiladas. Large portions, plus plenty of booze at the bar.

Le Cedre (Map pp74-5; ☎ 216336; St 278; mains US$3-7; ☯ 11am-11pm) Phnom Penh's first Lebanese restaurant boasts an atmospheric setting and a chef from Beirut.

La Croisette (Map p79; ☎ 220554; 241 Sisowath Quay; mains US$3-7; ☯ 7am-late) The new-look Croisette is a stylish spot with a good range of Western and Asian favourites.

Mekong River Restaurant (Map p79; ☎ 991150; cnr St 118 & Sisowath Quay; mains US$3-9; ☯ 10am-11pm) Good value set menus with a generous selection of Asian and international choices. Plus tapas for inveterate snackers.

Sarika (Map pp74-5; ☎ 017 456116; 69 St 566, Tuol Kork District; mains US$5-15) This stylish new address has a large and leafy garden for alfresco dining, plus interior dining in a gorgeous wooden house. The menu includes Asian fusion and an outdoor grill.

Fast Food & Bar Food

The good news is that at present none of the big fast-food chains grace Phnom Penh, just a few copycats including **Lucky Burger** (Map p79; 160 Sihanouk Blvd; ☯ 7am-9pm), but KFC is on its way (Khmer Fried Chicken?).

More popular than the copycats are the Khmer burger joints opening around town that pull in students between and after classes. There is a whole strip of them on Samdech Sothearos Blvd south of the Royal Palace, including **Mondo Burger** (Map p79; Sothearos Blvd). BB World in Sorya Shopping Centre (Map p79) also has a children's playground for those seeking a diversion over lunch. Don't expect McDonalds, but at least the ingredients are fresh.

Many of the recommended bars have great food, including Green Vespa, Rising Sun, Pink Elephant, Gym Bar, Talkin' to a Stranger and Teukai Bar: see Drinking (p104) for more options. One place that has particularly excellent bar food and could equally be at home under Eating or Drinking is **Freebird** (Map p79; ☎ 224991; 69 St 240; mains US$3-7; ☯ 7am-midnight), an American-style bar-diner with a great selection of burgers, wraps, salads and Tex-Mex.

Cafés

Corner 33 (Map p79; ☎ 092-998850; 33 Sothearos Blvd; mains US$1-4; ☯ 7am-late) A smart new café near the National Museum and riverfront, the elegant interior makes it a relaxing place to pass the time. Cakes, coffees and shakes, free wi-fi, plus free internet for those without a laptop.

El Mundo Café (Map p79; ☎ 012 520775; 219 Sisowath Quay; mains US$2-5; ☯ 6.30am-10.30pm) A mellow riverfront establishment, some say this has the best coffee in town. The menu includes a range of global food, ice cream and pastries, plus there's an upstairs lounge for movies.

Le Jardin (Map pp74-5; ☎ 011 723399; 16 St 360; mains US$2-5; ☯ 7am-6pm, closed Mon) Taking full advantage of the garden, this is a family-oriented café with a giant sandpit, a playhouse and toys for little boys and girls. Snacks and salads for adults, pastas and tidbits for kids, and everyone loves the ice cream.

The Shop (Map p79; ☎ 986964; 39 St 240; mains US$2-5; ☯ 7am-7pm) If you are craving the local deli back home, then make for this haven, which has a changing selection of sandwich and salad specials. The pastries and cakes are delectable and worth the indulgence. The team has opened **The Chocolate Shop** (35 St 240; ☯ 8am-8pm), highly dangerous for recovering chocoholics.

Java Café (Map p79; ☎ 987420; 56 Sihanouk Blvd; mains US$2-7; ☯ 7am-10pm) One of the most popular café-restaurants in the city, thanks to a breezy balcony and air-conditioned interior. The creative menu includes crisp salads, homemade sandwiches, towering burgers and daily specials. Plus health drinks, fruit shakes and coffee from several continents.

Garden Center Café (Map p79; ☎ 997850; 60 St 108; mains US$3-7; ☯ 7am-10pm, closed Mon) Relocated to a new home, there is less garden than before, but it remains an expat favourite thanks to the big breakfasts and huge portions of home-cooked food. Most mains come with a side salad, plus there are Sunday roasts, some Thai favourites and tasty desserts.

Fresco (Map p79; ☎ 224891; cnr Sts 51 & 306; mains US$3-10; ☯ 7am-7pm) A chic new café in the popular NGO district, there is an air-con interior, a breezy rooftop, plus a kiddies' play area. Sandwiches and salads dominate, plus some good value lunch combos. Wi-fi is free from 3pm to 5pm. There is a second smaller branch beneath FCC (p101).

Café culture doesn't stop there:

Café Sentiment (Map p79; ☎ 221922; 64 Monivong Blvd; mains US$1-4; ☯ 7am-11pm) Popular new café set over several floors on a busy Monivong junction. Great value pastries, snacks and coffees.

Jars of Clay (Map pp74-5; ☎ 300281; 39 St 155; cakes US$1, mains US$2-3; ☯ 9am-5.30pm Tue-Sat) If the Russian Market (p107) is too much, this little café is a great escape. Thirst-quenching drinks, light bites and home-baked cakes.

The Living Room (Map p79; ☎ 726139; 9 St 306; mains US$2-4; ☼ 7am-6.30pm Tue-Thu, to 9.30pm Fri-Sun, closed Mon) Family-friendly place with garden and playroom, plus a healthy menu and organic coffee. Free wi-fi.

Backpacker Cafés

There are few backpacker cafés of the sort so popular in nearby Vietnam, unless you include all the restaurants in the more popular guesthouses. Or try the Lazy Gecko Café (p102), which has a great vibe.

Mama's Restaurant (Map p79; 10C St 111; mains 2000-6000r; ☼ 7am-9.30pm) This long-running little place turns out cheap specials in steaming pots and is one of the best deals in town; includes a bit of Khmer, Thai, French and even African.

Bites (Map p79; 240 St 107; mains US$1-2.50; ☼ 7am-10pm) Mixing Malaysian, Padang and some international options, this is a clean little restaurant in a popular budget area of town.

Bakeries

Kiwi Bakery (Map p79; ☎ 215784; Sisowath Quay) Now boasting a great riverfront location, the Kiwi Bakery offers fresh bread, cakes and pies. Owned by a Khmer family who ran a bakery in New Zealand, it has everything from Eccles cakes to éclairs.

Among the aforementioned restaurants and cafés, the Shop (p103) has a great selection of breads and pastries, as does Comme a la Maison (p100).

Most of the city's finest hotels also operate bakery outlets with extravagant pastries, but prices are higher than elsewhere. Drop in after 6pm when they offer a 50% discount, and gorge away. The larger supermarkets also stock their own range of breads and cakes, freshly baked on the premises.

Self-Catering

Self-catering is easy enough in Phnom Penh, but it often works out considerably more expensive than eating like the locals. The markets are well stocked with fruit and vegetables, fish and meat, all at reasonable prices if you are prepared to bargain a little. Local baguettes are widely available, and start from 500r. Phnom Penh's supermarkets are remarkably well stocked. Imported items aren't that expensive as taxes aren't always paid, so for just US$2 to US$4 there are treats such as German meats, French cheeses and American snacks.

Lucky Supermarket (Map p79; 160 Sihanouk Blvd; ☼ 7am-9pm) Affectionately known as the unlucky market by some, this is the biggest supermarket chain in town with a serious range of products, including several branches, including one in the Sorya Shopping Mall (p107) on St 63.

Pencil Supermarket (Map p79; St 214; ☼ 7am-9pm) This popular Thai-run place is one of the largest supermarkets in town and is well stocked.

Bayon Market (Map p79; 133 Monivong Blvd) It may be a smaller supermarket, but Bayon Market has a good range of products, including some nice surprises that don't turn up elsewhere in the city.

Thai Huot Supermarket (Map p79; 103 Monivong Blvd) This is the place for French travellers who are missing home, as it stocks almost exclusively French products, including Bonne Maman jam and creamy chocolate.

Many petrol stations include shops with a good selection of imported products; most Starmart shops at Caltex petrol stations on major junctions in the city are now open 24 hours. La Boutique shops located at Total petrol stations are also worth keeping an eye out for.

DRINKING

Phnom Penh has some great bars and it's definitely worth at least one big night on the town when staying here. Many popular bars are clustered along the riverfront, but one or two of the best are tucked away in the back streets. Most bars are open until midnight and beyond.

Should it survive the developer's wrecking ball, the lakeside is a great place for sunset drinks. Laze in a hammock and watch the sun burn red – this is a must. Two of the more popular backpacker bars up here are the Drunken Frog and the Magic Sponge, but neither are on the water.

Keep an eye out for happy hours around town as these include two-for-one offers and the like that can save quite a bit of cash. Standard drink prices are US$1 to US$2 for a beer and US$3 to US$4 for a glass of wine. The happy hour at FCC (p101) from 5pm to 7pm is particularly popular.

Elephant Bar (Map p79; St 92; ☼ 2pm-midnight) This place has been drawing journalists, politicos and the rich and famous for 80 years. This sophisticated spot offers two-for-one happy hours between 4pm and 8pm, plus there's accompanying snacks and a pool table.

Pink Elephant (Map p79; 343 Sisowath Quay; 11am-midnight) A long-running riverfront bar, it pulls the punters thanks to top tunes, bargain beer and filling food. The only drawback are the hordes of 'soo-sine, Bangkok Poh, you wan buy flower, one doll-aah' kids passing by all night. Enter into the spirit (or imbibe it) and it's all good fun.

Green Vespa (Map p79; 95 Sisowath Quay; 6am-late) One of the most welcoming bars in town, the Vespa has a huge drinks collections, including some serious single malts. There's also hearty pub grub, an eclectic music collection and some devilish promotions, adding up to a popular place day or night.

Huxley's Brave New World (Map p79; 30 St 136; 10am-2am) The first upmarket British pub to open its doors in town, it occupies a laudable location near the riverfront. Think modern bar more than country pub, but it has one of the biggest drinks collections in Cambodia, and upstairs dining.

Talkin to a Stranger (Map p79; 012-798530; 21B St 294; 5pm-late, closed Mon) A lovable little garden bar, the congenial hosts have earned the place a loyal following with their killer cocktails and dinner specials. Regular events include quiz nights and live music.

Flavour (Map p79; 21B St 278; 7am-late) Located on the corner of up-and-coming St 278, this place was always destined to be popular and has rapidly become a darling of the NGO crowd, with cheap draft beer, cocktails and a menu which travels the world.

Revolution (Map p79; 9 St 51; 11am-late) Nearby, Revolution is a new spot with cheeky cocktails and an open jukebox (read: computer).

Equinox Bar (Map p79; 012 586139; 3A St 278) Popular place with a welcoming outdoor bar downstairs, plus a pool table and an intimate upstairs. Friendly service, cheap drinks, good food and a happy hour from 5pm to 8pm.

Zeppelin Café (Map p79; St 51; 4pm-late) Who says vinyl is dead? It lives on here in the Cambodian capital, thanks to the owner of this old-skool rock bar manning the turntables every night.

Rubies (Map p79; cnr Sts 240 & 19; 5.30pm-late, closed Mon) If you prefer the grape to the grain, then make for this small wine bar with a big personality. Lined with wood and spilling out onto the pavement, the lengthy wine list includes the best of the new world wines.

Elsewhere Bar (Map p79; 175 St 51; 10am-late, closed Tue) Why go Elsewhere? Ambient vibes, a lush garden setting, a great drinks menu, brilliant bar staff and a beckoning plunge pool, that's why. Hit the happy hour at 5pm and take a dip, or forget your worries over an 'amnesia' cocktail.

Gasolina (Map pp74-5; 56-58 St 57; 6pm-late, closed Mon) This stylish garden bar specialises in the sensual sounds of South America and even offers Salsa lessons (Tuesday and Thursday nights). Rum punches, cheap beers and a tasty bar menu round things off.

Gym Bar (Map p79; 42 St 178; 11am-late) The only workout going on here is raising glasses, as this is the number one sports bar in town. You won't find a better selection of big – no, make that giant – screens in this part of the world. Cold beer, pub grub and a rowdy crowd for the big ball games.

Salt Lounge (Map p79; 217 St 136; 6pm-late) Sleek, modern and minimalist, this cool cocktail bar is one of the most gay-friendly in town. The original interior draws a mixed crowd, making for a great spot.

Blue Chilli (Map p79; 36 St 178; 6pm-late) Another leading gay bar in town that draws all-comers, the original interior design includes tropical aquariums and some quiet corners.

Pontoon Lounge (Map p79; Tonlé Sap River, end of St 108; 11.30am-late) This place floats everyone's boat thanks to its unique location on the waters of Tonlé Sap River. One of the *in* spots, there are DJs at the weekend and happy hours every day from 5pm to 8pm. Aboard the attached boat is a smart new fusion restaurant called the Galley.

Riverhouse Lounge (Map p79; cnr St 110 & Sisowath Quay; 4pm-2am) Almost a club as much as a pub, this atmospheric lounge bar has DJs and live music through the week. It's chic and cool, as this is where young royals hang out.

Heart of Darkness (Map p79; 26 St 51; 8pm-late) More like the Heart of Business these days, it's evolved into a nightclub more than a bar, but remains a place to see and be seen thanks to the alluring Angkor theme. Be very wary of large gangs of rich young Khmers here…some are children of the elite and rely on their bodyguards to do their dirty work.

Other admired establishments with liquid menus:

Broken Bricks (Map p79; cnr Sts 130 & 5; 11am-2am) Atmospheric little bar set in a decaying colonial house near the riverfront.

'LOVE YOU LONG TIME'

There are lots of 'hostess' bars or 'girlie' bars in Phnom Penh. They are pretty welcoming to guys and girls, although 'I love you long time' should be taken with a pinch of salt. Some of them are quite smart and well-run, others are super-sleazy and little more than brothels with beer. Some of the girls are out-and-out prostitutes, others are more traditional bar staff and some are just fishing for boyfriends. Opinions are divided on these places. A certain breed of male expat can't get enough of them, while the NGO crowd can't stand them. While it's undoubtedly exploitation and the girls wouldn't choose this line of work if they were from wealthy families, it's nowhere near as scary or dangerous as the local prostitution scene where girls are virtual slaves and gang rapes are common. That said, it's a rocky road and once some of these girls cross the line there is no going back. Still, at least these places are in the public eye, the girls are free to pick and choose their customers and some make good money compared with unregulated underground brothels. If you want to join the circus, St 104, St 136 and St 51 are popular haunts with plenty of places. Some well-known spots around town:

Martini (Map pp74-5; 45 St 95) The original girlie bar; there's a big beer garden showing movies, plus a dark dance space.

Rose Bar (Map p79; 8 St 104) The place that kick-started the 104 strip, the food here is worth the diversion even if the girls are not your thang.

Sharky's (Map p79; 126 St 130) Plenty of pool tables and plenty more working girls. The bar food is some of the best in town.

Howie's Bar (Map p79; 32 St 51; 🕑 7pm-6am) Friendly and fun place that is the perfect spillover when the Heart of Darkness is packed.

Rising Sun (Map p79; 20 St 178; 🕑 7am-11pm) English pub meets backpacker bar with affordable drinks and top pub grub.

Rory's Pub (Map p79; 33 St 178; 🕑 7am-midnight, later at weekends) Popular Irish pub in an inviting central location.

Teukei Bar (Map p79; 23 St 111; 🕑 5pm-late, closed Sun) Funky little bar with signature rum punches, ambient sounds and reggae classics. Close to the Psar O Russei guesthouses.

ENTERTAINMENT

For news on what's happening here while you are in town, grab a copy of *AsiaLife Phnom Penh*, check the back page of the Friday edition of the *Cambodia Daily*, or look at the latest issue of the *Phnom Penh Post*.

Nightclubs

There aren't many out-and-out nightclubs in Phnom Penh and the few that there are tend to be playgrounds of the privileged, attracting children of the country's political elite who aren't always the best-behaved people to hang out with. The volume is normally cranked up to 11 and drinks are pretty expensive. Among the many bars listed earlier, the best dance spots are Heart of Darkness (p105) on any night of the week, Pontoon

(p105) or the classy Riverhouse Lounge (p105) on weekends.

Other clubbing options to see Cambodians at play:

Casa (Map p79; St 47; admission depends on event; 🕑 late) Rejuvenated Casa is back with guest DJs, themed nights and local celebs.

Manhattan Club (Map pp74-5; St 84; admission free; 🕑 until daylight) Cambodia's longest running full-on club with banging techno and a big crowd.

Rock (Map pp74-5; Norodom Blvd; admission depends on event; 🕑 late) Looks like a gigantic Home Depot, but Khmers go crazy for the place.

Spark (Map pp74-5; Mao Tse Toung Blvd; admission depends on event; 🕑 late) Owned by the daughter of Prime Minister Hun Sen, security should be tight.

Cinemas

There has been a renaissance of the cinema scene in Phnom Penh, following an appeal for the reopening of certain historic cinemas by King Sihanouk in 2001. There are almost no English-language films on offer, just a steady diet of low-budget Khmer films about zombies, vampires and ghosts.

Many lakeside guesthouses show movies every night, particularly those with a Cambodian connection such as the heart-wrenching *The Killing Fields*.

The French Cultural Centre (p77) has frequent movie screenings in French during the week, usually kicking off at 6.30pm. Check at the centre, where a monthly programme is available.

The Mekong River Restaurant (p103) screens two original films in English, one covering the Khmer Rouge and the other on the subject of land mines. Showings are hourly from 11am to 9pm and cost US$3.

Meta House (Map p79; www.meta-house.com; 6 St 264; 6pm-midnight, closed Mon) is a night gallery that has a great programme of films, documentaries and shorts about Cambodia (usually with English subtitles), including presentations by some of those involved.

Classical Dance & Arts

Apsara Arts Association (990621; www.apsara-art.org; 71 St 598) Alternate performances of classical dance and folk dance (US$5) are held every Saturday at 7.30pm. Visitors are also welcome from 7.30am to 10.30am and from 2pm to 5pm Monday to Saturday to watch the students in training (donations accepted). However, it is important to remember that this is a training school – noise and flash photography should be kept to a minimum.

Sovanna Phum Arts Association (Map pp74-5; 987564; 111 St 360) Impressive traditional shadow puppet performances and classical dance shows are held here at 7.30pm on Friday and Saturday nights. Tickets are usually US$5.

Check the latest information on performances at the **Chatomuk Theatre** (Map pp74-5; Sisowath Quay), just north of the Hotel Cambodiana. Officially, it has been turned into a government conference centre, but it's occasionally the venue for displays of traditional dance.

Live Music

Live music is pretty limited in Phnom Penh compared with the bigger Asian capitals. Several of the larger hotels have lobby bands from the Philippines, including the Intercontinental Hotel (p95) and Hotel Cambodiana (p95), but it can be more muzac than music.

Memphis Pub (Map p79; 3 St 118; 5pm-1am) It's not closed, it just has soundproof doors. This is the leading live-music venue in Phnom Penh, with live rock'n'roll from Tuesday to Saturday, including a Wednesday jam session.

Art Café (Map p79; www.artcafé-phnom-penh.com; 84 St 108; 11am-11pm) This cultured café and art space, offering German and Central European fare, is a big promoter of live music and plays

host to blues, classical and traditional Khmer musicians on Friday and Saturday nights. See the website for performances.

Miles (Map pp74-5; 011 698470; cnr Sts 113 & 310; 4pm-midnight Tue-Sun) Relocated to a rooftop near Tuol Sleng, this chilled out jazz café offers live sessions on Friday and Sunday.

Riverside Bistro (p101), a mainstay of the riverfront scene, often has bands jamming away in the back room.

SHOPPING

There is some great shopping to be had in Phnom Penh, but don't forget to bargain in the markets or you'll have your 'head shaved', local-speak for being ripped off. Most markets are open from around 6.30am to 5.30pm. Some shops keep shorter hours by opening later, while tourist-oriented stores often stay open into the evening.

As well as the markets, there are now some shopping malls in Phnom Penh. While these may not be as glamorous as the likes of the Siam Paragon in Bangkok, they are good places to browse thanks to the air-con. **Sorya Shopping Centre** (Map p79; cnr Sts 63 & 154) is currently pick of the crop with a good range of shops and superb views over the more traditional Psar Thmei.

Art Galleries

There are plenty of shops selling locally produced paintings along St 178, opposite the National Museum. It used to be a pretty sorry selection of the amateurish Angkor paintings seen all over the country, but now with a new generation of artists coming up, the selection is much stronger. It is necessary to bargain. There are also lots of reproduction busts of famous Angkorian sculptures available along this stretch – great for the mantelpiece back home.

Many of the leading hotels and restaurants dedicate some space to art or photographic exhibitions. There are several galleries and art spaces of note to seek out around the city:

Art Café (Map p79; 84 St 108; 11am-11pm) Café and gallery with changing exhibitions of local and international artists.

Asasax Art Gallery (Map p79; 192 St 178; 9am-8pm) High-end gallery featuring the striking work of local artist Asasax.

Java Café (Map p79; 56 Sihanouk Blvd; 7am-10pm) Strong supporter of the art scene in Cambodia with challenging exhibitions.

SHOPPING FOR A CAUSE

There are a host of tasteful shops selling handicrafts and textiles to raise money for projects to assist disadvantaged Cambodians. These are a good place to spend some dollars, as it helps to put a little bit back into the country.

Cambodian Craft Cooperation (Map p79; www.cambodian-craft.com; 1 Norodom Blvd; 9am-8pm) Just to the southeast of Wat Phnom, this lovely boutique showcases exquisite silk from Takeo, silver from Kompong Loung, pottery from Kompong Chhnang and wicker work from Kratie.

Cambodian Handicraft Association (Map p79; 40 St 160; 8am-6pm) This well-stocked showroom and workshop sells fine handmade clothing, scarves, toys, bags and photo albums.

Colours of Cambodia (Map p79; 373 Sisowath Quay; 9am-6pm) Tucked away underneath FCC, this is a popular fair-trade gift shop supporting NGO craft projects. Lines include silk, wood carvings, T-shirts and jewellery.

Friends & Stuff (Map p79; 215 St 13; noon-9pm Mon to Fri, 9am-6pm Sat) The closest thing to a charity shop or thrift store in Phnom Penh, with a good range of new and secondhand products sold to generate money to help street children.

Khemara Handicrafts (Map p79; 18 St 302; 8am-6pm) Run by a local NGO and women's self-help groups, this is a relaxing place for hassle-free browsing through the silk and other handicrafts.

Khmer Life (Map pp74-5; St 113; 8am-5pm) Close to Tuol Sleng, this shop is linked to the Khmer Village Homestay (p274) and sells handicrafts.

NCDP Handicrafts (Map p79; 213734; 3 Norodom Blvd; 8am-6pm) This shop was set up by the National Centre for Disabled Persons (NCDP). The collection includes exquisite silk scarves, throws, bags and cushions. Other items include *kramas* (scarves), shirts, wallets and purses, notebooks and greeting cards.

Nyemo (Map p79; 33 St 310; 7.30am-4.30pm) Helping disadvantaged women return to work, Nyemo's focus is on quality silk. It has a convenient new outlet next door to Rajana in Psar Tuol Tom Pong.

Rajana Main store (Map pp74-5; 170 St 450; 10am-6pm); Market store (Map pp74-5; Psar Tuol Tom Pong) There are two convenient branches of Rajana, both aimed at promoting fair wages and training. They have a beautiful selection of cards, some quirky metalware products, quality jewellery, bamboo crafts and a range of condiments from Cambodia.

Sobbhana (Map p79; 23 St 144; 9am-noon, 2.30-6pm) Established by Princess Marie, the Sobbhana Foundation is a not-for-profit organisation training women in traditional weaving. Beautiful silks in a stylish boutique.

Tabitha (Map pp74-5; St 51; 7am-6pm) This is another NGO shop with a good collection of silk bags, tableware, bedroom decorations and children's toys. Proceeds go towards rural community development, such as well drilling.

The Shop (off Map pp74-5; Stung Mean Chey; 8am-5pm Mon-Fri) Small shop at the Pour un Sourire d'un Enfant site, with silk, clothing, jewellery and toys made by families living around the Stung Mean Chey dump.

Villageworks (Map pp74-5; 118 St 113; 8am-6pm) Opposite Tuol Sleng Museum, this shop has the inevitable silk, as well as some delightful handmade cards and coconut shell utensils.

Wat Than Artisans (Map pp74-5; 180 Norodom Blvd; 7.30-noon, 1.30-5pm) Located in the grounds of Wat Than, this handicrafts shop is similar to NCDP, with an emphasis on products made from Khmer silk. Proceeds go to help land-mine and polio victims.

Meta House (Map p79; www.meta-house.com; 6 St 264; 6pm-midnight, closed Mon) Contemporary art space and night gallery with local exhibitions, international collections and photography.

Reyum (Map p79; 217149; www.reyum.org; 47 St 178) If you happen to be browsing St 178, drop in on Reyum, a nonprofit institute of arts and culture that hosts regular exhibitions on all aspects of Cambodian culture.

Designer Boutiques

There are several boutiques specialising in silk furnishings and stylish clothing, as well as glam accessories.

Ambre (Map p79; 217935; 37 St 178) Leading fashion designer Romyda Keth has turned this striking French-era mansion into an ideal showcase for her stunning silk collection.

Bliss Boutique (Map p79; 29 St 240) Attractive home decoration and interior design in silk and textiles, plus some casual clothing.

Couleurs D'Asie (Map p79; 33 St 240) Specialising in sumptuous silks for the home, this is the place for hangings, bedspreads and throws.

Jasmine (Map p79; 73 St 240) Popular boutique specialising in elegant evening wear and sartorial silk, there are some bold creations here.

Kambuja (Map p79; 165 St 110) Blending the best of Cambodian materials with innovative international designs, the Cambodian and American designers have quickly made a name for themselves.

Tuol Sleng Shoes (Map p79; 144 St 143) Scary name, but there's nothing scary about the price of these handmade shoes.

Water Lily (Map p79; 37 St 240) Popular jewellery and accessory shop with strikingly original designs.

Markets

Bargains, and bargaining sessions, await in Phnom Penh's lively markets – put on your haggling hat and enter the fray.

PSAR THMEI
ផ្សារថ្មី

A landmark building in the capital, the Art Deco **Psar Thmei** (Central Market; Map p79; north of St 63) is often called the Central Market, a reference to its location and size. The huge domed hall resembles a Babylonian ziggurat and some claim it ranks as one of the largest domes in the world. The design allows for maximum ventilation, and even on a sweltering day the central hall is cool and airy. The market has four wings filled with stalls selling gold and silver jewellery, antique coins, dodgy watches, clothing and other such items. For photographers, the fresh food section affords many opportunities. There are a host of food stalls for a local lunch, located on the western side, which faces Monivong Blvd.

Psar Thmei is undoubtedly the best market for browsing. However, it has a reputation among Cambodians for overcharging on most products. The French government is currently assisting with renovations to restore it to its former glory.

PSAR TUOL TOM PONG
ផ្សារទួលទំពូង

More commonly referred to by foreigners as the Russian Market (it is where the Russians shopped during the 1980s), **Psar Tuol Tom Pong** (Map pp74–5; south of Mao Tse Toung Blvd) is the best place in town for souvenir and clothes shopping. It has a large range of handicrafts and antiquities (many fake), including miniature Buddhas, woodcarvings, betel-nut boxes, silks, silver jewellery, musical instruments and so on. Bargain hard as thousands of tourists pass through here each month.

This is also the market where all the Western clothing made in garment factories around Phnom Penh turns up, all at just 10% of the price back home. Popular brands include Banana Republic, Billabong, Calvin Klein, Colombia, Gap, Gant and Next, but other names are contracting to Cambodia as time goes on. There are also fakes floating around, so be suspicious of labels like Kevin Clein.

This is the one market all visitors should come to at least once during a trip to Phnom Penh.

PSAR O RUSSEI
ផ្សារអូរ៉ុស្សី

Not to be confused with the Russian Market (left), **Psar O Russei** (Map p79; St 182) sells luxury foodstuffs, costume jewellery, imported toiletries, secondhand clothes and everything else you can imagine from hundreds of stalls. The market is housed in a huge labyrinth of a building that looks like a shopping mall from the outside.

Also worth checking out:

Phnom Penh Night Market (Map p79; Sisowath Quay; 4pm–midnight) A cooler alfresco version of Psar Tuol Tom Pong, this night market takes place every Friday, Saturday and Sunday evening, if rain doesn't stop play. Bargain vigorously, as it already has something of a reputation for overcharging.

Psar Chaa (Map p79; St 108) This is a scruffy place that deals in household goods, clothes and jewellery. There are small restaurants, food vendors and jewellery stalls, as well as some good fresh-fruit stalls outside.

Psar Olympic (Map pp74–5; St 310) Items for sale include bicycle parts, clothes, electronics and assorted edibles. This is quite a modern market set in a covered location.

GETTING THERE & AWAY
Air

For information on international and domestic air services to/from Phnom Penh, see p324.

Boat

There are numerous fast-boat companies that operate from the tourist boat dock (Map p79; Sisowath Quay) at the eastern end of St 104. Boats go to Siem Reap up the Tonlé Sap River and then Tonlé Sap Lake, but there are no longer services up the Mekong from Phnom Penh. For details on the international boat services connecting Phnom Penh with Chau Doc and the Mekong Delta in Vietnam, see p327.

The fast boats to Siem Reap (US$20 to US$25, five to six hours) aren't as popular as they used to be now that the road is in such good condition. When it costs US$5 for an air-conditioned bus or US$20 to be bundled on the roof of a boat, it is not hard to see why. It is better to save your boat experience for elsewhere in Cambodia if you have the choice.

Several companies have daily services departing at 7am and usually take it in turns to make the run. The first stretch of the journey along the river is scenic, but once the boat hits the lake, the fun is over as it is a vast inland sea with not a village in sight.

Express services to Siem Reap are overcrowded, and often appear to have little in the way of safety gear. Most tourists prefer to sit on the roof of the express boats, but don't forget a head covering and sunscreen as thick as paint. Less-nimble travellers or fair-skinned folk might prefer to be inside. Unfortunately, not everyone can sit inside, as companies sell twice as many tickets as there are seats! In the dry season, the boats are very small and dangerously overcrowded, to the point that one or two have sunk.

Bus

Bus services have improved dramatically with the advent of revitalised roads in Cambodia, and most major towns are now accessible by air-conditioned bus from Phnom Penh. Most buses leave from company offices, which are generally clustered around Psar Thmei or located near the northern end of Sisowath Quay.

Leading bus companies:

Capitol Transport (Map p79; ☎ 217627; 14 St 182) Services to Battambang, Poipet, Siem Reap & Sihanoukville.

GST (Map p79; ☎ 012 895550; Psar Thmei) Services to Battambang, Poipet, Siem Reap, Sihanoukville & Sisophon.

Hua Lian (Map pp74-5; ☎ 880761; 217 Monireth Blvd) Far-flung services include Ban Lung and Sen Monorom in the northeast, plus Battambang, Kampot, Kompong Cham, Kratie, Poipet, Siem Reap, Sihanoukville, Svay Rieng and Takeo.

Mai Linh (☎ 211888; 391 Sihanouk Blvd) Vietnamese company with buses to Siem Reap, plus Ho Chi Minh City.

Mekong Express (Map p79; ☎ 427518; 87 Sisowath Quay) Upmarket services to Battambang and Siem Reap (both US$9) complete with in-drive hostesses. Plus Ho Chi Minh City.

Neak Krohorm (Map p79; ☎ 219496; 24 St 108) Services to Battambang, Poipet, Siem Reap and Sisophon.

Paramount Angkor Express (Map p79; ☎ 427567; 127 St 108) Double-decker buses to Siem Reap and Sihanoukville.

Phnom Penh Sorya Transport (Map p79; ☎ 210359; Psar Thmei) Most established company serving Battambang, Kampot, Kep, Kompong Cham, Kompong Chhnang, Kratie, Neak Luong, Poipet, Siem Reap, Sihanoukville, Stung Treng and Takeo.

RAC Limousine Bus (Map p79; ☎ 884179; 81 St 130) Luxury limousine bus serving Siem Reap (from US$10).

Rith Mony Transport (☎ 991329; 137 St 118) Buses to Kompong Cham, Kratie, Siem Reap, Sihanoukville and Stung Treng.

Virak Buntham (Map p79; ☎ 012 322302; St 106) Buses to Krong Koh Kong via NH48 and Cardamom gateway communities.

Most buses charge a similar price, with the exception of premium services. The following list of destinations includes price, duration and frequency: Ban Lung (US$17.50, 12 hours, one daily), Battambang (US$4, five hours, frequent until midday), Kampot (US$3, three to four hours, several per day), Kompong Cham (US$2.50, two hours, frequent until 4pm), Kompong Chhnang (US$1.50, two hours, frequent), Kratie (US$5, five hours, several in the morning), Neak Luong (US$1.25, two hours, frequent), Poipet (US$7, eight hours, several early departures), Sen Monorom (US$10, 10 hours, one daily), Siem Reap (US$5, six hours, frequent until midday), Sihanoukville (US$4, four hours, frequent until midday), Stung Treng (US$9, seven hours, twice daily) and Takeo (US$2, two hours, frequent).

Most of the long-distance buses drop off and pick up in major towns along the way, such as Kompong Thom en route to Siem Reap or Pursat on the way to Battambang. However, it is necessary to buy tickets in advance to ensure a seat, plus a premium is usually charged for this service.

For more details on bus services between Phnom Penh and Ho Chi Minh City in Vietnam, see p331.

Taxi, Pick-up & Minibus

Taxis, pick-ups and minibuses leave Phnom Penh for destinations all over the country, but have lost a lot of ground to cheaper and more comfortable buses as the road network continues to improve. Vehicles for Svay Rieng and Vietnam leave from Chbah Ampeau taxi park (Map pp74–5) on the eastern side of Monivong Bridge in the south of town, while those for most other destinations leave from around Psar Thmei. Different vehicles run different routes depending on the quality of the road, but the fast share taxis are more popular than the bumpy pick-ups and overcrowded minibuses. The following prices are those quoted for the most commonly used vehicle on that particular route, but are indicative rather than definitive, as even Khmers have to bargain a bit.

Share taxis run to Sihanoukville (20,000r, 2½ hours), Kampot (15,000r, two hours), Kompong Thom (15,000r, 2½ hours), Siem Reap (30,000r, five hours), Battambang (25,000r, four hours), Pursat (20,000r, three hours), Kompong Cham (12,000r, two hours) and Kratie (30,000r, five hours).

It is also possible to hire share taxis by the day. Rates start at US$25 for around Phnom Penh and nearby destinations, and then go up according to distance and the language skills of the driver.

Pick-ups still take on some of the long-distance runs to places such as Mondulkiri (US$12, nine hours), but it is better to cover the good roads by bus and then switch to pick-ups for the shorter bumpy legs.

Minibuses aren't much fun and are best avoided when there are larger air-con buses or faster share taxis available, which is pretty much everywhere.

Train

There are currently no passenger services operating on the Cambodian rail network, but this should be seen as a blessing in disguise, given that the trains are extremely slow, travelling at about 20km/h. Yes, for a few minutes at least, you can outrun the train!

Just for reference, Phnom Penh's train station (Map p79) is located at the western end of St 106 and St 108, in a grand old colonial-era building that is a shambles inside.

GETTING AROUND

Being such a small city, Phnom Penh is quite easy to get around, although traffic is getting worse by the year and traffic jams are common around the morning and evening

rush hour, particularly around Monivong and Norodom Blvds.

To/From the Airport

Phnom Penh International Airport is 7km west of central Phnom Penh, via Russian Blvd. Official taxis from the airport to the city centre cost US$7 and unofficial taxis are no longer allowed to wait at the terminal. Taxi drivers will take you to only one destination for this price, so make sure that they take you to where you want to go, not where they want you to go. Official *motos* into town have been fixed at US$2, but if you walk outside the airport you can pick up a regular *moto* for more like US$1 to US$1.50. The journey usually takes about 30 minutes.

Heading to the airport from central Phnom Penh, a taxi should cost no more than US$5 to US$6 and a *moto* between US$1 and US$1.50. *Remorque-motos* can be had for about US$4.

Bicycle

It is possible to hire bicycles at some of the guesthouses around town for about US$1 a day, but take a look at the chaotic traffic conditions before venturing forth. Once you get used to the anarchy, it can be a fun way to get around, if a little dusty.

Bus

Local buses don't exist in Phnom Penh. Most Cambodians use *motos* or *cyclos* to get around the city. With the long, straight boulevards crisscrossing the city, it would be perfect for trams or trolley buses, but developments like these are still some years away.

Car & Motorcycle

Car hire is available through travel agencies, guesthouses and hotels in Phnom Penh. Everything from cars (from US$25) to 4WDs (from US$60) are available for travelling around the city, but prices rise if you venture beyond.

There are numerous motorbike hire places around town. Bear in mind that motorbike theft is a problem in Phnom Penh, and if the bike gets stolen you will be liable. Ask for a lock and use it, plus only leave the bike in guarded parking areas where available, such as outside popular markets (300r). The best places for motorbike hire are **Lucky! Lucky!** (Map p79; ☎ 212788; 413 Monivong Blvd) and **New! New!** (Map p79; 417 Monivong Blvd), right next door to each other on the main drag in town. A 100cc Honda costs US$4 per day or US$25 per week and 250cc dirt bikes start at US$9 per day or US$50 a week.

Riverside Moto (Map p79; ☎ 223588; www.riverside motorcycletours.com; 30 St 118) More-serious adventurers should consider coming here, as this place specialises in upcountry touring, has well-serviced bikes and can provide a tool kit and spares.

Cyclo

They are still common on the streets of Phnom Penh, but *cyclos* have lost a lot of ground to the *moto*. Travelling by *cyclo* is a more relaxing way to see the sights in the centre of town, but they are just too slow for going from one end of the city to another. For a day of sightseeing, think around US$6 to US$10 depending on exactly where you go and how many hours of pedalling it includes. Late at night, *cyclos* would have to be considered a security hazard for all but the shortest of journeys, but most drivers are asleep in their *cyclos* at this time anyway. Costs are generally similar to *moto* fares, although negotiate if picking one up at popular spots around town.

It's also possible to arrange a *cyclo* tour through the **Cyclo Centre** (☎ 991178; www.cyclo .org.uk), dedicated to supporting cyclo drivers in Phnom Penh. This is a good cause, and themed trips are available such as pub crawls or cultural tours.

Moto

These are generally recognisable by the baseball caps favoured by the drivers. In areas frequented by foreigners, *moto* drivers generally speak English and sometimes a little French. Elsewhere around town it can be difficult to find anyone who understands where you want to go – see the boxed text, opposite. Most short trips are about 1000r to 2000r and more again at night, although if you want to get from one end of the city to the other, you have to pay up to US$1. Prices were once rarely negotiated in advance when taking rides, but with so many tourists paying over the odds, it may be sensible to discuss the price first. For those staying in a luxury hotel, negotiation is essential. Likewise, night owls taking a *moto* home from popular drinking holes should definitely negotiate to avoid an expensive surprise.

Many of the *moto* drivers who wait outside the popular guesthouses and hotels have good English and are able to act as guides for a daily rate of about US$6 to US$8 depending on the destinations.

Remorque-moto

Also commonly known as *tuk tuks,* these motorbikes with carriages have hit Phnom Penh in the past few years and are here to stay. They come in every shape and size from China, India and Thailand, plus the home-grown variety such as in Siem Reap. Average fares are about double those of *motos,* and increase if you pack on the passengers.

Taxi

Phnom Penh has no metered taxis of the sort found in Thailand or Vietnam. **Bailey's Taxis** (☎ 012 890000) and **Taxi Vantha** (☎ 012 855000) offer taxis 24 hours a day, but have a limited number of cars. They do the run from town to the airport for US$5 and charge about US$1 per kilometre elsewhere. Note the price for the journey from the airport to town is fixed at US$7.

Private taxis tend to wait outside popular nightspots, but it is important to agree on a price in advance.

AROUND PHNOM PENH

There are several attractions around Phnom Penh that make good day trips, although they are kind of low key when compared with what's on offer in other parts of the country. The Angkorian temple of Tonlé Bati and hilltop pagoda of Phnom Chisor are best visited in one trip, and can be built into a journey south to either Takeo (p228) or Kampot (p215). Udong, once the capital of Cambodia, is also a potential day trip and can be combined with a visit to Kompong Chhnang (p234), known for being a 'genuine' Cambodian town.

There is a clean, comfortable and cheap bus network operated by Phnom Penh Sorya Transport (p110) covering most of the following places. For experienced riders, motorcycles (p111) are another interesting way to visit these attractions, as there are plenty of small villages along the way. If time is more important than money, you can rent a taxi to whisk you around for between US$35 and US$50 a day, depending on destination.

WE'RE ON A ROAD TO NOWHERE

Taking a ride on a *remorque-moto, moto* or *cyclo* is not as easy as it looks. Drivers who loiter around guesthouses, hotels, restaurants and bars may speak streetwise English and know the city well, but elsewhere the knowledge and understanding required to get you to your destination dries up fast. Flag one down on the street or grab one from outside the market, and you could end up pretty much anywhere in the city. You name your destination, and they nod confidently, eager for the extra money a foreigner may bring, but not having the first clue of where you want to go. They start driving or pedalling furiously down the road and await your instructions. You don't give them any instructions, as you think they know where they are going. Before you realise it, you are halfway to Thailand or Vietnam. The moral of the story is always carry a map of Phnom Penh and keep a close eye on the driver unless he speaks enough English to understand where on earth you want to go.

Some of the more popular guesthouses offer inexpensive tours, with or without a guide, to most of the places covered here.

KIEN SVAY
កៀនស្វាយ

Kien Svay is a very popular picnic area on a small tributary of the Mekong. Hundreds of bamboo huts have been built over the water and Khmers love to come here on the weekend and sit around gossiping and munching.

Kien Svay is a peculiarly Cambodian institution, mixing the universal love of picnicking by the water with the unique Khmer fondness for lounging about on mats. It works like this: for 5000r an hour, picnickers rent an area on a raised open hut covered with reed mats. Be sure to agree on the price *before* you rent a space and note that it should only be about 2000r if you buy food from the family. The tiny boat trip to the huts should be included in the price.

All sorts of food is sold at Kien Svay, although it is necessary to bargain to ensure a fair price. Prices generally seem reasonable thanks to the massive competition – there are perhaps 50 or more sellers here. Popular dishes include grilled chicken and fish, river lobster and fresh fruit. The area is pretty deserted during the week, but this can make it a calmer time to picnic.

Getting There & Away

Kien Svay is a district in Kandal Province, and the actual picnic spot is just before the small town of Koki, about 15km east of Phnom Penh. To get here from Phnom Penh, turn left off NH1, which links Phnom Penh with Ho Chi Minh City, through a wat-style gate at a point 15km east of the Monivong Bridge.

You will know you are on the right track if you see plenty of beggars and hundreds of cars. Buses regularly depart for Kien Svay from Psar Thmei and cost just 2000r. The local way to get there would be to take a *remorque-moto* from the Chbah Ampeau taxi park, just east of the Monivong Bridge. This would cost around 1000r or so, but the trip is very slow, if somewhat amusing. A round-trip *moto* should cost about US$5.

UDONG
ភ្នំឧដុង្គ

Udong (the Victorious) served as the capital of Cambodia under several sovereigns between 1618 and 1866, suggesting 'victorious' was an optimistic epithet, as Cambodia was in terminal decline at this time. A number of kings, including King Norodom, were crowned here. The main attractions today are the two small humps of Phnom Udong, which have several stupas on them. Both ends of the ridge have good views of the Cambodian countryside dotted with innumerable sugar palm trees. Udong is not a leading attraction, but for those with the time it's worth the visit.

The smaller ridge has two structures and several stupas on top. **Ta San Mosque** faces westward towards Mecca. Across the plains to the south of the mosque you can see **Phnom Vihear Leu**, a small hill on which a *vihara* stands between two white poles. To the right of the *vihara* is a building used as a prison under Pol Pot's rule. To the left of the *vihara* and below it is a pagoda known as **Arey Ka Sap**.

The larger ridge, Phnom Preah Reach Throap (Hill of the Royal Fortune), is so named because a 16th-century Khmer king is said to have hidden the national treasury here during a war with the Thais. The most impressive structure on Phnom Preah Reach Throap is **Vihear Preah Ath Roes**. The *vihara* and the statue of Buddha, dedicated in 1911 by King Sisowath, were blown up by the Khmer Rouge in 1977; only sections of the walls, the bases of eight enormous columns and the right arm and part of the right side of the original Buddha statue remain. The Buddha has been reconstructed and the roof is currently being rebuilt.

About 120m northwest of Vihear Preah Ath Roes is a line of small *viharas*. The first is **Vihear Preah Ko**, a brick-roofed structure that contains a statue of Preah Ko, the sacred bull; the original statue was carried away by the Thais long ago. The second structure, which has a seated Buddha inside, is **Vihear Preah Keo**. The third is **Vihear Prak Neak**, its cracked walls topped with a thatched roof. Inside this *vihara* is a seated Buddha who is guarded by a *naga*. (*Prak neak* means 'protected by a *naga*'.)

At the northwestern extremity of the ridge stand four large stupas. The first is the cement **Chet Dey Mak Proum**, the final resting place of King Monivong (r 1927–41). Decorated with *garudas* (mythical half-man, half-bird creatures), floral designs and elephants, it has four faces on top. The middle stupa, **Tray Troeng**, is decorated with coloured tiles; it was built in 1891 by King Norodom to house the ashes of his father, King Ang Duong (r 1845–59). But some say King Ang Duong was in fact buried next to the Silver Pagoda in Phnom Penh. The third stupa, **Damrei Sam Poan**, was built by King Chey Chetha II (r 1618–26) for the ashes of his predecessor, King Soriyopor. The fourth stupa was relocated in 2002 from in front of Phnom Penh railway station and contains a relic of the Buddha, believed to be an eyebrow hair.

An east-facing staircase leads down the hillside from the stupa of King Monivong. Just north of its base is a **pavilion** decorated with graphic murals depicting Khmer Rouge atrocities.

At the base of the ridge, close to the road, is a **memorial** to the victims of Pol Pot that contains the bones of some of the people who were buried in approximately 100 mass graves, each containing about a dozen bodies. Instruments of torture were unearthed along with the bones when a number of the pits were disinterred in 1981 and 1982.

Getting There & Away

Udong is 41km from the capital. Head north out of Phnom Penh on NH5 and turn left (south) at the signposted archway. Udong is 3.5km south of the turn-off; the access road goes through the village of Psar Dek Krom, and passes by a memorial to Pol Pot's victims and a structure known as the Blue Stupa, before arriving at a short staircase.

A cheap and convenient way to get to Udong is by air-con local bus (4000r, one hour) from Phnom Penh. Buses depart from near Psar Thmei and run regularly throughout the day. The bus drivers can drop you at the access road to Udong, from where you can arrange a *moto* to the base of the hill for US$1. Buses to/from Kompong Chhnang (p234) also stop here, so you can combine your visit to the temples with a visit to a Cambodian town that sees few tourists.

A taxi for the day trip from Phnom Penh will cost around US$40. *Moto* drivers also run people to Udong for about US$10 for the day, but compared with the bus this isn't the most pleasant way to go, as the road is pretty busy and very dusty.

TONLÉ BATI
ទន្លេបាទី

Tonlé Bati (admission incl a drink US$3) is the collective name for a pair of old Angkorian-era temples and a popular lakeside picnic area. Anyone who has already experienced the mighty temples of Angkor can probably survive without a visit, but if Angkor is yet to come, these attractive temples are worth the detour.

TA PROHM
តាព្រហ្ម

The laterite temple of Ta Prohm was built by King Jayavarman VII (r 1181–1219) on the site of an ancient 6th-century Khmer shrine. Today the ruined temple is surrounded by colourful flowers and plants, affording some great photo opportunities.

The main sanctuary consists of five chambers; in each is a *linga* (phallic symbol) and all show signs of the destruction wrought by the Khmer Rouge.

Entering the sanctuary from the east gate, 15m ahead on the right is a bas-relief depicting a woman, and a man who is bowing to another, larger woman. The smaller woman has just given birth and failed to show proper respect for the midwife (the larger woman).

The new mother has been condemned to carry the afterbirth on her head in a box for the rest of her life. The husband is asking that his wife be forgiven.

YEAY PEAU
យាយពៅ

Yeay Peau temple, named after King Prohm's mother, is 150m north of Ta Prohm in the grounds of a modern pagoda. Legend has it that Peau gave birth to a son, Prohm. When Prohm discovered his father was King Preah Ket Mealea, he set off to live with the king. After a few years, he returned to his mother but did not recognise her and, taken by her beauty, asked her to become his wife. He refused to believe Peau's protests that she was his mother. To put off his advances she suggested a contest…for the outcome of this legend, see p283.

LAKEFRONT

About 300m northwest of Ta Prohm, a long, narrow peninsula juts into Tonlé Bati. It used to be packed at weekends with vendors selling food and drink, but their high prices have led most Phnom Penh residents to give the place a miss or bring picnics.

Getting There & Away

The access road heading to Ta Prohm is signposted on NH2 at a point 31km south of Phnom Penh. The temple is 2.5km from the highway.

Buses leave for Takeo at fairly regular intervals throughout the day and can drop passengers at the access road. The fare is 3500r. The first bus from Phnom Penh leaves at 7am and there are hourly services until 4pm. Buses returning from Takeo pass the turn-off regularly throughout the day. If you are heading to the wildlife sanctuary at Phnom Tamao, these services also apply.

PHNOM TAMAO WILDLIFE SANCTUARY
ភ្នំតាម៉ៅ

Cambodia's foremost wildlife sanctuary, **Phnom Tamao** (www.cambodianwildliferescue.org; admission US$5) is a home for animals confiscated from traffickers or saved from poachers traps. It occupies a vast site south of the capital and its animals are kept in varying conditions that are rapidly improving with help from international wildlife NGOs. Spread out as it is, it feels like a zoo crossed with a safari park. The

way things are developing, Phnom Tamao is set to become one of the region's best-run animal sanctuaries in the coming years.

Popular enclosures include huge areas for the large tiger population, and there are elephants that sometimes take part in activities such as painting. There is also a walk-through area with macaques and deer and a huge menagerie, including some rare birds from around Cambodia.

The centre is home to the world's largest captive collections of pileated gibbons and Malayan sun bears, as well as other rarities such as Siamese crocodiles and greater adjutant storks. Wherever possible animals are released back into the wild once they have recovered and the centre operates breeding programs for a number of globally threatened species.

Cambodia's wildlife is usually very difficult to spot, as larger mammals inhabit remote and inhospitable areas of the country. Phnom Tamao is the perfect place to discover more about the incredible variety of animals in Cambodia.

If you don't like zoos, you probably won't like this wildlife sanctuary, but remember that these animals have been rescued from traffickers and poachers and need a home. Visitors that come here will be doing their own small bit to help in the protection and survival of Cambodia's varied and wonderful wildlife.

Free the Bears (Map p79; ☎ 017 794291; www .freethebears.org.au; 16A St 310) has just launched a 'bear keeper for the day' initiative to allow visitors a better understanding of the Asian black bear and Malayan sun bear. The full day visit includes the chance to feed and wash the young bears in their care.

Betelnut Jeep Tours (Map p79; ☎ 012 619924; www.betelnuttours.com; per person US$30), based at the Lazy Gecko Café, offers day trips here from Tuesday to Saturday, including entry, a guided tour and a chance to meet some of the residents.

Getting There & Away

Phnom Tamao is about 44km from Phnom Penh, down NH2. Take a left turn after the sign for the zoo (37km), and it is 6km further down a sandy track. On weekends, you can combine an air-con bus ride with a *remorque-moto*, but on weekdays it may be easier to rent a motorbike or charter a taxi. See opposite for details on bus times and prices.

PHNOM CHISOR
ភ្នំជីសូរ

A temple from the Angkorian era, **Phnom Chisor** (admission US$3) is set upon a solitary hill in Takeo Province (p227). Try to get to Phnom Chisor early in the morning or late in the afternoon, as it is a very uncomfortable climb in the heat of the midday sun.

The main temple stands on the eastern side of the hilltop. Constructed of laterite and brick with carved lintels of sandstone, the complex is surrounded by the partially ruined walls of a 2.5m-wide gallery with windows.

Inscriptions found here date from the 11th century, when this site was known as Suryagiri. The wooden doors to the sanctuary in the centre of the complex, which open to the east, are decorated with carvings of figures standing on pigs. Inside the sanctuary are statues of Buddha.

On the plain to the east of Phnom Chisor are the sanctuaries of **Sen Thmol**, just below Phnom Chisor, **Sen Ravang** and the former sacred pond of **Tonlé Om**. All three of these features form a straight line from Phnom Chisor in the direction of Angkor. During rituals held here 900 years ago, the king, his Brahmans and their entourage would climb a monumental 400 steps to Suryagiri from this direction.

There is a spectacular view of the temples and plains from the roofless gallery opposite the wooden doors to the central shrine. Near the main temple is a modern Buddhist *vihara* that is used by resident monks.

Curiously the US$3 charge is not levied at the bottom of the hill, but at the temple, so it is technically free to visit if you pass on the old brick structure.

Getting There & Away

The eastward-bound access road to Phnom Chisor is signposted on the left about 52km south of central Phnom Penh and 27km north of Takeo town. It's about 5km from the highway to the base of the hill.

The cheapest way to get to Phnom Chisor is to take a Takeo-bound bus from Phnom Penh and ask to be let off at the turn-off from NH2. This costs 5000r and from here you can take a *moto* to the bottom of the hill for US$1. Alternatively, you can charter a taxi for about US$40 to visit both Phnom Chisor and Tonlé Bati, or a motorcycle in Phnom Penh.

KIRIROM NATIONAL PARK
ឧទ្យានជាតិគីរីរម្យ

The hill station of **Kirirom** (entry US$5), set amid lush forest and pine groves, has been established as a national park. It is popular with Khmers at weekends as it is 675m above sea level with a climate notably cooler than Phnom Penh. There are several small **waterfalls** in the park, which are popular picnic spots for Khmers, and a number of basic walking trails. For a more substantial walk, consider hooking up with a ranger (US$5 or so) for a two-hour hike up to **Phnom Dat Chivit** (End of the World Mountain) where an abrupt cliff-face offers an unbroken view of the **Elephant Mountains** and **Cardamom Mountains** to the west. It is often possible to see wildlife on this trail, including black bears scavenging the pine trees for honey.

Kirirom is one of the few national parks to have a nearby community tourism programme. Set just beyond the park boundaries, **Chambok Community-based Ecotourism** (☎ 012 355272; ccben_cam@yahoo.com; www.geocities.com/chambokcbet/; entry per adult/child US$3/1) programme is based in Chambok village, where attractions include a 40m-high waterfall, traditional ox-cart rides (Cambodia's original 4WDs) and nature walks. It is also possible to sample traditional Cambodian country fare at the small restaurant or arrange a local homestay with a bit of notice. Originally established by local NGO **Mlup Baitong** (☎ 023-214409; mlup@online.com.kh), a percentage of the proceeds is pumped back into the local community.

Sleeping

There are two options for staying at Kirirom and they are poles apart. The very basic **Kirirom Guesthouse** (☎ 012 957700; r US$20) is pretty run-down for such a stunning location, but the rooms have clean sheets, a fan and attached bathroom. However, the restaurant here is more memorable with outdoor pavilions offering superb views over the forest.

Kirirom Hillside Resort (☎ 023-982394; www.kiriromresort.com; camping incl tent US$15, r from US$40, bungalow from US$55; ❄ ▢ ▣) is located just beneath the entrance to the national park. At first glance this is a kitsch place aimed at local and regional tourists wanting a taste of country life. The castlelike entrance and plastic dinosaurs put off most Westerners, but for families with children it offers plenty of activities such as biking, horse-riding and kayaking. Hidden away at the back in the spacious grounds are some Scandinavian-style bungalows in various shapes and sizes, all well appointed with TV, minibar and hot showers. Facilities include a swimming pool, sauna and several restaurants. Budget travellers can get back to basics with a night in a tent.

Getting There & Away

Kirirom National Park is 112km southwest of Phnom Penh, located about 20km to the west of NH4. Unless you have your own transport, it is not that easy to get here. One possibility is to catch a bus going to Sihanoukville and ask to be let off at Kirirom or Preah Suramarit Kossomak National Park (the full name in Khmer). However, it still requires a *moto* to get around the park itself. The best way to visit is to hire a motorcycle in Phnom Penh or get a group together and charter a taxi for about US$60. Coming under your own steam, the turn-off for the park is about 85km from Phnom Penh, and is marked by a large sign on the right of the highway.

Siem Reap
សៀមរាប

Back in the 1960s, Siem Reap (*see*-em ree-*ep*) was the place to be in Southeast Asia and saw a steady stream of the rich and famous. After three decades of slumber, it's well and truly back and one of the most popular destinations on the planet right now. The life-support system for the temples of Angkor, Cambodia's eighth wonder of the world, Siem Reap was always destined for great things, but few people saw them coming this thick and this fast. It has reinvented itself as the epicentre of the new Cambodia, with more guesthouses and hotels than temples, world-class wining and dining and sumptuous spas.

At its heart, Siem Reap is still a little charmer, with old French shop-houses, shady tree-lined boulevards and a slow-flowing river. But it is expanding at breakneck speed with new houses and apartments, hotels and resorts sprouting like mushrooms in the surrounding countryside. The tourist tide has arrived and locals are riding the wave. Not only is this great news for the long-suffering Khmers, but it has transformed the town into a pulsating place for visitors. Forget the naysayers who mutter into their beers about Siem Reap in the 'old days', now is the time to be here, although you may curse your luck when stuck behind a jam of tour buses on the way back from the temples.

Angkor is a place to be savoured, not rushed, and this is the base to plan your adventures. Still think three days at the temples is enough? Think again with Siem Reap on the doorstep.

HIGHLIGHTS

- Encounter some of the world's rarest large water birds at the sanctuary of **Prek Toal** (p138)
- Explore the flooded forest of **Kompong Phhluk** (p139), an incredible village of bamboo skyscrapers
- Discover the quiet temples of Angkor, hidden away in the modern pagodas of **Wat Athvea** and **Wat Preah Inkosei** (p123)
- Dive into **Bar Street** (p134), the drink capital of Siem Reap, and discover nearby restaurants and bars
- Learn the secrets of Khmer cuisine with a **cooking course** (p125), the perfect way to impress friends back home

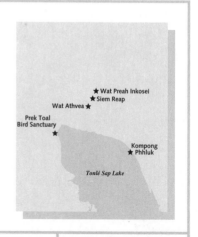

- TELEPHONE CODE: 063   - POPULATION: 800,000   - AREA: 10,299 SQ KM

HISTORY

The name Siem Reap means 'Siamese Defeated', hardly the most tactful name for a major city near Thailand. Imagine Birmingham with the name 'Germany Defeated'. The empire of Angkor once included much of modern-day Thailand, but there's a touch of irony about the name, given that Thailand ultimately defeated Cambodia and controlled Siem Reap and Angkor from 1794 to 1907.

Siem Reap was little more than a village when French explorers discovered Angkor in the 19th century. With the return of Angkor to Cambodian, or should that be French, control in 1907, Siem Reap began to grow, absorbing the first wave of tourists. The Grand Hotel d'Angkor opened its doors in 1929 and the temples of Angkor remained one of Asia's leading draws until the late 1960s, luring visitors including Charlie Chaplin and Jackie Kennedy. With the advent of war and the Khmer Rouge, Siem Reap entered a long slumber from which it only began to awake in the mid-1990s.

Tourism is the lifeblood of Siem Reap and without careful management it could become Siem Reapolinos, the not so Costa-del-Culture of Southeast Asia. However, there are promising signs that developers are learning from the mistakes that have blighted other regional hot spots, with restrictions on the height of hotels and bus sizes. Either way, Angkor is centre stage on the world travel map right now and there is no going back for its supply line, Siem Reap.

ORIENTATION

Siem Reap is still a small town at heart and easy enough to navigate in an hour or two. The centre is around Psar Chaa (Old Market), the administrative district is along the western bank of the river, and accommodation is spread throughout town. National Hwy 6 (NH6) cuts across the northern part of town, passing Psar Leu (Main Market) in the east of town and the Royal Residence and the Grand Hotel d'Angkor in the centre, and then heads to the airport and beyond to the Thai border. Stung Siem Reap (Siem Reap River) flows north–south through the centre of town, and has enough bridges that you won't have to worry too much about being on the wrong side. Like Phnom Penh, however, street numbering is haphazard to say the least, so take care when hunting down specific addresses.

Angkor Wat and Angkor Thom are only 6km and 8km north of town respectively, while the Roluos Group of temples is 13km east along NH6 – see the map on pp142–3 for the location of these and other places beyond the city centre.

Buses and share taxis usually drop passengers off at the taxi park about 3km east of the town centre, from where it is a short *moto* (small motorcycle with driver) ride to nearby guesthouses or hotels. Fast boats from Phnom Penh and Battambang arrive at Phnom Krom, about 11km south of town, and most places to stay include a free transfer by *moto* or minibus. Siem Reap airport is 7km west of town and there are plenty of taxis and *motos* available for transfers to the town centre. For more details, see p138.

INFORMATION

Pick up a copy of the *Siem Reap Angkor Visitors Guide* (www.canbypublications.com), which is packed with listings and comes out quarterly. For further insights into the restaurant and bar scene in Siem Reap, pick up the *Siem Reap Drinking & Dining* guide, produced by the Pocket Guide (www.cambodiapocketguide.com).

Bookshops

Cheap books on Angkor and Cambodia are hawked by kids around the temples, and by amputees trying to make a clean start in Siem Reap. Be aware that many are illegal photocopies and the print quality is poor.

Carnets d'Asie (Map p120; 333 Sivatha St) Boutique bookstore specialising in French editions, plus English coffee-table books.

D's Books (Map p120; Bar St; 🕑 9am-10pm) The largest chain of second-hand bookshops in Cambodia, this is conveniently located for night browsing.

Monument Books (Map p120; FCC Angkor) Well-stocked new bookstore with a branch at FCC Angkor and at Siem Reap International Airport in both international and domestic terminals.

Siem Reap Book Center (Map p120; Pithnou St) Large selection of new titles on Angkor and beyond.

Emergency

Tourist police (Map pp142-3; ☎ 012 969991) There's an office at the main ticket checkpoint for the Angkor area. This is the place to come and complain if you encounter any serious problems while in Siem Reap.

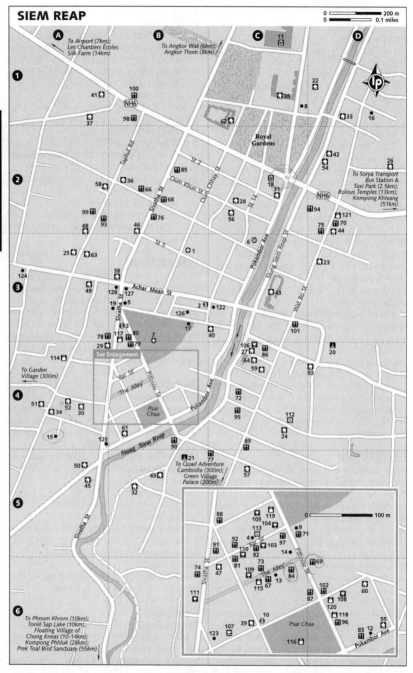

SIEM REAP

0   200 m
0   0.1 miles

A To Airport (7km);
Les Chantiers Écoles
Silk Farm (14km)

B To Angkor Wat (6km);
Angkor Thom (8km)

C

D

1

41 100 NH6 37 98

11

22

35 8 33 16

Royal Gardens

62

42 54

26 To Sorya Transport
Bus Station &
Taxi Park (2.5km);
Rolous Temples (13km);
Kompong Khleang
(51km)

2

58 36 66 St 2 85 Oum Khun St Oum Chhay St 68 St 14 76 28 56 18 31 NH6 94 121 75 70 44

99 93 48

25 63

St 5 46 1 6

23

3

124 38 49 128 127 Achar Mean St 19 5 Svatha St 78 117 80 29 79 114 2 126 17 3 7 40 122 43 101 106 27 64 59 86 20 53

To Garden
Village (300m)

Bar St The Alley

4

51 34 52 30 Pithnou Ave 61 125 Psar Chaa 72 95 89 112 24 Polambor Ave Stung Siem Reap

15

90

50 45 65 32 21 To Quad Adventure
Cambodia (300m);
Green Village
Palace (200m) 77 57

5

0   100 m

88 105 119 104 113 4 103 97 9 71

92 91 110 82 14 69

74 47 81 109 67 115 13 84 102 60 108 87 120 118 96 55 83 12

111 The Alley Bar St Sivatha St Pithnou St

6

To Phnom Khrom (10km);
Tonlé Sap Lake (10km);
Floating Village of
Chong Kneas (10-14km);
Kompong Phhluk (28km);
Prek Toal Bird Sanctuary (55km)

10 39 107 123 116 Psar Chaa Pokambor Ave

See Enlargement

Internet Access

Internet shops have spread through town like wildfire and your nearest online fix will never be far away. Prices are US$0.50 to US$1 per hour and most places also offer cheap internet-based telephone calls. The greatest concentration is along Sivatha St and around the Psar Chaa area. Many guesthouses and hotels also offer affordable access or free services for guests. Many of the leading restaurants and bars, as well as many midrange hotels, offer free wi-fi.

Medical Services & Pharmacies

Siem Reap now has an international-standard hospital for emergencies. However, any serious complications will still require relocation to Bangkok.

Angkor Children's Hospital (Map p120; ☎ 963409; ☽ 24hr) An international-standard paediatric hospital, the place to take your children if they fall sick. Will assist in any emergency for up to 24 hours. Donations accepted.

Royal Angkor International Hospital (Map pp142-3; ☎ 761888; www.royalangkorhospital.com; Airport Rd) A new international facility, affiliated with the Bangkok Hospital.

U-Care Pharmacy (Map p120; ☎ 965396; Pithnou St; ☽ 8am-9pm) Smart pharmacy and shop like Boots in Thailand (and the UK). English spoken.

Money

For cash exchanges, markets are faster and less bureaucratic than the banks.

ANZ Royal Bank (Map p120; ☎ 023 726900; Achar Mean St) Provides free credit-card advances and can change travellers cheques in most major currencies. International ATMs all over town.

Canadia Bank (Map p120; ☎ 964808; Sivatha St) Offers free credit-card cash advances and changes travellers cheques in most major currencies at a 2% commission. International ATM.

Union Commercial Bank (Map p120; ☎ 964703; Psar Chaa) Charges 2% commission for travellers cheques and offers free Visa advances.

Post

The **main post office** (Map p120; ☽ 7am-5.30pm) is along the river, 500m south of the Grand Hotel d'Angkor. Services are more reliable these days, but it doesn't hurt to see your stamps franked; many people have reported mail going astray in the past. For urgent shipping requirements, there are several courier services in town:

DHL (Map p120; ☎ 964949; Central Market)

EMS (Map p120; ☎ 760000; main post office)

Telephone & Fax

Making international calls is straightforward. The cheapest way is to use the major internet cafés, with calls starting at about US$0.10 per minute, but there can be some delay. The cheapest 'unblemished' calls can be arranged with the purchase of an M Fone tourist sim, working out at US$0.25 per minute. Or use one of the many private booths advertising these telephone services. There are a few public phone booths around town, including some around Psar Chaa. Phone cards are sold at shops and hotels. For domestic calls, it is cheaper to call from a private booth. Hotels impose hefty surcharges on calls, so check the rates before you dial.

If you need to send or receive faxes and are not based in a hotel that offers this service, try one of the many reasonably priced internet cafés in the Psar Chaa area.

Tourist Information

The Tourism Office in Siem Reap is in a white building opposite the Grand Hotel d'Angkor. There's a sign saying 'Tourist Information', but this is a little optimistic unless you come as a paid-up client on one of its private tours. Guesthouses and hotels are often a more reliable source of information, as are fellow travellers who have been in town for a few days.

DANGERS & ANNOYANCES

Siem Reap is a pretty safe city, even at night. However, if you rent a bike, don't keep your bag in the basket, as it will be easy pickings for a drive-by snatch. Likewise, lone females should try to walk home with travelling companions when leaving late-night spots, particularly if heading to poorly lit areas.

There are a lot of commission scams in Siem Reap that involve certain guesthouses and small hotels paying *moto* and taxi drivers to deliver guests. Ways to avoid the scam include booking ahead via the internet and arranging a pick-up, or sticking with a partner guesthouse if you are coming from Phnom Penh. Alternatively, just go with the flow and negotiate with the hotel or guesthouse on arrival.

For more on the commission scams facing those travelling to Siem Reap by land from Bangkok, see the boxed text on p330.

There are a lot of beggars around town and some visitors quickly develop beggar fatigue. However, try to remember that with no social security network and no government support, life is pretty tough for the poorest of the poor in Cambodia. There is no need to give to everybody, but there is also no need to treat them as pariahs. In the case of children, it is often better not to encourage begging, but if you are compelled to help then offer food, as money usually ends up being passed on to someone else.

Out at the remote temple sites beyond Angkor, stick to clearly marked trails. There are still land mines at locations such as Phnom Kulen and Kbal Spean. For more information about Cambodia's land mines, see p312.

SIGHTS

Visitors come to Siem Reap to see the temples of Angkor. The sights in and around the town pale in comparison, but they are a good diversion for those who find themselves templed out after a few days. That said, some of the best are…yet more temples!

Pagodas

Modern pagodas around Siem Reap offer an interesting contrast to the ancient sandstone structures of Angkor. **Wat Bo** (Map p120; 6am-6pm) is one of the town's oldest temples and has a collection of well-preserved wall paintings from the late 19th century depicting the *Reamker*, Cambodia's interpretation of the *Ramayana*. Another wat to consider is **Wat Preah Inkosei** (Map pp142-3; 6am-6pm), built on the site of an early Angkorian brick temple north of town, which still stands today at the rear of the compound.

South of the city centre, **Wat Athvea** (Map pp142-3; 6am-6pm) is an attractive pagoda on the site of an ancient temple. The old temple is still in very good condition and sees far fewer visitors than the main temples in the Angkor area, making it a peaceful spot in the late afternoon.

On the left fork of the road to Angkor Wat, **Wat Thmei** (Map p142-3; 6am-6pm) has a small memorial stupa containing the skulls and bones of victims of the Khmer Rouge. It also has plenty of young monks wanting to practise their English.

Wat Dam Nak (Map p120; 6am-6pm) was formerly a royal palace during the reign of King Sisowath, hence the name *dam nak* (palace). Today it is home to the **Centre for Khmer Studies** (www.khmerstudies.org), an independent institution promoting a greater understanding of Khmer culture with a drop-in research library on site.

Artisans d'Angkor

Siem Reap is the epicentre of the drive to revitalise Cambodian traditional culture, which was dealt such a harsh blow by the Khmer Rouge and the years of instability that followed its rule.

Les Chantiers Écoles (Map p120) is a school specialising in teaching wood- and stone-carving techniques to impoverished youngsters. On the premises the school has a beautiful shop called **Artisans d'Angkor** (Map p120; 380354; www.artisansdangkor.com), which sells everything from elegant stone and wood reproductions of Angkorian-era statues to household furniture. Tours are available daily from 7.30am to 5.30pm to learn more about traditional techniques. Tucked down a side road, the school is well signposted from Sivatha St.

ANGKOR NATIONAL MUSEUM

Looming large on the road to Angkor is the **Angkor National Museum** (Map pp142-3; 966601; www.angkornationalmuseum.com; 968 Charles de Gaulle Blvd; admission US$12, under 1.20m US$6; 6am-6pm), a state-of-the-art showpiece on the Khmer civilisation and the majesty of Angkor. Displays are themed by era, religion and royalty as visitors move through the impressive galleries. After a short presentation, visitors enter the zenlike 'Gallery of a Thousand Buddhas', which has a fine collection of images. Other collections include the pre-Angkorian period of Funan and Chenla, the great Khmer kings, Angkor Wat, Angkor Thom and the inscriptions.

Presentations include touch-screen video, epic commentary and the chance to experience a panoramic sunrise at Angkor Wat, but for all the technology there seems to be a scarcity of sculpture compared with the National Museum (p84) in Phnom Penh or even Angkor Conservation (p148). It is almost a triumph of style over substance, as if the curators are overcompensating for the shallowness of the collection with the depth of information. That said, it remains a very useful experience for first-time visitors to put the story of Angkor and the Khmer empire in context before exploring the temples. The downside is the price, which at US$12 is simply too high, given that US$20 buys admission to all the temples at Angkor. Visitors also have to pay a US$2 camera fee, but can't snap everywhere and an audio tour is available for US$3. Attached to the museum is a 'Cultural Mall', lined with shops, galleries and cafés.

SIEM REAP

There is also a second shop opposite Angkor Wat in the Angkor Café (p150) and outlets at Phnom Penh and Siem Reap international airports. Profits from sales go back into funding the school and bringing more teenagers into the training programme.

Les Chantiers Écoles Silk Farm

Les Chantiers Écoles (see Artisans d'Angkor above) also maintains a silk farm, which produces some of the best work in the country, including clothing, interior design products and accessories. All stages of the production process can be seen here, from the cultivation of mulberry trees through the nurturing of silk worms to the dyeing and weaving of silk. Free tours are available daily between 7am and 5pm and there is a free shuttle bus departing Les Chantiers Écoles at 9.30am and 1.30pm. The farm is about 16km west of Siem Reap, just off the road to Sisophon in the village of Puok.

National Centre for Khmer Ceramics Revival

This **ceramics centre** (Map pp142-3; ☎ 761519; www .khmerceramics.com; near Airport Rd; ⏱ 8am-6pm) is dedicated to reviving the Khmer tradition of pottery, which was an intricate art during the time of Angkor. The centre has recreated an ancient Khmer kiln that is eight metres long and is helping to breathe new life into this old art. It is possible to visit the centre and try your hand at the potter's wheel. There are plenty of elegant items on sale at the site and the centre is working with **Heritage Watch** (www .heritagewatch.org) to offer a sustainable livelihood to remote villagers. The centre is located down a left-hand side road, just before the roundabout near the airport.

Shadow Puppets

The creation of leather *sbei tuoi* (shadow puppets) is a traditional Khmer art form, and the figures make a memorable souvenir. Characters include gods and demons from the *Reamker*, as well as exquisite elephants with intricate armour. These are a very Cambodian keepsake. The House of Peace Association makes these puppets, and small puppets start from US$15 while larger pieces can be as much as US$150. One workshop is located at Wat Preah Inkosei (Map pp142–3) and a second (Map pp142–3) about 4km down NH6 on the way to the airport. La Noria

Guesthouse (p135) hosts shadow puppet shows on Wednesday evening.

Miniature Replicas of Angkor's Temples

One of the more quirky places in town is the **garden** (Map p120; admission US$1.50) of a local master sculptor, which houses miniature replicas of Angkor Wat, the Bayon, Banteay Srei and other temples. It is a bluffer's way to get that aerial shot of Angkor without chartering a helicopter, although the astute might question the presence of oversized insects in the shot.

Tonlé Sap Exhibition

North of town, Krousar Thmey – a nongovernmental organisation (NGO) supporting orphans – has an interesting **exhibition** (Map pp142-3; admission free) about Tonlé Sap Lake. The exhibition contains photos, models and fishing equipment from around the lake, as well as an informative video. After viewing the exhibition you can indulge in a massage to help the blind (opposite).

Cambodian Cultural Village

It may be kitsch, it may be kooky, but it is very popular with Cambodians and some Asian visitors, and provides a diversion for families travelling with children. This is the **Cambodian Cultural Village** (Map pp142-3; ☎ 963836; www.cambodianculturalvillage.com; Airport Rd; admission US$9; ⏱ 8am-7pm), which tries to represent all of Cambodia in a whirlwind tour of recreated houses and villages. The visit begins with a wax museum and includes homes of the Cham, Chinese, Kreung and Khmer people, as well as miniature replicas of landmark buildings in Cambodia. There are dance shows and performances throughout the day, but it still doesn't add up to a turn-on for most foreign visitors, unless they have the kiddies in tow. It is located about midway between Siem Reap and the airport.

Cambodia Land Mine Museum

Established by DIY de-miner Aki Ra, the **Land Mine Museum** (Map pp142-3; ☎ 12 598951; www .cambodialandminemuseum.org; admission US$1; ⏱ 7am-6pm) is very popular with travellers thanks to its informative displays on the curse of land mines in Cambodia. The museum includes an extensive collection of mines, mortars, guns and weaponry used during the civil war in Cambodia. The site includes a mock minefield so that visitors can attempt to locate the deactivated mines. Not only a weapon of war, land mines are a weapon against peace and proceeds from the museum are ploughed into mine awareness campaigns and support an on-site orphanage, rehabilitation centre and training facility. The museum is about 25km from Siem Reap in Banteay Srei and is easily combined with a visit to Banteay Srei temple, about 6km beyond.

For those wanting to learn more about the after-effects of an amputation, it is possible to visit the **Physical Rehabilitation Centre** (Map p120) in Siem Reap, run by **Handicap International** (www.handicapinternational.be). There are informative displays including a variety of homemade prosthetics that it has replaced with international-standard artificial limbs, plus it is possible to meet some of the locals receiving assistance here.

ACTIVITIES
Cooking Courses
Cooking classes have really taken off in Siem Reap with a number of restaurants and hotels now offering an introduction to the secrets of Cambodian cooking, including many of the top-end places. Some classes with a good reputation:

Angkor Palm (Map p120; ☎ 761436; www.angkorpalm .com; Pithnou St; ✆ 8am-5pm). This popular restaurant has just opened a new country villa near Banteay Srei temple offering informal cooking classes at just US$5 per dish.

Cooks in Tuk Tuks (Map pp142-3; ☎ 963400; www .therivergarden.info; US$18-25). Starts at 10am daily with a visit to Psar Leu market, then returns to the peaceful River Garden for a professional class.

Le Tigre de Papier (Map p120; ☎ 760930; letigrede papier@hotmail.com; Bar St; US$11). Starts at 10am daily and includes a visit to the market. Proceeds go to supporting Sala Bai Hotel and Restaurant School (p127), making it great value and a good cause.

Golf
Siem Reap has two international-standard golf courses. **Phokheetra Country Club** (Map pp142-3; ☎ 964600; www.sofitel.com) hosts the first tournament to be held in Cambodia on the Asian tour every December and includes an ancient Angkor bridge amid its manicured fairways and greens. The **Angkor Golf Resort** (Map pp142-3; ☎ 761139; www.angkor-golf.com) was designed by legendary British golfer Nick Faldo and is world class. Greens fees for both are around US$100, plus more for a caddy, clubs and carts.

Horse Riding
Yee-haa, ride 'em cowboy! The **Happy Ranch** (Map pp142-3; ☎ 012 920002; www.thehappyranch.com; US$15-80) offers the chance to explore Siem Reap on horseback, taking in surrounding villages and secluded temples. This is a calm way to experience the countryside, far from the traffic and crowds elsewhere. Riding lessons are also available for children or beginners, and for seriously horsier types there are a couple of stable rooms available to stay in.

Massage & Spa
You may well need a massage if you have been exploring the rollercoaster roads of Preah Vihear province. Deserving of support is **Seeing Hands Massage 4** (Map p120; ☎ 012 836487; 324 Sivatha St; per hr fan/air-con $5/7), which trains blind people in the art of massage. Watch out for copycats, as some of these are just exploiting the blind for profit. **Krousar Thmey** (Map pp142-3; massage US$6) also has massage by the blind at its interesting Tonlé Sap Exhibition.

Foot massage is a big hit in Siem Reap – not surprising given all those steep stairways at the temples. If your feet are feeling frumpy, head to the strip running northwest of Psar Chaa where there are half a dozen or more places offering a massage for about US$6 an hour, including **Islands Massage** (Map p120; ☎ 964402) and the brilliantly named **Dr Feet** (Map p120; ☎ 965034).

There are also some indulgent spas to pamper that inner princess:

Bodia Spa (Map p120; ☎ 761593; Pithnou St; ✆ 10am-midnight) Sophisticated spa near Psar Chaa offering a full range of scrubs, rubs and natural remedies, including its own line of herbal products.

Bodytune (Map p120; ☎ 764141; Pokambor Ave; massages US$12-37; ✆ 10am-10pm) Lavish outpost of a popular Thai spa, this is a fine place to relax and unwind on the riverfront.

Frangipani (Map p120; ☎ 964391; ✆ 10am-10pm) Located down a narrow alley between Psar Chaa and Bar St, this delightful little place offers massage and a whole range of spa treatments.

Many top-end hotels have in-house spas that are open to all. Those with the best reputation include **Angkor Spa** (Map pp142–3) at Sofitel Phokheetra Royal Angkor (p130), **Sanctuary Spa** (Map p120) at Shinta Mani (p129), voted second best in Asia by readers of the *Spa Asia* magazine, and **Visaya Spa** (Map p120) at FCC Angkor (p129).

Quad Biking

Quad biking has finally come to Siem Reap thank to **Quad Adventure Cambodia** (Map p120; ☎ 092 787216; www.quad-adventure-cambodia.com; US$19-76). For those who haven't tried it, all-terrain biking is serious fun and all rides include a short introductory lesson. Rides around Siem Reap involve sunset over the rice fields, pretty temples and back roads through traditional villages where children wave and shout. Quad Adventure Cambodia is well signposted in the Wat Dam Nak area.

Swimming

It's hot work clambering about the temples and there is no better way to wind down than with a dip in swimming pool. Pay by the day at most hotels for use of the swimming pool and/or gym, ranging from just US$5 at some of the midrange hotels to US$20 at the five-star palaces. More and more of the cheaper hotels and resorts are putting in pools and this can be a worthwhile splash for weary travellers.

Or head to **Aqua** (Map pp142-3; www.aquacambodia.com; 7 Makara St; swimming US$2), where there is a large pool and a lively little bar-restaurant. Locals like to swim in the waters of the Western Baray (p173) at the weekend.

Tours

Most visitors are in Siem Reap to tour the temples of Angkor. See p152 for more on temple tours and p333 for a list of recommended Cambodian tour operators.

SIEM REAP FOR CHILDREN

Siem Reap is a great city for children these days thanks to a range of activities beyond the temples. Many of the temples themselves will appeal to older children, particularly the Indiana Jones atmosphere of Ta Prohm and Beng Mealea, the sheer size and scale of Angkor Wat or the weird faces at the Bayon.

Other activities that might be popular include boat trips on the Tonlé Sap to visit the incredible floating village of Chong Kneas (p139) or the flooded forest of Kompong Phhluk (p139); swimming at a hotel or resort (above); exploring the countryside on horseback (p125) or quad bike (above); goofing around at the Cambodian Cultural Village (p124); or just enjoying the cafés and restaurants of Siem Reap at a leisurely pace, such as Butterflies Garden Restaurant (p131), with its incredible collection of fluttering butterflies.

SLEEPING

Siem Reap has the best range of accommodation in Cambodia. A vast number of family-run guesthouses charging US$3 to US$15 a room cater for budget travellers, while those looking for midrange accommodation can choose upmarket guesthouses from US$15, or small hotels from US$20 per room. Those wanting air-con at a budget price may find better value at cheap hotels and upmarket guesthouses than in the budget guesthouses offering only a few air-con rooms.

There are plenty of midrange to top-end hotels around town, and as the construction boom continues unabated, these will soon be supplemented by further arrivals. In the low season (April to September), it may be possible to negotiate discounts at many of these places. Top-end hotels usually publish high- and low-season rates.

Check out the website of **Siem Reap Angkor Hotel & Guesthouse Association** (www.angkorhotels .org) for a complete listing of guesthouses and hotels.

Budget

Touts for budget guesthouses wait at the taxi park, Phnom Krom (where the fast boat from Phnom Penh docks) and at the airport. Even if you have not yet decided where to stay in Siem Reap, do not be surprised to see a noticeboard displaying your name, as most guesthouses in Phnom Penh either have partners up here or sell your name on to another guesthouse! This system usually involves a free ride into town. There is no obligation to stay at their guesthouse if you don't like the look of it, but the 'free lift' might suddenly cost US$1 or more.

Apart from the guesthouses listed here, many places around town offer rooms from US$3. Many offer small discounts for those planning longer stays.

PSAR CHAA AREA

Popular Guesthouse (Map p120; ☎ 963578; chom@camnet .com.kh; r US$3-14; 🐱 🖳) Popular by name, popular by nature, this ever-expanding guesthouse has more than 70 well-tended rooms. There's a rooftop restaurant with great food.

Mandalay Inn (Map p120; ☎ 963960; www.mandalayinn.com; 148 Sivatha St; r US$7-20; 🐱 🖳) Promising Burmese hospitality meets Khmer smiles at this smart lodging with spotless rooms plus free wi-fi and a rooftop gym.

our pick **Shadow of Angkor Guesthouse** (Map p120; ☎ 964774; www.shadowofangkor.com; 353 Pokambor Ave; r US$8-25; 🔁 🖳) Boasting a choice setting in a grand old French-era building overlooking the river, this friendly place offers budget fan rooms, affordable air-con and free internet. Downstairs is a bustling riverfront restaurant with happy hours from 5pm to 9pm.

Other options near the market:

Ivy Guesthouse 2 (Map p120; ☎ 012 602930; r US$6-8) An inviting guesthouse with a chill-out area and bar, the Ivy is a fun place to stay.

Red Lodge (Map p120; ☎ 012 707048; www.redlodge angkor.com; r US$6-12; 🔁 🖳) Hidden in a maze of backstreets. Rooms are bright and spacious. Prices include free bicycles, but not to keep!

SIVATHA STREET AREA

our pick **Garden Village** (Map pp142-3; ☎ 012 217373; www.gardenvillage-angkor.com; dm US$1, r US$3-12; 🔁 🖳) This sprawling place offers some of the cheapest beds in town; choose from eight-bed dorms or US$3 cubicles with shared bathroom. The bargains don't stop there, with US$0.50 beer available at the rooftop bar. Nice.

Smiley Guesthouse (Map p120; ☎ 012 852955; r US$6-15; 🔁) One of the first guesthouses to undergo a hoteltastic makeover, this place has more than 70 rooms set around a flourishing garden courtyard.

Sala Bai Hotel & Restaurant School (Map p120; ☎ 963329; www.salabai.com; r US$10-25; 🔁) Immerse yourself in the intimate surrounds of this training school hotel, where the super staff are ever-helpful. Rooms include silk wall hangings, woven throw pillows and wicker wardrobes.

A few more friendly, family-run options:

Naga Guesthouse (Map p120; ☎ 963439; naga_gh@ hotmail.com; r US$4-10; 🔁) One of the original budget crashpads, extras include a pool table and free wi-fi.

Mommy's Guesthouse (Map p120; ☎ 012 941755; r US$4-15; 🔁) This homely villa has large rooms with air-con, as well as cheap digs with cold showers.

AIRPORT ROAD

Jasmine Lodge (Map p120; ☎ 760697; www.jasminelodge .com; NH6; r US$2-15; 🔁 🖳) Offering a home away from home, this long-running guesthouse boasts cheapies with shared bathroom and a range of smarter options. The elevated bar-restaurant includes a pool table.

our pick **Earthwalkers** (Map pp142-3; ☎ 012 967901; www.earthwalkers.no; off NH6; dm US$5, s/d from US$9/12; 🔁 🖳 🐾) The original backpacker

hostel in town, Earthwalkers just got better thanks to the signature 'footprint' swimming pool. Dorms include breakfast and private rooms come with fan or air-con to suit all budgets. Popular bar-restaurant, plus great travel information.

Phoum Khmer Guesthouse (Map pp142-3; ☎ 965197; khmerreservation@gmail.com; off NH6; r from US$15; 🔁 🖳 🐾) Barely scraping into the budget category, this attractively designed guesthouse has expressive rooms complete with silks and smart fittings.

More, you want more? Try these:

Prince Mekong Villa (Map pp142-3; ☎ 012 437972; www.princemekong.com; s/tw from US$4/6) Satisfied guests buzz about the range of services provided here: free laundry, breakfast, bicycle and good travel info.

Hello Guesthouse (Map p120; ☎ 012 920556; r US$4-15; 🔁) Linked to Okay Guesthouse in Phnom Penh, the rooms here are tempting value. The restaurant includes handy Khmer phrases plastered all over the wall.

WAT BO AREA

Mahogany Guesthouse (Map p120; ☎ 760909; proeun@ online.com.kh; Wat Bo St; r US$5-15; 🔁 🖳) There's still a hint of mahogany in long-running Mahogany Guesthouse. Hit the old house for cheap rooms or continue to the newer block for rooms with whistles and bells. Good travel info available.

Rithy Rin Villa (Map p120; ☎ 800488; rithyrin_villa@ yahoo.com; r US$8-15; 🔁) A large modern villa in a quiet part of town, the Rithy Rin is a friendly spot with a good range of rooms, all with TV, fridge and hot water.

Angkor Thom Hotel (Map p120; ☎ 964862; Wat Bo St; r US$10-15; 🔁) Consistently good value, this place is a cut above the guesthouse competition. Satellite TV, fridge and hot water are standard and the prices drop as the stairs rise.

And the budget beat goes on…

Rosy Guesthouse (Map p120; ☎ 965059; Stung Siem Reap St; r US$7-15; 🔁) Sensibly priced rooms here, plus it's not far to the bustling bar downstairs.

Wat's Up Guesthouse (Map p120; ☎ 012 675881; r US$8-15; 🔁 🖳) A smart new place with a memorable name in a quieter part of town.

Midrange

Great deals are available thanks to an explosion in Siem Reap's midrange options. Most rates include a free transfer from the airport or boat dock. Don't be afraid to venture 'further afield' (p129), as some of the most atmospheric places are away from the centre.

SIEM REAP

PSAR CHAA AREA

Molly Malone's Guesthouse (Map p120; ☎ 963533; www
.mollymalonescambodia.com; Bar St; r US$20-40; 🔀 🖳)
If you want to be in the thick of things, this
smart B&B above a popular Irish pub (p134)
has a small selection of guestrooms, crea-
tively finished with four-poster beds. Try for
a higher-priced room with balcony.

Golden Banana (Map p120; ☎ 012 885366; www
.golden-banana.com; r US$23-58; 🔀 🖳 🖳)Memorable
name for a memorable place. All the rooms
are set in pagoda-style bungalows. The old
wing is a cheaper, but newer suites are set
on two floors with swing chairs and a pool
view. Gay-friendly.

Ta Prohm Hotel (Map p120; ☎ 380117; www.taprohm
hotel.com; r US$30-70; 🔀) One of the oldest hotels
in town, Ta Prohm keeps earning a commen-
dation for very reasonable rates. The rooms
are huge and the location great, helping it keep
up with cooler new places.

Steung Siem Reap Hotel (Map p120; ☎ 965167; www
.steungsiemreaphotel.com; s/d from US$70/80; 🔀 🖳 🖳)
In keeping with the French colonial air around
Psar Chaa, this hotel has high ceilings, louvre
shutters and wrought-iron balconies. Three-
star rooms feature a smart wooden trim. The
location is hard to beat.

Or check out some cheaper deals:

EI8HT Rooms (Map p120; ☎ 012 800860; www
.ei8htrooms.com; r US$15-20; 🔀) Smart little boutique
guesthouse with bright silks, DVD player and free internet.
Actually 16 rooms now.

Ivy Guesthouse (Map p120; ☎ 012 800860; ivyasia@
hotmail.com; r US$15-20; 🔀) Well-established and right
in the middle of the action; rooms have TV, hot water and
decorative detail.

SIVATHA ST AREA

our pick Golden Temple Villa (Map p120; ☎ 012 943459;
www.goldentemplevilla.com; r US$8-30; 🔀 🖳)Readers
love this place thanks to its funky décor and
fun outlook. Rooms are painted in vivid colours and include cable TV. The modern villa
is surrounded by a lush garden, and a bar-
restaurant is downstairs. Free internet.

Ancient Angkor Guesthouse (Map pp142-3; ☎ 012
772862; www.ancient-angkor.com; r US$10-30; 🔀 🖳 🖳)
A newer pad offering tidy rooms. The
small pool is inviting on a hot day, as is the
free internet.

Villa Siem Reap (Map p120; ☎ 761036; www.thevilla
siemreap.com; 153 Taphul St; r US$20-50; 🔀 🖳)Homely
service in intimate surrounds make this a
popular place. Rooms are nicely finished and

include a safe and minibar. Good tours are
available to some of the far-flung sights.

Mekong Angkor Palace (Map p120; ☎ 963636; www
.mekongangkorpalace.com; Sivatha St; r US$30-40; 🔀) Set
in spacious grounds away from the main drag,
this hotel offers large, bright rooms with all the
amenities, but little flourish. The pool makes
up for such minor shortcomings, however.

Auberge Mont Royal (Map p120; ☎ 964044; www
.auberge-mont-royal.com; r US$30-55; 🔀) Set in a clas-
sic colonial-style villa, the auberge has smart
rooms at a smart price, with the swimming
pool and spa taking it to another level.

Other places in and around the popular
Sivatha strip:

Dead Fish Inn (Map p120; ☎ 963060; www.deadfish
tower.com; r US$5-25; 🔀) Once visited, not forgotten
thanks to a wicked sense of humour that sees all rooms
named after luxury hotel chains like Hilton and Sofitel.

Green Garden Home Villa (Map p120; ☎ 963342;
www.greengardenhome.com; r US$15-50; 🔀) It keeps
on growing and now boasts an inviting swimming pool
and smarter rooms in a wat-style wing.

Red Piano Guesthouse (Map p120; ☎ 963240; www
.redpianocambodia.com; r US$16-30; 🔀) Popular guest-
house with signature carved wooden beds and colourful
wall hangings, plus TV and hot water.

NH6 WEST AREA

Paul Dubrule Hotel & Tourism School (École d'Hôtellerie
et de Tourisme Paul Dubrule; Map pp142-3; ☎ 963673; www
.ecolepauldubrule.org; r US$15-30; 🔀) Paul Dubrule
co-founded the Accor hotel group, so it's
no surprise his tourism school hotel offers
slick service and smart rooms. Proceeds are
ploughed into maintaining the training centre.
The rooms are a great deal.

WAT BO AREA

Many of the hotels here are on or near the east
riverbank, a pleasant, shaded area of town.

our pick Green Village Palace (off Map p120;
☎ 760623; www.greenvillagepalace.com; Wat Dam Nak St;
r US$15-30; 🔀 🖳) It is something of a palace for
this sort of money, as the smart rooms include
sweeping silks, plus there's a small swimming
pool and a gym.

Siem Reap Hostel (Map p120; ☎ 964660; www
.thesiemreaphostel.com; 10 Makara St; dm US$10, r US$30-45;
🔀 🖳) Angkor's latest backpacker hostel is
pretty slick, catering to the budget backpacker
and the aspiring flashpacker, but the dorms
are pricey given US$10 will buy an air-con
room elsewhere. Smart rooms, free bicycles
and a lively bar-restaurant.

Soria Moria Hotel (Map p120; ☎ 964768; www
.thesoriamoria.com; Wat Bo St; r US$40-75; ✗ ☀) A
hotel with a heart, promoting local causes
to help the community, this boutique place
has attractive rooms with smart bathroom
fittings. Fusion restaurant downstairs, sky
Jacuzzi upstairs.

La Noria Guesthouse (Map p120; ☎ 964242; www
.angkor-hotel-lanoria.com; s/d US$41/44; ✗ ☐ ☀)
Lovely La Noria is set in a lush tropical garden
with a pretty swimming pool. Rooms have a
traditional trim and include a veranda but no
TV or fridge.

Viroth's Hotel (Map p120; ☎ 761720; www.viroth-hotel
.com; r US$70; ✗ ☐ ☀) Minimalist and modern,
this small boutique property has seven rooms
finished in contemporary chic. Facilities include a pool, a Jacuzzi and off-peak wi-fi.

Other recommendations:

Golden Orange Hotel (Map p120; ☎ 965389; www
.goldenorangehotel.com; r US$25-35; ✗ ☐) Spacious
rooms, some with big bathtubs, plus free wi-fi/internet
for all guests.

City River Hotel (Map p120; ☎ 763000; www
.cityriverhotel.com; r from US$50; ✗ ☐ ☀) Smart,
modern rooms in a great riverside location, now with a
swimming pool.

FURTHER AFIELD

Lotus Lodge (Map pp142-3; ☎ 966140; www.lotuslodge
cambodia.com; r US$15-35; ✗ ☐ ☀) A new re-
sort, the Lotus offers a great deal for those
wanting a peaceful retreat after a day at the
temples. Rooms are clean and comfortable,
plus there is a spacious swimming pool with
a welcoming restaurant-bar.

our pick **The River Garden** (Map pp142-3; ☎ 963400;
www.therivergarden.info; r US$44-66; ✗ ☐ ☀)
Invitingly set amid an enchanting garden,
this wooden resort has a small selection of
atmospheric rooms, some with large balconies
and deep baths. Relax by the pool, indulge in
an ice-cream buffet or join their cooks in *tuk
tuks* culinary class (p125).

Pavillon Indochine (Map pp142-3; ☎ 012 849681;
www.pavillon-indochine.com; r US$50-55, ste US$65-75;
✗ ☐ ☀) The expanded Pavillon offers
charming colonial chic rooms set around a
small swimming pool. The trim includes bil-
lowing mosquito nets and a safe. The doors
have just opened on the new Pavillon d'Orient
(St 60), a higher-end boutique resort with MP4
movies on wide-screen TVs, plus a spa.

Hanumanalaya (Map pp142-3; ☎ 760582; www
.hanumanalaya.com; r US$60-90; ✗ ☐ ☀) A beaut-

iful boutique retreat, Hanumanalaya is set
around a lush garden and pretty swimming
pool. Rooms are decorated in antiques and
handicrafts, but include modern comforts
like cable TV, a minibar and safe. Also home
to the indulgent Sita Spa and the authentic
Reahoo Restaurant.

More for the mix:

Mysteres d'Angkor (Map pp142-3; ☎ 963639; www
.mysteres-angkor.com; r US$49-74; ✗ ☐ ☀) Set
behind Wat Po Langka, the rooms are set amid a verdant
garden with pool.

Antune Angkor Villa (Map pp142-3; ☎ 965230;
www.antanue.com; r US$50-90; ✗ ☐ ☀) Smart
rooms, garden bungalows and a swimming pool here, plus
a recommended Japanese restaurant.

Top End

Most of the hotels in this range levy an additional
10% government tax, 2% tourist tax, and sometimes an extra 10% for service, but breakfast is included. It is essential to book ahead at most places
from November through to March, particularly
for the glamorous spots. Competition in this sector
can be fierce, meaning some tempting low season
discounts. Booking online or through a travel
agent can save considerable money on the
walk-in rate.

La Maison d'Angkor (Map pp142-3; ☎ 965045; www
.lamaisondangkor.com; Airport Rd; r US$80-115; ✗ ☐ ☀)
These pretty white bungalows are set around
a tempting swimming pool in a leafy garden.
Features include contemporary bathrooms,
thoughtful detail and a safety-deposit box.

Angkor Village (Map p120; ☎ 965561; www.angkor
village.com; r US$89-139; ✗ ☐ ☀) This beautiful
bungalow resort is set in stunningly sculpted
water gardens and has made a name for
itself as a haven of peace and tranquillity. The
rooms include four-poster beds and Sino-
Khmer furnishings but no TV, and breakfast
is extra.

Shinta Mani (Map p120; ☎ 761998; www.shintamani
.com; Oum Khun St; s/d/tr from US$90/100/110; ✗ ☐ ☀)
Established as a training institute to give disadvantaged youth a helping hand into the
tourism industry, this hotel's 18 rooms feature designer bathrooms and sleigh beds, as
well as a small pool. Shinta Mani has won
several international awards for responsible
tourism practices and has lots of community programmes. The restaurant here is also
highly regarded.

FCC Angkor (Map p120; ☎ 760280; www.fcccambodia
.com; Pokambor Ave; s/d from US$130/150; ✗ ☐ ☀)

This funky hotel is a member of Design Hotels and wouldn't look out of place in any chic European capital. However, there are Khmer touches, and rooms feature large bathtubs, Cambodian silks and wi-fi throughout. The black-tiled swimming pool and Visaya Spa complete the picture.

Victoria Angkor Hotel (Map p120; ☎ 760428; www .victoriahotels-asia.com; s/d from US$140/150; ✖ ☐ ☎) The Victoria is a popular choice for those craving the French touch in Indochine. The classy lobby is the perfect introduction to one of the most impressive courtyard pools in town. The rooms are well-finished and many include a striking pool view.

Angkor Village Resort (Map pp142-3; ☎ 963561; Phum Traeng St; r US$169; ✖ ☐ ☎) Smarter still is the Angkor Village, out towards Angkor, with a snaking pool that wends its way through the grounds like a river. The rooms are more spacious and include elegant bathrooms and mod cons such as TVs.

ourpick La Résidence d'Angkor (Map p120; ☎ 963390; www.pansea-angkor.com; Stung Siem Reap St; r from US$190; ✖ ☐ ☎) These open-plan, all-wooden rooms are among the most inviting in town, complete with huge Jacuzzi-sized tubs. Wander through the subtle reception to a stunning swimming pool, which is perfect for laps. Memorable indeed.

Hotel de la Paix (Map p120; ☎ 966000; www.hotel delapaixangkor.com; Sivatha St; r from US$300; ✖ ☐ ☎) This is the sort of hotel you either love or hate, thanks to its contemporary design, trendy interiors and minimalist style. We happen to love it, including the open-plan bathrooms, the iPods in each room and the cutting-edge cuisine. Traditionalists be warned.

Sofitel Phokheetra Royal Angkor (Map pp142-3; ☎ 964600; www.sofitel.com; Vithei Charles de Gaulle; r from US$355; ✖ ☐ ☎) For a touch of Thai islands on the road to Angkor, this resort hotel is a smart option. It has one of the largest lagoon pools in town, plus a renowned spa, and rooms are signature Sofitel.

Grand Hotel d'Angkor (Map p120; ☎ 963888; www .raffles-grandhotelangkor.com; r from US$360; ✖ ☐ ☎) The hotel with history on its side, this place has been welcoming guests since 1929, including Charlie Chaplin, Charles de Gaulle, Jackie Kennedy and Bill Clinton. Ensconced in such opulent surroundings, you can imagine what it was like to be a tourist in colonial days. Rooms include classic colonial-era touches and a diz-

zying array of bathroom gifts. Currently being refitted, it will offer more exclusivity and suites than ever as it rolls out the new rooms.

Amansara (Map p120; ☎ 760333; www.amanresorts .com; r from US$675; ✖ ☐ ☎) Aman junkies just can't get enough of the Aman chain and will fly to the ends of the earth to experience unashamed luxury. Set in the old guest villa of Norodom Sihanouk, the superb suites here are among the largest in town and some include a private plunge pool. Rates include tours around the main Angkor temples, but not meals and far-flung sights. Former guests already include a Who's Who of the rich and famous, such as Mick Jagger and Brad Pitt.

Other ideas for indulging:

Lotus Angkor Hotel (Map pp142-3; ☎ 965555; www .lotusangkor.com; Airport Rd; r from US$80; ✖ ☐ ☎) Popular with tour groups thanks to smart rooms and a full-sized pool.

Day Inn Angkor Resort (Map p120; ☎ 760500; www.dayinnangkor.com; Oum Khun St; s/d US$80/90; ✖ ☐ ☎) Bamboo- and rattan-clad rooms here are attractively set around an inviting pool.

Tara Angkor Hotel (Map pp142-3; ☎ 966661; www .taraangkorhotel.com; r from US$110; ✖ ☐ ☎) A new boutique hotel on the road to Angkor; the décor is cool and minimalist.

Angkor Palace Spa Resort (Map pp142-3; ☎ 760511; www.angkorpalaceresort.com; off Airport Rd; r US$180; ✖ ☐ ☎) This Balinese-style resort is a huge place with lovely open-plan rooms and a huge swimming pool. Good value.

Heritage Suites Hotel (Map pp142-3; ☎ 969100; www.relaischateaux.com/heritage; r from US$235, ste US$520; ✖ ☐ ☎) Designed in the colonial style, the suites here are spectacular and open plan.

EATING

The dining scene in Siem Reap is something to savour, offering a superb selection of street dining, Asian eateries and sumptuous restaurants. The range encompasses something from every continent, with new temptations constantly on offer. Sample the subtleties of Khmer cuisine in Siem Reap, or simply indulge in home comforts or gastronomic delights prior to – or after – hitting the remote provinces.

Tourist numbers mean many top restaurants are heaving during high season. But with so many places to choose from, keep walking and you'll find somewhere more tranquil. The restaurants reviewed here represent just a fraction of the food on offer.

DINING (OR DRINKING) FOR A CAUSE

These are some fabulous restaurants that support worthy causes or assist in the training of Cambodia's future hospitality gurus with a subsidised ticket into the tourism industry. If you dine at the training places, it gives the trainees a good opportunity to hone their skills with real customers.

Butterflies Garden Restaurant (Map p120; ☎ 761211; www.butterfliesofangkor.com; mains US$3-7; ☺ 9am-10pm) Set in a blooming garden that provides a backdrop for more than 1000 butterflies, this is dining with a difference. The menu includes Khmer flavours with an international touch, some classics from home and indulgent desserts. Supports good causes, including Cambodian Living Arts, and sells handicrafts to help communities affected by HIV/AIDS.

Sala Bai Hotel and Restaurant School (Map p120; ☎ 963329; www.salabai.com; set lunch US$5; ☺ noon-2pm Mon-Fri Nov-Jun) This school trains young Khmers in the art of hospitality and serves an affordable menu of Western and Cambodian cuisine.

Les Jardins des Delices (Map pp142-3; ☎ 963673; Paul Dubrule Hotel & Tourism School; NH6; set lunch US$8; ☺ noon-2pm Mon-Fri) Enjoy Sofitel standards at a snip with a three-course meal of Asian and Western food prepared by students training in the culinary arts.

Joe-To-Go (Map p120; ☎ 092 532640; www.theglobalchild.org; ☺ 5am-3pm) Gourmet coffee is the main draw here, a good wake-up call before sunrise at the temples. Proceeds support education for street children and help to house them in a safer environment.

Singing Tree Café (Map p120; ☎ 965210; www.singingtreecafe.com; mains US$1.50-3; ☺ closed Mon) This garden café serves scrumptious muffins, coffee with a kick and health food. It doubles as a community centre, yoga studio and gallery, committing a percentage of profits to wildlife conservation and helping street children.

Some of the budget guesthouses have good menus offering a selection of local dishes and Western meals; while it's easy to order in-house food, it hardly counts as the full Siem Reap experience. Several of the midrange hotels and all the top-end places have restaurants, some excellent. For details on dinner and a performance of classical dance, as featured at several hotels and restaurants around town, see Entertainment (p135).

For more on the lunch options available in and around Angkor, see the boxed text on p150.

Khmer

When it comes to cheaper Khmer eats, **Psar Chaa** (Map p120; ☺ 7am-9pm) has plenty of food stalls on the northwest side, all with signs and menus in English. These are atmospheric places for a local meal at local-ish prices. Some dishes are on display, others are freshly flash fried to order, but most dishes are just US$1 to US$2. Another good strip of local diners sits opposite Wat Damnak, and you can judge the quality and value by the number of *motos* and *remorque-motos* parked outside.

By night, lots of street strips turn out bargain meals: try the strip at the end of Bar St, opposite Molly Malone's. Alternatively, ask a *moto* driver to recommend the best hole-in-the-walls, as these guys know the rub.

Socheata II Restaurant (Map p120; ☎ 761416; Pithnou St; mains US$1.50-5; ☺ 7am-10pm) A blink-and-you'll-miss-it Khmer restaurant that offers a big range of Cambodian classics including very tasty salads such as banana leaf, pomelo and watercress.

Khmer Kitchen Restaurant (Map p120; ☎ 964154; The Alley; mains US$2-4; ☺ 11am-10pm) Can't get no (culinary) satisfaction? Then follow in the footsteps of Sir Mick and try this popular place, which offers an affordable selection of Khmer and Thai favourites.

Angkor Palm (Map p120; ☎ 761436; Pithnou St; mains US$3-6; ☺ 10am-10pm) This award-winning Cambodian restaurant offers the authentic taste of Cambodia. Even Khmers go crazy for the legendary *amoc* (baked fish in banana leaf) here. Cooking classes are also available at its new Banteay Srei location (p125).

Sugar Palm (Map p120; ☎ 964838; Taphul Rd; mains US$4-7; ☺ 11am-late) Set in a beautiful wooden house in the west of town, the Sugar Palm is the place to sample traditional flavours infused with herbs and spices. Popular cocktail bar to warm-up or wind-down.

Café Indochine (Map p120; Sivatha St; mains US$4-7; ☺ 10am-3pm & 5-11pm) One of the few remaining traditional Khmer houses in town, this attractive restaurant offers a blend of Asian and European flavours. Enjoy the ambience by dining later to dodge the crowds.

Madame Butterfly (Map pp142-3; ☎ 016 909607; Airport Rd; mains US$4-8; 6-11pm) This traditional wooden house has been sumptuously decorated with fine silks and billowing drapes. The menu is Khmer and a fusion of Asian cuisines. There are plenty of private rooms and hidden corners for a romantic night.

Amarapura (Map pp142-3; ☎ 761844; off Airport Rd; mains US$4-8; lunch & dinner) This garden restaurant offers an original combination of Khmer and Burmese cuisine, but has just been put up for sale as we go to press, so there may be changes afoot.

Amok (Map p120; ☎ 012 800309; The Alley; mains US$4-9; 5-11pm) The name pays homage to Cambodia's national dish, *amoc* (or *amok*), and this is indeed a fine place to try baked fish curry in banana leaf. It is in the heart of the Alley.

L'Escale des Arts & des Sens (Map p120; ☎ 761442; www.escale-arts-sens.com; Oum Khun St; mains US$5-20; 6.30am-10pm) Established by Sofitel superchef Didier Corlou, this striking villa offers new Asian cuisine. Try the wonderful tapas platters that include a selection of teasing tasters and are washed down with rice wine. Mains include beef cooked seven ways, inspired by a royal recipe for tiger meat, thankfully not on the menu.

Cambodian BBQ (Map p120; ☎ 965407; The Alley; mains US$7-9; dinner) This is another tasty option along the Alley, which is wall-to-wall with good Cambodian restaurants, many family owned. Take a stroll and see what takes your fancy. Cambodian BBQ uses crocodile, snake, ostrich and kangaroo to add a twist to the traditional *phnom pleung* (hill of fire) grills.

Some good Khmer restaurants cater to tour groups:

Bayon Restaurant (Map p120; ☎ 012 855219; Wat Bo St; mains US$2-5; lunch & dinner) Set around an inner courtyard, this place has slick service and a deserved reputation for tasty food.

Samapheap Restaurant (Map p120; Stung Siem Reap St; mains US$2-5; lunch & dinner) A typical garden restaurant, the range of food here is excellent with hundreds of dishes.

Viroth's Restaurant (Map p120; ☎ 016 951800; Wat Bo St; mains US$3-7; lunch & dinner) A sophisticated garden restaurant near Wat Bo, this is where Khmer cuisine meets Balinese design.

Other Asian

Soup Dragon (Map p120; ☎ 964933; Bar St; Vietnamese mains US$1-4, Western mains US$4-7; 6am-11pm) This three-level restaurant has a split personality: the ground floor serves up classic Asian breakfasts like *pho* (Vietnamese rice-noodle soup) for under US$1 – just the recipe for tackling the temples – while upstairs serves a diverse menu of Asian and international dishes, including Italian and Moroccan.

Dead Fish Tower (Map p120; Sivatha St; mains US$2-4; 7am-late) Looking more like an adventure playground than a restaurant at first glance, this place has floor dining and tree-trunk tables. The restaurant promises '…we don't serve dog, cat, rat or worm', so bad luck if you like any of those. However, it does keep crocodiles on site, which might put off some.

Hong Kong Restaurant (Map p120; ☎ 012 966226; Pithnou St; mains US$2-4; 9am-10pm) A new Chinese restaurant specialising in authentic *dim sum* at a reasonable price. Try the spicy *mopor tofu* (minced pork with tofu).

Curry Walla (Map p120; ☎ 965451; Sivatha St; mains US$2-4; 10.30am-11pm) For good value Indian food, this place is hard to beat. The *thalis* (set meals) are a bargain and the owner knows his share of spicy secrets from the subcontinent.

Chivit Thai (Map p120; ☎ 012 830761; 130 Wat Bo St; mains US$2-6; 7am-10pm) The most atmospheric Thai place in town, this is set in a beautiful wooden villa surrounded by a lush garden. Choose between floor dining on Thai cushions or table dining. The food includes a delicious *laab* (spicy Thai salad with fish or meat).

Kama Sutra (Map p120; ☎ 017 824474; Bar St; mains US$2.50-7; noon-late) Enjoy it in 80 different positions; ahem, that's Indian food and seating arrangements we're talking about here. This stylish Indian restaurant offers a delicious array of curries at surprisingly affordable prices. Delectable daals, creamy curries and regional flavours make it a must.

In Touch (Map p120; ☎ 963240; Bar St; mains US$3-6; 11am-late) Located on a prime corner at the end of Bar St, In Touch has spectacular lighting to set the mood. The flavours are mainly Thai, but dine early unless you want to be serenaded by the resident band.

Kobe (Map pp142-3; ☎ 012 985038; Airport Rd; mains US$5-15; lunch & dinner) This cube could be confused with a mausoleum at first glance, but it's actually an uber-trendy new Japanese restaurant.

Ginga (Map pp142-3; ☎ 963366; mains US$6-15; 🕑 lunch & dinner) This popular Japanese restaurant draws the Tokyo crowd for traditional Japanese cuisine. The menu includes some affordable sashimi and sushi sets, plus combo boxes at lunchtime.

International

A lot of the guesthouses around town offer affordable international dishes for those on a budget.

Blue Pumpkin (Map p120; ☎ 963574; Pithnou St; mains US$1.50-5; 🕑 6am-10pm) Downstairs it looks like any old café, albeit with a delightful selection of cakes, breads and homemade ice cream. Upstairs is another world of white minimalism with beds to lounge on and free wi-fi. Light bites, great sandwiches, filling specials, ice-cream creations and divine shakes, what more can you ask for?

Red Piano Restaurant (Map p120; ☎ 963240; Bar St; mains US$3-5) Strikingly set in a restored colonial gem, there is a big balcony for watching the action unfold on the streets below. The menu has a great selection of Asian and international food, all at reasonable prices. Former celebrity guest Angelina Jolie even has a cocktail named in her honour.

Le Grand Café (Map p120; ☎ 012 414375; mains US$2-6; 🕑 8am-midnight) Housed in a lovingly restored French house near Psar Chaa, this elegant restaurant offers an enticing blend of French and Khmer flavours. Highlights include succulent duck, tender steaks and an indulgent ice-cream menu.

Funky Munky (Map p120; ☎ 017 824553; www.funky-munkycambodia.com; mains US$3-7; 🕑 noon-late, closed Mon) This great little bar-restaurant turns out brilliant build-your-own burgers, including the slightly scary 'Cardiac Arrest'. The eclectic menu will satisfy any global nomad and it is well worth dropping by on Thursday for the quiz; all proceeds are donated to local causes. Truly funky décor, with artsy film posters, and a cocktail menu created for cheeky monkeys.

Carnets d'Asie (Map p120; ☎ 760278; 333 Sivatha St; mains US$4-12; 🕑 lunch & dinner) This courtyard restaurant offers refined dining, mixing the exotic from Asia with the familiar from Europe. Particularly good fish and seafood selection.

Les Orientalistes (Map p120; ☎ 760278; 613 Wat Bo St; mains US$4-12; 🕑 lunch & dinner) A bright and exotic restaurant with voluptuous archways and Turkish rugs, this place conjures up the

souks of the Maghreb. It serves an international mix of Khmer, French and Moroccan cuisine, including tasty tapas.

FCC Angkor (Map p120; ☎ 760280; mains US$5-15; 🕑 7am-midnight) This bold building draws people in from the riverside thanks to a reflective pool, torch-lit dining and a garden bar. Inside, the colonial chic continues with lounge chairs and an open kitchen turning out a range of Asian and international food. Daily set menus are available from US$15.

Other internationally inclined places:

Viva (Map p120; ☎ 012 209154; Pithnou St; mains US$2-5; 🕑 11.30am-late) Spice up your life with Mexican food and margaritas. Great location.

Kampuccino Pizza (Map p120; ☎ 012 970896; Pokambor Ave; mains US$2-6; 🕑 7am-midnight) A popular restaurant near Psar Chaa; the international menu offers something from every corner of the globe.

Tell Restaurant (Map p120; ☎ 963289; Sivatha St; mains US$2-10; 🕑 10am-10pm; 🅰) Soak up the air-con on a hot day; this place has cheap Asian eats and some creative Central European dishes.

French

Abacus (Map p120; ☎ 012 644286; mains US$5-10; 🕑 11am-late) The French menu here is one of the most original in town, combining traditional treats like entrecote and duck breast with new world additions like ostrich and smoked salmon. Lovely setting in an old wooden house with a verdant garden.

Le Malraux (Map p120; ☎ 966041; mains US$5-12; 🕑 7am-midnight) A good spot for gastronomes, this classy Art Deco café-restaurant offers fine French food. Try the combination salmon *tartare* and *carpaccio* to start, followed by a quality cut from the selection of steaks.

Damnak Alliance Café (Map p120; ☎ 964242; mains US$5-15; 🕑 10am-10pm) This classy French restaurant also pays homage to its Cambodian context, with starters that include a rare lotus salad. Try scallops on a bed of spinach and graduate to duck breast in a passion sauce, but remember to save space for dessert.

Italian

Happy Herb's Pizza (Map p120; ☎ 092 838134; Pithnou St; pizzas US$3-7; 🕑 7am-11pm) The Siem Reap outpost of a Phnom Penh institution, the 'happy' in question is a somewhat illegal herb that leaves diners on a high. Nonhappy pizzas also available.

Pissa Italiana (Map p120; ☎ 012 440382; Bar St; pizzas US$4-8; 🕑 11am-11pm) Turning out tasty Italian food, this is a good place to watch the action warming up. Pizzas are thin-crust and come in some original combinations, plus there are pastas and daily specials.

L'Oasi Italiana (Map pp142-3; ☎ 092 418917; meals US$4-10; ☺ 11am-2pm & 6-10pm, closed Mon lunch) This really is something of an oasis, hidden away in a forest near Wat Preah Inkosei. Expats swear by the gnocchi and homemade pasta, so venture forth.

Cafés

Some very good cafés are covered under the 'Dining (or Drinking) for a Cause' boxed text (p131).

Le Café (Map p120; ☎ 092 271392; Wat Bo area; snacks US$2-4; ☺ 7.30am-9pm) Run in partnership with the Paul Dubrule Hotel School (p131), this café brings five-star sandwiches, salads and shakes to the French Cultural Centre.

our pick **Café de la Paix** (Map p120; Hotel de la Paix; Sivatha St; meals US$3-5; ☺ 6am-10pm) Sounds unlikely, but the opulent de la Paix is home to an affordable café serving up a superb selection of sandwiches, salads and Lavazza coffees. The ice cream is among the best in town, including a divine passionfruit. Free wi-fi.

Self-Catering

The markets are well stocked with fruit and fresh bread. For more substantial treats like cheese and chocolate, try the local supermarkets. Eating in the market usually works out cheaper than self-catering, but some folks like to make up a picnic for longer days on the road.

Try these outlets:

Angkor Market (Map p120; Sivatha St) A steady supply of international eats and treats.

Starmart (Map p120; Caltex Starmart, NH6 west) Has a good selection of imports, including ice creams.

DRINKING

Siem Reap rocks. The transformation from sleepy overgrown village to an international destination for the jetset has been dramatic and Siem Reap is now firmly on the nightlife map of Southeast Asia. The Psar Chaa area is a good hunting ground, with one street even earning the moniker Bar St – dive in, crawl out! Bar St is closed to traffic every evening. However, the floodgates open around midnight.

A great spot running parallel to Bar St is the Alley, where the volume control is just a little lower. There are plenty more places around town, so make sure you plan at least one big night out.

Most of the bars here have happy hours, but so do some of the fancier hotels, which is a good way to sample the high life even if you are not staying at those places, although the atmosphere can be a little austere.

As well as the storming selection of bars below, some of the aforementioned restaurants double-up as lively bars by night, including atmospheric Abacus (p133), Aqua (p126) with its tempting swimming pool, classic FCC Angkor (p133), the very Funky Munky (p133), the popular Red Piano (p133) and the rooftop Soup Dragon (p132), which donates 7% of the take to the Angkor Children's Hospital, so you are helping someone's liver if not your own.

The Warehouse (Map p120; Psar Chaa area; ☺ 10.30am-3am) One of the most popular bars in town, it occupies a strategic corner that simply sucks you in. Rockin' tunes, table football and devilish drinks keep them coming. There's great bar food and international bites, plus free wi-fi at all hours.

Laundry Bar (Map p120; Psar Chaa area; ☺ 6pm-late) One of the most alluring bars in town thanks to low lighting and discerning décor – put your cleanest undies on for a trip here. It gets busy on weekends or when guest DJs crank up the volume, but is worth a visit anytime. Happy hour until 9pm.

Angkor What? (Map p120; Bar St; ☺ 6pm-late) Siem Reap's original bar is still serving up serious hangovers every night. The happy hour (to 8pm) – with bargain buckets of Mekong whiskey and cheap Anchor pitchers – lightens the mood for later when everyone's bouncing along to indie anthems, sometimes on the tables.

Temple Club (Map p120; Bar St; ☺ 10am-late) The only worshipping going on at this temple is 'all hail the ale'. With a popular restaurant, this place starts moving early and doesn't stop. The loud tunes and some liberally minded locals draw a dance crowd. Insane happy hours from 10am to 10pm.

Le Tigre de Papier (Map p120; Bar St; ☺ 24hr) Established spot on Bar St offering big-screen sports and movies and a great menu of Italian, international and Asian food, plus the chance to slake the midnight munchies as it is open 24 hours.

Molly Malone's (Map p120; Bar St; ☺ 7.30am-midnight) Siem Reap's first Irish pub brings the sparkle of the Emerald Isle to homesick Irish and a whole host of other honorary Dubliners. Serves up Powers whiskey, Guinness and steaming stews. It also hosts occasional live bands.

Linga Bar (Map p120; The Alley; 5pm-late) This chic gay bar is attracting all-comers thanks to a relaxed atmosphere, a cracking cocktail list and some big beats, which draw a dancing crowd later into the night.

Chilli Si-Dang (Map p120; ☎ 012 723488; Stung Siem Reap St; 7am-late) Boasting a tranquil riverside location and balcony views, this is a relaxed wine bar from which to quaff some vintages or sample some cocktails. Happy hour 5pm to 8pm and free wi-fi.

X Bar (Map p120; Sivatha St; 4am-sunrise) Currently *the* late-night spot in town, X Bar draws revellers for the witching hour when other places are closing up. Early-evening movies on the big screen, pool tables and rumours of a skateboard pipe…mind the cocktails.

Other places to imbibe:

Banana Leaf (Map p120; Bar St) Spread along the sidewalk, this place is good for people watching, and watching football, thanks to a giant screen.

Blue Chilli Too (Map p120; the New Alley) A small gay bar, tucked away in the new alley area north of Bar St.

Island Bar (Map p120; Angkor Night Market; 4am-late) Lurking at the back of the night market, this is a great spot to relax after a shopping spree. Happy hour until 8pm.

Ivy Bar (Map p120; Psar Chaa area) A long-running and deservedly popular bar with excellent food and a friendly crowd.

World Lounge (Map p120; Bar St) Formerly known as Buddha Lounge, this is a good spot to while away an evening.

ENTERTAINMENT

Several restaurants and hotels offer cultural performances during the evening, and for many visitors such shows offer the only opportunity to see Cambodian classical dance. While they may be aimed at tourists and nowhere near as sophisticated as a performance of the Royal Ballet in Phnom Penh, to the untrained eye it is nonetheless graceful and alluring. Prices usually include a buffet meal. Look out for special performances to support cultural organisations and orphanages, as these can be a good way to assist the local community.

The best deal is at **Temple Club** (Map p120; Bar St), which offers a free traditional dance show upstairs from 7.30pm, providing

punters order some food and drink from the very reasonably priced menu. In a similar vein, Dead Fish Tower (p132) offers a nightly performance from 7pm. Butterflies Garden Restaurant (p131) also hosts regular cultural performances.

The most atmospheric show is at **Apsara Theatre** (Map p120; admission US$25) at Angkor Village (p129), as the setting is a striking wooden pavilion finished in the style of a wat, but the set menu is uninspiring. There are two shows per night. The Grand Hotel d'Angkor (p130) has an attractive performance stage behind its swimming pool, but admission is a hefty US$32. Better than both of these is the performance at the **Dining Room** (Map p120; free performance Tue, Thu & Sat), the restaurant (mains US$10 to US$25) at La Residence d'Angkor (p130), as you can dine á la carte in the garden.

Tonlé Sap Restaurant (Map p120; ☎ 963388; NH6 west; show US$12; 7.30pm) and **Koulen II Restaurant** (Map p120; ☎ 012 630090; Sivatha St; show US$12; 7pm) both offer major shows that pull in the big tour groups who chow down on a wide spread of buffet dishes.

For something a bit different, try the Wednesday evening shadow-puppet show with classical dance at **La Noria Restaurant** (Map p120; ☎ 964242; mains US$3-6), which includes a set-dinner. Part of the fee is donated to a charity supporting local children.

Beatocello (Map pp142-3; www.beatocello.com; 7.15pm Thu & Sat), better known as Dr Beat Richner, performs original and Bach cello compositions at Jayavarman VII Children's Hospital. Entry is free, but donations are welcome, as they assist the hospital in its mission to give free medical treatment to the children of Cambodia.

SHOPPING

Much of what you see on sale in the markets of Siem Reap can also be purchased from children and vendors throughout the temple area. Some people get fed up with the endless sales pitches as they navigate the ancient wonders, while others enjoy the banter and a chance to interact with Cambodian people.

It's often children out selling, and some visitors will argue that they should be at school instead. However, most do attend school at least half of the time, if their families can afford it.

Items touted at the temples include postcards, T-shirts, temple bas-relief rubbings,

---

SHOPPING FOR A CAUSE

There are several shops that support Cambodia's disabled and disenfranchised through their production process or their profits. Consider spending some money at one of these worthy places:

Artisans D'Angkor (Map p120; ☎ 380354; www.artisansdangkor.com; ⏰ 7.30am-7pm) High-quality reproduction carvings and exquisite silks are available. Impoverished youngsters are trained in the arts of their ancestors.

Krousar Thmey (Map pp142-3; Charles de Gaulle Blvd; ⏰ 8am-5.30pm) Small shop selling shadow puppets, traditional scarves, paintings and postcards, all to assist blind children in Cambodia.

Nyemo (Map p120; Sivatha St; ⏰ 8am-9pm) Beautiful silk products such as cushions, hangings and throws, plus children's toys. Proceeds used to help HIV/AIDS sufferers and vulnerable women generally. Located in Carnets d'Asie.

Rajana (Map p120; Sivatha St; ⏰ 9am-9pm, closed Sun) Sells quirky wooden and metalware objects, well-designed silver jewellery and handmade cards. Rajana promotes fair trade and employment opportunities for Cambodians.

Rehab Craft (Map p120; Pithnou St; ⏰ 10am-7pm) This shop specialises in quality silk products such as wallets, handbags and the like. Profits train and sustain the disabled community.

Senteurs d'Angkor (Map p120; ☎ 964801; Pithnou St; ⏰ 8.30am-9.30pm) Opposite Psar Chaa, this shop has an eclectic collection of silk and carvings, as well as a superb range of traditional beauty products and spices, all made locally.

Tabitha Cambodia (Map p120; ☎ 760650; Sivatha St; ⏰ 7am-6pm) Attractive range of silk scarves, cushion covers and throws to choose from. Proceeds go towards Tabitha projects like house building and well drilling.

---

curious musical instruments, ornamental knives and crossbows – the latter may raise a few eyebrows with customs should you try to take one home! Bargain, but not too hard, as you can't bargain at the fixed price shops in town.

When it comes to shopping in town, **Psar Chaa market** (Map p120) is well stocked with anything you may want to buy in Cambodia, and lots you don't. Silverware, silk, wood carvings, stone carvings, Buddhas, paintings, rubbings, notes and coins, T-shirts, table mats…the list goes on. There are bargains to be had if you haggle patiently and humorously. Avoid buying old stone carvings that vendors claim are from Angkor. Whether or not they are real, buying these artefacts serves only to encourage their plunder and they will usually be confiscated by customs. Buy modern replicas and bury them in the garden for a few months – they will soon look the same.

Angkor Night Market (Map p120; near Sivatha St; ⏰ 4pm-midnight) is the latest addition to the Siem Reap shopping scene. It is packed with stalls selling a variety of handicrafts, souvenirs and silks and is well worth a browse to take advantage of cooler temperatures.

There are now lots of memorable shops in Siem Reap. Some of the standout places:

Boom Boom Room (Map p120; Pithnou St; ⏰ 10am-10pm) No, not that sort of boom boom! Dedicated to selling iPods, downloads, accessories and T-shirts.

Jasmine (Map p120; ☎ 760610; Pokambor Ave; ⏰ 9am-10pm) Located in FCC Angkor, this boutique produces stylish silk clothing.

McDermott Gallery (Map p120; ☎ 012 615695; www.mcdermottgallery.com; The Alley; ⏰ 10am-10pm) Calendars, cards and striking sepia images of the temples, plus regular exhibitions.

Samatoa (Map p120; ☎ 012 285930; Pithnou St; ⏰ 8am-11pm) Designer clothes finished in silk with the option of a tailored fit in 48 hours. Promotes fair trade.

There are also several venues showcasing contemporary local art. Check out the Arts Lounge in Hotel de la Paix (p130) and the Damnak Alliance Café (p133).

Quality photos can be printed cheaply in Siem Reap, and digital shots downloaded onto DVD. One of the most reliable photographic shops is **Siem Reap Thmei Photo** (Map p120; Wat Bo St), a large Fuji lab.

GETTING THERE & AWAY
Air

There are direct international flights to Bangkok in Thailand; Vientiane, Luang Prabang and Pakse in Laos; Ho Chi Minh

City (Saigon) and Hanoi in Vietnam; Hong Kong; Kuala Lumpur in Malaysia; Kunming in China; Seoul in South Korea; Singapore; and Taipei in Taiwan. For more information on international flights to and from Siem Reap, see the Transport chapter (p324).

Domestic links are currently limited to Phnom Penh and only Siem Reap Airways (US$75/120 one way/return) currently offers this route. Demand for the limited number of flights is high during peak season, so book as far in advance as possible. There were flights to Sihanoukville for a short time and these may well resume some time soon.

Airline offices around town:

Angkor Airways (Map p120; ☎ 964166; www .angkorairways.com; Achar Mean St)

Bangkok Airways (Map pp142-3; ☎ 380191; www .bangkokair.com; Airport Rd)

China Eastern Airlines (Map p120; ☎ 965229; www .ce-air.com; Tep Vong St)

Jetstar Asia (Map pp142-3; ☎ 964388; www.jetstarasia .com; Siem Reap Airport)

Lao Airlines (Map p120; ☎ 963283; www.laos-airlines .com) Behind Center Market.

Malaysia Airlines (Map pp142-3; ☎ 964135; www .malaysia-airlines.com; Siem Reap Airport)

Siem Reap Airways (Map pp142-3; ☎ 380191; www .siemreapairways.com; Airport Rd)

Vietnam Airlines (Map pp142-3; ☎ 964488; www .vietnamairlines.com; Airport Rd)

Boat

There are daily express boat services between Siem Reap and Phnom Penh (US$20 to US$25, five to six hours) or Battambang (US$15, three to eight hours depending on the season). The boat to Phnom Penh is a bit of a rip-off these days, given it is just as fast by road and about one-quarter the price. The Battambang trip is seriously scenic, but breakdowns are *very* common. See the Phnom Penh (p109) and Battambang (p245) listings for more details.

Boats from Siem Reap leave from the floating village of Chong Kneas near Phnom Krom, 11km south of Siem Reap. The boats dock in different places at different times of the year; when the lake recedes in the dry season, both the port and floating village move with it. A Korean company is currently building an all-weather road and, somewhat incongruously, a marina.

Most of the guesthouses in town sell boat tickets. Buying the ticket from a guesthouse

usually includes a *moto* or minibus ride to the port. Otherwise, a *moto* out here costs about US$1 to US$2, a *remorque-moto* about US$4. A taxi is more like US$10.

Bus, Car & Taxi

The road linking Siem Reap to Phnom Penh is now surfaced all the way, and air-con buses thunder up and down daily. The road west to Sisophon, Thailand and Battambang is in a messy state in places, but is finally being overhauled. It is served by some buses and plenty of share taxis.

There are several companies operating buses between Phnom Penh and Siem Reap, and services depart between 6.30am and 12.30pm. The average cost of a bus ticket is US$5, depending on the company. Tickets can be bought at guesthouses or ticket booths in town. Leading companies include **Capitol Transport** (Map p120; ☎ 963883), **GST** (Map p120; ☎ 012 888981; Sivatha St), **Neak Krohorm** (Map p120; ☎ 964924) near Psar Chaa, and **Sorya Transport** (Off Map p120; ☎ 760103). **Mekong Express** (Map p120; ☎ 963662; Central Market; US$9) and **Paramount Angkor Express** (☎ 963662; Tep Vong St; US$8) both offer a slightly more upmarket service with an in-drive hostess and a snack. All buses now arrive and depart from the bus station and taxi park, about one kilometre east of Psar Leu on NH6 towards Phnom Penh. Watch out for over-eager *moto* and *remorque* drivers on arrival at Siem Reap bus station; it's like stepping off the bus and into a rugby scrum.

Share taxis are a faster way to travel between Siem Reap and the capital. They usually cover the distance in just four hours and charge about US$7 per person or US$45 for the whole car.

The 152km run to Thailand can take as little as three hours, but in the wet season you should double that and add some more on an off day. Buses through to Bangkok cost about US$10 to US$12 and can take from 10 to 14 hours. It is faster to go your own way. Share taxis run to Poipet (US$6 per seat, US$40 for the car, three to four hours) for those travelling independently, or to Sisophon (US$4), for connections to Battambang. For more on the overland trip between Bangkok and Siem Reap, including the 'scam bus', see p330.

Share taxis and pick-ups depart from the taxi park about 3km out of town on NH6 towards Phnom Penh.

GETTING AROUND

For more on transport around Angkor, see p152. Following are insights on the most common forms of transport used for getting around Siem Reap.

To/From the Airport

Siem Reap International Airport is 7km from the town centre. Many hotels and guesthouses in Siem Reap have a free airport pick-up service if you have booked in advance. Official taxis are available next to the terminal for US$5. A trip to the city centre on the back of a *moto* is US$1.50. *Remorque-motos* are available outside the terminal; negotiate for about US$4, depending on the hotel or guesthouse location.

Bicycle

Some of the guesthouses around town hire out bicycles, as do a few shops around Psar Chaa, usually for US$1 to US$2 a day. Try to support the **White Bicycles** (www.thewhitebicycles .org) project to help the local community (see p153).

Car & Motorcycle

Most hotels and guesthouses can organise car hire for the day, with a going rate of US$20 to US$30. Upmarket hotels may charge more. Foreigners are forbidden to rent motorcycles in and around Siem Reap. If you want to get around on your own motorcycle, you need to hire one in Phnom Penh and ride it to Siem Reap.

Moto

A *moto* with a driver will cost about US$6 to US$8 per day. The average cost for a short trip within town is 1000r to 2000r, more to places strung out along the roads to Angkor or the airport. It is probably best to negotiate in advance these days, as a lot of drivers have got into the habit of overcharging with the tourism boom.

Remorque-moto

These sweet little motorcycles with carriages (commonly called *tuk tuks* around town) are a nice way for couples to get about Siem Reap, although drivers like to inflate the prices. Try for US$1 on trips around town, although drivers may charge US$2 for a trip to the edges of town at night. Prices rise if you pile in more people!

AROUND SIEM REAP

PREK TOAL BIRD SANCTUARY
ជំរកបក្សីប្រែកទួល

Prek Toal is one of three biospheres on Tonlé Sap Lake, and the establishment of the bird sanctuary makes Prek Toal the most worthwhile and straightforward to visit. It is an ornithologist's fantasy, with a significant number of rare breeds gathered in one small area, including the huge lesser and greater adjutant storks, the milky stork and the spot-billed pelican. Even the uninitiated will be impressed, as these birds have a huge wingspan and build enormous nests.

Visitors during the dry season (December to May) will find the concentration of birds like something out of a Hitchcock film. As water starts to dry up elsewhere, the birds congregate here. Serious twitchers know that the best time to see birds is early morning or late afternoon and this means an early start or an overnight at Prek Toal's environment office, where there are basic beds for US$7. For real enthusiasts, it may be best to head out of Siem Reap after lunch, to get to the sanctuary at around 4pm for an afternoon viewing. Stay overnight and view the birds in the morning before returning to town.

One company in Siem Reap, **Osmose** (☎ 012 832812; www.osmosetonlesap.net), runs organised day trips to help promote responsible tourism in Cambodia, and contributes to the conservation of the area. The day trips cost US$80 per person with a minimum group of four. Tours offered by this nonprofit agency include transportation, entrance fees, guides, breakfast, lunch and water, making it a very reasonable deal. They can arrange overnight trips for serious enthusiasts. Proceeds go towards educating children and villagers about the importance of the birds and the unique flooded-forest environment, and the trip includes the chance to visit one of the local communities. Day trips include a hotel pick-up around 6am and a return by nightfall.

Binoculars are available at Prek Toal for those who don't carry their own. Sunscreen and head protection are essential, as it can get very hot in the dry season. The guides are equipped with booklets with the bird names in English, but they speak little English themselves, hence the advantage of travelling with Osmose.

Getting to the sanctuary under your own steam requires you to take a 20-minute *moto* (US$1 or so) or taxi (US$10) ride to the floating village of Chong Kneas and then a boat to the environment office (around US$40 return, one hour each way). From here, a small boat (US$20 including a guide) will take you into the sanctuary, which is about one hour beyond.

ANG TRAPENG THMOR RESERVE

There is another bird sanctuary, **Ang Trapeng Thmor Reserve** (admission US$10), just across the border in the Phnom Srok region of Banteay Meanchey Province, about 100km from Siem Reap. It's one of only two places in the world where it is possible to see the extremely rare sarus crane, as depicted on bas-reliefs at Bayon. These grey-feathered birds have immensely long legs and striking red heads. The reserve is based around a reservoir created by forced labour during the Khmer Rouge regime, and facilities are very basic, but it is an incredibly beautiful place. Bring your own binoculars, however, as none are available. To reach here, follow the road to Sisophon for about 72km before turning north at Prey Mon. It's 22km to the site, passing through some famous silk-weaving villages. The **Sam Veasna Centre** (☎ 761597; www.samveasna.org) arranges birding trips out here, which is probably the easiest way to undertake the trip. It also arranges specialist birding trips to remote parts of northwestern Cambodia (p267 and p267).

FLOATING VILLAGE OF CHONG KNEAS
ភូមិបណ្ដែតចុងឃ្នាស

This famous floating village is now extremely popular with visitors wanting a break from the temples, and is an easy excursion to arrange yourself. Visitors arriving by fast boat get a preview, as the floating village is near Phnom Krom, where the boat docks. It is very scenic in the warm light of early morning or late afternoon and can be combined with a view of the sunset from the hilltop temple of Phnom Krom (p174). The downside is that tour groups tend to take over, and boats end up chugging up and down the channels in convoy.

Visitors should also check out the **Gecko Centre** (www.tsbr-ed.org; ☺ 8.30am-5.30pm), an informative centre that is located in the floating village and helps to unlock the secrets of the Tonlé Sap. It has displays on flora and fauna of the area, as well as information on communities living around the lake.

The village moves depending on the season and you will need to rent a boat to get around it properly. A local cooperative has fixed boat prices at US$10 per person to visit the floating village, a touch on the cheeky side for what is a short trip. On top of this, the Koreans are charging for the new road and the local police for security, all-in-all a bit of a scam. If you are travelling by boat between Phnom Penh and Siem Reap, you get to see it for free anyhow.

To get to the floating village from Siem Reap costs US$1.50 or so by *moto* each way (more if the driver waits), or US$10 by taxi. The trip takes 20 minutes.

FLOODED FOREST OF KOMPONG PHHLUK
ព្រៃលិចទឹកកំពង់ភ្លុក

More memorable than Chong Kneas, but harder to reach, is the village of Kompong Phhluk, an other-worldly place built on soaring stilts. Nearby is a flooded forest, inundated every year when the lake rises to take the Mekong's overflow. As the lake drops, the petrified trees are revealed. Exploring this area by wooden dugout in the wet season is very atmospheric. The village itself is a friendly place, where most of the houses are built on stilts of about 6m or 7m high, almost bamboo skyscrapers. It looks like it's straight out of a film set.

There are two ways to get to Kompong Phhluk. One is to come via the floating village of Chong Kneas, where a boat (one hour) can be arranged for about US$30 round trip, and the other is to come via the small town of Roluos by a combination of road (about US$5 by *moto*) and boat (US$7). All said the road/boat route will take up to two hours, but it depends on the season – sometimes it's more by road, sometimes more by boat!

KOMPONG KHLEANG
កំពង់ឃ្លាំង

One of the largest communities on the Tonlé Sap, Kompong Khleang is almost a floating town, complete with several large pagodas. Like Kompong Phhluk, most of the houses here are built on towering stilts to allow for a dramatic change in water level. Few tourists have visited here, but it is not that difficult to reach from Siem Reap. It is possible to get here by road via the town of Dam Dek or by boat from the floating village of Chong Kneas.

Temples of Angkor

Welcome to the heart and soul of Cambodia. The temples of Angkor are a source of inspiration and national pride to all Khmers as they struggle to rebuild their lives after years of terror and trauma. Today, the temples are a point of pilgrimage for all Cambodians, and no traveller to the region will want to miss their extravagant beauty.

Angkor is the perfect fusion of creative ambition and spiritual devotion. The Cambodian 'god-kings' of old each strove to better their ancestors in size, scale and symmetry, culminating in the world's largest religious building, Angkor Wat. The hundreds of temples surviving today are but the sacred skeleton of the vast political, religious and social centre of Cambodia's ancient Khmer empire; a city that, at its zenith, boasted a population of one million when London was a scrawny town of 50,000. The houses, public buildings and palaces of Angkor were constructed of wood – now long decayed – because the right to dwell in structures of brick or stone was reserved for the gods.

Some visitors assume they will be templed out within a day or two, but soon discover the sheer diversity in design among the temples that switches dramatically from one god-king to another. Come face to face (quite literally) with Bayon, one of the world's weirdest buildings; experience the excitement of the first European explorers at Ta Prohm, where nature runs riot; or follow the sacred river of a thousand lingas like pilgrims of old. If these holy sites were anywhere else in the region they would have top billing. One day at Angkor? Sacrilege! Don't even consider it.

Jayavarman II spent his formative years on the island of Java, at the court of the Shailendras Kingdom, and may have been inspired by the Hindu temples of Prambanan and the great Buddhist temple of Borobodur.

HISTORY
Early Years

The Angkorian period spans more than 600 years from AD 802 to 1432. This incredible period of history saw the construction of the temples of Angkor and the Khmer empire consolidate its position as one of the great powers in Southeast Asia. This era encompasses periods of decline and revival, and wars with rival powers in Vietnam, Thailand and Myanmar. This brief history deals only with the periods that produced the temples that can be seen at Angkor.

The Angkorian period began with the rule of Jayavarman II (r 802–50). He was the first to unify Cambodia's competing kingdoms before the birth of Angkor. His court was situated at various locations, including Phnom

---

ANGKOR EXPERIENCES

- See the sun rise over the holiest of holies, **Angkor Wat** (p154), the world's largest religious building

- Contemplate the serenity and splendour of the **Bayon** (p161), its 216 enigmatic faces staring out into the jungle

- Witness nature reclaiming the stones at the mysterious ruin of **Ta Prohm** (p166), the *Tomb Raider* temple

- Stare in wonder at the delicate carvings adorning **Banteay Srei** (p175), the finest seen at Angkor

- Trek deep into the jungle to discover the River of a Thousand Lingas at **Kbal Spean** (p176)

TOP 10 KINGS OF ANGKOR

A mind-numbing array of kings ruled the Khmer empire from the 9th century AD to the 14th century. All of their names include the word *'varman'*, which means 'armour' or 'protector'. Forget the small fry and focus on the big fish in our Top 10:

- **Jayavarman II** (r 802–50) Founder of the Khmer empire in AD 802
- **Indravarman I** (r 877–89) Builder of the first *baray* (reservoir), and of Preah Ko and Bakong
- **Yasovarman I** (r 889–910) Moved the capital to Angkor and built Lolei and Phnom Bakheng
- **Jayavarman IV** (r 928–42) Usurper king who moved the capital to Koh Ker
- **Rajendravarman II** (r 944–68) Builder of Eastern Mebon, Pre Rup and Phimeanakas
- **Jayavarman V** (r 968–1001) Oversaw construction of Ta Keo and Banteay Srei
- **Suryavarman I** (r 1002–49) Expanded the empire into much of Laos and Thailand
- **Udayadityavarman II** (r 1049–65) Builder of the pyramidal Baphuon and the Western Mebon
- **Suryavarman II** (r 1112–52) Legendary builder of Angkor Wat and Beng Mealea
- **Jayavarman VII** (r 1181–1219) The king of the god-kings, building Angkor Thom, Preah Khan and Ta Prohm

Kulen (p177), 40km northeast of Angkor Wat, and Roluos (p173; known then as Hariharalaya), 13km east of Siem Reap.

Jayavarman II proclaimed himself a *devaraja* (god-king), the earthly representative of Hindu god Shiva. Jayavarman built a 'temple-mountain' at Phnom Kulen, symbolising Shiva's dwelling place of Mt Meru, the holy mountain at the centre of the universe. This set a precedent that became a dominant feature of the Angkorian period and accounts for the staggering architectural productivity of the Khmers at this time.

Indravarman I (r 877–89) is believed to have been a usurper, and probably inherited the mantle of *devaraja* through conquest. He built a 6.5 sq km *baray* (reservoir) at Roluos and established Preah Ko (p174). The *baray* was the first stage of an irrigation system that created a hydraulic city, the ancient Khmers mastering the cycle of nature to water their lands. It also had religious significance as, according to legend, Mt Meru is flanked by lakes. As is often the case, form and function work together in harmony. Indravarman's final work was Bakong (p174), a pyramidal representation of Mt Meru.

Indravarman I's son Yasovarman I (r 889–910) looked further afield to celebrate his divinity and glory in a temple-mountain of his own. He first built Lolei (p174) on an artificial island in the *baray* established by his father, before beginning work on the Bakheng. Today this hill is known as Phnom Bakheng (p168), a favoured spot for viewing the sunset over Angkor Wat. A raised highway was constructed to connect Phnom Bakheng with Roluos, 16km to the southeast, and a large *baray* was constructed to the east of Phnom Bakheng. Today it is known as the Eastern Baray (p172), but has entirely silted up. Yasovarman I also established the temple-mountains of Phnom Krom (p174) and Phnom Bok (p175).

After the death of Yasovarman I, power briefly shifted from the Angkor region to Koh Ker (p264), around 80km to the northeast, under another usurper – Jayavarman IV (r 928–42). In AD 944 power returned again to Angkor under the leadership of Rajendravarman II (r 944–68), who built the Eastern Mebon (p172) and Pre Rup (p173). The reign of his son Jayavarman V (r 968–1001) produced the temples Ta Keo (p169) and Banteay Srei (p175), the latter built by a Brahman rather than the king.

For Indian Hindus, the Himalayas represent Mt Meru, the home of the gods, while the Khmer kings of old adopted Phnom Kulen as their symbolic Mt Meru.

TEMPLES OF ANGKOR

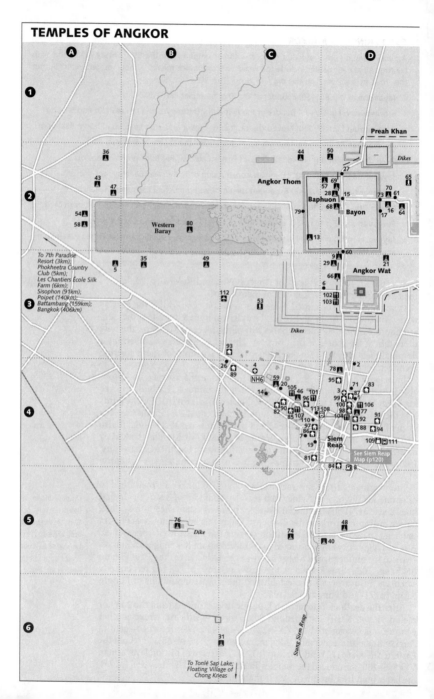

Preah Khan

Dikes

Angkor Thom

Baphuon

Bayon

Western Baray

To 7th Paradise Resort (3km); Phokheetra Country Club (5km); Les Chantiers Ecole Silk Farm (6km); Sisophon (91km); Poipet (140km); Battambang (159km); Bangkok (406km)

Angkor Wat

Dikes

NH6

Siem Reap

See Siem Reap Map (p120)

Dike

Stung Siem Reap

To Tonlé Sap Lake; Floating Village of Chong Kneas

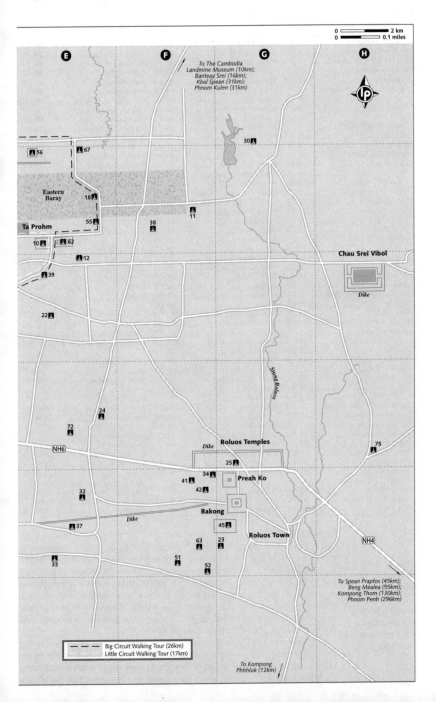

0 ———— 2 km
0 ———— 0.1 miles

E **F** **G** **H**

To The Cambodia
Landmine Museum (10km);
Banteay Srei (16km);
Kbal Spean (31km);
Phnom Kulen (31km)

56
67
30

Eastern
Baray
18
55
11
38

Ta Prohm
10
62
12
39

Chau Srei Vibol

Dike

22

Stung Roluos

24
72

Roluos Temples

NH6
Dike
25

75

34
41
Preah Ko
42
32
Bakong
37
Dike
45
Roluos Town
NH4

33
63
23
51
52

To Spean Praptos (45km);
Beng Mealea (55km);
Kompong Thom (130km);
Phnom Penh (296km)

– – – Big Circuit Walking Tour (26km)
——— Little Circuit Walking Tour (17km)

To Kompong
Phhluk (12km)

Classical Age

The temples that are now the highlight of a visit to Angkor – Angkor Wat and those in and around the walled city of Angkor Thom – were built during the classical age. The classical appellation conjures up images of a golden age of abundance and leisurely temple construction, but while this period is marked by fits of remarkable productivity, it was also a time of turmoil, conquests and setbacks. The great city of Angkor Thom owes its existence to the fact that the old city of Angkor – which stood on the same site – was destroyed during the Cham invasion of 1177.

Suryavarman I (r 1002–49) was a usurper to the throne who won the day through strategic alliances and military conquests. Although he adopted the Hindu cult of the god-king, he is thought to have come from a Mahayana Buddhist tradition and may even have sponsored the growth of Buddhism

Check out the website of Heritage Watch at www .heritagewatch.org to learn more about sustainable initiatives to involve the local community in the tourism boom in Angkor.

in Cambodia. Buddhist sculpture certainly became more commonplace in the Angkor region during his time.

Little physical evidence of Suryavarman I's reign remains at Angkor, but his military exploits brought much of southern Thailand and southern Laos under the control of Angkor. His son Udayadityavarman II (r 1049–65) embarked on further military expeditions, extending the empire once more, and building Baphuon (p163) and the Western Mebon (p173).

From 1066 until the end of the century, Angkor was again divided as rival factions contested the throne. The first important monarch of this new era was Suryavarman II (r 1112–52), who unified Cambodia and extended Khmer influence to Malaya and Burma (Myanmar). He also set himself apart religiously from earlier kings through his devotion to the Hindu deity Vishnu, to whom he consecrated the largest and arguably most magnificent of all the Angkorian temples, Angkor Wat (p154).

The reign of Suryavarman II and the construction of Angkor Wat signifies one of the high-water marks of Khmer civilisation. However, there were signs that decline was waiting in the wings. It is thought that the hydraulic system of reservoirs and canals that supported the agriculture of Angkor had by this time been pushed beyond its limits, and was slowly starting to silt up due to overpopulation and deforestation. The construction of Angkor Wat was a major strain on resources, and, on top of this, Suryavarman II led a disastrous campaign against the Dai Viet (Vietnamese) late in his reign.

In 1177 the Chams of southern Vietnam, then the Kingdom of Champa and long annexed by the Khmer empire, rose up and sacked Angkor. They burned the wooden city and plundered its wealth. Four years later Jayavarman VII (r 1181–1219) struck back, emphatically driving the Chams out of Cambodia and reclaiming Angkor.

Jayavarman VII's reign has given scholars much to debate. It represents a radical departure from the reigns of his predecessors. For centuries the fount of royal divinity had reposed in the Hindu deity Shiva (and, occasionally, Vishnu). Jayavarman VII adopted Mahayana Buddhism and looked to Avalokiteshvara, the Bodhisattva of Compassion, for patronage during his reign. In doing so he may well have been converting to a religion that already enjoyed wide popular support among his subjects. It may also be that the destruction of Angkor was such a blow to royal divinity that a new religious foundation was thought to be needed.

During his reign, Jayavarman VII embarked on a dizzying array of temple projects that centred on Baphuon, which was the site of the capital city destroyed by the Chams. Angkor Thom (p159), Jayavarman VII's new city, was surrounded by walls and a moat, which became another component of Angkor's complex irrigation system. The centrepiece of Angkor Thom was Bayon (p161), the temple-mountain studded with faces that, along with Angkor Wat, is the most famous of Cambodia's temples. Other temples built during his reign include Ta Prohm (p166), Banteay Kdei (p169) and Preah Khan (p170). Further away, he rebuilt vast temple complexes such as Banteay Chhmar (p255) and Preah Khan (p262), making him by far the most prolific builder of Angkor's many kings.

Jayavarman VII also embarked on a major public-works programme, building roads, schools and hospitals across the empire. Remains of many of these roads and their magnificent bridges can be seen across Cambodia. Spean Praptos at Kompong Kdei, 60km southeast of Siem Reap on National Hwy 6 (NH6), is the most famous, but there are many more lost in the forest on the old Angkorian road from Beng Mealea to the great Preah Khan.

After the death of Jayavarman VII around 1219, the Khmer empire went into decline. The state religion reverted to Hinduism for a century or more

When the Chams attacked Angkor in 1177, it caught the Khmers completely by surprise, as they attacked by sea, river and lake rather than the traditional land routes.

While Suryavarman II may have planned Angkor Wat as his funerary temple or mausoleum, he was never buried there and it is believed he may have died after returning from a failed expedition to subdue the Dai Viet (Vietnamese).

The King's Last Song by Geoff Ryman weaves together the story of Jayavarman VII with a contemporary drama involving kidnapping and the Khmer Rouge.

The glorious Siamese capital of Ayuthaya, which enjoyed a golden age from the 14th to 18th centuries, was in many ways a recreation of the glories of Angkor from which the Thai conquerors drew inspiration.

and outbreaks of iconoclasm saw Buddhist sculpture adorning the Hindu temples vandalised or altered. The Thais sacked Angkor in 1351 and again with devastating efficiency in 1431. The Khmer court moved to Phnom Penh, only to return fleetingly to Angkor in the 16th century; in the meantime it was abandoned to pilgrims, holy men and the elements.

Angkor Rediscovered

Henri Mouhot was French by birth, but was married to an English-woman. His 'journey of discovery' to Angkor was actually funded by the Royal Geographic Society of London.

The French 'discovery' of Angkor in the 1860s made an international splash and created a great deal of outside interest in Cambodia. But 'discovery', with all the romance it implied, was something of a misnomer. When French explorer Henri Mouhot first stumbled across Angkor Wat it included a wealthy, working monastery with monks and slaves. Moreover, Portuguese travellers in the 16th century encountered Angkor, referring to it as the Walled City. Diogo do Couto produced an accurate description of Angkor in 1614, but it was not published until 1958.

Still, it was the publication of *Voyage à Siam et dans le Cambodge* by Mouhot in 1868 that first brought Angkor to the public eye. Although the explorer himself made no such claims, by the 1870s he was being posthumously celebrated as the discoverer of the lost temple-city of Cambodia. In fact, a French missionary known as Charles-Emile Bouillevaux had visited Angkor 10 years before Mouhot and had published his own account of his findings. However, the Bouillevaux account was roundly ignored and it was Mouhot's account, with its rich descriptions and tantalising pen-and-ink colour sketches of the temples, that turned the temple ruins into an international obsession.

GUIDE TO THE GUIDES

Countless books on Angkor have been written over the years, with more and more new titles coming out every year, reflecting Angkor's rebirth as one of the world's cultural hotspots. Here are just a few of them.

- *A Guide to the Angkor Monuments* (Maurice Glaize) – the definitive guide to Angkor, downloadable for free at www.theangkorguide.com
- *A Passage Through Angkor* (Mark Standen) – one of the best photographic records of the temples of Angkor
- *A Pilgrimage to Angkor* (Pierre Loti) – one of the most beautifully written books on Angkor, based on the author's 1910 journey
- *Ancient Angkor* (Claudes Jacques) – written by one of the foremost scholars on Angkor, this is the most readable guide to the temples, with photos by Michael Freeman
- *Angkor: an Introduction to the Temples* (Dawn Rooney) – probably the most popular contemporary guide available
- *Angkor: Millennium of Glory* (various authors) – a fascinating introduction to the history, culture, sculpture and religion of the Angkorian period
- *Angkor – Heart of an Asian Empire* (Bruno Dagens) – the story of the 'discovery' of Angkor, complete with lavish illustrations
- *Angkor: Splendours of the Khmer Civilisation* (Marilia Albanese) – Beautifully photographed guide to the major temples, including some of the more remote places in northern Cambodia
- *Khmer Heritage in the Old Siamese Provinces of Cambodia* (Etienne Aymonier) – Aymonier journeyed through Cambodia in 1901 and visited many of the major temples
- *The Customs of Cambodia* (Chou Ta Kuan) – the only eyewitness account of Angkor, from a Chinese emissary who spent a year at the Khmer capital in the late 13th century

From the time of Mouhot, Angkor became the target of French-financed expeditions and, in 1901, the **École Française d'Extrême-Orient** (EFEO; www.efeo.fr) began a long association with Angkor by funding an expedition to the Bayon. In 1907, Angkor was returned to Cambodia, having been under Thai control for almost 150 years, and the EFEO took responsibility for clearing and restoring the whole site. In the same year, the first foreign tourists arrived in Angkor – an unprecedented 200 of them in three months. Angkor had been 'rescued' from the jungle and was assuming its place in the modern world.

Architect Lucien Fournereau travelled to Angkor in 1887. He produced plans and meticulously executed cross-sections that were to stand as the best available until the 1960s.

ARCHAEOLOGY OF ANGKOR

With the exception of Angkor Wat, which was restored for use as a Buddhist shrine in the 16th century by the Khmer royalty, the temples of Angkor were left to the jungle for many centuries. The majority of temples are made of sandstone, which tends to dissolve when in prolonged contact with dampness. Bat droppings took their toll, as did sporadic pilfering of sculptures and cut stones. At some monuments, such as Ta Prohm, the jungle had stealthily waged an all-out invasion, and plant-life could only be removed at great risk to the structures it now supported in its web of roots.

Initial attempts to clear Angkor under the aegis of the EFEO were fraught with technical difficulties and theoretical disputes. On a technical front, the jungle tended to grow back as soon as it was cleared, and on a theoretical front, scholars debated the extent to which temples should be restored and whether later additions, such as Buddha images in Hindu temples, should be removed.

It was not until the late 1920s that a solution came along – anastylosis. This was the method the Dutch had used to restore Borobodur in Java. Put simply, it was a way of reconstructing monuments using the original materials and in keeping with the original form of the structure. New materials were permitted only where the originals could not be found, and were to be used discreetly. An example of this method can be seen on the causeway leading to the entrance of Angkor Wat, as the right-hand side was originally restored by the French.

A 17th-century Japanese pilgrim drew a detailed plan of Angkor Wat, though he mistakenly recalled that he had seen it in India.

The first major restoration job was carried out on Banteay Srei in 1930. It was deemed such a success that many more extensive restoration projects were undertaken elsewhere around Angkor, culminating in the massive Angkor Wat restoration in the 1960s. Large cranes and earth-moving machines were brought in, and the operation was backed by a veritable army of surveying equipment.

The Khmer Rouge victory and Cambodia's subsequent slide into an intractable civil war resulted in far less damage to Angkor than many had assumed, as EFEO and Ministry of Culture teams had removed many of the statues from the temple sites for protection. Nevertheless, turmoil in Cambodia resulted in a long interruption of restoration work, allowing the jungle to grow back and once again resume its assault on the monuments. The illegal trade of *objets d'art* on the world art market has also been a major threat to Angkor, although it is the more remote sites that have been targeted recently. Angkor has been under the jurisdiction of the UN Educational Scientific and Cultural Organisation (Unesco) since 1992 as a World Heritage site, and international and local efforts continue to preserve and reconstruct the monuments. In a sign of real progress, Angkor was removed from Unesco's endangered list in 2003.

Between 1970 and 1973, the front line of fighting between Lon Nol forces and Khmer Rouge/North Vietnamese soldiers was midway between Siem Reap and Angkor Wat. Archaeologists were allowed to cross back and forth to continue their work restoring temples.

Many of Angkor's secrets remain to be discovered, as most of the work at the temples has concentrated on restoration efforts above ground rather than archaeological surveys below. Underground is where the real story of Angkor and its people lies – the inscriptions on the temples give us only a partial picture of the gods to whom each structure was dedicated, and the kings who built them.

HIDDEN RICHES, POLITICAL HITCHES

Angkor Conservation is a Ministry of Culture compound on the banks of the Stung Siem Reap, about 400m east of the Sofitel Phokheetra Royal Angkor Hotel. The compound houses more than 5000 statues, *lingas* (phallic symbols) and inscribed steles, stored here to protect them from the wanton looting that has blighted hundreds of sites around Angkor. The finest statuary is hidden away inside Angkor Conservation's warehouses, meticulously numbered and catalogued. Unfortunately, without the right contacts, trying to get a peek at the statues is a lost cause. Some of the statuary is now on public display in the Angkor National Museum (p123) in Siem Reap, but it is only a fraction of the collection. In a further development, the Thai consortium behind the new museum now has control over Angkor Conservation.

Formerly housed at Angkor Conservation, but now going it alone in offices throughout Siem Reap, is Apsara Authority (Authority for the Protection and Management of Angkor and the region of Siem Reap). This organisation is responsible for the research, protection and conservation of cultural heritage around Angkor, as well as urban planning in Siem Reap and tourism development in the region. Quite a mandate, quite a challenge – especially now that the government is taking such a keen interest in its work. Angkor is a money-spinner; it remains to be seen whether Apsara will be empowered to put preservation before profits.

ARCHITECTURAL STYLES

From the time of the earliest Angkorian monuments at Roluos, Khmer architecture was continually evolving, often from the rule of one king to the next. Archaeologists therefore divide the monuments of Angkor into nine separate periods, named after the foremost example of each period's architectural style.

The evolution of Khmer architecture was based around a central theme of the temple-mountain, preferably set on a real hill, but artificial if there weren't any mountains to hand. The earlier a temple was constructed, the closer it adheres to this fundamental idea. Essentially, the mountain was represented by a tower mounted on a tiered base. At the summit was the central sanctuary, usually with an open door to the east, and three false doors at the remaining cardinal points of the compass.

By the time of the Bakheng period, this layout was being embellished. The summit of the central tower was crowned with five 'peaks' – four at the points of the compass and one in the centre. Even Angkor Wat features this layout, though on a grandiose scale. Other features that came to be favoured included an entry tower and a causeway lined with *naga* (mythical serpent) balustrades leading up to the temple.

As the temples grew in ambition, the central tower became a less-prominent feature, although it remained the focus of the temple. Later temples saw the central tower flanked by courtyards and richly decorated galleries. Smaller towers were placed on gates and on the corners of walls, their overall number often marking a religious or astrological significance.

These refinements and additions eventually culminated in Angkor Wat, which effectively showcases the evolution of Angkorian architecture. The architecture of the Bayon period breaks with tradition in temples such as Ta Prohm and Preah Khan. In these temples, the horizontal layout of the galleries, corridors and courtyards seems to completely eclipse the central tower.

The curious narrowness of the corridors and doorways in these structures can be explained by the fact that Angkorian architects never mastered the flying buttress to build a full arch. They engineered arches by laying blocks on top of each other, until they met at a central point; known as false arches, they can only support very short spans.

To learn more about Unesco's activities at Angkor and the incredible diversity of World Heritage sites, visit http://whc.unesco.org.

John Thomson was a Scottish photographer who took the first photographs of the temples in 1866. He was the first to posit the idea that they were symbolic representations of the mythical Mt Meru.

The seven-headed *naga*, which is a feature at many temples, represents the rainbow which acts as a bridge between heaven and earth.

ORIENTATION

Heading north from Siem Reap, Angkor Wat is the first major temple, followed by the walled city of Angkor Thom. To the east and west of this city are two vast reservoirs, which helped to feed the huge population. Further east are temples including Ta Prohm, Banteay Kdei and Pre Rup. North of Angkor Thom is Preah Khan and way beyond in the northeast, Banteay Srei, Kbal Spean, Phnom Kulen and Beng Mealea. To the southeast of Siem Reap is the Roluos Group of early Angkorian temples.

Maps

There are several free maps covering Angkor, including the *Siem Reap Angkor 3D Map,* available at certain hotels, guesthouses and restaurants in town. River Books of Thailand publishes a foldout *Angkor Map,* which is one of the more detailed offerings available.

INFORMATION
Admission Fees

While the cost of entry to Angkor is relatively expensive by Cambodian standards, the fees represent excellent value. Visitors have a choice of a one-day pass (US$20), a three-day pass (US$40) or a one-week pass (US$60). Passes cannot be extended and days run consecutively, so plan your visit in advance. Purchase the entry pass from the large official entrance booth on the road to Angkor Wat. Passes include a digital photo snapped at the entrance booth, so queues can be quite long. Visitors entering after 5pm get a free sunset, as the ticket starts from the following day. The fee includes access to all the monuments in the Siem Reap area, but does not currently include the sacred mountain of Phnom Kulen or the remote complexes of Beng Mealea and Koh Ker.

Entry tickets to the temples of Angkor are controlled by local hotel chain Sokha Hotels, part of a local petroleum conglomerate called Sokimex, which in return for administrating the site takes 17% of the revenue. A mere 10% goes to Apsara Authority (see the boxed text, opposite), the body responsible for protecting and conserving the temples, and the lion's share is returned to the black hole that is the Finance Ministry.

Most of the major temples now have uniformed guards to check the tickets, which has reduced the opportunity for scams (although many would argue that the current arrangement with Sokha is the biggest scam of all). A pass is not required for excursions to villages around or beyond Angkor, but you still have to stop at the checkpoint to explain your movements to the guards.

ITINERARIES

Back in the early days of tourism, the problem of what to see and in what order came down to two basic temple itineraries: the Small (Petit) Circuit and the Big (Grand) Circuit, both marked on the Temples of Angkor map (Map pp142–3). It's difficult to imagine that anyone follows these to the letter

Stung Siem Reap, the river that runs from the foothills of Phnom Kulen to Tonlé Sap Lake, was diverted to run through most of the major temples and *barays* of Angkor.

WARNING!
Visitors found inside any of the main temples without a ticket will be fined a whopping US$100.

WHEN NATURE CALLS

Angkor is now blessed with some of the finest public toilets in Asia. Designed in wooden chalets and complete with amenities such as electronic flush, they wouldn't be out of place in a fancy hotel. The trouble is that the guardians often choose not to run the generators that power the toilets, meaning it is pretty dark inside the cubicles (but thankfully you can flush manually, too!). Entrance is free if you show your Angkor pass, and they are found near most of the major temples.

Remember, in remote areas, don't stray off the path – being seen in a compromising position is infinitely better than stepping on a land mine.

ANGKORIN' FOR LUNCH

Most of the tour groups buzzing around Angkor head back to Siem Reap for lunch. This is as good a reason as any to stick around the temples, taking advantage of the lack of crowds to explore some popular sites and enjoy a local lunch at one of the many stalls. Almost all the major temples have some sort of nourishment available beyond the walls. Anyone travelling with a *moto* or *remorque-moto* should ask the driver for tips on cheap eats, as these guys eat around the temples every day. They know the best spots, at the best price, and should be able to sort you out (assuming you are getting along well).

The most extensive selection of restaurants is lined up opposite the entrance to Angkor Wat. It includes several restaurants, such as Khmer Angkor Restaurant and Angkor Reach Restaurant, with dishes ranging from US$3 to US$6. There is also now a handy branch of **Blue Pumpkin** (Map pp142-3; dishes US$2-4) turning out sandwiches, salads and ice creams, as well as the usual divine fruit shakes, all to take away if required. **Chez Sophea** (Map pp142-3; ☎ 012 858003; meals US$10-20) offers barbecued meats and fish, accompanied by a cracking homemade salad, but prices are at the high end.

There are dozens of local noodle stalls just north of the Bayon, which are a good spot for a quick bite to eat. Other central temples with food available include Ta Prohm, Preah Khan and Ta Keo. Further afield, Banteay Srei has several small restaurants, complete with ornate wood furnishings cut from Cambodia's forests. Further north at Kbal Spean, food stalls at the bottom of the hill can cook up fried rice or a noodle soup, plus there is the excellent Borey Sovann Restaurant (meals US$3 to US$5), which is a great place to wind down before or after an ascent. There are also stop-and-dip stalls (dishes US$1 to US$3) near the entrance to Beng Mealea temple.

Water and soft drinks are available throughout the temple area, and many sellers lurk outside the temples, ready to pounce with offers of 'You wanna buy cold drink?' Sometimes they ask at just the right moment; on other occasions it is the 27th time in an hour that you've been approached and you are ready to scream. Try not to – you'll scare your fellow travellers and lose face with the locals.

Take a virtual tour of Angkor in 360 degrees on the *World Heritage Tour* website at www.world -heritage-tour.org.

any more, but in their time they were an essential component of the Angkor experience and were often undertaken on the back of an elephant.

For tips on the best times to visit particular temples, the best locations for sunrise and sunset and avoiding the hordes see the boxed text, opposite.

Small Circuit

The 17km Small Circuit begins at Angkor Wat and heads north to Phnom Bakheng, Baksei Chamkrong and Angkor Thom (including the city wall and gates, the Bayon, the Baphuon, the Royal Enclosure, Phimeanakas, Preah Palilay, the Terrace of the Leper King, the Terrace of Elephants, the Kleangs and Prasat Suor Prat. It exits from Angkor Thom via the Victory Gate in the eastern wall, and continues to Chau Say Tevoda, Thommanon, Spean Thmor and Ta Keo. It then heads northeast of the road to Ta Nei, turns south to Ta Prohm, continues east to Banteay Kdei and Sra Srang, and finally returns to Angkor Wat via Prasat Kravan.

Big Circuit

The 26km Big Circuit is an extension of the Small Circuit: instead of exiting the walled city of Angkor Thom at the east gate, the Big Circuit exits at the north gate and continues to Preah Khan and Preah Neak Poan, east to Ta Som then south via the Eastern Mebon to Pre Rup. From there it heads west and then southwest on its return to Angkor Wat.

One Day

If you have only one day to visit Angkor, then bad luck, but a good itinerary would be Angkor Wat for sunrise and then stick around to explore the mighty temple while it is quieter. From there continue to the tree roots of Ta Prohm before breaking for lunch. In the afternoon, explore the temples within the walled city of Angkor Thom and the beauty of the Bayon in the late afternoon light.

Two Days

A two-day itinerary allows time to include some of the other big hitters around Angkor. Spend the first day visiting petite Banteay Srei, with its fabulous carvings, and stop at Banteay Samré on the return leg. In the afternoon, visit immense Preah Khan, delicate Preah Neak Poan and the tree roots of Ta Som, before taking in a sunset at Pre Rup. Spend the second day following the one-day itinerary to Angkor Wat, Ta Prohm and Angkor Thom.

DODGING THE CROWDS

Angkor is on the tourist trail and is getting busier by the year but, with a little planning, it is still possible to escape the hordes. One important thing to remember, particularly when it comes to sunrise and sunset, is that places are popular for a reason, and it is worth going with the flow at least once.

A curious lore of itineraries and times for visiting the monuments developed at Angkor when tourism first began early in the 20th century. It is received wisdom that as Angkor Wat faces west, one should be there for late afternoon, and in the case of the Bayon, which faces east, in the morning. Ta Prohm, most people seem to agree, can be visited in the middle of the day because of its umbrella of foliage. This is all well and good, but if you reverse the order, the temples will still look good – and you can avoid some of the crowds.

The most popular place for sunrise is Angkor Wat. Most tour groups head back to town for breakfast, so stick around and explore the temple while it's cool and quiet. The Bayon sees far fewer visitors than Angkor Wat in the early hours. Sra Srang is usually pretty quiet, and sunrise here can be spectacular thanks to reflections in the extensive waters. Phnom Bakheng could be an attractive option, because the sun comes up behind Angkor Wat and you are far from the madding crowd that gathers here at sunset. Ta Prohm is an alternative option, with no sight of sunrise, but a mysterious and magical atmosphere.

The definitive sunset spot is the hilltop temple of Phnom Bakheng, but this has been getting well out of control lately, with as many as 1000 tourists clambering around the small structure. Better to check it out for sunrise or early morning and miss the crowds. Staying within the confines of Angkor Wat for sunset is a rewarding option, as it can be pretty peaceful when most tourists head off to Phnom Bakheng around 4.30pm or so. Pre Rup is popular with some for an authentic rural sunset over the surrounding rice-fields, but this is starting to get busier (although nothing like the circus at Bakheng). Better is the hilltop temple of Phnom Krom, which offers commanding views across Tonlé Sap Lake, but involves a long drive back to town in the dark. The Western Baray takes in the sunset from the eastern end, across its vast waters, and is generally a quiet option.

When it comes to the most popular temples, the middle of the day is consistently the quietest time. This is because the majority of the large tour groups head back to Siem Reap for lunch. It is also the hottest part of the day, which makes it tough going around relatively open temples such as Banteay Srei and the Bayon, but fine at well-covered temples such as Ta Prohm, Preah Khan and Beng Mealea, or even the bas-reliefs at Angkor Wat. The busiest times at Angkor Wat are from 6am to 7am and 3pm to 5pm; at the Bayon from 7.30am to 9.30am; at Banteay Srei mid-morning and mid-afternoon. However, at other popular temples, such as Ta Prohm and Preah Khan, the crowds are harder to predict, and at most other temples in the Angkor region it's just a case of pot luck. If you pull up outside and see a car park full of tour buses, you may want to move on to somewhere quieter. The wonderful thing about Angkor is that there is always another temple to explore.

Three to Five Days

If you have three to five days to explore Angkor, it is possible to see most of the important sites. One approach is to see as much as possible on the first day or two (as covered earlier) and then spend the final days combining visits to other sites such as the Roluos temples and Banteay Kdei. Better still is a gradual build-up to the most spectacular monuments. After all, if you see Angkor Wat on the first day, then a temple like Ta Keo just won't cut it. Another option is a chronological approach, starting with the earliest Angkorian temples and working steadily forwards in time to Angkor Thom, taking stock of the evolution of Khmer architecture and artistry.

It is well worth making the trip to the River of a Thousand Lingas at Kbal Spean for the chance to stretch your legs amid natural and manmade splendour, or making a trip to the remote, vast and overgrown temple of Beng Mealea; both can be combined with Banteay Srei in one long day.

The average stay at Angkor is still just 2½ days, which barely allows enough time to see the major temples, let alone enjoy the action-packed town of Siem Reap.

One Week

Those with the time to spend a week at Angkor will be richly rewarded. Not only is it possible to fit all the temples of the region into an itinerary, but a longer stay also allows for non-temple activities, such as relaxing by a pool, indulging in a spa treatment or shopping around Siem Reap. Check out the aforementioned itineraries for some ideas on approach, but relax in the knowledge that you'll see it all. You may also want to throw in some of the more remote sites such as Koh Ker (p264), Prasat Preah Vihear (p268) or Banteay Chhmar (p255).

TOURS

Most budget and midrange travellers not on package tours prefer to take in the temples at their own pace. However, visitors who have only a day or two at this incredible site may prefer something organised locally.

It is possible to link up with an official tour guide in Siem Reap. The **Khmer Angkor Tour Guides Association** (☎ 964347; khmerang@camintel.com) represents all of Angkor's authorised guides. English- or French-speaking guides can be booked from US$20 to US$30 a day; guides speaking other languages, such as Italian, German, Spanish, Japanese and Chinese, are available at a higher rate as there are fewer of them.

For an organised tour around Angkor, check out the recommended Cambodian operators under Tours (p332) in the Transport chapter. Other good Siem Reap–based companies:

Buffalo Trails (☎ 012-297506; buffalotrails@online.com.kh) Promotes homestays, birdwatching, traditional fishing techniques and Cambodian cooking classes.

La Villa (☎ 092-256691; www.thevillasiemreap.com) Small group trips to the more remote spots like Beng Mealea temple and Kompong Phhluk village, plus lifestyle visits beyond the temples.

Paneman (☎ 063-761759; www.paneman.org) A specialist ecotourism company that operates bio-diesel boats on Tonlé Sap Lake and arranges remote temple, lifestyle and specialist trips around the Angkor area.

Terre Cambodge (☎ 063-964391; www.terrecambodge.com) Offers trips to a variety of remote sites around Angkor, some by bicycle, plus boat trips on Tonlé Sap Lake aboard its wooden sampan.

GETTING THERE & AROUND

Visitors heading to the temples of Angkor – in other words pretty much everybody coming to Cambodia – need to consider the most suitable way to travel between the temples. Many of the best-known temples are no more than a few kilometres from the walled city of Angkor Thom, which is just 8km from Siem Reap, and can be visited using anything from a car or motorcycle to a sturdy pair of walking boots. For the independent traveller there is a daunting range of alternatives to consider.

Bicycle

A great way to get around the temples, bicycles are environmentally friendly and are used by most locals living around the area. There are few hills and the roads are good, so there's no need for much cycling experience. Moving about at a slower speed, you soon find that you take in more than from out of a car window or on the back of a speeding *moto*.

White Bicycles (www.thewhitebicycles.org; per day US$2) is supported by some guesthouses around town, with proceeds from the US$2 hire fee going towards community projects. Many guesthouses and hotels in town rent bikes for around US$1 to US$2 per day. There are also electric bicycles for hire and these cost about US$3 to US$4 a day, although make sure the battery is fully charged before setting off.

Car & Motorcycle

Cars are a popular choice for getting about the temples. The obvious advantage is protection from the elements, be it rain or the punishing sun. Shared between several travellers, they can also be an economical way to explore. The downside is that visitors are a little more isolated from the sights, sounds and smells as they travel between temples. A car for the day around the central temples is US$25 to US$30 and can be arranged with hotels, guesthouses and agencies in town.

Motorcycle rental in Siem Reap is currently prohibited, but some travellers bring a motorcycle from Phnom Penh. If you manage to get a bike up here, leave it at a guarded parking area or with a stallholder outside each temple, otherwise it could get stolen.

4WD

People planning adventures further afield to the remote temples in Preah Vihear Province (p261) will need to arrange a 4WD if they don't want to be on a motorcycle for several long days. Rates are higher the further you plan to go and the fancier the vehicle. Think US$80 and up per day.

Elephant

Travelling by elephant was the traditional way to see the temples way back in the early days of tourism at Angkor, at the start of the 20th century. It is once again possible to take an elephant ride between the south gate of Angkor Thom and the Bayon (US$10) in the morning, or up to the summit of Phnom Bakheng for sunset (US$15). The elephants owned by the **Angkor Village** (www.angkorvillage.com) resort group are very well looked after. A half-day mahout course was recently introduced. It costs US$50 per person and includes learning some elephant commands, a ride around Angkor Thom and a chance to bathe the elephant.

Helicopter

For those with plenty of spending money, there are tourist flights around Angkor Wat (US$75) and the temples outside Angkor Thom (US$130) with **Helicopters Cambodia** (Map p120; ☎ 012 814500; www.helicopterscambodia.com), which has an office near the Psar Chaa in Siem Reap. The company also offers charters to remote temples such as Prasat Preah Vihear and Preah Khan, with prices starting at around US$1800 per hour plus 10% sales tax. Call the bank manager first. Newcomer **Sokha Helicopters** (Map p120; ☎ 017 848891; www.sokhahelicopters.com) has slightly cheaper sightseeing flights.

For the ultimate Angkor experience, try a pick and mix approach, with a *moto, remorque-moto (tuk tuk)* or car for one day to cover the remote sites, a bicycle to experience the central temples, and an exploration on foot for a spot of peace and serenity.

Hot-Air Balloon

For a bird's eye view of Angkor Wat, try the **Angkor Balloon** (Map pp142-3; ☎ 012 844049; per person US$11). The balloon carries up to 30 people, is on a fixed line and rises 200m above the landscape.

Minibus

Minibuses are available from various hotels and travel agents around town. A 12-seat minibus costs from US$50 per day, while a 25- or 30-seat coaster bus is around US$80 to US$100 per day.

Moto

Many independent travellers end up visiting the temples by *moto*. *Moto* drivers accost visitors from the moment they set foot in Siem Reap, but they often end up being knowledgeable and friendly, and good companions for a tour around the temples. They can drop you off and pick you up at allotted times and places and even tell you a bit of background about the temples as you zip around. Those on a really tight budget can just take individual *moto* rides from temple to temple and this may end up cheaper than the US$7 to US$8 a day most drivers charge.

Remorque-moto

A motorcycle with a twee little hooded carriage towed behind, these are also known as *tuk tuks*. They are a popular way to get around Angkor as fellow travellers can still talk to each other as they explore (unlike on the back of a *moto*). They also offer some protection from the rain. As with *moto* drivers, some *remorque* drivers are very good companions for a tour of the temples. Prices start run from US$10 to US$20 for the day, depending on the destination and number of passengers.

Transport will be more expensive to remote temples such as Banteay Srei or Beng Mealea, due to extra fuel costs.

Walking

Why not forget all these new-fangled methods and simply explore on foot? There are obvious limitations to what can be seen, as some temples are just too far from Siem Reap. However, it is easy enough to walk to Angkor Wat and the temples of Angkor Thom, and this is a great way to meet up with villagers in the area. Those who want to get away from the roads should try the peaceful walk along the walls of Angkor Thom. It is about 13km in total, and offers access to several small, remote temples and a lot of birdlife. Another rewarding walk is from Ta Nei to Ta Keo through the forest.

ANGKOR WAT

អង្គរវត្ត

Angkor Wat is the largest and undoubtedly the most breathtaking of the monuments at Angkor, and is widely believed to be the largest religious structure in the world. It is simply unique, a stunning blend of spirituality and symmetry, an enduring example of man's devotion to his gods. Relish the very first approach, as that spine-tickling moment when you emerge on the inner causeway will rarely be felt again. It is the best-preserved temple at Angkor, as it was never abandoned to the elements, and repeat visits are rewarded with previously unnoticed details. It was probably built as a funerary temple for Suryavarman II (r 1112–52) to honour Vishnu, the Hindu deity with whom the king identified.

There is much about Angkor Wat that is unique among the temples of Angkor. The most significant fact is that the temple is oriented towards the

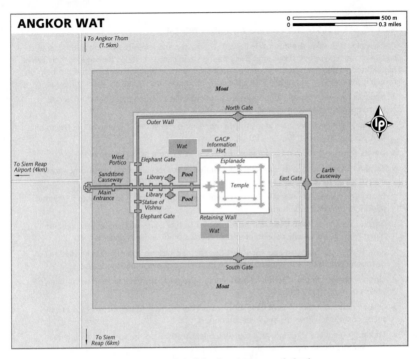

west. West is symbolically the direction of death, which once led a large number of scholars to conclude that Angkor Wat must have existed primarily as a tomb. This idea was supported by the fact that the magnificent bas-reliefs of the temple were designed to be viewed in an anticlockwise direction, a practice that has precedents in ancient Hindu funerary rites. Vishnu, however, is also frequently associated with the west, and it is now commonly accepted that Angkor Wat most likely served both as a temple and a mausoleum for Suryavarman II.

Angkor Wat is famous for its beguiling *apsaras* (heavenly nymphs). Many of these exquisite *apsaras* were damaged during Indian efforts to clean the temples with chemicals during the 1980s, the ultimate bad acid trip, but they are now being restored by the teams with the **German Apsara Conservation Project** (GACP; www.gacp-angkor.de). The organisation operates a small information booth in the northwest corner of Angkor Wat, near the wat, where beautiful black-and-white postcards and images of Angkor are available.

There are more than 3000 *apsaras* carved into the walls of Angkor Wat, each of them unique, and there are more than 30 different hairstyles for budding stylists to check out.

SYMBOLISM

Visitors to Angkor Wat are struck by its imposing grandeur and, at close quarters, its fascinating decorative flourishes and extensive bas-reliefs. Holy men at the time of Angkor must have revelled in its multilayered levels of meaning in much the same way a contemporary literary scholar might delight in James Joyce's *Ulysses*.

Eleanor Mannikka explains in her book *Angkor Wat: Time, Space and Kingship* that the spatial dimensions of Angkor Wat parallel the lengths of the four ages (Yuga) of classical Hindu thought. Thus the visitor to Angkor Wat who walks the causeway to the main entrance and through the courtyards to

MOTIFS, SYMBOLS & CHARACTERS AROUND ANGKOR

The temples of Angkor are intricately carved with myths and legends, symbols and signs, and a cast of characters in their thousands. Deciphering them can be quite a challenge, so here we've highlighted some of the most commonly seen around the majestic temples. For more help unravelling the carvings of Angkor, pick up a copy of *Images of the Gods* by Vittorio Reveda.

- **Apsaras** Heavenly nymphs or goddesses, also known as *devadas*; these beautiful female forms decorate the walls of many temples.
- **Asuras** These devils feature extensively in representations of the Churning of the Ocean of Milk, such as at Angkor Wat (p158).
- **Devas** The 'good gods' in the creation myth of the Churning of the Ocean of Milk.
- **Essai** A Hindu wise man or ascetic; these bearded characters are often seen sitting cross-legged at the base of pillars or flanking walls.
- **Flame** The flame motif is found flanking steps and doorways and is intended to purify the pilgrim as they enter the temple.
- **Garuda** Vehicle of Vishnu; this half-man-half-bird features in some temples and was combined with his old enemy *naga* to promote religious unity under Jayavarman VII.
- **Kala** The temple guardian appointed by Shiva; he had such an appetite that he tried to devour his own body and appears only as a giant head above many doorways.
- **Linga** A phallic symbol of fertility, *lingas* would have originally been located within the towers of most Hindu temples.
- **Lotus** Another symbol of purity, the lotus features extensively in the shape of towers, the shape of steps to entrances and in decoration.
- **Makara** A giant sea serpent with a reticulated jaw; features on the corner of pediments, spewing forth a *naga* or some other creature.
- **Naga** The multiheaded serpent, half-brother and enemy of *garuda,* who controls the rains and, therefore, prosperity of the kingdom; seen on causeways, doorways and roofs.
- **Nandi** The mount of Shiva; there are several statues of Nandi dotted about the temples, although many have been damaged or stolen by looters.
- **Vine** Yet another symbol of purity, the vine graces doorways and lintels and is meant to help cleanse the visitor on their journey to this heaven on earth, the abode of the gods.
- **Yama** God of death who presides over the underworld and passes judgement on whether people continue to heaven or hell.
- **Yoni** Female fertility symbol that is combined with the linga to produce holy water infused with fertility.

the final main tower, which once contained a statue of Vishnu, is metaphorically travelling back to the first age of the creation of the universe.

Like the other temple-mountains of Angkor, Angkor Wat also replicates the spatial universe in miniature. The central tower is Mt Meru, with its surrounding smaller peaks, bounded in turn by continents (the lower courtyards) and the oceans (the moat). The seven-headed *naga* becomes a symbolic rainbow bridge for man to reach the abode of the gods.

ARCHITECTURAL LAYOUT

Angkor Wat is surrounded by a 190m-wide moat, which forms a giant rectangle measuring 1.5km by 1.3km. It makes the moats around European castles look like kid's play. From the west, a sandstone causeway crosses the moat. The sandstone blocks from which Angkor Wat was built were quarried more than 50km away (from the district of Svay Leu at the eastern foot of Phnom Kulen) and floated down the Stung Siem Reap on rafts. The logistics of such an operation are mind-blowing, consuming the labour of thousands – an unbelievable feat given the lack of cranes and trucks that we take for granted in contemporary construction projects.

The rectangular outer wall, which measures 1025m by 800m, has a gate on each side, but the main entrance, a 235m-wide porch richly decorated with carvings and sculptures, is on the western side. There is a statue of Vishnu, 3.25m in height and hewn from a single block of sandstone, located in the right-hand tower. Vishnu's eight arms hold a mace, a spear, a disc, a conch and other items. You may also see locks of hair lying about. These are offerings from both young people preparing to get married and by pilgrims giving thanks for their good fortune.

An avenue, 475m long and 9.5m wide and lined with *naga* balustrades, leads from the main entrance to the central temple, passing between two graceful libraries (the northern one restored by a Japanese team) and then two pools, the northern one a popular spot from which to watch the sunrise.

The central temple complex consists of three storeys, each made of laterite, which enclose a square surrounded by intricately interlinked galleries. The Gallery of a Thousand Buddhas used to house hundreds of Buddha images before the war, but many of these were removed or stolen, leaving just the handful we see today.

The corners of the second and third storeys are marked by towers, each topped with symbolic lotus bud towers. Rising 31m above the third level and 55m above the ground is the central tower, which gives the whole ensemble its sublime unity. The stairs to the upper level are immensely steep, because reaching the kingdom of the gods was no easy task. Apsara Authority is currently building large wooden staircases that will make life easier for modern-day pilgrims.

Once at the central tower, the pilgrimage is complete; soak up the breeze, take in the views and then find a quiet corner in which to contemplate the symmetry and symbolism of this Everest of temples.

> Most of the major sandstone blocks around Angkor include small circular holes. These originally held wooden stakes that were used to lift and position the stones during construction before being sawn off.

BAS-RELIEFS

Stretching around the outside of the central temple complex is an 800m-long series of intricate and astonishing bas-reliefs. The following is a brief description of the epic events depicted on the panels. They are described in the order in which you'll come to them if you begin on the western side and keep the bas-reliefs to your left. The majority of them were completed in the 12th century, but in the 16th century several new reliefs were added to unfinished panels.

(A) The Battle of Kurukshetra

The southern portion of the west gallery depicts a battle scene from the Hindu *Mahabharata* epic, in which the Kauravas (coming from the north) and the Pandavas (coming from the south) advance upon each other, meeting in furious battle. Infantry are shown on the lowest tier, with officers on elephant-back and chiefs on the second and third tiers. Some of the more interesting details (from left to right): a dead chief lying on a pile of arrows, surrounded by his grieving parents and troops; a warrior on an elephant who, by putting down his weapon, has accepted defeat; and a mortally wounded officer, falling from his carriage into the arms of his soldiers. Over the centuries, some sections have been polished (by the millions of hands that fall upon them) to look like black marble. The portico at the southwestern corner is decorated with sculptures representing characters from the *Ramayana*.

> According to inscriptions, the construction of Angkor Wat involved 300,000 workers and 6000 elephants, yet was still not fully completed.

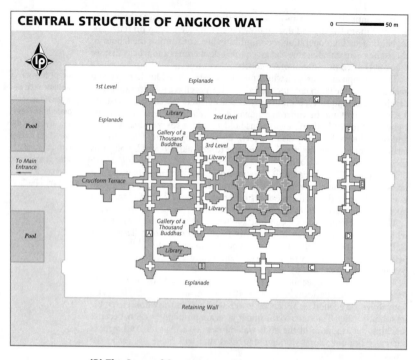

CENTRAL STRUCTURE OF ANGKOR WAT

0 ▭▭▭ 50 m

1st Level
Esplanade
Library
2nd Level
Esplanade
Pool
Gallery of a
Thousand
Buddhas
3rd Level
To Main
Entrance
Library
Cruciform Terrace
Library
Library
Gallery of a
Thousand
Buddhas
Pool
Library
Esplanade
Retaining Wall

Originally, the central
sanctuary of Angkor
Wat held a gold statue
of Vishnu mounted on a
garuda (a mythical half-
man, half-bird creature)
that represented the
deified god-king Surya-
varman II.

(B) The Army of Suryavarman II

The remarkable western section of the south gallery depicts a triumphal battle-
march of Suryavarman II's army. In the southwestern corner about 2m from
the floor is Suryavarman II on an elephant, wearing the royal tiara and armed
with a battle-axe; he is shaded by 15 parasols and fanned by legions of servants.
Further on is a procession of well-armed soldiers and officers on horseback;
among them are bold and warlike chiefs on elephants. Just before the end of
this panel is the rather disorderly Siamese mercenary army, with their long
headdresses and ragged marching, at that time allied with the Khmers in their
conflict with the Chams. The Khmer troops have square breastplates and are
armed with spears; the Thais wear skirts and carry tridents.

(C) Heaven & Hell

The eastern half of the south gallery depicts the punishments and rewards of
the 37 heavens and 32 hells. On the left, the upper and middle tiers show fine
gentlemen and ladies proceeding towards 18-armed Yama (the judge of the
dead) seated on a bull; below him are his assistants, Dharma and Sitragupta.
On the lower tier, devils drag the wicked along the road to hell. To Yama's right,
the tableau is divided into two parts by a horizontal line of *garudas:* above, the
elect dwell in beautiful mansions, served by women and attendants; below, the
condemned suffer horrible tortures that might have inspired the Khmer Rouge.
The ceiling in this section was restored by the French in the 1930s.

(D) Churning of the Ocean of Milk

The southern section of the east gallery is decorated by the most famous
of the bas-relief scenes at Angkor Wat, the Churning of the Ocean of Milk.

This brilliantly executed carving depicts 88 *asuras* on the left, and 92 *devas*, with crested helmets, churning up the sea to extract from it the elixir of immortality. The demons hold the head of the serpent and the gods hold its tail. At the centre of the sea, the serpent is coiled around Mt Mandala, which turns and churns up the water in the tug of war between the demons and the gods. Vishnu, incarnated as a huge turtle, lends his shell to serve as the base and pivot of Mt Mandala. Brahma, Shiva, Hanuman (the monkey god) and Lakshmi (the goddess of beauty) all make appearances, while overhead a host of heavenly female spirits sing and dance in encouragement. Luckily for us the gods won through, as the *apsaras* above were too much for the hot-blooded devils to take.

> The bas-reliefs at Angkor Wat were once sheltered by the cloister's wooden roof, which long ago rotted away except for one original beam in the western half of the north gallery. The other roofed sections are reconstructions.

(E) The Elephant Gate
This gate, which has no stairway, was used by the king and others for mounting and dismounting elephants directly from the gallery. North of the gate is a Khmer inscription recording the erection of a nearby stupa in the 18th century.

(F) Vishnu Conquers the Demons
The northern section of the east gallery shows a furious and desperate encounter between Vishnu, riding on a *garuda,* and innumerable devils. Needless to say, he slays all comers. This gallery was completed at a later date, most likely in the 16th century, and the later carving is notably inferior to the original work from the 12th century.

> Check out the images of Suryavarman II on the southern gallery and compare him with the image of Rama in the northern gallery and you'll notice an uncanny likeness that helped reinforce the aura of the god-king.

(G) Krishna and the Demon King
The eastern section of the north gallery shows Vishnu incarnated as Krishna riding a *garuda.* He confronts a burning walled city, the residence of Bana, the demon king. The *garuda* puts out the fire and Bana is captured. In the final scene Krishna kneels before Shiva and asks that Bana's life be spared.

(H) Battle of the Gods and the Demons
The western section of the north gallery depicts the battle between the 21 gods of the Brahmanic pantheon and various demons. The gods are featured with their traditional attributes and mounts. Vishnu, for example, has four arms and is seated on a *garuda,* while Shiva rides a sacred goose.

(I) Battle of Lanka
The northern half of the west gallery shows scenes from the *Ramayana.* In the Battle of Lanka, Rama (on the shoulders of Hanuman), along with his army of monkeys, battles 10-headed, 20-armed Ravana, seducer of Rama's beautiful wife Sita. Ravana rides a chariot drawn by monsters and commands an army of giants.

> The rectangular holes seen in the Army of Suryavarman II relief were created when, long ago, pieces of the scene containing inscriptions (reputed to possess magical powers) were removed.

ANGKOR THOM

អង្គរធំ
The fortified city of Angkor Thom (Great Angkor, or Great City), is on an epic scale, some 10 sq km in size. It was built by Angkor's greatest king, Jayavarman VII (r 1181–1219), who came to power following the disastrous sacking of the previous Khmer capital by the Chams. At the city's height, it may have supported a population of one million people in the surrounding region. Centred on the Bayon, Angkor Thom is enclosed by a *jayagiri* (square

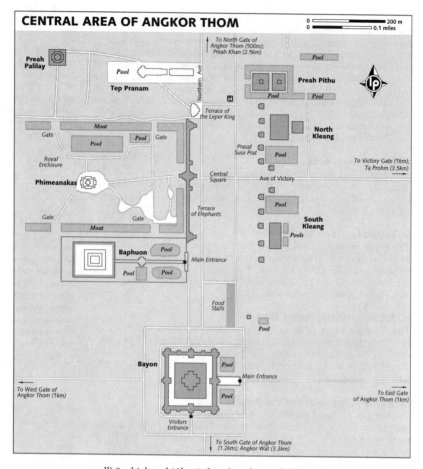

CENTRAL AREA OF ANGKOR THOM

wall) 8m high and 12km in length and encircled by a 100m-wide *jayasindhu* (moat) . (The moat is said to have been inhabited by fierce crocodiles.) This architectural layout is yet another monumental expression of Mt Meru surrounded by the oceans.

The city has five immense gates, one each in the northern, western and southern walls and two in the eastern wall. The gates are 20m in height, decorated with stone elephant trunks and crowned by four gargantuan faces of Avalokiteshvara, the Bodhisattva of Compassion, facing the cardinal directions. In front of each gate stands giant statues of 54 gods (to the left of the causeway) and 54 demons (to the right of the causeway), a motif taken from the story of the Churning of the Ocean of Milk. The south gate is most popular with visitors, as it has been fully restored and many of the heads (usually copies) remain in place. The gate is on the main road into Angkor Thom from Angkor Wat, and it gets very busy. More peaceful are the east and west gates, found at the end of uneven trails. The east gate was used as a location in *Tomb Raider* where the bad guys broke into the 'tomb' by pulling down a giant (polystyrene!) *apsara*.

The causeway at the west gate of Angkor Thom has completely collapsed, leaving a jumble of ancient stones sticking out of the soil like victims of a terrible historical pile-up.

In the centre of the walled enclosure are the city's most important monuments, including the Bayon, the Baphuon, the Royal Enclosure, Phimeanakas and the Terrace of Elephants.

BAYON
ប្រាសាទបាយ័ន

Unique, even among its cherished contemporaries, Bayon epitomises the creative genius and inflated ego of Cambodia's legendary king, Jayavarman VII. It's a place of stooped corridors, precipitous flights of stairs and, best of all, a collection of 54 gothic towers decorated with 216 coldly smiling, enormous faces of Avalokiteshvara that bear more than a passing resemblance to the great king himself. These huge heads glare down from every angle, exuding power and control with a hint of humanity – this was precisely the blend required to hold sway over such a vast empire, ensuring the disparate and far-flung population yielded to his magnanimous will. As you walk around, a dozen or more of the heads are visible at any one time – full-face or in profile, almost level with your eyes or staring down from on high.

Bayon is now known to have been built by Jayavarman VII, though for many years its origins were unknown. Shrouded in dense jungle, it also took researchers some time to realise that it stands in the exact centre of the city of Angkor Thom. There is still much mystery associated with Bayon – such as its exact function and symbolism – and this seems only appropriate for a monument whose signature is an enigmatic smiling face.

The eastward orientation of Bayon leads most people to visit early in the morning, preferably just after sunrise, when the sun inches upwards, lighting face after face. Bayon, however, looks equally good in the late afternoon, and if you stay for the sunset you get the same effect as at sunrise, in reverse. A Japanese team is restoring several outer areas of the temple.

Architectural Layout

Unlike Angkor Wat, which looks impressive from all angles, the Bayon looks rather like a glorified pile of rubble from a distance. It's only when you enter the temple and make your way up to the third level that its magic becomes apparent.

The basic structure of the Bayon is a simple three levels, which correspond more or less to three distinct phases of building. This is because Jayavarman VII began construction of this temple at an advanced age, so was never confident it would be completed. Each time one phase was completed, he moved on to the next. The first two levels are square and adorned with bas-reliefs. They lead up to a third, circular level, with the towers and their faces.

Bas-Reliefs

Bayon is decorated with a total of 1.2km of extraordinary bas-reliefs incorporating more than 11,000 figures. The famous carvings on the outer wall of the first level depict vivid scenes of everyday life in 12th-century Cambodia. The bas-reliefs on the second level do not have the epic proportions of those on the first level and tend to be fragmented. The reliefs described are those on the first level. The sequence assumes that you enter the Bayon from the east and view the reliefs in a clockwise direction.

Some say that the Khmer empire was divided into 54 provinces at the time of Bayon's construction, hence the all-seeing eyes of Avalokiteshvara (or Jayavarman VII) keeping watch on the kingdom's outlying subjects.

(A) CHAMS ON THE RUN

Just south of the east gate is a three-level panorama. On the first tier, Khmer soldiers march off to battle; check out the elephants and the ox carts, which are almost exactly like those still used in Cambodia today. The second tier depicts the coffins being carried back from the battlefield. In the centre of

BAYON

0 ⊏⊏⊏⊏⊏⊏⊏⊏⊏ 50 m

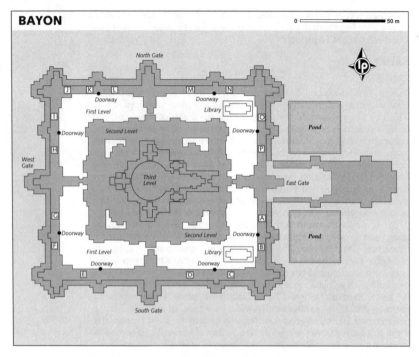

the third tier, Jayavarman VII, shaded by parasols, is shown on horseback followed by legions of concubines (to the left).

(B) LINGA WORSHIP
The first panel north of the southeastern corner shows Hindus praying to a *linga* (phallic symbol). This image was probably originally a Buddha, later modified by a Hindu king.

(C) NAVAL BATTLE
The next panel has some of the best-carved reliefs. The scenes depict a naval battle between the Khmers and the Chams (the latter with head coverings) and everyday life around Tonlé Sap Lake, where the battle was fought. Look for images of people picking lice from each other's hair, of hunters and, towards the western end of the panel, a woman giving birth.

(D) THE CHAMS VANQUISHED
In the next panel, scenes from daily life continue and the battle shifts to the shore where the Chams are soundly thrashed. Scenes include two people playing chess, a cockfight and women selling fish in the market. The scenes of meals being prepared and served are in celebration of the Khmer victory.

(E & F) MILITARY PROCESSION
The last section of the south gallery, depicting a military procession, is unfinished, as is the panel showing elephants being led down from the mountains. Brahmans have been chased up two trees by tigers.

(G) CIVIL WAR

This panel depicts scenes that some scholars maintain is a civil war. Groups of people, some armed, confront each other, and the violence escalates until elephants and warriors join the melee.

(H) THE ALL-SEEING KING

The fighting continues on a smaller scale in the next panel. An antelope is being swallowed by a gargantuan fish; among the smaller fish is a prawn, under which an inscription proclaims that the king will seek out those in hiding.

(I) VICTORY PARADE

This panel depicts a procession that includes the king (carrying a bow). Presumably it is a celebration of his victory.

(J) THE CIRCUS COMES TO TOWN

At the western corner of the northern wall is a Khmer circus. A strong man holds three dwarfs, and a man on his back is spinning a wheel with his feet; above is a group of tightrope walkers. To the right of the circus, the royal court watches from a terrace, below which is a procession of animals. Some of the reliefs in this section remain unfinished.

(K) A LAND OF PLENTY

The two rivers, one next to the doorpost and the other a few metres to the right, are teeming with fish.

(L, M & N) THE CHAMS RETREAT

On the lowest level of this unfinished three-tiered scene, the Cham armies are being defeated and expelled from the Khmer kingdom. The next panel depicts the Cham armies advancing, and the badly deteriorated panel shows the Chams (on the left) chasing the Khmers.

(O) THE SACKING OF ANGKOR

This panel shows the war of 1177, when the Khmers were defeated by the Chams, and Angkor was pillaged. The wounded Khmer king is being lowered from the back of an elephant and a wounded Khmer general is being carried on a hammock suspended from a pole. Directly above, despairing Khmers are getting drunk. The Chams (on the right) are in hot pursuit of their vanquished enemy.

For the filming of *Tomb Raider,* an elaborate floating village was constructed on the northern pond of Angkor Wat; Angelina Jolie came ashore here before borrowing a mobile phone from a local monk.

(P) THE CHAMS ENTER ANGKOR

This panel depicts another meeting of the two armies. Notice the flag bearers among the Cham troops (on the right). The Chams were defeated in the war, which ended in 1181, as depicted on panel A.

BAPHUON
បាពួន

Baphuon would have been one of the most spectacular of Angkor's temples in its heyday. Located 200m northwest of Bayon, it's a pyramidal representation of mythical Mt Meru. Construction probably began under Suryavarman I and was later completed by Udayadityavarman II (r 1049–65). It marked the centre of the city that existed before the construction of Angkor Thom.

Baphuon was the centre of EFEO restoration efforts when the Cambodian civil war erupted and work paused for a quarter of a century. The temple was taken apart piece by piece, in keeping with the anastylosis method of renovation, but all the records were destroyed during the Khmer Rouge years, leaving experts with the world's largest jigsaw puzzle. The EFEO resumed a 10-year restoration programme in 1995, which is running behind schedule but will see the temple reopen some time during the lifetime of this book. Baphuon is approached by a 200m elevated walkway made of sandstone, and the central structure is 43m high.

On the western side of the temple is the retaining wall of the second level. The wall was fashioned – apparently in the 15th or 16th century – into a reclining Buddha 60m in length. The unfinished figure is quite difficult to make out, but the head is on the northern side of the wall and the gate is where the hips should be; to the left of the gate protrudes an arm. When it comes to the legs and feet – the latter are entirely gone – imagination must suffice. This huge project was undertaken by the Buddhist faithful around 500 years ago, which reinforces the fact that Angkor was never entirely abandoned.

TIP

Clamber under the elevated causeway leading to Baphuon for an incredible view of the hundreds of pillars supporting it.

ROYAL ENCLOSURE & PHIMEANAKAS
ភិមានអាកាស

Phimeanakas stands close to the centre of a walled area that once housed the royal palace. There's very little left of the palace today except for two sandstone pools near the northern wall. Once the site of royal ablutions, these are now used as swimming holes by local children. It is fronted to the east by the Terrace of Elephants. Construction of the palace began under Rajendravarman II, although it was used by Jayavarman V and Udayadityavarman I. It was later added to and embellished by Jayavarman VII (who else?) and his successors.

Phimeanakas means 'Celestial Palace', and some scholars say that it was once topped by a golden spire. Today it only hints at its former splendour and looks a little worse for wear. The temple is another pyramidal representation of Mt Meru, with three levels. Most of the decorative features are broken or have disappeared. Still, it is worth clambering up to the second and third levels for good views of Baphuon.

PREAH PALILAY
ព្រះប៉ាលីឡៃ

Preah Palilay is one of the most atmospheric temples in Angkor Thom, located about 200m north of the Royal Enclosure's northern wall. It was erected during the rule of Jayavarman VII and originally housed a Buddha, which has long since vanished. There are several enormous trees looming large over the central sanctuary, which make for a fine photo.

TEP PRANAM
ទេព្យប្រណាម្យ

View the striking temples of Angkor Thom in a different light by checking out the sepia, infra-red images of John McDermott at www .mcdermottgallery.com or visit his gallery in Siem Reap (p136).

Tep Pranam, an 82m by 34m cruciform Buddhist terrace 150m east of Preah Palilay, was once the base of a pagoda of lightweight construction. Nearby is a Buddha that's 4.5m high, but it's a reconstruction of the original. A group of Buddhist nuns lives in a wooden structure close by.

PREAH PITHU
ព្រះពិធូ

Preah Pithu, which is across Northern Ave from Tep Pranam, is a group of 12th-century Hindu and Buddhist temples enclosed by a wall. It includes some beautifully decorated terraces and guardian animals in the form of elephants and lions.

TERRACE OF THE LEPER KING
ទីលានព្រះគម្ងង់

The Terrace of the Leper King is just north of the Terrace of Elephants. It is a 7m-high platform, on top of which stands a nude, though sexless, statue. It is yet another of Angkor's mysteries. The original of the statue is in Phnom Penh's National Museum (p84), and various theories have been advanced to explain its meaning. Legend has it that at least two of the Angkor kings had leprosy, and the statue may represent one of them. Another theory, and a more likely explanation, is that the statue is of Yama, the god of death, and that the Terrace of the Leper King housed the royal crematorium.

The front retaining walls of the terrace are decorated with at least five tiers of meticulously executed carvings of seated *apsaras;* other figures include kings wearing pointed diadems, armed with short double-edged swords and accompanied by the court and princesses, the latter adorned with beautiful rows of pearls. The terrace, built in the late 12th century between the construction of Angkor Wat and the Bayon, once supported a pavilion made of lightweight materials.

On the southern side of the Terrace of the Leper King (facing the Terrace of Elephants), there is access to the front wall of a hidden terrace that was covered up when the outer structure was built – a terrace within a terrace. The four tiers of *apsaras* and other figures, including *nagas,* look as fresh as if they had been carved yesterday, thanks to being covered up for centuries. Some of the figures carry fearsome expressions.

TERRACE OF ELEPHANTS
ទីលានដល់ដំរី

The 350m-long Terrace of Elephants was used as a giant viewing stand for public ceremonies and served as a base for the king's grand audience hall. As you stand here, try to imagine the pomp and grandeur of the Khmer empire at its height, with infantry, cavalry, horse-drawn chariots and elephants parading across the Central Sq in a colourful procession, pennants and standards aloft. Looking on is the god-king, crowned with a gold diadem, shaded by multitiered parasols and attended by mandarins and handmaidens bearing gold and silver utensils.

The Terrace of Elephants has five piers extending towards the Central Sq – three in the centre and one at each end. The middle section of the retaining wall is decorated with life-size *garudas* and lions; towards either end are the two parts of the famous parade of elephants, complete with their Khmer mahouts.

KLEANGS & PRASAT SUOR PRAT
ឃ្លាំង/ប្រាសាទសួរប្រាត

Along the east side of Central Sq are two groups of buildings, called Kleangs. The North Kleang and the South Kleang may at one time have been palaces. The North Kleang has been dated from the period of Jayavarman V (r 968–1001).

Along the Central Sq in front of the two Kleangs are 12 laterite towers – 10 in a row and two more at right angles facing the Ave of Victory – known as the Prasat Suor Prat or Temple of the Tightrope Dancers. Archaeologists believe the towers, which form an honour guard along Central Sq, were constructed by Jayavarman VII (r 1181–1219). It is likely that each one originally contained either a *linga* or a statue. It is said artists performed for the king on tightropes or rope-bridges strung between these towers.

TIP

As you follow the inner wall of the Terrace of the Leper King, notice the increasingly rough chisel marks on the figures, an indication that this wall was never completed, like many of the temples at Angkor.

According to Chinese emissary Chou Ta-Kuan, the towers of Suor Prat were also used for public trials of sorts – during a dispute the two parties would be made to sit inside two towers, one party eventually succumbing to disease and proven guilty.

AROUND ANGKOR THOM

TA PROHM
តាព្រហ្ម

Ta Prohm is undoubtedly the most atmospheric ruin at Angkor and should be high on the hit list of every visitor. Its appeal lies in the fact that, unlike the other monuments of Angkor, it has been swallowed by the jungle, and looks very much the way most of the monuments of Angkor appeared when European explorers first stumbled upon them. Well, that's the theory, but in fact the jungle is pegged back and only the largest trees are left in place, making it manicured rather than raw like Beng Mealea. Still, a visit to Ta Prohm is a unique, other-world experience. The temple is cloaked in dappled shadow, its crumbling towers and walls locked in the slow muscular embrace of vast root systems. If Angkor Wat, the Bayon and other temples are testimony to the genius of the ancient Khmers, Ta Prohm reminds us equally of the awesome fecundity and power of the jungle. There is a poetic cycle to this venerable ruin, with humanity first conquering nature to rapidly create, and nature once again conquering humanity to slowly destroy.

Built from 1186 and originally known as Rajavihara (Monastery of the King), Ta Prohm was a Buddhist temple dedicated to the mother of Jayavarman VII. It is one of the few temples in the Angkor region where an inscription provides information about the temple's dependents and inhabitants.

Ta Prohm is a temple of towers, closed courtyards and narrow corridors. Many of the corridors are impassable, clogged with jumbled piles

According to an inscription stele from Ta Prohm, close to 80,000 people were required to maintain or attend at the temple, among them more than 2700 officials and 615 dancers.

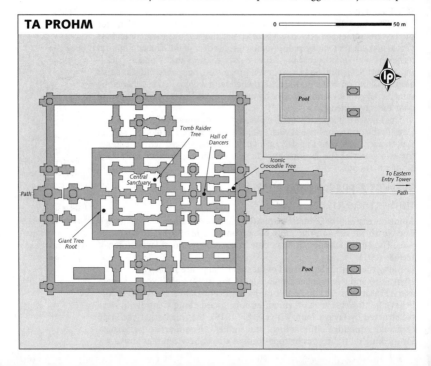

TA PROHM

0 — 50 m

Pool

Tomb Raider Tree

Hall of Dancers

Iconic Crocodile Tree

Central Sanctuary

To Eastern Entry Tower

Path

Path

Giant Tree Root

Pool

NHIEM CHUN   *Nick Ray*

Nhiem Chun is as much an icon of Angkor as the tangled roots that slowly choke the ancient stones of Ta Prohm. He will forever be known as the 'sweeper of Ta Prohm', as Nhiem Chun has dedicated his life to stemming the tide of nature, bent double, stooping low over the stones to sweep away the falling leaves each day.

I first met Nhiem back in 1995 when exploring Ta Prohm. He was more sprightly then, nimbly gliding over fallen pillars, tumbled stones and moss-clad lintels in search of his quarry, those ever-falling leaves. Nhiem's face was every bit as chiselled and characterful as the beautiful *devadas* that still lined the galleries.

Years later he was immortalised by Lonely Planet when his iconic image was selected as the cover shot for the fourth edition of this Cambodia guidebook (see p6). It is a definitive shot, Nhiem standing in front of the '*Tomb Raider* tree'. Nhiem soon became an A-list Angkor celebrity and crowds thronged around him wanting a photograph. At 86, Nhiem Chun is about the same age as King Sihanouk, although their lives could hardly be more different. He grew up tending buffalo and helping with the harvest, but thanks to a chance meeting with Angkor curator Henri Marchal in 1941 he began work as a labourer, helping with temple restoration at Angkor. It was the start of a lifelong love affair with the temples and Nhiem was destined to spend the next 65 years of his life working amid the sacred stones.

Nhiem's world crumbled around him when the Khmer Rouge came to power. 'In the 1970s, our lives were turned upside down. I could not do my job, I had to work the land,' says Nhiem. 'You had no choice. You would be killed.' More precious than his beloved temples, his two sons disappeared during the Khmer Rouge regime. 'When the fighting was over, my two sons were still missing,' he recalls. 'I was told they had been killed by the Khmer Rouge, their throats slit with sharpened sugar palm fronds.'

In 2006 the BBC came to Cambodia to film for the documentary series *Imagine...Who Cares About Art?* and Nhiem Chun, the ever-loyal guardian of Ta Prohm, was our subject. We spent several days with him, learning about his life, his loves, and his loss. 'The older I get the more I love this place. These temples are the spirit of the Cambodian nation,' muses Nhiem, wandering about Ta Prohm. 'I could have built this temple in a past life. If I did not have any connection, I would not be here to take care of it today.'

Nhiem is not getting any younger and frets about the future: 'I am old now. I can't take care of these temples any more,' he opines wistfully. 'But when I am gone, these stones will still be here. These temples are the symbols of our soul. We will not survive if we don't look after our temples.'

Like the ancient stones of Ta Prohm, like his beloved monarch Sihanouk, Nhiem Chun has experienced light and dark. A life lived among beauty and brilliance, he has also experienced the ugly side of mankind. But life goes on and the leaves continue to fall. 'If I don't sweep, the leaves will cover the temple. I must sweep,' he mutters. Nhiem Chun is a man for all seasons.

Nhiem Chun has finally hung up his brush to enjoy a well-earned retirement and lives with his grandchildren in a village near Ta Prohm. Some quotes taken from BBC film Imagine...Who Cares About Art?

of delicately carved stone blocks dislodged by the roots of long-decayed trees. Bas-reliefs on bulging walls are carpeted with lichen, moss and creeping plants, and shrubs sprout from the roofs of monumental porches. Trees, hundreds of years old – some supported by flying buttresses – tower overhead, their leaves filtering the sunlight and casting a greenish pall over the whole scene. The most popular of the many strangulating root formations is that on the inside of the easternmost *gopura* (entrance pavilion) of the central enclosure, nicknamed the Crocodile Tree. It used to be possible to climb onto the damaged galleries, but this is now prohibited to protect both the temple and visitor. Many of these precariously balanced stones weigh a tonne or more and would do some serious damage if they came down.

One of the most famous spots in Ta Prohm is the so-called '*Tomb Raider* tree' where Angelina Jolie's Lara Croft picked a jasmine flower before falling through the earth into...Pinewood Studios.

BAKSEI CHAMKRONG
បក្សីចាំក្រុង

Located southwest of the south gate of Angkor Thom, Baksei Chamkrong is one of the few brick edifices in the immediate vicinity of Angkor. A well-proportioned though petite temple, it was once decorated with a covering of lime mortar. Like virtually all of the structures of Angkor, it opens to the east. In the early 10th century, Harshavarman I erected five statues in this temple: two of Shiva, one of Vishnu and two of Devi.

PHNOM BAKHENG
ភ្នំបាក់ខែង

Located around 400m south of Angkor Thom, the main attraction at Phnom Bakheng is the photo op of a sunset view of Angkor Wat. Unfortunately, the whole affair has turned into something of a circus, with crowds of tourists ascending the slopes of the hill and jockeying for space once on top. Coming down can be even worse as there is nothing at all in the way of lighting. Still, the sunset over the Western Baray is very impressive from the hill. To get a decent picture of Angkor Wat in the warm glow of the late afternoon sun you will need at least a 300mm lens, as the temple is 1.3km away.

Phnom Bakheng also lays claim to being home to the first of the temple-mountains built in the vicinity of Angkor. Yasovarman I (r 889–910) chose Phnom Bakheng over the Roluos area, where the earlier capital (and temple-mountains) had been located.

The temple-mountain has five tiers, with seven levels (including the base and the summit). At the base are – or were – 44 towers. Each of the five tiers had 12 towers. The summit of the temple has four towers at the cardinal points of the compass as well as a central sanctuary. All of these numbers are of symbolic significance. The seven levels, for example, represent the seven Hindu heavens, while the total number of towers, excluding the Central Sanctuary, is 108, a particularly auspicious number and one that correlates to the lunar calendar.

It is now possible to arrange an elephant ride up the hill (one way US$15; see p153). It is advisable to book in advance, as the rides are very popular with tour groups.

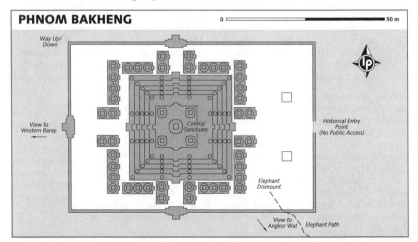

PHNOM BAKHENG   0 ⌈━━━━━━━━━━⌉ 50 m

Way Up/Down

View to Western Baray

Central Sanctuary

Historical Entry Point (No Public Access)

Elephant Dismount

View to Angkor Wat   Elephant Path

THE LONG STRIDER

One of Vishnu's best-loved incarnations was when he appeared as the dwarf Vamana, and proceeded to reclaim the world from the evil demon-king Bali. The dwarf politely asked the demon-king for a comfortable patch of ground upon which to meditate, saying that the patch need only be big enough so that he could easily walk across it in three paces. The demon agreed, only to see the dwarf swell into a mighty giant who strode across the universe in three enormous steps. From this legend, depicted at Prasat Kravan, Vishnu is sometimes known as the 'long strider'.

PRASAT KRAVAN
ប្រាសាទក្រវាន់

Prasat Kravan is famous for its interior brick carvings concealed within its towers. The five brick towers of Prasat Kravan, which are arranged in a north–south line and oriented to the east, were built for Hindu worship in AD 921. The structure is unusual in that it was not constructed by royalty; this accounts for its slightly distant location, away from the centre of the capital. Prasat Kravan is just south of the road between Angkor Wat and Banteay Kdei.

Prasat Kravan was partially restored in 1968, returning the brick carvings to their former glory. The images of Vishnu in the largest central tower show the eight-armed deity on the back wall; taking the three gigantic steps with which he reclaimed the world on the left wall (see above); and riding a *garuda* on the right wall. The northernmost tower displays bas-reliefs of Vishnu's consort, Lakshmi.

For a great online photographic resource on the temples of Angkor, look no further than www.angkor-ruins.com, a Japanese website with an English version.

BANTEAY KDEI & SRA SRANG
បន្ទាយក្ដី និង ស្រះស្រង់

Banteay Kdei, a massive Buddhist monastery from the latter part of the 12th century, is surrounded by four concentric walls. The outer wall measures 500m by 700m. Each of its four entrances is decorated with *garudas*, which hold aloft one of Jayavarman VII's favourite themes: the four faces of Avalokiteshvara. The inside of the central tower was never finished and much of the temple is in a ruinous state due to hasty construction. It is considerably less busy than nearby Ta Prohm and this alone can justify a visit.

East of Banteay Kdei is an earlier basin, Sra Srang (Pool of Ablutions), measuring 800m by 400m, reserved for the king and his wives. A tiny island in the middle once bore a wooden temple, of which only the stone base remains. This is a beautiful body of water from which to take in a quiet sunrise.

TA KEO
តាកែវ

Ta Keo is a stark, undecorated temple that undoubtedly would have been one of the finest of Angkor's structures, had it been finished. Built by Jayavarman V (r 968–1001), it was dedicated to Shiva and was the first Angkorian monument built entirely of sandstone. The summit of the central tower, which is surrounded by four lower towers, is almost 50m high. This quincuncial arrangement (with four towers at the corners of a square and a fifth tower in the centre) is typical of many Angkorian temple-mountains.

No-one is certain why work was never completed, but a likely cause may have been the death of Jayavarman V.

According to inscriptions, Ta Keo was struck by lightning during construction, which may have been a bad omen and led to its abandonment.

TA NEI
តានី

Ta Nei, 800m north of Ta Keo, was built by Jayavarman VII (r 1181–1219). There is something of the spirit of Ta Prohm here, albeit on a lesser scale, with moss and tentacle-like roots covering outer areas of this small temple. The number of visitors are also on a lesser scale, making it very atmospheric. It now houses the Apsara Authority's training unit and can be accessed by walking across the French-built dam. To get to the dam, take the long track on the left, just after the Victory Gate of Angkor Thom when coming from Siem Reap.

TIP

It is possible to walk from Ta Nei to Ta Keo through the forest, a guaranteed way to leave the crowds behind.

SPEAN THMOR
ស្ពានថ្ម

Spean Thmor (Stone Bridge), of which an arch and several piers remain, is 200m east of Thommanon. Jayavarman VII, the last great builder of Angkor, constructed many roads with these immense stone bridges spanning watercourses. This is the only large bridge remaining in the immediate vicinity of Angkor. The bridge vividly highlights how the water level has changed course over the subsequent centuries and may offer another clue to the collapse of Angkor's extensive irrigation system. Just north of Spean Thmor is a large water wheel.

There are more-spectacular examples of these ancient bridges elsewhere in Siem Reap Province, such as Spean Praptos, with 19 arches, in Kompong Kdei on NH6 from Phnom Penh; and Spean Ta Ong, a 77m bridge with a beautiful *naga,* forgotten in the forest about 25km east of Beng Mealea.

CHAU SAY TEVODA
ចៅសាយទេវតា

Just east of Angkor Thom's east gate is Chau Say Tevoda. It was probably built during the second quarter of the 12th century, under the reign of Suryavarman II, and dedicated to Shiva and Vishnu. It is under renovation by the Chinese to bring it up to the condition of its twin temple, Thommanon.

THOMMANON
ធម្មនន្ទ

Thommanon is just north of Chau Say Tevoda. Although unique, the temple complements its neighbour, as it was built to a similar design around the same time. It was also dedicated to Shiva and Vishnu. Thommanon is in much better condition than Chau Say Tevoda thanks to extensive work by the EFEO in the 1960s.

PREAH KHAN
ព្រះខ័ន្ឋ

The temple of Preah Khan (Sacred Sword) is one of the largest complexes at Angkor – a maze of vaulted corridors, fine carvings and lichen-clad stonework. It is a good counterpoint to Ta Prohm and generally sees slightly fewer visitors. Preah Khan was built by Jayavarman VII and probably served as his temporary residence while Angkor Thom was being built. Like Ta Prohm it is a place of towered enclosures and shoulder-hugging corridors. Unlike Ta Prohm, however, the temple of Preah Khan is in a reasonable state of preservation thanks to the ongoing restoration efforts of the **World Monuments Fund** (WMF; www.wmf.org).

The central sanctuary of the temple was dedicated in AD 1191 and a large stone stele tells us much about Preah Khan's role as a centre for worship and learning. Originally located within the first eastern enclosure, this stele is now housed safely at Angkor Conservation. The temple was dedicated to 515 divinities and during the course of a year 18 major festivals took place here, requiring a team of thousands just to maintain the place.

Preah Khan covers a very large area, but the temple itself is within a rectangular enclosing wall of around 700m by 800m. Four processional walkways approach the gates of the temple, and these are bordered by another stunning depiction of the Churning of the Ocean of Milk, as in the

Preah Khan is a genuine fusion temple, the eastern entrance dedicated to Mahayana Buddhism with equal sized doors, and the other cardinal directions dedicated to Shiva, Vishnu and Brahma with successively smaller doors, emphasising the unequal nature of Hinduism.

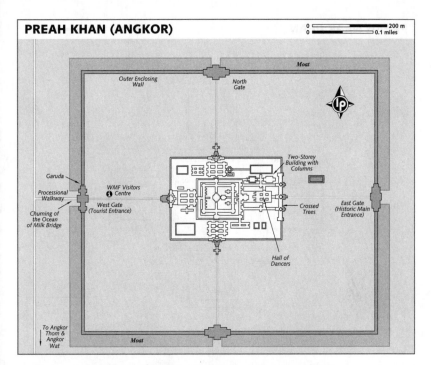

PREAH KHAN (ANGKOR)

Map labels: Moat; Outer Enclosing Wall; North Gate; Two-Storey Building with Columns; Garuda; WMF Visitors Centre; Processional Walkway; West Gate (Tourist Entrance); Churning of the Ocean of Milk Bridge; Crossed Trees; East Gate (Historic Main Entrance); Hall of Dancers; To Angkor Thom & Angkor Wat; Moat; 0 200 m; 0 0.1 miles

approach to Angkor Thom, although most of the heads have disappeared. From the central sanctuary, four long, vaulted galleries extend in the cardinal directions. Many of the interior walls of Preah Khan were once coated with plaster that was held in place by holes in the stone. Today, many delicate reliefs remain, including *essai* and *apsara* carvings.

The main entrance to Preah Khan is in the east but most tourists enter at the west gate near the main road, walk the length of the temple to the east gate before doubling back to the central sanctuary, and exit at the north gate. This is reason enough to rip up the rule book and enter from the original entrance in the east. Approaching from the west, there is little clue to nature's genius, but on the outer retaining wall of the east gate is a pair of trees with monstrous roots embracing, one still reaching for the sky. There is also a curious Grecian-style two-storey structure in the temple grounds, the purpose of which is unknown, but it looks like an exile from Athens.

PREAH NEAK PEAN
ព្រះនាគព័ន្ធ

The Buddhist temple of Preah Neak Poan (Intertwined Nagas; pronounced preah neak *po*-an) is a petite yet perfect temple constructed by…surely not him again…Jayavarman VII in the late 12th century. It has a large square pool surrounded by four smaller square pools. In the middle of the central pool is a circular 'island' encircled by the two *nagas* whose intertwined tails give the temple its name. Although it has been centuries since the small pools were last filled with water, it's a safe bet that when the Encore Angkor casino is eventually but inevitably developed in Las Vegas, Preah Neak Poan will provide the blueprint for the ultimate swimming complex.

Preah Neak Pean was once in the centre of a huge 3km-by-900m *baray* serving Preah Khan, known as Jayataka, now dried up and overgrown.

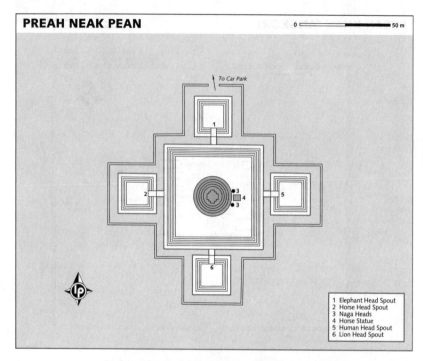

PREAH NEAK PEAN

0 ____ 50 m

To Car Park

1 Elephant Head Spout
2 Horse Head Spout
3 Naga Heads
4 Horse Statue
5 Human Head Spout
6 Lion Head Spout

In the pool around the central island there were once four statues, but only one remains, reconstructed from the debris by the French archaeologists who cleared the site. The curious figure has the body of a horse supported by a tangle of human legs. It relates to a legend that Avalokiteshvara once saved a group of shipwrecked followers from an island of ghouls by transforming into a flying horse. A beautiful replica of this statue decorates the main roundabout at Siem Reap Airport.

Water once flowed from the central pool into the four peripheral pools via ornamental spouts, which can still be seen in the pavilions at each axis of the pool. The spouts are in the form of an elephant's head, a horse's head, a lion's head and a human head. The pool was used for ritual purification rites.

TA SOM
តា សោម

Ta Som, which stands to the east of Preah Neak Pean, is yet another of the late-12th-century Buddhist temples of Jayavarman VII, the Donald Trump of ancient Cambodia. The central area of Ta Som is in a ruinous state, but restoration by the WMF is close to completion.

EASTERN BARAY & EASTERN MEBON
បារាយណ៍ខាងកើត/មេបុណ្យខាងកើត

The enormous one-time reservoir known as the Eastern Baray was excavated by Yasovarman I (r 889–910), who marked its four corners with steles. This basin, now entirely dried up, was the most important of the public works of Yasodharapura, Yasovarman I's capital, and is 7km by 1.8km. It was originally fed by the Stung Siem Reap.

TIP

The most impressive feature at Ta Som is the huge tree completely overwhelming the eastern *gopura*, providing one of the most popular photo opportunities in the Angkor area.

The Hindu temple known as the Eastern Mebon, erected by Rajendravarman II (r 944–68), would have been on an islet in the centre of the Eastern Baray, but is now very much on dry land. This temple is like a smaller version of Pre Rup, which was built 15 to 20 years later and lies to the south. The temple-mountain form is topped off by the now familiar quincuncial arrangement of towers. The elaborate brick shrines are dotted with neatly arranged holes, which attached the original plasterwork. The base of the temple is guarded at its corners by perfectly carved stone figures of elephants, many of which are still in a very good state of preservation.

Eastern Mebon is flanked by earthen ramps, a clue that this temple was never finished and a good visual guide to how the temples were constructed.

PRE RUP
ប្រែរូប

Pre Rup, built by Rajendravarman II, is about 1km south of the Eastern Mebon. Like its nearby predecessor, the temple consists of a pyramid-shaped temple-mountain with the uppermost of the three tiers carrying five lotus towers. The brick sanctuaries were also once decorated with a plaster coating, fragments of which still remain on the southwestern tower; there are some amazingly detailed lintel carvings here. Several of the outermost eastern towers are perilously close to collapse and are propped up by an army of wooden supports.

Pre Rup means 'Turning the Body' and refers to a traditional method of cremation in which a corpse's outline is traced in the cinders, first in one direction and then in the other; this suggests that the temple may have served as an early royal crematorium.

TIP

Pre Rup is one of the most popular sunset spots around Angkor, as the view over the surrounding rice-fields of the Eastern Baray is beautiful.

BANTEAY SAMRÉ
បន្ទាយសំរែ

Banteay Samré dates from the same period as Angkor Wat and was built by Suryavarman II (r 1112–52). The temple is in a fairly healthy state of preservation due to some extensive renovation work, although its isolation has resulted in some looting during the past two decades. The area consists of a central temple with four wings, preceded by a hall and also accompanied by two libraries, the southern one remarkably well preserved. The whole ensemble is enclosed by two large concentric walls around what would have been the unique feature of an inner moat, sadly now dry.

Banteay Samré is 400m east of the Eastern Baray, which in practical terms means following the road to Banteay Srei to the village of Preah Dak and continuing straight ahead rather than following the tarmac to the left. A visit here can be combined with a trip to Banteay Srei or Phnom Bok.

WESTERN BARAY & WESTERN MEBON
បារាយខាងលិច និងមេបុណ្យខាងលិច

The Western Baray, measuring an incredible 8km by 2.3km, was excavated by hand to provide water for the intensive cultivation of lands around Angkor. Just for the record, these enormous *barays* weren't dug out, but were huge dykes built up around the edges. In the centre of the Western Baray is the ruin of the Western Mebon temple, where the giant bronze statue of Vishnu, now in the National Museum (p84) in Phnom Penh, was found. The Western Mebon is accessible by boat from the dam on the southern shore.

The Western Baray is the main local swimming pool around Siem Reap. There is a small beach of sorts at the western extreme (complete with picnic huts and inner tubes for rent), which attracts plenty of Khmers at weekends.

ROLUOS TEMPLES
រលួស

The monuments of Roluos, which served as Indravarman I's (r 877–89) capital, Hariharalaya, are among the earliest large, permanent temples built by the Khmers and mark the dawn of Khmer classical art. Before the construction of Roluos, generally only lighter (and less-durable) construction materials such as brick were employed.

The temples can be found 13km east of Siem Reap along NH6 near the modern-day town of Roluos.

PREAH KO
ប្រះគោ

Preah Ko was erected by Indravarman I in the late 9th century, and was dedicated to Shiva. The six *prasats* (stone halls), aligned in two rows and decorated with carved sandstone and plaster reliefs, face east; the central tower of the front row is a great deal larger than the other towers. Preah Ko has some of the best surviving examples of plasterwork seen at Angkor and is currently under restoration by a German team. There are elaborate inscriptions in the ancient Hindu language of Sanskrit on the doorposts of each tower.

The towers of Preah Ko (Sacred Ox) feature three *nandis* (sacred oxen), all of whom look like a few steaks have been sliced off them over the years. Preah Ko was dedicated by Indravarman I to his deified ancestors in AD 880. The front towers relate to male ancestors or gods, the rear towers to female ancestors or goddesses. Lions guard the steps up to the temple.

BAKONG
បាគង

The sanctuary on the fifth level of Bakong temple was a later addition during the reign of Suryavarman II, in the style of Angkor Wat's central tower.

Bakong is the largest and most interesting of the Roluos Group temples, and has an active Buddhist monastery just to the north of the east entrance. It was built and dedicated to Shiva by Indravarman I. It's a representation of Mt Meru, and it served as the city's central temple. The east-facing complex consists of a five-tier central pyramid of sandstone, 60m square at the base, flanked by eight towers (or their remains) of brick and sandstone and by other minor sanctuaries. A number of the eight towers below the upper central tower are still partly covered by their original plasterwork.

The complex is enclosed by three concentric walls and a moat. There are well-preserved statues of stone elephants on each corner of the first three levels of the central temple. There are 12 stupas – three to a side – on the third tier.

LOLEI
លលៃ

The four brick towers of Lolei, an almost exact replica of the towers of Preah Ko (although in much worse shape) were built on an islet in the centre of a large reservoir – now rice-fields – by Yasovarman I (r 889–910), the founder of the first city at Angkor. The sandstone carvings in the niches of the temples are worth a look and there are Sanskrit inscriptions on the doorposts. According to one of the inscriptions, the four towers were dedicated by Yasovarman I to his mother, his father and his maternal grandparents on 12 July 893.

AROUND ANGKOR

PHNOM KROM
ភ្នំក្រោម

The temple of Phnom Krom, 12km south of Siem Reap on a hill overlooking Tonlé Sap Lake, dates from the reign of Yasovarman I in the late 9th or early 10th century. The name means 'Lower Hill' and is a reference to its geographic location in relation to its sister temples of Phnom Bakheng and Phnom Bok. The three towers, dedicated (from north to south) to Vishnu, Shiva and Brahma, are in a ruined state, but Phnom Krom remains one of the more tranquil spots from which to view the sunset, complete with an active wat. The fast boats from Phnom Penh dock near here, but it is not possible to see the temple from beneath the hill. If coming here by *moto* or car, try to get the driver to take you to the summit, as it is a long, hot climb otherwise.

PHNOM BOK
ភ្នំបុក

Making up the triplicate of temple-mountains built by Yasovarman I in the late 9th or early 10th century, this peaceful but remote location sees few visitors. The small temple is in reasonable shape and includes two frangipani trees growing out of a pair of ruinous towers – they look like some sort of extravagant haircut when in full flower. However, it is the views of Phnom Kulen to the north and the plains of Angkor to the south from this 212m hill that make it worth the trip. The remains of a 5m *linga* are also visible at the opposite end of the hill and it's believed there were similar *linga* at Phnom Bakheng and Phnom Krom. Unfortunately, it is not a sensible place for sunrise or sunset, as it would require a long journey in the dark to get here or get back.

There is a long, winding trail (not suitable for bikes) snaking up the hill, which takes about 20 minutes to climb, plus a new faster cement staircase, but the latter is fairly exposed. Avoid the heat of the middle of the day and carry plenty of water, which can be purchased near the base of the mountain.

Phnom Bok is about 25km from Siem Reap and is clearly visible from the road to Banteay Srei. It is accessible by continuing east on the road to Banteay Samré for another 6km. It is possible to loop back to Siem Reap via the temples of Roluos by heading south instead of west on the return journey, and gain some rewarding glimpses of the countryside.

CHAU SREI VIBOL
ចៅស្រីវិបុល

This petite hilltop temple sees few visitors, as it is difficult to access. The central sanctuary is in a ruined state, but is nicely complemented by the construction of a modern wat nearby. Surrounding the base of the hill are laterite walls, each with a small entrance hall in reasonable condition. To get here, turn east off the reasonable dirt road between Phnom Bok and Roluos at a point about 8km north of NH6, or 5km south of Phnom Bok. From this point, the trail deteriorates and crosses several small, rickety bridges, helping to explain why tour buses don't make it here. The path also crosses a small Angkorian bridge, built at the end of the 12th century, complete with *naga* balustrades. The route is easy to lose, so keep asking locals for directions at junctions and eventually you will find yourself in a monastic compound at the base of the small hill.

BANTEAY SREI
បន្ទាយស្រី

Banteay Srei is considered by many to be the jewel in the crown of Angkorian art. A Hindu temple dedicated to Shiva, it is cut from stone of a pinkish hue and includes some of the finest stone carving seen anywhere on earth. It is one of the smallest sites at Angkor, but what it lacks in size it makes up for in stature. It is wonderfully well preserved and many of its carvings are three-dimensional.

Construction on Banteay Srei began in AD 967 and it is one of the few temples around Angkor not to be commissioned by a king, but by a Brahman, who may have been a tutor to Jayavarman V. The temple is square and has entrances at the east and west, the east approached by a causeway. Of interest are the lavishly decorated libraries and the three central towers, which are decorated with male and female divinities and beautiful filigree relief work.

Classic carvings at Banteay Srei include delicate women with lotus flowers in hand and traditional skirts clearly visible, as well as breathtaking recreations of scenes from the epic *Ramayana* adorning the library pediments (carved inlays above a lintel). However, the sum of the parts is no greater than the whole – almost every inch of these interior buildings is covered in decoration. Standing watch over such perfect creations are the mythical guardians, all of which are copies of originals stored in the National Museum (p84).

Banteay Srei was the first major temple-restoration undertaken by the EFEO in 1930 using the anastylosis method. The project, as evidenced today, was a major success and soon led to other larger projects such as the restoration of the Bayon.

When Banteay Srei was first rediscovered, it was assumed to be from the 13th or 14th centuries, as the refined carving must have come at the end of the Angkor period. It was later dated to AD 967, from inscriptions found at the site. However, some scholars are once again calling for a revision of this date, given that the style of this temple and its carvings are unlike anything else seen in the 10th century. New theories suggest that like the great cathedrals of Europe, some Angkorian temples may have been destroyed and then rebuilt, or altered beyond recognition, and that the inscription stele at Banteay Srei relates to an earlier structure on the site, not the delicate flower of a temple we see today.

Banteay Srei is 21km northeast of Bayon or about 32km from Siem Reap. It is well signposted and the road is surfaced all the way – a trip from Siem Reap should take about one hour. *Moto* and *remorque* drivers will want a bit of extra cash to come out here, so agree on a sum first. It is possible to combine a visit to Banteay Srei with a trip to the River of a Thousand Lingas at Kbal Spean and Beng Mealea, or to Banteay Samré and Phnom Bok.

KBAL SPEAN
ក្បាលស្ពាន

Kbal Spean is a spectacularly carved riverbed, set deep in the jungle to the northeast of Angkor. More commonly referred to in English as the 'River of a Thousand Lingas', the name actually means 'bridgehead', a reference to the natural rock bridge at the site. *Lingas* have been elaborately carved into the riverbed, and images of Hindu deities are dotted about the area.

It is a 2km uphill walk to the carvings, along a pretty path that winds its way up into the jungle, passing by some interesting boulder formations along the way. Carry plenty of water up the hill, as there is none available beyond the parking area. The path eventually splits to the waterfall or the river carvings. There is an impressive carving of Vishnu on the upper section of the river, followed by a series of carvings at the bridgehead itself, many of which have been tragically hacked off in the past few years. This area is now roped off to protect the carvings from further damage.

Following the river down, there are several more impressive carvings of Vishnu, and Shiva with his consort Uma, and further downstream hundreds of *linga* appear on the riverbed. At the top of the waterfall, there are many animal images, including a cow and a frog, and a path winds around the boulders to a wooden staircase leading down to the base of the falls. Visitors between January and June will be disappointed to see very little water here. The best time to visit is between September and December.

Banteay Srei means 'Citadel of the Women' and it is said that it must have been built by a woman, as the elaborate carvings are too fine for the hand of a man.

In 1923 Frenchman André Malraux was arrested in Phnom Penh for attempting to steal several of Banteay Srei's major statues and pieces of sculpture. Ironically, Malraux was later appointed Minister of Culture under Charles de Gaulle.

TIP

When exploring Kbal Spean it is best to start with the river carvings and work back down to the waterfall to cool off.

> **LAND MINE ALERT!**
>
> At no point during a visit to Kbal Spean or Phnom Kulen should you leave well-trodden paths, as there may be land mines in the area.

Nearby is the **Angkor Centre for Conservation of Biodiversity** (www.accb-cambodia.org), committed to rescuing, rehabilitating and reintroducing threatened wildlife. Tours of the centre can be arranged daily at 1pm.

Kbal Spean is about 50km northeast of Siem Reap or about 18km beyond the temple of Banteay Srei. The road is sometimes good, sometimes bad, sometimes ugly, but it should be surfaced in the near future because it continues north to Anlong Veng (p258) near the Thai border.

Moto drivers will no doubt want a bit of extra money to take you here – a few extra dollars should do, or US$10 to US$15 for the day, including a trip to Banteay Srei. Likewise, *remorque* drivers will probably up the price to US$20. A surcharge is also levied to come out here by car. Admission to Kbal Spean is included in the general Angkor pass and the last entry to the site is at 3.30pm.

PHNOM KULEN
ភ្នំគូលែន

Phnom Kulen is considered by Khmers to be the most sacred mountain in Cambodia and is a popular place of pilgrimage during weekends and festivals. It played a significant role in the history of the Khmer empire, as it was from here in AD 802 that Jayavarman II proclaimed himself a *devaraja* (god-king) and announced independence from Java, giving birth to modern-day Cambodia. There is a small wat at the summit of the mountain, which houses a large **reclining Buddha** carved into the sandstone boulder upon which it is built. Nearby is a large **waterfall** and above it are smaller bathing areas and a number of carvings in the riverbed, including numerous *lingas*. The bad news is that a private businessman bulldozed a road up here back in 1999 and charges a US$20 toll per foreign visitor, an ambitious fee compared with what you get for your money at Angkor. None of the toll goes towards preserving the site.

The new road winds its way through some spectacular jungle scenery, emerging on the plateau after a 20km ascent. The road eventually splits: the left fork leads to the picnic spot, waterfalls and ruins of a 9th-century temple; the right fork continues over a bridge and some riverbed carvings to the reclining Buddha. This is the focal point of a pilgrimage here for Khmer people, so it is important to take off your shoes and any head covering before climbing the stairs to the sanctuary. The views from the 487m peak are tremendous, as you can see right across the forested plateau.

The waterfall is an attractive spot, but could be much more beautiful were it not for all the litter left here by families picnicking at the weekend. Near the top of the waterfall is a jungle-clad temple known as **Prasat Krau Romeas**, dating from the 9th century.

There are plenty of other Angkorian sites on Phnom Kulen, including as many as 20 minor temples around the plateau, the most important of which is **Prasat Rong Chen**, the first pyramid or temple-mountain to be constructed in the Angkor area. Most impressive of all are the giant stone animals or guardians of the mountain, known as **Sra Damrei** (Elephant Pond). These are very difficult to get to, with the route passing through mined sections of the mountain (stick to the path!) and the trail impossible in the wet season. The few people who make it, however, are rewarded with a life-size replica of a stone elephant – a full 4m long and 3m tall – and smaller statues of lions, a

Kbal Spean was 'discovered' in 1969, when EFEO ethnologist Jean Boulbet was shown the area by an *essai;* the area was soon off-limits due to the civil war, only becoming safe again in 1998.

TIP

It is possible to buy a cheaper entrance ticket to Phnom Kulen for US$12 from the City Angkor Hotel in Siem Reap.

frog and a cow. These were constructed on the southern face of the mountain and from here there are spectacular views across the plains below. Getting here requires taking a *moto* from Wat Preah Ang Thom for about 12km on very rough trails through thick forest before arriving at a sheer rock face. From here it is a 1km walk to the animals through the forest. Don't try to find it on your own; expect to pay the *moto* driver about US$6 (with some hard negotiating) and carry plenty of water, as none is available.

Before the construction of the private road up Phnom Kulen, visitors had to scale the mountain and then walk across the top of the plateau to the reclining Buddha. This route takes more than two hours and is still an option. About 15km east of the new road, the trail winds its way to a small pagoda called Wat Chou, set into the cliff face from which a *tuk chou* (spring) emerges. The water is considered holy and Khmers like to bottle it to take home with them. This water source eventually flows into Tonlé Sap Lake and is thought to bless the waterways of Cambodia.

Phnom Kulen is a huge plateau around 50km from Siem Reap and about 15km from Banteay Srei. To get here on the new toll road, take the well-signposted right fork just before Banteay Srei village and go straight ahead at the crossroads. Just before the road starts to climb the mountain, there is a barrier and it is here that the US$20 charge is levied. It is only possible to go up before 11am and only possible to come down after midday, to avoid vehicles meeting on the narrow road.

To walk to the site, head east along the base of the mountain from the major crossroads. After about 15km, there is a wat-style gate on the left and a sandy trail. Follow this to a small community from where the climb begins. It is about a 2km climb and then an hour or more in a westerly direction along the top of the plateau. This route of the pilgrims of old should cost nothing if you arrive after midday, although it takes considerably longer.

Moto drivers are likely to want about US$15 or more to bring you out here, and rented cars will hit passengers with a surcharge, more than double the going rate for Angkor; forget coming by *remorque* as the hill climb is just too tough.

BENG MEALEA
បឹងមាលា

The filming of *Two Brothers* (2004) included some locations in Beng Mealea and the production worked with 20 tigers of all ages for continuity throughout the story.

Beng Mealea is a spectacular sight to behold. It's one of the most mysterious temples at Angkor, as nature has well and truly run riot. Built to the same floorplan as Angkor Wat, exploring this titanic of temples is Angkor's ultimate Indiana Jones experience. Built in the 12th century under Suryavarman II (r 1112–52), Beng Mealea is enclosed by a massive moat measuring 1.2km by 900m, much of which has dried up today.

The temple used to be utterly subsumed by jungle, but some of the dense foliage has been cut back in recent years. Entering from the south, visitors wend their way over piles of masonry, through long dark chambers and between hanging vines to arrive at the central tower, which has completely collapsed. Hidden away among the rubble and foliage are several impressive carvings, as well as a well-preserved library in the northeastern quadrant. The temple is a special place and it is worth taking the time to explore it thoroughly. There is also a large wooden walkway to the centre, originally constructed for the filming of Jean-Jacques Annaud's *Two Brothers* (2004).

Beng Mealea is at the centre of an ancient Angkorian road connecting Angkor Thom and Preah Khan in Preah Vihear Province. A small Angkorian bridge just west of Chau Srei Vibol temple is the only remaining trace of the old Angkorian road between Beng Mealea and Angkor Thom; between Beng Mealea and Preah Khan there are at least 10 bridges abandoned in the forest.

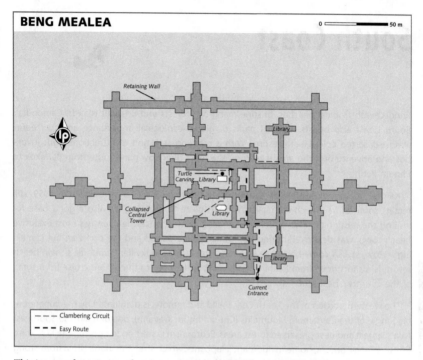

BENG MEALEA

Retaining Wall

Library

Turtle Carving *Library*

Collapsed Central Tower *Library*

Library

Current Entrance

– – – Clambering Circuit

– – – Easy Route

This is a way for extreme adventurers to get to Preah Khan temple (p262); however, don't undertake this journey lightly.

It now costs US$5 to visit Beng Mealea and there are additional small charges for cars and motorcycles – make sure you work out in advance who is paying this. It is best to undertake a long day trip combining Beng Mealea, Kbal Spean and Banteay Srei.

Beng Mealea is about 40km east of Bayon (as the crow flies) and 6.5km southeast of Phnom Kulen. By road it is about 70km from Siem Reap and is a 1½ hour trip.

The shortest route is via the small town of Dam Dek, located on NH6 towards Phnom Penh. Turn north immediately after the market and continue on this road for about 35km. The entrance to the temple lies just beyond the left-hand turn to Koh Ker.

For the second, longer route, take the road towards Banteay Srei and follow the right fork to Phnom Kulen, continuing right at the major crossroads along the base of the holy mountain. Follow this route for about 25km until you leave Kulen behind and come to a T-junction where you turn left on to the tarmac for the final 10km to Beng Mealea. This is another private road and partly privatised temple, where profit takes precedence over preservation. It usually costs US$2.50 for a car, US$1 for a motorbike, but that is each way, believe it or not!

Take a virtual photographic tour of the remote temples of Cambodia before you leave home to work out which places you want to visit: http://angkor .main.jp.

REMOTE ANGKORIAN SITES

Information on the following remote Angkorian sites is found in the Northwestern Cambodia chapter: Banteay Chhmar (p255), Koh Ker (p264), Preah Khan (p262) and Prasat Preah Vihear (p268).

South Coast

Fringed with tropical beaches, pristine mangrove forests and unspoilt islands, Cambodia's South Coast also boasts national parks of global ecological importance and two eerie, almost-deserted colonial-era resorts. With a cracking selection of attractions both luxurious and adventurous, the area is now on the most direct overland route from Bangkok to Phnom Penh.

Kampot, Cambodia's principal seaport until the founding of Sihanoukville in 1959, still retains some of its French-era charm. A great place to chill out, it's also a good base for visiting the misty highlands of Bokor National Park. Kep, once the country's most exclusive beach town, was destroyed during the Khmer Rouge period and the civil war, but is making a slow, stylish come-back. The booming city of Sihanoukville, Cambodia's main beach resort, is a short drive from Ream National Park and a one- to three-hour cruise from some of the country's best scuba diving.

The western portion of the South Coast, wild and remote, is dominated by the impenetrable jungle of the Cardamom Mountains (Chuor Phnom Kravanh), one of mainland Southeast Asia's largest and best-preserved forest areas. Ecotourism is starting to open up the Koh Kong Conservation Corridor, home to tigers and elephants, which stretches along NH48 from Krong Koh Kong, near the Thai frontier, to the Gulf of Kompong Som, north of Sihanoukville.

Near the Vietnamese border are some fabulous cave-temples and the Angkor Borei region, 5th-century birthplace of ancient Cambodian civilisation.

HIGHLIGHTS

- Explore the uninhabited islands, isolated beaches, pristine rainforests, mangrove-lined rivers and remote waterfalls of the **Koh Kong Conservation Corridor** (p186), which is just opening up to ecotourism

- Soak up the sun in **Sihanoukville** (p193), home to blissful beaches, tropical islands, scuba diving and a lively nightshift

- Journey up to cool, mist-enveloped **Bokor National Park** (p219), with its abandoned casino and breathtaking coastal views

- Kick back in quiet **Kampot** (p215), a pretty river town with some of Cambodia's best-preserved French architecture

- Explore remote islands and dine on fresh seafood around **Kep** (p224), the mid-century mecca of Cambodia's jet set

■ ELEVATION: 0-1800M   ■ POPULATION: 2.6 MILLION   ■ AREA: 27,817 SQ KM

SOUTH COAST

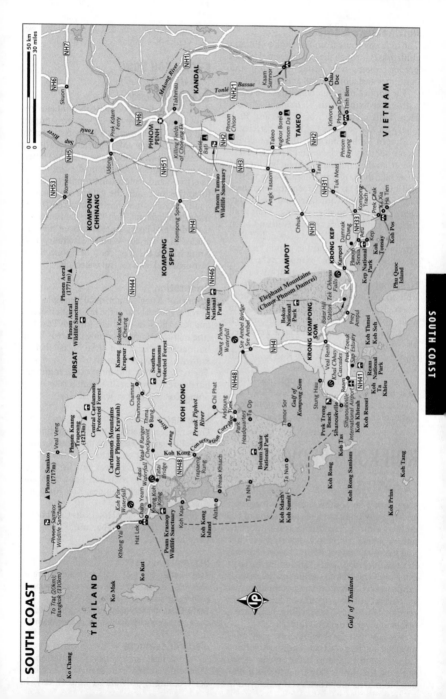

Getting There & Around

The highway route from Bangkok to Phnom Penh passes through the Cham Yeam–Hat Lek border crossing near Krong Koh Kong and continues east along NH48 and then NH4.

The South Coast region now has two international crossings with Vietnam, at Phnom Den–Tinh Bien, south of Takeo; and Prek Chak–Xa Xia, southeast of Kep at Ha Tien.

Phnom Penh is linked with Sihanoukville by NH4; buses are cheap and frequent. NH3 goes from the capital to Kampot, but for now buses take the long way around via Kep (NH3 and then NH31). NH2, recently upgraded, links Phnom Penh with Takeo and the Phnom Den–Tinh Bien border crossing. Almost all the area's other roads are unpaved and often become degraded in the wet season. In Takeo Province, boats are almost as popular a form of wet-season transport as motor vehicles.

Until 2003, when the Thai army carved NH48 out of the jungle, it was nearly impossible to get from Krong Koh Kong to anywhere else in Cambodia by land. The area will undergo a second transport revolution when NH48's four slow ferry crossings are replaced by bridges sometime in 2008. For now, at least, a daily ferry links Krong Koh Kong with Koh Sdach and Sihanoukville.

Sights in this chapter are organised from west to east, perfect if you're coming from Thailand. If you're starting in Phnom Penh just read the listings in reverse order.

KOH KONG PROVINCE
ខេត្តកោះកុង

Cambodia's far southwestern province, vast and sparsely populated, shelters some of the country's most remarkable and important natural sites. Incredible deserted beaches line the west coast of Botum Sakor National Park and nearby islands – including the largest, Koh Kong Island – while inland are lush rainforests with ecotourism potential as vast as their mountains, streams and hamlets are remote. Diving and snorkelling, too, have a bright and very colourful future.

The best base for exploring the province's untamed jungle, spread out along the Koh Kong Conservation Corridor, is the riverine town of Krong Koh Kong, 8km from the Thai border. From here, motorboats can whisk you to rushing waterfalls, secluded islands, sandy coves and Venice-like fishers' villages on stilts.

KRONG KOH KONG
ក្រុងកោះកុង

☎ 035 / pop 29,500

Once Cambodia's Wild West, its frontier economy dominated by smuggling, prostitution and gambling, Krong Koh Kong has recently taken big steps towards respectability. The city centre is still scruffy but new midrange hotels are going up, especially along the landscaped riverfront, and ecotourism promises to transform the town into the gateway to some of Southeast Asia's most breathtaking coastal and mountain habitats. Koh Kong Conservation Corridor highlights accessible from here include Peam Krasaop Wildlife Sanctuary, Koh Kong Island, the west coast of Botum Sakor National Park and several waterfalls.

Orientation

Krong Koh Kong's commercial heart is located near the roundabout at the intersection of St 3 and St 8, and south of there, towards Psar Leu (the market). A big shopping centre is being built at the intersection of St 5 – as NH48 is known as it passes through town – and St 3. The ferry landing and most of the midrange hotels are on or near St 1, which runs along Stung Koh Poi, a 2km-wide estuary.

Information

Guesthouses, hotels and pubs – including the Oasis Bungalow Resort and the Sauna Garden Bar – are the best places to get the local lowdown. You can also check out Koh Kong's unofficial website, www.koh-kong.com, and two free rival pocket guides, *Koh Kong* and *Koh Kong Guide*.

The Koh Kong City Hotel sells Cambodian SIM cards (US$12). Thai mobile phones work here.

INTERNET ACCESS

Asean Hotel (☎ 936667; St 1) Internet access (per hour 60B to US$2) is available here, as well as next to Rasmey Buntam Guesthouse and along St 2 near Psar Leu.

Sokha Computer Technologies (St 2; ☼ 6am-10pm) One of a number of mom-and-pop internet places along St 2.

MEDICAL SERVICES

In a medical emergency, evacuation to Thailand via the Cham Yeam–Hat Lek border crossing is possible 24 hours a day. In

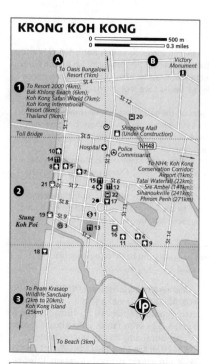

KRONG KOH KONG

Thailand there's a hospital in Trat, 92km from the border.

Pharmacie Koh Kong (St 3) A reliable pharmacy.

Visal Sok Clinic (☎ 011 988586; St 3; ⏰ 6am-9pm) The clinic of choice for NGO staff with minor medical problems. There's no English sign but staff speak English and French.

MONEY

Thai baht are widely used so there's no need to buy riels. *Moto* drivers who offer to help you change money are probably setting you up for a rip-off. There are exchange shops around the southeast corner of Psar Leu.

The nearest ATMs are at the Cham Yeam–Hat Lek border crossing, a few metres inside Thailand. They can be accessed without visa formalities – just mosey on over to the Thai immigration counter, explain that you need an ATM and leave them your passport.

Acleda Bank (St 9) Handles Western Union transfers and may get an ATM in 2008. Will soon move to new quarters a few blocks north.

Sights & Activities

The best nearby **beach** is on the eastern (ie city centre) side of Stung Koh Poi about 4km south of the bridge at the tip of the peninsula. You can get there along the river on foot or by *moto*; by car you have to loop around to the east.

Across the estuary from town and about 2km south of the bridge, **Resort 2000** has a grassy beach area and eating options that are popular with Khmers. Further south, **Bak Khlong Beach** has cheap fish and seafood.

The **pool** at the **Oasis Bungalow Resort** (☎ 092-228342, 016 331556) is open to nonguests for US$2 a day. The Oasis also has details on Krong Koh Kong's first **dive school** (it's planning to offer PADI courses, reef dives and jungle river dives), **canoe rental** options and three-hour **boat trips** (1600B) to observe endangered **Irrawaddy dolphins**.

For information on natural sites around Krong Koh Kong, see Koh Kong Conservation Corridor (p186).

Sleeping

Most of the city's accommodation options are near the ferry landing, though some of the cheapies are a long block or two southeast of the roundabout on St 3. Many places pay *moto* drivers a commission, leading to a whole lot of Sihanoukville-type shenanigans (see p213).

SOUTH COAST

SOUTH COAST

THE TREPID TIGER TRAINER *Daniel Robinson*

I'd heard that animal welfare may not be the primary consideration at **Koh Kong Safari World** (☎ 016 800811; admission for foreigners US$12, for kids 90cm to 140cm US$8; ☺ 8am-5pm), run by Koh Kong International Resort (the casino-hotel a few kilometres away at the border), but the Disneyesque gateway – in a style that Bavaria's mad King Ludwig II would have found irresistible – didn't hint at anything sinister.

The park has the usual zoo animals but it also puts on the sort of live-animal shows banned in most countries, with performances reminiscent of a 19th-century circus sideshow. Every morning, and into the early afternoon, birds ride tiny bicycles, orang-utans dressed up as boxers throw punches and a man puts his head inside a crocodile's mouth.

While wandering around I ran into a slight, soft-spoken Khmer fellow who looked a bit lost – a park employee, as it turned out. 'I see there's a sea lion show', I said, pointing to a notice board. 'No', he replied, not any more, 'sea lion dead'. Not a good sign.

'What's your job here?' I continued, guessing that he worked in ticket sales. 'I the tiger trainer', he replied. Intrigued – I'd never met a tiger trainer before – I enquired if Safari World would soon be adding tiger shows to its animalian repertoire. 'No', he shook his head sadly, 'I not work; I afraid'.

The woman who lies on top of the crocodile – another Safari World hit – is probably similarly untrained and terrified but I'm guessing she needs her salary too badly to go on strike.

Neptune Guesthouse (☎ 011 984512; r 100B) The cheapest place in town, the Neptune has nine very basic rooms with plank beds, mosquito nets, bare neon lights and sinkless bathrooms.

Blue Moon Guesthouse (☎ 016 575741; r US$4-10; ☒) Run by a friendly former park ranger, this modest place has nine medium-sized rooms with spring mattresses and compact bathrooms. Air-con rooms come with hot water.

KRONG KOH KONG – KICKBOXING POWERHOUSE

Traditional Khmer kickboxing – similar to Thailand's Muay Thai, which Khmers insist is in fact Cambodian – is especially popular in Krong Koh Kong, and many of the country's top boxers, including the national champion, Eh Phouthong, hail from here.

Matches (40B) are sometimes held in Krong Koh Kong on Saturday nights, especially in the dry season. The hugely enthusiastic crowds include quite a few women and the provincial governor who, it is said, never misses a match. Locals are joined by Thai punters from across the border.

For details on times, ask someone to translate what's being said when you see an old pick-up driving around town with its loudspeakers blaring.

Rasmey Buntam Guesthouse (☎ 016 207771; r 150-400B; ☒ ▣) A decent 14-room place with so many colourful tiles you'll think you're in Tunisia. The same family runs a bus company (Virak-Buntham) and an internet café.

Phou Mint Koh Kong Hotel (☎ 936221; St 1; r US$5-15; ☒) In a great riverside location, this hostelry – painted light blue – has 20 spacious rooms, including the best-value fan rooms in town. The US$15 rooms have both hot water and a fridge; otherwise a fridge costs US$1 extra.

Bopha Koh Kong Hotel (☎ 936073; http://bpkhotel .netkhmer.com; St 6; r with fan/air-con from 200B/300B; ☒) Once the top dog in town, the 40 rooms here are impersonal but comfortable and come with TV and fridge. VIP rooms have two huge beds and an all-wood living-room corner.

Asean Hotel (☎ 936667; http://aseanhotel.netkhmer .com; St 1; r US$10-20; ☒ ▣) The new hotel across the street blocks river views but the rooms here are spacious and comfortable, with proper bathrooms and endearingly tacky wall lamps. Pricier rooms have hot water.

Koh Kong City Hotel (☎ 936777; St 1; http://kkcthotel .netkhmer.com; d US$15-20; ☒ ▣) Opened in late 2006, this welcoming, professionally run place – right on the water – has 56 rooms with snazzy tub-equipped bathrooms, cable TV, hot water and fridges. Good value for money. Guests get 15 minutes of free internet.

our pick Oasis Bungalow Resort (☎ 092 228342; 016 331556; http://oasisresort.netkhmer.com; tr US$20;

$\boxed{?}$ $\boxed{P}$) In a quiet rural area 1.5km north of the city centre, this delightful oasis of calm, run sustainably, has five cheerful, spacious bungalows with all the amenities. To get there from the corner of St 3 and St 4, follow the blue signs north for 1.2km. Call ahead and they'll arrange transport from town or the border.

Koh Kong International Resort Club (☎ 016 700790, Thai number +66-39588173; www.kohkonginter.com; r 1600B-2500B, ste 7000B-35,000B; $\boxed{?}$ $\boxed{?}$) Cambodia's borders are littered with casinos that cater to Thai gamblers (gambling is banned in Thailand) and this monster resort, next to the Cham Yeam–Hat Lek crossing, is one of the biggest. It's got a whopping 509 rooms and, next door, an imposing new casino – neoclassical with baroque touches – that looks like it was flown in from Baden-Baden. Accommodation and food are free if you play 20,000B a day. An 18-hole golf course is planned.

Eating & Drinking

Thai food is more common here than in most parts of Cambodia. There are cheap **food stalls** around the perimeter of Psar Leu – have a look along St 2 and north of the market along St 3.

Hotels with well-regarded restaurants include the Asean Hotel and the Bopha Koh Kong Hotel.

Baan Peakmai (☎ 393906; St 6; mains 60-150B; ☽ 7am-10pm) A relaxing Thai-style garden restaurant that's a real hit with Thai expats. The monster menu includes several dozen vegetarian choices and a fair spread of seafood.

Sauna Garden Bar (☎ 015 601633, Thai number +66-78082286; codgerbojer@yahoo.com; St 3) Both a relaxing sauna and a garden restaurant with good Khmer, Thai and Western food, this place is something of an expat hang-out and is also a good source of local information.

Riverfront Restaurant (☎ 011 943497; St 1; mains 100B-200B; ☽ 7am-9pm) Across St 1 from the Asean Hotel, this Thai and Khmer place specialises in reasonably priced seafood and soups (150B), including delicious tom yam. Four breezy pavilions out over the water afford truly romantic sunset views.

Moto Bar (☎ 936220; St 3; mains 80B-200B) More geared-up for the Pattaya expat on a visa run than for the average backpacker.

Bob's Bar (☎ 016 326455; mains 100B-150B; ☽ 9am-9pm or later) Breakfast is available all day long at this cheery, Aussie-run restaurant-bar.

Serves Western dishes and the best espresso in town.

Sunset Bar (☎ 016 326455; St 1; ☽ 8am-8pm or 9pm or later) Right on the waterfront nestled in a row of fishers' houses, this mellow bar – an ideal spot to watch the sun go down – is the best place in town for a laid-back beer. It's hidden down an alleyway – look for the 'Bar' sign.

Getting There & Away

When NH48 finally gets its four new bridges, ending the frustrating traffic jams at the ferries, travel times will plummet and transport options to Sihanoukville (220km) and Phnom Penh (290km) are likely to mushroom.

Krong Koh Kong is linked to the Thai border by a dual carriageway of sorts – not only does it lack lines, lanes, signs, reflectors and verges/shoulders, but some locals drive as if it were two parallel two-lane highways! The 1.9km bridge over Stung Koh Poi, built and run by the Thais, costs 4800r/44B each way for a car and 1200r/11B for a motorbike; bicycles and pedestrians cross for free.

Flights from Bangkok to Krong Koh Kong are planned.

BOAT

Passenger ferries link Krong Koh Kong with Sihanoukville's ferry port (4½ hours) at 8am; departures from Sihanoukville are at 9.30am. Khmers pay 50,000r or 500B, foreigners are charged US$20. The route is handled by two vessels, the **Royal** (☎ 016 851934) and the **Khemara** (Kamra; ☎ 016 852223). Immigration police check passports before boarding. Tickets in both directions can be booked through guesthouses and hotels. When you arrive in Krong Koh Kong, be prepared for a rugby scrum of *moto* drivers hoping to take you to the border.

A word of warning: the sea can be dangerously rough and these boats were designed for river travel, not sailing the open seas.

It's not clear if this service will survive the easy land transport that will be possible once the NH48 bridges are opened.

BUS & TAXI

Rith Mony (☎ 015 404085; St 3) and **Virak-Buntham** (☎ 016 2077771; St 9) run buses (you have to change vehicles at each crossing) and faster minibuses to Sihanoukville (300B, five hours by minibus) and Phnom Penh (300B, seven hours by minibus). Capital Transport is planning to add a service to Krong Koh Kong. Guesthouses and hotels sell tickets.

On the northeast edge of town, Krong Koh Kong's **bus and taxi station** (St 12) has an unpaved parking lot and a tin-roofed waiting area. Buses tend to stop in town, so the only reason to come out here is to find share taxis – most numerous in the morning – to Andoung Tuek (300B), Sihanoukville (400B) and Phnom Penh (400B). Prices will surely drop as the bridges come on line. Share taxis can also be found around the northwest corner of Psar Leu.

To the Thai border, a private taxi costs 200B to 250B (plus the 44B bridge toll) while a *moto* costs 70B (plus the 11B toll). A *moto* from the border is cheaper – just 50B (plus the toll).

Getting Around

As we go to press, boats for excursions to destinations such as Peam Krasaop Wildlife Sanctuary, Koh Kong Island and Tatai Waterfall can be hired near the intersection of St 1 and St 9, but at some point the dock is slated to move across the river.

Motos are the most popular form of local transport; short hops in town cost 1000r/10B.

The Sauna Garden Bar and the Neptune Guesthouse rent 250cc dirt bikes (500B); the former also hires out jeeps (2000B).

The Oasis Bungalow Resort and Virak-Buntham bus company can arrange nine-person minibuses for local touring or travel around the country.

KOH KONG CONSERVATION CORRIDOR

The fabled Cardamom Mountains, an area of breathtaking beauty and astonishing biodiversity, cover 20,000 sq km of southwestern Cambodia. Their remote peaks – up to 1800m high – and river valleys are home to at least 59 globally threatened animal species, including tigers, Asian elephants, bears, Siamese crocodiles (p190), pangolins (p189) and eight species of tortoises and turtles. Botanically the area is something of a cipher because basic research has yet to be carried out, but so far more than 100 species of endemic plants have been identified.

The second-largest virgin rainforest on mainland Southeast Asia, the Cardamoms are one of only two sites in the region where unbroken forests still connect mountain summits with the sea (the other is in Burma). Some highland areas receive up to

5m of rain a year. Conservationists hope the Cardamoms will soon be declared a Unesco World Heritage Site.

While forests and coastlines elsewhere in Southeast Asia were being ravaged by greedy developers and well-connected logging companies, the Cardamom Mountains and the adjacent mangrove forests – the most extensive on mainland Southeast Asia – were protected from the worst ecological outrages by their sheer remoteness and, at least in part, by Cambodia's long civil war. As a result, much of the area is still in pretty good shape, ecologically speaking, so the potential for ecotourism is huge – akin, some say, to that of Kenya's game reserves.

The Koh Kong Conservation Corridor stretches along both sides of NH48 from Krong Koh Kong to the Gulf of Kompong Som (the bay north of Sihanoukville). It encompasses many of Cambodia's most outstanding natural sites, including the mangrove forests of Peam Krasaop Wildlife Sanctuary, the pristine beaches of Koh Kong Island, Botum Sakor National Park and two huge, noncontiguous protected areas: the Southern Cardamoms Protected Forest, whose southern boundary is NH48, and the Central Cardamoms Protected Forest further north.

The next few years will be critical in determining the future of the Cardamom Mountains. NGOs such as **Conservation International** (CI; www.conservation.org), **Fauna & Flora International** (FFI; www.fauna-flora.org) and the **Wildlife Alliance** (formerly WildAid; www.wildlifealliance .org) are working night and day to help protect the area's 16 distinct ecosystems from loggers and poachers. But ecotourism, too, can play a role in generating income for local people and spurring sustainable development.

For information on the northern side of the Cardamom Mountains, accessible from Pursat and Pailin, see p238 and p252 respectively.

Tours

The Rainbow Lodge (opposite), 20km east of Krong Koh Kong on the Tatai River, arranges guided jungle treks and boat trips.

In Krong Koh Kong, a number of establishments organise land and sea tours in the Koh Kong Conservation Corridor and can go via Peam Krasaop Wildlife Sanctuary:

Blue Moon Guesthouse (☎ 016 575741) Run by a former park ranger, this outfit offers boat trips to Koh Kong Island, island overnights and land excursions to nature sites.

Neptune Guesthouse (☎ 016 575741) Has a 20-person boat and runs dry-season excursions to Koh Kong Island and up the river.

Oasis Bungalow Resort (☎ 092 228342, 016 331556; http://oasisresort.netkhmer.com) Organises boat trips to Koh Kong Island, Koh Por Waterfall and other destinations. Oasis Bungalow is also an excellent source of up-to-date information.

Sauna Garden Bar (☎ 015 601633, Thai number +66-78082286; codgerbojer@yahoo.com; St 3) Can arrange day trips into the jungle and, for those willing to rough it, two- and three-day camping expeditions into the Cardamom Mountains.

Sunset Lounge Tours (☎ 016 548977) Rents boats 'for island and dolphin tours'.

Ecologically and socially responsible travel companies planning adventure tours in the Central Cardamoms Protected Forest in partnership with Conservation International:

Intrepid Travel (www.intrepidindochina.com)
Peregrine (www.peregrineadventures.com)

Getting There & Around

All buses, minibuses and share taxis travelling between Krong Koh Kong and points east, including Phnom Penh and Sihanoukville, take NH48. Thanks to the efforts of environmental groups, including the Wildlife Alliance, agricultural development and land speculation along NH48 – a common sight, hundreds of metres deep, along new roads everywhere else in the country – have been strictly forbidden.

For details on transport options, see Getting There & Away under each listing.

A very rough road goes north through the wild Cardamoms to Pailin and Battambang, passing by remote mountain towns such as Veal Veng, O Som (where there's a ranger station) and Promoui (the main town in the Phnom Samkos Wildlife Sanctuary – see p239). It should be attempted only in the dry season by dirt bikers with oodles of off-road experience. Near Krong Koh Kong, the turn-off is on the old road to Phnom Penh past the airport, a few hundred metres beyond the army base. There's no public transport.

Motorcycles are loud, scaring birds and animals and making it impossible for the rider to hear their calls. By contrast, mountain bikes, which can go anywhere motorcycles can and some places they can't, are silent, letting you hear and feel the forest as you ride. Bike tours of the Cardamoms, and local bike-rental

options, are sure to sprout up over the next few years, including in Chi Phat.

Koh Por Waterfall

Upriver from Krong Koh Kong, these rapids pour over a stone shelf in a lovely jungle gorge. It's great to clamber around here in the dry season, as there are immense boulders to use as stepping stones.

A speedboat from Krong Koh Kong (one hour) costs about 1600B. By long-tail boat the trip takes three hours each way and costs 1200B. See left.

Tatai River & Waterfall

When driving east from Krong Koh Kong along NH48, the first bridge you come to – after about 20km – spans the Tatai River (Stung Tatai).

Set in a lushly forested gorge a bit upstream from the bridge, **Tatai Waterfall** is a thundering set of rapids in the wet season, plunging over a 4m rock shelf. In the dry season, when water levels drop, you can walk across much of the ledge and take a dip in the gently-flowing river. The water is fairly pure, as it comes down from the high Cardamoms where there are very few human settlements.

To get to the falls from Krong Koh Kong, you can either take a *moto* (the turn-off from NH48 is a couple of kilometres west of the Tatai River bridge) or a gorgeous motorboat ride via Peam Krasaop Wildlife Sanctuary (US$60, one hour). Boats can also be hired at the Rainbow Lodge.

The tranquil **Rainbow Lodge** (☎ 017 602585; http://greenescape.netkhmer.com; s/d US$30/40), a new eco-lodge on the Tatai River, has seven bungalows with fans and mosquito nets. Built using local labour and materials, its electricity is generated by solar panels and the wash-water arrived as rain. Whenever possible, waste is recycled and ingredients for meals (room rates include three a day) are purchased from local farmers. The lodge is a 10-minute boat ride from the Tatai River bridge – call ahead to arrange to be picked up.

Peam Krasaop Wildlife Sanctuary

Home to millions of magnificent mangroves, the sanctuary's numerous alluvial islands (some no larger than a house) are separated by a maze of bays and channels. Anchored by multiple roots in the briny sea, the trees, with their foliage just above the high-water mark,

SOUTH COAST

dissipate wave energy and protect the coast from erosion, especially during storms.

The mangroves also serve as a vital breeding and feeding ground for fish, shrimp and shellfish and are home to birds such as the broad-billed sandpiper and Nordman's greenshank. The area is all the more valuable from an ecological standpoint because similar forests in Thailand have been trashed by short-sighted development.

The sanctuary, which covers 260 sq km, is largely uninhabited, though you may come upon a few **fishing hamlets**, whose residents use spindly traps to catch fish, which are then kept alive till market time in partly submerged nets attached to floating wooden frames. Further out, on some of the more remote mangrove islands, you pass utterly isolated little **beaches** where you can land and lounge.

The main gateway to Peam Krasaop is the settlement of Boeng Kayak, where the local community has built a 1km-long **mangrove walk** that consists of a series of elevated walkways, picnic platforms, a suspension bridge and a 15m-high observation tower offering brilliant panoramic views. The best time to come is early in the morning. In Boeng Kayak you can also hire boats for **bird watching**, **fishing** and – an hour or two after sunset – **firefly watching**.

On the sanctuary's west coast, along both banks of a channel, is the Venice-like village of **Koh Kapi**. Each of the fishers' houses – held aloft by stilts – has a blue or green wooden boat docked outside. Ask around to find a local family willing to prepare a fresh fish or seafood meal.

Endangered **Irrawaddy dolphins** can sometimes be seen early in the morning (6.30am or 7am) around the entrance to the Stung Koh Poi estuary, and occasionally the gentle marine mammals even swim upriver to Krong Koh Kong.

Much of Peam Krasaop is on the prestigious **Ramsar List of Wetlands of International Importance** (www.ramsar.org).

GETTING THERE & AWAY

The best way to see Peam Krasaop is by boat from Krong Koh Kong, perhaps on the way to Tatai Waterfall or Koh Kong Island.

Because 40-horsepower outboard motors really slurp up the petrol, the cost of boat travel is largely a function of how far you go. An open motorboat costs US$65 to US$75 for a day trip to Koh Kong Island (right) and

back, including a meander through Peam Krasaop; more if you'd like to circumnavigate the island and stop at one of the mainland beaches near Preak Khsach, on the coast of Botum Sakor National Park.

It's best to set out early in the morning as the sea, often smooth as glass at 7am, tends to get choppy in the afternoon. Bring sunscreen, a hat and plenty of bottled water (for some unknown reason, one local brand is called Porn Marina). Make sure your vessel has life vests on board – and don't count on being able to summon rescuers with your mobile (cell) phone, as many offshore areas, including Koh Kong Island's west coast, lack coverage.

Koh Kong Island

Cambodia's largest island, about 25km south of Krong Koh Kong, towers over seas so crystal clear you can make out individual grains of sand in a couple of metres of water. Its **seven pristine beaches**, all of them along the western coast, get so few visitors that sand crabs scamper obliviously up and down the beach and the shoreline is dotted with colourful shells of the sort you usually see only in souvenir shops.

There's a police post near the 20km-long island's northern end, above the second beach you come to, so skippers may be reluctant to stop nearby – or even stick around the area too long. It's forbidden to explore the thickly forested interior. The island is not part of any national park or wildlife sanctuary and thus has few protections against rampant development.

Several of the beaches – lined with coconut palms and lush vegetation, just as you'd expect in a tropical paradise – are at the mouths of little streams. At the **sixth beach** from the north, a narrow channel leads to a genuine *Gilligan's Island*–style lagoon.

On Koh Kong Island's eastern side, half-a-dozen forested hills – the highest towers 407m above the sea – drop steeply to the mangrove-lined coast. The fishing village of **Alatan**, the island's only settlement (for now), is on the southeast coast facing the northwest corner of Botum Sakor National Park.

For details on getting to Koh Kong Island by boat (the northern tip is about one hour from Krong Koh Kong if you sail direct), see Peam Krasaop Wildlife Sanctuary (p186) and details on Koh Kong Conservation Corridor tours (p186).

SOUTH COAST

> **'THAT PLACE WAS PARADISE UNTIL LONELY PLANET MENTIONED IT'**
>
> If Koh Kong Island is truly such an untouched paradise, why is Lonely Planet recklessly exposing its heretofore hidden charms? Won't publicity hasten the island's ruin?
>
> Cambodia and its people desperately need economic growth, so it's inevitable that natural resources such as Koh Kong Island – hardly a secret either to locals or to Phnom Penh investors – will be developed. The question is, how? Will developers be allowed to construct massive resorts for package tourists interested only in sun, sand and creature comforts, chopping down trees and destroying the island's delicate ecosystem in the process? Or will local residents and the people in charge – in the provincial and national governments – realise that, in the long term, sustainable development that preserves the island's rare natural beauty is the way to go?
>
> Each time you visit an ecotourism site, marvelling at its flora and fauna and unspoilt habitats, you're casting a vote for sustainable development, backed up by cash in local pockets.

Southern Cardamoms Protected Forest

In an effort to protect the southern Cardamom Mountains (from poaching, logging and encroachment) by turning the forest into a source of jobs and income for local people, the **Wildlife Alliance** (www.wildlifealliance.org) is launching a project to transform the Southern Cardamoms Protected Forest (1443 sq km), whose southern boundary is NH48 between Krong Koh Kong to Andoung Tuek, into a world-class ecotourism destination.

Over the next few years, the Wildlife Alliance – with Dutch government funding – plans to:

- establish two visitors centres – built of natural materials (except wood!) – with displays on the Cardamoms' geography, flora and fauna. They will be situated on the Tatai River and at Andoung Tuek.
- build two ecotourism lodges, a 'forest retreat' near the Tatai River and a 'spa retreat centre' near Chi Phat.
- assist locals in organising boat tours along the area's many rivers.
- help establish community-based homestays and guesthouses in villages such as Andoung Tuek and Trapaeng Rung and along the Tatai River.
- provide microloans so local people can set up small businesses hiring out mountain bikes and kayaks.
- expand ecotourism facilities in the Chi Phat area (see p191).

Central Cardamoms Protected Forest

The Central Cardamoms Protected Forest (CCPF; 4013 sq km) encompasses three of Southeast Asia's most threatened ecosystems: lowland evergreen forests, riparian forests and wetlands.

The rangers and military policemen who protect this vast area from illegal hunting and logging, with the help of Conservation International, are based in seven strategically sited ranger stations, including one in **Thma Bang**, where they run a **guesthouse** (☎ to coordinate a visit 012 256777; ccp.kimsan@everyday.com.kh; per person US$8). Opened in 2008, its four double rooms have outside bathrooms and electricity from 6pm to 9pm (there are plans to install solar panels). Meals are US$2. Bring warm clothes as temperatures can drop as low as 10°C. Thma Bang lacks mobile phone coverage but the station has radio contact with the **Veal II ranger checkpoint** (☎ 092 269440).

Thma Bang District has the lowest population density (1.35 people per sq km) and the highest levels of poverty in Koh Kong Province. Mostly covered with dense rainforest, it is perfect for bird-watching or hiking – perhaps to a waterfall – with a local guide

> **END OF THE LINE FOR THE PANGOLIN?**
>
> In China and Vietnam, the meat of the Malayan (Sunda) pangolin – a kind of nocturnal anteater whose only food is ants and termites – is considered a delicacy, and the creature's blood and scales are believed to have healing powers. As a result, villagers in the Cardamom Mountains, who often hunt with dogs, are paid a whopping US$40 per kilo for live pangolins (the price rises to US$70 in Vietnam and US$100 in China) and pangolin populations have been in freefall. Enforcement rangers are doing their best to crack down on poaching before it's too late.

SOUTH COAST

TEN PERCENT

In 2007 researchers found 23 Siamese crocodile eggs in a nest on the Areng River, in the Central Cardamoms Protected Forest. They took 12 eggs to a protected site where, 45 days later, all hatched; after being blessed by monks, they were released back into the river. Observations confirmed that all 11 eggs left behind also hatched. It's hard to believe but these 23 hatchlings represent 10% of the entire global population of wild Siamese crocodiles!

(rangers can help you find one). The nearby **Areng River Valley**, some of whose inhabitants belong to the Khmer Daeum minority community, is home to the dragonfish (Asian arowana), almost extinct in the wild, and the world's most important population of critically endangered Siamese crocodiles (above), toothy critters that don't eat people.

The truly intrepid can hire guides for the trek from Thma Bang north to **Kravanh** (p239), which takes at least a week, or from **Chamnar** (linked to Thma Bang by road) over the mountains to Kravanh, a five-day affair. These treks are possible only in the dry season.

An easier option is the three-day hike from **Chumnoab**, east of Thma Bang, eastwards to **Roleak Kang Cheung**, linked to Kompong Speu by road. Between the two is **Knong Krapeur** (1000m), set amid high-elevation grassland and pines. Inhabited five centuries ago, the area is known for its giant ceramic funeral jars, still filled with human bones.

It may also be possible to accompany enforcement rangers on an overnight or three-day **patrol** – contact the Thma Bang guesthouse for details.

GETTING THERE & AWAY

Few roads of any sort penetrate the Cardamom Mountains, ideal if you're trying to protect the natural habitat – roads, even rudimentary ones, tend to attract loggers, poachers and encroachers – but a bit of a problem if you'd like to visit.

The southern reaches of the CCPF are easiest to reach from the south. It takes about two hours to drive from Krong Koh Kong to Thma Bang (wet-season travel may be difficult or impossible). Turn off NH48 about 10km east of the Tatai River bridge; from the Veal II

(Veal Pii) ranger checkpoint, where a user fee may be collected, it's a further 50 minutes.

Thma Bang is linked to Chi Phat (opposite) by a difficult trail that can be handled by motorbike, but just barely.

The CCPF's northern sections can be accessed, to the degree that they're accessible at all, from Pursat (see p238).

Botum Sakor National Park

Occupying almost the entirety of the 35km-wide peninsula across the Gulf of Kompong Som from Sihanoukville, this 1834-sq-km national park, encircled by mangroves and beaches, is home to a profusion of wildlife, including elephants (about 20 of them, according to recent camera-trap evidence), tigers, deer, leopards and sun bears. The highest point is a 402m hill in the park's almost inaccessible interior.

Although a road is being built down the park's eastern side (it will eventually go all the way round the peninsula's coastline), the best way to see Botum Sakor is by boat. To get to the mangrove forests on the east coast and the almost deserted **beaches** on the park's southeastern tip, you can hire a long-tail boat in Andoung Tuek (opposite) or Sihanoukville. The west coast, with its many kilometres of fine beaches, is easiest to reach by boat from Koh Sdach (opposite). There are more **beaches** across the strait from Koh Kong Island, south of the picturesque fishers' village of **Preak Khsach**; for these destinations you can hire a boat in Krong Koh Kong (p185).

Small boats can be taken up into four mangrove-lined streams that are rich in wildlife, including the pileated gibbon, long-tailed macaque and black-shanked douc langur: **Ta Op**, the largest, on the east coast; **Ta Nun** in the middle of the south coast; and **Ta Nhi** and **Preak Khsach** on the east coast.

Grandiose tourist development seems to be on the cards for the park's west coast. A Chinese company has plans to build seven new cities (no, that's not a typo), an airport, golf courses and lots of hotels, though things are on hold while a three-year study is carried out. Another potential threat to the area comes from offshore oil rigs.

Botum Sakor is not yet geared up for tourism but at the park headquarters, on NH48 about 3km west of Andoung Tuek, it should be possible to arrange a hike with a ranger (US$5 a day) or a boat excursion.

SOUTH COAST

The nearest guesthouses are in Andoung Tuek, on the Tatai River and on Koh Sdach. On the south coast, it may be possible to overnight at the **Ta Nun ranger station** or in a basic guesthouse in **Thmor Sor**, an east coast fishing village linked by ferry with Sihanoukville.

Koh Sdach

Just off Botum Sakor National Park's southwest tip, this island has a small fishing port, a couple of sandy **beaches**, some modest eateries and a seaside bungalow outfit called **Mean Chey Guesthouse** (☎ 011 983806; r US$5). It's linked to both Sihanoukville and Krong Koh Kong by ferry (p185), which costs US$10 (2 hours from either city).

There are some fine **coral reefs** – excellent for diving or snorkelling – around some of the nearby islands. This is a good place to hire a boat to explore the wonderful beaches along the west coast of Botum Sakor National Park (opposite).

Andoung Tuek

On the western side of the highway bridge over Preak Piphot, this river port can be used as a jumping-off point for a boat trip along the east coast of Botum Sakor National Park (opposite) and for an excursion upriver to Chi Phat (below). Andoung Tuek is on NH48, 98km from Krong Koh Kong and 191km from Phnom Penh.

Botum Sakor Guesthouse (☎ 016 732731; r without/with bathroom 10,000r/20,000r) West of the bridge 250m, this has six basic rooms with bright pink mosquito nets. The bad news is that there's some dodgy electric wiring in the bathrooms; the good news is that you can get electrocuted only from 6pm to 10pm, when the town has electricity. One recent guest found a painted bullfrog in the shower, which was carefully redistributed outside.

Chi Phat

Chi Phat's pioneering community-based ecotourism project (p192), though at press time still a work in progress, gives hardy travellers a unique opportunity to explore the Cardamom ecosystem while contributing in a small way to its protection.

Chi Phat, though hardly the most beautiful village in Cambodia, is an excellent base for a variety of outdoor activities. Visitors can swim in the river, cycle (or take a *moto*) to several sets of rapids, hike in the forest (perhaps with

a former poacher as a guide; US$6 to US$10 per day) and play volleyball with the locals. Monkeys, hornbills and other rainforest creatures can often be seen along the banks of **Stung Proat**, an unlogged tributary of the Preak Piphot River accessible by boat. According to a village elder, the last time a tiger was seen in these parts was 1975.

Longer-term ecotourism plans for the Chi Phat area call for kayaking, overnight camping, mountain-bike day trips to nearby waterfalls, river excursions on traditional wooden boats, bird- and animal-watching from observation towers and hides, rainforest canopy walks, aerial ziplines through the forest canopy and an elephant rescue centre where visitors will be able to help out. Also on the cards are one- to five-night mountain-bike trips and jungle treks (US$10 to US$30 per person per day) deep into the Cardamoms.

For now, the accommodation on offer is quite basic. **Phuong Vanny Guesthouse** (☎ 016 617183; r US$4-5), run by a dynamic village woman, has six rooms (there are plans to add nine more) with hardwood floors and mosquito nets. The shared bathrooms have a barrel shower. The office of the **Wildlife Alliance** (☎ 016 951426), which oversees the project and can coordinate your visit, is next door. Homestays (US$3 per person per night) may become available.

In the small **covered market**, a bowl of noodles costs 2000r. The riverfront has two little **eateries**, one of which doubles as a pool hall (yes, right here in Preak Piphot River City!). Meals at the communal restaurant cost $US1.50 to US$4.

By the time you read this the area may have mobile phone coverage.

GETTING THERE & AWAY

Chi Phat is on the Preak Piphot River 21km upriver from Andoung Tuek. The best way to get there from Andoung Tuek is to charter a **fast motorboat** (☎ 016 348860, 016 565054; for 3/6 people US$25/40) or a slower **wooden long-tail motorboat** (☎ 016 399134; US$12). The fast boat takes 40 minutes and the slow 1½ hours. The ride is especially enchanting just after dawn, when the water is often smooth as glass. Much cheaper cargo boats (5000r, two hours) make daily merchandise runs, leaving Chi Phat at 8am or 8.30am and Andoung Tuek sometime between noon and 2pm.

SOUTH COAST

CHI PHAT: AN ECOTOURISM CASE STUDY

Chi Phat's 500 families have long supplemented their meagre agricultural income with products from the nearby forests. Gathering non-timber forest products (known in development lingo as NTFPs) and small quantities of firewood can be ecologically sustainable, but around Chi Phat the wholesale forest destruction carried out during 'the logging time' – the anarchic 1990s – left the whole ecosystem, and villagers' livelihoods, way out of whack. For many, poaching endangered animals became a way of life.

When the **Wildlife Alliance** (www.wildlifealliance.org) came on the scene in 2002 in a last-ditch effort to save the southern Cardamoms, local villagers and outsiders were encroaching on protected land, destroying the forest by illegal logging, and hunting endangered animals for local consumption and sale on the black market. The only way to prevent ecological catastrophe – and, among other things, to save monkeys from being trapped, sold for US$75 and sent to Vietnam to be eaten – was to send in teams of enforcement rangers to crack down on 'forestry and wildlife crimes'.

But enforcing the law constricted local people's ability to earn money to feed their children (or buy motorbikes), generating a great deal of resentment. Many didn't see that environmental degradation – caused, in part, by their own unsustainable activities – would leave them far worse off in a few years' time, though most everyone noticed that animals were getting harder and harder to find.

The Wildlife Alliance realised that in order to save the Cardamom forests, it needed the cooperation of locals – and that such cooperation would be forthcoming only if income-generating alternatives to poaching and whacking trees were available. In such a remote area, one of the only resources is the forest itself, and one of the few ways to earn money from plants and animals without destroying them is ecotourism.

Thus the Wildlife Alliance launched what's known in NGO parlance as a community-based ecotourism (CBET) project. Coordinated by an Israeli former-ranger experienced in collective endeavours from his kibbutz upbringing, the first step was empowering the local community. A committee of villagers was established to assess positive and negative impacts (eg of contact with Western culture), set goals and manage the project. Many of those who joined as 'stakeholders' were former loggers and hunters.

As we go to press, the Chi Phat CBET project is still in its pioneering phase, but initially sceptical locals are warming to the idea and are beginning to see the Wildlife Alliance, and forest conservation, in a different light. A trickle of tourists has begun coming up to Chi Phat and the income generated – income that goes both into villagers' pockets and into a community development fund – is starting to make a difference.

Groups working to support sustainable, low-impact CBET projects like that in Chi Pat have banded together to form the **Cambodia Community-Based Ecotourism Network** (CCBEN; www .ccben.org) – their website has details on other such initiatives around the country.

By *moto* the trip from Andoung Tuek is a hard – and, in the wet season, muddy – slog along a forest track (30,000r, 1½ hours).

Stung Phong Roul Waterfall

Although off the beaten path, this is one of Cambodia's most spectacular waterfalls, with five big drops arrayed around a vertiginous curve in the river. Clambering around is tough but worth it, as there are some good swimming holes at the right time of year.

The uppermost waterfall is a dramatic 10m high. Flat rock ledges border clear and surprisingly cool pools, and are ideal for a romantic picnic. If you sit quietly with your

feet in the water, little fish (goodness knows how they got up here) may nibble your toes.

GETTING THERE & AWAY

Stung Phong Roul Waterfall is about 20km northeast of Sre Ambel in the foothills of the Cardamom Mountains. As the crow flies, Kirirom National Park (p116) is 20km further to the northeast.

In the dry season you can get to the falls by motorbike, though be warned: there are potholes big and deep enough to swallow an entire motorcycle, and getting around the rotted-out bridges can be a wet affair. From just northwest of the Sre Ambel bridge, turn northeast off NH48 and follow the dirt road to the Bailey bridge. From there, an arrow-straight one-time logging road heads east and then north-northeast to a cleft in the forested hills. A 20-minute walk up the slope takes you to the uppermost waterfall.

In Sre Ambel, you can hire a *moto* (US$15 return, one hour to the base of the mountain). In the wet season it's possible to go most of the way by boat. The falls are rarely visited even by locals so it may be hard to find someone who knows the way.

Sre Ambel

Since ferry service to Krong Koh Kong ended a few years ago, the only reason to come to this charmless smugglers' port, 150km from Phnom Penh, is to use it as a base for a trip to Stung Phong Roul Waterfall.

A few blocks down the hill and to the right from the market, there's a **guesthouse** (☎ 016 798956; r US$5) with nine simple, me-dium-sized rooms and, next door, a simi-lar 10-room **guesthouse** (r US$5-12; ❄) with a partly Chinese sign. **Pohak Restaurant** (mains 6000r), across the street, serves – according to the nicely laminated menu – some unique delicacies, including odoriferous soup, salad Vietnamese girl, chickens with three legs, cow haunts water, eel falling in love and frontline troop open the way. For less martial fare, try the **small eateries** near the market.

GETTING THERE & AWAY

To get to Sre Ambel from Krong Koh Kong, take any vehicle heading to Phnom Penh or Sihanoukville and get off the NH48 either at the eastern end of the bridge (a *moto* from here to town costs 3000r) or at the oblique junction a few kilometres further east (from here the 5km *moto* ride costs 5000r).

Buses, minibuses and share taxis travel-ling between Phnom Penh and Sihanoukville stop at the intersection of NH4 and NH48, a 10km *moto* ride southeast of town.

KOMPONG SOM PROVINCE

Sandwiched between Kampot and Koh Kong Provinces, this tiny province is dominated by its main city, the dynamic beach resort and port of Sihanoukville.

Nearby islands, some with fine beaches, afford superb diving and snorkelling, and a few now offer bungalows. Other natural sites include Ream National Park, situated 18km east of Sihanoukville, and the Kbal Chhay Cascades.

SIHANOUKVILLE

ក្រុងព្រះសីហនុ

☎ 034 / pop 155,000

Surrounded by white-sand beaches and un-developed tropical islands, the port city and beach resort of Sihanoukville (Krong Preah Sihanouk), also known as Kompong Som, is the closest thing you get to the Costa del Cambodia. Visitor numbers have risen steadily in recent years – and are likely to skyrocket if flights to Siem Reap are resumed – but for the time being, despite the boomtown rents, the city and its sandy bits remain pretty laid-back.

Named in honour of the then-king, Sihanoukville was hacked out of the jungle in the late 1950s to create Cambodia's first and only deep-water port, considered vital so the country's international trade would no longer have to pass through Vietnam. During the 1960s the city experienced a small tourism boom.

The big attractions around here are the four beaches ringing the headland. None of them qualify as the region's finest but on weekdays it's still possible to have stretches of sand to yourself. On weekends and holidays Sihanoukville is extremely popular with well-to-do Phnom Penhers.

Orientation

The scruffy city centre, where the bus station and most businesses are located, is spread out along and north of Ekareach St. It is roughly equidistant from the two main beach areas, the Serendipity-Occheuteal area, 2km to the south, and Victory Beach, 2.5km to the northwest.

Serendipity Beach – as the northwestern tip of Occheuteal Beach is known – is linked to the Golden Lions Roundabout by an unpaved access road, Serendipity St, and the Road to Serendipity, the area's commercial and culinary heart. Victory Hill (Weather Station Hill, also known as 'The Hill'), once the main backpacker haven, is up the hill from Victory Beach.

Boats to/from Krong Koh Kong dock about 3km north of town.

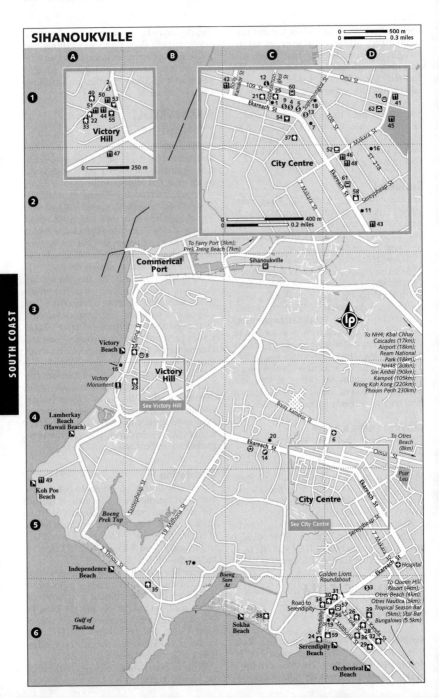

Information

Sihanoukville is a centre that's developing so fast it's hard to keep track of all the new establishments and activities sprouting up around town.

BOOKSHOPS

Casablanca Books (☎ 012 484051; Road to Serendipity; ◷ 8am-10pm) Next to Mick & Craig's, this bookshop sells new and used English paperbacks.

Mister Heinz Books (☎ 017 802721; 219 Ekareach St, City Centre; ◷ 9am-6pm or later) Stocks 6000 books in 10 languages, including lots of used English paperbacks and titles on Cambodian history. Most can be sold back for 50% of what you paid.

Q&A (☎ 012 342720; 95 Ekareach St, City Centre; ◷ 7.30am-7.30pm) A secondhand bookshop that doubles as a café (mains cost US$2 to US$4.50).

Starfish Bakery & Café (☎ 012 952011; down alley, 62 7 Makara St, City Centre; ◷ 7am-6pm) Used books to sell and swap, mainly in English and Swedish.

INTERNET ACCESS

Internet access (per hour 3000r to 5000r) is easy to find in the city centre – there are internet cafés at 173, 193 and 236A Ekareach

St, inside the NGO-run Starfish Bakery & Café, and both inside and across the street from the Angkor Inn Guesthouse.

In the Serendipity area, internet outfits are sprinkled along the Road to Serendipity and can be found inside the Seaside Hotel and in the minimarket at the Koh Meas Guesthouse.

LAUNDRY

Lots of places around Serendipity Beach offer to do laundry for 3000r per kilo.

Laundry Express (☎ 016 988483; 157 Ekareach St, City Centre; ◷ 7am-8pm) Costs US$1 per kilo with a 24-hour turnaround; double that if you need your clothes in three hours.

MEDICAL SERVICES

Travellers have reported that a few guesthouses charge exorbitant rates for house calls by doctors.

CT Clinic (☎ 934222; ct_clinic@yahoo.com; 47 Boray Kamakor St, City Centre; ◷ 24hr for emergencies) All the expats and NGO workers head here when they need care, including emergency trauma treatment and rabies shots. Staff will tell you if you need to be evacuated to Phnom

Penh and will help you contact your embassy. Has a reliable in-house pharmacy.

MONEY

Most of the banks are in the city centre (on or near Ekareach St), though there are now several ATMs near Serendipity Beach and one on Victory Hill.

ANZ Royal (215 Ekareach St, City Centre) Has a 24-hour ATM. Also runs ATMs at Victory Hill and near Serendipity at 15 Ekareach St and in the Golden Sand Hotel.

Canadia Bank (☎ 933490; 197 Ekareach St, City Centre) Has a 24-hour ATM. Changes non-US-dollar travellers cheques.

Union Commercial Bank (195 Ekareach St, City Centre) Has an ATM.

POST

Post Office (19 7 Makara St, City Centre) Over the road from Psar Leu.

TOURIST INFORMATION

Guesthouses and bars are generally the best source of information and can equip you with the free *Sihanouk Ville Visitors Guide* (www .canbypublications.com), a useful pocket guide issued quarterly. The *Sihanoukville Advertiser* lives up to its name.

Tourist Office (☎ 933894; cnr Sopheakmongkol & 109 Sts, City Centre; ☟ 8.30-11am & 2-5pm Mon-Fri) Friendly but pretty useless.

TRAVEL AGENCIES

Eco-Trek Tours (☎ 012 987073; ecotrektourscambodia@ yahoo.com; Road to Serendipity; ☟ 8am-10pm) Next to Mick & Craig's, this agency runs snorkelling trips (US$10), excursions to Koh Russei and Koh Preus (US$10, including meals) and trips to Ream National Park (US$15 to US$25).

Diving and More (Tourist Information Center; ☎ 934220; www.divingandmore.com; cnr Sophamongkol & 108 Sts, City Centre) Catty-corner from the bus station, this travel agency handles land tours and diving excursions.

VISAS

Ana Internet & Travel (☎ 933929; cnr Ekareach & Sopheakmongkol Sts, City Centre) Can help extend Cambodian visas.

Samudera Supermarket (☎ 933441; 64 7 Makara St, City Centre; ☟ 7am-9pm) Ditto.

Vietnamese consulate (☎ 934039; Ekareach St, City Centre; ☟ 8am-noon & 2-4pm Mon-Sat) Issues some of the fastest Vietnamese visas (US$35) in the world; staff can normally turn one around in 15 minutes or, at the latest, the same afternoon.

Dangers & Annoyances

Sihanoukville is not as dicey, security-wise, as its reputation of recent years may imply, but crime is certainly not unknown here. The most common problem is theft on the beaches while people are out swimming, often by drug addicts or children. Don't take anything valuable to the beach unless you have someone to keep an eye on it at all times.

Lone women should exercise caution when walking on Occheuteal and Otres Beaches after dark, as there have been assaults and at least one highly-publicised rape in recent years. There have also been a number of violent incidents along Victory Hill's main drag.

As in Phnom Penh, drive-by bag snatchings happen and are especially dangerous when you're riding a *moto*. Shoulder bags are an attractive target, so on a *moto* it's common sense to hold them tightly in front of you, especially at night. Never put a bag or purse in the front basket of a motorbike. Motorcycle theft is also a popular pastime in Sihanoukville. If you rent wheels, make sure they come with a padlock.

Night-time robberies sometimes occur, particularly around the 'chicken farm' red-light district near the container port and on the poorly lit parts of Ekareach St between the city centre and Victory Hill.

Take care with the currents off Occheuteal during the wet season as they can be deceptively strong.

One annoyance for locals is underdressed foreigners wandering about town. Cambodia is not Thailand; Khmers are generally more conservative than their neighbours. Just look at the Cambodians frolicking in the sea – most are fully dressed. Wearing bikinis on the beach is fine but cover up elsewhere. Topless or nude bathing is a definite no-no.

Sights & Activities
BEACHES

Sihanoukville's beaches are in a state of flux as developers move in and murky leases are signed to cash in on the tourism boom.

The best all-rounder is **Occheuteal Beach**, whose northwestern end – a tiny, rocky strip – has emerged as a popular travellers' hangout known as **Serendipity Beach**. Some of the city's best restaurants and pubs are a few hundred metres up the hill along the Road to Serendipity.

THE LAST BATTLE OF THE VIETNAM WAR

The final bloody confrontation of the Vietnam War took place far from Vietnam – in fact, off the coast of Sihanoukville.

On 12 May 1975, a month after the fall of Phnom Penh, Khmer Rouge forces using captured US-made Swift boats seized an American container ship, the SS *Mayagüez* (named after a city in Puerto Rico) while it was on a routine voyage from Hong Kong to Thailand. The vessel was anchored 50km southwest of Sihanoukville off Koh Tang – now a popular scuba-diving destination – while the 39 crew members were taken to Sihanoukville.

Determined to show resolve in the face of this 'act of piracy', President Gerald Ford ordered that the ship and its crew be freed. Naval planes from the US aircraft carrier *Coral Sea* bombed Sihanoukville's oil refinery and the Ream airbase, and marines prepared for their first hostile boarding of a ship at sea since 1826.

On 15 May marines stormed aboard the *Mayagüez* like swashbuckling pirates but found it deserted. In parallel, airborne marine units landed on Koh Tang. Thought to be lightly defended, the island turned out to have been fortified in anticipation of a Vietnamese attack (Vietnam also claimed the island). In the course of the assault, most of the US helicopters were destroyed or damaged and 15 Americans were killed.

Early on 15 May the Khmer Rouge had placed the crew of the *Mayagüez* aboard a Thai fishing boat and set it adrift, but they weren't discovered by US ships until after the assault on Koh Tang had begun. In the chaotic withdrawal from the island, three marines were accidentally left behind and, it is believed, were later executed by the Khmer Rouge.

The Vietnam War Memorial in Washington, DC lists the war dead chronologically, which is why the names of the men who perished in the *Mayagüez* Incident appear last.

Occheuteal's sand, backed by a row of casuarina trees, stretches for about 4km. In addition to sitting under parasols on rented chairs, you can hire an inner tube (2000r), charter a banana boat (US$10) or ruin everyone else's peace of mind with a jetski (US$60 per hour). The ramshackle restaurant shacks, convenient for a drink (beers go for US$0.50) or a grilled meal (Khmer mains cost US$2 to US$4), are on short-term leases and may be removed by government bulldozers at any time. Much of the southern section of the beach, about 1.5km of prime waterfront, is now walled off pending its transformation into another exclusive Sokha resort complex. If you see a low-flying helicopter, it's probably landing at Prime Minister Hun Sen's huge Hollywood-style mansion.

At the southern end of Occheuteal Beach, go up and over the small headland and you'll get to **Otres Beach**, a seemingly infinite strip of casuarinas and almost-empty white sand that can definitely give southern Thailand a run for its money. Sadly, Otres has recently been sold so much is likely to change during the lifetime of this book. But as we go to press, the area is still gloriously quiet, with just a few little restaurants and small bungalow places and, for kayak and catama-

ran rental and snorkelling excursions, Otres Nautica (p198).

To get to Otres Beach, follow the road fronting Occheuteal Beach, go around the closed section and drive up and over the headland (note: the descent is impassable to cars). From the city centre, you can follow Omui St from Psar Leu east out of town for about 7km. Both are pretty rough tracks.

Victory Beach was the original backpacker beach but has lost much of its buzz because, frankly, it's not the city's best strip of sand. However, investors seem to think the area has a midrange future. These investors include the Russian guy who created a restaurant under the wings of a real Antonov-24 turboprop (a true blessing to air travellers everywhere, as no-one is trying to fly the thing any more). The beach's southwestern section, around a small headland, is also known as **Hawaii Beach** and, after the old hotel near here, **Lamherkay Beach**. The island 800m offshore, **Koh Pos** (Snake Island), was going to be turned into a US$300-million tourist resort until the Russian investor was arrested on child sex charges in October 2007.

Further southwest is tiny **Koh Pos Beach**, on the tip of Sihanoukville's headland; nice and shady but with rough waters.

Southeast of here, **Independence Beach** (7-Chann Beach), named after the hotel that has dominated the area since the 1960s, is a good stretch of clean sand but lacks shade and facilities.

Midway between here and Serendipity lies **Sokha Beach**, perhaps Sihanoukville's prettiest, which is now the exclusive property of the Sokha Beach Resort (p209). Except on particularly crowded high-season days, non-guests can spend the day here – and use the hotel's huge pool – on weekdays/weekends for US$4/6 (50% off for children under 12). Confiscating the beach may have been an act of robbery perpetrated on the entire Cambodian public, but your stuff will be safe while you swim – there aren't any small-time criminals here.

About 7km northeast of the ferry port is casuarina-lined **Prek Treng Beach**, also known as Hun Sen Beach. Largely deserted (for now), it is marked by a number of Khmer-style open pavilions.

DIVING & SNORKELLING

The reefs around Sihanoukville are rich in corals, sponges and all sorts of sea life, from eels to anemones and stingrays to dolphins. Some of the best diving is around **Koh Tang** and **Koh Prins**, which require an overnight trip, though there's also decent diving closer in near **Koh Tas** (Koh Kaong Kang) and **Koh Rung Samloem** (two hours one-way).

Excellent snorkelling locales include coral-rich **Koh Khteah**, about 2km off Otres Beach.

Reliable operators include the following:

Claude Diving Centre (☎ 012 824870; above 2 Thnou St) Claude has been exploring the waters off Sihanoukville for 15 years now and specialises in longer trips to distant reefs.

Coasters (☎ 933776; www.cambodia-beach.com; Serendipity St) Offers PowerDive snorkel diving excursions (full-day US$29) and, daily at 10am, boat tours to Koh Russei (US$6).

Diving and More (☎ 934220; www.divingandmore .com; cnr Sophamongkol & 108 Sts, City Centre) A diving outfit offering PADI and SSI courses.

EcoSea Dive (☎ 934347; www.ecoseadive.com; 225 Ekareach St, City Centre; ☯ 7.30/8am-7pm) Offers PADI and SSI courses, one-/two-dive packages (US$39/59) and one-/two-day snorkelling trips (US$15/49). Has a second office on the Road to Serendipity.

Otres Nautica (☎ 092 230065; otres.nautica@yahoo .com; Otres Beach; ☯ 8am-6/7pm) Situated 1km south of the Queen Hill Resort, this laid-back, French-run outfit

rents sea kayaks (per hour/day US$3/15) and HobiCat sailing catamarans (US$8/40) and can arrange snorkelling excursions on a fishing boat (half/whole day US$30/50).

Scuba Nation Diving Center (☎ 012 604680; www .divecambodia.com; Serendipity St) The only PADI five-star dive centre in Cambodia. Highly professional, multilingual instructors with first-class equipment offer classes in English, Swedish, French and Dutch.

MASSAGE

There are loads of dodgy massage parlours in Sihanoukville but also some legitimate venues staffed by disabled locals:

Seeing Hands Massage 3 (☎ 012 799016; 95 Ekareach St; per hr US$4; ☯ 8am-9pm) As elsewhere in Cambodia, Seeing Hands–trained masseurs are blind. Income from Seeing Hands Massage helps the local visually impaired community.

Starfish Bakery & Café (☎ 012 952011; 62 7 Makara St, City Centre; per hr US$6; ☯ 7am-6pm) Blind and disabled masseurs, trained by Western massage therapists, perform Khmer, Thai, foot, oil and Indian head massages. Profits go towards social projects.

COOKING

Traditional Khmer Cookery (☎ 092 738615; khmer cookery@hotmail.com; 335 Ekareach St; per person US$25; ☯ 10am-Mon-Sat) Teaches traditional culinary techniques in daily classes with a maximum of eight participants. Special requests (eg veggie) are happily accommodated. Cooking is done on a shaded, rain-proof terrace with plenty of counter space. Book a day ahead.

FITNESS

The French-run **Centre de Fitness et de Boxe Asiatique** (☎ 016 394276; St 118; per day US$2.50; ☯ 5am-9pm) is a fully outfitted fitness club with 165 machines, free weights, late-afternoon aerobics and Khmer and Thai boxing classes (per class US$3.50, personal coaching US$6).

Sleeping

These days the most happening backpacker and midrange area is Serendipity Beach, including the beachfront, Serendipity St (the dirt access road to Serendipity Beach) and the Road to Serendipity (linking Serendipity St with the Golden Lions Roundabout).

A long block or two southeast of the Serendipity area, budget and midrange places offering excellent value for money can be found along the streets that parallel Occheuteal Beach, including 23 Tola St.

Development will soon bring big changes to Otres Beach, Sihanoukville's most pristine, but for now it's perfect for a romantic seaside getaway – if you don't mind being 4km or 5km out of town (US$1.50 or US$2 by *moto* from Occheuteal Beach).

Victory Hill (Weather Station Hill), the original backpackers' area up the slope from Victory Beach, has recently lost much of its popularity (except with French travellers), although the places listed below are far from the hullabaloo of The Hill's somewhat sleazy main strip.

The lively city centre, preferred by many long-termers, is very convenient if you're travelling by bus and has lots of banks and businesses as well as the main market. Of course, getting to the beaches requires a short commute (3000r to 4000r by *moto*).

Prices quoted below are for the high season, which runs from November to March.

BUDGET
Serendipity Beach

There are lots of guesthouses along the water, on Serendipity St and along the Road to Serendipity. Some are on land leased from the military police, an arrangement that may ensure their survival as nearby areas are snapped up by investors.

Monkey Republic Bungalows (☎ 012 490290; monkeyrepubliccambodia@yahoo.co.uk; Road to Serendipity; r US$7) A favourite hang-out of the young backpacker crowd, this establishment has 26 bright-blue bungalows (12 of them added in 2007) set around two banana-shaded garden courtyards. All have simple furnishings, mozzie nets and verandas.

Mick & Craig's (☎ 012 727740; mccraigs@yahoo.com; Road to Serendipity; r US$8-20; 🕸) Attached to a restaurant of the same name, this guesthouse has 16 simple, eminently serviceable rooms with mosquito nets. In the heart of Serendipity's dining and nightlife strip.

Occheuteal Beach

A five-minute walk from Serendipity, this area's budget places offer solid value for money.

Sovann Phoum Guesthouse (☎ 012 504537; 1 Kanda St; r US$5-12; 🕸) This family-run place, set around a quiet paved courtyard, consists of 17 well-kept, compact rooms with tile bathrooms. The guesthouse will arrange free pickup at the bus station if you call ahead.

Koh Meas Guesthouse (☎ 934337; kohmeas@hotmail .com; 23 Tola St; r US$8-13; 🕸) Opened in 2007, this laid-back, family-run guesthouse – the name means 'golden island' – has 12 rooms (more are planned) with simple but serviceable bathrooms. Air-con rooms have hot water.

Lucky Guesthouse (☎ 016 837146; 23 Tola St; r US$8-15; 🕸) A step up in terms of comfort and security from most budget establishments, this family-friendly place is quiet except when Prime Minister Hun Sen's helicopter lands next door. The 26 rooms are fairly large and come with practical decor. Singapore-accented English spoken.

Otres Beach

Star Bar Bungalows (☎ 934245; www.starbungalow.com; bungalow US$10) Lapping waves are the loudest sound you'll hear at Star Bar, where the eight rustic bungalows – with cement floors, grass mat walls, thatch ceilings and mosquito nets – are just 10m from the waterline. Situated 1.4km south of the Queen Hill Resort.

Victory Hill

Rainy Season Guesthouse (☎ 092 583372; rainyseason cambodia@yahoo.com; r US$5) Attached to a restaurant with décor reminiscent of Tahiti, this French-run guesthouse, named after an album by the American singer-songwriter Elliot Murphy, has just four very basic rooms; prices include breakfast, so they're really almost free.

Sunset Garden Guesthouse (☎ 012 562004; d US$5-10; 🕸) Run by an enthusiastic woman in her late 50s, this spotless, family-run hostelry, in an Italianate house surrounded by a neatly tended garden, has 16 spacious and spotless rooms.

Bungalow Village (☎ 012 490293; bungalowvillage@ hotmail.com; r US$5-10) Set in a parklike, hillside garden shaded by tropical trees, this complex is just 200m from the beach and has an old-fashioned chill-out zone and nine basic bungalows with wood-plank walls and glassless windows; the more expensive bungalows come with sea views.

Blue Frog Guesthouse (☎ 012 838004; www.blue froghotel.com; r US$12-30; 🕸) This quiet wooden house, just up the slope from Victory Beach ('three minutes down, 10 minutes up'), is run by a friendly Swedish-Thai couple. Its seven rooms – wooden upstairs, cement and tile downstairs – have bright bathrooms and king-size beds.

City Centre

These places are a two-minute walk from the bus station.

Angkor Inn Guesthouse (☎ 016 896204; angkor inn99@yahoo.com; Sopheakmongkol St; r US$5-10; ✦) Cheap and a little bit gloomy, this is a firmly established budget deal. Large TVs and small bathrooms are standard, as are super-soft foam mattresses. The best rooms have street-facing windows.

Freedom Hotel (☎ 012 257953; Sopheakmongkol St; d US$5-12; ✦) Behind the bright-yellow façade, the whole 20-room place feels a bit jerry-rigged and the halls could use some sprucing up, but the set-up is quite functional and each room is fairly large and has a fridge. Has a restaurant with hearty Western breakfasts. Guests get a free beer at the downstairs bar.

our pick **Small Hotel** (☎ 012 716385; thesmallhotel@ yahoo.com; r US$10-15; ✦ 💻) Neat and organised in the best Scandinavian tradition, this super-welcoming guesthouse – run by a Swedish-Khmer couple – has a cheerful lounge and 11 spotless rooms, all with air-con and fridge; the US$15 rooms also have hot water. The giant spider on the wall above the lounge is made out of old weapons bent and welded into art. Often full, so book ahead.

MIDRANGE

With the exception of weekends, when Khmers head down from Phnom Penh, there's generally a glut of midrange rooms, a circumstance that translates into some good deals.

Serendipity Beach

Coasters (☎ 933776; www.cambodia-beach.com; Serendipity St; r US$10-15, with air-con & hot water US$25-35; ✦ 💻) The 20 solid rooms and bungalows, many with verandas for some quality contemplation, are spread across the hillside above the beach, although the bar and restaurant run right to the water's edge. Situated 100m up an alley from the bottom of Serendipity St.

our pick **Reef Resort** (☎ 934281; www.reefresort.com .kh; Road to Serendipity; d US$35-45, q US$60) Offering excellent value, this professionally run hotel has 14 good-sized rooms with views of the 12.5m pool, surrounded by a patio and lots of luscious purple orchids. Prices include breakfast. Bus station pick-up is available.

Occheuteal Beach

Orchidée Guesthouse (☎ 933639; www.orchidee-guest house.com; 23 Tola St; d US$13-30, tr US$40; ✦ 💻 🍴)

A delightful 10m pool surrounded by chairs and palms is the centrepiece of this restful, family-friendly place. Popular with adventure groups, its 45 spotless rooms – some pool-side – have air-con, hot water, a fridge and well-designed bathrooms (rare in these parts). Prices include breakfast (except for the US$13 rooms). Excellent value.

Seaside Hotel (☎ 933662; www.seasidehotel .com.kh; 14 Milthona St; r US$20-50; ✦ 💻) One of Occheuteal's most established hotels, with professional staff and 83 spacious rooms featuring lots of solid wood. Housed in an imposing Khmer-style building. Prices include breakfast (except for the US$20 rooms).

Golden Sand Hotel (☎ 933607; goldensand hotel@gmail.com; 23 Tola St; r US$27.50-44, ste US$55-66; ✦ 💻 🍴) The swishest place near Occheuteal, this 111-room hotel offers almost four-star comfort. Lobby highlights include elaborately carved wooden dragon chairs and a marble sea maiden with strategically long hair.

Otres Beach

Queen Hill Resort (☎ 011 937373; www.queenhill resortbungalows.com; Otres Beach; r US$15-30; ✦) Sihanoukville's most romantic getaway is spectacularly situated atop the isolated bluff between Occheuteal and Otres Beaches. Surrounded by crystal-clear waters, it has 22 all-wood bungalows, many with sea views, and 12 rooms. Sea breezes usually make air-con unnecessary. We've recently had reports of visitors being treated less than courteously.

Victory Beach

Holiday Palace (☎ 933808; www.holidaypalace.com; Krong St; r US$25-35, ste US$40-50; ✦ 💻) The first casino complex to set up shop in Sihanoukville, this six-storey hotel – just 100m from the seafront – keeps its rates low to draw in the punters. The spacious rooms are almost four-star quality and the suites are so enormous that, per square metre, they're probably cheaper than many US$5 bungalows.

Independence Beach

Sea Breeze Guesthouse (☎ 934205; www.seabreezesite .com; 2 Thnou St; r US$15-45; ✦ 💻) Across the road from the beach and equidistant (3.5km) from the city centre, Victory Beach and Serendipity Beach, this family-friendly, Aussie-run place is a good choice for a bit of peace and quiet.

(Continued on page 209)

SOUTH COAST

COLOURS OF CAMBODIA

Travelling through Cambodia reveals a vivid palette of colour. Rural rice fields glimmer like emeralds; Buddhist monks' saffron robes shimmer in the sunlight. Cambodia's ancient temples are hewn from sandstone, but are cloaked in green moss or drip with dappled shadows. Khmer food is as striking in colour as it is in flavour. Even the arts are bright, with exquisite dance costumes. But the people of Cambodia bring most colour of all, their beautiful smiles and warm welcome an enduring memory of any visit.

'Angkor is heaven on earth – the home of the gods, cast in stone'

Temple-Hopping

Cambodia is the undisputed temple capital of Asia and we are not just talking about the awesome Angkor Wat, the mother of all temples. Angkor is heaven on earth – the home of the gods, cast in stone – but all over the country, hidden away in the jungles, lie monuments that attest to the glories of the Khmer empire.

① Angkor Wat

Follow in the footsteps of pilgrims of old along the immense causeway of the 'temple that is a city', the holiest of holies, the one and only Angkor Wat (p154).

② Koh Ker

Discover the rival capital of Koh Ker (p264), carved out of the jungles in the 10th century and home to some of the most epic sculptures from the Angkorian era.

③ Preah Khan

Experience spiritual harmony in the ultimate fusion-temple, Preah Khan (p170), which is dedicated to the Hindu trinity of Shiva, Vishnu and Brahma, as well as the Buddha.

④ Banteay Chhmar

Venture off the trail to the 'narrow fortress' of Banteay Chhmar (p255), one of the monumental creations of Jayavarman VII, complete with the signature faces of Avalokiteshvara, the Bodhisattva of Compassion.

⑤ Jungle Temples

Iconic Ta Prohm (p166) is the original jungle temple, with serpentine root systems slowly strangling the life out of the stones. Further afield lies Beng Mealea, smothered then swallowed by the voracious jungle.

⑥ Life Before Angkor

Cambodia didn't begin and end with Angkor. There are vestiges of the powerful pre-Angkorian kingdoms of Funan and Chenla all over the country, including Sambor Prei Kuk (p272), the first temple-city in Southeast Asia.

People & Culture

The Khmer people have opened their arms to the world and make any visit to the kingdom a humbling lesson in the endurance of the human spirit. The past is not forgotten in devotion to their ancestors and pilgrimages to pagodas, but the future is embraced, as youngsters seize the day. Share the adventure with a local meal, a traditional performance or a meeting with the minorities.

1 Buddhist Monks
Witness the rebirth of the Buddhist faith (p50), so nearly destroyed during the Khmer Rouge regime, as saffron-clad monks wander the streets of towns and cities across Cambodia.

2 A Culinary Adventure
Cambodia is not only a feast for the senses. An epicurean journey into a little-known cuisine (p63), it is on the culinary crossroads of Asia, combining the best of Thailand, Vietnam, India and China.

3 The Living Arts
The royal ballet (p52), folk dance and shadow puppetry are a tangible link with the glorious days of Angkor, recounting myths and legends from an earlier, Hindu past.

4 Country Life
The majority of Cambodians still live in the countryside, eeking out a living from farming or fishing, while an incredible 50% of the population is under the age of 16 (p48).

5 Multiculturalism
Sitting in the heart of Asia, it's no surprise to discover that Cambodia is home to a diverse array of peoples (p48), including the majority Khmers, ethnic Chinese, Vietnamese and Chams, and minority hilltribes in the remote northeast.

6 Handicrafts
The ancient artisans of Angkor were incredibly skilled carvers and the tradition is alive and well today (p318), with a range of stone sculpture, wood carving and intricate silver available, as well as exquisite silk and delicate lacquerware.

Natural Wonders

Wiped off the map for more than three decades by war and revolution, there are plenty of unexplored wilds in Cambodia that are now beginning to draw visitors. Explore the meandering Mekong as it wends through the country, penetrate the vast wilderness of the Cardamoms, trek in nascent national parks, take the plunge in the waterfalls and lakes of the northeast, or beachcomb like Robinson Crusoe. Cambodia and adventure go hand-in-hand.

① The Wild East

Head to the hills of Mondulkiri (p298) or Ratanakiri (p291), where elephants are still a regular means of transport, to explore a different Cambodia of dense jungle, hidden waterfalls and shy minority peoples.

② Tonlé Sap Lake

Take to the waters of the largest lake in Southeast Asia to explore floating villages and flooded forest. Tonlé Sap (p57) acts as a natural flood barrier for the Mekong River.

③ The Caves of Kampot

Go underground around Kampot (p215) to discover the many caves that pepper this region of limestone karst, some containing ancient Hindu temples that look like they were built yesterday.

④ Deserted Beaches

Comb the coast of Cambodia to discover pristine tropical beaches and deserted paradise hideaways, including the islands off Sihanoukville (p193) and Kep (p224), and the national parks of Koh Kong Province (p182).

⑤ The Mekong

Go with the flow and follow the mighty Mekong, the mother river, on its meander through the heart of Cambodia, with the chance to see rare freshwater Irrawaddy dolphins (p288) along the way.

⑥ Cardamom Mountains

Venture into one of Asia's last great wildernesses, the untamed Cardamom Mountains (p186), where dense jungle tumbles down from mountain peaks to the crystal-clear waters of the Gulf of Thailand.

(Continued from page 200)

Has 20 capacious rooms, a steak restaurant and a motorboat; offers free pick-up and free transport to/from anywhere in town. A swimming pool is planned.

TOP END
An immense new luxury resort complex with 1.5km of private – formerly public – beach is being built along most of the southern half of Occheuteal Beach.

Sokha Beach Resort (☎ 935999; www.sokhahotels .com; 2 Thnou St; r US$200-1000; ❄ 🖥 🏊) Cambodia's first five-star beach resort, this stunning Khmer-style complex has 166 super-elegant rooms and suites. Amenities include a spa, fitness centre, children's playground and huge pool, but better yet is the 1.5km private beach, long considered the best in town. Prices include breakfast.

Eating
There's a healthy selection of restaurants and cafés in all parts of Sihanoukville. Victory Hill's main drag, though sleazifying, still claims a dozen worthwhile restaurants, but the centre of gravity has definitely shifted to Serendipity Beach (a good spot for beachside barbecues) and the nearby Road to Serendipity. The centre of town has a number of worthwhile places, especially useful before or after a bus trip or during a night on the town.

Most beaches attract vendors selling everything from pineapples and quail eggs to freshly grilled prawns and fish. You may find it all a bit of a hard sell if you're just trying to relax on the sand, but provided you bargain, this can be an inexpensive way to snack your way through the day.

SERENDIPITY & OCCHEUTEAL BEACHES
Many of this area's best restaurants are along the Road to Serendipity but lots of visitors end up dining right on Serendipity Beach, as the beachfront tables with candles are hard to beat for atmosphere, especially around sunset. The Reef Resort has an authentic Mexican place.

our pick **Happa** (☎ 012 728901; Road to Serendipity; mains US$3.50-6; ❄ 5pm-10pm) Authentic meat, fish, seafood and vegetable teppanyaki, with a variety of sauce options, is served amid tropical decor accented with Japanese touches. Under the same roof, Ku Kai (☎ 012 593339) serves sashimi and tempura dishes.

Mick & Craig's (☎ 012 727740; Road to Serendipity; mains US$4-10; ❄ 7am-11pm) Set under a thatched roof, this open-air restaurant has Western grub including pizzas, hearty vegetarian options, popular daily specials and a good selection of breakfasts.

New Sea View Villa (☎ 092-759753; 2-course meal US$6.50) Just a few metres back from Serendipity Beach, this place serves up an incredible selection of food that's among the area's tastiest. Starters include scallops and an authentic tomato-moz-basil salad, while main courses range from a seafood platter to vegetarian dishes.

A number of small, **good-value restaurants** (mains US$3-4), calmer and more hygienic than the beachside shacks, can be found a block inland from Occheuteal Beach along 23 Tola St.

VICTORY HILL
Even if you're staying elsewhere in town, it's worth checking out this lively area for its wide range of tasty and inexpensive cuisines, including French. Despite what the bloggers say, this area still has some of its old-time hippy vibe.

Koh Lin (☎ 012 588625; mains 5000r-16,000r; ❄ 10am-11.30pm) Its name a play on a play on the French word *colline* (hill), this unpretentious eatery has just five candle-lit tables and serves good-value Cambodian, Vietnamese and French bistro classics. Dessert options include profiterole, crème caramel and crèpes.

Indian Curry Pot (☎ 934040; dishes US$2-4; ❄ 7am-11pm or later) The best place in Sihanoukville for North Indian and Pakistani specialities, both vegetarian and non-veggie (the latter are 100% halal). A cooling raita costs US$1.

Tutti Frutti (☎ 016 464360; mains US$2-4; ❄ 7am-10pm or 11pm) Brightly painted in yellow, orange and red, this cheerful eatery serves light meals, including Breton crèpes, panini and salads.

Snake House (☎ 012 673805; www.snake-house .com in Russian; mains US$3-10; ❄ 8am-11pm) The best place in town for Russian mains (pelmeny, manty, chicken Kiev) and soups (red and green borsht, solyanka); it also serves seafood. In a unique, slithering twist, diners sit at glass-topped tables with live serpents – many venomous – inside. The jungle-enveloped complex includes a bar, a guesthouse and a crocodile farm: one false step and the crocs will eat as well as you did.

XXL (☎ 092 738641; mains US$7-11; ⏰ 7am-11pm) The Belgian chef prepares classy, French-style *cuisine du marché* (dishes based on what's available fresh in the markets) and will be happy to uncork a bottle of French wine.

OTHER BEACHES

Treasure Island (☎ 012 755335; Koh Pos Beach; mains US$3-8; ⏰ 10am-2pm & 5-9.30pm) In an isolated spot in the middle of nowhere, this big, informal seafoodery is popular with Khmers and Asian tourists with a hankering for its 'Hong Kong-style' fish and seafood. Most everything is fresh and housed in tanks, just point to what you want and the staff will pluck it out. Prices are generally reasonable but read the fine print – some items are sold by weight.

CITY CENTRE

The city centre, including Ekareach St towards Serendipity, has more than its fair share of worthy restaurants.

Holy Cow (☎ 012 478510; 83 Ekareach St; mains US$2-4.50; ⏰ 9.30am-11pm) At this attractive, chic-funky café-restaurant, options include pasta, sandwiches on homemade bread (US$1.50 to US$2.50) and a good selection of veggie options, including two vegan desserts, both involving chocolate. The small shop sells M'lop Tapang products (opposite).

Starfish Bakery & Café (☎ 012 952011; 62 7 Makara St; mains US$2.50-4; ⏰ 7am-6pm) Tucked down a red-earth alley, this attractive, NGO-run garden café serves filling Western breakfasts, light lunches (sandwiches, quiche, tortillas, salads) and teatime treats such as brownies and apple tarts. Veggie options are legion. Income goes to help poor Cambodians get medical care, housing and microloans.

Happy Herb Pizza (☎ 012 632198; 81 Ekareach St; most mains US$3-5; ⏰ 8am-11pm) A pizzeria with a breezy, tropical twist. In addition to Khmer dishes, options include garlic bread (US$1), salads (US$1.50 to US$3.50) and pasta (US$2 to US$4). Free delivery available.

Small Hotel (☎ 012 716385; mains US$3.50-6; ⏰ 7am-10pm) The best place in town for authentic Swedish specialities such as Swedish meatballs with mashed potatoes (US$4.75), *falukorr scan* (Swedish sausage; US$6) and *pyt i panna* (Swedish hash; US$4.50). Also has delicious fish *amoc* (US$5).

In the evening, **food stalls** (cnr Omui & 7 Makara Sts; mains 2500r) set up one block north of Psar Leu, the city's jerry-built main market that went up in flames – under highly suspicious circumstances – in January 2008. Options include barbeque chicken, rice porridge or noodles with chicken, and a variety of Cambodian desserts.

SELF-CATERING

In the city centre, fruit and veggie stalls can be found at Psar Leu (opposite the post office) and at the southern end of Boray Kamakor St.

Samudera Supermarket (☎ 933441; 64 7 Makara St, City Centre; ⏰ 7am-9pm) Stocks everything from cheese and wine to fishing rods.

Koh Meas Mini-Mart (23 Tola St, Occheuteal Beach; ⏰ 7am-10pm or 11pm) Underneath the Koh Meas Guesthouse, this market carries wine, ice cream and things to spread on bread, including peanut butter.

Drinking

Late-night bars can be found on Victory Hill, along Serendipity Beach and in the city centre.

With the Angkor Brewery located right on the outskirts of town, beer is very cheap, starting at just US$0.50.

VICTORY HILL

The Victory Hill nightlife scene has recently gone a bit sleazy and now includes half-a-dozen open-front bars where Western men come to shoot pool and make the acquaintance of much younger Cambodian women working freelance. Tame stuff compared with Thailand but a real turn-off to many backpackers.

The battle for the soul of Victory Hill has been joined. On one side are the 'girlie bars' owners, who dream of creating a Cambodian Pattaya, and on the other the fighting-mad owners of the area's legitimate businesses, whose receipts have been plummeting. One sign of progress: brash solicitation has stopped, so children out with their parents no longer whisper quizzically to their mothers, 'Why are all the ladies saying hello to Daddy?'

Among the nightspots in the area worth a look:

Mojo Bar (☎ 016 307704; ⏰ 11am-1am or later) The only place in town you're likely to hear world music, including Raï, this unpretentious, rough-hewn bar has over 20 kinds of rum, screens English football matches and hosts jam sessions on Thursdays.

Rainy Season (☎ 092 583372; ⏰ to 1am) Has a BBQ buffet, a tropical-style bar and (sometimes) live music.

Retox Bar (☎ 012 819451; ☽ 5pm-2.30am or later) Often has live music (from 8pm) and jam sessions – guests are welcome to play instruments they keep on hand (keyboard, guitar, drums, etc).

CITY CENTRE

Espresso Kampuchea (☎ 012 478139; Sopheakmongkol St, two shops north of 235 Ekareach St; ☽ 7am-8pm) Appreciated for its excellent coffee, this café – just five tables and a tiny bar – is something of a hang-out for expats. Breakfast is served all day. The soundtrack is jazz and blues.

Gelato Italiano (49 7 Makara St; ☽ 7am-8pm) Run by students from Sihanoukville's Don Bosco Hotel School, this modern, Italian-style café serves espresso, latte, ice coffee and banana splits (US$2), as well as its creamy namesake. Affords panoramic views of downtown Sihanoukville.

ourpick Paco's (☎ 092 542095; 198 Ekareach St; ☽ noon-11pm or midnight) The décor and music will whisk you off to Iberia at this Spanish tapas bar, presided over by a genuine Madrileño. Tapas is US$1 to US$1.50, and mains run from US$2.50 to US$4. Paco's also serves paella and mini-*bocatas* (small sandwiches; US$2).

BEACHES

Many of Sihanoukville's most popular backpacker pubs and beach bars are along Serendipity Beach and the Road to Serendipity. Places to check out include the bar at the **Monkey Republic Bungalows** (☎ 012 490290) and **Utopia** (☎ 934319; cnr Road to Serendipity & 14 Milthona St), a garden bar that's home to the 24-hour party people and offers free dorm accommodation.

Options on the sand at Otres Beach include the **Tropical Season Bar** (☎ 092 583372; ☽ 7am-1am), which doubles as a restaurant.

Entertainment

Popular night-time activities include hanging out in the shacks and pubs along Serendipity and Occheuteal Beaches, in the nightspots on the Road to Serendipity and in the bars of Victory Hill, some of which host jam sessions and live music.

In the evening there's lots to watch at **Top-Cat** (☎ 011 617799; Road to Serendipity; ☒), a clean, wholesome 'entertainment centre' where you can see moving images (or play Xbox 360-for-two) on a state-of-the-art, 8m hi-def screen.

Down the slope from Victory Hill, Bungalow Village has an open-air cinema.

Shopping

Khmer Artisans (☎ 012 615111; 101B Ekareach St; ☽ 8am-8pm) This shop, like its Phnom Penh flagship, has a good selection of creative, high-quality handicrafts, including exquisite textiles, silk items (purses, cushions) and embroidery.

M'lop Tapang (☎ 934072; Serendipity St; www .mloptapang.org) Run by a local NGO that works with at-risk children, this shop sells items made by street kids, so that they can attend school instead of peddling on the beach.

Rajana (www.rajanacrafts.org; down the alley, 62 7 Makara St; ☽ 7am-6pm) This nonprofit shop – upstairs at the Starfish Bakery & Café – sells fair-trade jewellery, clothing, accessories and crafts. Profits are invested in teaching handicraft skills to young Cambodians.

Getting There & Away

National Highway 4 (NH4), the 230km highway between Sihanoukville and Phnom Penh, is in excellent condition but is quite dangerous due to the prevalence of high-speed overtaking on blind corners. It's doubly dicey around dusk and at night, when all intercity road travel is best avoided.

NH3 to Kampot (105km) is also in tip-top shape.

Taking NH48 to Krong Koh Kong and the Cham Yeam–Hat Lek border crossing will be a breeze once the four ferry crossings are replaced by bridges, an engineering landmark that should happen sometime in 2008.

AIR

Sihanoukville International Airport is 18km east of town near Ream National Park. Temple-beach combo holidays have been much touted for years, but air service to Sihanoukville was suspended in mid-2007 after a plane went down near Bokor Hill Station. Siem Reap Airways is looking into reinstating the service.

BOAT

For details on the ferry to Krong Koh Kong, see p185.

BUS

The bus station – little more than a big parking lot – is in the city centre a block north of Ekareach St. Almost all companies charge foreigners a bit more than Khmers; prices quoted below are for foreigners. Bookings

SOUTH COAST

can be made in person or via guesthouses and hotels, which take a commission.

Companies with services to Phnom Penh (four hours) include **Phnom Penh Sorya** (☎ 933888), Cambodia's largest bus company, which has six per day at US$4.50; **Mekong Express** (☎ 934189), whose limousine buses have toilets, two per day at US$6; **Rith Mony** (RMN; ☎ 934161), four per day at US$3.50; **GST Express** (☎ 933826), four per day at US$3.50 to US$4.50; and **Paramount Angkor Express** (☎ 017 525366), US$5. All have offices at the bus station with schedules posted. Departures are plentiful in the morning but peter out by about 2pm.

Phnom Penh Sorya can get you to Kampot (US$3.50, two hours, one daily), as can a minibus company based at Sihanoukville's G'day Mate Guesthouse (US$6.50); see p218.

Buses to Krong Koh Kong also leave from the bus station. Virak-Buntham has services to Krong Koh Kong and the nearby Cham Yeam–Hat Lek border crossing (US$14; likely to drop as ferry crossings are replaced by bridges) and can get you to Bangkok (US$31), Ko Samet (US$31) and Ko Chang (US$26). Rith Mony can also get you to Krong Koh Kong (US$14). We've received reports of wild driving by some minibus drivers on this route.

It's a long haul to Siem Reap but if you don't mind spending 10 hours on the road it can be done, generally via Phnom Penh. Companies to contact include Mekong Express (US$16).

SHARE TAXI

Many share-taxi drivers seem to think they're Michael Schumacher, so if you don't like blind overtaking you may want to wait for a bus.

Taxis to Phnom Penh (four hours) set out from the bus station. Expect to pay US$5 for a cramped seat (US$7.50 with just four passengers) or US$30 to US$35 for a taxi to call your own. In Phnom Penh, Sihanoukville-bound taxis can be found near Psar Dang Kor or Psar Thmei.

Share taxis to Kampot (US$3.50, two hours) leave from an open lot across 7 Makara St from Psar Leu. Chartering your own costs about US$20.

Eco-Trek Tours (p196) can arrange English-speaking taxis.

Getting Around

Some hotels and guesthouses offer free pick-up at the bus station if you book ahead.

BICYCLE

Cycling is a pleasant and environmentally friendly way to get around Sihanoukville. Some guesthouses offer rentals, as do two bookshops, **Mister Heinz Books** (☎ 012 342720; 95 Ekareach St, City Centre; ⏱ 7.30am-7.30pm), which hires out bikes for US$2 per day, and **Q&A** (☎ 017 802721; 219 Ekareach St, City Centre; ⏱ 9am-6pm or later).

MOTO & TUK TUK

Sihanoukville's *moto* drivers are notorious for aggressively touting passers-by and – more than anywhere else in Cambodia – ripping you off, so haggle hard over the price before setting out. Expect to pay a bit more than in Phnom Penh.

From the city centre, daytime rates are 2000r to Victory Hill, 3000r or 4000r to Serendipity, Occheuteal and Victory Beaches and US$1.50 or US$2 to the ferry dock. Expect to pay 1000r

---

MOTORBIKE RENTAL BAN

At press time, local authorities were not allowing foreigners to rent motorcycles, officially for safety reasons (half-a-dozen foreigners die around Sihanoukville each year in motorbike accidents). A few places are known to defy the rental ban – ask around for the latest at guesthouses, restaurants and bars.

As well as the rental ban, some police have been pulling over foreigners who've rented motorbikes in other towns for not having a valid Cambodian driver's licence. In many cases, US$5 will get you out of trouble. Favourite spots for surprise police roadblocks – rarely seen in rainy weather, Sihanoukville expats note – are the Golden Lions Roundabout and the Caltex petrol station on Ekareach St.

Electric bicycles (per half/whole day US$2/3), which can go for 40km to 80km between charges, are one way to get around the rental ban. They can be hired at the Monkey Republic Bungalows and the Orchidée Guesthouse.

SINS OF COMMISSION, SINS OF OMISSION

At Sihanoukville's bus station, you may encounter high prices being quoted for a *moto*. When a bus arrives, a *motodup* (*moto* driver) is assigned to each foreigner. Bargaining is futile – if you don't agree to the set price (usually 6000r to 8000r to the beaches) no other driver will take you.

Walk out to the main street, though, and you'll find a *motodup* who'll accept the market rate (3000r to 4000r to the beaches). *Tuk tuks* – ideal for travel with a big pack – can also be found on nearby streets.

Some guesthouses pay drivers handsome commissions to send custom their way, so if you've just arrived, getting your *motodup* to take you where *you* want may turn into a battle of wills. If your chosen hostelry is one that won't ante up, don't be surprised to hear that it's closed, has contaminated water or is 'full of prostitutes'.

---

or 2000r more at night. *Tuk tuks* generally charge about double the *moto* rates.

TAXI

At the bus station, the posted taxi fares are US$6 to Victory, Serendipity and Occheuteal Beaches and US$7 to the ferry port. This is a couple of dollars more than the going rate but the *motodup* cartel enforces higher prices to keep a lid on competition.

AROUND SIHANOUKVILLE

For details on what to see and do in Kirirom National Park, located midway between Sihanoukville and the capital, see p116.

Islands

More than a dozen islands – some with gorgeous, blissfully empty beaches – dot the waters off Sihanoukville. As we go to press, a number of exclusive island resorts are on the drawing boards.

Crescent-shaped **Koh Russei** (Bamboo Island), about an hour offshore, has several restaurant-bars, including QQ, and three basic beachfront bungalow groupings. One, with shared bathrooms, is run by **Coasters** (r without fan US$10); see p200. Nearby **Bimbamboo** (r US$10-12) offers private bathrooms. With no electricity and no hawkers, this is a good place to completely relax.

Koh Rong, two hours from the mainland, has a fantastic beach on the southwestern coast, stretching for 5km or more. This 15km-long island has other fine beaches, too, and there's a bustling fishing community on the southeast coast with basic supplies available, plus fresh fish and crab. If one place is set to become the Ko Samui of Cambodia, this is it! For now, you can stay at **Lazy Beach Bungalows** (☎ 017 879552; r US$10-15).

Koh Rong Samlon, just south of Koh Rong and 10km from end to end, includes a large heart-shaped bay with some shellfish cultivation, as well as good beaches on its north coast. EcoSea Dive (p198) has four bungalows here, usually used by divers on overnight trips.

Nearer the coast and to the south of Sihanoukville are several smaller islands that are an option if the open waters to Koh Rong are too choppy. **Koh Khteah** is the nearest (Otres Nautica runs snorkelling trips out here – see p198), while **Koh Ta Khieu** has better beaches but is near Ream Naval Base, Cambodia's navy headquarters.

Day trips to the islands, some with snorkelling, can be arranged by many Sihanoukville guesthouses and travel agencies (p196). See p198 for details on dive companies.

Ream National Park
ឧទ្យានជាតិរាម

Just 18km east of Sihanoukville, Ream National Park – also known as Preah Sihanouk National Park – comprises 150 sq km of primary forests (mostly lowland evergreen forest and mangrove swamps) and 60 sq km of marine habitats. It's home to breeding populations of a number of regionally and globally endangered birds of prey, including the Brahminy kite, grey-headed fish-eagle and white-bellied sea-eagle – look for them soaring over **Prek Toeuk Sap Estuary**, which is salty in the dry season and freshwater in the wet season. Endangered birds that feed on the mudflats include the lesser adjutant, milky stork and painted stork. The park's more common feathered residents include the great egret, little egret, woolly-necked stork, black-capped kingfisher and stork-billed kingfisher.

Ream's profusion of colourful butterflies includes multiple species of Hesperiidae,

Lycaenidae, Nymphalidae, Papilionidae and Pieridae. All sorts of gleaming damselflies make their home in the park, too.

SIGHTS, ACTIVITIES & SLEEPING

Fascinating **jungle walks** led by rangers – most, but not all, speak English – are easy to arrange (hiking unaccompanied is not allowed) at the **park headquarters** (☎ 016 767686, 012 875096; ☺ 9am–5pm). A two- to three-hour walk from the Keng Kong Recreation Site (9.5km south of the park's HQ) to the Andoung Tuek Cascades costs US$6 per person. Pond swimming is possible during the wet season. A five- or six-hour hike into the park's mountainous interior costs US$2 per hour per participant. It's best (but not obligatory) to call ahead. The income generated goes to help protect the park.

Ranger-led **boat trips** (1-5 people US$35 or US$40) on the Prek Toeuk Sap Estuary and its mangrove channels are another option. You can often spot monkeys, dolphins and lots of birds, in addition to sunbathing, swimming and snorkelling (equipment hire costs US$2).

In the coconut-shaded fishers' village of **Thmor Thom** – reachable by boat (US$30 return for up to four people; 1¼ hours each way) – the national park has a ranger post known as Dolphin Station because, from November to March, you can often see dolphins in the morning and evening. Two-hour dolphin-watching boat trips costs US$20 for up to four people. It's possible to overnight here – the village is a 25-minute walk from **Koh Sampoach Beach** – in an over-the-water **bungalow** (per person US$5); meals are available from villagers.

Ream National Park's territory includes two islands with some fine snorkelling, **Koh Thmei** and – just off Vietnam's Phu Quoc Island – **Koh Seh**. In the dry season, if it's not too windy, you can get out there by wooden motorboat (US$40 or US$50) from the Prek Toeuk Sap ranger station.

Travel agencies offering day trips to Ream National Park include Eco-Trek Tours (p196; US$15 to US$25, including lunch).

GETTING THERE & AWAY

To get to Ream National Park, 18km east Sihanoukville, take NH4 to Sihanoukville International Airport; the park headquarters is 700m south of NH4 across the road from the new green-roofed terminal building. Boats leave from Prek Toeuk Sap Ranger Station,

about 3km further out along NH4 (at the bridge). A coastal road linking the park with Otres Beach and Sihanoukville is planned.

A return trip by *moto* should cost US$5 to US$10; the price depends on how well the driver speaks English and how long you stay. A private taxi costs about US$25 for the day.

Kbal Chhay Cascades

Thanks to their appearance in *Pos Keng Kong* (The Giant Snake; 2000), the most successful Cambodian film of the post-civil war era, these **cascades** (admission US$1) on the Prek Toeuk Sap River draw huge numbers of domestic tourists. That's why there are so many raised **picnicking platforms** (per day 5000r, more on holidays) and so much litter.

From the parking area, a rough log **toll bridge** (for locals/tourists 300r/500r), a miniature version of Cambodia's user fee-based highway system, leads to several miniature sandy coves, more lounging areas and some perilous rapids. The best spot for a safe, refreshing dip – by children as well as adults – is across another bridge, on the far bank of a cool, crystal-clear tributary of the brown-tinted main river. Free changing booths are available. Not much water flows here in the dry season.

The cascades are about 17km from the centre of Sihanoukville. To get there, head east along NH4 for 9km and then, at the sign, north along a wide dirt road for 8km. By *moto* a return trip should cost US$5.

KAMPOT PROVINCE

ខេត្តកំពត

Kampot Province has emerged as one of Cambodia's most popular destinations for tourists – both foreign and domestic – thanks to an alluring combination of old colonial towns, abundant natural attractions and easy intra-regional transport. Highlights include Bokor National Park and its abandoned hill station, the caves around Kompong Trach and, in an adjacent mini-province of its own, the enchanting – if dilapidated – seaside resort of Kep (p224). Visitors often end up staying in the sleepy, atmospheric provincial capital of Kampot longer than planned.

Kampot Province is renowned for producing some of the world's finest pepper.

Indeed, before the war no Paris restaurant worth its salt would be without Kampot pepper on the table. Durian haters be warned: Kampot is Cambodia's main producer of this stinky fruit.

KAMPOT
កំពត
☎ 033 / pop 33,000

More and more visitors are discovering the sleepy riverside town of Kampot, a charming place with a relaxed atmosphere and a fine, if run-down French architectural legacy. Eclipsed as a port when Sihanoukville was founded in 1959, Kampot makes an excellent base for exploring Bokor National Park and the verdant coast east towards Vietnam, including Kep and a number of superb cave-temples.

Orientation

Commercial activity is centred around 7 Makara St, which stretches from the Central Roundabout to River Rd, and the padlocked old market. The main transport hub is around the Total petrol station, linked to the old market (Psar Leu) by a broad avenue.

Information

As of this writing, the tourist office doesn't have much to offer the public – guesthouses and hotels are a far better source of information.

Acleda Bank (cnr 7 Makara St & Central Roundabout) Can change travellers cheques and has a 24-hour ATM.

Canadia Bank Handles travellers cheques and credit-card cash advances. One block northwest of Central Roundabout.

Epic Arts Café (☼ 7am-6pm) Has a small selection of English paperback books for US$2.

Kampot Network (7 Makara St; per hr 3000r; ☼ 7am-10pm) One of a few internet cafés along 7 Makara St.

Sok Lim Tours (☎ 012 719872; www.soklimtours.com) An established, professional outfit with reasonably priced trips to Bokor National Park, Kep and other South Coast sites. May also be able to organise cycling trips. Guides speak English and French. Bookings can be made through guesthouses.

Sy Internet (7 Makara St) Another internet café.

Sights & Activities

Kampot's most enjoyable activity is **strolling** along streets that evoke days long gone. Blocks lined with decrepit French-era shops can be found in the triangle delineated by 7 Makara

KAMPOT

INFORMATION	
Canadia Bank	1 C2
Epic Arts Café	(see 16)
Kampot Network	2 C2
Main Post Office	3 C3
Sy Internet	4 C2
Tourist Office	5 D3

SIGHTS & ACTIVITIES	
Kampot Massage By Blind	(see 7)
Kampot Traditional Music School	6 C2
Seeing Hands Massage 5	7 C2

SLEEPING	
Blissful Guesthouse	8 D2
Bokor Mountain Lodge	9 C2
Kampot Guesthouse	10 D2
Little Garden Bar	(see 18)
Long Villa Guesthouse	11 C1
Orchid Guesthouse	12 D2
Rikitikitavi	(see 20)
Ta Eng Guesthouse	13 D3

EATING	
Bakery 333	14 C2
Bamboo Light Café	15 C2
Bokor Mountain Lodge	(see 9)
Epic Arts Café	16 C2
Heng Dy Grocery	17 C2
Little Garden Bar	18 C2
Mittapheap Restaurant	19 C1
Rheaj's Burger House	(see 7)
Sarveestablishment	20 C3
Ta Eou Restaurant	21 B1

DRINKING	
Bonkers	(see 9)

TRANSPORT	
Cheang Try Motorbike Rental	22 C2
Hour Lean Bus Office	(see 23)
Phnom Penh Sorya Bus Office	23 D2
Sean Ly Motorcycle Shop	24 C2
Share Taxis	25 D2

Map labels:
To Les Manguiers (2km)
To Train Station (1km); Phnom Penh (148km)
Psar Leu
To Bokor National Park (41km); Sihanoukville (105km)
New Bridge
St 713
River Rd
White Obelisk
7 Makara St
To Phnom Chhnork (8km); Phnom Sorsia (15km); Kep (23km); Kompong Trach (37km)
Total Petrol Station
Four Nagas Roundabout
To Bodhi Villa (2km); Tek Chhou Zoo (6km)
Old Bridge
Prek Kampong Bay
Old Market
Vietnam-Cambodia Friendship Monument
Lily Pad Pond
To Riverfront Promenade; Hang Guesthouse (500m)
0 200 m
0 0.1 miles

SOUTH COAST

THE COST OF KEEPING COOL

Due to the underdeveloped state of Cambodia's electricity system – many towns get their mains supply from antiquated diesel generators – Cambodians pay considerably more for electricity than do vastly wealthier people in the West. In Kampot, for example, 1kWh of electricity costs a whopping 1200r. That's seven times the price in the UK, 10 times what you'd pay in the USA and 14 times what consumers are charged in Australia or Canada. To put it another way, an Australian earning minimum wage has to work for 18 seconds to buy one kWh of electricity while your *average* Cambodian has to work 1½ hours – 300 times as long! That's why Cambodians have adopted power-saving fluorescent light bulbs so much faster than people in the West.

When you run your hotel room's air-con unit, just three hours of coolness cost about US$1 – what many Cambodians earn in a day. And it costs almost as much to keep a hot-water boiler on for an hour. That's why air-con rooms cost so much more than ones with fans – no-one is getting rich except, perhaps, the well-connected owners of the local electricity company.

The expense of diesel electricity is one of the reasons that quite a few hydroelectric projects are being planned, despite their environmental costs. Near Kampot, for instance, a dam being built upstream from Tek Chhouu Falls will soon flood parts of Bokor National Park.

St, the Central Roundabout and the post office. The **old bridge** is quite a sight: destroyed during the Khmer Rouge period, it has been repaired in a mishmash of styles.

Kampot's riverside location makes it an excellent place to begin a **boat excursion**, either to scenic areas upstream or – at around 5pm, when the fishing boats head out to sea – downstream. Enquire at your guesthouse or ask around along the river. You should be able to arrange a seaworthy vessel for about US$10 an hour.

Les Manguiers, a riverside guesthouse 2km north of town, rents out **river kayaks** for two hours/half-day/full day for US$3/5/8 (marginally more for two-person boats).

Visitors are welcome to drop by and observe the students of the **Kampot Traditional Music School** (8-11am & 6.30-9pm Mon-Fri), which trains orphaned and disabled children in traditional music and dance. There's no charge but donations are welcome.

Blind masseurs and masseuses offer soothing bliss – especially pleasurable after a day of bone-jarring motorbike travel – at **Seeing Hands Massage 5** (012 503012; per hr US$4; 7am-10pm) and **Kampot Massage by the Blind** (012 421043; River Rd; per hr US$4).

Sleeping

It's worth bearing in mind that after a chilly day trip up to Bokor, a hot shower might be a welcome treat.

BUDGET

Ta Eng Guesthouse (012 330058; r US$3-6) A few blocks from the centre on a street lined with 1960s row houses, this place has expanded from a family homestay into a popular guesthouse with 10 well-kept rooms and rooftop views. The gracious owner speaks French and English.

Long Villa Guesthouse (012 210820; longvilla guesthouse@yahoo.com; 75 St 713; s US$3, d US$4-8;) In a quiet spot near bustling Psar Leu, this family-run backpacker sanctuary, opened in 2006, has 15 smallish, good-value rooms. Offers Bokor and Kep tours and motorbike rental.

Blissful Guesthouse (012 513024; www.blissful guesthouse.com; blissfulguesthouse@yahoo.com; r US$4-8) Surrounded by a lovely garden, this atmospheric old wooden house has 11 rooms, four with shared bathroom. Danish-owned, it's got a popular bar-restaurant and, upstairs, a great chill-out area.

Bodhi Villa (012 728884; bodhivilla@mac.com; dm US$2, r US$4-8) Situated 2km towards Tek Chhouu Falls from town (a few hundred metres upriver from the rail bridge), this happy hideaway – with four bungalows – is tucked away behind a luxuriant garden on the banks of the river and is a good base for water sports. A *moto* from town should cost 3000r. A larger version is planned on an island just downriver from the falls.

Orchid Guest House (092 226996; orchidguesthouse kampot@yahoo.com; s US$4, d US$10-15;) Set in a manicured garden full of orchids, this hostelry has 10 comfortable rooms and a fish pond out back. Pricier rooms come with air-con and hot water. Offers Bokor and Kep tours.

Kampot Guesthouse (012 512931; thean22@gmail .com; r US$5-15;) Has 26 spacious rooms with soaring ceilings and TV. The garden restaurant offers good value.

Hang Guesthouse (☎ 932170; www.hang.esmartweb .com; r US$10) Situated on the waterfront 800m downriver from the post office (300m south of the southern end of the riverfront promenade), this serene, family-run place is ideal if you want to get away from it all. The three bungalows face a quiet garden. Bicycles are free, so it's easy to get into town.

Little Garden Bar (☎ 012 256901; www.littlegarden bar.com; River Rd; r with fan/air-con from US$10/16; 🐾) This relaxing garden restaurant has six functional, spacious rooms, some with river views and hot water. More rooms are planned.

MIDRANGE

our pick **Les Manguiers** (☎ 092 330050; www.mango mango.byethost18.com; mango@camshin.com.kh; r US$10-15, bungalow US$20-35) This family- and child-friendly complex, 2km north of the new bridge, is set in a grassy sugar palm garden right on the river. Run by a friendly Khmer-French couple, it has three rooms and six simple but tasteful wooden bungalows (without hot water for now), a children's playground, badminton and pétanque courts, and two over-the-water gazebos. Use of canoes and basic bicycles is free. Serves *table d'hôte*–style meals. A *moto* from town should cost 2000r to 3000r. Call ahead for free pick-up.

Rikitikitavi (☎ 012 235102; www.rikitikitavi-kampot .com; River Rd; r US$25-35; 🐾 💻) This classy riverfront restaurant has five tasteful and very comfortable rooms, all with hot water.

Bokor Mountain Lodge (☎ 932314; www.bokorlodge .com; River Rd; r US$25-35; 🐾) A majestic French-era building facing the river has been turned into Kampot's most evocative hostelry. The five spacious rooms have 3½-metre ceilings and all the amenities; pricier ones come with a river view. Rates include breakfast.

Eating

Kampot now has quite a variety of decent dining options. There's a row of local eateries along 7 Makara St.

Rheaj's Burger House (☎ 012 333361; River Rd; mains US$1.50-2.50; 🕙 7am-9pm) Run by a woman from New Hampshire and her Khmer husband, this eatery serves thick, juicy burgers and does surprisingly good hot dogs, as well as sandwiches, salads, pizza and home-made pasta.

Ta Eou Restaurant (☎ 932422; River Rd; mains US$1.50-5; 🕙 10am-2pm & 6-10pm) Built on stilts

over the river, this is a top place for a sunset meal, with views across to Bokor. The menu is extensive and includes fresh seafood (crab with peppercorns is a favourite), veggie dishes and local broths.

Epic Arts Café (www.epicarts.org.uk; mains US$2-3.25; 🕙 7am-6pm) A great place for breakfast (US$2.50), home-made cakes or tea, this mellow eatery – staffed by deaf and disabled young people – can also pack a bagel lunch for a trip up to Bokor. Sometimes it hosts dance performances. Profits fund dance, music and art workshops for deaf and disabled Cambodians.

Mittapheap Restaurant (☎ 012 330105; mains US$2-4) An establishment facing the market that's long been a favourite thanks to its great soups and Khmer and Chinese staples, all at fair prices.

Bamboo Light Café (☎ 016 936543; River Rd; curries US$2.50-4.50; 🕙 7am-11pm) One of two rival Sri Lankan restaurants in Kampot. Local expats rave about the fine subcontinental flavours, the many veggie options and the riverfront terrace.

Little Garden Bar (☎ 012 256901; River Rd; mains US$4; 🕙 breakfast, lunch & dinner) Set in the garden of an old French-period property, this tranquil little haven serves Khmer and international dishes, including pizzas (US$5.50), and wine by the glass. The rooftop terrace affords superb river views.

Bokor Mountain Lodge (☎ 932314; River Rd; most mains US$4-6) Not just a hotel, this French-era place has an atmospheric restaurant. Serves a good selection of mainly European dishes, including salads, deli sandwiches and pizzas.

Rikitikitavi (☎ 012 235102; River Rd; mains US$4.50-9.75; 🕙 7am-10pm) Named after the mongoose in Rudyard Kipling's *The Jungle Book*, this stylish terrace restaurant affords unsurpassed river views and is known for its generous portions. Specialities include Kampot pepper chicken, imported beefsteak, sandwiches, burgers, burritos, salads, apple pie and plenty of veggie options. Serves wine by the glass.

Several hostelries have popular restaurants, including **Kampot Guesthouse** (🕙 breakfast, lunch & dinner) and **Blissful Guesthouse** (mains US$2.50-4; 🕙 7.30am-9.30pm), which serves Danish and Mexican dishes.

SELF-CATERING

Bakery 333 Around the corner from the Epic Arts Café, this is the best place in town for fresh baguettes (500r). Look for the piles of split wood (for the oven) out front.

Heng Dy (☎ 932925; Central Roundabout) A key address if you're heading off to explore Bokor, this grocery has a decent selection of imported goods, including chocolate, wine, cheese (in the freezer), canned goods and even peanut butter.

Drinking

Hostelries with popular bars include **Blissful Guesthouse** (☿ to midnight or later), with its happening little downstairs bar, and Bokor Mountain Lodge, a convivial 'gourmet pub' with a vaguely colonial ambiance, wine by the glass and a good selection of single-malt whiskies.

Bonkors (☎ 011 598176; River Rd; ☿ 1pm-midnight or later; ⊞) Run by an English couple, this bar has air-con, the best loos in town and 400 cocktails, as well as homemade ice cream, cheese cake and meat pies. Cigarettes and water are free. In case you're wondering, the name is a play on 'Bokor'.

Getting There & Away

NH3, these days in sharp shape, links Kampot with both Phnom Penh (148km, two hours) and Sihanoukville (105km).

Both Phnom Penh Sorya Transport and **Hour Lean** (☎ 012 939917) run two buses daily to midday to/from Phnom Penh (US$4, four to five hours). Both companies take the long way around – via Kep (US$2, 40 minutes) and Angk Tasaom (the gateway to Takeo; US$2.50) – because the Bailey bridges on NH3 aren't bus-friendly. Both companies have ticket desks around Sokhoda Restaurant (facing the Total petrol station).

Other options to Phnom Penh, via Angk Tasaom, include share taxi (US$4) and crowded-to-the-gills minibus (US$3). Both leave from a stand near the Total petrol station and are easiest to find between 7.30am and 10am.

A *moto/tuk tuk*/taxi to Kep should cost about US$3/6/10.

To Sihanoukville, Phnom Penh Sorya has a bus (US$3.50, 1½ hours) at 8.30am. Share taxis cost US$3.50, minibuses are US$3, and a private taxi is about US$20. Sihanoukville's G'day Mate Guesthouse operates a safe, reliable **minibus service** (☎ 017 707857; US$6.50) between Kampot and Sihanoukville on Monday and Friday, with plans to make the service

daily. The service is door-to-door, with pick-up and drop-off at your guesthouse or hotel.

There is talk of establishing a regular boat service from Kampot to the Vietnamese island of Phu Quoc.

Getting Around

The average fare for a *moto* ride around town is 2000r (3000r in the evening). *Tuk tuk*s, the latest addition to the local transport scene, cost about US$1 in town.

Ta Eng Guesthouse can arrange *motos/tuk tuk*s with drivers for US$4/10 a day. **Long Villa Tours** (☎ 012 626698), based at Long Villa Guesthouse, rents out bicycles for US$1 a day and motorbikes for US$4 a day (US$5 for a new one). **Orchid Guesthouse** hires out 250cc motorbikes for US$12 a day.

Two excellent shops rent out motorbikes, cars and pick-ups:

Sean Ly Motorcycle Shop (☎ 012 944687; ☿ 7am-8pm) Rents out 125cc bikes for US$3 a day (US$5 for a new one) and 250cc trail bikes for US$10. Can also arrange a car/pick-up with a driver for US$30/60 a day.

Cheang Try Motorbike Rental (☎ 012 974698; ☿ 7am-8pm) Small bikes cost US$3 a day, new 125cc Hondas are US$6 a day. A car/4WD pickup cost US$30/70 a day, including a driver. The owner speaks good English and often guides tourists himself.

AROUND KAMPOT

The limestone hills east towards Kep are honeycombed with caves, some of which can be explored with the help of local kids and a reliable torch/flashlight. Phnom Chhnork, surrounded by blazingly beautiful countryside, is a real gem and can easily be visited in an afternoon along with Phnom Sorsia.

Phnom Chhnork

The base of **Phnom Chhnork** (Phnom Chngouk; admission US$1) is a short walk through the rice fields from Wat Ang Sdok, where a monk will collect the entry fee and a gaggle of friendly local kids will offer their services as guides. A well-tended staircase leads up the hillside and down into a cavern as graceful as a Gothic cathedral. There you'll be greeted by a **stalactite elephant**, with yet another elephant outlined on the flat cliff face to the right. Nearby is a formation that looks like a **calf's head**. Tiny chirping bats live up near two natural chimneys that soar towards the blue sky, partly blocked by foliage of an impossibly green hue.

Inside the cave's main chamber stands a remarkable 7th-century (Funan-era) **brick temple**, dedicated to Shiva. The temple's brickwork is in superb condition thanks to the protection afforded by the cave. Poke your head inside and check out the ancient stalactite that serves as a linga.

Phnom Chhnork occupies a bucolic site surrounded by rice paddies and meticulously tended vegetable plots. The view from up top, and the walk to and from the wat, is especially magical in the late afternoon and around sunset.

Phnom Chhnork is about 8km from Kampot. A bit past the rhino statue in the middle of NH33, turn northeast – across the road from the Cham mosque look for a sign reading 'Phnom Chhngok Resort'. A *moto/tuk tuk* from Kampot should cost about US$5/7 return.

Phnom Sorsia

Less interesting than Phnom Chhnork, **Phnom Sorsia** (admission free) has a gaudily painted modern temple and several natural caves.

From the parking area in front of the school, a stairway leads up the hillside to a colourful temple. From there, steps lead left up to **Rung Damrey Saa** (White Elephant Cave), named not for a failed mega-project but rather for a mineral formation situated to the right of the two Buddha statues. A bit past a slippery, sloping passage where one false step will send you into the abyss, a hand-sized hole leads to a **hidden pool** filled with refreshingly cool water. Nearby you can glimpse a peep show of tiny terraced paddy fields. Shine your flashlight up and you may spot bats.

From the colourful temple, steps angle up to the right to the **Bat Cave**. Inside, countless bats flutter and chirp overhead, flying out to the forest and back through a narrow natural chimney. Bamboo poles are used to hunt the creatures by swatting them out of the air. The circuit ends near a hilltop **stupa** with impressive views.

The local kids who guide tourists – and insistently ask for huge tips – are not likely to keep much of what you pay them. As soon as visitors hand over the cash, adults swoop down and confiscate most it.

The turn-off to Phnom Sorsia is on NH33 13.5km southeast of Kampot and 2.5km northwest of the statue of the white horse at the Kep junction. Look for a sign reading

'Phnom Sorsia Resort' – from there a dirt road leads about 1km northeast through the rice fields.

Tek Chhouu Falls

ទឹកឈូរ

Hugely popular with locals, this pleasant bathing spot is likely to disappoint fans of sheer curtains of tumbling water as the 'falls' are really just a series of small rapids that don't even move all that rapidly in the dry season. However, the site has lots of little eateries and picnicking platforms, a prerequisite for any proper Khmer day out. A bouncy pedestrian suspension bridge leads to an island whose far side has some tiny strips of sand where you can swim.

The privately owned **Tek Chhouu Zoo** (Teok Chhou Zoo; ☎ 011 768470; admission for locals/foreigners 3000r/US$4), several kilometres towards Kampot from the falls, is small but clean and well-kept. The entrance is marked by twin statues of roaring tigers.

A *moto* to Tek Chhouu Falls from Kampot (8km each way), past the durian fields, should cost about US$4 or US$5 return.

BOKOR NATIONAL PARK

ឧទ្យានជាតិបូកគោ

This **national park** (admission US$5) – officially called Preah Monivong National Park – comprises 1581 sq km of protected land, most of it primary forest, that's particularly rich in endemic flora and provides a home to globally endangered fauna such as the tiger (recently photographed with camera traps), chestnut-headed partridge and green peafowl. In addition to the rainforest itself, with its unceasing insect and bird calls, the park's main attractions are Popokvil Falls and the abandoned French hill station of Bokor.

Bokor's moist evergreen forests – with dry dipterocarp and mixed deciduous forests in the north – shelter a wide variety of rare and threatened animals, including the Indian elephant, leopard, Asiatic black bear, Malayan sun bear, pileated gibbon, pig-tailed macaque, slow loris, red muntjac deer, lesser mouse deer, pangolin (p189), yellow-throated martin, small Asian mongoose and various species of civet, porcupine, squirrel and bat. Over 300 species of bird, including several types of hornbill, also live here. Don't expect to see much wildlife, though – most of the animals are nocturnal and survive by staying in more remote parts of the park.

SOUTH COAST

CHEY YUTHEARITH *Daniel Robinson*

Chey Yuthearith is a modest man with a very tough job: director of Bokor National Park (p219). In a country in which short-term profit – from clear-cutting ancient rainforests, for instance – often matters to those in power more than long-term sustainability or saving endangered species, working from within the system to bring about incremental change requires consummate political skill and a great deal of perseverance and patience.

It also requires no small degree of courage. Winner of a 2004 Clark R Bavin Wildlife Law Enforcement Award, given by the **Species Survival Network** (www.ssn.org), Chey's citation mentions not only that he is 'a shining example of what a dedicated and honest official can achieve' and that Bokor has become 'a model protection project for Cambodia', but also that 'in the line of duty, he has received numerous threats against his life and has been the target of gunfire. Several of his staff have had hand grenades thrown at them and have suffered injuries as a result.' None of this was even hinted at during our conversation.

Chey was born in Phnom Penh in 1958. In April 1975, at the age of 17, he was marched out of the capital along with the rest of the population and was sent to Nereay Commune in Chhuk District, just east of what is now Bokor National Park. 'During the Pol Pot regime, I go to work in the fields, same as all the Cambodian people', he relates. 'No school, no market, no everything. Very hard job, not enough food'. When Chey took the reins of Bokor National Park, there was 'a lot of illegal activity like logging and hunting, and the local people and armed forces don't know' – or care – 'about the national park and the environment'. From 1996 to 1998, 'in the southeast of the park, every day we can hear the chainsaws. When we come here [to the ranger station at the park entrance] in 1997, we have only 10 rangers to protect the whole park, very big park.' He now has 56 rangers in eight stations and substations – but even this is 'not enough'.

Complicating his plans is a massive development programme being undertaken by the powerful, well-connected Sokha company – the same people who run the entry-fee concession at Angkor and managed to gain exclusive control of 3km along two of Sihanoukville's finest beaches. 'I worry about the investor, worry they cutting the forest, but I try to explain to them. I suggest that they make a study tour to Africa, learn from Africa how to make ecotourism. Maybe Kenya, where they don't build big buildings in a national park. I suggest to Sokha to build the same way here.'

The original Sokha plan was to construct a casino, a guesthouse and a golf course atop Phnom Bokor, in effect re-establishing the old French hill station. Chey gently explained to the men from Sokha that it's 'not possible to make a golf course because over there very foggy, cannot play'. Maybe, he jokes, 'put light inside the golf balls so people can play'.

Chey hopes that Sokha will think again about the golf course and that the investment will result in more, not less, protection for the park, especially its more remote areas. 'I want to make ecotourism here for the local people so they can earn money', he explains. 'I told the director of Sokha to help the local people living around the park, give them jobs so they can earn money so there's no need to go to the forest to hunt, cut the trees.' Until now, a Bokor tree was just a tree. Perhaps when it becomes a Sokha tree, valuable because the forests are the park's big draw, it will get better protection than before. Perhaps.

Chey Yuthearith has been director of Bokor National Park since 1997, and is also the deputy director of Kampot Province's Department of the Environment.

Long kept off the tourist map due to Khmer Rouge activity, Bokor National Park is still threatened by poaching and illegal logging, especially in the north, as well as by squatters, development and, in the southeast, the Kamchay hydropower project. In the 1990s there was talk of making the park a World Heritage site but, sadly, the government's inability to protect the site put an end to the initiative.

On the frontline of the never-ending battle to protect Bokor is a group of dedicated foresters and enforcement rangers, paid in part by admission fees and assisted by expertise and funding from the Wildlife Alliance, an NGO based in San Francisco. At the park entrance, an informative (if low-budget) visitors centre has text and charts about Bokor's rare animals and the challenges of protecting the area's ecosystems.

As we went to press, plans were underway to re-establish some sort of a luxury resort atop Phnom Bokor. Whether this huge project – being carried out by the well-connected fellow who owns all those Sokimex petrol stations and holds the entry-fee concession at Angkor – will contribute to preserving the national park or endanger its rainforest ecosystem remains to be seen. Conservationists are hoping that judicious tourism development, especially ecotourism, can provide income both for local communities and for the enlightened management of the park.

The national park, including the hill station, are believed to be free of land mines, but as always in Cambodia, do the sensible thing and stick to well-worn paths.

Sights & Activities
BOKOR HILL STATION
ស្ថានីយនៃភ្នំបូកគោ

The eerie ruins of the old French hill station of Bokor, high atop Phnom Bokor (1080m), are known for their cool, even chilly, mountain climate and dramatic vistas of the coastal plain, one vertical kilometre below.

The road up to Bokor was built from 1917 to 1921 by Cambodian indentured labourers, many of whom perished. By the early 1920s a French holiday settlement had been established and a grand hotel-casino, the Bokor Palace, was inaugurated in 1925.

The hill station was twice abandoned: first when Vietnamese and Khmer Issarak (Free Khmer) forces overran it in the late 1940s while fighting for independence from France, and again in 1972 when the Lon Nol regime left it to the Khmer Rouge forces that were steadily taking over the countryside. It has been uninhabited ever since – except for the presence of either Vietnamese troops or Khmer Rouge guerrillas during much of the '80s and '90s. Because of its commanding position, the site was strategically important to all sides during the long years of conflict and was one location the Vietnamese really had to fight for during their 1979 invasion. The Khmer Rouge held out for several months, with one unit holed up in the Catholic church while the Vietnamese shot at them from the Bokor Palace, 500m away.

Today, Bokor Hill Station and its abandoned buildings have an eerie, ghost-town feel accentuated by a bright-orange lichen that carpets the exterior walls, giving them

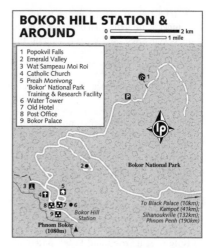

BOKOR HILL STATION & AROUND

1 Popokvil Falls
2 Emerald Valley
3 Wat Sampeau Moi Roi
4 Catholic Church
5 Preah Monivong 'Bokor' National Park Training & Research Facility
6 Water Tower
7 Old Hotel
8 Post Office
9 Bokor Palace

an otherworldly cast. Mountain mists float through the abandoned buildings, and the sea views are either breathtaking or a complete white-out. The foggy showdown that ends the Matt Dillon crime thriller *City of Ghosts* (2002) was filmed here.

The old **Catholic church** looks like the priest locked it up only yesterday. Inside, bits of glass still cling to the corners of the windows and the altar remains intact; drawings of what appear to be Khmer Rouge fighters adorn the walls. Near the kitchen, one window holds the rusty outline of a cross. A bit up the hill, past the rusted green base of some Khmer Rouge military hardware, a sheer drop overlooks virgin rainforest.

The highlight of a visit to the hill station is the shell of the **Bokor Palace**, which has been stripped of everything of value. You can explore all four levels and the rooftop terrace, from which there's a magnificent view over dense jungles that stretch almost to the sea. It's possible to wander up and down the corridors, around the kitchens and through the ballroom to the suites above, past variegated ceramic floors, tiled bathrooms and a giant fireplace where cocksure colonial French and wealthy Khmers could warm up on a nippy night. On cold, foggy days it can get pretty creepy up here as mists drop visibility to nothing and the wind howls through the building.

Other structures dotted around include an abandoned **post office** reached via a handrailless footbridge; a **water tower** that looks like a spacecraft straight out of *Close Encounters* *of the Third Kind;* and, across the lake from the ranger station, the shell of a modest **hotel**. Four decades too late, we recommend the rooms out back, which come with views.

About 250m northwest of the church, a road leads through a three-towered gate to lichen-caked **Wat Sampeau Moi Roi**, known as Five Boats Wat because some say the five oddly-sculpted rocks nearby resemble boats (although what they were smoking at the time is up for debate). Built in 1924, it affords tremendous views over the jungle to the coastline below, including Vietnam's Phu Quoc Island. Four cement supports that once anchored a Khmer Rouge radar station still stand just outside.

Debate rages over whether to redevelop the hill station. Some preservationists say it should be left untouched, while entrepreneurs salivate over its tried and tested potential. The mainstream environmentalist position is that it's most sensible to compromise, allowing limited redevelopment of the hill station area in order to generate much-needed funds to help protect the actual national park, much of which remains remote and relatively defenceless.

BLACK PALACE

As you drive up from Kampot, the first buildings you come to atop Phnom Bokor are Sihanouk's villa complex, known as the Black Palace. Inside the blotchy, windowless villas, you can still find rooms with elegant marble floors and bathrooms partly tiled in mid-century shades of pink and brown.

From here the final 10km pass through grassy scenery that's decidedly different from the lush forests along the hillside. Check out the lush **Emerald Valley**, visible to the left of the main road just before you reach the hill station.

POPOKVIL FALLS
ពពកវិល

This two-tiered waterfall is a fine place to bathe on a sunny day. The lower falls, the best place to swim, are 14m high. The upper falls, 18m high, can be reached by a path and a wooden stairway. The name translates as 'Swirling Clouds' and much of the time mists do indeed whorl just above the falls.

A shady, 11km trail links Wat Sampeau Moi Roi with Popokvil Falls. This route, which takes four or five hours, should not be undertaken without a guide, as there's always the possibility of an unexpected encounter with a three-legged female tiger nicknamed Tripod, who has been known to roam the ridge along here.

From the hill station, the falls are about 15 minutes by road. At the time of writing a bridge was out so the last 2km had to be covered on foot.

TREKKING

Hiking has a lot of potential at Bokor but as yet there is little in the way of organised trekking. The park charges US$20 for the services of a **ranger** (☎ 012 705245, 016 881540, 012 937666; US$20) who will be experienced but won't necessarily speak English.

Tours

One of the most popular ways to visit Bokor is with a group tour (generally US$8 to US$10 including lunch, plus the US$5 park fee), organised through one of the guesthouses in Kampot. Many concentrate on the old French hill station, so if you'd like to spend the day hiking through the rainforest make sure the itinerary is clear ahead of time.

Sok Lim Tours (p215) is a reliable outfit whose Bokor excursions (US$10 plus the admission fee) include a sunset river cruise on the way back. The company also offers two-day jungle treks (US$50 per person). Wild Orchid Adventure Tours, based at the Orchid Guesthouse (p216), and **Long Villa Tours** (☎ 012 626698), based at Long Villa Guesthouse (p216), are also good bets. Now that Sokimex has started building a new road up to Bokor, only certain tour operators seem to have permission to work in the park.

Sleeping & Eating

It's possible to overnight near the old hill station at the **Preah Monivong 'Bokor' National Park Training & Research Facility** (☎ 012 705245; dm US$5, r US$20-25), a national ranger training centre whose green Khmer-style roofs are easy to spot. The simply adorned rooms have comfortable beds (up to four) and hot water. Air-con and fans are not necessary up here, though extra layers may be, as temperatures can plummet as low as 12°C at night. Signs ask you not to open the window because the wind can get so fierce that it blows the dropped ceiling panels out of place! It's a good idea to call ahead for reservations.

The station generally offers a limited menu of the noodle or rice variety but some visitors prefer to bring edibles up from Kampot. Kitchen facilities are available.

Getting There & Away

Bokor National Park is 41km from Kampot, 132km from Sihanoukville and 190km from Phnom Penh. The access road begins 7km west of Kampot. Motorbikes, cars and pick-ups can be hired or rented in Kampot (p218).

As part of the hill station's redevelopment, the legendarily rough road up to Bokor – whose minibus-sized potholes make the Paris–Dakar Rally look like a Sunday drive in the country – is finally being upgraded. Rumour has it that while roadwork is underway, the only way to the top will be on foot or by Sokha-owned helicopter (US$2500 from Phnom Penh), but according to other rumours the road *will* be open but not all day, every day.

Mountain biking is a truly hardcore option. There are no decent bikes to rent as yet but they may come. If the 1km vertical climb appears too ugly, it's possible to put the bike in the back of a pick-up, cut out the hard part and enjoy an adrenaline-fuelled descent, taking serious care on the corners.

KOMPONG TRACH
កំពង់ត្រាច

The dusty town of Kompong Trach has little to recommend it except that it's near Kampot Province's fabled pepper fields and not far from a spectacular cave-temple, and makes an easy stopover if you're travelling from Vietnam's Ha Tien border crossing to Kep or Kampot.

Wat Kirisan (Wat Phnom; admission US$1) is a Buddhist temple built at the foot of **Phnom Sor** (White Mountain), a karst formation riddled with over 100 caverns and passageways and said by locals to resemble a dragon. Even without its modern religious shrines, the site would be worth a visit for its dramatic natural beauty. There's definitely rock-climbing potential here.

From the wat, an underground passage leads to the centre of the karst formation, where the sheer, vine-draped cliffs of a **hidden valley** unfold before you. This is the sort of place where you'd hardly be surprised to see a dinosaur munching on foliage or, à la *Jurassic Park,* chewing on a lawyer.

From here, other caves – some flooded during the wet season – lead through the hill. In one, there's a greenish stalactite that looks like the head of an eel, while nearby caves shelter **formations** that really do resemble the head of a crocodile, the body of a turtle, the dangling tongue (or perhaps tonsil) of a dragon, a military boot and a hillside of miniature rice terraces. The reclining Buddha was inaugurated in 1999 to replace one destroyed by the Khmer Rouge.

The only way to spot the most interesting formations, and avoid walking right by most of the passageways, is to hire a guide. Fortunately, friendly local kids with torches/flashlights, eager to put their evening-school English to use, are likely to spot you even before you get to the blue gate, where the entry fee is collected. Make sure your tip is big enough to cover the cost of batteries.

Near the wat, a tiny **café** serves water and sugarcane juice.

About 300m around the mountain from the wat, behind a lone tree-like bush, a narrow path, over loose stones and then up carved steps, leads to a tiny triangular opening, where an old concrete ladder descends 5m into the darkness (warning: the second-to-top and bottom two rungs are missing). Two more wooden ladders lead ever deeper into the slimy, slippery depths of the **cave**, where a guide – essential here – can point out slumbering bats and surprising limestone formations, one of which looks like a jackfruit.

Sleeping

In Kompong Trach, **Kiri Sela Guesthouse** (☎ 012 993317) is just west of the temple.

Getting There & Away

Kompong Trach, on NH33 15km north of the Ha Tien border crossing, is 37km east of Kampot and 23km northeast of Kep, and makes an easy day trip from both towns by *moto* or motorbike. From Kep Beach (one hour), take the coastal road east and then north and hang a right at the NH33.

To get to Wat Kirisan from Kompong Trach, turn onto the dirt road opposite the Acleda Bank – look for the yellow Western Union insignia and a white-on-blue sign reading 'Phnom Kompong Trach Resort' – and continue for 2km to the foot of the sheer karst outcrop. Follow the road to the

SOUTH COAST

right (through the blue gate) and the wat is a few hundred metres ahead on the left.

KRONG KEP

Krong Kep is a province-level municipality that consists of little more than the town of Kep and Kep National Park.

KEP

ក្រែប

☎ 036 / pop 4000

The seaside resort of Kep-sur-Mer, famed for its spectacular sunsets and splendid seafood, was founded as a colonial retreat for the French elite in 1908. Cambodian high rollers continued the tradition, flocking here to enjoy gambling and water sports, and in the 1960s it was home to Cambodia's leading zoo.

The Khmer Rouge – radical Maoists who loathed the bourgeoisie – were known to harbour a particular hatred for the town and the destruction they wrought was nearly total. Today, dozens of Kep's luxurious pre-war villas are still just blackened shells, poignant reminders of the long years of Khmer Rouge rule and civil war. Inhabited by squatters, the mansions – remnants of a once-great (or at least rich and flashy) civilisation that met a sudden and violent end – have a post-apocalyptic feel.

After several false starts, Kep finally seems to be rising from (or among) the ruins. It's again popular, especially on weekends and holidays, with the wealthy elite of Phnom Penh. Drawn by the languid, Riviera-like atmosphere, they drive down in SUVs to picnic and frolic on the scruffy beaches (even before the war, white sand was shipped in from Sihanoukville to keep up appearances). If you want to see the town before big money transforms it, you'd better hurry.

Orientation

From the roundabout at Kep's northern edge, turning east takes you up the slope to a bunch of hillside guesthouses, while turning west brings you to the Crab Market. Go straight (south) from the roundabout, or take the coastal road from the Crab Market, and you'll get to a second roundabout just up the slope from Kep Beach. The boat dock is further east, past Coconut Beach.

Information

Kep Tourism Office Not much seems to be going on inside this fine building, which is across from the roundabout next to Kep Beach.

Sunny Tour (☎ 012 548273, 012 870465) Run by a small group of *moto* drivers, this travel agency – at the northern end of the Crab Market – offers bus tickets and tours.

Sights & Activities

From Kep's northern roundabout, NH33A heads north past the mildewed shells of handsome **mid-20th-century villas** that speak of happier, carefree times – and of the truly terrible Khmer Rouge years. Built according to the precepts of the modernist style, with clean lines, lots of horizontals and little adornment, they once played host to glittering jet-set parties and may do so again someday, though for the time being many shelter squatters (and, some say, ghosts). Don't even think of buying one – they were all snapped up for a song in the mid-1990s by speculators well-connected in Cambodia's murky corridors of military and civilian power.

Kep Beach, which faces south and is thus not great for sunsets, is sandy but narrow and strewn with little rocks. The eastern end of the shaded **promenade** is marked by a **nude statue** of a fisher's wife. A **waterfront promenade** to the Crab Market was under construction as we went to press.

On top of the hill northwest of Kep Beach is a **palace** built by King Sihanouk in the early 1990s. Before his overthrow in 1970, Kep was one of his favourite spots and he used to entertain visiting foreign dignitaries on an outlying island nicknamed Île des Ambassadeurs. The king may have harboured thoughts of retirement here but his poor health and Cambodia's political instability meant that he never actually stayed at the palace, which remains unfurnished. Access is from the east; it's usually possible to walk around the grounds – after tipping the guard, if necessary.

Coconut Beach is a few hundred metres southeast of Kep Beach, just past the **giant crab statue** and across the NH33A from two gilded statues that locals say – with a great deal of justification – look like oversized chickens.

Sailboats (but, mercifully, not jet skis) may soon be available for rent at a restaurant-equipped **beach club** being built just north of the Kep Seaside Guesthouse.

Kep National Park, despite its protected status, is in a sad state. Occupying the interior of Kep

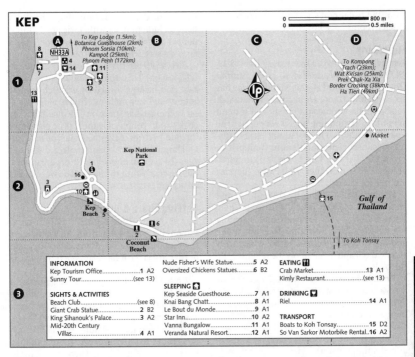

KEP

0 — 800 m
0 — 0.5 miles

To Kep Lodge (1.5km);
Botanica Guesthouse (2km);
Phnom Sosia (10km);
Kampot (25km);
Phnom Penh (172km)

To Kompong
Trach (23km);
Wat Kirisan (25km);
Prek Chak-Xa Xia
Border Crossing (38km);
Ha Tien (49km)

Market

Kep National
Park

Gulf of
Thailand

Kep
Beach

Coconut
Beach

To Koh Tonsay

INFORMATION		Nude Fisher's Wife Statue...........**5** A2	EATING
Kep Tourism Office...................**1** A2		Oversized Chickens Statues........**6** B2	Crab Market...........................**13** A1
Sunny Tour............................(see 13)			Kimly Restaurant.....................(see 13)
		SLEEPING	
SIGHTS & ACTIVITIES		Kep Seaside Guesthouse...........**7** A1	DRINKING
Beach Club...........................(see 8)		Knai Bang Chatt.......................**8** A1	Riel...................................**14** A1
Giant Crab Statue....................**2** B2		Le Bout du Monde....................**9** A1	
King Sihanouk's Palace.............**3** A2		Star Inn................................**10** A2	TRANSPORT
Mid-20th Century		Vanna Bungalow.....................**11** A1	Boats to Koh Tonsay.................**15** D2
Villas..............................**4** A1		Veranda Natural Resort............**12** A1	So Van Sarkor Motorbike Rental..**16** A2

SOUTH COAST

headland, it has no guest facilities. Access is via an 8km road open to 4WD vehicles. Kep Lodge may be able to arrange a half-day hike through the park as well as snorkelling excursions, fishing trips and seaborne visits to coastal mangrove forests.

Tours

If you're based in Kampot, **Sok Lim Tours** (p215) offers day trips (US$10 per person, minimum four people) to Kep, Koh Tonsay (p227), the caves of Kompong Trach (p223), a pepper plantation and salt ponds.

Sleeping

Both along the shore and on the verdant hillside east of the Crab Market, the cheap guesthouses of old are giving way to pricier accommodation, including several self-enclosed mini-resorts. Few have TVs because, as of this writing, reception is limited to stations from Vietnam.

BUDGET

Kep Seaside Guesthouse (☎ 012 684241; admin@bnckh .com; r with fan/air-con from US$6/15; 🔀) So close to

the shore you can hear the waves (though there isn't exactly a sandy beach here), this three-storey place – dormitory-like in appearance – has 26 clean, simply furnished rooms. There's a small premium for upstairs rooms; Room 20 even has a full-frontal sea view. Often fills up with domestic tourists, especially on weekends and holidays.

Botanica (☎ 016 562775; www.kep-botanica.com; r US$7) Opened in late 2007, this Belgian-owned place has five bungalows set in a flowery garden (thus the name) and a 'world kitchen' restaurant. Situated about 2km north of the Riel bar on the main road to Kampot.

Le Bout du Monde (☎ 012 242166; r US$7-10) The last cheapie on the hill, this French-run garden guesthouse is basic but atmospheric. The rather flimsy bungalows, which are showing signs of age, have woven cane walls, split-wood floors, brick-walled loos and mosquito nets.

Vanna Bungalow (☎ 012 755038; www.vanna bungalows.com; r US$10-20; 🔀) Popular with in-the-know expats, this mellow place has 17 solidly built, tasteful bungalows – all with fridges – set in pleasant gardens. The sunset sea views from the restaurant's veranda are gorgeous. Pricier rooms have hot water and air-con.

MIDRANGE

Kep Lodge (☎ 092 435330; www.keplodge.com; r US$15-28) On a quiet hillside 2km towards Kampot from the Crab Market, this friendly place has six bungalows (more are planned) with thatch roofs, tile floors, mosquito nets and tasteful verandas. A swimming pool is supposed to be installed in 2008. The restaurant has breathtaking sunset views and Phnom Penh prices. From the Riel bar, Kep Lodge is 1km north along NH33A and then 700m east. Bicycles are free for guests.

Star Inn (☎ 016 743701; r US$25-35; 🕸) At the western end of Kep Beach, this brand new hotel has a lovely location and glorious sea views but the 30 rooms lack hot water and are decked out like a karaoke bar, with recessed red and green fluorescent lights over the beds.

Veranda Natural Resort (☎ 012 888619; www .veranda-resort.com; r with fan/air-con from US$25/45; 🕸) Spread across the hill above town, this 15-bungalow complex – built of wood, bamboo and stone – is a memorable spot for a romantic getaway. The all-wood restaurant and bar afford stunning sunset views. Internet connections are planned.

TOP END

Knai Bang Chatt (☎ 012 879486; www.knaibangchatt.com; r US$168-392) A boutique hotel whose 11 rooms occupy three vintage villas, this chic getaway has a waterfront infinity pool, breathtaking views and staff who wait on you hand and foot – the ultimate in luxury and exclusivity. Book well in advance.

Eating & Drinking

Dining in Kep is all about fresh seafood. For the best deals head to the Crab Market, a row of wooden waterfront shacks where you can tuck into mouth-watering grilled prawns, crab, squid and fish. In case you're interested, crabs – kept alive in pens tethered a few metres off the pebbly beach – costs 20,000r to 30,000r a kilo.

All of Kep's guesthouses and hotels have restaurants. The Veranda Natural Resort and Vanna Bungalows offer drop-dead gorgeous views along with Phnom Penh prices.

Kimly Restaurant (☎ 017 904077; mains medium/ large 15,000r/20,000r; 🕙 8am-9pm or 10pm) Perhaps the best of the Crab Market eateries, specialities here include prawns with sprigs of Kampot pepper and fresh crab. Mains come with a tasty dessert: fried tarrow root in sugar.

Riel (☎ 017 902771; www.kep-riel-bar.com; 🕙 breakfast & 6pm-late) This unpretentious bar, restaurant and bakery, owned by a Dutch sound engineer and his Khmer wife, occupies a hangar-like space outfitted with wicker chairs and a couple of hammocks. Specialities include pastries, cakes, German beer bread and home-made ice cream confected without eggs (to avoid salmonella). Prices are quoted only in riels – thus the name. The website has an activities calendar.

Getting There & Away

Kep is 25km from Kampot, 172km from Phnom Penh and 49km from the Vietnamese town of Ha Tien. The Cambodia–Vietnam border at Ha Tien has been open to tourists since mid-2007.

Both Phnom Penh Sorya Transport and Hour Lean run Phnom Penh–Kampot buses that pass through Kep (they also serve Angk Tasaom, near Takeo). On Phnom Penh Sorya, the fare to Kampot (40 minutes) is US$2; arrival times from Phnom Penh are variable. Buses stop at Kep Beach, where *motos* await, but you can ask to get off near the Riel bar or Kep Lodge. Ticketing is handled by guesthouses or Sunny Tour.

To get to Kampot by *moto/tuk tuk*/taxi, count on paying US$3/6/10 one-way (a bit more if the driver speaks English). Drivers hang out at the northern end of Kep Beach and at the Crab Market, but it's easiest to have your guesthouse make arrangements.

Getting Around

Kep has almost no street lighting – the town only got mains electricity in early 2007, when it was linked to the Vietnamese grid – so a flashlight/torch helps if you'll be walking around at night.

Kep's *moto* drivers are a cooperative bunch: they all know each other and many have long-standing ties to this or that guesthouse. A ride from the Crab Market to Kep Beach costs 2000r. Hiring a *moto* for the day costs about US$10 (more to Kompong Trach).

So Van Sarkor (Sovann Sakor; ☎ 012 608345; 🕙 6am-late year-round), 50m west of the roundabout above Kep Beach, rents out 100cc motorbikes (US$5 for a 12-hour day) and bicycles

SOUTH COAST

(US$2.50 a day). A 250cc bike may be available for US$15 a day.

Botanica Guesthouse rents bicycles/mountain bikes to nonguests for 3500r/8000r.

AROUND KEP

Kep makes a good base for visiting several delightful cave-temples, including **Wat Kirisan** near Kompong Trach (p223), **Phnom Chhnork** (p218) and **Phnom Sorsia** (p219).

Rumour has it that there may soon be a boat link from Kep to the unspoiled beaches of **Phu Quoc Island**, 25km to the southwest, whose loss to Vietnam is still bitterly resented by many Cambodians.

Koh Tonsay
កោះទន្សាយ

Koh Tonsay (Rabbit Island), said to have the nicest beaches of any Kep-area island (except Vietnam's Phu Quoc), is so named because locals say it resembles a rabbit, an example of what too much local brew can do to your imagination. If you like rusticity, come now before the island is changed forever by development.

At the 250m-long, tree-lined **main beach**, which faces west towards the setting sun, you can dine on seafood, lounge around on raised bamboo platforms and stay in thatched bungalows. North American travellers of a certain age may be tempted to hum the theme tune from *Gilligan's Island*. Many people say Koh Tonsay is a 'tropical paradise' but don't expect the sanitised resort version – this one has shorefront flotsam, flies, chickens, packs of dogs and wandering cows.

From the southern end of the main beach, a 10-minute walk takes you to a fishers' hamlet and two more sand **beaches**, one on either side of the island's narrow southern tip. It's possible to walk all the way around Koh Tonsay.

The island's interior is forested and, except along the beaches, trees grow right up to the water's edge. On the **hilltop** you can see the remains of a one-time Khmer Rouge bunker.

Other Kep-area islands include **Koh Pos** (Snake Island; about 20 minutes past Koh Tonsay), which some say Chinese investors plan to turn into a resort, and beachless **Koh Svai** (Mango Island), whose summit offers nice views.

SLEEPING & EATING

Strung out along the main beach, the island's five rudimentary guesthouses – all family-run and all with tiny open-air restaurants – include **Thi Am** (☎ 012 343759) and **Nyan Voyet Mai** (☎ 012 893102), which charge US$5 for a raised bungalow with a mosquito net and, across the yard, a sit-down toilet. Meals cost US$3/5 for a small/large portion of fish, crab, squid, shrimp or free-range chicken. (The latter may wander under your table and one traveller reports having his feet well hen-pecked!) The English menus look like they could have been nicked from an eatery on the mainland.

GETTING THERE & AWAY

Boats from Kep's boat dock to Koh Tonsay (20 minutes) cost US$15 return, including a US$5 tax. *Moto* drivers often offer to arrange boat rides for US$5 per person, so for groups of four or more it may be cheaper to handle the booking yourself. If you'd like to stay all day or overnight, arrange a time to be picked up. Guesthouses can help make arrangements. Especially in the late afternoon, keep an eye out for schools of little silver fish jumping out of the water in unison.

TAKEO PROVINCE
ខេត្តតាកែវ

Often referred to as 'the cradle of Cambodian civilisation', Takeo Province includes several important pre-Angkorian sites built between the 5th and 8th centuries. The whole area was part of what Chinese annals called 'water Chenla', no doubt a reference to the extensive annual floods that still blanket much of the province. An important kingdom among several smaller states that existed at the time, its principal centre was at Angkor Borei, with other religious foci at Phnom Chisor and Phnom Bayong. Centuries later, sites such as Phnom Chisor continued to exert a strong pull on the kings of Angkor and many came to pay tribute to their ancestors in elaborate ceremonies.

Today, Takeo is a poor, rural province whose economy is based on farming and fishing. The temples of Tonlé Bati (p114) and Phnom Chisor (p116), near Phnom Penh, get a healthy number of visitors each year, but few foreigners spend much time in the provincial capital, Takeo, gateway to Angkor

SOUTH COAST

Borei, where it's easy to score a slice of real Cambodian life.

TAKEO
តាកែវ

☎ 032 / pop 39,000

Takeo, the quiet, lakeside provincial capital, is an excellent base from which to take a zippy motorboat ride to the pre-Angkorian temples in the Angkor Borei area, and is an easy stop if you're travelling between Phnom Penh and Kampot. Little visited by foreigners, it lacks the architectural charm of some provincial towns but does retain some of its French-era legacy, especially around Psar Nat.

Cycling groups en route from the Mekong Delta to Phnom Penh, via the Phnom Den–Tinh Bien border crossing, often stop off here because NH2 has luxuriously wide, paved verges/shoulders.

Orientation

Laid out on a grid, Takeo is hemmed in by a large *boeung* (lake) to the north and a huge flood zone to the east. The old town centre is around partly occupied Psar Nat (Meeting Market). The town's main commercial strip stretches along NH2 (St 20) from Independence Monument to the bustling main market, Psar Thmei (New Market), next to the bus and taxi station.

Information

You can surf and check emails at the Mittapheap Hotel, next to the Sotheavy Guesthouse and perhaps at Bayong Tours.

Acleda Bank (☎ 931246; NH2) Takeo's only bank can change travellers cheques and has a 24-hour ATM.

Bayang Tours (☎ 931193, 012 971411; sunsophal@ yahoo.com; St 14) An English-speaking travel agency that opened in 2007.

Soch Tith Internet (NH2; per hr 3000r; ☒ 6am-8pm) A proper internet café facing Psar Thmei.

Takeo Tourism (☎ 931323; ☒ 7am-noon & 2-5pm Mon-Fri) Facing Psar Nat, the provincial tourist office has helpful staff who can supply you with photocopied maps and may be able to arrange an English- or French-speaking guide to Angkor Borei and Phnom Da.

Sights

Psar Nat, an ugly concrete structure built after the overthrow of the Khmer Rouge in 1979, is surrounded by streets partly lined with arcaded, French-era buildings. One block east of the market, **boats** travelling along Canal No 15

to Angkor Borei leave from St 9, which runs along the water.

The **lakefront promenade** along the northern edge of town is a popular late-afternoon hang-out for local youth and a favourite backdrop for wedding photos. At its western end, a cement **pier** (St 3 btwn St 15 & St 17) that's seen better days attracts young couples in the mood to commune with lily pads and frogs – and each other. The area is especially romantic at sunset.

The brand-new **Provincial Museum** (St 4), built in the style of a Khmer temple, is supposed to open its exhibits on local archaeology and culture in 2008.

Takeo Province's most notorious native son, Ta Mok – AKA 'The Butcher' – served as the Khmer Rouge's chief-of-staff in the 1960s and was later commander of the Southwestern Zone, where he presided over horrific atrocities. Ta Mok was paranoid about his personal security and had an elaborate house built in the middle of the lake. It is said that he had the architects and builders executed upon completion of each floor, which included hidden rooms and escape passages. Today, **Ta Mok's House**, which is about 1km north of town at the end of a causeway, is occupied by a police training facility but can be viewed from the outside. Ta Mok, who had two more residences near Anlong Veng (p259 and p260), died in prison in mid-2006 awaiting trial for genocide and crimes against humanity.

Sleeping

At one of the less-than-spotless guesthouses facing Psar Nat, one recent visitor had his cupcake snatched by a rodent!

Boeung Takeo Guesthouse (☎ 931306; cnr Sts 3 & 14; r US$5-10; ☒) Boasting the most romantic location in town, including a balcony overlooking the lakefront promenade, this quiet place – owned by a member of the National Assembly – has 19 spacious, clean rooms with TV and cold water. Ask for a room with a view, as it's no more expensive.

Phnom Da Guesthouse (☎ 016 826083; St 9; r US$5-10; ☒) Facing the lake near the boat dock, this newly renovated, family-run hostelry has 10 cold-water rooms with high ceilings and carved wooden doors and a spacious, grille-enclosed balcony with watery views. Ask for a room with a window (not all have one) and, if possible, a lake view.

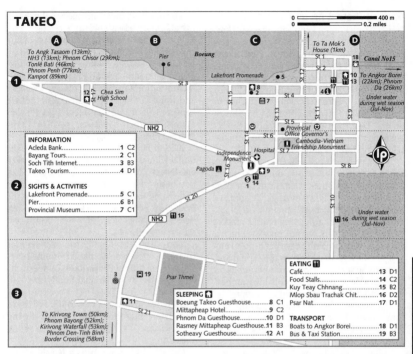

TAKEO

INFORMATION
Acleda Bank	1 C2
Bayang Tours	2 C1
Soch Tith Internet	3 B3
Takeo Tourism	4 D1

SIGHTS & ACTIVITIES
Lakefront Promenade	5 C1
Pier	6 B1
Provincial Museum	7 C1

SLEEPING
Boeung Takeo Guesthouse	8 C1
Mittapheap Hotel	9 C2
Phnom Da Guesthouse	10 D1
Rasmey Mittapheap Guesthouse	11 B3
Sotheavy Guesthouse	12 A1

EATING
Café	13 D1
Food Stalls	14 C2
Kuy Teay Chhnang	15 B2
Mlop Sbau Trachak Chit	16 D2
Psar Nat	17 D1

TRANSPORT
Boats to Angkor Borei	18 D1
Bus & Taxi Station	19 B3

Soteavy Guesthouse (☎ 016 869482, 012 935133; NH2 at St 17; d US$5-10; ✷) A new establishment about 1km towards Phnom Penh from the centre, this yellow, four-storey structure – surrounded by balconies – has 27 smallish rooms with low ceilings, ceramic tile floors, compact bathrooms and air-con you can really crank up.

Mittapheap Hotel (☎ 931205, 012 341744; St 20; d US$5-15; ✷) Facing Independence Monument about midway between the bus station and Psar Nat, this place has 35 darkish rooms in four buildings arrayed around a coconut-shaded back yard. Staff speak some English. Pricier rooms have hot water.

Rasmey Mittapheap Guesthouse (☎ 016 882362; NH2) Facing Psar Thmei, this place – run by the Mittapheap Hotel – is convenient to public transport.

Eating & Drinking

There are plenty of food stalls around Independence Monument. By night, this is the place to snack on Cambodian desserts or enjoy a *tukalok* (fruit shake).

Psar Nat (St 10; ☽ early morning-dusk) This grimy market shelters a handful of basic food stalls

that are great for coffee, tea or traditional Khmer breakfast soup (2000r). Also has a few vegetable sellers.

Café (St 9; ☽ closed evening) This unpretentious place, run by an exceptionally tall lad, serves Takeo's best ice coffee (1500r) – but no food – under a tin roof.

Kuy Teay Chhnang (☎ 011 618868; NH2; ☽ breakfast, lunch & dinner) Likely to fulfil the promise implied in its name, which means *bon appétit*, this spotless eatery specialises in Chinese soups (3000r), which are lip-smackingly tasty early in the morning. It also has lots of rice-based Khmer dishes. There's no English sign; look for neatly parked motorbikes out front and a fake brick façade.

Mlop Sbau Trachak Chit (☎ 011 974040; St 10; mains 5000r; ☽ 9am-9pm) Offering better value than some of the places in town, this restaurant – outdoors under a thatch roof – and its delicious Khmer dishes are hugely popular with the locals, especially in the evening. Neither the menu nor the sign are in English; from St 10 walk through a gate with an Anchor Beer sign over it and follow the wooden walkway to the restaurant.

Getting There & Around

NH2 linking Phnom Penh with Takeo (77km) is in reasonable condition, with just a few potholes to slow things down. **Phnom Penh Sorya Transport** (☎ in Phnom Penh 012 631545) runs air-con buses between Phnom Penh's Psar Thmei (7500r, 2¼ hours, six a day till 3.30pm) and Takeo's bus and taxi station, which is in front of Takeo's own Psar Thmei. These buses go past Tonlé Bati and Phnom Chisor. By six-passenger share taxi or crammed minibus, the trip from Phnom Penh costs about US$2.

If you're heading south, the easiest destination to get to is Kampot. Buses, taxis (1¼ hours) and minibuses (US$3) can be picked up 13km west of Takeo at Angk Tasaom, an ugly, chaotic transport junction on NH3, where you'll find hawkers, eateries, a market and even two hotels, but precious few English speakers. Phnom Penh Sorya Transport runs just two buses a day between the capital and Kampot, so searching for a taxi or minibus on the west side of the NH3 is probably your best bet. Traffic peters out by mid-afternoon.

The best way to get to Kep is to hop on a minibus or share taxi to Kampot, though a few Kep-bound buses pass by Angk Tasaom in the morning.

To get from Takeo to Angk Tasaom, you can take a *remorque-moto* (without/with a shade roof 1500r/2000r) from Psar Thmei, a *tuk tuk* (8000r) from Psar Thmei or the hospital, or a *moto* (5000r) wherever you spot one.

Within Takeo, a *moto* from Psar Thmei to Psar Nat should cost 1000r.

AROUND TAKEO

For details on the temples around Phnom Chisor, see p116; for those around Tonlé Bati, see p114. Both are in Takeo Province.

Angkor Borei & Phnom Da

អង្គរបុរី និង ភ្នំដា

Known as Vyadhapura when it served as the capital of 'water Chenla' in the 8th century, Angkor Borei – founded in the 5th century – is one of the earliest pre-Angkorian sites in Cambodia.

Today, Angkor Borei is a small, impoverished riverine town surrounded by an ancient wall. The local economy is based on dry-season rice cultivation, year-round fishing and raising the chickens and pigs that forage on the unpaved streets.

The modest, new **archaeological museum** (☎ 012 201638; admission US$1; ☼ officially 7-11am & 2-4pm, unofficially open all day), a bit east of the road bridge, occupies a Khmer-style building set to open in 2008. Featured are locally discovered Funan- and Chenla-era artefacts, including human bones, pottery, jewellery and stone carvings. The dark-red statues are copies of important works now in Phnom Penh's National Museum (p84) or Paris' Musée Guimet.

A local family has turned part of a traditional Khmer home into the signless **Srey Pao Guesthouse** (☎ 012 383094; per person 10,000r). The two basic rooms come with mosquito nets and shared bathroom. To get there from the bridge, go north one block and then go left (west) for 100m – it's next to the wooden stall selling schoolbooks.

You can grab a bite at the rudimentary psar (market), a few blocks inland from the river.

The twin hills of **Phnom Da** (US$2), spectacularly isolated by the annual floods, are 3km south of Angkor Borei. The rocky slopes shelter five artificial caves, built as Hindu and, later, Buddhist shrines and, during the Vietnam War, used as hideouts by the Viet Cong.

On top, 142 steps up, is a **temple** whose foundations date from the 6th century. Rebuilt in the 11th century, it's 12 sq m and 18m high. The entrance faces due north, with blind doors – decorated with bas-relief *nagas* – on the other three sides. The lower section is laterite, while the upper reaches are made of red bricks. The finest carvings have been taken to museums in Angkor Borei, Phnom Penh and Paris.

About 50m northeast of the temple, a huge **'floating boulder'** sits balanced on just three points. Vietnam can be seen 8km to the southeast.

Nearby, on a second hillock, is **Wat Asram Moha Russei**, a smaller, restored Hindu sanctuary, made of sandstone, that's 5.5 sq m and 8m high.

At the dock, a couple of very basic cafés serve coconut milk and soft drinks.

GETTING THERE & AWAY

Angkor Borei and Phnom Da are about 20km east of Takeo town along Canal No 15, built in the 1880s to connect Takeo with the Tonlé Bassac and the Mekong Delta. Clearly delineated in the dry season, the waterway is surrounded by flooded rice fields the rest of the year.

For great, bracing, open-air fun, zip along the canal in a fibreglass motorboat (US$25 return, 35 minutes to Angkor Borei, 10 to 15 minutes more to Phnom Da) or, in the dry season, a smaller wooden motorboat (US$15 return), both available for hire at Takeo's boat dock. All but a small part of what you pay will be spent on fuel. In the wet season the water can get rough in the afternoon, so it's a good idea to head out early. Bring sunscreen, a hat and, in the wet season, rain gear. Many of the heavily laden boats you pass are bringing terracotta tiles and smuggled fuel from Vietnam.

Larger boats (3000r per person, two hours) depart from Takeo's boat dock at 1pm or 2pm and from Angkor Borei at about 7.30am. Another cheap option is to wait around for enough locals to fill a share motorboat (8000r per person).

Phnom Da used to be an island during the wet season but a causeway now assures year-round land access. From Angkor Borei, wooden long boats (3000r per person) travel frequently to Phnom Da, or you can take a *moto* (US$2 return).

Angkor Borei can also be visited on an overland day trip from Phnom Penh. By car, take NH2; drive east on Highway 107, which passes south of Phnom Chisor; and then turn south at Prey Lvea.

Phnom Bayong
ភ្នំបាយ៉ង

Affording breathtaking views of Vietnam's pancake-flat Mekong Delta, the cliff-ringed summit of Phnom Bayong (313m) is graced by a 7th-century **Chenla temple** built to celebrate a victory over Funan. The *linga* originally in the inner chamber is now in Paris' Musée Guimet but a number of flora- and fauna-themed **bas-relief panels** can still be seen, eg on the lintels of the three false doorways and carved into the brickwork. The site, once surrounded by two concentric walls (remnants are still visible), still attracts pilgrims and is tended by Buddhist nuns who live nearby in basic huts.

The steep walk up to the temple takes about 2½ hours return. The trail is not clearly marked, so it's a good idea to hire a local lad (or five) with a machete (5000r or 10,000r). Along the way you're likely to see locals out collecting leaves and roots for the preparation of traditional medicines. Bring plenty of water and thick eyebrows (or at least a handkerchief to wipe the sweat from your forehead). The descent over smooth rocky inclines will help prepare your leg muscles for the next ski season.

In Kirivong town, **Tran Hout Guesthouse** (☎ 016 500033; NH2; r US$5-8) is friendly but its 17 tiny rooms are lightless and have poor ventilation.

Further west along the Phnom Bayong access road is **Phnom Tchea Tapech**, whose summit is marked by a jumbo standing Buddha reached by a monumental staircase. This new temple complex was inaugurated in late 2006.

Kirivong Waterfall, 2.5km west of the southern edge of Kirivong town, is popular with locals, especially on warm weekends, but it's nothing to write home about – unless you like telling your friends about all the litter you've seen. Until it's cleaned up (there are plans…), the only reason to head out there is to check out the market stalls selling the area's most famous product: topaz and quartz, either cut like gems or carved into tiny Buddhas and *nagas*.

GETTING THERE & AWAY
Kirivong town is on the nicely paved NH2, 50km south of Takeo and 8km north of the Phnom Den–Tinh Bien border crossing. Phnom Bayong is about 3km west of the northern edge of Kirivong town; the turn-off is marked by a painted panel depicting the temple.

From Takeo, a *moto* costs about 30,000r return. It's cheaper to take a share taxi or a bus to Kirivong town and then hop on a *moto* at the turn-off.

From the border, it's easy to catch a *remorque-moto* or a *moto* to Kirivong, whence minibuses go to Takeo and Phnom Penh. Catching a taxi at the border may involve phoning to have one sent from Kirivong town.

SOUTH COAST

Northwestern Cambodia

Offering a blend of highway accessibility and outback adventure, Northwestern Cambodia covers a broad swath of the country, running all the way around Tonlé Sap Lake, extending from Kompong Chhnang west to the Thai frontier and north to the Dangkrek Mountains (Chuor Phnom Dangkrek), which mark Cambodia's northern border with Thailand. (In this book, Siem Reap and the Temples of Angkor have their own chapters.)

Of the region's municipalities, Battambang – Cambodia's second-largest city – attracts the most visitors thanks to an alluring blend of classic colonial architecture and excellent day trip options. Other towns serve as gateways to some of the country's most captivating corners – Kompong Thom is a good base for a visit to the temples of Sambor Prei Kuk, Pursat makes a fine jumping-off point for the wilds of the northern Cardamoms, and Anlong Veng is a short *moto* ride from a string of eerie Khmer Rouge sites.

The remote jungles conceal some of Cambodia's most inspired temples, forgotten to all but the intrepid for decades. Preah Khan and Prasat Preah Vihear are sublime spots but are only for those with a serious thirst for adventure. Koh Ker is more accessible than ever thanks to a new road and Banteay Chhmar now has a pioneering community-based homestay project.

The Northwest is where you'll find some of Cambodia's most important wilderness areas, most well off the beaten track. The Cardamom Mountains in the southwest are home to pristine jungle and rare wildlife, while the forests and marshes of Preah Vihear Province provide ideal habitat for endangered birds such as the giant ibis, Cambodia's national bird.

HIGHLIGHTS

- Soak up colonial-era charm in the riverside town of **Battambang** (p240), surrounded by lush countryside and hilltop temples
- Explore Southeast Asia's first temple city, the impressive pre-Angkorian ruins of **Sambor Prei Kuk** (p272)
- Journey to the 10th-century capital of **Koh Ker** (p264), its massive temples forgotten in the forests for a thousand years
- Make an adventurous overland pilgrimage to the majestic mountaintop temple of **Prasat Preah Vihear** (p268)
- Sail out to the colourful **floating villages** at Kompong Luong (p239) and Kompong Chhnang (p234)

Prasat Preah ★ Vihear

★ Koh Ker

★ Battambang

Sambor Prei Kuk ★

Kompong Luong ★
Kompong Chhnang ★

| ▪ ELEVATION: 5-1500M | ▪ POPULATION: 3.5 MILLION | ▪ AREA: 71,157 SQ KM |

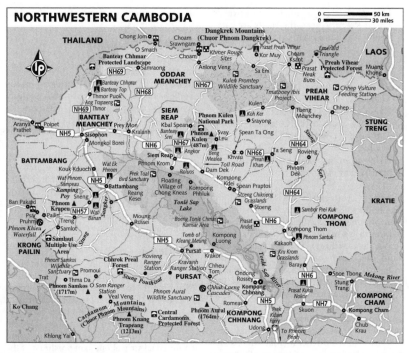

Getting There & Away

Northwestern Cambodia has an ever-increasing number of international border crossings with Thailand:

- Poipet–Aranya Prathet (p329), on the recently upgraded NH5 48km west of Sisophon and 153km west of Siem Reap. This is Cambodia's most popular land crossing with Thailand.
- Psar Pruhm–Ban Pakard (p331), 22km west of Pailin and 102km southwest of Battambang via a churned-up dirt road.
- Choam–Choam Srawngam (p331), 16km north of Anlong Veng and 134km north of Siem Reap.
- O Smach–Chong Jom (p330), a punishing 40km northeast of Samraong and 120km north of Kralanh (on NH6).

Within Cambodia, the obvious gateways to the region are Siem Reap (p118) and Phnom Penh (p72). A memorable boat service links Siem Reap with Battambang. It should be possible to disembark from one of the Siem Reap–Phnom Penh fast boats at Kompong Chhnang.

Getting Around

The sights in this chapter can be visited on a giant loop around Tonlé Sap Lake.

SOUTH OF THE TONLÉ SAP

You can visit the towns along NH5 (including Kompong Chhnang, Kompong Luong, Pursat and Battambang) en route between Phnom Penh and either the Poipet–Aranya Prathet border crossing to Thailand, or – if you loop around via Sisophon – Siem Reap. Heavily potholed dirt roads lead from Pursat southeast into the Cardamom Mountains and from Battambang southwest to Pailin (NH57) and the Psar Pruhm–Ban Pakard crossing to Thailand.

NORTH OF THE TONLÉ SAP

NH6 links Phnom Penh with Kompong Thom, Siem Reap and Sisophon. Roads leading north from NH6 include the following:

- NH64 from Kompong Thom to Tbeng Meanchey, at press time in a ruinous state.
- A decent toll road from Dam Dek via Beng Mealea and Koh Ker to Tbeng

NORTHWESTERN CAMBODIA

Meanchey. North of there, towards Prasat Preah Vihear, the roads are catastrophic and are often impassable in the wet season.

■ The recently upgraded NH67 from Siem Reap to Anlong Veng and the Choam-Choam Srawngam border crossing to Thailand.

■ NH68 from Kralanh to Samraong. From there the road to the O Smach–Chong Jom border crossing to Thailand is in a terrible state.

■ NH69 from Sisophon via Banteay Chhmar to Samraong.

Doing a loop north of Angkor along Cambodia's northern border with Thailand – from Sisophon (on NH6) to Banteay Chhmar, Samraong, Anlong Veng, Sa Em (near Prasat Preah Vihear), Tbeng Meanchey and Kompong Thom (on NH6) – is challenging in the dry season and virtually impossible in the wet, when the trip could be dubbed 'the Churning of the Ocean of Mud'.

Commercial and passenger traffic to and from each of these towns is oriented southward, towards NH6, rather than east or west, the result being that there's little vehicular traffic – and no public transport – from Banteay Chhmar northeast to Samraong, from there east to Anlong Veng, and from there east to Sa Em. In general, your only option for these segments – *if* the road is motorable – is to hire a *moto* or a taxi, pricey because the driver will probably have to head back empty. *Motos* have an easier time of it than cars (generally, amazingly hardy Toyota Camrys) or 4WDs, which have to find two parallel grooves rather than just one. For the hardy traveller, though, this route, past minefields and through areas so remote they're being homesteaded only now, is one of Cambodia's most challenging outback journeys.

KOMPONG CHHNANG PROVINCE

ខេត្តកំពង់ឆ្នាំង

Kompong Chhnang is a relatively wealthy province thanks to its proximity to the capital and its fishing and agricultural industries, which are supported by abundant water resources.

KOMPONG CHHNANG

កំពង់ឆ្នាំង

☎ 026 / pop 42,000

Kompong Chhnang (Clay Pot Port), on the Tonlé Sap River, is a tale of two cities: the leafy centre, its focal point a grassy park, and the bustling dockside. Nearby sights include two floating villages and a hamlet famous for its distinctive pottery.

By land, the town is a straightforward stop on the way from Phnom Penh to Battambang, or an easy day trip from the capital, perhaps combined with a visit to Udong (p113). You can also get to Kompong Chhnang by water; usually it's possible to get off the Phnom Penh–Siem Reap fast boat here.

Orientation

The city centre's civic focal point is a grassy park stretching from Independence Monument to the Cambodia-Vietnam Friendship Monument. Just north of the park is the bus and taxi station and a commercial district anchored by Psar Leu (Central Market). Kompong Chhnang has a second commercial strip about 3km northeast of the centre, around Psar Krom (Lower Market) and the waterfront.

Information

Acleda Bank (☎ 988748; NH5) Changes travellers cheques and should have an ATM by the time you read this.
Canadia Bank (NH5) Expected to get an ATM in 2008.
Internet Phone (per hr US$2; ☼ 6am-8pm) Fifty metres north of the western end of Psar Leu.
Internet Terminals (per hr 10,000r; ☼ 7am-8pm) Two mobile-phone shops are situated across the street from the bus and taxi station, 30m north of Acleda Bank.

Sights & Activities

A short sail from Kompong Chhnang's **waterfront** takes you to two colourful floating villages, **Phoum Kandal** to the east and **Chong Kos** to the northwest. Much less commercial than Kompong Luong (p239), they have all the amenities of a mainland village – houses, machine tool shops, veggie vendors, a mosque, a petrol station – except that almost everything floats. Many of the people are ethnic Vietnamese.

From the Tourism Port, you can charter a **big wooden boat** with space for eight (US$8) for

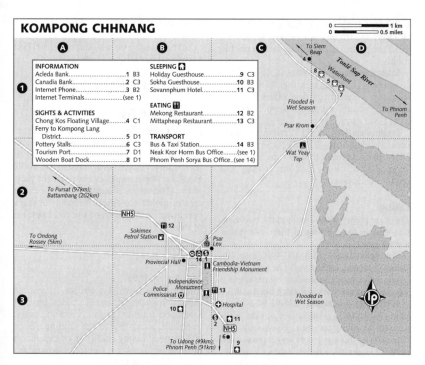

KOMPONG CHHNANG

INFORMATION
Acleda Bank.................................1 B3
Canadia Bank...............................2 C3
Internet Phone.............................3 B2
Internet Terminals....................(see 1)

SIGHTS & ACTIVITIES
Chong Kos Floating Village.........4 C1
Ferry to Kompong Lang
  District.....................................5 D1
Pottery Stalls...............................6 C3
Tourism Port................................7 D1
Wooden Boat Dock......................8 D1

SLEEPING
Holiday Guesthouse....................9 C3
Sokha Guesthouse.....................10 B3
Sovannphum Hotel....................11 C3

EATING
Mekong Restaurant...................12 B2
Mittapheap Restaurant.............13 C3

TRANSPORT
Bus & Taxi Station....................14 B3
Neak Kror Horm Bus Office........(see 1)
Phnom Penh Sorya Bus Office..(see 14)

a one-hour excursion. A cheaper, quieter and more ecological option, available about 300m to the west, is to get around like the floating villagers do: on a **narrow wooden boat** rowed standing up (US$1 for a 20-minute trip).

For a cheap river cruise, you can hop on a **ferry** (2000r, 45 minutes, hourly to 4pm) to Kompong Lang District, about 6km away. The vessels, which have space for several dozen people, dock 100m west of the Tourism Port.

Across the Tonlé Sap River are several rather dilapidated brick-built **temples** dating from the Chenla period, including **Prasat Srei**.

The quiet village of **Ondong Rossey**, where the area's famous red pottery is made under every house, is a delightful 7km ride west of town through serene rice fields dotted with sugar palms, most with bamboo ladders running up the trunk. The unpainted pots, decorated with etched or appliqué designs, are either made with a foot-spun wheel (for small pieces) or banged into shape with a heavy wooden spatula (for large ones). Artisans are happy to show you how they do it.

The golden-hued mud piled up in the yards is quarried at nearby **Phnom Krang Dai Meas** and

pounded into fine clay before being shaped and fired; only at the last stage does it acquire a pinkish hue. Pieces (from 1000r), including piggy banks, can be purchased at the **Pottery Development Center**. In Kompong Chhnang, several **stalls** selling Ondong Rossey pottery can be found on NH5 towards Phnom Penh from the centre.

A visit to Ondong Rossey can be combined with **Phnom Santuk**, a rocky hillock behind Wat Santuk, a few kilometres southwest of Kompong Chhnang. The boulder-strewn summit affords fine views of the countryside, including the Tonlé Sap, 20km to the north.

By bicycle or *moto,* combining Ondong Rossey and Phnom Santuk makes for a truly magical circuit, especially early in the morning or late in the afternoon. There are no road signs, so it's a good idea to go with a local.

Sleeping

There are several cheap guesthouses on NH5 within 1km of the Cambodia-Vietnam Friendship Monument, towards both Battambang and Phnom Penh.

Holiday Guesthouse (☎ 988802; NH5; r US$3-10; ❄) Run by a friendly teacher and his family, this basic place has 10 slightly claustrophobic rooms.

Sokha Guesthouse (☎ 988622; r US$5-10; ❄) A favourite of NGO workers, this 30-room hostelry, set in a shady garden, offers the most charming accommodation in town. Hot water costs US$2 extra.

Sovannphum Hotel (☎ 989333; sovannphumkchotel@ yahoo.com.kh; NH5; r US$10-15; ❄ 🖵) Opened in late 2006, this is a proper tourist-class hotel. The 30 good-sized rooms have 4m ceilings and modern bathrooms.

Eating

There are plenty of food stalls at the two markets and, in the evening, at the western end of Psar Leu.

Mekong Restaurant (☎ 012 374154; NH5; mains 5000-13,000r; ✲ breakfast, lunch & dinner) The small menu includes the basic Cambodian hit parade and a good interpretation of French beefsteak.

Mittapheap Restaurant (☎ 012 949297; NH5; mains 6000-20,000r; ✲ 5am-8pm) Popular with Khmers travelling between Phnom Penh and Battambang, this airy eatery serves good-sized portions of mainly Khmer dishes.

Getting There & Around

The ferries linking Phnom Penh with Siem Reap pass right by Kompong Chhnang. If you'd like to get off here, inform the boat company in advance and they should be able to arrange for a local launch to pull up alongside the ferry and whisk you ashore.

From the bus and taxi station, **Phnom Penh Sorya** (☎ 012 631545) has services to Phnom Penh (7500r, 91km, five or more a day to 3.30pm), Pursat (8000r, 97km, six a day till 4pm), Battambang (20,000r, 202km, two or 2½ hours, five a day till 2.30pm) and Poipet (30,000r, two a day in the morning).

Sam Phoas Mobile Phone Shop, across the street from the bus and taxi station, sells westbound tickets issued by **Neak Kror Horm** (☎ 012 900190). Departures to Battambang (17,000r), Sisophon (20,000r) and Poipet (24,000r) are hourly from about 8.15am to 3.30pm.

You can also get to Phnom Penh by share taxi (8000r or 9000r, 1¾ hours, departures till early evening) or minibus (8000r). A pick-up to Pursat is 5000r.

Moto drivers charge 1000r for short hops around town. Hiring a *moto* for a day trip to Ondong Rossey and Phnom Santuk costs US$6.

Sokha Guesthouse rents out bicycles (US$1 a day) and motorbikes (US$5 a day).

PURSAT PROVINCE
ខេត្តពោធិ៍សាត់

Pursat, Cambodia's fourth-largest province, stretches from the remote forests of Phnom Samkos, on the Thai border, eastwards to the fishing villages and marshes of Tonlé Sap Lake. It encompasses the northern parts of the Cardamom Mountains, a huge forest area of global ecological importance that's becoming accessible from the relaxed town of Pursat.

PURSAT
ពោធិ៍សាត់

☎ 052 / pop 57,000

This mellow town, known for its marble carvers and oranges, makes an ideal base for a bamboo train excursion, visits to several waterfalls, a day trip to the floating village of Kompong Luong (p239) or an expedition into the wilds of the Central Cardamoms Protected Forest (p238).

Orientation

Pursat's main commercial street, St 3, is two blocks west of St 1, which runs along the riverfront. Both streets are perpendicular to the NH5.

Information

Internet cafés are concentrated along the southern stretch of St 1. Money can be changed at any of the gold shops near the market or at Lim Hoeurn Grocery.

Acleda Bank (☎ 951434; NH5) Changes travellers cheques and may get an ATM in 2008.

Chruy Rithy Web (St 1; per hr 3000; ✲ 6am-10pm) Internet access.

Department of Tourism (☎ 012 838854; ✲ 7-11am & 2-5pm Mon-Fri) Has maps and photos of province highlights on the walls and a few handouts.

Pheng Ky Computer (St 1; per hr 2000r; ✲ 6am-8pm or 9pm) Internet access.

Sights & Activities

A pleasant few hours can be spent strolling north along St 1 and then south along the east bank of the river.

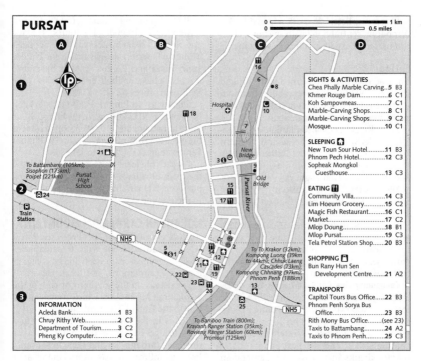

PURSAT

0 ———————— 1 km
0 ———————— 0.5 miles

SIGHTS & ACTIVITIES
Chea Phally Marble Carving..**5** B3	
Khmer Rouge Dam..............**6** C1	
Koh Sampovmeas...............**7** C1	
Marble-Carving Shops.........**8** C1	
Marble-Carving Shops.........**9** C2	
Mosque..............................**10** C1	

SLEEPING
New Toun Sour Hotel..........**11** B3	
Phnom Pech Hotel...............**12** C3	
Sopheak Mongkol Guesthouse..................**13** C3	

EATING
Community Villa..................**14** C3	
Lim Hoeurn Grocery............**15** C2	
Magic Fish Restaurant.........**16** C1	
Market...............................**17** C2	
Mlop Doung........................**18** B1	
Mlop Pursat........................**19** C3	
Tela Petrol Station Shop......**20** B3	

SHOPPING
Bun Rany Hun Sen Development Centre.......**21** A2	

TRANSPORT
Capitol Tours Bus Office....**22** B3	
Phnom Penh Sorya Bus Office..............................**23** B3	
Rith Mony Bus Office........(see 23)	
Taxis to Battambang..........**24** A2	
Taxis to Phnom Penh..........**25** C3	

INFORMATION
Acleda Bank........................**1** B3	
Chruy Rithy Web.................**2** C3	
Department of Tourism.........**3** C2	
Pheng Ky Computer..............**4** C2	

To Battambang (105km); Sisophon (173km); Poipet (221km)

Pursat High School

Hospital

New Bridge

Old Bridge

Pursat River

Train Station

NH5

NH5

To To Krakor (32km); Kompong Luong (39km to 44km); Chhuk Laeng Cascades (73km); Kompong Chhnang (97km); Phnom Penh (188km)

To Bamboo Train (800m); Kravanh Ranger Station (35km); Rovieng Ranger Station (60km); Promoui (125km)

Koh Sampovmeas, the town's answer to Singapore's Sentosa (though there's no cable car just yet), is an island park with manicured lawns, benches and Khmer-style pavilions. From the northern tip you can see a yellow, onion-domed **mosque** – topped with a star and crescent – eastward across the river.

A long block north, you can complete a vertiginous walk across the crumbling Khmer Rouge–era cement **dam**, part of a grandiose project intended to make it possible to grow rice in the dry season (the scheme never worked). On the rural east bank, walk south along the river road and you'll come upon a number of small **marble-carving shops**, where artisans make – and sell – everything from tiny tchotchkes to huge smiling Buddhas (also on sale in shops along NH5, including **Chea Phally Marble Carving**).You may also see groups of women making *naom banchok* (thick rice noodles) that they sell fresh in the market.

Pursat's own **bamboo trains** (p247) – much less tourist-oriented than their Battambang cousins – stop at the train crossing 800m south of NH5 along the road to Kravanh.

A three- or four-hour private excursion costs US$10, or you can hop on with the locals; departures are most frequent in the morning. For the best scenery, head towards Phnom Penh. One option is to get off at the village of **Chheu Tom** and catch a *moto* to **Chhuk Laeng Cascades** (Chroek Laeng Waterfall; one hour), situated 73km southeast of Pursat and 41km south of Krakor (on NH5 near Kompong Luong).

Sleeping

Sopheak Mongkol Guesthouse (☎ 012 483538; NH5; r with 1/2 beds US$3/5) A real cheapie but the 19 rooms, though TV-equipped, are barely larger than a bed and bathrooms lack sinks. Friendly, though, and a hub of activity, with pool and ping-pong tables in the courtyard.

New Toun Sour Hotel (Hotel Than Sour Thmey, Hotel Thmey Thansour; ☎ 951506; St 2; r US$6-12;) Its lobby chock full of carved wooden do-dads, this welcoming hotel has 43 large, pleasant rooms and a restaurant in the yard. Popular with the NGO crowd.

NORTHWESTERN CAMBODIA

Phnom Pech Hotel (☎ 951515; St 1; r US$6-13; 🔀) A modern, central hotel with spacious, clean rooms. Don't expect an effusive welcome.

Eating

The **market** (St 1), which burned to the ground in April 2007 but is being rebuilt, has both daytime eateries and a night market, as well as the usual fruit and veggie stalls.

For self-caterers, **Lim Hoeurn Grocery** (🕑 6am-8pm) stocks wine, soft cheese and Western snack food. The **Tela Petrol Station shop** (NH5; 🕑 6am-8.30pm) sells ice cream, wine, cookies and sometimes even yoghurt.

Mlop Pursat (☎ 012 928586; St 1; 🕑 6-11am) Serves, in its shady garden, the best breakfast soup (2000r) in town.

Magic Fish Restaurant (☎ 951537; St 1; mains 3000-15,000r; 🕑 9am-9pm) Affording fine river views from the balcony, this place – just north of the dam – serves tasty Khmer dishes and has the best roasted salt peanuts in town.

Community Villa (☎ 951483; mains 4500-10,000r; 🕑 to early evening) Run by a Cambodian NGO that gives job skills to at-risk young people, this place just off St 2 serves Khmer dishes, including ginger fish; Western meals, including salads; and the best pancakes and *tukalok* drinks in town. Most Cambodian restaurants have geckos that eat insects; this one has fearless frogs, so watch where you step at night.

Mlop Doung (☎ 951760; mains 5000-10,000r; 🕑 approx noon-midnight) Said by some to serve Pursat's best cuisine, this garden restaurant – decked out in coloured fairy lights – serves Khmer specialities such as *dtray bong kachait* (fish with vegetables cooked at your table) in open-air thatched pavilions.

Shopping

The gift shop at the Community Villa restaurant sells silk items, *krama* and bags made by local women.

Bun Rany Hun Sen Development Centre(☎ 951606; St 9; 🕑 7-11am & 2-5pm Mon-Fri & Sat morning) Teaches cloth weaving, mat weaving, sewing, marble carving and other practical skills to young people and markets the items they make. Travellers are welcome to visit classes.

Getting There & Around

Lots of buses run by lots of companies pass through Pursat. Destinations include Phnom Penh (16,000r, three hours,

188km), Kompong Chhnang (8000r, 97km), Battambang (10,000r, 1½ hours, 105km) and Poipet (20,000r, 221km). The Sopheak Mongkol Guesthouse sells tickets for Phnom Penh Sorya and Ponleu Angkor buses and serves as a bus stop (both companies also have their own offices on NH5).

Share taxis to Phnom Penh (15,000r) can be found on NH5 just east of the bridge, while those to Battambang (10,000r) stop in front of the old train station. A private taxi to Phnom Penh should cost US$25 or US$30.

Pursat's big local transport news for 2007: the town now has two *tuk tuks*! These hang out along NH5 in the day and along the river in the evening.

NORTHERN CARDAMOM MOUNTAINS

As the Central Cardamoms Protected Forest (CCPF) and adjacent wildlife sanctuaries slowly open up to ecotourism, Pursat is emerging as the Cardamoms' northern gateway.

For details on the southern reaches of the Cardamom Mountains, which stretch all the way to the Gulf of Thailand, see p186.

Roads in the area are heavily rutted and some bridges have holes big enough for a car tire to fall through. To find a taxi to Kravanh, Rovieng or Promoui, ask around in Pursat or enquire at a hotel or guesthouse.

Central Cardamoms Protected Forest

For information on the CCPF and road access to its southern sections, see p189.

The CCPF, which is not contiguous with the Southern Cardamoms Protected Forest (p189), is flanked by two at-risk areas: **Phnom Samkos Wildlife Sanctuary** to the west (opposite); and **Phnom Aural Wildlife Sanctuary** (2538 sq km) to the east, where Cambodia's highest peak, Phnom Aural (1764m), and the country's only hot springs are found. Sadly, the latter is rapidly being destroyed from the south and the east by corruption-spurred land speculation and rampant illegal logging.

The CCPF's enforcement ranger teams get technical and financial support from **Conservation International** (CI; www.conservation.org). To coordinate a visit, arrange a guide and perhaps stay at a ranger station (eg Kravanh, Rovieng or O Som), contact CI's **Ouk Kimsan** (☎ 012 256777; ccp.kimsan@everyday.com.kh).

Areas in and near the CCPF are still being de-mined, so stay on roads and well-trodden trails.

KRAVANH RANGER STATION

The Forest Administration rangers (in tan uniforms) and armed military policemen (in dark-green uniforms) based at this CCPF ranger station, about an hour south of Pursat, play an unending game of cat and mouse with loggers, poachers and encroachers – a game with life-and-death consequences for the rainforest and for Cambodia's biodiversity. Evidence of recent successes fills the station's yard: dozens of confiscated Toyota Camrys, crammed to the gills with raw luxury timber, are kept here as evidence for future trials. On a bulletin board, photos show rangers impounding snares, chain saws and guns. Teams based here often go out on long-range foot patrols, sleeping rough under tarps for a week or more.

Nearby attractions – popular with Khmers on holidays – include the **Chheu Tok Cascades**, a bit to the southeast, and **Odar Rapids**, 26km to the southwest. For information on trans-CCPF treks to/from Kravanh, see p189.

If you contact CI in advance, it may be possible to stay at Kravanh, where life has the pace and feel of a remote military outpost. Another option is to arrange a homestay with a local family.

ROVIENG RANGER STATION

Another impressive collection of seatless cars and ox carts loaded with illegal wood fills the yard at Rovieng, but the most valuable contraband here is aromatic *moras preuv* oil, extracted from the roots of the endangered *Disoxylon loureiri* tree and kept in scores of plastic jerry cans. It has a delightful, sandalwood-like scent and keeps away both mossies and rats but interests smugglers because it can be used to make the drug ecstasy. Other impounded objects stored here include chainsaws, snares (including some specially designed to catch pangolins; see p189) and guns.

Bulletin-board photos show clandestine sawmills, stills used to make *moras preuv* oil, confiscated bush meat and animals observed by rangers while on patrol, including leopards, foxes, crocodiles, monkeys, pangolins, deer, manchettes and wild pigs.

One nearby sight is **L'Bak Kamronh Rapids**, which on attracts holidaying Khmers; the river eventually flows into the Tonlé Sap. About 25km west of Rovieng, in Promoui Commune, is the primary **Chhrok Preal Forest**, which can be visited with a guide.

The land on either side of the road to Rovieng was deforested by the Vietnamese to prevent ambushes and later settled by destitute homesteaders, in some cases before anyone checked for mines. In many areas clear-cut a few years ago but now protected, the forest is growing back – a hopeful sign of regeneration.

By car, Rovieng is an hour from Kravanh and two hours from Pursat. Contact CI to see if it's possible to overnight here.

Phnom Samkos Wildlife Sanctuary

Sandwiched between the CCPF and the Thai frontier, the Phnom Samkos Wildlife Sanctuary (3338 sq km) is well and truly out in the sticks. Its northern flanks are under pressure because of a copper mining concession and proposed hydroelectric dams.

Boasting Cambodia's second-highest peak, **Phnom Samkos** (1717m), the sanctuary's main town is **Promoui**, 125km and 4½ hours from Pursat over a ruinous road (via Rovieng). An even worse track heads south via **O Som** (where there's a CCPF ranger station) and **Veal Veng** (where there are several guesthouses) to Krong Koh Kong and the Koh Kong Conservation Corridor (see p187). The area is administered by the Ministry of the Environment with help from **Flora & Fauna International** (FFI; www.fauna-flora.org).

KOMPONG LUONG
កំពង់ឡួង
pop 10,000

Kompong Luong has all the amenities you'd expect to find in an oversized fishing village – except that here everything floats! The result is an ethnic-Vietnamese Venice without the dry land. The cafés, shops, chicken coops, fish ponds, ice-making factory and crocodile farm are kept from sinking by boat hulls, barrels or bunches of bamboo, as are the Vietnamese pagoda (with bougainvilleas on the front porch), the blue-roofed church and the colourful houses, some with flower pots on their verandas – similar, perhaps, to terrestrial homes with aquariums. The cool teenagers zip around in boats with oversized motors while little old ladies paddle rhythmically the old-fashioned way. The only thing you can't do in Kompong Luong, it seems, is play pool – for obvious reasons, the nearest pool halls are on dry land.

In the dry season, when water levels drop and the Tonlé Sap shrinks, the entire aquapolis is towed, boat by boat, a few kilometres north. That's why there used to be a sign on NH5 indicating that the distance to Kompong Luong is a maximum of 7km, a minimum of 2km. Not much fun for the postman!

There is no guesthouse, so if you'd like to overnight ask around for a homestay.

The population of this fascinating and picturesque village is predominantly Vietnamese, so – reflecting their ambiguous status in Cambodian society – you may find the welcome here slightly more subdued than in most rural Cambodian towns, at least from adults. Khmer Rouge massacres of Vietnamese villagers living around Tonlé Sap Lake were commonplace during the first half of the 1990s, and even as late as 1998 more than 20 Vietnamese were killed in a pogrom near Kompong Chhnang.

GETTING THERE & AROUND
Kompong Luong is between 39km and 44km east of Pursat, depending on the time of year. Round-trip transport options include *moto* (one-way/return US$3/6, 45 minutes) and private taxi (US$25). The turn-off from NH5 is in Krakor next to the Sokimex petrol station.

From April to June, when Tonlé Sap Lake is very low, the small fast boats that ferry tourists between Phnom Penh and Siem Reap occasionally stop at Kompong Luong for refuelling…at one of the two floating petrol stations, of course!

The official tourist rate to charter a four-passenger wooden motorboat around Kompong Luong – posted on a bright-blue sign near the dock – is US$5 an hour (locals pay much less), but boatmen complain that fuel prices have skyrocketed since the sign was put up. Since you're paying by the hour expect a very leisurely cruise! Paddle-powered boats, available a few hundred metres north of the motorboat dock, cost about half that per hour.

BATTAMBANG PROVINCE

ខេត្តបាត់ដំបង

Battambang (Bat Dambang), said by proud locals to produce Cambodia's finest rice, tastiest oranges and sweetest coconuts, has a long border with Thailand and a short stretch of the Tonlé Sap shoreline. Once Cambodia's largest and richest province, it was on the front lines of the civil war for much of the 1980s and 1990s and ceded territory to form two new provinces, Banteay Meanchey and Krong Pailin, but its fortunes are now looking up. The region has a long tradition of producing many of Cambodia's best-loved singers and actors.

Battambang has passed from Cambodia to Thailand and back again several times over the past few centuries. Thailand ruled the area from 1795 to 1907, and as recently as WWII (1941 to 1946), the Thais cut a deal with the Japanese and the Vichy French to take control again, resulting in five years of repression.

The provincial capital, Battambang, is emerging as Cambodia's fourth tourist destination (after Siem Reap, Phnom Penh and Sihanoukville), thanks in part to its colonial architecture and general liveliness. The city is an excellent base for delightful bicycle or *moto* trips to several hilltop temples.

BATTAMBANG
បាត់ដំបង
☎ 053 / pop 140,000

Cambodia's second-largest city is an elegant riverside town, home to some of the best-preserved French-period architecture in the country and to warm and friendly inhabitants. The city itself is developing fast but timeless hilltop temples and scenic villages can be seen on leisurely day-trips. The most scenic river trip in the country links Battambang with Siem Reap.

Battambang has more Hindu representations (eg roundabout statues) than you find in most parts of Cambodia and has long had a sizeable Christian minority.

Orientation
The focal point of Battambang's city centre, on the west bank of Stung Sangker, is Psar Nat (Meeting Market). The city has only five named streets. In the city centre, St 1 runs along the riverfront, St 2 is one block inland and St 3 serves as the main commercial thoroughfare. The liveliest street on the up-and-coming East Bank is Old NH5, linked to the west bank by the Old Stone Bridge (in fact made of concrete). The two banks are also linked by NH5, which passes over the New Stone Bridge.

Information

Available at selected hotels and restaurants, *Around Battambang* (US$10; updated in 2006) by Ray Zepp has details on Angkorian temples, wats and excursions in the Battambang and Pailin areas. Proceeds go to monks and nuns working to raise awareness of HIV/AIDS and to help AIDS orphans.

Centre Culturel Français (☎ 952897; www.ccf -cambodge.org) The French Cultural Centre has a *médiathèque* with books, CDs and DVDs, and screens films – some with English subtitles – at 7pm on Friday.

Money changers can be found along the southern and western sides of Psar Nat. In the city centre, internet options are most numerous along St 3 and St 1; an hour online generally costs 1500r.

Acleda Bank On the east bank of the river. Changes travellers cheques and has an ATM.

ANZ Royal (☎ 953830; St 1) Has ATMs.

Canadia Bank (☎ 952267) Near Psar Nat. Has ATMs.

Emergency Surgical Centre for War Victims (☎ 370065; emergency@online.com.kh; ✆ 24hr for emergencies) This 106-bed surgical hospital, free-of-charge thanks to donors in Italy, *cannot* help with tropical diseases or routine illness but may be able to save your life if you need emergency surgery, eg for trauma or appendicitis. Has two ambulances. Located off NH5 on East Bank.

Green Net (St 1; ✆ 6am-7pm or later) Internet access.

KCT Internet Café (✆ 6.30am to 9pm or 10pm) Just off St 2 next to White Rose restaurant.

Polyclinique Visal Sokh (☎ 952401; NH5; ✆ 24hr) For minor medical problems, including snake bites, malaria and rabies shots. Doctors speak French and some English. Has a pharmacy and two ambulances. Near Vietnamese consulate.

SP Internet (St 3; ✆ 6.30am-9pm) A few doors south of the Chhaya Hotel

Tourist Office (☎ 730217; St 1; ✆ 7-11am & 2-5pm Mon-Fri) In an early-20th-century French-style villa facing the old Governor's Residence, which is worth a look inside. Has little in the way of handouts.

Union Commercial Bank (☎ 952552; St 1) Has ATMs.

Vietnamese Consulate (☎ 952894; ✆ 8-11am & 2-4pm) Issues visas (US$35) in 10 minutes, provided the consul general is in town.

Sights

Much of Battambang's special charm lies in its early-20th-century French architecture. Some of the finest **colonial buildings** are along the waterfront, especially along the two blocks of St 1 south of **Psar Nat**, itself an architectural monument, albeit a modernist one. The four-faced clock tower is worth a look. There are also some old **French shop houses** along St 3, eg just east of the train station.

The two-storey **Governor's Residence**, with its balconies and wooden shutters, is another handsome legacy of very early 1900s. The interior is closed but it should be possible to stroll the grounds. Except for the neo-Khmer laterite gate, the intersection out front looks much as it did in the 1930s – check out the French-only distance marker, the neat lawns and the **New Iron Bridge**, now reserved for pedestrians and motorbikes.

Two elegant – though as yet nameless – **avenues**, with parkland down the middle, grace the city centre. One goes by the Centre Culturel Français (one block north of NH5), while the other stretches west from the worthwhile **Battambang Museum** (St 1; admission US$1; ✆ 8-11am & 2-5pm Mon-Fri). Highlights include fine Angkorian lintels and statuary from all over Battambang Province, including Phnom Banan and Sneng. Signs are in Khmer, English and French.

Battambang's many temples, which survived the Khmer Rouge period relatively unscathed thanks to a local commander who ignored orders, include **Wat Phiphétaram**, a long block north of Psar Nat, built in 1888; **Wat Damrey Sar**, west of the Battambang Museum; and **Wat Kandal** on the East Bank, once famed for its library. A number of the monks at all three wats speak English and are glad for a chance to practise; they're often around in the late afternoon.

In the area around the **old train station** – where the time is always 8.02, according to the clock – and along the tracks just south of there, you can explore a treasure trove of crumbling, French-era repair sheds, warehouses and rolling stock, evocative of times long gone. Check out the wagons' constructor's plates: some read '1930 Köln' (Cologne, Germany). German reparations from WWI, perhaps? Or maybe the wagons were confiscated after WWII and shipped out here in the last days of French Indochina?

Activities

For details on day trips from Battambang, see p246.

Always wanted to learn how to prepare authentic family-style Khmer dishes? Daily from 9.30am to 1pm, **Smokin' Pot** (☎ 012 821400; vannaksmokingpot@yahoo.com) offers **cooking classes**

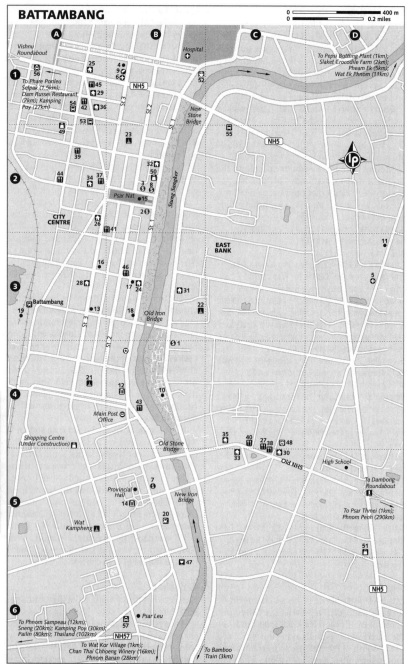

(US$8) that start with a trip to the local market and include a three-course lunch (you eat what you cook). Reserve a day ahead.

Phare Ponleu Selpak (☎ 952424; www.phareps .org), a multi-arts centre for disadvantaged children, puts on circus shows and dance performances. From Monday to Friday, it's often possible to observe the drawing, music, dance and circus students practising and see an exhibition of students' art. To get there from the Vishnu Roundabout on NH5, head west for 900m and then turn right (north) and continue for 600m.

In New York or London they may be achieving inner harmony with tai chi, but here in Battambang they're burning off the rice carbs doing classic Western **aerobics** (500r), held each evening from about 5.30pm to 7pm on the East Bank north of the Old Stone Bridge. Led by a local hunk with a portable sound system, just five minutes of working out should be enough to teach you how to count in Khmer – at least up to four.

You can swim and use the fitness machines at the **Victory Club** (☎ 092 621616; per day US$4; ☺ 6am-8pm), a sports club popular with Battambang's *jeunesse dorée* (golden youth). The lockers are lockable but not secure enough for valuables.

At **Seeing Hands Massage** (☎ 012 724714; per hr US$5; ☺ 7am-10pm), trained blind masseurs and

masseuses offer Japanese-style therapeutic massage and other soothing work-overs.

For as little as US$2, you can pose in traditional Khmer costume and have your photo taken at two shops along the waterfront, **Tourism Photo Shop** (☎ 012 853840; 10 St 1) and **Nikon Photo Studio** (☎ 012 365987; 23 St 1). Prices include makeup and a suitably kitschy background.

If you'd like to see rural development projects in action, contact **Agricultural Development Action** (☎ 952551; ans.ada.btg@online .com.kh) a day or two ahead to arrange an all-day (7am to 7pm) tour by 4WD (US$150 for up to three people, including translator and meals).

Sleeping
CITY CENTRE
Most of the city's veteran hotels are within a few bustling blocks of Psar Nat. The rival Royal and Chhaya Hotels dominate the backpacker market and can help arrange guides and transport.

There are quite a few hotels and guesthouses strung out all along NH5.

Golden River Hotel (☎ 730165; 234 St 3; r with fan/air-con from US$5/8; ☒) An old-style guesthouse with dim hallways and 38 serviceable, though somewhat spartan, rooms. Not the place for a romantic getaway. Has the city's cheapest air-con.

NORTHWESTERN CAMBODIA

Royal Hotel (☎ 016 912034; www.asrhotel.com; r with fan/air-con from US$5/13; ✇ ▯) A real hit with independent travellers, the 45-room Royal has the city's widest range of rooms. The worthy rooftop restaurant has panoramic urban views. The same company runs two new hotels on St 3, the Hotel Asie and the plusher Star Hotel.

Chhaya Hotel (☎ 952170; chhayahotel-bb@hotmail .com; 118 St 3; s/d/tr US$4/5/7, r with air-con US$8-10; ✇) This sprawling, shambolic establishment, long a leading backpacker choice, has 84 uninspiring but serviceable rooms. Tourists generally stay in the new building, away from the sometimes rowdy male Khmer clients.

Monorom Guesthouse (☎ 012 921374; 75 St 1; s/d/tr US$4.50/5/7, r with air-con US$10; ✇) The no-frills rooms at this big, riverfront establishment are a touch fusty, but the price is right for such a popular location.

Angkor Hotel (☎ 952310; St 1; r US$6-11; ✇) Boasting a prime riverfront location, this hotel – a fine example of what was considered the height of modernity in 1973 – has 27 clean rooms with beat-up furniture; ask for one of the seven with river views.

Banan Hotel (☎ 953242; bananhotel@yahoo.com; NH5; r US$15-30; ✇) Opened in 2006, this modern place combines three-star comfort with Khmer-style décor. The 30 rooms come with all the mod-cons and there's plenty of parking out back.

EAST BANK

Most of Battambang's new hotels are on the up-and-coming East Bank.

Spring Park Hotel (☎ 730999; www.springpark hotelbtb.com; Old NH5; r with fan/air-con from US$6/11; ✇ ▯) Opened in 2005, this place boasts Battambang's only lift and 90 comfortable rooms, all with either a proper shower stall or a bathtub. Excellent value all around.

Khemara Battambang Hotel (☎ 732727; www .kmrbb.com; Old NH5; US$12-25; ✇ ▯) With its apricot exterior, tile roof and sandstone-floored hallways, this brand new hotel – the doors opened in late 2007 – stands out. The 32 three-star-comfort rooms tastefully mix Khmer and modern design and come with Western-standard bathrooms.

Golden Palace Hotel (☎ 953901; www.goldenpalace hotels.com; gph-sale@hotmail.com; Old NH5; r US$13-20; ▯) Businesslike in the best sense of the word, this modern place has 50 spotless, nicely laid-out rooms and a business centre with free internet

terminals. Offers solid value and free pick-up from bus stops or the ferry landing.

our pick **La Villa** (☎ 730151; www.lavilla-battambang .com; s/d US$45/50; ✇ ▯) One of the most romantic and evocative boutique hotels in Cambodia, this delightful seven-room hostelry, in a French-era villa built by a rich Sino-Khmer merchant, was totally renovated in vintage 1930s style. Room prices include breakfast. A pool and four more rooms may be added in 2008. Often full, so reserve ahead.

Eating
CITY CENTRE

Cheap dining is available in and around Psar Nat (eg in the space between the two market buildings), but be aware that some places specialise in what can only be described as 'unusable bits' soup.

Riverside night market (St 1; mains 4000-6000r; ⏱ 5-9pm) Locals in the mood for good-value Khmer food flock to about a dozen neon-lit eateries across the street from the Battambang Museum.

Fresh Eats Café (☎ 953912; mains US$1-1.50; ⏱ 6.30am-9pm) Run by an NGO that helps children whose families have been affected by HIV/AIDS, this little place serves Western breakfasts, including bagels, and holds dance performances (US$3) from 7pm to 9pm on Friday and Saturday.

Sunrise Coffee House (☎ 953426; mains US$1-3; ⏱ 6.30am-5pm Mon-Sat) Caffeine is blended into a variety of delicious forms here and can be enjoyed with fresh-baked goodies, California-style snacks, pancakes, sandwiches and salads.

Smokin' Pot (☎ 012 821400; mains 4500-10,000r; ⏱ 7am-about 11pm) Popular with the younger NGO crowd, this cheery, laid-back restaurant serves good Khmer, Thai and Western food – burgers and fried beef with ginger are favourites. Doubles as a cooking school (see p241).

White Rose (☎ 012 693855; St 2; mains 5000-9000r; ⏱ 6.30am-10pm) Has a mammoth menu of good-value Khmer, Vietnamese and Chinese dishes, including soups, veggie options and marvellous *tukalok* (fruit shakes).

EAST BANK

A lively restaurant scene is developing on the East Bank, especially on Old NH5 between the Old Stone Bridge and Khemara Battambang Hotel.

Green House Café (☎ 012 467313; Old NH5; mains US$1.25-2; ☻ 6.30am-8.30pm) Serves coffee, shakes, Khmer-style rice and noodle favourites, salads and exotic dishes – the menu has photographs so clients know what they're getting – such as pizza, hamburgers and doughnuts. Popular with students from the nearby colleges.

Cold Night Restaurant (☎ 012 994746; NH5; mains US$2-4; ☻ 6am-11pm or midnight) With 175 menu items, there are plenty of Asian and Western options, including sandwiches (tuna salad, club), burgers and pasta, plus a local version of pizzas. The name refers to the cold beer on offer.

La Villa (☎ 730151; mains US$4-7.50; ☻ noon-2.30pm & 6-9pm; ☒) An island of civilised charm, Battambang's finest restaurant, attached to its best hostelry, serves family-style Khmer, French and Italian dishes accompanied by wines from around the world. Specialities include *amoc*, lasagne, French onion soup and *filet de bœuf* (beef filet).

VEGETARIAN

our pick **Vegetarian Foods Restaurant** (☎ 012 501408; mains 1500-2000r; ☻ 6.30-11am or noon) Run by an ideologically vegetarian ethnic-Chinese family, this informal eatery serves home-made soy milk and delicious noodle soup breakfasts and brunches made with tofu or mushrooms. Recipes are Khmer, Chinese and Vietnamese.

Mercy House (☎ 012 243402; mains 2000-4800r; ☻ 6.30am-7pm) Serves Western breakfasts, noodle dishes, fruit-based beverages and even veggie hamburgers (2800r) amid flowery tablecloths and struggling potted plants.

SELF-CATERING

Psar Nat has oodles of food stalls.

Chea Neang Grocery (St 3; ☻ 8am-7pm) Facing Psar Nat, Chea Neang stocks Western products, including cheese, wine, yoghurt and Wall's ice cream.

Lux-Tang Bakery (St 3; ☻ 6am-9pm) Facing Chhaya Hotel, this bakery sells baguettes and French pastries.

San Long International Bakery (☎ 012 530155; St 1; ☻ 6am-7pm or later) Next to the ferry dock, San Long sells baguettes and bread made without sugar.

Drinking & Entertainment

A number of beer gardens and Khmer nightclubs can be found on the East Bank north and east of La Villa.

Riverside Balcony Bar (☎ 730313; St 1; mains US$2.50-4; ☻ 4pm-midnight Tue-Sun) Set in a gorgeous wooden house high above the riverfront, this is the most atmospheric bar in town. Renowned for its burgers but also serves pasta, burritos and enchiladas

La Villa (☎ 730151; ☻ to 9pm or 9.30pm; ☒) A Hemingwayesque bar with an elegant colonial ambiance. One of the few places in the world that serves Cambodian cognac, distilled just outside town.

Sky Disco (☎ 012 862777; ☻ 8pm-1am) Just north of the Khemara Battambang Hotel, this is Battambang's hottest dance venue. The DJs play everything from traditional Khmer melodies to hip-hop.

Shopping

Boeung Chhouk Market has a whole section selling pre-worn clothes from Thailand for 500r. Quality varies, but finds are always a possibility.

Fresh Eats Café (☎ 953912; ☻ 6.30am-9pm) Sells purses, *kramas,* stuffed animals and other handicrafts made by vulnerable women.

Rachana Handicrafts (☎ 952506; ☻ 8am-5.30pm Mon-Fri, sometimes Sat & Sun mornings) This NGO-run sewing workshop trains disadvantaged women and sells purses, stuffed toys, *kramas* and cotton and silk accessories.

Heng Maly (☎ 952270; St 1) Sells massive hardwood furniture as well as more portable Khmer-style carved-wood items.

Getting There & Away

Battambang is 290km from Phnom Penh along the heavily trafficked NH5. Travelling after dark is best avoided for safety reasons. Boat and bus tickets can be arranged through hotels and guesthouses.

NH57 to Pailin (80km) is still sometimes referred to by locals as NH10.

BOAT

The boat to Siem Reap (US$15, daily at 7am), arguably Cambodia's most spectacular boat journey, follows narrow waterways, scrapes marshland trees and passes through protected wetlands – a birdwatcher's paradise – but can take anywhere from five to nine or more hours, depending on the water level. Run by **Angkor Express** (☎ 012 601287) and **Chann Na** (☎ 012 354344), boats have room for 25 to 40 people.

In the dry season, passengers sometimes have to be driven to a navigable section of the

NORTHWESTERN CAMBODIA

river. It's possible to arrange to get off at the Prek Toal Bird Sanctuary (p138) and then be picked up there the next day (US$5 extra).

BUS & TAXI

Half-a-dozen bus companies have offices and stops on or near NH5, most of them west of the river. All serve Phnom Penh (US$4, five hours), Pursat (US$2.50 or US$3, two hours), Sisophon (US$2, one hour) and Poipet (US$4, three hours). Booking through a hotel may incur a US$1 commission.

Capitol Tours (☎ 953040) Praised by expats and cheaper than the competition. Has hourly buses to Phnom Penh until 2.30pm and, via Poipet, to Bangkok (US$10).

Neak Kror Horm (☎ 953838) Can get you to Siem Reap (US$4, six hours, one daily) and Bangkok (US$15, seven hours, two daily).

Phnom Penh Sorya (☎ 092 181804; NH5) Situated 100m east of the bridge.

Ponleu Angkor Khmer (☎ 092 517792) Has four buses a day going east (towards Phnom Penh) and one a day going west (towards Poipet).

Rith Mony (☎ 092 888847; St 1) Next to the ferry landing. Has hourly buses to Pursat and Phnom Penh until about 3pm and two morning buses to Sisophon and Poipet.

At the **taxi station** (NH5), share taxis to Poipet (US$5), Sisophon (100B or US$3) and Siem Reap (250B or US$6) leave from the north side while taxis to Pursat (15,000r) and Phnom Penh (25,000r) leave from the southeast corner. Pickups to Sisophon (100B in the front seat, 60B out back) stop nearby.

For details on getting to Pailin, see p251. A private taxi to Phnom Penh costs US$38.

Getting Around

A *moto* ride costs 1000r if you stay on one bank of the river, 1500r if you cross the river and 2000r at night. Battambang's very first *tuk tuk*s hit the tarmac in 2007.

Hiring a *moto* driver who speaks English or French costs US$5 for a half-day in and around town and US$6 to US$9 (depending on the distance) for an all-day trip out of the city. Many of the *moto* drivers who hang out at the Royal Hotel, and their bitter rivals at the Chhaya Hotel, speak decent English and are good sources of information on things to see and do. Equally competent are the friendly, English-speaking *moto* drivers you'll run into elsewhere around town, though they may avoid picking you up in

front of either hotel as the house drivers jealously protect their turf.

Bicycles are a great way to get around and can be ridden along either bank of the river in either direction. The Chhaya Hotel rents bicycles to nonguests for US$1.50 a day; the Royal Hotel charges US$2.

Guesthouses can often arrange motorbike rental – the Chhaya Hotel, for instance, charges guests or nonguests US$5 or US$6 a day. They can also arrange taxi rentals, which are handy during the wet season when a motorbike may leave you drenched.

AROUND BATTAMBANG

Before setting out on trips around Battambang, try to link up with an English-speaking *moto* driver, as it really adds to the experience. For details on lots of sites not mentioned below, check out the guidebook *Around Battambang* (p241).

Admission to Phnom Sampeau, Phnom Banan and Wat Ek Phnom costs US$2. If you purchase a ticket – sold by the Tourist Police – at one site it's valid all day long at the other two.

Local geography lends itself to a number of enjoyable day-trip itineraries. A visit to Phnom Sampeau can be turned into a loop via Phnom Banan, perhaps with a bamboo train ride (opposite) on the way back. Kamping Poy can be combined with Phnom Sampeau and, perhaps, Phnom Banan too. Wat Phnom Sampeau and Sneng (Sneung) can be visited on the way to Pailin.

Depending on the distance, a *moto* to a single site should cost US$4 (Wat Ek Phnom) or US$5 (Phnom Banan), while a full-day trip ranges from US$6 to US$9.

Wat Ek Phnom
វត្តឯកភ្នំ
Wat Ek Phnom (Aek Phnum; admission US$2) an atmospheric, partly collapsed, 11th-century temple situated 11km north of Battambang, measures 52m by 49m and is surrounded by the remains of a laterite wall and an ancient *baray* (reservoir). A lintel showing the **Churning of the Ocean of Milk** can be seen above the east entrance to the central temple, whose upper flanks hold some fine bas-reliefs. Construction of the giant Buddha statue next door has been stopped by the government because, they say, it mars the site's timeless beauty. This is a very

---

ALL ABOARD, EVERYONE OFF, ALL ABOARD, EVERYONE OFF!

The **bamboo train** is one of the world's all-time classic rail journeys. From O Dambong, on the east bank 3.7km south of Battambang's Old Stone Bridge, the train runs southeast to O Sra Lav, via half an hour of clicks and clacks along warped, misaligned rails and vertiginous bridges left by the French.

Each bamboo train – known in Khmer as a *norry* (*nori*) – consists of a 3m-long wood frame, covered lengthwise with slats made of ultra-light bamboo, that rests on two barbell-like bogies, the aft one connected by fan belts to a 6HP gasoline engine. Pile on 10 or 15 people or up to three tonnes of rice, crank it up and you can cruise along at about 15km/h.

The genius of the system is that it offers a brilliant solution to the most ineluctable problem faced on any single-track line: what to do when two trains going opposite directions meet. In the case of bamboo trains, the answer is simple: one car is quickly disassembled and set on the ground beside the tracks so the other can pass. The rule is that whichever car has fewer passengers has to cede priority, though motorbikes pull rank, so if you bring one along – or have a convincing inflatable *moto* decoy – you'll get VIP treatment.

What happens, you may ask, when a bamboo train meets a real train barrelling down the track? First, Cambodian trains don't barrel, they crawl. Second, bamboo train conductors know the real train's schedule. And third, the real train can be heard tooting its horn from a great distance, providing more than enough time to dismount and disassemble.

Hiring a private bamboo train from O Dambong to O Sra Lav costs US$8, though it's much cheaper to take a share-*norry* with locals transporting veggies, charcoal or wood to market.

Sadly, rumour has it that bamboo trains will soon be banned, especially if the rail line to Phnom Penh is – as planned – upgraded.

---

popular picnic and pilgrimage destination for Khmers at festival times.

On the way from Battambang by bicycle or *moto*, it's possible to make a number of interesting stops. About 1.2km north of Battambang's ferry landing is a 1960s **Pepsi bottling plant**, its logo faded but otherwise hardly changed since production ceased abruptly in 1975. You can still see the remains of the old production line and, in a warehouse out back, thousands of dusty empties – bearing Pepsi's old script logo – whose contents quenched someone's thirst back when Nixon was in the White House.

Drive 700m further and turn left (west) and after 200m you'll get to a signless house behind which is the **Slaket crocodile farm**. It's open all day, including mealtimes – the crocs are always happy to have tourists for lunch.

Return to the main road and drive another 3.5km, past several wats, to the village of **Pheam Ek**, whose speciality is making rice paper for spring rolls. All along the road, in family workshops, you'll see rice paste being steamed and then placed on a bamboo frame for drying in the sun. The income earned is meagre – 100 rice sheets sell for just 2500r. The coconuts grown in this area are said to be especially sweet. Wat Ek Phnom is 5.5km further on.

The nonprofit **Cambodian Education Center** in Pheam Ek, which provides free English instruction to local kids, is always looking for volunteer teachers. For details contact **Racky Thy** (☎ 017 829450; rith_gentleman@yahoo.com).

GETTING THERE & AWAY

Wat Ek Phnom is 11km from Battambang's ferry landing by the shortest route and 21km if you go via the Pepsi plant and Pheam Ek. Combining both makes for a nice 32km circuit.

Phnom Banan

វត្តបាណន់

Exactly 358 stone steps lead up a shaded slope to **Prasat Banan** (admission US$2), whose five towers are reminiscent of the layout of Angkor Wat. Indeed, locals claim it was the inspiration for Angkor Wat!

Udayadityavarman II, son of Suryavarman I, built Prasat Banan in the 11th century, and its hillside location offers incredible views across the surrounding countryside. There are impressive carved lintels above the doorways to each tower and bas-reliefs on the upper parts of the central tower. Many

RACKY THY *Daniel Robinson*

Racky Thy's earliest memories are of the Khmer Rouge. Born in 1973 in Bay Damram village near Wat Banan (p247), he was of kindergarten age when the Khmer Rouge split up his rice-growing family, forcing his parents to relocate to single-sex encampments and the children to move to a 'children's site', run with an iron hand – and no small degree of sadism – by revolutionary true believers who were almost children themselves. This is the story of his survival, as told in the shade of the timeless ruins of Wat Ek Phnom.

'Each child had to collect 10kg of cow dung and 10kg of plants to make compost fertiliser. If a child cannot, they will give punishments, like don't give porridge water to drink, give more hard work to do. One day, when I come back, nothing to eat. I was very hungry so I went to a big tamarind tree and pick a lot of fruit to eat. Later I got much diarrhoea.

'I got very sick, no strength, cannot stand up. But the children's leaders think that I'm pretending to be ill so they want to teach me a lesson. They force me to pick the tamarind fruit for them. Because the base of the tree was big and I have no strength, I could not climb up the tree. They threatened me, "If you cannot, maybe I kill you under this tree". I pray to Buddha for help. Finally, I could climb up the tree and picked a lot of tamarind fruit for them.'Then the cadres don't let me climb down – they cut the lower branches of the tree, cover the base of the tree with thorns and burn [set fire to] the base of the tree. And then they laugh and go away. At that time, I feel this is my final time, my death day is coming. But fortunately there was a little rain that put out the fire. So I climbed down from the tree. I was very happy and walked back to the children's site. When they [the leaders] saw me they were surprised that a little boy can survive their cruel and violent activities. I tell them a lie, that I jumped down through the fire.

'As punishment, they take me to another place for me to jump down, from a cliff into a river with fast-flowing water. The height is around 10m so I feel I die before I jump down. I pray to Buddha and Buddha look after me and he guide me to catch the branch of a tree. And the water flow over my head with air bubbles, they did not see me but I could breathe in and breathe out. Because my body colour is similar to water they think, "he already die", and they go back.

'Then I run fast across the forest. I keep a long time running. Finally I could find my grandfather's place, I cry a lot at that time, and my grandfather carry me into the house and find a way to hide me by digging a hiding hole under the house and he let me breathe in and breathe out with a papaya branch, like a straw. Some of the children's leaders come to find me at the house, many times coming but did not see me. When they came I live in the hole – for around three months [this went on], my grandfather told me later.

'After that I came out from the hole and came to live as other children and change the [family] name so nobody know me, and my grandfather send me to another children's site. The next site is better than the first site but the leader is more strict than the first one, never let children go visit parents, never let children cry at night, never let children urinate at night. If one of the children cry or urinate at night, they bring to kill – they threatened this at mealtimes. So we just cry in [our] mind, never let our tears outside the eyes.'

Racky Thy lives in Battambang with his wife and two young daughters. He is a tour guide and runs a nonprofit English-language school.

of this temple's best carvings are now in the Battambang Museum (p241).

From the temple, 28km south of Battambang, a narrow stone staircase leads south down the hill to **three caves**, two of which are not mined and can thus be visited with a torch-/flashlight-equipped local guide. At the first, 25m up the slope from the papaya orchard, you have to crouch to get through the first 5m, but you eventually get to a soaring chamber with a skylight high overhead. At the second, a few hundred metres west, you clamber over giant boulders to a cavernous space with some Buddhist statues and, way above you, a skylight and chirping bats. A path leads from the caves around the hill to the parking area.

On the way to Phnom Banan, on the river's west bank 1.7km south of Battambang's Riverside Balcony Bar, you can stop at **Wat Kor Village**, which is known for its 21 **Khmer heritage houses**. Built of now-rare hardwoods almost a century ago and surrounded by orchard gardens, they sport wide verandas and the ambiance of another era. Signs in Khmer, English and French explain each building's history. It's possible to stay in some of the houses – ask around to see who's got a guest room. **Ox-cart rides** may be available just south of the rail bridge.

About 15km further, through an area famous for its hot red chillies, you can visit Cambodia's only winery, **Chan Thai Chhoeng** (☎ 012 665238). Local connoisseurs express more enthusiasm for the owner's pioneering spirit than for her reds and rosés, though her cognac-like grape brandy gets better reviews.

Phnom Sampeau
ភ្នំសំពៅ

At the summit of this fabled limestone outcrop, 12km southwest of Battambang along NH57 (towards Pailin), a complex of **temples** (admission US$2) – several built recently thanks to donations from overseas Khmers – affords gorgeous views of the surrounding plains and, to the south, Phnom Banan. Some of the macaques that live around the summit, dining on bananas left as offerings, are pretty ornery.

Between the summit and the mobile-phone antenna, a **deep canyon** – its vertical sides cloaked in greenery – descends steeply through a natural arch to a 'lost world' of stalactites, creeping vines, air roots, bats and statues of two Angkorian warriors.

In the area between the two sets of antennas stand two government **artillery pieces**, one with markings in Russian, the other in German. They still point westwards towards **Phnom Krapeu** (Crocodile Mountain), a one-time Khmer Rouge stronghold.

About half-way up the cement access road to the summit, a turn-off leads 250m up the hill to the **Killing Caves of Phnom Sampeau**. An enchanted staircase, flanked by greenery, leads into a cavern where a golden reclining Buddha lies peacefully next to a glass-walled memorial, dedicated in 2007, filled with the bones and skulls of some of the people bludgeoned to death by Khmer Rouge cadres before being thrown through the overhead skylight. Nearby is the **old memorial**, a rusty cage made of chicken wire and cyclone fencing.

At the base of the hill, a 15m-high **Buddha** is being carved out of the cliff face, starting with the head. While more funds are raised,

local macaques treat the scaffolding like a giant jungle gym.

Food stalls sell edibles at the base of the hill; snacks are available up top.

GETTING THERE & AWAY
From Battambang, a return *moto* ride costs about US$5 (including wait time). To get to the top, you can either walk through the gate and up the stairs, or take the 1km cement road by foot or by *moto* (US$3 return with an English-speaking guide).

Kamping Poy
កំពីងពួយ

Kamping Poy (Poi or Puoy), also known as the Killing Dam, was one of the Khmer Rouge's many grand, futile irrigation schemes. Some locals claim the hand-built dam, stretching 8km between two distant hillsides, was intended as a sort of final solution for enemies of the revolution, who were to be invited to its inauguration and then drowned following the detonation of dynamite charges. More likely, it was an extravagant Khmer Rouge attempt to re-create the complex irrigation network that helped Cambodia prosper under the kings of Angkor. Whatever the truth, as many as 10,000 Cambodians are thought to have perished during its construction, worked to death under the shadow of executions, malnutrition and disease.

Despite its grim history – and the fact that there's little to see except the sluice gates – the lake is today a popular excursion for locals on weekends and holidays. You can take a boat rowed by local kids to the far shore but they sometimes demand exorbitant prices.

GETTING THERE & AWAY
Kamping Poi is 27km from Battambang (if you go via NH5). To get there from the north, turn southwest off NH5 7km northwest of Battambang (across from the much-beloved **Dam Russei Restaurant**) and follow the Khmer Rouge–built irrigation canal. From the south, turn northwest off NH57 2km past Phnom Sampeau.

Sneng
ស្នឹង

This nondescript town on the way to Pailin, on NH57 20km southwest of Battambang, is home to two small yet interesting temples. The Hindu **Prasat Yeay Ten** dates from the end of the 10th century and, although little more than a neat pile of blocks, has above its doorways three delicately carved lintels that somehow survived the ravages of time and war. Dedicated to Shiva, it is on the east side of the highway so close to the road that you can't miss it.

Behind Prasat Yeay Ten, 200m to the east, is a contemporary wat, and tucked away at the back of this compound are three **brick sanctuaries**, which have some beautifully preserved carvings around the entrances. The sanctuaries look like pre-Angkorian Chenla temples, but given the limited Chenla presence in western Cambodia, it is possible that they date from the same period as Prasat Kravan (p169) at Angkor, ie the early 10th century.

KRONG PAILIN

The province-level municipality of Krong Pailin is best known for its gem mines (which are now exhausted), land mines (which are still being removed) and for an equally sinister ideological *mein* – the Khmer Rouge version of *Mein Kampf*.

During the civil war, the Pailin area's gem and timber resources – sold to the world with the help of Thai army generals – served as the economic crutch that kept the Khmer Rouge hobbling along. In the mid-1990s, it was a staging area for regular dry-season offensives that overran government positions as far east as Phnom Sampeau.

DON'T STRAY FROM THE PATH!

Krong Pailin, nearby areas along the Thai frontier and the Battambang Province district of Samlot are some of the most heavily mined places in the world. On the front lines for years, districts such as Treng and Ratanak Mondul (the Sdau area) also have huge quantities of unexploded ordnance lying around. In 2006 and 2007, Krong Pailin had more casualties from mines and unexploded ordnance, per square kilometre, than any province in Cambodia.

The upshot is that you should stick to well-used roads and paths. Carelessness in this part of the country could cost you a leg or your life.

In 1996 the Khmer Rouge supremo in these parts, Ieng Sary (Brother Number Three), defected to the government side, bringing with him 3000 fighters and their dependants. His reward: amnesty and free reign in Krong Pailin, created in 2001 from land carved out of Battambang Province. Only in late 2007 were Ieng and his wife arrested for war crimes and crimes against humanity. Around the same time, two other Khmer Rouge retirees were taken into custody from their homes in Pailin: Khieu Samphan, the Khmer Rouge's one-time head-of-state, and Nuon Chea (Brother Number Two), the group's chief ideologue. Ieng's son, Ieng Vuth, currently serves as deputy governor of Pailin.

The border crossing 22km northwest of Pailin is likely to get more business when, and if, the road to Battambang is paved.

PAILIN
ប៉ៃលិន
☎ 053 / pop 22,000
The fly-blown, Wild West town of Pailin has little to recommend it except a particularly colourful hilltop temple. However, it can serve as a base for visits to the Samlaut Protected Area.

Information
There are no ATMs but money can be changed at **Canadia Bank** (NH57) and **Acleda Bank** (NH57); the latter takes travellers cheques.

The only internet café in town is run by **Buddhism for Development** (NH57; per hr US$1; ☯ 7am-noon & 2-7pm).

Sights & Activities
The southern gateway to Pailin is marked by a tree-covered hillock, **Phnom Yat**. From NH57, stairs lead through a garish gate – the *nagas* are bubblegum pink, spearmint green and sunflower yellow – up to the equally psychedelic **Wat Phnom Yat**. The temple is centred on an ancient *po* tree and a life-sized cement **tableau** showing butt-naked sinners (about the only nudity you'll see in Cambodia) being heaved into a cauldron, de-tongued (for liars) and forced to climb a spiny tree (for adulterers). Medieval European triptychs never made hell seem so uninviting! Nearby, the repentant pray for forgiveness, which is a highly pertinent message given who lives around here. From Phnom Yat there are clear views across Pailin,

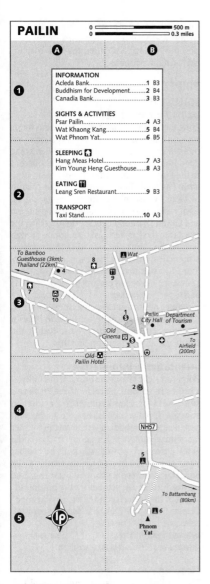

PAILIN

0 ——————— 500 m
0 ——————— 0.3 miles

INFORMATION
Acleda Bank.....................................1 B3
Buddhism for Development.........2 B4
Canadia Bank.................................3 B3

SIGHTS & ACTIVITIES
Psar Pailin.....................................4 A3
Wat Khaong Kang........................5 B4
Wat Phnom Yat...........................6 B5

SLEEPING
Hang Meas Hotel.........................7 A3
Kim Young Heng Guesthouse.....8 A3

EATING
Leang Sren Restaurant.................9 B3

TRANSPORT
Taxi Stand...................................10 A3

To Bamboo Guesthouse (3km); Thailand (22km)

Wat

Pailin City Hall
Department of Tourism

Old Cinema

Old Pailin Hotel

To Airfield (200m)

NH57

To Battambang (80km)

Phnom Yat

and this is a top spot for enjoying a sunrise or sunset.

At the base of the hill, an impressive gate from 1968 leads to **Wat Khaong Kang**, an important centre for Buddhist teaching before the Khmer Rouge madness.

Moto drivers can take you to several **waterfalls** outside town.

A few stalls in **Psar Pailin** (Psar Pahi; Pailin Market) still sell rubies and sapphires, many of inferior quality.

Sleeping

Just inside Cambodia at the Psar Pruhm–Ban Pakard border crossing are three casino hotels set up to milk cash from Thai gamblers. The Diamond Crown, the **Caesar Casino** (☎ 017 482414) and the **Pailin Flamingo** (☎ from Thailand 081 5635511) offer comfortable rooms for 400B to 600B.

Kim Young Heng Guesthouse (☎ 012 978430; r with fan/air-con from US$4/10; 🗙) A remnant of Pailin's boomtown days, this is a proper guesthouse whose 72 rooms are clean and come with hot water.

Hang Meas Hotel (☎ 012 640763; r US$5-10; 🗙) Once Pailin's best hotel, this establishment – like the town – has seen more prosperous days. The 55 smallish, institutional rooms come with TV and fridge.

Bamboo Guesthouse (☎ 012 405818, from Thailand 01-2799725; r US$12-15; 🗙) This little neighbourhood of bungalows, on the northwestern outskirts of town about 3km from the centre, consists of 20 bungalows with air-con, hot water and cable TV. Pricier units, made entirely of rare, reddish and no-longer-available *beng* wood, have a forest-lodge feel.

Eating

There are food stalls along the northwest and southeast edges of Psar Pailin.

Leang Sren Restaurant (☎ 016 842115; 🕑 6am-9pm) This informal, open-fronted eatery is known for its soups (big/small 80/150B). The name means 'laughing cow'.

Bamboo Guesthouse (mains 35-150B; 🕑 6am-10pm) Serves Pailin's best Khmer and Thai food in shaded outdoor pavilions.

Getting There & Away

NH57 from Battambang to Pailin (80km, 2½ hours), which passes through fields used to grow corn for the Thai market, is finally being upgraded – and the land alongside is finally being de-mined. Transport options include share taxis (200B; departures are from Battambang's Psar Leu, at the far southern end of St 3) and pick-ups (120/80B inside/out back). If you wish to make stops along the way at places such as Phnom Sampeau and Sneng, take a private taxi (US$35 to US$40 one-way, US$60 to US$70 return).

NORTHWESTERN CAMBODIA

The Psar Pruhm–Ban Pakard border crossing to Thailand is 22km northwest of Pailin. A share taxi, available just past passport control, costs 5000r/50B to Pailin and US$6.50 to Battambang. Khmers pay 100B for a *moto* from the border to Pailin, but foreigners are hit up for double that.

For details on the rough track from Treng District to Krong Koh Kong, see p187.

SAMLAUT

The northernmost tip of the Cardamom Mountains – a truly remote area that's home to elephants, gibbons, pangolins, hornbills and many other endangered creatures – covers the southern half of Krong Pailin (pretty much everything south of NH57). Known as the **Samlaut Multiple Use Area** (600 sq km; highest point 1164m), this expanse of forested mountains is contiguous with two Thai parks, including Namtok Klong Kaew National Park, and is administered and patrolled with help from the **Maddox Jolie-Pitt Foundation** (MJP; www.mjpasia .org), named after the adopted Cambodian-born son of its founder and president, the American actress Angelina Jolie.

In 2006 the Samlaut administration signed a sister-park agreement with Sequoia National Park in California, coincidentally not far from Fresno, home to one of the largest Cambodian communities in the United States.

MJP is developing plans to run rough-and-ready, **ranger-led tours** of the Samlaut forests using Pailin as a base. For updates see the MJP website or write to info@mjpasia.org.

BANTEAY MEANCHEY PROVINCE

ខេត្តបន្ទាយមានជ័យ

Sandwiched between the casinos of Poipet, Cambodia's most important border crossing with Thailand, and the glories of Angkor, agricultural Banteay Meanchey (Fortress of Victory) – which claims to grow Cambodia's best rice – often gets overlooked by travellers rushing on to Siem Reap or Battambang. But those with an inclination to get off the beaten track can take in the Angkorian temples around Banteay Chhmar, observe

rare birds at Ang Trapeng Thmor Reserve (p139) and visit a wat-based fish conservation project near Sisophon, the best base for exploring the province.

POIPET
ប៉ោយប៉ែត
☎ 054 / pop 45,000

Long the armpit of Cambodia, notorious for its squalor, scams and sleaze, Poipet (pronounced poi-*peh* in Khmer) has recently applied some deodorant, at least in the casino zone adjacent to the Poipet–Aranya Prathet border crossing with Thailand. Based mainly on the custom of Thais, whose own country bans gambling, eight casino resorts with names like Tropicana and Grand Diamond City are helping turn the town into the Las Vegas of Cambodia, though outside the casino zone it's still a trash-strewn strip mall sprinkled with dodgy massage parlours. In a sign that Poipet is starting to attract Khmers, it has begun hosting outdoor concerts of Khmer pop music.

Poipet offers a lively, chaotic welcome to Cambodia, the Khmers' gentle side little in evidence, but don't worry – the rest of the country does not carry on like this.

Orientation & Information

Poipet stretches from the border (the filthy O Chrou stream) and the casino zone eastwards along NH5 for a few kilometres. Cambodian visas are issued at the Visa Service, to the right as you enter Cambodian territory (the counter faces the ceremonial Kingdom of Cambodia gate). Prices are posted, so don't buy a visa from any of the touts on either side of the border. Passports are stamped a few hundred metres further on, just before the big roundabout at the eastern edge of the casino zone.

Canadia Bank (☎ 967107; NH5) About 1km east of the casino zone. Has a 24-hour ATM.

Internet Shop (NH5; per hr 40B; ⏱ 7.15am-9pm) Internet access 250m east of the roundabout.

Sleeping

There's little reason to spend the night in Poipet, although hotels in the casino zone advertise rooms for 500B to 1500B – good value given the facilities. Cheap guesthouses, some of them brothels, are strung out along NH5 and around the bus station.

Ngy Heng Hotel (☎ 967101; nopnadadr@yahoo .com; NH5; r 200-400B; ❄) Situated 100m west of the sidestreet leading to the bus station, this hotel's rooms are more than adequate, though not by much.

Orkiday Angkor Hotel (Orchidée Angkor Hotel; ☎ 012 767676; oa_tour@online.com.kh; NH5; r 400-600B; 🕃) Just outside the casino zone on the north side of the roundabout. Rooms at this newish, pink, four-storey place have terracotta floors, large beds and hot water. Although there's no lift, the lower floors are cheaper.

Ly Heng Chhay Hotel (☎ 967136, Thai mobile 081 6649317; lyfen_poipet@yahoo.com; NH5; r US$15; 🕃) Popular with NGO workers, this comfortable, seven-storey establishment is on the north side of the highway about 1km east of the roundabout.

Eating

Many of the casino-hotels offer all-you-can-eat buffets; culinary options include Thai (200B at Grand Diamond City) and Japanese (300B).

The cheapest eats are inside the market (near the bus station) and along NH5.

Getting There & Away

For details on travelling between Thailand and Cambodia via Poipet, see p329.

A rail line from Poipet to Sisophon – planned by the French but never built – is supposed to be constructed as part of the Trans-Asia Rail Link, which by 2015 may make it possible to take the train all the way from Singapore to Western Europe.

Thanks to the prestige at stake when Cambodia hosted its first international golf tournament, held near Siem Reap in November 2007, the heavily trafficked NH5 between Sisophon and Poipet is *finally* being paved! Poipet is 48km from Sisophon and 153km from Siem Reap.

BUS

All buses depart from the bus station. To get there from the casino zone, go east along NH5 for 1.5km and then turn left (north) for 200m. Bus companies, including **GST** (☎ 012 727721), **Neak Kror Horm** (☎ 012 970067, Thai mobile 01-9825610), **Phnom Penh Sorya**, **Ponleu Angkor Khmer** and **Rith Mony** (☎ 012 579943), have a roadside office along NH5 near the bus station. Word has it that the OSP bus and taxi monopoly, which forced tourists to pay double local prices, has been abolished.

Destinations by bus include Sisophon (10,000r/100B, one hour), Battambang

(15,000r/150B, 2½ hours) and Phnom Penh (22,000r/220B, 7½ hours). All buses leave early in the morning (between 6.15am and 8am) and all take NH5, which runs south of the Tonlé Sap, so for now the only way to get to Siem Reap is via Sisophon or by taxi. However, direct buses to Siem Reap are planned.

TAXI

Share taxis – some of them Thai right-hand-drives that provide front-seat passengers the thrill of seeing oncoming traffic before the driver can – are available all day long, either at the big roundabout just past passport control or along NH5 near the bus station.

Destinations include Sisophon (100B, one hour), Siem Reap (250B, three hours) and Battambang (US$5, two hours). Private taxis can be hired for as little as US$20 to Battambang and US$35 or US$40 to Siem Reap, though the usual fee is six times the single-seat fare (Cambodian share taxis pack two passengers in front and four in back). Be prepared for a cheerfully chaotic rugby scrum of taxi touts and negotiate hard (smiling helps) or you'll pay above the odds.

Packed-to-the-gills pickups, which stop along NH5, are a bit cheaper, in part because riding in back is so dangerous (even in a minor accident everyone goes flying).

Getting Around

Free shuttles take you from the Visa Service (at the border) through the casino zone to passport control, though it's easy enough to walk. From there, larger buses (US$1) take you 1.5km to the bus station. For local hops, *moto* drivers wait at the roundabout just beyond passport control.

SISOPHON

ស៊ីសុផុង

☎ 054 / pop 98,000

Strategically situated at northwest Cambodia's great crossroads, the intersection of NH5 and NH6, Sisophon (often called Svay by locals) makes a convenient first stop in Cambodia if you're coming from Poipet. It's also a good base for exploring the Angkorian temples of Banteay Chhmar and Banteay Top, about 50km north of town, and Ang Trapeng Thmor Reserve (p139), a bird sanctuary 56km (1½ to two hours by car) to the northeast.

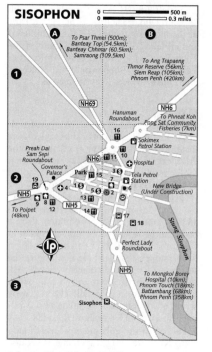

SISOPHON

0 — 500 m
0 — 0.3 miles

To Psar Thmei (500m);
Banteay Top (54.5km);
Banteay Chhmar (60.5km);
Samraong (109.5km)

To Ang Trapaeng
Thmor Reserve (56km);
Siem Reap (105km);
Phnom Penh (420km)

NH69

Hanuman
Roundabout

NH6

To Phneat Koh
Pong Sat Community
Fisheries (7km)

Sokimex
Petrol Station

Preah Dai
Sam Sepi
Roundabout

NH6

Hospital

Governor's
Palace

Park

Tela Petrol
Station

New Bridge
(Under Construction)

NH5

To Poipet
(48km)

NH5

Perfect Lady
Roundabout

NH5

To Mongkol Borey
Hospital (10km);
Phnom Touch (18km);
Battambang (68km);
Phnom Penh (358km)

Sisophon

Stung Sisophan

INFORMATION
Acleda Bank..**1** A2
Bayon Web...**2** B2
Canadia Bank...**3** B2
Eng Sovannara Clinic...............................**4** A2
Lao Puoy Kheang Exchange.....................**5** A2
Peng Chann Internet..........................(see **4**)

SIGHTS & ACTIVITIES
École d'Art et de Culture Khmers.............**6** B2

SLEEPING ⚐
Golden Crown Hotel.................................**7** B2
Phnom Svay Hotel....................................**8** A2
Roeung Rong Hotel..................................**9** A2

EATING ⏏
Arun Reas Restaurant.............................**10** B2
Food Stalls..**11** B2
Phkay Preuk Restaurant.........................**12** A2
Psar Sisophon..**13** A2
Sok Yi Grocery..**14** A2
Sorm Rethy Bakery.............................(see **10**)
Suon Kamsan Restaurant.......................**15** A2
Vichet Pizza Shop...................................**16** B2

TRANSPORT
Bus Station...**17** B2
New Bus Station.....................................**18** B2
Share Taxis to Poipet.............................**19** A2

Orientation & Information

NH6 (from Siem Reap and Phnom Penh) intersects NH5 (from Battambang and Phnom Penh) at the western tip of the triangular town centre.

In a medical emergency, evacuation across the border to Thailand is possible 24 hours a day. The new **Mongkol Borey Hospital**, donated by the Japanese, is about 10km from Sisophon towards Battambang.

Acleda Bank (☎ 958821) Has a 24-hour ATM.

Bayon Web (per hr 2500r; ☾ 7am-7.30pm) Internet access across from the Golden Crown Hotel.

Canadia Bank (☎ 958989) Changes travellers cheques and can do cash advances at the counter. An ATM is planned.

Eng Sovannara Clinic (☎ 012 852877; NH6; ☾ 24hr) Can treat minor medical problems. Works with international NGOs.

Lao Puoy Kheang Exchange (☾ 6am-6pm) A reliable exchange place that accepts a wide variety of currencies.

Peng Chann Internet (NH5; per hr 2000r; ☾ 6.30am-9pm) Internet access.

Sights

The **École d'Art et de Culture Khmers** (School of Khmer Art & Culture; ☾ 7-11am & 2-5pm Mon-Fri, 7-11am Sat)

has classes in traditional music, *apsara* dancing, painting, sculpture and shadow puppetry. It's often possible to observe a class or see students practising. Drop by to find out when.

At the **Phneat Koh Pong Sat Community Fisheries**, a community-based fish sanctuary run by monks 8km east of town, you can feed schools of fat, frisky fish from a peaceful riverside pavilion on the grounds of a wat. Monks sell food pellets and dry bread (500r). It makes a delightful excursion by bicycle, *moto* or car, especially in the late afternoon.

Phnom Touch, 18km towards Battambang on the west side of NH5, has several temples on and around it and affords gorgeous views.

Sleeping

As we go to press, the **Phnom Svay Hotel** (NH5) is being totally renovated.

Roeung Rong Hotel (☎ 092 260515; NH5; r US$5-10; ⊠) A family-run place with 24 recently renovated rooms. The goings-on out back in and around the private 'karaoke rooms' are kept separate from the hotel.

Golden Crown Hotel (☎ 958444; r US$5-15; ⊠) A big hit with the NGO crowd and Khmers of the car-owning class, this new place has 39 rooms with soaring ceilings and fridges; hot water is US$1 extra. Excellent value.

Eating

Inexpensive **food stalls** can be found at Psar
Sisophon (Sisophon Market), especially for
breakfast and lunch, and in the evening along
the north side of the park on NH6.

Arun Reas Restaurant (☎ 012 350321; NH6; mains
3000-10,000r; ☼ 6.30am-8.30pm) Popular with de-
miners and other NGO workers, this airy
place has cute café tables and excellent green
curry and fried rice.

Suon Kamsan Restaurant (☎ 012 829006; mains
6000-8000r; ☼ 5am-11pm) A big, popular place
with Western and Khmer breakfasts, reliable
Khmer mains and some Thai dishes. The
Khmer menus are up on the wall. Crooners
perform nightly from 6pm to 11pm.

Phkay Preuk Restaurant (☎ 012 838934; NH5; mains
US$2-4; ☼ 6.30am-10pm) An enormous and ener-
getic place with Khmer and Thai cuisine and
a few Western dishes, including breakfast favourites. It may look closed from the front but
head on in – the dining goes on out back.

Vichet Pizza Shop (☎ 012 529820; NH6; ☼ 5am-
10pm) Sisophon's first and only pizzeria. The
enterprising owner learned how to make pizza
by doing research on the internet!

SELF-CATERING

Sorm Rethy Bakery (NH6; ☼ 8am-5pm) Has bread
and super sponge cake (1000r per slice).

Sok Yi Grocery (☼ 6am-7pm) Half-a-block south
of Psar Sisophon, this grocery stocks fresh
milk and yoghurt from Thailand, wine, cheese
and ice cream.

Getting There & Away

Sisophon is 48km east of Poipet, 105km west
of Siem Reap, 61km south of Banteay Chhmar
and 68km northwest of Battambang. In terms
of driving time, it's about midway between
Bangkok and Phnom Penh (five or six hours
from each).

Long-haul buses and most share taxis stop
at the bus station (a new bus station is being
built near the old one). Companies includ-
ing **Capitol Tour** (☎ 012 525782), **Rith Mony** (☎ 012
637271) and **Neak Kror Horm** serve Phnom Penh
(20,000r), Siem Reap (15,000r to 20,000r),
Battambang (8000r) and Poipet (5000r). Neak
Kror Horm can get you to Bangkok. Most
departures, except to Poipet, are early in
the morning.

Share taxis link the bus station with Phnom
Penh (30,000r), Siem Reap (15,000r to 20,000r)
and Battambang (10,000r). Share taxis to Poipet

(100r, one hour) stop on NH5 across the street
from the Roeung Rong Hotel. Share taxis north
to Thmor Puok and Banteay Chhmar leave
from near Psar Thmei on NH69, 1km north of
NH6. Private taxis cost six times the share taxi
fare. A place on a pickup costs 50% less than a
share taxi (30% less if you sit inside).

Pickups to Phnom Srok District (near Ang
Trapeng Thmor Reserve) stop on NH6 near
the Hanuman statue.

A *moto* ride around town costs 1000r.

BANTEAY CHHMAR & BANTEAY TOP
បន្ទាយឆ្មារ & បន្ទាយទ័ព

The temple complex of **Banteay Chhmar** (admission
US$5) was constructed by Cambodia's most pro-
lific builder, Jayavarman VII (r 1181–1219), on
the site of a 9th-century temple. There is debate
over its origins, with some scholars suggesting
it was built in tribute to Jayavarman VII's son
Indravarman and the Cambodian generals responsible for defeating the Chams, while others
propose it was intended as a funerary temple
for the king's grandmother.

Originally enclosed by a 9km-long wall,
the temple housed one of the largest and
most impressive Buddhist monasteries of the
Angkorian period. Today, it is one of the few
temples to feature the enigmatic, Bayon-style
visages of Avalokiteshvara, with their mysterious –
and world famous – smiles.

On the temple's east side, a huge **bas-relief**
on a partly-toppled wall dramatically depicts
naval warfare between the Khmers (on the left)
and the Chams (on the right), with the dead –
some being devoured by crocodiles – at the
bottom. Further south (to the left) are scenes
of land warfare with infantry and elephants.
There are more martial bas-reliefs along the
exterior of the temple's south walls.

The once-grand entry gallery is now a
jumble of fallen sandstone blocks, though
elsewhere a few intersecting galleries have
withstood the ravages of time, as have some
almost-hidden 12th-century inscriptions. All
the remaining *apsaras* (nymphs) have been
decapitated by looters.

Banteay Chhmar was deservedly renowned for its intricate carvings, including
scenes of daily life in the Angkorian period
similar to those at Bayon. Unique to Banteay
Chhmar was a sequence of eight **multi-armed
Avalokiteshvaras** on the outside of the southern
section of the temple's western ramparts, but

six of these were hacked out and trucked into Thailand in a brazen act of looting in 1998. Still, the two that remain – one with 22 arms, the other with 32 – are spectacular.

There are as many as a dozen smaller temples in the vicinity of Banteay Chhmar, all in a ruinous state. These include Prasat Mebon, Prasat Ta Prohm, Prasat Prom Muk Buon, Prasat Yeay Choun, Prasat Pranang Ta Sok and Prasat Chiem Trey.

At the headquarters of the **Banteay Chhmar Protected Landscape** (☎ 017 971225), 2km towards Sisophon from town, it may be possible to hire a guide (non-English speaking) for a nature walk.

Through Agir Pour le Cambodge (see below), you can participate in **traditional activities** such as honey collecting and the hunting of frogs and rice-field crabs (US$10 for a group). It may also be possible to visit local silk weavers. A ride out to Banteay Top costs US$5 by ox-cart or US$6 by *koyun* (tractor). Renting a bicycle costs US$1.50 a day.

Banteay Top (Fortress of the Army), set among rice paddies southeast of Banteay Chhmar, may only be a small temple but there's something special about the atmosphere here. Constructed around the same time as Banteay Chhmar, it may be a tribute to the army of Jayavarman VII, which confirmed Khmer dominance over the region by conclusively defeating the Chams. One of the damaged towers looks decidedly precarious, like a bony finger pointing skyward. The turn-off from NH69, marked by a stone plinth with gold inscription, is 9km south of Banteay Chhmar.

Sleeping & Eating

A French-based NGO, **Agir Pour le Cambodge** (www.agirpourlecambodge.org in French; aplc@online.com.kh), has launched a pioneering community-based **homestay project** (☎ 017 782156 or 012 435660; d US$7) in Banteay Chhmar. Situated both in town and in three nearby hamlets, the homes – marked with handsome brown and yellow signs – offer rooms with mosquito nets, fans that run when there's electricity (6pm to 10pm), and downstairs bathrooms. Breakfast/lunch/dinner cooked by local women costs US$2/3/4. Forty percent of revenues go into a community development fund.

A couple of small private guesthouses are being built in Banteay Chhmar.

For now, the nearest rooms with private bathrooms are in Thmor Puok, about 15km south of Banteay Chhmar. **Ly Hour Guesthouse** (☎ 012 622218; r 200B), on the southern edge of the village, has 10 simple rooms with Western toilet and bucket showers.

Getting There & Away

After having its bridges washed out by floods, NH69 – which links Banteay Chhmar with Sisophon (61km to the south; two hours) and Samraong (to the northeast; 1½ hours) – is getting a serious upgrade.

From Sisophon, most northbound pickups only go as far as Thmor Puok, where you can hire a *moto* to the temple (US$5 return). Or you can take a *moto* all the way from Sisophon (about US$10 return). Hotels in Sisophon may be able to rent you a motorbike. There's no public transport from Banteay Chhmar to Samraong.

By car, it's possible to get out here on a very long day trip from Siem Reap.

ODDAR MEANCHEY PROVINCE

ខេត្តឧត្តរមានជ័យ

The remote, dirt-poor province of Oddar Meanchey (Otdar Mean Chey), created from parts of Siem Reap Province that the government didn't control for much of the 1980s and 1990s, produces very little apart from opportunities for aid organisations. From a touristic standpoint there are two rather dim bright spots: the seldom-used international border crossings of Choam–Choam Srawngam and O Smach–Chong Jom and, around Anlong Veng, the presence of Khmer

> ### LAND MINE ALERT!
>
> Banteay Meanchey and Oddar Meanchey are among the most heavily mined provinces in Cambodia. In 2006 and 2007, mines claimed more victims in Banteay Meanchey than in any other province in Cambodia, and Oddar Meanchey wasn't far behind. Do not, under any circumstances, stray from previously trodden paths. If you've got your own wheels, travel only on roads or trails regularly used by locals.

Rouge sites that are starting to attract visitors appalled and fascinated by evil and its banality. Illegal logging was rampant for a few years but seems to have stopped for now.

Getting around the province is no picnic during the dry season and tougher during the wet, as there are virtually no sealed roads. NH67 from Siem Reap to Anlong Veng and Choam was recently upgraded with Thai assistance.

SAMRAONG
សំរោង

There are towns called Samraong throughout Cambodia – the name means 'dense jungle', sadly a rarity in this area today. This Samraong, the provincial-backwater capital of Oddar Meanchey, is emerging very slowly from decades of isolation, a legacy of its frontline position in the long civil war. There's nothing for foreigners to see or do up here unless they happen to be in development work – something much in demand around here. There's a border crossing with Thailand 40km to the north at O Smach.

It's worth noting that in 2006 and 2007, mines and unexploded ordnance injured more people in Samraong District than in any other district in Cambodia.

The **Acleda Bank**, facing the scruffy little market, changes travellers cheques.

The best place to stay is the **Meanchey Hotel** (☎ 011 700099; r US$5-10; 🟦), often used by NGO workers, which has 24 simply furnished rooms. Air-con rooms have hot water.

In the evening food stalls pop up around the market. Next to the Meanchey Hotel, **Heng Heng Restaurant** (☎ 012 983083; mains 4000-6000r) is hardly more than a shed with red plastic chairs, but the food is decent.

Getting There & Away

To get to most places from Samraong, a long and bumpy journey over terrible roads is in order. Before 8am, share taxis (250B; four hours) and pickups (inside/outside 15,000r/10,000r) to Siem Reap, via NH68 and Kralanh (80km due south on NH6), depart from the market. There may also be a bus (170B).

For details on getting to/from O Smach, see right.

There's no public transport along NH69 to Banteay Chhmar; hiring a *moto* costs 500B, a car 1200B. The backwoods road east towards Anlong Veng, although passable year-round,

is even less travelled; hiring a *moto* costs 500B to 650B.

O SMACH
អូរស្មាច់

Only a trickle of foreign visitors uses the O Smach–Chong Jom border crossing (see p330), which is pretty remote on the Thai side and in the middle of nowhere on the Cambodian side. At the frontier there's a zone of Thai-style modernity, with two big casino-hotels, a paved dual carriageway a few hundred metres long and a modern market. But from there south you're in outback Cambodia. The road meanders between minefields and at one point you have the choice of paying 20B/2000r for a dodgy private toll bridge built of logs by enterprising locals or driving through a river. All along the way, you pass motorbikes so overloaded with fruit, cheap household items and petrol smuggled in from Thailand that they often topple over.

O Smach shot to fame in July 1997 as Funcinpec forces regrouped here after the coup. Perched on the mountain, soldiers under the command of General Neak Bun Chhay were able to hold out against the superior forces of the Cambodian People's Party (CPP) until a peace agreement was brokered that allowed the 1998 elections to go ahead.

With the advent of peace, the military moved in and cleared locals off safe land to sell it to a casino developer. Meanwhile, the locals who were evicted were forced to relocate to mined land that the military claimed to have cleared. As happens all too often in Cambodia, the strong exploited the weak, but this episode was particularly heartless and brought to international attention the issue of military land grabs in 'peacetime' Cambodia.

The 30-room **Chay Na Guesthouse** (☎ 011 940533; r 300-500B; 🟦), a bit over 1km from the border at the top of the hill near the antennas, is built in a style that can only be described as part neoclassical, part Spanish and part Khmer. For something fancier, you can stay on the border at the Royal Hill Hotel or the O Smach Resort, its entrance flanked by two decommissioned Soviet armoured cars.

About 50m inside Cambodian territory, tens of *motos* and a few taxis await passengers or freight. To Samraong (40km, 1½ to two hours), a *moto* costs 250B, a private taxi 1200B. And once you get to Samraong, where are you? Nowhere.

DEADLY LEGACY OF WAR

Although peace treaties were signed a decade ago, Cambodia's civil war is still claiming new victims: civilians who have stepped on a mine or been injured by unexploded ordnance (UXO).

The first massive use of mines came in the mid-1980s, when Vietnamese forces – using forced local labour – constructed a 700km-long minefield along the entire Cambodian-Thai border. After the Vietnamese withdrawal, more mines were laid by the Cambodian government to prevent towns, villages, military positions, bridges, border crossings and supply routes from being over-run, and by Khmer Rouge forces to protect areas they had captured. Lots more government mines were laid in the mid-1990s in offensives against Khmer Rouge positions around Anlong Veng and Pailin.

Today, Cambodia has one of the world's worst landmine problems and the highest number of amputees per capita of any country – over 25,000 Cambodians have lost limbs due to mines and other military explosives. Despite extensive mine awareness campaigns, an average of 30 victims are injured or killed every month. This is a vast improvement on the mid-1990s, when the figure was more like 300, but it's still wartime carnage in a country officially at peace.

To make matters more complicated, areas that seem safe in the dry season can become danger-ous in the wet season as the earth softens. It's not uncommon for Cambodian farmers to settle on land during the dry season, only to have their dreams of a new life shattered a few months later when a family member has a leg blown off.

A number of groups are working to clear mines, whacking through the undergrowth square metre after laborious square metre. If you travel in the more remote parts of provinces such as Banteay Meanchey, Battambang, Krong Pailin, Oddar Meanchey, Preah Vihear, Pursat and Siem Reap, you're likely to see de-mining teams run by the **Cambodian Mine Action Centre** (CMAC; www.cmac.org.kh), the **HALO Trust** (www.halotrust.org) and the **Mines Advisory Group** (MAG; www.mag.org.uk) in action.

Some sage advice about mines that's worth bearing in mind in rural Cambodia:

■ Always check with locals that paths are not mined.

■ Never leave a well-trodden path in remote areas.

■ Never touch anything that looks remotely like a mine or munitions.

■ If you find yourself accidentally in a mined area, retrace your steps only if you can clearly see your footprints. If not, stay where you are and call for help – as advisory groups put it, 'better to spend a day stuck in a minefield than a lifetime as an amputee'.

■ If someone is injured in a minefield do not rush in to assist even if they are crying out for help – find someone who knows how to safely enter a mined area.

■ Do not leave the roadside in remote areas, even for the call of nature. Your limbs are more important than your modesty.

Since 1997 more than 150 countries have signed the Ottawa Convention banning the production, stockpiling, use and sale of land mines. Details are available from the **International Campaign to Ban Landmines** (ICBL; www.icbl.org), co-winner of the 1997 Nobel Peace Prize.

ANLONG VENG
អន្លង់វែង

For almost a decade this was the ultimate Khmer Rouge stronghold: home to Pol Pot, Nuon Chea, Khieu Samphan and Ta Mok, among the most notorious leaders of Democratic Kampuchea. Anlong Veng fell to government forces in April 1998 at the same time as Pol Pot died mysteriously nearby.

Soon after, Prime Minister Hun Sen ordered that NH67 be bulldozed through the jungle to ensure that the population didn't have second thoughts about ending the war.

Today Anlong Veng is a poor, dusty town with little going for it except the nearby Choam–Choam Srawngam border crossing, which takes you to a pretty isolated part of Thailand. The average visitor will find little to see or do here, but for those with a keen interest in contemporary Cambodian history its Khmer Rouge sites are an important – if troubling and enigmatic – part of the picture.

Orientation & Information

Anlong Veng's focal point is the Dove of Peace Monument – a gift of Hun Sen – in the middle of a roundabout. From here, roads lead north to the Choam border crossing, east to Sa Em and Prasat Preah Vihear, and south to Siem Reap (along NH67).

There's nowhere to access the internet. Acleda Bank, the only bank in town, handles travellers cheques.

Sights & Activities

Most of Anlong Veng's sights are connected with the terrible Khmer Rouge years.

PILE OF RUBBLE

An **Angkorian temple** used to stand in the southeast corner of the yard behind Hun Sen Anlong Veng Primary School – formerly Ta Mok Primary School – but it was turned into a jumble of laterite and sandstone blocks by Ta Mok and his army in their search for ancient statues to sell to the Thais. The school is 600m east of the roundabout.

TA MOK'S HOUSE & GRAVE

To his former supporters, many of whom still reside around Anlong Veng, Ta Mok (Uncle Mok, AKA Brother Number Five) was harsh but fair, a benevolent builder of orphanages and schools, and a leader who kept order in stark contrast to the anarchic atmosphere that prevailed once the government took over. But to most Cambodians, Pol Pot's military enforcer, responsible for thousands of deaths in successive purges during the terrible years of Democratic Kampuchea, was best known as 'The Butcher'. Arrested in 1999, he died in July 2006 in a Phnom Penh hospital, awaiting trial for genocide and crimes against humanity.

Ta Mok's house (admission US$2), on a peaceful lakeside site, is a Spartan structure with a bunker in the basement, five childish wall murals downstairs and three more murals upstairs, including a map and an idyllic wildlife scene. About the only furnishings that weren't looted are the **floor tiles** – on these very bits of ceramic, the men who killed 1.7 million Cambodians planned offensives, passed death sentences and joked with friends. The trees

around the house have been growing quietly since Khmer Rouge times, oblivious to the horrific events swirling around them.

The swampy lake was created on Ta Mok's orders but the water killed all the trees, their skeletons a fitting monument to the devastation he and his movement left behind. In the middle of the lake, due east from the house, is a small brick structure – an outhouse, all that remains of **Pol Pot's residence** in Anlong Veng.

To get to Ta Mok's house, head north from the Dove of Peace Roundabout for about 2km, turn right and continue 200m past the Tourism Information hut, whose posters promote local curiosities such as 'Ta Mok's mango field'. The admission price includes a tour with a knowledgeable English-speaking guide.

From the turnoff to Ta Mok's house, driving a further 7km north takes you to Tumnup Leu, where a right turn and 400m brings you to **Ta Mok's grave**. Situated next to a very modest pagoda and the concrete foundations of **Ta Mok's sawmill**, it is protected from the elements by a blue roof. The tomb has no name or inscription of any sort but this doesn't seem to bother the locals who stop by to light incense sticks – and, in a bizarre new local tradition, hope his ghost grants them a winning lottery number.

ALONG THE THAI FRONTIER

Further north, atop the escarpment of the Dangkrek Mountains, are a number of other key Khmer Rouge sites, each marked with a light blue Ministry of Tourism sign. For years the world wondered where Pol Pot and his cronies were hiding out – the answer was right here, close enough to Thailand that they could flee across the border if government forces drew nigh.

About 2km before the frontier, where the road splits to go around a house-sized boulder, look out for a group of **statues** – hewn entirely from the surrounding rock by the Khmer Rouge – depicting a woman carrying bundles of bamboo sticks on her head and two uniformed Khmer Rouge soldiers, since decapitated by government forces. Now a macabre place of popular pilgrimage, local people come here to leave offerings of fruit and incense to honour the souls of dead Khmer Rouge soldiers.

At the pass (a few hundred metres before the frontier), turn right (east) next to a new, cream-coloured, three-storey building and then, after 50m, hang a left. In front of you,

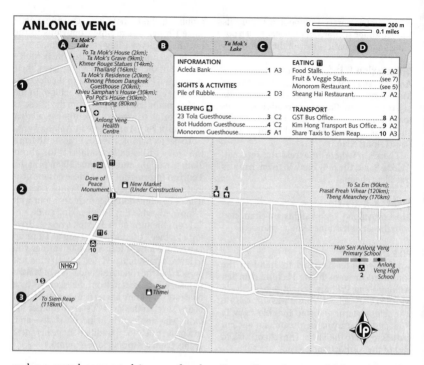

ANLONG VENG

INFORMATION		
Acleda Bank	1	A3
SIGHTS & ACTIVITIES		
Pile of Rubble	2	D3
SLEEPING		
23 Tola Guesthouse	3	C2
Bot Huddom Guesthouse	4	C2
Monorom Guesthouse	5	A1
EATING		
Food Stalls	6	A2
Fruit & Veggie Stalls	(see 7)	
Monorom Restaurant	(see 5)	
Sheang Hai Restaurant	7	A2
TRANSPORT		
GST Bus Office	8	A2
Kim Hong Transport Bus Office	9	A2
Share Taxis to Siem Reap	10	A3

under a rusted corrugated iron roof and surrounded by rows of partly buried glass bottles, is the **cremation site of Pol Pot**, who was hastily burned in 1998 on a pile of old tyres and rubbish – a fitting end, some say, given the suffering he inflicted on millions of Cambodians.

Bizarre as it may sound, Pol Pot is remembered with affection by some locals, and people sometimes stop by to light incense. According to neighbours, every last bone fragment has been snatched from the ashes by visitors in search of good luck charms – Pol Pot, too, is said to give out winning lottery numbers.

In 1997 Pol Pot ordered that former Khmer Rouge defence minister Son Sen – who was trying to reach a settlement with the government – and his family be murdered and their bodies run over by trucks. This incident led to Pol Pot's overthrow and arrest by Ta Mok, followed by his Khmer Rouge show trial (held near the cremation site) and his mysterious death, ostensibly because of a heart attack.

A few hundred metres north, next to a ramshackle **smugglers' market**, is the old

Choam–Choam Srawngam border crossing (for more information see p331). A bit to the west, right on the nicely paved main road, the Thais have built a spiffy new crossing, but the Cambodians say it's on Cambodian territory – yet another Thai land grab. So for now, with no end to the dispute in sight, the old facilities will have to do.

From the smugglers' market, a dirt road heads east between minefields, parallel to the escarpment. After about 4km you come to the overgrown brick walls and cement floor of another **Ta Mok residence**, shaded by mango, jackfruit and tamarind trees. Nearby is the cement shell of the Khmer Rouge's **radio station** and **Peuy Ta Mok** (Ta Mok's Cliff), where domestic tourists come to enjoy spectacular views of Cambodia's northern plains. Some stay at the six-room **Khnong Phnom Dankrek Guesthouse** (☎ 012 444067; r 30,000r), from which a path leads a few hundred metres east, through the cliffside jungle, to a **waterfall** (dry except in the west season). In late 2007, this area was being de-mined by the Halo Trust.

From here the road continues northeast past minefields, slash-and-burn homesteads and some army bases where soldiers wearing bits and pieces of uniforms sometimes demand that tourists pay bribes. A half-hour *moto* ride takes you to **Khieu Samphan's house**, buried in the jungle on the bank of a stream, from where it's a few hundred metres along an overgrown road to **Pol Pot's house**. Both are marked by signs. Surrounded by a cinderblock wall, the jungle hideout of Brother Number One was comprehensively looted, though you can still see a low brick building whose courtyard hides an underground bunker. Many of the courtyard's tiles have been carted off, revealing the frozen-in-cement footprints of the trusted Khmer Rouge cadres who built the place.

Sleeping

Bot Huddom Guesthouse (Bot Uddom; ☎ 011 500507; r US$5-15; 🔀) Owned by the family of the deputy governor, this establishment – 300m east of the roundabout – has 12 spacious, well-kept rooms with massive hardwood beds.

23 Tola Guesthouse (☎ 012 975104; r US$6-15; 🔀) Built alongside the owners' family residence, this new place sports hallways tiled in Delft blue and 27 rooms with light-yellow walls.

Monorom Guesthouse (☎ 012 603339; r US$7-15; 🔀) Anlong Veng's finest hostelry, with 20 big, modern rooms; some of the air-con rooms have hot water. Pay when you check in.

Eating

South of the roundabout there's a row of food stalls, some with pots you can peer into, others with blazing braziers barbecuing chicken, fish and eggs on skewers. There are **fruit and veggie stalls** (🕐 6am-about 6pm) around Sheang Hai Restaurant.

Sheang Hai Restaurant (☎ 012 786878; mains 5000-12,000r; 🕐 5.30am-9pm or 10pm) Named after the Chinese city of Shanghai (the owner's nickname), this all-wood, mess hall–like place serves Chinese and Khmer dishes, including fried rice and tom yam soup.

Monorom Restaurant (mains 8500r; 🕐 6am-9pm) Next to the Monorom Guesthouse, this brightly lit place is the town's fanciest eatery. If you order a beer, you get hot oily peanuts you can try to eat with chop sticks.

Getting There & Around

Anlong Veng is 118km north of Siem Reap (along NH67), 16km south of the Choam border crossing, 80km northeast of Samraong and 90km west of Sa Em.

Both **GST** (☎ 012 531490), whose office and bus stop is across from the Sheang Hai Restaurant, and **Kim Hong Transport** (☎ 012 306862), 70m south of the roundabout, have early morning buses to Siem Reap (15,000r, four hours). A share taxi to Siem Reap (US$5, 2½ hours) is available a few hundred metres south of the roundabout; a private taxi is US$30.

A *moto* to/from the Choam border crossing costs 8000r to 10,000r. At the border there aren't any taxi touts but officials should be able to summon a taxi for you.

Precious few vehicles, and no public transport, take the passable dirt road southwest to Samraong, though it's possible to get there by *moto* (US$20, 1¾ hours) or private taxi (US$40).

If you're heading east to Sa Em (the turnoff to Prasat Preah Vihear), the transport situation is as dire as the state of the dirt road, with through-traffic virtually nonexistent. A bum-bruising *moto* ride costs US$20 (three hours) in the dry season, more during the rainy season. In the dry season, hiring a private taxi may be an option but expect to pay through the nose.

To get to Ta Mok's house, locals pay 1000r for a *moto* but foreigners are charged more. A *moto* circuit to the border costs US$5 (US$10 including a tour of Pol Pot's House).

PREAH VIHEAR PROVINCE

ខេត្តព្រះវិហារ

Bordering Thailand and Laos to the north, vast Preah Vihear Province – much of it heavily forested and extremely remote – remains desperately poor. This is in part because many areas were under Khmer Rouge control until 1998, and in part because of the catastrophic state of the infrastructure – there's not a single paved road in the entire province!

However, Preah Vihear is home to three of Cambodia's most impressive legacies of the Angkorian era. Prasat Preah Vihear, high atop the Dangkrek Mountains escarpment, is truly stunning, though for now this temple is much easier to get to from Thailand than from the provincial capital, Tbeng Meanchey. The trip from the Cambodian side involves a tough overland journey and, in the wet season, the distinct possibility of a night in the forest. The mighty Preah Khan isn't as far north but is reachable only in the dry season. Fortunately, there's good news regarding the 10th-century capital of Koh Ker, now an easy toll-road drive from Siem Reap (via Beng Mealea).

Hidden Cambodia (www.hiddencambodia.com) operates dirt-bike tours to these temples during the dry season. For something more upmarket, try the temple safari offered by **Hanuman Tourism** (www.hanumantourism.com).

Getting There & Around

For now, travel around Preah Vihear is only for the most resilient of souls. The province's main transport artery, the north–south oriented NH64 from Kompong Thom to Tbeng Meanchey (157km), is in a truly miserable state. Consequently, most people with their own wheels get to Koh Ker and Tbeng Meanchey by taking the new toll road (10,000r for a car, free for motorbikes) from Dam Dek, on NH6 115km northwest of Kompong Thom and 35km southeast of Siem Reap. This road opened up previously inaccessible areas – some of them mined – to settlement and at many points you can see impoverished peasants setting up homesteads. The police in these parts carry AK-47s.

The morass of potholes and ruts linking Tbeng Meanchey with Choam Ksant and Sa Em (near Prasat Preah Vihear) to the north is passable for only half the year, and that's stretching the definition of passable.

Roadworks are underway – or promised – all over the province, including NH64 (thanks to a World Bank loan). By the time you read this the situation may have improved, though we all know what the road to hell is paved with.

PREAH KHAN
ប្រាសាទព្រះខ័ន

Covering almost 5 sq km, **Preah Khan** (admission US$5) is the largest temple enclosure constructed during the Angkorian period – quite a feat when you consider the competition. Thanks to its back-of-the-beyond location, the site is astonishingly quiet and peaceful.

Preah Khan's history is shrouded in mystery, but it was long an important religious site and some of the structures here date back to the 9th century. Both Suryavarman II, builder of Angkor Wat, and Jayavarman VII

lived here at various times during their lives, suggesting that Preah Khan was something of a second city in the Angkorian empire. Originally dedicated to Hindu deities, it was reconsecrated to Mahayana Buddhist worship during a monumental reconstruction undertaken by Jayavarman VII in the late 12th and early 13th centuries.

At the eastern end of the 3km-long *baray* (reservoir) is a small pyramid temple called **Prasat Damrei** (Elephant Temple). On the remaining entrance wall, there are several impressive carvings of *devadas* (goddesses). At the summit of the hill, two of the original exquisitely carved elephants can still be seen; two others are at Phnom Penh's National Museum (p84) and Paris' Musée Guimet.

In the centre of the *baray* is **Prasat Preah Thkol** (known by locals as Mebon), an island temple similar in style to the Western Mebon (p173) at Angkor. At the *baray's* western end stands **Prasat Preah Stung** (known to locals as Prasat Muk Buon – Temple of the Four Faces), perhaps the most memorable of the structures here because its central tower is adorned with four enigmatic Bayon-style faces.

It is a further 400m southwest to the walls of Preah Khan itself, which are surrounded by a moat similar to the one around the walled city of Angkor Thom. Entering through the eastern *gopura* (entrance pavilion), there is a **dharmasala** (pilgrims' rest house). Much of this central area is overgrown by forest, giving it an abandoned feel, though local authorities are undertaking a clearing programme.

The central structure, which included libraries and a pond for ablutions, has been devastated by looting in recent years. As recently as the mid-1990s, it was thought to be in reasonable shape, but some time in the second half of the decade thieves arrived seeking buried statues under each *prang* (temple tower). Assaulted with pneumatic drills and mechanical diggers, the ancient temple never stood a chance and many of the towers simply collapsed in on themselves, leaving the depressing mess we see today. Once again, a temple that had survived so much couldn't stand the onslaught of the 20th century and its all-consuming appetites.

Among the carvings found at Preah Khan was the bust of Jayavarman now in Phnom Penh's National Museum and widely copied as a souvenir for tourists. The body of the statue was discovered a few years ago by locals

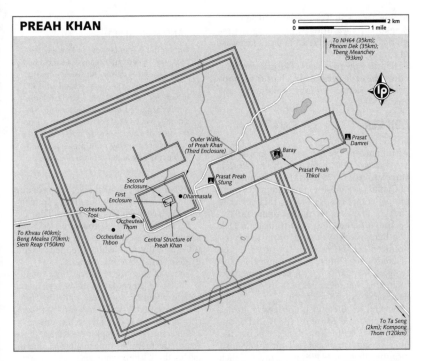

PREAH KHAN

0 ——————— 2 km
0 ——————— 1 mile

To NH64 (35km);
Phnom Dek (35km);
Tbeng Meanchey
(93km)

Outer Walls
of Preah Khan
(Third Enclosure)

Prasat
Damrei

Baray

Second
Enclosure

Prasat Preah
Thkol

First
Enclosure

Prasat Preah
Stung

Dharmasala

Occheuteal
Tooi

Occheuteal
Thom

To Khvau (40km);
Beng Mealea (70km);
Siem Reap (150km)

Occheuteal
Thbon

Central Structure of
Preah Khan

To Ta Seng
(2km); Kompong
Thom (120km)

who alerted authorities, making it possible for a joyous reunion of head and body in 1999.

Locals say there are no land mines in the vicinity of Preah Khan, but stick to marked paths just to be on the safe side.

Sleeping & Eating

Getting the most out of a visit to Preah Khan really requires an overnight stay. With a hammock and mosquito net, it's possible to camp within the Preah Khan complex (coordinate your location with the tourist police, who will appreciate a small tip for keeping an eye on you), or you can stay in a private house (US$3 per person, including a meal) in the nearby village of Ta Seng, where there's some electricity, a small restaurant and basic supplies.

Getting There & Away

Unless you enjoy travelling by ox cart, it is extremely difficult to get to Preah Khan between May and November. The best time to visit is from February to April, as the trails are reasonably dry then.

There's no public transport to Preah Khan, so your best bet is to hire a *moto* or a pickup truck in Kompong Thom (120km, five hours), Phnom Dek (on NH64, 35km east of the temple along an execrable road) or Tbeng Meanchey (four or five hours). If you've got more cash, you might consider chartering a 4WD.

Only *very* experienced bikers should attempt to get to Preah Khan on rental motorcycles, as conditions are extremely tough from every side. Take a wrong turn in this neck of the woods and you'll end up in the middle of nowhere, so consider bringing along a knowledgeable *moto* driver (US$15 a day plus petrol).

Coming from Siem Reap there are several options. By car, the easiest route may soon be to take a planned toll road heading due east from Beng Mealea. Until then, take NH6 to Stoeng and then head north. By motorcycle, you can take NH6 to Kompong Kdei, head north to Khvau and then ride 40km east on a miserable ox-cart track. An amazing, exhausting alternative is to approach from Beng Mealea along the ancient Angkor road (Cambodia's own Route 66 – NH66), which in places vanishes into a rough ox-cart track to nowhere. You'll cross about 10 splendid Angkorian *naga* bridges, including the remarkable 77m-long **Spean Ta Ong**, 7km west of Khvau.

If hitting the road seems like just too much effort, head for the skies: charter a chopper from Siem Reap for the ultimate view (see p153).

KOH KER
កោះកេរ្តិ៍

Abandoned to the forests of the north, **Koh Ker** (admission US$10), capital of the Angkorian empire from AD 928 to AD 944, was long one of Cambodia's most remote and inaccessible temple complexes. However, this has now changed thanks to recent de-mining and the opening of a new toll road from Dam Dek (via Beng Mealea) that puts Koh Ker (pronounced kah-*kei*) within day-trip distance of Siem Reap. But to really appreciate the temples – the area has 42 major structures in an area that measures 9km by 4km – it's necessary to spend the night.

Several of the most impressive pieces in the National Museum (p84) in Phnom Penh come from Koh Ker, including the huge *garuda* (mythical half-man, half-bird creature) that greets visitors in the entrance hall and a unique carving depicting a pair of wrestling monkey-kings.

Most visitors start at **Prasat Krahom** (Red Temple), the second-largest structure at Koh Ker, which is named for the red bricks from which it is constructed. Sadly, none of the carved lions for which this temple was once known remain, though there's still plenty to see – stone archways and galleries lean hither and thither and impressive stone carvings grace lintels, doorposts and slender window columns. A *naga*-flanked causeway and series of sanctuaries, libraries and gates lead past trees and vegetation-covered ponds. Just west of Prasat Krahom, at the far end of a half-fallen colonnade, are the remains of an impressive statue of Nandin.

The principal monument at Koh Ker is **Prasat Thom** (Prasat Kompeng), a 55m-wide, 40m-high sandstone-faced pyramid with seven tiers that's just west of Prasat Krahom. This striking structure, which looks like it could almost be a Mayan site somewhere on the Yucatan Peninsula, offers some spectacular views across the forest from its summit. Look out for the giant *garuda* under the collapsed

chamber at the top of the vertigo-inducing stairs. Some 40 inscriptions, dating from 932 to 1010, have been found at Prasat Thom.

South of this central group is a 1185m-by-548m *baray* (reservoir) known as the **Rahal**. It is fed by Stung Sen, which supplied water to irrigate the land in this arid area.

Some of the largest Shiva *linga* (phallic symbols) in Cambodia can still be seen in four temples about 1km northeast of Prasat Thom. The largest is in **Prasat Thneng**, and **Prasat Leung** (Prasat Balang) is similarly well endowed.

Other interesting temples: **Prasat Bram** (Prasat Pram), the first you come to after passing the toll booths (it'll be on your left), which is named in honour of its five towers, two of which are smothered by strangler figs; **Prasat Neang Khmau** (Prasat Nean Khmau), a bit further north and on your right, with some fine lintels decorating its otherwise bland exterior; and **Prasat Chen** (Prasat Chhin), about halfway from the toll booths to Prasat Krahom, where the statue of the wrestling monkeys was discovered.

Koh Ker is one of the least-studied temple areas from the Angkorian period. Louis Delaporte visited in 1880 during his extensive investigations into Angkorian temples. It was surveyed in 1921 by the great Henri Parmentier for an article in the *Bulletin de l'École d'Extrême Orient*, but no restoration work was ever undertaken here. Archaeological surveys were carried out by Cambodian teams in the 1950s and 1960s, but all records vanished during the destruction of the 1970s, helping to preserve this complex as something of an enigma.

Young people in dark khaki uniforms, members of the Apsara Authority's Community Heritage Patrol (www.autoriteapsara.org), keep an eye on the site, which is refreshingly clean and orderly. **Ox-cart tours** of the temples, lasting an hour-and-a-half, cost US$12; proceeds go into a community development fund. For information on preservation and sustainable development plans for Koh Ker, visit www.heritagewatch.org.

Sleeping & Eating

If you bring a hammock and mosquito net, it's possible to sleep near Prasat Krahom – ask a police official for a good spot. There are a few **small eateries** (morning-about 5pm) near Prasat Krahom. It should also be possible to find a homestay in the hamlet of Koh Ker, a few hundred metres north of the main pyramid.

Basic guesthouses can be found in the quiet, wood-built village of Srayong, which has electricity from 6pm to 10pm. To get there from the toll plaza, go 1km south and then 1km east. **Ponloeu Preah Chan Guesthouse** (012 489058; r US$5), run by a friendly family, has 12 well-kept but small rooms – there's just enough space for a double bed – with wooden plank floors, walls and ceilings. Toilets and showers are out back, across a covered courtyard. One room has an en suite bathroom with a squat toilet.

Another option is **Kohke Guesthouse** (011 578258; r US$4-5), a two-storey wood building on tall concrete stilts. As is usual in Khmer homes, the bedrooms are upstairs while the bathrooms are downstairs.

There are a few tiny eateries in the market area. Local families are happy to cook meals upon request.

Rumour has it that the two-storey building 200m south of the Koh Ker toll plaza will soon become a guesthouse.

Getting There & Away

Koh Ker is 127km northeast of Siem Reap (2½ hours by car) and 72km west of Tbeng Meanchey (two hours). There are plans to pave the toll road from Dam Dek to Koh Ker, which passes by Beng Mealea (p178), 61km southwest of Koh Ker; one-day bus excursions from Siem Reap often visit both temple complexes. Admission fees are paid at a brand new toll plaza 7km south of Prasat Krahom.

From Siem Reap, hiring a private car for a day trip to Koh Ker costs US$60 to US$70. It's a long way by *moto* (US$15 to US$20) but travelling this way is possible if you've got a hardy behind and steely nerves.

From Tbeng Meanchey, a private taxi costs US$70 return, a *moto* US$10. There may be occasional pickups from Tbeng Meanchey to Kulen, 40km to the west, though to get from there to Srayong, 23km further west, locals tend to use motorbikes. A minibus from Tbeng Meanchey to Srayong may be in the works.

TBENG MEANCHEY
ត្បូងមានជ័យ

 064 / pop 22,000

Tbeng Meanchey (pronounced tbai man-*chey*), often referred to by locals as Preah Vihear (not to be confused with Prasat Preah Vihear), is one of Cambodia's more out-of-the-way provincial capitals. Sprawling and dusty-red (or muddy-red, depending on the season), it has the grid layout of a large city but, in fact, consists of little more than two parallel main roads, running north to south, on which dogs lounge in the middle of the day. There's very little to see or do here, but the town makes a good staging post for the long haul to the mountaintop temple of Prasat Preah Vihear, 110 punishing kilometres further north.

Until 1999, because of Khmer Rouge activity, the only way in or out of Tbeng Meanchey was by air.

Orientation & Information

The centre of town, insofar as there is one, is around the taxi park and the market, Psar Kompong Pranak.

Acleda Bank (012 289851) The only place in the province that changes travellers cheques.

Danik Internet (092 476872; NH64; per hr US$2) The first internet café in the province, linked with the web by satellite.

Tourist Office (NH64) Doesn't yet have much to offer tourists.

Sights

The **Weaves of Cambodia** (092 346415; www .villagefocus.org, www.joomnoon.com) silk-weaving centre, known locally as Chum Ka Mon, was established by the Vietnam Veterans of

---

LAND MINE ALERT!

Preah Vihear Province is one of the most heavily mined provinces in Cambodia. Do not, under any circumstances, stray from previously trodden paths. Those with their own transport should travel only on roads or trails regularly used by locals.

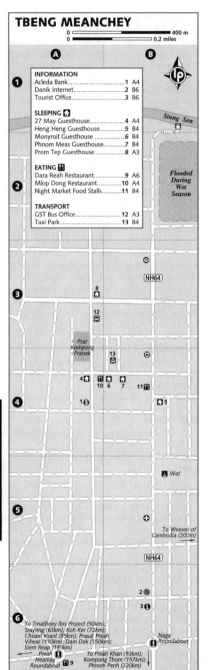

TBENG MEANCHEY

0 — 400 m
0 — 0.2 miles

INFORMATION
Acleda Bank...........................1 A4
Danik Internet........................2 B6
Tourist Office.........................3 B6

SLEEPING
27 May Guesthouse.................4 A4
Heng Heng Guesthouse...........5 B4
Monyroit Guesthouse 6 B4
Phnom Meas Guesthouse........7 B4
Prom Tep Guesthouse.............8 A3

EATING
Dara Reah Restaurant.............9 A6
Mlop Dong Restaurant...........10 A4
Night Market Food Stalls.........11 B4

TRANSPORT
GST Bus Office......................12 A3
Taxi Park.............................13 B4

Stung Sen

Flooded
During
Wet
Season

NH64

Psar
Kompong
Pranak

Wat

To Weaves of
Cambodia (200m)

NH64

Naga
Roundabout

To Tmatboey Ibis Project (50km);
Srayong (63km); Koh Ker (72km);
Choam Ksant (85km); Prasat Preah
Vihear (110km); Dam Dek (150km);
Siem Reap (185km)

Preah
Nеаreаy
Roundabout

To Preah Khan (93km);
Kompong Thom (157km);
Phnom Penh (320km)

America Foundation (VVAF) to rehabilitate amputees injured by land mines. Its artisans – who are at their hand looms from 7am to 11am Monday to Saturday – produce fine silk scarves and sarongs for export to Australia, Japan and the USA. To get there from the hospital on NH64, head four blocks east and half-a-block south.

Sleeping

27 May Guesthouse (☎ 011 905472; r US$5-15;) The cheapies with shared bathroom (US$3) are little more than cells but for US$2 more you can bed down in the motel-like two-storey section.

Phnom Meas Guesthouse (☎ 012 632017; r US$5-15;) Near the taxi park and a number of cheapie guesthouses, this hotel-like establishment has 26 comfortable, mid-sized units with foam mattresses, tile floors, simple furnishings and squat toilets.

Prom Tep Guesthouse (☎ 012 964645; r US$5-15;) Large enough to be a hotel, this three-storey place – on a broad avenue that may one day be fashionable – has 28 big, impersonal rooms, all with cable TV and Western toilets, some with fridge.

Monyroit Guesthouse (☎ 012 789955; r US$6-15;) Opened in 2007, this three-storey place has 12 spacious rooms with lots of windows, high ceilings, solid wood beds and cold water. Good value.

Heng Heng Guesthouse (☎ 011 994055; NH64; r US$7-15;) Opened in late 2007, this enthusiastically run, nine-room place offers the best accommodation deal in town. An internet satellite link is planned.

Eating

Lots of cattle are raised in these parts, so beef is a tasty – if tough – dining option.

There are several small eateries around Psar Kompong Pranak and a row of night-market food stalls on NH64 just north of the Heng Heng Guesthouse, whose capacious restaurant serves tasty dishes.

Mlop Dong Restaurant (☎ 011 207451; mains 4000-8000r; 6am-9pm) This timber-shed eatery serves up the standard Khmer favourites, including fried veggies. Mornings are atmospheric as locals drop by for a quick noodle soup, while after dinner this is about the closest thing Tbeng Meanchey has to a pub.

Dara Reah Restaurant (mains 8000-12,000r; 7am-9pm) Popular with well-to-do locals, this large garden restaurant has two airy pavilions and generous portions of good grub. Specialities include a sizzling plate of rather chewy sliced beef.

Getting There & Around
Tbeng Meanchey is 157km north of Kompong Thom via NH64, which is in such execrable condition that the trip takes at least five hours. The government has promised to upgrade – or at least grade – this artery in 2008, cutting travel time in half. In other directions, the city is 185km northeast of Siem Reap, 150km northeast of Dam Dek (three hours), 72km east of Koh Ker and 110km south of Prasat Preah Vihear.

GST (☎ 012 200128) sends one early morning bus a day to Kompong Thom (US$5) and Phnom Penh (US$8.75).

Share taxis, which leave from the taxi park, go to Kompong Thom (US$9 or US$10) and, much less frequently, to Choam Ksant (US$9, three hours) and Prasat Preah Vihear (US$10, 4½ hours). Private taxis can be hired to Siem Reap (US$65 one-way), Kompong Thom (US$60 one-way), Koh Ker (US$70 return), Choam Ksant (US$90 one-way or return) and Prasat Preah Vihear (US$90 one-way or return).

For more information on getting to Prasat Preah Vihear and Koh Ker, see p269 and p265 respectively.

Tbeng Meanchey is so far off the tourist track that it's sometimes hard to find a *moto* driver.

TMATBOEY IBIS PROJECT
Cambodia's remote northern plains, the largest remaining block of deciduous dipterocarp forest, seasonal wetlands and grasslands in Southeast Asia, have been described as the region's answer to Africa's savannas. Covering much of northwestern Preah Vihear Province, they are one of the last places on earth where you can see Cambodia's national bird, the critically endangered **giant ibis** (nests from July to November).

In a last-ditch effort to ensure the survival of this majestic bird, protect the only confirmed breeding sites of the **white-shouldered ibis** (nests from December to March), and save the habitat of other globally endangered species, including the Sarus crane (breeds June to October) and greater adjutant, the **Wildlife Conservation Society** (www.wcs.org) has set up a pioneering community ecotourism project. Situated in the isolated village of Tmatboey (Thmat Baeuy) in **Kulen Promtep Wildlife Sanctuary**, the initiative – a winner of Wild Asia's **2007 Responsible Tourism Award** (www.wildasia.net) – provides local villagers with education, income generated by work in the tourism sector, and a concrete incentive to do everything possible to protect the ibis. Visitors agree in advance to make a donation to a village conservation fund, but only if they actually *see* one or more of the birds. Other rare species that can be spotted here include the woolly-necked stork, white-rumped falcon, green peafowl, Alexandrine parakeet, grey-headed fish eagle and no less than 16 species of woodpecker, as well as owls and raptors. Birds are easiest to see from December to March

Tmatboey is about four to five hours from Siem Reap (via Beng Mealea and Koh Ker) and one hour north of Tbeng Meanchey. The site is accessible year-round, though at the height of the wet season the only way to get there may be by *moto*. To arrange a tailor-made visit, which costs approximately US$65 per person per night (including accommodation, guides and food), contact the Siem Reap–based **Sam Veasna Centre for Wildlife Conservation** (☎ 063 761597; www.samveasna.org). Visitors sleep in wooden bungalows with en suite bathrooms.

CHHEP VULTURE FEEDING STATION
In an effort to save the critically endangered white-rumped vulture and slender-billed vulture, the **Wildlife Conservation Society** (WCS; www.wcs.org) has set up a 'vulture restaurant' at Chhep, on the edge of the ultra-remote **Preah Vihear Protected Forest**. At the feeding station, with at least a week's advance coordination, visitors can observe these almost-extinct carrion-eaters dining on the carcass of a domestic cow – and, through fees, contribute to the project's funding.

The feeding station, accessible only in the dry season and even then only by 4WD, is about 45km northeast of Tbeng Meanchey (as the endangered crow flies) and 75km southeast of Choam Ksant along Rd 211. From Tbeng Meanchey, the trip takes about six bone-jarring hours. For details, contact the Siem Reap–based **Sam Veasna Centre for Wildlife Conservation** (☎ 063 761597; www.samveasna.org). Accommodation is at a forest camp maintained by the WCS.

NORTHWESTERN CAMBODIA

CHOAM KSANT
ជាំក្សាន្ត

Choam Ksant, an overgrown village with an end-of-the-line feel, survives in part thanks to petty trade with Thailand via Anh Seh, 20km north in the Dangkrek Mountains. The crossing is closed to foreigners and there's nothing of interest to see up there except some big views. Someday, though, the town may become a gateway to wild places further east, including temples such as the historically important (though heavily mined) **Prasat Neak Buos**, visitable by *moto* or bicycle in the dry season, and the remote **Preah Vihear Protected Forest**, which hugs the Laotian frontier near the so-called **Emerald Triangle** (the point where the Cambodian, Thai and Laotian borders meet).

As far as accommodation is concerned, the best of a sorry lot is **Sok San Guesthouse** (☎ 012 350187; r US$3), across the street from the health centre. Sok San has about a dozen very basic, all-wood rooms with shared bathroom. There's electricity from 6pm to 10pm.

There are a few basic food stalls near the market, which is one block north of the Acleda Bank.

Road connections are open year-round west towards Prasat Preah Vihear (1½ hours) and Anlong Veng but are wretched south to Tbeng Meanchey (three hours by car), especially in the wet season, though only a few of the potholes are deeper than 50cm or larger than a car. In places, the road has been washed out and provisionally repaired with rows of rough logs.

PRASAT PREAH VIHEAR
ប្រាសាទព្រះវិហារ

The most dramatically situated of all the Angkorian monuments, 800m-long **Prasat Preah Vihear** (elevation 730m; admission 10,000r) perches high atop the south-facing cliff face of the Dangkrek Mountains. The views are

---

LAND MINE ALERT!

Prasat Preah Vihear was the scene of heavy fighting as recently as 1998 and countless land mines were used by the Khmer Rouge to defend this strategic summit against government forces. In late 2007 mine clearance around the temple was continuing, so do not stray from marked paths – several locals have been killed or maimed in recent years.

---

breathtaking: lowland Cambodia, 550m below, stretching as far as the eye can see, with the holy mountain of Phnom Kulen (p177) looming in the distance.

Prasat Preah Vihear, an important place of pilgrimage during the Angkorian period, was built by a succession of seven Khmer monarchs, beginning with Yasovarman I (r 889–910) and ending with Suryavarman II (r 1112–1152), builder of Angkor Wat. Like other temple-mountains from this period, it was designed to represent Mt Meru and was dedicated to the Hindu deity Shiva.

Start a visit at the **monumental stairway**, if possible from the bottom (near the market and the crossing from Thailand). As you walk south, you come to four cruciform *gopuras* (sanctuaries), decorated with a profusion of exquisite carvings and separated by esplanades up to 350m long. At the entrance to the **Gopura of the Third Level**, look for an early rendition of the Churning of the Ocean of Milk, a theme later depicted awesomely at Angkor Wat. The **Central Sanctuary** and its associated structures and galleries, in a remarkably good state of repair, are right at the edge of the cliff, which affords **stupendous views** of Cambodia's northern plains – this is a fantastic spot for a picnic.

For more on the carvings of Prasat Preah Vihear and the temple's history, look out for market vendors selling *Preah Vihear* by Vittorio Roveda, a readable souvenir book accompanied by some attractive photographs.

Sleeping & Eating

The only way to enjoy both a spectacular sunset and a magnificent sunrise from atop Prasat Preah Vihear is to stay at the very basic **guesthouse** (☎ 012 472846; r US$5) in the southeast corner of the border market, situated at the bottom of the monumental stairway. The eight all-wood rooms have glassless windows, shared bathrooms and electricity from 6pm to 10pm. The market has several food stalls.

Kor Muy, the village at the base of the hill, has two rudimentary guesthouses. **Ponleu Pech Mean Lap Guesthouse** (☎ 012 472795; r US$3) is an all-wood building whose bathroom is at the end of a long hallway. The 20 2½m-by-2½m cubicles come with mosquito nets. The 10-room **Raksaleap Guesthouse** (☎ 092 224838) is a bit more comfortable.

The options in the gritty junction hamlet of Sa Em, a half-hour south of Kor Muy,

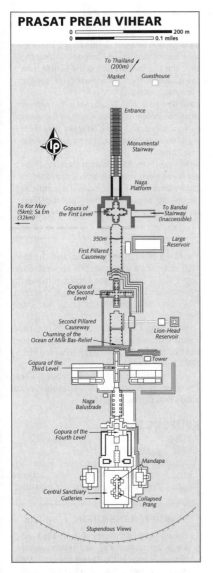

PRASAT PREAH VIHEAR

0 ————— 200 m
0 ————— 0.1 miles

To Thailand (200m)

Market

Guesthouse

Entrance

Monumental Stairway

Naga Platform

To Kor Muy (5km); Sa Em (32km)

Gopura of the First Level

To Bandai Stairway (Inaccessible)

350m

Large Reservoir

First Pillared Causeway

Gopura of the Second Level

Second Pillared Causeway

Churning of the Ocean of Milk Bas-Relief

Lion-Head Reservoir

Gopura of the Third Level

Tower

Naga Balustrade

Gopura of the Fourth Level

Mandapa

Central Sanctuary Galleries

Collapsed Prang

Stupendous Views

GOOD INTENTIONS

As we go to press, Chinese surveyors and engineers are working to upgrade the road from Koh Ker to Prasat Preah Vihear, a project that – if and when it's completed – will revolutionise access to the temple.

Getting There & Away

The easy way to get to Prasat Preah Vihear – known as Khao Phra Wiharn (Sacred Monastery) to the Thais – is from Thailand, as there are paved roads right up to the Cambodian border market and the adjacent monumental stairway. Anyone coming this way will no doubt be armed with a copy of Lonely Planet *Thailand,* which supplies all the details on getting here via the town of Kantharalak.

Note that Prasat Preah Vihear is not an international border crossing – visitors enter Cambodia without a visa and must return to Thailand by 5pm the same day. Tourist visas for onward travel into Cambodia are *not* available here. It costs US$10 to visit from the Thai side – US$5 goes to the Thais for visiting the 'national park' and US$5/200B goes to the Khmers as the temple fee.

Since the border-crossing agreement is reciprocal, tourists coming from the Cambodian side can go a few hundred metres into Thailand to shop at the border market. Cambodian authorities charge 10B to cross.

Getting to Prasat Preah Vihear from the Cambodian side is a unique and challenging adventure. It can generally be done only between mid-November and May because in the wet season many of the roads in this part of the country are impassable. When you finally reach the temple, you'll have the satisfaction of knowing that you've completed a modern-day pilgrimage almost the equal of any undertaken at the height of the Angkorian empire. On the downside, you'll have to deal with the disheartening sight of hundreds of Thai-side tourists who have zipped up to the temple in air-conditioned coaches along a sealed superhighway – they'll never know what you've been through.

From Tbeng Meanchey, 110km to the south, you can either take a share taxi (US$10, 4½ hours) or hire a private taxi (US$90 one-way or return). Often share taxis and pickups only go as far as Sa Em (Sra Em), 27km south

NORTHWESTERN CAMBODIA

are hardly better. The second house north of the roundabout – a signless, two-storey grey building – serves as an eight-room **guesthouse** (☎ 012 435763; r US$3). The grim bathroom is out in the trash-strewn back yard. Across the roundabout, the tin-roofed **Phoum Sra Em Restaurant** caters to truckers – or you can eat at the guesthouse with the family.

NEIGHBOURLY RELATIONS

For generations, Prasat Preah Vihear has been a source of tension between Cambodia and Thailand. This area was ruled by Thailand for several centuries but retroceded to Cambodia during the French protectorate, under the treaty of 1907. In 1959 the Thai military seized the temple from Cambodia and then-Prime Minister Sihanouk took the dispute to the International Court, gaining worldwide recognition for Cambodian sovereignty in a 1962 ruling.

The next time Prasat Preah Vihear made international news was in 1979, when the Thai military pushed more than 40,000 Cambodian refugees across the border in what was then the worst case of forced repatriation in UN history. The area was mined and many refugees died from injuries, starvation and disease before the occupying Vietnamese army could cut a safe passage and escort them on the long walk south to Kompong Thom.

Prasat Preah Vihear hit the headlines again in May 1998 because the Khmer Rouge regrouped here after the fall of Anlong Veng and staged a last stand that soon turned into a final surrender.

With peace came an agreement between the Cambodians and Thais to open the temple to tourism. The Thais built a huge road up the mountain and began work along the ill-defined border. Today, a large visitors centre and car park stand on what was – not so long ago – Cambodian land.

---

of Prasat Preah Vihear, from which it's a 30-minute *moto* ride (3000r) along a remarkably good dirt road to Kor Muy (Koh Muy) at the base of the escarpment. From there you have two options: hire a *moto* (US$5 return) for a hair-raising, 20-minute ride up gradients of up to 35%; or take a 5km, two-hour walk up the same steep road (bring plenty of water).

For onward transport, you can try to score a ride at Kor Muy, but you'll probably have better luck in the junction village of Sa Em. Arriving at the roundabout from the temple, the road to the right goes west to Anlong Veng while the road to the left goes southeast to Choam Ksant and Tbeng Meanchey. Only to Tbeng Meanchey is there anything resembling regular traffic, including the occasional share taxi. Virtually no vehicles head west to Anlong Veng – from which there's transport south to Siem Reap – so your only option may be to hire a *moto* (US$20). See p261 for details.

To get a bird's-eye view of the temple – and arrive in style – take a helicopter from Siem Reap. For more information, see p153.

KOMPONG THOM PROVINCE

ខេត្តកំពង់ធំ

Kompong Thom, Cambodia's second-largest province, is starting to draw more visitors thanks to the pre-Angkorian temples of Sambor Prei Kuk, an easy day trip from

the town of Kompong Thom, and the bird-rich marshes and grasslands around Tonlé Sap Lake. The province's most noteworthy geographical feature is Stung Sen, a serpentine river that eventually joins the Tonlé Sap River.

Kompong Thom came under US bombardment in the early 1970s in an effort to reopen the Phnom Penh–Siem Reap road severed by the Khmer Rouge.

Almost all the sights in Kompong Thom Province are along NH6, or accessible via local roads that intersect NH6.

KOMPONG THOM

កំពង់ធំ

☎ 062 / pop 66,000

A bustling commercial centre, Kompong Thom is situated on NH6 midway between Phnom Penh and Siem Reap. It's an ideal

---

SEARCH FOR THE BENGAL FLORICAN

The northeastern shores of Tonlé Sap Lake are home to scores of bird species, some of them – such as the Bengal florican – endangered. Sites in Kompong Thom Province that are gaining popularity with twitchers include the **Stoeng Chikrieng grasslands** and the **Boeng Tonlé Chmar Ramsar Area**, both straddling the border between Kompong Thom Province and Siem Reap Province, and the **Kru Krom grasslands**, 25km due south of Kompong Thom town.

base from which to explore the pre-Angkorian Chenla capital of Sambor Prei Kuk.

Parallel to the **old French bridge** over Stung Sen, the **new steel bridge**, opened in 1997, was built with Australian assistance. That's why it's decorated with hopping kangaroos at each end.

Information

Acleda Bank (NH6) An ATM is said to be coming.
Department of Tourism (Prachea Thepatay St; ☯ 8-11am & 2-5pm) Upstairs in an old wooden building. May have handouts.
Internet pharmacy (NH6; per hr 3000-4000r; ☯ 6am-8pm) Internet access one block north of the market.
Po Sothea Internet (cnr NH6 & St 5; per hr 4000r; ☯ 7am-9pm) A pharmacy with two computers.

Sleeping

There are bargain basement guesthouses on Dekchau Meas St, but some make more money as brothels and are opposite the taxi park, which means early morning horn action.

Mittapheap Hotel (☎ 961213; NH6; r US$5-10; ☒) In a neat yellow building just north of the bridge, this smart hotel has 23 comfortable rooms at the right price.

Arunras Hotel (☎/fax 961294; 46 Sereipheap Blvd; r US$5-13; ☒) Occupying a seven-storey corner building, this place – with Kompong Thom's only elevator – has 58 smart, good-value rooms. It also runs the cheaper Arunras Guesthouse next door, where fan/air-con rooms start at US$3/8.

Stung Sen Royal Garden Hotel (☎/fax 961228; Stung Sen St; d/tr US$20/30; ☒) Not as plush as the name implies but still comfortable, though showing its age. This place has 32 rooms, some of them huge.

Eating

There are plenty of snack stalls and *tukalok* vendors just north of the river and around the new market, which is supposed to open sometime in 2008.

Araska Restaurant (☎ 092 289238; mains 5000-12,000r) Run by a Finnish-Khmer couple, this new establishment serves tasty Khmer dishes and good shakes but is best known for its hearty Western fare, including breakfasts, pizza, pasta, hamburgers and veggie options.

Arunras Restaurant (☎ 012 187107; 46 Sereipheap Blvd; mains US$1.50-4; ☯ 6am-11pm) Popular with people passing through and has a wide range

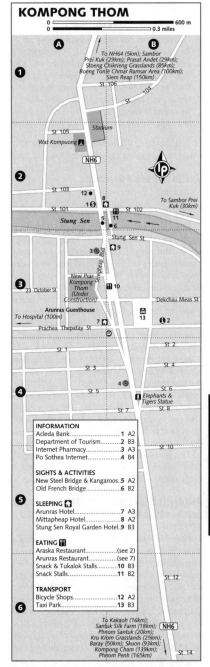

NORTHWESTERN CAMBODIA

SUSTAINABLE LIVELIHOODS

Cooperation for the Development of Cambodia (CDC; ☎ 012 481924; codeckt@ yahoo.com), a Kompong Thom–based NGO that works to help the rural poor increase their incomes in a sustainable way, is looking for volunteers who can spend at least two months here.

of Cambodian, Chinese and veggie dishes. Don't expect solicitous service.

Getting There & Around

Kompong Thom is on NH6 165km north of Phnom Penh and 150km southeast of Siem Reap.

Bus companies running between Phnom Penh (14,000r, four hours) and Siem Reap often drop off and pick up passengers when passing through. The Arunras Hotel sells tickets – lots of buses stop out front – but they take a commission, so it's cheaper to flag a bus down yourself and pay on board. Share taxis, which leave from the taxi park, are faster and cost US$4 or US$5 to either Phnom Penh (2½ hours) or Siem Reap. Minibuses are slightly cheaper but more crowded.

Heading north to Tbeng Meanchey (often referred to as Preah Vihear by locals) along the atrocious NH64, pickups (15,000/10,000r inside/on the back, six hours) are the most common form of transport, but share taxis also do occasional runs (20,000r to 30,000r). Both can be found at the taxi park. For more on the unholy road conditions, see p267.

The Araska Restaurant rents bicycles and motorbikes. It may also be possible to rent a bicycle at one of the bike shops on St 103.

AROUND KOMPONG THOM
Sambor Prei Kuk
សំបូរ៍ប្រៃគុក

Sambor Prei Kuk (admission US$3), Cambodia's most impressive group of pre-Angkorian monuments, encompasses more than 100 mainly brick temples scattered through the forest, among them some of the oldest structures in the country. Originally called Isanapura, Sambor Prei Kuk was the capital of Chenla during the reign of the early-7th-century King Isanavarman and continued to be an important learning centre during the Angkorian era.

The main temple area consists of three complexes, each enclosed by the remains of two concentric walls. Their basic layout – a central tower surrounded by shrines, ponds and gates – may have served as an inspiration for the architects of Angkor five centuries later.

Forested and shady, Sambor Prei Kuk has a serene and soothing atmosphere, enhanced by a recent anti-litter campaign, and the sandy paths make for a pleasant stroll. Past the ticket booth, the **Isanborei Crafts Shop** sells a worthwhile English brochure (2000r), high-quality, handcrafted basket and wood items, and T-shirts with original designs. Nearby, **small eateries** sell drinks and chicken or beef with rice.

The principle temple group, **Prasat Sambor**, is dedicated to Gambhireshvara, one of Shiva's many incarnations (the other groups are dedicated to Shiva himself). Several of Prasat Sambor's towers retain brick carvings in pretty good condition, and there is a series of large *yonis* (female fertility symbols) around the central tower that appear to date from a later period, demonstrating the continuity between pre-Angkorian and Angkorian culture.

Prasat Yeay Peau (Prasat Yeai Poeun) is arguably the most atmospheric complex, as it feels lost in the forest. The eastern gateway is being both held up and torn asunder by an ancient tree, the bricks interwoven with the tree's extensive, probing roots. A truly massive tree shades the western gate.

Prasat Tao (Lion Temple), the largest of the Sambor Prei Kuk structures, boasts two excellent examples of Chenla carving in the form of two large, elaborately coiffed stone lions.

In the early 1970s, Sambor Prei Kuk was bombed by US aircraft in support of the Lon Nol government's doomed fight against the Khmer Rouge. Some of the craters can still be seen.

GETTING THERE & AWAY
If you're interested in the chronological evolution of Cambodian temple architecture, you might want to see Sambor Prei Kuk before heading to Angkor.

To get here from Kompong Thom, follow NH6 north for 5km before continuing straight on NH64 towards Tbeng Meanchey (the paved road to Siem Reap veers left). After 11km (look for an elaborate laterite sign) turn right and continue for 14km. Another option is to head east out of Kompong Thom on

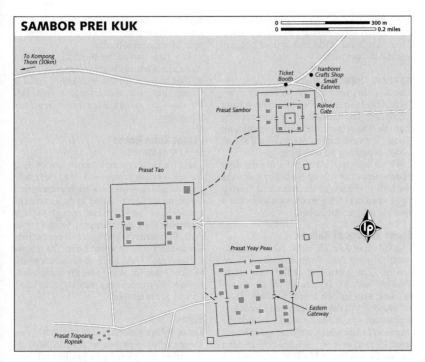

SAMBOR PREI KUK

To Kompong Thom (30km)

Ticket Booth

Isanborei Crafts Shop Small Eateries

Prasat Sambor

Ruined Gate

Prasat Tao

Prasat Yeay Peau

Eastern Gateway

Prasat Trapeang Ropeak

St 102 – some *moto* drivers prefer this quiet, circuitous route through the countryside.

From Kompong Thom, a *moto* ride out here (under an hour) should cost US$7 or US$8 (US$10 including Phnom Santuk). By car the trip takes about an hour.

Prasat Andet
ប្រាសាទអណ្តែត

Dating from the same period as Sambor Prei Kuk (7th century), this small, ruined brick temple is set amid the grounds of a modern wat. Prasat Andet would have been the focal point of an important commercial centre trading on the Tonlé Sap, and some researchers believe it continued to play such a role during the time of Angkor. Today, very little remains and it is only worth a visit for dedicated temple-trackers with time on their hands. It is 29km northwest of Kompong Thom and about 2km south of NH6.

Phnom Santuk
ភ្នំសន្ទុក

Phnom Santuk (Phnom Sontuk; 207m), its flanks decorated with Buddha images and a series of pagodas, is the most important holy mountain in this region and a site of Buddhist pilgrimage. It's attractively set high above the surrounding countryside, which means there are lots of stairs to climb – 809, in fact. These wind their way up through a forest and emerge at a colourful **pagoda** that has many small shrines quite unlike others around Cambodia. Balanced around the wat are a number of interesting sandstone boulders into which images of Buddha have been carved. Just beneath the southern summit of the mountain are several large **reclining Buddhas** – some modern incarnations cast in cement, others carved into the mountain itself centuries ago.

Phnom Santuk has an active wat and the local monks are always interested in receiving foreign tourists. For travellers spending the night in Kompong Thom, Phnom Santuk is a good place from which to catch a magnificent sunset over the rice fields, though this means coming down in the dark.

The parking fee, which is clearly not being spent on litter pickup, depends on who's collecting it and who you are. Khmer motorbike/taxi drivers generally pay 500r/2000r; foreigners are hit up for more. There are food stalls and lots of beggars around the car park.

GETTING THERE & AWAY

The 2km dirt road to Phnom Santuk intersects NH6 18km towards Phnom Penh from Kompong Thom; look for a sign reading 'Santuk Mountain Site'. From Kompong Thom, a round trip by *moto* costs US$4 to US$5, depending on wait time.

Those with trail bikes and a healthy dose of experience can ride up the hill by following the trail to the left of the stairs and veering right when the trail goes up what looks like a rocky dried-out streambed.

Stone Masons of Kakaoh

The village of Kakaoh, along NH6 16km towards Phnom Penh from Kompong Thom (about 2km northwest of the turn-off to Phnom Santuk), is famous for its stonemasons, who fashion Buddha statues, decorative lions and the like with hand tools and a practised eye. It's fascinating to watch the creation of these works, which range in height from 15cm to over 5m. A 2.5m-high Buddha carved from a single block of stone will set you back about US$2000, not including airline overweight fees.

Santuk Silk Farm

Situated on the other side of NH6 from the access road to Phnom Santuk, the **Santuk Silk Farm** (☎ 012 906604; budgibb@yahoo.com; admission free) is one of the few places where you can see the entire silk production cycle, starting with the seven-week lifecycle of the silkworm, a delicate creature that feeds only on mulberry leaves and has to be protected from predators such as geckos, ants and mosquitos. Although most of the raw silk used here comes from China and Vietnam, the local worms produce 'Khmer golden silk', so-called because of its lush golden hue. You can watch local artisans

weaving scarfs (US$15 to US$25) and other items by hand from 7am to 11am and 1pm to 5pm Monday to Saturday.

The farm is run by Budd Gibbons, an American Vietnam War veteran who's lived in Cambodia since the mid-1990s, and his Cambodian wife. To arrange a visit, call the day – or at least a few hours – before, if possible.

Prasat Kuha Nokor

ប្រាសាទគុហានគរ

This 11th-century temple, constructed during the reign of Suryavarman I, is in extremely good condition thanks to a lengthy renovation before the civil war. It is set in the grounds of a modern wat and is an easy enough stop for those with their own transport. From Phnom Penh, the journey takes about two hours, from Kompong Thom about an hour. The temple is signposted from NH6 about 22km north of Skuon and is 2km from the main road. From NH6, you can get a *moto* (US$2 to US$3 return) to the temple.

Baray

Khmer Village Homestay (☎ 092 776067; www .khmerhomestay.com; per person for 1/2 days US$20/35), an operation that ploughs its profits back into the local community, lets you experience a slice of traditional Khmer village life while enjoying modern toilet and shower facilities. Surrounded by rice fields and sugar palms, guests stay in bamboo, palm leaf or wood chalets and can explore the environs by pony cart and ox cart, meet village families, help the local fishers catch dinner and even have a go at weaving. Prices include activities and full board; breakfast options include noodles at the local market.

The homestay is in Baray, on NH6 about 120km north of Phnom Penh and 50km southeast of Kompong Thom. All the buses and share taxis linking Phnom Penh (two hours) with Siem Reap (195km; three hours) pass by here.

Eastern Cambodia

Eastern Cambodia is home to a diversity of landscapes and peoples, shattering the illusion that the country is all paddy fields and sugar palms. There are plenty of those in the lowland provinces, but in the northeast they yield to the forested mountains of Mondulkiri and Ratanakiri, both up-and-coming ecotourism areas. This is a vast region, stretching from the dragon's tail where the borders of Cambodia, Laos and Vietnam meet, to near enough the dragon's mouth where the mighty Mekong continues its journey into the delta and on to the South China Sea. The river and its tributaries snake through the land, breathing life into the fields, blanketing the landscape in dazzling greens and providing a livelihood for millions of people.

If it is a walk on the wild side that fires your imagination, then the northeast is calling. The rolling hills and lush forests provide a home to many ethnic minority groups known as Khmer Leu (Upper Khmer) or *chunchiet* (ethnic minorities). With different dialects, lifestyles and looks, these people are a world away from their lowland Khmer neighbours. Peppering the area are thundering waterfalls, crater lakes and meandering rivers. Trekking, biking, kayaking and elephant rides are all activities beginning to take off in this remote corner of Cambodia, making it a must for adrenaline seekers.

The 'Wild East' atmosphere doesn't stop there. This is also home to rare wildlife such as tigers, leopards and elephants, although the chances of seeing some of these are about as likely as the kouprey – a wild ox and the country's national symbol – still living in the forests. The Mekong is home to dwindling numbers of the rare freshwater Irrawaddy dolphin, which can be viewed year-round near Kratie. Do the maths: it all adds up to an amazing experience.

HIGHLIGHTS

- Catch a glimpse of the rare freshwater Irrawaddy dolphin in the Mekong River near **Kratie** (p288)
- Experience a different Cambodia with a homestay in **Mondulkiri** (p298) and learn about the life of the hardy Pnong people
- Dive into the crystal-clear waters of the crater lake of **Boeng Yeak Lom** (p296) in Ratanakiri, the best natural swimming pool in the country, surrounded by lush forest
- Learn how to be a mahout for the day at the Elephant Valley Project in **Mondulkiri** (p302)
- Soak up the charms of **Kompong Cham** (p280), a bustling town on the Mekong and gateway to historic temples, lush countryside and friendly locals

- ELEVATION: 5-1500M
- POPULATION: 6 MILLION
- AREA: 68,472 SQ KM

EASTERN CAMBODIA

EASTERN CAMBODIA

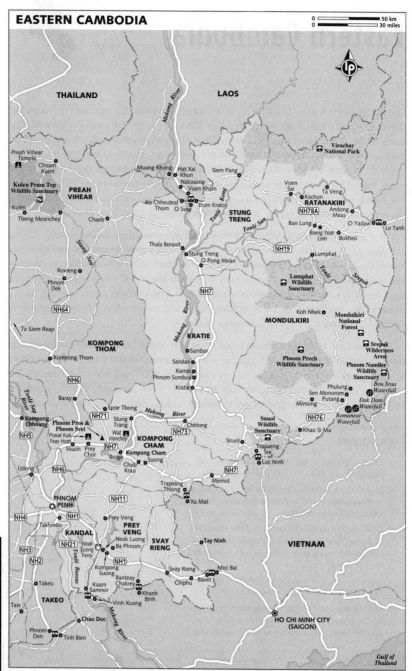

0   50 km
0   30 miles

THAILAND

LAOS

Mekong River

Tonlé Kong

Virachay
National Park

Preah Vihear
Temple
Choam
Ksant

Muang Khong
Hat Xai
Khun
Nakasong
Voen Kham
Siem Pang

Voen
Sai
Ta Veng
Kachon

Kulen Prum Tep
Wildlife Sanctuary

PREAH
VIHEAR

Ko Chheuteal
Thom
O Svay
Dom Kralor

STUNG
TRENG

RATANAKIRI
NH78A
Andong
Meas

Kulen

Ban Lung
O Yadaw
Le Tanh

Tbeng Meanchey
Chaeb

Thala Boravit

Boeng Yeak
Lom
Bokheo

Stung Sen

Tonlé San

NH19

Rovieng

Stung Treng
O Pong Moan

Lumphat

Phnom
Dek

NH64

Tonlé Srepok

NH7

Lumphat
Wildlife
Sanctuary

To Siem Reap

KOMPONG
THOM

KRATIE

Koh Nhek

MONDULKIRI

Mondulkiri
National
Forest

Kompong Thom

Mekong River

Sambor

Phnom Prech
Wildlife Sanctuary

Srepok
Wilderness
Area

NH6

Sandan
Kampi
Phnom Sombok
Kratie

Phnom Namlier
Wildlife
Sanctuary

Baray

Tonlé San River

Spoe Tbong

Mekong River

Phulung
Sen Monorom
Mimong
Putang

Bou Sraa
Waterfall

Kompong
Chhnang

NH71
Stung
Trang
Wat
Hanchey

Chhlong

Snuol
Wildlife
Sanctuary

NH76

Dak Dam
Waterfall

Romanear
Waterfall

NH5

Phnom Pros &
Phnom Srei

Prasat Kuh
Yeay Hom

Skuon
Prey
Chor

NH7
Bridge

KOMPONG
CHAM

NH73

Suong

Snuol

Khao Si Ma

Trapaeng
Sre
Loc Ninh

Udong

NH6

Chub
Krau

NH7

Memot

Takhmau

PHNOM
PENH

NH11

Trapaeng
Thlong

Xa Mat

NH4
NH1

Prey Veng

KANDAL

NH21
Neak
Luong Ferry

NH3
NH2

Neak Luong
Ba Phnom

PREY
VENG

SVAY
RIENG

Tay Ninh

VIETNAM

Kompong
Suong
NH1

Takeo

Kaam
Samnor

Banteay
Chakrey

Svay Rieng

Moc Bai

Tani

TAKEO

Vinh Xuong

Khanh
Binh

Chiphu
Bavet

Tonlé Bassac

Chau Doc

Mekong River

Phnom
Den
Tinh Bien

HO CHI MINH CITY
(SAIGON)

Gulf of
Thailand

History

In the 1960s Vietnamese communist forces sought sanctuary in eastern Cambodia to escape the fire power and might of the US army, and much of the area was heavily under the influence of the Vietnamese. Prince Sihanouk became increasingly anti-American as the '60s progressed, and cut a deal to tacitly supply the Vietnamese communists with weapons from the Chinese, via the port of Sihanoukville. By the end of the decade, as the USA began its bombing raids and incursions, the Vietnamese communists had moved deep into the country. Following the overthrow of Sihanouk, Lon Nol demanded that all Vietnamese communist forces withdraw from Cambodia within one week, an ultimatum they could not possibly meet, and open war erupted. In just a few months, much of eastern Cambodia fell to the Vietnamese communists and their Khmer Rouge allies.

During much of the rule of the Khmer Rouge, the eastern zones were known to be more moderate than other parts of the country and it wasn't until 1977 that Pol Pot and the central government tried to impose their will on the east. Militarily, eastern Cambodia was independent and strong, and the crackdown provoked what amounted to a civil war between Khmer Rouge factions. This tussle lingered until December 1978, when the Vietnamese invasion forced the Khmer Rouge leadership to flee to the Thai border. The east became one of the safest areas of the country during much of the 1980s, as the Khmer Rouge kept well away from areas that were close to the Vietnamese border.

These days the region is experiencing an economic renaissance as the rubber industry bounces back and staple commodity prices soar.

Getting There & Away

Eastern Cambodia is home to several important international border crossings between Cambodia and its neighbours. The Mekong River border at Dom Kralor–Voen Kham shared with Laos to the north is an ever-more popular route for adventurous travellers. East of Phnom Penh are plenty of border crossings with Vietnam, including the old favourite Bavet–Moc Bai crossing on the road to Ho Chi Minh City, and the evocative Mekong River crossing at Kaam Samnor–Vinh Xuong. See p328 for more on border crossings in this region.

For those already in Cambodia, Phnom Penh is the usual gateway to the region, with a host of reliable roads fanning out to the major cities, plus irregular flights between the capital and the popular province of Ratanakiri.

As overland travel takes off in Cambodia, it is possible to reach almost any destination in the region in one day, unthinkable just a few years ago. A round trip from Phnom Penh to Ratanakiri by land can take just six days (if you set a fast pace). Mondulkiri is more straightforward and, with good connections, a round trip can be done in four days. But be aware that you still sometimes end up stranded in the wet season.

Getting Around

Eastern Cambodia is one of the more remote parts of the country and conditions vary widely between wet and dry seasons. Getting around the lowlands is easy enough, as many of the roads have been upgraded and buses, minibuses and taxis ply the routes. National Highway 1 (NH1) to Vietnam is in fine shape all the way to the border. NH7 has been rebuilt all the way to Stung Treng and the Lao border.

The northeast is a different matter, as the punishing rains of the wet season leave many of the roads in a sorry state. A good road can turn bad in a matter of months and journey times become hit and miss.

SVAY RIENG PROVINCE
ខេត្តស្វាយរៀង

This small province occupies a jut of land sticking into Vietnam, an area known as the parrot's beak. During the Vietnam War, American forces were convinced that this was where the Vietnamese communists' version of the Pentagon was situated. While there were undoubtedly a lot of Vietnamese communists hiding in Cambodia during much of the war, there was no such thing as a Pentagon. In 1969 the Americans began unauthorised bombing in this area and in 1970 joined forces with the South Vietnamese for a ground assault.

Svay Rieng is considered one of Cambodia's poorest provinces because of the poor quality of its land. Most of the population eke out a subsistence living based on farming and fishing. There is really nothing to attract visitors here, which is why 99.99% zoom through it on their way to Vietnam.

SVAY RIENG
ស្វាយរៀង
☎ 044 / pop 21,000

Svay Rieng is a blink-and-you'll-miss-it provincial capital that many travellers whistle past when making the journey between Phnom Penh and Ho Chi Minh City. There is quite literally nothing to do here, but winding its way through town is Tonlé Wayko, a tributary of the Mekong.

Information
Acleda Bank (☎ 945545), a few blocks west of the Independence Monument, is the place to change travellers cheques. Internet access is intermittently available in telephone shops along the main drag.

Sleeping & Eating
Samaki Guesthouse (☎ 011 888412; St 113; r with/without bathroom US$4/3) Clustered around a central junction is a group of guesthouses and this is the best of a mediocre bunch. The family are friendly enough, but cheaper rooms involve taking a chance with a share bathroom.

Tonlay Waikor Hotel (☎ 945718; NH1; r US$10; 🕸) The only real hotel in town, the rooms are basic but comfortable and include cable TV. Security should be pretty good here, as it's owned by the National Police Chief.

Boeng Meas Restaurant (NH1; mains US$1; 🕑 6.30am-9.30pm) Well located on stilts near the riverside, this wooden restaurant is consistently popular with Khmers passing through town. Service is sharp and the menu includes a healthy selection of Khmer favourites.

There are cheap food stalls around Psar Svay Rieng (Svay Rieng Market) for those wanting the local touch, as well as some snack stalls along the river at night that sell cold beer.

Getting There & Away
Share taxis for Svay Rieng leave from Phnom Penh's Chbah Ampeau taxi park in the southeast of the city. The cost is about 10,000r per person. Hua Lian operates buses direct from Phnom Penh to Svay Rieng (8000r, three hours, one departure a day).

Travelling to Svay Rieng from the Bavet border crossing with Vietnam may be more difficult because taxi drivers prefer the more lucrative option of taking foreigners all the way to Phnom Penh. Stuff yourself into a taxi with other travellers and ask to be dropped off at Svay Rieng (US$2). Taxis usually drop people off near Psar Svay Rieng.

PREY VENG PROVINCE
ខេត្តព្រៃវែង

Prey Veng is a small but heavily populated agricultural region nestled on the east bank of the Mekong. Rubber played a large part in Prey Veng's prewar economy, but most of the plantations are only just being redeveloped. There is little of significance to be seen in the province today, but it may have played a significant role in Cambodian history, as one of the earliest pre-Angkorian kingdoms was located in the area around Ba Phnom. It is a province that has experienced few visitors; the provincial capital is a sleepy place on NH11, a pretty road with light traffic linking NH1 and NH7.

PREY VENG
ព្រៃវែង
☎ 043 / pop 55,000

Few travellers make it to Prey Veng, a sleepy backwater between Neak Luong and Kompong Cham. Not a lot happens here and most of the population is tucked up in bed by 9pm. But for those who want to escape their fellow tourists, it offers an alternative route between Phnom Penh and Kompong Cham.

There are a few decaying colonial structures around town, attesting to a once-important centre. During most of the year a vast lake marks the western edge of town, but from March to August this evaporates and the local farmers cultivate rice.

Information
Acleda Bank (☎ 944555) represents Western Union for those needing quick transfers, and can cash US dollar travellers cheques.

Sleeping & Eating
Angkor Thom Hotel (☎ 393929; r US$5-10; 🕸) One of the taller buildings in low-rise Prey Veng, this is the smartest hotel in town, offering 27 spotless rooms. All include hot-water showers and cable TV.

Mittapheap Hotel (☎ 012 997757; r US$3-10; ❄) Occupying a prime position on the central crossroads in town, this is the elder statesmen among Prey Veng's hotels. The friendly owners run a clean establishment and it's good value.

Mittapheap Restaurant (☎ 011 939213; mains 3000-4000r) Under the same ownership as the aforementioned Mittapheap Hotel, this restaurant has an ebullient manager who ensures speedy service. The menu is packed with inexpensive Khmer, Chinese and Vietnamese dishes.

Getting There & Away

Prey Veng is 90km east of Phnom Penh and 78km south of Kompong Cham. Share taxis link Phnom Penh with Prey Veng (10,000r, two hours); minibuses (7000r) depart when full. Prey Veng and Kompong Cham are also connected by minibus (5000r, 1½ hours) and share taxi (8000r).

NEAK LUONG

អ្នកលើង

☎ 043 / pop 22,000

Neak Luong is the point at which travellers speeding between Phnom Penh and the Vietnamese border have to slow to a stop to cross the mighty Mekong River. The car ferry chugs back and forth giving kids ample time to try to sell you strange-looking insects and other unidentifiable food on sticks. Coming from Vietnam, it is an overwhelming welcome to Cambodia. The first bridge to span the Mekong's girth in Cambodia is in Kompong Cham. Construction on a second at Neak Luong has long been discussed but work is yet to begin.

The most straightforward way to get here is to take an air-con bus (4500r, hourly) from Psar Thmei in Phnom Penh and pay the foot-passenger toll (100r) to cross the Mekong on the ferry. From Neak Luong, it is possible to continue east to Svay Rieng (64km), north to Prey Veng (30km) or south to Kaam Samnor (45km), gateway to Vietnam and the Mekong Delta. For more on the route between Phnom Penh and Chau Doc, see p328.

BA PHNOM

ប្រាំភ្នំ

Ba Phnom is one of the earliest religious and cultural sites in Cambodia, dating back to the 5th century AD and the time of the mysterious Funan. Some scholars consider it the birthplace of the Cambodian nation, in the same way that Phnom Kulen is revered as the first capital of Angkor. It remained an important place of pilgrimage for kings of the subsequent empires of Chenla and Angkor and continued to be a place of spiritual significance into the 19th century, but its past conceals a darker side: according to French records, human sacrifices were carried out here and were only finally stamped out in 1872.

Today there is little left to see considering the site's extensive history. At the eastern extremity of the small group of hills lie the kitsch ruins of an 11th-century temple known as **Preah Vihear Chann**. The temple was evidently destroyed by the ravages of time, but has been rebuilt by the local monastery using a few original blocks and a whole lot of cement, all set under a corrugated roof.

There is a modern **wat** at the base of the hill and a series of concrete steps lead up the slope to some small **pagodas** on the summit. It is only really worth the detour for those who have a keen interest in early Cambodian history; for the casual visitor there is unfortunately little to see.

To get to Ba Phnom from Phnom Penh, head east on NH1 and turn north at Kompong Suong, about 9km east of Neak Luong. Follow

---

THE BOMBING OF NEAK LUONG

Neak Luong is depicted in the opening sequences of *The Killing Fields* (1984), the definitive film about the civil war and genocide. In August 1973, American B-52s mistakenly razed the town to the ground in an attempt to halt a Khmer Rouge advance on Phnom Penh. The intensive bombardment killed 137 civilians and wounded 268. The US government tried to cover it up by keeping the media out, but Sydney Schanberg, played by Sam Waterstone in the film, managed to travel to the city by river and publicise the true scale of the tragedy. The US ambassador offered compensation of US$100 per family and the navigator of the B-52 was fined US$700, which pretty much summed up the American attitude to the price of Cambodian lives in this most miserable of sideshows.

this dirt road for 3km before turning right and bearing east along the base of the hill. After another 7km, turn left under a wat-style arch and head to the bottom of the hill. Those without wheels can engage the services of a *moto* in Neak Luong for about US$5 round trip.

KOMPONG CHAM PROVINCE

ខេត្តកំពង់ចាម

Kompong Cham draws a growing number of visitors thanks to its role as a gateway to the northeast. Attractions include several pre-Angkorian and Angkorian temples, as well as some pleasant riverbank rides for cyclists or motorbikers. The provincial capital offers an accessible slice of the real Cambodia and the surrounding countryside is very pretty. Getting about has became a lot easier thanks to the excellent condition of NH7 all the way to Kratie. Beyond the main roads, travel is not too bad, as the large population has helped to prioritise secondary road improvements.

The most heavily populated province in Cambodia, Kompong Cham has also supplied a steady stream of Cambodia's current political heavyweights including Prime Minister Hun Sen and Senate Head Chea Sim. Most Kompong Cham residents enjoy quieter lives, living off the land or fishing along the Mekong River. Rubber was the major prewar industry and there are huge plantations stretching eastwards from the Mekong. Some of Cambodia's finest silk is also produced in this province and most of the country's *kramas* (scarves) originate here.

KOMPONG CHAM

កំពង់ចាម

☎ 042 / pop 46,000

Kompong Cham is a gateway to the real Cambodia, a land of picturesque villages, pretty wats and fishing communities. More a quiet town than a bustling city, it is a peaceful provincial capital spread along the banks of the Mekong. It was an important trading post during the French period, the legacy evident as you wander through the streets of chastened yet classic buildings.

Long considered Cambodia's third city after Phnom Penh and Battambang, lately Kompong Cham has been somewhat left in the dust by the fast-growing tourist towns of Siem Reap and Sihanoukville. Kompong Cham remains an important travel hub and acts as the gateway to eastern and northeastern Cambodia. This role has grown thanks to the first bridge to span the Mekong's width in Cambodia, dramatically cutting journey times to popular destinations like Kratie and Mondulkiri.

Orientation

Kompong Cham may be one of Cambodia's larger cities, but that doesn't make it very big. Navigating on foot is straightforward. Arriving from Phnom Penh, all roads east end up at the Mekong, near many of the guesthouses and hotels. The market is a few blocks west of the river.

Information

Mr Vannat is an experienced local guide, and if you sip an evening drink overlooking the Mekong, he'll likely find you before long. He speaks English and French and his children are now continuing the family trade.

KRAMA CHAMELEON

The colourful checked scarf known as the *krama* is almost universally worn by rural Khmers and is still pretty popular in the cities. The scarves are made from cotton or silk and the most famous silk *kramas* come from Kompong Cham and Takeo Provinces.

Kramas have a multitude of uses. They are primarily used to protect Cambodians from the sun, the dust and the wind, and it is for this reason many tourists end up investing in one during a visit. However, they are also slung around the waist as mini-sarongs, used as towels for drying the body, knotted at the neck as decorations, tied across the shoulders as baby carries, placed upon chairs or beds as pillow covers, used to tow broken-down motorbikes and stuffed inside motorbike tyres in the advent of remote punctures – the list is endless.

Kramas are sold in markets throughout Cambodia and are an essential purchase for travellers using pick-up trucks or taking boat services. They have become very much a symbol of Cambodia and for many Khmers, wearing one is an affirmation of their identity.

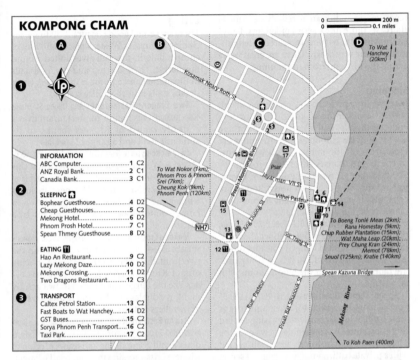

KOMPONG CHAM

ABC Computer (11 Ang Duong St; per hr US$1) Internet
access.

ANZ Royal Bank (Preah Monivong Blvd) International
banking in Kompong Cham (the times they are a changin'),
plus a working ATM.

Canadia Bank (Preah Monivong Blvd) Can handle cash
and travellers cheques in various currencies, Visa and
MasterCard cash advances and MoneyGram transfers.

Sights
WAT NOKOR
វត្តនគរ

The original fusion temple, **Wat Nokor** (entry
US$2) is a modern Theravada Buddhist pagoda
squeezed into the walls of an 11th-century
Mahayana Buddhist shrine of sandstone
and laterite. It is a kitsch kind of place and
many of the older building's archways have
been incorporated into the new building as
shrines for worship. On weekdays there are
only a few monks in the complex and it is
peaceful to wander among the many alcoves
and their hidden shrines. There is also a large
reclining Buddha.

To get here, head out of town on the road
to Phnom Penh, and take the left fork at the

large roundabout about 1km from town. The
temple is at the end of this pretty dirt road.

KOH PAEN
កោះប៉ែន

Koh Paen is a rural island in the Mekong River,
connected to the southern reaches of Kompong
Cham town by an elaborate bamboo bridge
in the dry season or a local ferry in the wet
season. The bamboo bridge is an attraction
in itself, totally built by hand each year and
looking like it is made of matchsticks from afar.
There are plenty of local wats on the island and
locals make a living fishing, as well as growing
tobacco and sesame. During the dry season,
several sandbars, the closest thing to a beach
in this part of Cambodia, appear around the
island. The best way to get about the island is
by bicycle, which is possible to arrange through
some of the budget guesthouses in town.

OLD FRENCH LIGHTHOUSE
បមទន្លេបិទ

Looming over the Mekong River opposite
town is an old French lighthouse. For years it
was an abandoned shell, but has recently been

renovated, including an incredibly steep metal staircase, more like a series of ladders. Don't attempt the climb if you are scared of heights, as it is a long way down. There are great views across the Mekong from the summit.

Sleeping

Many visitors prefer to stay on the riverfront, with a view over the Mekong. There are several guesthouses and a hotel here, but there is a lot of noise as soon as the sun comes up. One street off the market has a whole row of cheap guesthouses advertising rooms for 5000r, although most 'guests' seem to pay by the hour, so it could get noisy. Rooms are cells, but if money's too tight to mention, consider taking one for a night.

Bophea Guesthouse (☎ 012 796803; Vithei Pasteur; r US$2-4) It's bare bones, but then what do you expect for this kind of budget? Cheaper rooms have a share bathroom, so it is worth splashing that extra cash for the bigger rooms with an ensuite.

Spean Thmey Guesthouse (☎ 012 831329; 95 Preah Bat Sihanouk St; s/tw US$4/5) The name means 'new bridge', so it's hardly surprising to find this guesthouse has sweeping views over the Mekong bridge. The rooms are all fan-cooled with a private bathroom. The restaurant serves a reasonable range of food, including pizzas.

Mekong Hotel (☎ 941536; Preah Bat Sihanouk St; r US$6-12; ✷) It's hard to beat this hotel, with a prime riverfront location and good value rooms, although they are beginning to age. All rooms include satellite TV, but 10 bucks will guarantee air-con and hot water. Ask for a Mekong view. The corridors are so vast, they are begging for a fusball football tournament.

Phnom Prosh Hotel (☎ 941444; Kosamak Neary Roth St; r US$6-12; ✷) A large hotel in the centre of town, this place is owned by a nephew of Samdech Hun Sen, Cambodia's prime minister, so security should be one less thing to worry about. The rooms include all the trimmings such as satellite TV, fridge and hot water.

Rana Homestay (☎ 012 686240; www.rana-cambodia .blogspot.com; one night US$16, two nights or more US$14 per night) Located in the countryside beyond Kompong Cham, this homestay offers an insight into life in rural Cambodia. The price includes all meals and tours of the local area. They only have capacity for five guests, so book ahead.

Eating

There are several good restaurants in town, including a couple of Western places, and a lot of cheaper hole-in-the-wall dives dotted around the market. There are stop-and-dip food stalls in the market and a number of *tukalok* (fruit shake) stalls near the police station.

Two Dragons Restaurant (Ang Duong St; mains 4000-10,000r) This family-run restaurant draws a steady crowd of Khmers thanks to its authentic food and a range of specials.

Lazy Mekong Daze (Preah Bat Sihanouk St; mains 4000-12,000r) A Western spot on the riverfront, this is – as the name suggests – a relaxing place to while away some time. The menu includes Khmer and Thai classics, plus a selection of home-comfort food. Plus beer – it's run by a Brit after all.

Mekong Crossing (☎ 012 427432; Preah Bat Sihanouk St; mains US$2-4) Now on a prime corner on the riverfront, this old favourite serves an enticing mix of Khmer curries and Western favourites like big burgers and tasty sandwiches. By night, it doubles as a bar and draws a trickle of travellers in town.

Hao An Restaurant (☎ 941234; Preah Monivong Blvd; mains 4000-20,000r) The original Kompong Cham diner is still going strong and draws a legion of Khmers criss-crossing the country. The menu includes a mix of Khmer and Chinese favourites and service is slick, including beer girls who plug their brands at any time of day.

The advent of the bridge over the Mekong has brought a whole rash of restaurants on stilts to the other side of the river. Many are mini versions of those huge restaurants across the Chruoy Changvar Bridge in Phnom Penh. Some have live bands, others go for karaoke and all have a good range of Khmer favourites. Try the **Boeng Tonlé Meas** (NH7; US$2-5), regarded by many locals as the best of the bunch.

In the early evening, locals gather on the waterfront outside the Mekong Hotel, where a number of stalls sell cheap drinks and cold beers.

Getting There & Away

Kompong Cham is 120km northeast of the capital and the road is in good shape. Phnom Penh Sorya Transport (Sorya; p110) and GST (p110) offer air-con buses between Kompong Cham and the capital (10,000r, two hours, hourly). Overcrowded minibuses also do the run (8000r), as do super-fast share taxis (12,000r).

INCY WINCY SPIDER

Locals in the small Cambodian town of Skuon (otherwise known affectionately as Spiderville) eat eight-legged furry friends for breakfast, lunch and dinner. Most tourists travelling between Siem Reap and Phnom Penh pass through Skuon without ever realising they have been there. This is hardly surprising, as it has nothing much to attract visitors, but it is the centre of one of Cambodia's more exotic culinary delights – the deep-fried spider.

Buses usually make a bathroom stop in Spiderville, so take a careful look at the eight-legged goodies the food sellers are offering. The creatures, decidedly dead, are piled high on platters, but don't get too complacent as there are usually live samples lurking nearby.

The spiders are hunted in holes in the hills to the north of Skuon and are quite an interesting dining experience. They are best treated like a crab and eaten by cracking the body open and pulling the legs off one by one, bringing the juiciest flesh out with them – a cathartic experience indeed for arachnophobes. They taste a bit like…mmm chicken. Alternatively, for a memorable photo, just bite the thing in half and hope for the best. Watch out for the abdomen, which seems to be filled with some pretty nasty-tasting brown sludge, which could be anything from eggs to excrement; spider truffles, perhaps?

No-one seems to know exactly how this micro-industry developed around Skuon, although some have suggested that the population may have developed a taste for these creatures during the years of Khmer Rouge rule, when food was in short supply.

NH7 to Kratie and Stung Treng is in great shape. Sorya has bus services from Phnom Penh to Memot and Kratie that pick up punters in Kompong Cham if space allows, as does Hua Lian. The buses to Kratie (17,000r, three hours) pass through around 10am.

There are no longer any passenger boat services running on the Mekong, but it may be possible to arrange passage on a cargo boat. However, given the speed at which they travel and the number of stops they make, this isn't the smoothest way to get about.

Motorbikers travelling north to Kratie should consider following the Mekong route for a slice of rural river life. See p287 for more details.

Getting Around

Most *moto* journeys around town are only 1000r or so; a little more at night. Bicycle or motorcycle rental can be arranged through negotiations with staff at your guesthouse or hotel.

AROUND KOMPONG CHAM
Phnom Pros & Phnom Srei
ភ្នំប្រុសភ្នំស្រី

'Man hill' and 'Woman Hill' are the subjects of local legends with many variations, one of which describes a child taken away at infancy only to return a powerful man who falls in love with his own mother. Disbelieving her protestations, he demanded her hand in marriage.

Desperate to avoid this disaster, the mother cunningly devised a deal; a competition between her team of women and his team of men to build the highest hill by dawn. If the women won, she would not give her hand. As they toiled into the night, the women built a fire with the flames reaching high into the sky. The men, mistaking this for sunrise, lay down their tools and the impending marriage was foiled. Locals love to relay this tale, each adding their own herbs and spices as the story unfolds.

A short distance from here lies **Cheung Kok** village, home to a local ecotourism initiative aimed at introducing visitors to rural life in Kompong Cham. Run by the NGO **Amica** (www .amica-cambodge.org, in French), villagers can teach visitors about harvesting rice, sugar palm and other crops. There is also a small shop in the village selling local handicraft products.

Phnom Srei has good views of the countryside during the wet season and a very strokeable Nandin (sacred bull that was Shiva's mount) statue. Phnom Pros is a good place for a cold drink, among the inquisitive monkeys that populate the trees. The hills are about 7km out of town on the road to Phnom Penh and can be reached by *moto* for about US$4 (round trip) depending on wait time.

Wat Maha Leap
វត្តមហាលាភ

Wat Maha Leap is one of the most sacred temples in Cambodia, as it is one of the last remaining wooden pagodas left in the country. More than a century old, it was only spared devastation by the Khmer Rouge because they converted it into a hospital. Many of the Khmers who were put to work in the surrounding fields perished here; 500 bodies were thrown into graves on site, now camouflaged by a tranquil garden.

The pagoda itself is beautiful. The wide columns supporting the structure are complete tree trunks, resplendent in gilded patterns and royal blue. The Khmer Rouge painted over the designs to match their austere philosophies, but the monks have since stripped it back to its original glory. Up above, the ceiling is adorned with colourful frescos depicting scenes of Buddha and his teachings.

It is necessary to remove your shoes to enter a temple, but this one is carpeted in thick pigeon poop. So unless you want a special souvenir, it is advisable to wear some old socks.

Wat Maha Leap is pretty difficult to find without a guide or some knowledge of Khmer, as there are lots of small turns along the way. It is about 20km from Kompong Cham on the other side of the Mekong River.

Prey Chung Kran Weaving Village
ភូមិប្រែកចង្រ្កាន

Kompong Cham is famous for its high-quality silk. The tiny village of Prey Chung Kran is set on the banks of the river and nearly every household has a weaving loom. Under the cool shade provided by their stilted homes, they work deftly to produce *kramas* of fashion and tradition. The most interesting thing to watch is the dyeing process as the typical diamond and dot tessellations are formed at this stage. Prey Chung Kran is about 4km from Wat Maha Leap.

Wat Hanchey
វត្តហាន់ជ័យ

Wat Hanchey is a hilltop pagoda that was an important centre of worship during the Chenla period, and today offers some of the best Mekong views in Cambodia. As well as a large, contemporary wat, there is a brick sanctuary dating from the 8th century and the foundations of several others. During the time of the Chenla empire, this may have been an important transit stop on journeys between the ancient cities of Thala Boravit (near Stung Treng to the north) and Angkor Borei (near Takeo to the south), and Sambor

Prei Kuk (near Kompong Thom to the west) and Banteay Prei Nokor (near Memot to the east).

The simplest way to get to Wat Hanchey is to charter an outboard from near the Mekong Hotel (p282) in Kompong Cham. Boats with a 15HP engine cost around 60,000r, while faster boats with a 40HP engine are 80,000r.

Local expats like to cycle up here in the dry season through the pretty riverbank villages. If you can get your hands on a decent bicycle, this could be a good way to pass a day.

Rubber Plantations
ចំការកៅស៊ូ

Kompong Cham was the heartland of the Cambodian rubber industry and rubber plantations still stretch across the province. Many of them are back in business and some of the largest plantations can be visited. Using an extended scraping instrument, they graze the trunks until the sap appears, dripping into the open coconut shells on the ground. In 1921, it was discovered that rich soils from Chup Hill were ideal for the cultivation of rubber and **Chup Rubber Plantation**, about 15km east of Kompong Cham, remains the most popular spot to visit.

MEMOT
មេមត់

☎ 042 / pop 35,000

Pronounced more like 'may-*moot'*, this is a surprisingly large town set amid the rubber plantations of eastern Kompong Cham Province. Very few visitors stop here as there is little of interest unless you happen to work for Michelin, but plenty pass through on the way to Mondulkiri.

There is one small attraction in town for those with a keen interest in prehistory, namely the **Memot Centre of Archaeology** (NH7; admission free; ☷ 8-11am & 2-5pm). It houses a small exhibition on Iron Age circular earthwork villages, many of which have been discovered in the Memot region. It's only really for the initiated, but breaks the long overland journey east if you have your own transport. The gate may look closed, but the guardians can usually let you in.

There is no real need to stay here, with the new and improved road connections, but those that get stuck should hit the **Reaksmey Angkor Chum Guesthouse** (☎ 012 317272; NH7; r US$4-10; ☒), a smart place with cheap, clean fan rooms with TV, optional air-con and a central location.

The most reliable restaurant in town is the **Soy Try Restaurant** (☎ 012 708095; mains 3000-8000r), with an inexpensive range of Khmer standards.

Buses connect Memot with Kompong Cham (7000r, 1½ hours, several a day), but faster and more frequent are share taxis (10,000r). Heading on to Snuol, where you can connect to Mondulkiri, a seat in a share taxi should cost about 6000r.

KRATIE PROVINCE
ខេត្តក្រចេះ៖

A pretty province spanning the Mekong, much of Kratie's population makes its living from the mother river's waters. Beyond the river it's a remote and wild land that sees few outsiders. Most visitors are drawn to the rare freshwater Irrawaddy dolphins found 15km north of the provincial capital. The town of Kratie is a little charmer and makes a good base from which to explore the surrounding countryside.

This was one of the first areas to fall to Khmer Rouge control in the civil war, although for several years it was in fact the Vietnamese communists who were running the show. It was also one of the first provincial capitals to fall to the liberating Vietnamese forces in the overthrow of the Khmer Rouge on 30 December 1978.

In the past, getting about was easier by boat than by road, as most roads in the province were pretty nasty. However, Kratie is now connected by NH7 to Kompong Cham and Phnom Penh to the south and Stung Treng and the Lao border to the north, making it a major cultural crossroads.

KRATIE
ក្រចេះ៖

☎ 072 / pop 79,000

Kratie is a thriving travel hub and the natural place to break the journey when travelling overland between Phnom Penh and Champasak in southern Laos. It is *the* place in the country to see the rare Irrawaddy dolphins, which live in the Mekong River in ever-diminishing numbers. A lively riverside town, Kratie (pronounced kra-*cheh*) has an expansive riverfront and some of the best Mekong sunsets in Cambodia. There is

a rich legacy of French-era architecture, as it was spared the war-time bombing that destroyed so many other provincial centres. It was one of the first towns to be 'liberated' by the Khmer Rouge (actually it was the North Vietnamese, but the Khmer Rouge later took the credit) in the summer of 1970.

Information

Telephone services are available at kiosks around the market, plus there are several internet shops in the vicinity of the market.

Acleda Bank (☎ 971707; ✆ 7.30am-4pm Mon-Fri) can change cash and travellers cheques (US dollars and euros) and has relocated to a swish new branch on Rue Preah Sihanouk.

There is a **tourist office** (✆ 8-11.30am & 2-5pm) by the river in the south of town, but don't count on the (theoretical) opening hours!

For general information on getting around the province, the recommended budget guesthouses are pretty switched on with a wealth of information available.

Sights & Activities

The main activity that draws visitors to Kratie is the chance to spot the elusive Irrawaddy river dolphin (p288).

Lying just across the water from Kratie is the island of **Koh Trong**, an almighty sandbar in the middle of the river. Cross here by boat with a bicycle in tow and enjoy a slice of rural island life. This could be the Don Khong of Cambodia in years to come and attractions include an **old stupa** and a small **floating village**, as well as the chance to encounter one of the rare **Mekong mud turtles** who inhabit the western shore. Catch the little ferry from the port (500r) or charter a local boat (US$2) to get here.

Wat Roka Kandal (www.cambodian-craft.com; ✆ 8am-5pm) is a beautiful little temple dating from the early 19th century, one of the oldest in the region. The roof is in the classic Khmer style and the interior has been turned into a showroom for local wicker handicrafts. Baskets, bags, slippers and more are available at giveaway prices, all to help local women in the province. The temple is about 2km south of Kratie on the road to Chhlong.

It is also possible to arrange a visit to the handicraft village of **Chheu Tiel Ploch Krom** near Chhlong, an almost medieval-looking cluster of wooden houses on the banks of the Mekong.

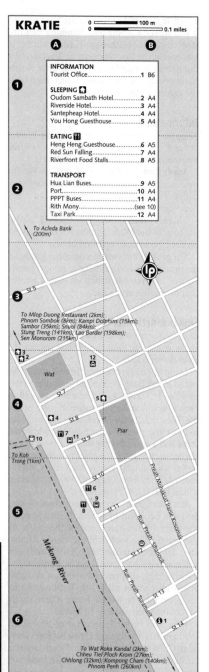

KRATIE

0 — 100 m
0 — 0.1 miles

INFORMATION
Tourist Office.....................1 B6

SLEEPING
Oudom Sambath Hotel.............2 A4
Riverside Hotel....................3 A4
Santepheap Hotel..................4 A4
You Hong Guesthouse.............5 A4

EATING
Heng Heng Guesthouse............6 A5
Red Sun Falling....................7 A4
Riverfront Food Stalls.............8 A5

TRANSPORT
Hua Lian Buses....................9 A5
Port..............................10 A4
PPPT Buses.......................11 A4
Rith Mony......................(see 10)
Taxi Park.........................12 A4

To Acleda Bank
(200m)

St 5

To Mlop Duong Restaurant (2km);
Phnom Sombok (8km); Kampi Dolphins (15km);
Sambor (35km); Snuol (84km);
Stung Treng (141km); Lao Border (198km);
Sen Monorom (215km)

Wat

St 7

St 8

To Koh
Trong (1km)

Psar

St 9

St 10

St 11

Mekong River

St 12

Preah Monivong/Preah Kossamak

Rue Preah Sihanouk

St 13

Rue Preah Suramarit

St 14

To Wat Roka Kandal (2km);
Chheu Tiel; Ploch Krom (27km);
Chhlong (32km); Kompong Cham (140km);
Phnom Penh (260km)

Sleeping

The cheapest places to stay in Kratie are the guesthouses clustered around the market.

You Hong Guesthouse (☎ 012957003; youhong_kratie@ yahoo.com; 91 St 8; r US$3-5; 🖳) A great little guesthouse overlooking the bustling market, try and bag a room at the front with a view. Higher priced rooms include a TV and triples are just US$5. Downstairs is a lively little restaurant and bar, plastered wall-to-wall with travel info. It also has a reliable internet connection (per hr US$1).

Riverside Hotel (☎ 012 779255; Rue Preah Sumarit; r US$5-12; 🗮) A new riverfront property, the rooms here are enticing thanks to a real bath, hot water and cable TV. It was expanding during our visit, so looks set for bigger things.

Oudom Sambath Hotel (☎ 971502, fax 971503; 439 Rue Preah Sumarit; r US$5-15; 🗮) Another smart hotel on the riverfront, this hotel has large rooms with air-con, hot water and cable TV for those with the cash. There is a lively restaurant downstairs for those wanting an early breakfast.

Santepheap Hotel (☎ 971537; santepheaphotel@ yahoo.com; Rue Preah Sumarit; r US$5-20; 🗮) The don of hotels in Kratie, this large place has large fan rooms at the back for just US$5 with TV and bathroom. Air-con rooms come in various shapes and sizes, some with a plush wood trim and hot water. Popular with tour groups.

Wat Roka Kandal Bungalows (☎ 971729; Rue Preah Sumarit; r US$8-15; 🗮) And now for something completely different... Set on the banks of the Mekong, these wooden bungalows offer the perfect slice of river life. Hot water is a pleasant surprise and each has a balcony to soak up the sunset. The only drawback may be finding someone with a key.

There is also a high-end boutique hotel in Chhlong, 32km south of Kratie. See opposite for details.

Eating & Drinking

Cheap dining is available on the riverfront during the evening when food stalls set up shop overlooking the Mekong, and this area doubles up as a cheap spot for a sunset drink. By day, the *psar* (market) has the usual range of cheap food stalls hawking Cambodian, Chinese and Vietnamese dishes for next to nothing, including bargain breakfasts of *bobor* (rice porridge).

Mlop Duong Restaurant (NH7; mains US$1-3) It's a bit out of the way for riverfront aficionados, but if you have bolted down from the Lao border, this may be your first chance for a Khmer-style night out, complete with a local band and *rom vong,* the closest thing to line dancing in Cambodia.

Red Sun Falling (Rue Preah Sumarit; mains US$1-4) One of the liveliest little spots in town, this place kicks off when the owner puts on his party hat to play. A relaxed ambience, subtle tunes and a small bookshop by day, the kitchen turns out a solid selection of Asian and Western meals, including moist homemade brownies. By night, it's a bar and draws the drinkers.

Several guesthouses and hotels also have good restaurants attached. One of the most popular local restaurants is attached to the **Heng Heng Guesthouse** (Rue Preah Sumarit; meals US$1-3), with all the leading luminaries from the world of Cambodian and Chinese cooking.

Getting There & Away

NH7 puts Kratie 348km northeast of Phnom Penh and 141km south of Stung Treng. The road is surfaced all the way making the journeys straightforward. **SPPT** (☎ 092 181806) has buses to Phnom Penh (US$5, five hours) at 7.15am and 9am; and one to Stung Treng (18,000r, two hours) at 1.30pm. **Hua Lian** (☎ 012 535387) has buses to Phnom Penh (US$4, five hours) at 7.15/9/10.45am; the Lao border at Voen Kham (US$10, four hours) at 1.30pm; Sen Monorom (US$10, five hours) at 9am; and Banlung (US$12, six hours) at 12.30pm. **Rith Mony** (☎ 012 991663) has buses to Phnom Penh (US$5, five hours) at 7.30am and 9.30am; and one to Stung Treng (18,000r, two hours) at 1.30pm.

More frequent and faster are share taxis that cost about US$4 per place to Kompong Cham and US$7 to Phnom Penh. Most taxis take the dirt road south through Chhlong to Suong district to save money on petrol and that means just four hours to the capital.

For motorbikers, there is a more scenic dry-season route that follows the Mekong River. Take the river road north out of Kompong Cham as far as Stung Trang (pronounced Trong) district and cross the Mekong on a small ferry before continuing up the east bank of the Mekong through Chhlong to Kratie. This is a very beautiful ride through small rural villages and takes about four hours or so on a trail bike.

For the lowdown on getting from Kratie to Mondulkiri Province, check out p302.

Getting Around

A *moto* ride around Kratie town is the usual 1000r or so depending how far into the suburbs you venture. Most of the guesthouses and hotels can arrange motorbikes (with driver US$6 to US$10) and should also be able to set visitors up with a bicycle.

AROUND KRATIE
Phnom Sombok
ភ្នំសំបុក

Phnom Sombok is a small hill with an active wat, located on the road from Kratie to Kampi. The hill offers the best views across the Mekong on this stretch of the river and a visit here can easily be combined with a trip to see the dolphins for an extra dollar or so.

Sambor
សម្បូរណ៍

Sambor was the site of a thriving pre-Angkorian city during the time of Sambor Prei Kuk and the Chenla empire. Not a stone remains in the modern town of Sambor, which is locally famous for having the largest **wat** in Cambodia, complete with 108 columns. Known locally as Wat Moi Roi (Wat Sorsor Moi Roi; 100 Columns Temple), it was constructed on the site of a 19th-century wooden temple, a few pillars of which are still located at the back of the compound. This temple is a minor place of pilgrimage for residents of Kratie Province. To get to Sambor, follow the Kampi road north to Sandan, before veering left along a reasonable 10km stretch of road – it's about 35km in total.

CHHLONG
ឆ្លូង

Chhlong is a thriving riverside port with a wealth of beautiful old French buildings. French tourists sometimes make a diversion, but other visitors are few and far between. During the civil war, Chhlong somehow held out against the communists until 1975, probably a useful way for the Khmer Rouge to acquire arms from corrupt government forces.

Behind the market on the riverfront road are several grand old buildings from the 1920s, any of which would be prime real estate in Phnom Penh. Further north is the **house of a hundred pillars**, a huge old wooden Khmer residence that is one of the best preserved in the region.

EASTERN CAMBODIA

DOLPHIN-WATCHING AROUND KRATIE

The freshwater Irrawaddy dolphin *(trey pisaut)* is an endangered species throughout Asia, with shrinking numbers inhabiting stretches of the Mekong in Cambodia and Laos, and isolated pockets in Bangladesh and Myanmar. The dark blue to grey cetaceans grow to 2.75m long and are recognisable by their bulging foreheads and small dorsal fins. They can live in fresh or salt water, although they are seldom seen in the sea. For more on this rare creature, see the **Mekong Dolphin Conservation Project** (MDCP; www.mekongdolphin.org).

Before the civil war, locals say, Cambodia was home to as many as 1000 dolphins. However, during the Pol Pot regime, many were hunted for their oils and their numbers have plummeted.

Locals and experts alike believe there may be as few as 75 Irrawaddy dolphins left in the Mekong between Kratie and the Lao border near Don Khone. It is possible to see them at Kampi, about 15km north of Kratie, on the road to Sambor. A *moto* for the 30km round trip should be around US$4 depending on how long the driver has to wait.

There are local motorboats available to shuttle visitors out to the middle of the river to view the dolphins at close quarters. It costs US$3/2.50/2 per person for one/two/three people in the dry season; US$5/4/3 in the wet season, fixed price. Encourage the boat driver to use the engine as little as possible once near the dolphins, as the noise is sure to disturb them. It is also possible to see them at O Svay village (p290) in Stung Treng province, near the Dom Kralor border with Laos.

The old governor's residence has been given an ambitious renovation and is now **Le Relais de Chhlong** (☎ 012 501742; www.nicimex.com; r US$80-100; ✖ ⌘), an atmospheric boutique hotel with just six rooms. Set on the riverfront, facilities include an inviting swimming pool and a private restaurant. Rooms have high ceilings and are thoughtfully decorated, although the prices are pretty steep for the provinces.

Chhlong is easy enough to access by motorbike or car from Kratie or can make a sensible stop on the long road journey from Phnom Penh.

SNUOL
ស្នួល

☎ 072 / pop 19,000

This was a sorry little town before the coming of the road. It still feels a little like it has fallen off the map, but the new road provides a quick way out. A lot of folk end up having at least one meal here, as it is common to have to change vehicles when journeying between Mondulkiri Province and towns on the Mekong. It is easy enough to get a feed around the *psar* (market) where there are several local restaurants.

Snuol is approximately 125km southwest of Mondulkiri Province and 135km east of Kompong Cham. It is only about 15km north of the Vietnamese border and this remote crossing is now open to foreigners (see p331). Several pick-ups take on the road to

Sen Monorom (inside/on the back US$7/4, four hours). Buses and taxis connect Snuol with Kompong Cham (1½ hours) and Kratie (one hour).

STUNG TRENG PROVINCE
ខេត្តស្ទឹងត្រែង

Poor old Stung Treng is the neglected middle child, sandwiched between the luminary siblings of Ratanakiri Province and Champasak in southern Laos. While tourism is yet to take off, it is emerging as a major commercial crossroads for trade between Cambodia, Laos, Thailand and Vietnam. New roads have now plugged it into the rest of the country, but much of Stung Treng's traffic travels by water, as several major rivers traverse the province, including Tonlé Kong, Tonlé San, Tonlé Srepok and, of course, the Mekong.

Visitor attractions are limited for now, but as more travellers hit the overland route between Laos and Cambodia, it is possible that boat trips up the Mekong's tributaries, to places like Siem Pang, will be a different way to see some remote areas. Stung Treng is home to several minority groups and the western chunk of the massive Virachay National Park, accessible from Siem Pang – two factors that suggest there is definitely some tourism potential as the province's infrastructure develops. It is also taking off as an alternative location to view the rare Irrawaddy dolphins in the village of O Svay, near the Lao border.

STUNG TRENG
ស្ទឹងត្រែង
☎ 074 / pop 24,500

While new roads have helped to put Stung Treng back on the map, they have also made it easier to pass through and many travellers are no longer overnighting here. It is located on the banks of Tonlé San, which flows into the mighty Mekong on the western outskirts of the city. Some locals call Tonlé San the 'Tonlé Kong' or 'Tonlé Sekong', as these two rivers merge 10km east of town. There is now a major new bridge across the San, which is a key link in the new road between Kratie and the Lao border.

Information

Acleda Bank (☎ 973684), near the *psar* (market), can change travellers cheques and arrange Western Union money transfers. Stung Treng might also be the last chance to get rid of any excess Lao kip.

For telephone services, try the mobile phone kiosks sprinkled around the market. Internet access is available in shops around the *psar* at US$2 per hour.

Assuming you have a Lao visa in hand, there is no longer any need to arrange any paperwork to exit Cambodia into Laos. Anyone who tries to tell you otherwise is fishing for money.

There is a new **tourist office** (☎ 973967) located near the new bridge, not particularly convenient for the centre of town. Fellow travellers and local guesthouses are a more useful source of information.

Sights & Activities
THALA BORAVIT
ថ្លាបុរវិត

Thala Boravit was an important Chenla-period trading town on the river route connecting the ancient city of Champasak and the sacred temple of Wat Phu with the southern reaches of the Chenla empire, including the ancient cities of Sambor Prei Kuk (Isanapura) and Angkor Borei. For all its past glories, there is very little to see today. It is hardly worth the effort for the casual visitor, but temple

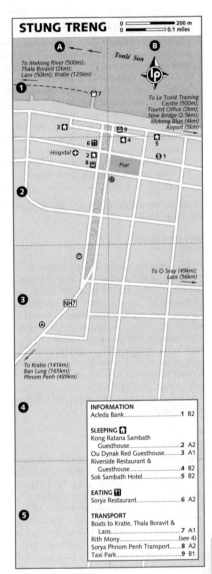

STUNG TRENG

INFORMATION	
Acleda Bank	1 B2

SLEEPING	
Kong Ratana Sambath Guesthouse	2 A2
Ou Dynak Red Guesthouse	3 A1
Riverside Restaurant & Guesthouse	4 B2
Sok Sambath Hotel	5 B2

EATING	
Sorya Restaurant	6 A2

TRANSPORT	
Boats to Kratie, Thala Boravit & Laos	7 A1
Rith Mony	(see 4)
Sorya Phnom Penh Transport	8 A2
Taxi Park	9 B1

fiends may feel the urge to tick it off. Thala Boravit is on the west bank of the Mekong River and irregular boats cross from Stung Treng throughout the day. It should be easy enough to wait for locals to fill up the regular boats (1000r), rather than charter an outboard (US$5 or so). It is from here that the jungle road to Kompong Thom or Tbeng Meanchey

---

MEKONG DISCOVERY TRAIL

Efforts are underway to open up the Mekong River for community-based tourism, particularly the wild and beautiful stretches in Stung Treng and Kratie Provinces. The **Mekong Discovery Trail** (www.mekongdiscoverytrail.com) is a new initiative to get visitors to spend more time visiting villages and learning about the local lifestyle in communities along the river between Voen Kham and Kratie. The project includes homestays in O Svay (below) and dolphin vists nearby, plus plans for homestays and pagoda-stays along the length of the trail. There are also plans for eco-friendly activities such as mountain biking on traditional islands like Koh Trong, opposite Kratie town, and kayaking pretty stretches of river renowned for their birdlife. The project is still in its infancy, but deserves support, as it intends to offer fishing communities an alternative income in order to protect the Irawaddy dolphin and other rare species on this stretch of river.

To stay up-to-date with the latest developments on the trail, including more homestays and kayaking options, check out the website.

---

starts via the village of Chaeb. See opposite for more details.

MEKONG BLUE
មេកុងប្ល៊ូ

A silk-weaving centre on the outskirts of Stung Treng, **Mekong Blue** (☎ 973977; www.mekong blue.com; ☼ 7.30-11.30am & 1.30-5pm Mon-Sat) is part of the Stung Treng Women's Development Centre. Mekong Blue specialises in exquisite silk products for sale and export. It is possible to see the dyers and weavers in action at this centre, most of whom come from vulnerable or impoverished backgrounds. There is a small showroom on site with a selection of silk on sale, plus a café. The centre is located about 4km east of the centre and moto drivers know the place.

O SVAY
អូរស្វាយ

This small village near the border with Laos is emerging as an alternative place to view the rare freshwater dolphins of the Mekong. As politics muddies the waters on the Lao side of the border, with the Cambodian and Lao authorities arguing over who has the right to profit from the dolphins, O Svay is stepping forward. A friendly village that also offers the chance for a homestay with a local family, it is possible to view the dolphins for just US$1 here. Boat rental is also available for about US$5 per hour, although for now the boats have no covers so bring a hat or scarf. O Svay is now part of the Mekong Discovery Trail (above) and it is possible to arrange a homestay here. Contact the **Culture & Environment Preservation Association** (☎ 973858, 011 724250; www.cepa-cambodia.org) for details.

Sleeping
Riverside Guesthouse (☎ 012 439454; r US$3-4; 🖵) Overlooking the riverfront area, this is a popular crossroads for travellers heading north and south, thanks to the lively little restaurant (US$1 to US$3) downstairs and cheap rooms. Rooms are pretty basic, but so are the prices. This place is also a reliable source of travel information.

Le Tonlé Training Centre (☎ 973638; www .tourismforhelp.org; r US$6) Located in a shady spot near the Tonlé Kong, this small guesthouse doubles as a training centre to give underprivileged locals a helping hand into the tourism industry. Rooms include mosquito net and fan, but involve a share bathroom. There is also an excellent restaurant.

Kong Ratana Sambath Guesthouse (☎ 012 964483; r US$5-14; 🐾) The name is a bit of a mouthful, but don't let that put you off, as the service is friendly and the welcome warm. Only the top-whack US$14 rooms include hot water.

Ou Dynak Red Guesthouse (☎ 011 963676; r US$7-25; 🐾) One of the new breed of guesthouses in town, the rooms here are naturally cool even before the air-con kicks in. More expensive rooms are more spacious and include hot water.

Sok Sambath Hotel (☎ 973790; r US$8-55; 🐾) Long the smartest hotel in town, this place was on the move during our last visit to a new location overlooking the river. The old place had hot water, cable TV and air-con, so the new place should only improve things, although prices may rise.

Eating
Sorya Restaurant (☎ 011 908584; US$1-3) Located near the market, this eatery offers a pick

and mix of Asian flavours from Cambodia, Thailand and China, plus a fair selection of beers to help wash the meal down.

Le Tonlé (☎ 973638; US$2-4) Part of Le Tonlé Training Centre, this restaurant offers a selection of affordable Khmer and international food. All proceeds go to helping the training programme for underprivileged youngsters.

Mekong Blue (☎ 973977; US$2-4) This relaxing café offers traditional Khmer flavours and is set in the countryside outside town. It is best to call ahead and make a booking for lunch and dinner, as they don't get that many drop-in diners.

Getting There & Away

NH7 south to Kratie (141km) is in great shape these days and the journey is a breeze. Sorya, Hua Lian and Rith Mony all operate buses to Phnom Penh (US$9/9/10, eight hours, 470km) that pass through Kratie (US$5), all leaving around 7am. Share taxis also make the run to Kratie (US$4, two hours).

For the scoop on the road between Stung Treng and Ban Lung in Ratanakiri, see p294. There is a minibus service to Ban Lung (US$8, three to four hours) which leaves around 7.30am daily and will pick up punters from their hotel.

For the inside story on the border crossing with Laos, see p328.

The adventurous can also charter small longtail rocket boats from Stung Treng to Kratie (US$100 or so, three hours), but the river can be perilous with rocks and sandbars appearing everywhere. Do not be talked into taking one of these boats in the afternoon, as they have no lights and travelling at high speeds on the Mekong in the dark is dicing with death. Several locals die on this stretch each year and several tourists have lost everything when their boats have collided with immovable objects.

There is also a trail that leads across northern Cambodia from Stung Treng to either Tbeng Meanchey or Kompong Thom. It is unwise for the average traveller to take this route, but for adventure addicts who don't mind a very long and bumpy bike ride it is an option. First, cross the Mekong to Thala Boravit from where a jungle trail leads west to the large village of Chaeb. If trail conditions are bad you may need to overnight in Chaeb in the wat or with some locals. From Chaeb, there is an old logging road west that joins with the main road from Kompong Thom to Tbeng Meanchey. A *moto* to or from Tbeng Meanchey should cost about US$20, as the drivers need to cover the cost of their return. This route should not be attempted in the wet season.

RATANAKIRI PROVINCE

ខេត្តរតនគិរី

Up-and-coming Ratanakiri is making a name for itself as diverse region of outstanding natural beauty that provides a remote home for a mosaic of minority peoples. The Jarai, Tompoun, Brau and Kreung are the Khmer Leu (Upper Khmer) people with their own languages, traditions and customs. There is also a large Lao population throughout the province and multiple languages will be heard in villages such as Voen Sai.

Adrenaline activities are plentiful. Swim in clear volcanic lakes, shower under waterfalls, glimpse an elephant or trek in the vast Virachay National Park – it's all here. Tourism is set to take off, but that is if the lowland politicians and generals don't plunder the place first. Ratanakiri is the frontline in the battle for land, and the slash-and-burn minorities are losing out thanks to their tradition of collective ownership. The forest is disappearing at an alarming and accelerating rate, replaced by rubber plantations and cashew-nut farms. It is to be hoped someone wakes up and smells the coffee – there's plenty of that as well – before it's too late.

Gem mining is big business in Ratanakiri, hardly surprising given the name actually translates as 'hill of the precious stones'. There is good quality zircon mined in several parts of the province as well as other semi-precious stones. The prices are low compared with the West, but don't get suckered into a dream deal, as gem scams are as old as the hills themselves.

Ratanakiri Province played its part in the country's contemporary tragedy, by serving as a base for the Khmer Rouge leadership during much of the 1960s. Pol Pot and Ieng Sary fled here in 1963 and established headquarters in Ta Veng in the north of the province.

Roads in Ratanakiri are not as impressive as the sights: the dry season means chewing on dust; the wet season, sliding about in

EASTERN CAMBODIA

mud… take your pick. The roads look like carrot soup during the wet season, so the ideal time to explore is December to February. Prepare to do battle with the dust of 'red earth Ratanakiri', which will leave you with a fake tan and orange hair.

Boats are a popular means of transport for scenic trips, but the province is too isolated to make river travel into Stung Treng a realistic option.

BAN LUNG
 បានលុង

☎ 075 / pop 25,000

Affectionately known as 'dey krahorm' (red earth) after its rust coloured affliction, Ban Lung provides a popular base for a range of Ratanakiri romps. It may look like autumn all year round, but it's just that the leaves, like everything else, are cloaked in a blanket of dust. The town itself isn't the most inspiring, but with attractions such as Boeng Yeak Lom just a short hop away, there is little room for complaint. Many of the minorities from the surrounding villages come to Ban Lung to buy and sell at the market, making it one of the more lively centres in the province.

The town was originally known as Labansiek before the civil war, but the district name of Ban Lung has gradually slipped into use among locals.

Information
Acleda Bank (☎ 974220), near the *psar* (market), can change travellers cheques and offers Western Union money transfers. There is a local ATM here, which may be upgraded to credit cards.

There is a **post office** on the road to Bokheo that offers international phone services, but the mobile-phone kiosks around the market are cheaper. Internet access is available in town but rates are high, speed low. Try **Redland Internet Café** (per hr 10,000r) or **Cyber Sophat** (per hr US$3).

There is a small provincial **tourist office** in the centre of town, but we have never seen it open in the last decade. Visitors will find their guesthouse or hotel to be of more use in the quest for knowledge. Check out www .yaklom.com for more ideas on what to do in Ratanakiri.

Activities
There are no real sights in town, but plenty beyond. For details on lakes, waterfalls, minority villages, national parks and gem mines beyond Ban Lung, see p296.

ELEPHANT RIDES
Most guesthouses and hotels can arrange short elephant rides from nearby villages to local waterfalls. One of the most popular rides is from the village of Kateung to the spectacular waterfall of Ka Tieng. The ride takes about one hour, passing through beautiful rubber plantations. The usual charge is US$10 per person per hour. For longer elephant rides, Mondulkiri Province (p301) remains the more popular option.

TREKKING
Trekking has really started to take off around Ratanakiri, but it is important to make clear arrangements with your guide to ensure you get what is expected out of a trip. There are lots of popular routes that take in minority villages and scenic spots around the province, including Kreung villages near the road to Ta Veng, and Jarai villages up in Andong Meas district, but with deforestation continuing apace you need to be sure of conditions along the way.

Many visitors opt for a trek into Virachay National Park, but be aware that some of these treks barely scrape the park itself, and spend much of the time in the park buffer zone. There are now multiday treks into the park, and these are a great way to explore one of the most wild and remote areas in Cambodia. See p297 for details. The cost depends on the route, but figure on US$15 to US$25 a day for a good guide and more for transport, food and lodging along the way. Budget travellers really need to link up with a group to make it affordable. The best places to arrange trekking are Terres Rouges (opposite) and Yaklom Hill Lodge (opposite). Recommended guesthouses can also help out with budget treks.

Sleeping
Ratanakiri is now firmly entrenched on the overland map of Cambodia and the choice of accommodation is growing by the year. Most places offer free pick-up from the airport if and when flights are operating.

Tribal Hotel (☎ 974074; tribalhotel@camintel.com; r US$3-20; ✱) There is nothing particularly tribal about this huge place, but there is a healthy selection of rooms catering to all budgets. Pricier rooms include hot water,

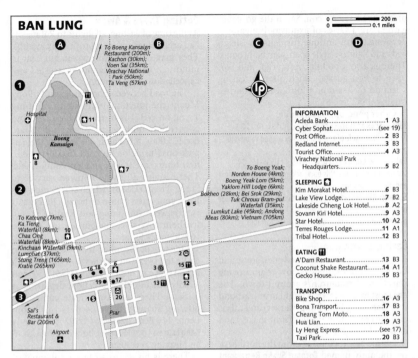

BAN LUNG

0 — 200 m
0 — 0.1 miles

To Boeng Kansaign
Restaurant (200m);
Kachon (30km);
Voen Sai (35km);
Virachay National
Park (50km);
Ta Veng (57km)

Hospital

Boeng
Kansaign

To Boeng Yeak;
Norden House (4km);
Boeng Yeak Lom (5km);
Yaklom Hill Lodge (6km);
Bokheo (28km); Bei Srok (29km);
Tuk Chrouu Bram-pul
Waterfall (35km);
Lumkut Lake (45km); Andong
Meas (80km); Vietnam (105km)

To Kateung (7km);
Ka Tieng
Waterfall (8km);
Chaa Ong
Waterfall (8km);
Kinchaan Waterfall (9km);
Lumphat (37km);
Stung Treng (165km);
Kratie (265km)

Sal's
Restaurant &
Bar (200m)

Psar

Airport

INFORMATION	
Acleda Bank	1 A3
Cyber Sophat	(see 19)
Post Office	2 B3
Redland Internet	3 B3
Tourist Office	4 A3
Virachey National Park Headquarters	5 B2

SLEEPING	
Kim Morakat Hotel	6 B3
Lake View Lodge	7 B2
Lakeside Chheng Lok Hotel	8 A2
Sovann Kiri Hotel	9 A3
Star Hotel	10 A2
Terres Rouges Lodge	11 A1
Tribal Hotel	12 B3

EATING	
A'Dam Restaurant	13 B3
Coconut Shake Restaurant	14 A1
Gecko House	15 B3

TRANSPORT	
Bike Shop	16 A3
Bona Transport	17 B3
Cheang Torn Moto	18 A3
Hua Lian	19 A3
Ly Heng Express	(see 17)
Taxi Park	20 B3

cable TV and a fridge, while budget rooms are dotted around the huge garden and include singles with bathroom for US$3. The garden includes a big restaurant (mains US$1 to US$3) with a good selection of Khmer and Asian cuisine.

Star Hotel (☎ 012 958322; r US$5-10; ✷) Run by the irrepressible Mr Leng, this cotton-candy structure was originally built as a home and has large rooms complete with hot-water bathrooms. There is plenty of travel information here and the lively restaurant is a good place for a beer or a signature *phnom pleung* (hill of fire), a beef-and-vegetable DIY tabletop barbecue.

ourpick Lakeside Chheng Lok Hotel (☎ 390063; www.chhenglok-hotel.com/index.htm; chhenglok@yahoo.com; r US$5-20; ✷) In a prime spot overlooking Boeng Kansaign, this is the best all-rounder in Ban Lung. Set in a lush garden, there is a choice of attractive garden bungalows or smart rooms. Hot water, cable TV, it's all here, and there is a local restaurant amid the flourishing plants.

Yaklom Hill Lodge (☎ 012 644240; www.yaklom.com; r incl breakfast US$10-22) For an alternative

experience to the places in town, make for Ratanakiri's only ecolodge. Set amid lush forest about 6km east of town, the wooden bungalows are thoughtfully decorated with ethnic minority handicrafts. There is no power during the day, but the fan and lights work through the night. There is an atmospheric restaurant (mains US$2 to US$4) serving Thai and Khmer food.

Norden House (☎ 012 880327; www.nordenhouse yaklom.com; r US$25; ✷ ▯) This new bungalow resort is exceptional value and sits in a peaceful location on the road to Boeng Yeak Lom. Rooms are stylish and include cable TV and a DVD player, plus there's free internet access. There is also a restaurant with Swedish specialities, plus dirt bikes (per day US$25) for hire.

Terres Rouges Lodge (☎ 974051; www.ratanakiri-lodge.com; r US$32-75; ✷ ▯) Undoubtedly one of the most atmospheric places to stay in provincial Cambodia, this former governor's residence has an imperious setting on the shores of Boeng Kansaign. There is a range of rooms in the main house, all finished with creative Khmer and Chinese touches, but only some have air-con. Set in the gorgeous garden are a series of exquisite bungalows, decorated with antique furnishings, sleigh beds and Balinese-style open-plan bathrooms. There is also a popular restaurant and bar, open to non-guests, which offers a teasing selection of Asian and European favourites (mains US$2 to US$5).

Other good options include:

Kim Morakat Hotel (☎ 974121; r US$5-10; ✷)
Right in the middle of town, this hotel is good value and popular with Khmers.

Lake View Lodge (☎ 092 785259; r US$5-15; ✷)
Located near the lake, this backpacker pad has eight rooms and good-value grub.

Sovann Kiri Hotel (☎ 974001; r US$5-15; ✷) A huge new hotel on the way into town, it is a riot of concrete but that ensures the rooms are smart and comfortable.

Eating & Drinking

As well as the aforementioned guesthouse and hotel restaurants, there is now an improving selection of restaurants around town. The cheapest food in town is found in and around Psar Ban Lung (Ban Lung Market) and this is also the area to find *tukalok* (fruit shakes) and desserts by night.

For the best coconut shake in the northeast, try the aptly named **Coconut Shake Restaurant** (☎ 012 416234; Boeng Kansaign; meals 4000-10,000r). Dare to try the friend frie or the friend toes (French toast?).

Gecko House (☎ 012 422228; mains US$1-4) A charming little restaurant with inviting sofas and soft lighting, this is a great place by day or night. The menu features Thai tastes, Khmer classics and some Western dishes such as pizza, pasta and sandwiches. After dark it doubles as a lively bar.

Sal's Restaurant & Bar (☎ 012 284377; mains US$1.50-5) This restaurant-bar, set in a traditional wooden house on the edge of town, is the place to come for comfort food from home, including Indian curries, spicy Mexican and great burgers. Service can be slow, but it's worth the wait.

Boeng Kansaign Restaurant (mains US$1-4) Relax and unwind on the shores of the lake at this local restaurant. Khmer and Chinese dishes make up the menu and the breeze across the water is blissful on a hot day.

A'Dam Restaurant (mains US$1-3) This local restaurant doubles up as a bar by night, thanks to one of the only pool tables in Ban Lung and a dart board… almost a British pub.

Getting There & Away

At the time of writing, all flights to Ratanakiri had been suspended for more than six months. They may start operating again, but bear in mind that schedules cannot be trusted and cancellations are common.

The road between Ban Lung and O Pong Moan (the junction 19km south of Stung Treng on NH7) is in reasonable shape and is currently undergoing renovation. Share taxi (25,000r, three hours) is the way to go as pick-ups (inside/on the back 25,000/15,000r, four hours) are slower and less comfortable. There is also a private minivan service to Stung Treng (US$8), which offers pick-ups from your guest house or hotel. Direct taxis run between Ban Lung and Kratie (30,000, five hours). Wet-season journey times can be considerably longer.

One way or the other, it is now possible to make the overland journey to Phnom Penh in just one day and Hua Lian (US$17.50) run a daily bus in either direction, departing at 6.15am. There are also private companies offering shared people carriers to Phnom Penh. Try **Bona Transport** (☎ 012 567161) or **Ly Heng Express** (☎ 012 724096), both costing US$15 and leaving at 6.30am.

There is no real road linking Ratanakiri to Mondulkiri, contrary to what older maps may show. There is a road as far south as Lumphat, but after crossing the Tonlé Srepok by ferry, it descends into a series of sandy ox-cart tracks until Koh Nhek in northern Mondulkiri Province. A handful of hardcore bikers have been using this route over the past few years, but only attempt it if you have years of biking experience or are an extremely hardy soul with an iron backside. Anyone seriously considering this option should link up with a local who knows the route, as there are lots of opportunities to get lost. A range of motorbike spares, copious amounts of water and a compass should make for a smoother journey. An increasing number of travellers are also coming this way on the back of a *moto*, but it's punishing. The Cambodian military have rebuilt the road from Sen Monorom to Koh Nhek, which makes the journey possible in one day, assuming you don't get lost. It is almost impossible in the wet season.

Getting Around

Motorbikes, cars and 4WDs are available for hire from most guesthouses in town.

Motorbikes are usually US$5 to US$8 a day. Cars are available from US$30 a day and 4WDs from about US$50 a day, but prices rise rapidly the further you want to travel. **Cheang Torn Moto** (☎ 012 960533) has some 250cc dirt bikes available for US$10 per day, but maintenance is an issue. Norden House

(p292) has reliable ones, but at US$25 a day. Local guides with motorbikes offer their services around the province and rates range from US$8 to US$15 depending on their experience, level of English and where you want to go.

For something cheaper and more environmentally friendly, consider a bicycle (US$1

THE JUNGLE GIRL OF RATANAKIRI   *Nick Ray*

In 1988, nine-year old Pnieng Rochum disappeared in a remote corner of Cambodia. In January 2007, she emerged from the jungle to be reunited with her family in O Yadaw village in Ratanakiri. When the story broke, the international press descended on this remote village and the story broke all over the world. I covered the story for the UK media and followed up with a visit to the family when researching this guidebook. This is her story.

For eighteen years, her mother Rochom Choy prayed for the safe return of her daughter. 'It was the happiest moment of my life,' she says. 'I looked into her eyes and knew this was my long lost daughter.' Her father, Lou Sal, a local policeman, was also certain it was his daughter. Filthy, naked and silent, instinct told him this was the little girl he had last seen during Cambodia's civil war. Back at the village, her mother bathed her. 'As I washed her, I saw a scar on her forearm,' she told me. 'I knew it was her because her sister accidentally cut her with a knife just before she disappeared.'

Early reports claimed she was with a wild man wielding a sword. 'She was alone. She came out of the jungle and I was afraid', says Cher Tam, the first person to set eyes on her for 18 years. 'She was naked and dirty and moving with a stoop,' continues the woodcutter from the nearby village of Ten. Pnieng Rochum and her young cousin vanished in 1988 when her mother had gone to collect some drinking water. The parents searched everywhere, wandering through the jungle and travelling from village to village. 'Some villagers saw some small footprints on the banks of a jungle stream near their rice fields,' says Rochom Chey. 'I thought we might find her but the jungle spirits did not want to let her go.' Ceremonies were held to pray to the spirits for her safe return. 'Money was no object to bring back my daughter,' says her father. 'I asked the spirits of the jungle to give back my daughter every night.'

When I first met Pnieng in January 2007, she sat and stared into space, traumatised and distant, almost autistic. She talked to herself at night, muttering noises that the family could not understand. 'She makes strange sounds like a small animal,' explained her mother. She was like a newborn baby, unable to take care of her most basic needs, spoon-fed, washed, and her every move watched.

Her parents were terrified she would return to the jungle, reclaimed by the powerful spirits in which they believe. Their fears were realised in the summer of 2007 when Pnieng vanished again for nine days. She was eventually found, a changed woman on her return. I met her again in November 2007 and she had put on weight, could barely contain her smile and sang songs. She also seemed to understand some language, particularly Vietnamese and Jarai, suggesting she may have spent some time across the border. Her parents believe she had made her peace with the spirits, or possibly said a final farewell to her jungle man companion.

The jungle girl story is baffling. There are more questions than answers. How does an eight-year old girl survive in the jungle for so many years? The Cambodian jungle is home to poisonous snakes, malaria and other dangers. It is an unforgiving place for anyone, particularly a young girl. Was she kidnapped by a jungle man and forced to forage with him, a Cambodian version of Tarzan and Jane? Did she stray across the border into Vietnam and end up forced into slavery for a time? What happened to her young cousin?

Even today, nobody knows. What is certain is that a little girl disappeared 18 years ago. The only person who knows the truth is Pnieng Rochum. For now she remains silent, but in time she may reveal her secret past.

Pnieng Rochum currently lives in O Yadaw village with her parents.

per day), available from some hotels and the bike shop on the main drag.

AROUND BAN LUNG

Try to link up with a responsible local guide when exploring Ratanakiri, as the minority people around the province are sensitive to outsiders just stomping in and out of their villages.

Boeng Yeak Lom
បឹងយក្សទ្រោម

At the heart of the protected area of **Yeak Lom** (admission US$1) is a beautiful blue crater-lake set amid the vivid greens of the towering jungle. The lake is believed to have been formed 700,000 years ago and some people swear it must have been formed by a meteor strike as the circle is so perfect. The indigenous minority people in the area have long considered Yeak Lom a sacred place and their legends talk of mysterious creatures that inhabit the waters of the lake. It is one of the most peaceful, beautiful locations Cambodia has to offer and the water is extremely clear. It is a great place to take a dip early in the morning or late in the afternoon, as there is a wooden pier on the water's edge, plus tubes for rent.

There is a small **visitors centre** (admission by donation) that has information on ethnic minorities in the province, local handicrafts for sale and suggested walks around the lake. The area is administered by the local Tompuon minority and proceeds from the entry fee go towards improving life in the nearby villages.

Boeng Yeak Lom is 5km east of Ban Lung. Turn right off the road to Bokheo at the statue of the minority family. *Motos* are available for around US$2 return, but expect to pay more if the driver has to wait around. It takes almost an hour to get to on foot from Ban Lung.

Waterfalls

There are numerous waterfalls in the province, but many are difficult to reach in the wet season and lacking much water in the dry season. The three most commonly visited are **Chaa Ong**, **Ka Tieng** and **Kinchaan**, all attracting a 2000r admission fee, and these are signposted from the main road towards Stung Treng, about 5km west of town. The most spectacular of the three is Chaa Ong, as it is set in a jungle gorge and you can clamber behind the waterfall or venture underneath for a power shower. Ka Tieng is the most enjoyable, as it drops over a rock shelf allowing you to clamber all the way behind. There are some vines on the far side that are strong enough to swing on for some Tarzan action.

Tuk Chrouu Bram-pul (O Sin Laer Waterfall; admission 2000r) is a popular waterfall with seven gentle tiers, located about 35km southeast of Ban Lung, but the trail to get here is tough at any time and pretty much impossible in the wet season. Access to the waterfall involves a gentle walk through the forest. A visit here can be combined with a visit to the current hot spot for **gem mining** in Bei Srok, with gem mines littering the roadside. Locals dig a large pit in the ground and then tunnel horizontally in their search for amethyst and zircon. Take a local guide for this combination trip, but check in Ban Lung that the mines are still active.

Voen Sai
វ៉ើនសៃ
pop 3000

Located on the banks of the Tonlé San, Voen Sai is a cluster of Chinese, Lao and Kreung villages. Originally, the town was located on the north bank of the river and known as Virachay, but these days the main settlement is on the south bank. The north side of the river is the most interesting, with an **old Chinese settlement** that dates back more than 100 years and several **Lao and chunchiet villages** nearby. It is possible to cross the river on a small ferry (500r) and walk west for a couple of kilometres, passing through the Khmer village, a Lao community and a small *chunchiet* area, before finally emerging on a wealthy Chinese village complete with large wooden houses and inhabitants who still speak Chinese. Check out how neat and tidy it is compared with the surrounding communities.

Voen Sai is about 35km northwest of Ban Lung on an average-to-poor road. It is easy enough to get to under your own steam on a motorbike or vehicle.

Chunchiet Cemeteries
កន្លែងបញ្ចុះសពពួកជនជាតិ

The *chunchiet* of Ratanakiri bury their dead amidst the jungle, carving effigies of the deceased to stand guard over the graves. There are many cemeteries scattered throughout the forests of Ratanakiri. **Kachon** is a one-hour boat ride east of Voen Sai and has an impressive **Tompuon cemetery** (admission US$1) in the forest beyond the village. When a lengthy period of mourning is complete, villagers hold a big celebration and add two carved wooden likenesses of elephant tusks to the structures. Some of these tombs date back many years and have been abandoned to the jungle. Newer tombs of wealthy individuals have been cast in concrete and show some modern touches like shades and mobile phones. Sadly, some unscrupulous art collectors and amateur anthropologists from Europe have reportedly been buying up the old effigies from poor villagers, something tantamount to cultural rape. Remember that this is a sacred site for local Tompuon people – touch nothing and act respectfully. Many other Tompuon and Jarai villages have small cemeteries; ask villagers or guides for suggested sites.

Expect to pay around US$15 for the boat trip from Voen Sai to Kachon, including a jaunt to the Chinese and Lao villages opposite Voen Sai. To get to the cemetery, walk through the health centre located at the riverbank and turn right. The cemetery is just a short distance from the village. It is also possible to get to Kachon by road – head south out of Voen Sai and turn left at the first major junction.

Lumkut Lake
បឹងលំគត

Lumkut is the new Boeng Yeak Loam, at least that is what some guides in Ban Lung would have you believe. Yes, it is a large crater lake and hemmed in by dense forest on all sides, but it is not as accessible as Yeak Loam and the old pier has already rotted into the water, making swimming a challenge. However, it's a beautiful spot and lies about 45km from Ban Lung to the south of Bokheo district.

Ta Veng
តាវែង

Ta Veng is an insignificant village on the southern bank of Tonlé San, but acts as an alternative gateway to Virachay National Park. It was in the Ta Veng district that Pol Pot, Ieng Sary and other leaders of the Khmer Rouge established their guerrilla base in the 1960s. Locals say nothing remains of the remote base today although, in a dismal sign of decline, they point out that Ta Veng had electricity before the war.

Ta Veng is about 57km north of Ban Lung on a rollercoaster road through the mountains that affords some of the province's better views.

The road passes through several **minority villages**, where it is possible to break the journey. There are some very steep climbs in sections and for this reason it wouldn't be much fun in the rain. Travel by motorbike or charter a vehicle.

It is possible to arrange small boats in Ta Veng for river jaunts; US$5 in the local area or US$30 for the three-hour trip to Voen Sai.

Andong Meas
អណ្ដូងមាស

pop 1500

Andong Meas district was growing in popularity thanks to a combination of minority villages, **Jarai cemeteries** and a short river trip, but there has been widespread deforestation in the last couple of years. There is a walkable trail from Andong Meas to a Jarai cemetery on the banks of the Tonlé San. From the cemetery it is possible to return to Andong Meas by river for about US$10 by boat. Andong Meas lies about 80km northeast of Ban Lung on a reasonable road taking three hours. Transport prices are slightly higher due to the distance involved.

Virachay National Park
ឧទ្យានជាតិវីរៈជ័យ

Virachay National Park is one of the largest protected areas in Cambodia, stretching for 3325 sq km east to Vietnam, north to Laos and west to Stung Treng Province. The park has never been fully explored and is likely home to a number of larger mammals, including elephants, leopards and tigers. Optimists speculate that there may even be isolated rhinoceroses or kouprey (wild oxen), but this is unlikely. Rangers also suggest there are **waterfalls**, some as high as 100m, but these are many days' hike from the park boundary. So important is the park to the Mekong region that it was designated an Asean Heritage Park in 2003.

Virachay has the most organised ecotourism programme in Cambodia, focusing on small-scale culture, nature and adventure trekking. The programme aims to involve and benefit local communities. There is a small visitor and information centre at the **Virachay National Park Headquarters** (☎ 974176; www.bpamp .org.kh) in Ban Lung, located at the Department of Environment. Visitors can book park excursions here, pay the necessary fees and find out the latest information. All visitors who wish to enter the park require an entry permit and must be accompanied by a park ranger and community guide.

TREKS IN VIRACHAY NATIONAL PARK

There are three main treks available in Virachay, from a gentle two-day trek to a week-long workout.

- **Kalang Chhouy Sacred Mountain Trek** (2 days/1 night; per person from US$40) This short trek starts from near Koklak village and includes a night by the Chai Chanang Waterfall. On the second day, continue to Phnom Gong, a sacred mountain for the Brau people, and swim at the Tju Preah rapids.

- **O'Lapeung River Valley Trek** (4 days/3 nights; per person from US$85) This trek starts from Ta Veng with a boat ride on the Tonlé San and O Tabok Rivers to the Brau village of Phum Yorn, where trekkers experience a homestay. The trek continues to the summit of Phnom Meive and into the O'Lapeung valley to a campsite. On the third day, the route passes along a section of the Ho Chi Minh Trail and it may be possible to see some war relics. After a second night in the Brau village, you return to Ta Veng by inflatable kayak.

- **Phnom Veal Thom Wilderness Trek** (8 days/7 nights; per person from US$170) The longest trek into Virachay starts from Ta Veng with an overnight homestay in a Brau village. The trek goes deep into the heart of the Phnom Veal Thom grasslands, an area rich in wildlife such as sambar deer, gibbon, langur, wild pig, bear and hornbill. Trekkers return via a different route and pass through beautiful areas of evergreen forest. Due to the terrain, trekkers need to be relatively fit.

The park is actually more accessible from the Stung Treng side, although it's all relative really. Siem Pang acts as the western gateway to the park and it can be easier to spot wildlife in this section. Siem Pang is accessible by motorbike in the dry season, about a three-hour ride from Voen Sai. It is also connected to Stung Treng by longtail rocket boat (30,000r), but have a look at how rocky the Tonlé Kong is before you sign up.

Lumphat
លំផាត់
pop 2000

The former provincial capital of Lumphat, on the banks of the Tonlé Srepok, is something of a ghost town these days thanks to sustained US bombing raids in the early 1970s. This is also the last gasp of civilisation, if it can even be called that, for hardcore bikers heading south on the tough trails to Mondulkiri Province.

The Tonlé Srepok is believed to be the river depicted in the seminal anti-war film *Apocalypse Now*, in which Martin Sheen's Captain Benjamin Willard goes upriver into Cambodia in search of renegade Colonel Kurtz, played by Marlon Brando.

To get here from Ban Lung, take the road to Stung Treng for about 15km before heading south. The 35km journey takes around an hour and pick-ups do a few runs from Ban Lung for 5000r.

MONDULKIRI PROVINCE
ខេត្តមណ្ឌលគិរី

A world apart from lowland Cambodia, Mondulkiri is the original Wild East of the country. Climatically and culturally, it's also another world, which comes as a relief after the heat of the plains. Home to the hardy Pnong people and their noble elephants, it is possible to visit traditional villages and learn how to be a mahout. The landscape is a seductive mix of pine clumps, grassy hills and windswept valleys that fade beguilingly into forests of jade green and hidden waterfalls. Wild animals, such as bears and tigers, are more numerous here than elsewhere, although chances of seeing them are about as good as winning the lottery.

Mondulkiri means 'Meeting of the Hills', an apt sobriquet for a land of rolling hills. In the dry season it is a little like Wales with sunshine; in the wet season, like Tasmania with more rain. At an average elevation of 800m, it can get quite chilly at night, so carry something warm.

Mondulkiri is the most sparsely populated province in the country, with just two people per sq km. Almost half the inhabitants come from the Pnong minority group, with other minorities making up much of the rest of the population. There has been an influx of migrants in recent years, drawn to the abundant land and benign climate. Fruit and vegetable plantations are popping up, but hunting remains the profession of choice for many minorities. Conservationists have grand plans for the province, creating wildlife sanctuaries and initiating sustainable tourism activities, but are facing off against speculators and industrialists queuing up for natural resources. BHP Billiton, one of the world's largest mining companies, is already digging around, literally.

Roads are pretty poor throughout the province, but the main highway to Phnom Penh is in pretty good shape most of the way, bringing journey times down to seven hours. The road to Koh Nhek is unrecognisable from the mess of bygone years. Improved access has fuelled an explosion of domestic tourists, so book ahead at weekends.

ȘEN MONOROM
សែនមនោរម្យ
☎ 073 / pop 7000

The provincial capital of Mondulkiri, Sen Monorom is little more than an overgrown village. A charming community set in the spot where the famous hills meet, the centre of town has two lakes, leading some dreamers to call it 'The Switzerland of Cambodia'. The area around Sen Monorom is peppered with minority villages and picturesque waterfalls, making it the ideal place to spend some time. Many of the Pnong people from nearby villages come to Sen Monorom to trade, and the distinctive baskets they carry on their backs makes them easy to distinguish from the immigrant lowlanders. Set at more than 800m, when the winds billow it's notably cooler than the rest of Cambodia, so bring some warm clothing.

Information

Hurrah, **Acleda Bank** has opened its doors on the main road from Phnom Penh and can change major currencies. Prices are slightly higher than in other parts of the country, as everything has to be shipped in from Phnom Penh or Vietnam.

Green House (www.thegreen-house.blogspot.com; per hour US$2) has the cheapest internet access in town and doubles as a lively little bar by night. Internet access is also available at the **Arun Reas II Hill Lodge** (per hr US$4). Telephone calls can be made from mobile phones around the town.

There is a small **tourist office** in town and staff speak good English and French. They can arrange elephant treks and overnight stays in minority villages, as can the leading guesthouses in town, such as Long Vibol Guesthouse (p301).

Sights & Activities

Not much happens in Sen Monorom itself but there's plenty to see and do nearby.

Trips out to the Pnong villages dotted across the province can be arranged through guesthouses and hotels, including an overnight stay with the community. Each guesthouse has a preferred village to send travellers to, which is a great way to spread the wealth.

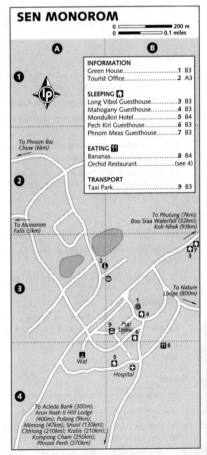

SEN MONOROM

INFORMATION	
Green House	1 B3
Tourist Office	2 A3

SLEEPING	
Long Vibol Guesthouse	3 B3
Mahogany Guesthouse	4 B3
Mondulkiri Hotel	5 B4
Pech Kiri Guesthouse	6 B3
Phnom Meas Guesthouse	7 B3

EATING	
Bananas	8 B4
Orchid Restaurant	(see 4)

TRANSPORT	
Taxi Park	9 B3

To Phnom Bai Chuw (6km)
To Monorom Falls (3km)
To Phulung (7km); Bou Sraa Waterfall (32km); Koh Nhek (93km)
To Nature Lodge (800m)
Psar Thmei
Wat
Hospital
To Acleda Bank (300m); Arun Reah II Hill Lodge (400m); Putang (9km); Mimong (47km); Snuol (130km); Chhlong (210km); Kratie (210km); Kompong Cham (250km); Phnom Penh (370km)

EASTERN CAMBODIA

TREAD LIGHTLY IN THE HILLS

Tourism can bring many benefits to highland communities: cross-cultural understanding, improved infrastructure, cheaper market goods, employment opportunities and tourist dollars supporting handicraft industries. However, there are also the negatives: the overtaxing of natural resources, increased litter and pollutants, dependency on tourist dollars, proliferation of drug use and prostitution and the erosion of local values and practices.

If you visit Cambodia's hill-tribe communities, make a positive contribution and ensure that the benefits of your stay outweigh the costs.

Interaction

- Be polite and respectful.
- Dress modestly.
- Minimise litter.
- Do not urinate or defecate near villagers' households; bury faeces.
- Do not take drugs – young children tend to imitate tourists' behaviour.
- Do not engage in sexual relationships with local people, including prostitutes.
- Try to learn something about the community's culture and language and teach something good about yours.

Gifts

- Do not give children sweets or money; it encourages begging and paves the way for prostitution for 'gifts' and money. Sweets also contribute to tooth decay.
- Do not give clothes – communities are self-sufficient.
- Don't give medicines – it erodes traditional healing practices and the medicine may not be correctly administered.
- Individual gifts create jealousy and create expectations. Instead make donations to the local school, medical centre or community fund.
- No matter how poor they are, villagers are extremely hospitable; however, feeding a guest can result in food shortages. If you accept an invitation to share a meal, be sure to bring a generous contribution.

Shopping

- Haggle politely and always pay the agreed (and fair) price for goods and services.
- Do not ask to buy a villager's personal household items or the jewellery or clothes they are wearing.
- Don't buy village treasures, such as altar pieces or totems.

Photographs

- Do not photograph without first asking permission – this includes children. Some hill tribes believe the camera will capture their spirit. Don't photograph altars.
- If you take a picture, do it quickly and avoid using a flash. If you promise to send copies, keep your word.

Travel

- Travel in small, less disruptive groups.
- Stay, eat and travel with local businesses.
- Try to book tours with responsible tourism outlets who employ hill-tribe people or contribute to community welfare.

Check out the observation deck of **Phnom Bai Chuw** (Raw Rice Mountain), 6km northwest of Sen Monorom, for a jaw-dropping view of the emerald forest. It looks as though you are seeing a vast sea of tree tops, hence the locals have named it **Samot Cheur** (Ocean of Trees).

ELEPHANT TREKS

The villages of Phulung, 7km northeast of Sen Monorom, and Putang, 9km southwest of town, are the most popular places to arrange an elephant trek. Most of the recommended guesthouses around town, as well as the tourist office, can arrange day treks for around US$30 or so, including lunch and transport to and from the village. It can get pretty uncomfortable up on top of an elephant after a couple of hours; carry a pillow to ease the strain.

It is also possible to negotiate a longer trek with an overnight stay in a Pnong village, costing from US$60 to US$80 per person with an overnight homestay or camping out by a waterfall.

For the complete elephant experience, head out of town to the Elephant Valley Project (see p302).

Sleeping & Eating

Electricity has finally come to Sen Monorom, lighting up the lives of residents and visitors alike. Hot water is more important in this part of the country, as the temperature can drop dramatically at night. Places without hot-water showers can usually provide flasks of boiling water for bathing. There is no need for air-conditioning in this neck of the woods.

Pech Kiri Guesthouse (☎ 012 932102; r US$3-10) Once upon a time, this was the only guesthouse in town and it is still going strong under the lively direction of Madame Deu. The place keeps expanding, with an oversized new wing underway, but there are still lots of bargain bungalows available.

ourpick Nature Lodge (☎ 230272; www.naturelodge cambodia.com; r US$4-10) Everyone will want to get back to nature once they discover this place. Located on a windswept hilltop near town, this quirky eco-resort has basic bungalow accommodation with shared hot showers and an incredible Swiss family Robinson-style chalet with sunken beds and hidden rooms. The inviting restaurant is decorated with abandoned tree trunks and roots and has a good range of

traveller fare. There's also a bar and pool table for night owls.

Arun Reah II Hill Lodge (☎ 012 856667; arunreah_mondulkiri@yahoo.com.kh; r US$5-10; 🖳) We still haven't worked out where Arun Reah I is, but never mind as this is a fine place to stay. This wooden lodge boasts some fine views across the hills of Mondulkiri. The bungalows are good value, including hot water and cable TV. There is a cavernous restaurant (mains US$1 to US$3) for a local bite, plus free bicycles for those that fancy a little workout.

Long Vibol Guesthouse (☎ 012 944647; r US$5-10) Vibol's is an attractive wooden resort set amid a lush garden. The rooms are clean and spacious and higher prices include hot water. Vibol is the elder statesman among the tour guides of Mondulkiri, making this a top spot for information and a reliable place to arrange trekking. The restaurant has a small selection of Cambodian favourites, with mains from US$1 to US$3.

Phnom Meas Guesthouse (☎ 012 929562; r US$5-10) Next door to Vibol's, the 'Golden Hill' has a verdant garden dotted with bungalows and huts. Most rooms include hot water and all have cable TV. Check out the curious triangular huts near the entrance.

Mahogany Guesthouse (☎ 017 999042; www.mondulkiri.info; r US$8-10) This small guesthouse in the middle of town has eight rooms, all with hot water, and they are steadily being upgraded. Better still is the excellent restaurant (mains US$3 to $7), serving some of the best pizzas and pastas in the province, plus an unexpected range of authentic Indian and Nepalese food. It's also a fine spot for international breakfasts, including quality coffees.

Mondulkiri Hotel (☎ 390139; r US$15-30; 🍴 🖳) It looks out of place in this pristine land of rolling hills, but the hulking concrete exterior conceals the most comfortable rooms in town. All are equipped with air-con, smart bathrooms, cable TV and fridge. There are also some bungalows and Pnong-style dwellings in the extensive gardens.

Aside from the guesthouse restaurants recommended above, there is also the inviting **Orchid Restaurant** (mains US$1-3) on the main drag, with some flavoursome Khmer and Chinese dishes on the menu. **Bananas** (☎ 092 412680; mains US$2-5) is a new restaurant-bar serving up Western favourites like shepherd's pie and Flemish stew, with a dose of expat insight on life in Cambodia. By night, beers and spirits flow.

THE ELEPHANT VALLEY PROJECT

For an original elephant experience, visit the **Elephant Valley Project** (☎ 017 613833; jackhighwood@yahoo.co.uk). Part of the **Elephants Livelihood Initiative Environment** (www .elie-cambodia.org), visitors can learn the art of the mahout for a day. The trip starts with a tour of the project before learning about the body language of elephants. Students are then given the chance to try a series of short elephant rides to build their confidence. After lunch, wannabee mahouts get the chance to experience a longer elephant ride to a nearby waterfall. After a dip in the water, it's possible to help wash down the elephants. The experience costs US$50 per person per day up to a maximum of four people, although this number may rise as more elephants are brought into the project. The price includes transport but not lunch. All proceeds are ploughed back into the project to help provide veterinary care for the working elephants of Mondulkiri. There are plans to build bungalows at the site, which may offer up the option of longer immersion courses with the elephants. Project coordinator Jack Highwood has also trained up some former hunters as trekking guides and these guys have inside knowledge of the birdlife and wildlife of the region.

Getting There & Away

The airstrip at Sen Monorom has been sold off and there are plans to develop a new airport at Putang. For now, visitors who want to get to this unique region have to come overland, and this is pretty straightforward thanks to a major dirt highway which is slowly being upgraded to bitumen.

There are two ways to get to Mondulkiri, both of which include the same section of old logging road from Snuol to Sen Monorom, and a third, harsh trail north to Ratanakiri – see p294 for more details on this hardcore route. The stretch from Snuol to Sen Monorom passes through some wild jungle after Khao Si Ma district and is one of the most dramatic and beautiful roads in Cambodia.

There is usually one bus daily between Phnom Penh and Sen Monorom (US$10, ten hours, 7.15am) in the dry season. However, locals say it is safer to take a car or pick-up due to steep hills and unexpected rains. There are also pick-ups heading from Phnom Penh to Sen Monorom (inside/on the back US$12/6, eight hours), leaving from Psar Thmei soon after 6am, but it's best to head to the market the day before you want to travel to arrange a seat with a driver, as places are limited.

Coming from Kompong Cham, there are few direct services to Sen Monorom, so it is usually necessary to first go to Snuol (12,000r by taxi, 1½ hours). From Snuol, there are pick-ups to Sen Monorom (inside/on the back 20,000/15,000r, three hours).

From Kratie there are direct pick-ups heading to Sen Monorom (inside/on the back 30,000/20,000r, five hours) early in the morning. Anyone leaving later will probably need to change vehicles in Snuol.

Getting from Mondulkiri Province to any of these destinations is generally easier, as most locals are going beyond Snuol and so no change is required, plus guesthouses can arrange for the pick-ups to collect.

Experienced bikers will find it a pretty straightforward run these days, on surfaced roads all the way to Snuol and then decent enough dirt roads through to Sen Monorom. If it doesn't sound challenging enough compared with the old days, don't worry: once you get to Mondulkiri there are still plenty of tough trails to be found.

Getting Around

Motorbikes cost from US$5 to US$10 to rent around town. Ask your guesthouse or hotel or negotiate with a *moto* driver. There are no 250cc dirt bikes available for rent here, so hire one in Phnom Penh (p111) if you want more muscle. Pick-up trucks and 4WDs can be chartered for the day. It costs about US$40 or so around Sen Monorom in the dry season, and more again in the wet season.

AROUND SEN MONOROM
Monorom Falls
ទឹកជ្រោះមនោរម្យ

This small waterfall is the closest thing to a public swimming pool for Sen Monorom. It has an attractive location in the forest, about 3km northwest of town. *Motos* can take people out here for about US$2 or so for the round trip. If walking, head straight on beyond

Sihanouk's abandoned villa and when the trail eventually forks, take the left-hand side.

Bou Sraa Waterfall
ទឹកជ្រោះប៊ូស្រា

Plunging into the dense Cambodian jungle below, this is one of the country's most impressive falls. Famous throughout the country, this double-drop waterfall has an upper tier of some 10m and a spectacular lower tier with a thundering 25m drop. To get to the bottom of the upper falls, take a left turn just before the river that feeds the falls. To get to the bottom of the lower falls, cross the river and follow a path to a precipitous staircase that continues to the bottom; it takes about 15 minutes to get down.

Bou Sraa is an easy 35km journey east of Sen Monorom, thanks to a new toll road to get out here, taking just 45 minutes. Prices are 3000r for a small motorbike, 5000r for a large motorbike and 15,000r for a car or 4WD. Hire a *moto* driver for the day or charter a car in a group. Basic snacks and drinks are available at the falls, but pack a picnic if you want something more sophisticated.

Other Waterfalls

Other popular waterfalls in Mondulkiri include **Romanear Waterfall**, 18km southeast of Sen Monorom, and **Dak Dam Waterfall**, 25km east of Sen Monorom. Both are very difficult to find without assistance, so it's best to take a *moto* driver or local guide. Romanear is a low, wide waterfall with some convenient swimming holes. There is also a second Romanear Waterfall, known rather originally as **Romanear II**, which is near the main road between Sen Monorom and Snuol. Dak Dam is similar to the Monorom Falls, albeit with a greater volume of water. The waterfall is several kilometres beyond the Pnong village of Dak Dam and locals are able to lead the way if you can make yourself understood.

MIMONG
ម៉ីម៉ុង

Welcome to the Wild East, where the gold rush lives on. Mimong district is famous for its **gold mines** and this has drawn speculators from as far away as Vietnam and China on the trail of wealth. The population of this overgrown village may actually be equal to that of Sen Monorom. Miners descend into the pits on ancient mine carts that are connected to dodgy-looking winches, sometimes going to a depth of 100m or more. It's not for the faint-hearted and several miners die in accidents each year.

The main problem is getting here, as the road is so bad that it takes about four hours to cover the 47km from Sen Monorom. The road improves slightly on the other side of Mimong and it is possible to carry on to link up with NH7 to Kratie to the west (taking another four hours). There is a major set of falls in the

---

MONDULKIRI PROTECTED FOREST: THE AFRICAN EXPERIENCE IN CAMBODIA

Before the civil war, the vast grasslands of northern Mondulkiri were home to huge herds of gaur, banteng and wild buffalo. Visitors lucky enough to witness their annual migrations compared the experience to the Serengeti and the annual wildebeest migrations. Sadly, the long civil war took its toll and like Uganda and other African countries, thousands of animals were killed for bush meat.

A project is currently underway to return this area to its former glory. An initiative from the **World Wide Fund for Nature** (WWF; www.wwf.org/cambodia), the Srepok Wilderness area is at the heart of the Mondulkiri Protected Forest, one of the largest protected areas in Cambodia that provides a home to tigers, leopards, bears, langurs, wild cow and rare birdlife. Plans are currently underway to develop ecotourism activities here during 2009, which will include homestays, elephant trekking, mountain biking, kayaking and bird watching. Villagers and rangers are currently undergoing training to prepare for visitors and part of the project will showcase minority cultures and lifestyles. There are also eventual plans for a high-end eco-lodge in the heart of the protected area. However, all this is some way off, so check in with the WWF website or the **Phnom Penh office** (☎ 023-218034) to find out the latest. Once it is up and running, access is possible via Sen Monorom and Koh Nhek, but it takes two days from Phnom Penh. If flights to Ratanakiri resume, then it will be faster to fly to Ban Lung and travel by road and trail from there.

Mimong area called **Tan Lung Waterfall**, but this is also a nightmare to reach.

KOH NHEK

កោះញែក

pop 6000

The final frontier as far as Mondulkiri goes, this remote village in the far north of the province is a strategic place on the challenging overland route between Sen Monorom and Ratanakiri Province. Friendly locals are willing to put up foreigners for 10,000r and can prepare some basic food for a small charge. There are also basic supplies in the village, including coldish beer – well-earned once you get here.

The road from Sen Monorom to Koh Nhek is in good shape and takes just a couple of hours to cover the 93km. After Koh Nhek, the road simply vanishes into a spider's web of ox-cart trails after Koh Nhek and it really requires a local to show the way to Ban Lung in Ratanakiri. For more on this route, see p294.

Directory

CONTENTS

BOOK YOUR STAY ONLINE

For more accommodation reviews and recommendations by Lonely Planet authors, check out the online booking service at www.lonelyplanet.com/hotels. You'll find the true, insider low-down on the best places to stay. Reviews are thorough and independent. Best of all, you can book online.

ACCOMMODATION

Accommodation in Cambodia has improved immensely during the past decade and everything is available, from the classic budget crash pad to the plush palace. Most hotels quote in US dollars, but some places in the provinces quote in riel, while those near the Thai border quote in baht. We provide prices based on the currency quoted to us at the time of research. In Phnom Penh, Siem Reap, Sihanoukville and Kep there are options to suit all wallets. Elsewhere around Cambodia, the choice is limited to budget and midrange options, but these places provide great value for money.

In this guide, budget accommodation refers to guesthouses where the majority of rooms are within the US$2 to US$15 range, midrange generally runs from US$15 up to US$75 and top end is considered US$75 and up, up, up.

Budget guesthouses used to be restricted to Phnom Penh, Siem Reap and Sihanoukville, but as tourism takes off in the provinces, they are turning up in most other provincial capitals such as Kampot, Kratie and Stung Treng. Costs hover around US$2 to US$5 for a bed. In many rural parts of Cambodia, the standard rate for cheap hotels is US$5, usually with bathroom and satellite TV. There may be a few places starting at 10,000r, but they tend to make more by the hour than they do by the night – don't count on much sleep!

In Phnom Penh, Sihanoukville and Siem Reap, which see a steady flow of tourist traffic, hotels improve significantly once you start spending more than US$10 a night. For US$15 or less it is usually possible to find an air-con room with satellite TV and attached bathroom. If you spend between US$20 and US$50 it is possible to arrange something very comfortable with the possible lure of a swimming pool. Most smaller provincial cities also offer air-conditioned comfort in the US$10 to US$20 range.

There are now a host of international-standard hotels in Siem Reap, several in Phnom Penh and a couple on the coast in Sihanoukville and Kep. Some are operated by familiar international brands such as Le Meridien, Raffles and Sofitel. Most quote hefty walk-in rates and whack 10% tax and 10% service on as well. Book through a travel agent for a lower rate including taxes and service.

Some guesthouses in Cambodia do not have hot water, but most places have at least a few more-expensive rooms where it is available. Smaller places in remote areas may have bathrooms where a large jar or cement trough is filled with water for bathing purposes. Don't climb into it – just sluice the water with the plastic scoop or metal bowl. However, most guesthouses have cold showers these days.

While many of the swish new hotels have lifts, older hotels often don't and the cheapest rooms are at the end of several flights of stairs. It's a win-win-win situation: cheaper rooms, a bit of exercise and better views!

There is often confusion over the terms 'singles', 'doubles', 'double occupancy' and 'twins'. A single contains one bed, even if two people sleep in it. If there are two beds in the room, that is a twin, even if only one person occupies it. If two people stay in the same room, that is double occupancy. In some hotels 'doubles' means twin beds, while in others it means double occupancy.

Homestays

Homestays are popping up in the provinces and offer a good way to meet the local people and learn about the Cambodian lifestyle. There are several organised homestays around the country in provinces like Kompong Cham and Kompong Thom, as well as lots of informal homestays in out-of-the-way places such as Preah Vihear. In the minority areas of Mondulkiri and Ratanakiri, it is often possible to stay with tribal villagers.

ACTIVITIES

Tourism in Cambodia is catching up fast and there are now more activities than ever to get that adrenaline buzz. Phnom Penh and Siem Reap remain the places with most of the action, but Sihanoukville and Kep are making a name for themselves for fun in the sun with water sports.

Bird-watching

Bird-watching is a big draw, as Cambodia is home to some of the region's rarest large water birds including adjutants, storks and pelicans. For more on the birds of Cambodia see p58, and for the low-down on bird sanctuaries and birding opportunities around Siem Reap, see p138.

Boat Trips

With so much water around the country, it is hardly surprising that boat trips are popular with tourists. Some of these are functional, such as travelling up the Tonlé Sap River from Phnom Penh to Siem Reap (p137), or along the Sangker River from Siem Reap to Battambang (p245). Others are the traditional tourist trips, such as those available in Phnom Penh (p88), Siem Reap (p139) and Sihanoukville (p211), or dolphin-spotting in Kratie (p288).

Cycling

As Cambodia's roads continue to improve, cycling tourists are an increasingly common sight. It's an adrenaline-packed adventure and brings visitors that much closer to the uber-friendly locals. Local kids will race you at any opportunity and families will beckon cyclists in for some fruit or hot tea. Some of the main roads are getting busier and others remain dusty, but there are some great routes for those willing to put in the effort. The south coast of Cambodia remains a rewarding region for cyclists, while the northeast holds future promise for serious mountain-bikers. The most popular place for cycling is around the majestic temples of Angkor where the roads are paved and the forest thick. Bikes are available for hire in most towns in Cambodia for US$1 to US$2 a day, but serious tourers need to bring their own wheels.

Dirt Biking

For experienced riders, Cambodia is one of the most rewarding off-road biking destinations in the world. The roads are generally considered some of the worst in Asia (or best in Asia for die-hard biking enthusiasts). There are incredible rides all over the country, particularly in the north and northeast, but it is best to stay away from the main highways as traffic and dust make it a choking experience. For more on dirt biking, see p327, including recommended motorcycle touring companies.

Diving & Snorkelling

Snorkelling and diving are available off the coast of Sihanoukville. The jury is still out about the dive sites, as much is still to be explored, but while it may not be as spectacular as Indonesia or the Philippines, there is plenty in the deep blue yonder. It is best to venture further afield to dive sites such as Koh Tang (p198) and Koh Prins (p198), staying overnight on a boat. There are many unexplored areas off the coast between Koh Kong and Sihanoukville that could one day put Cambodia on the dive map of Asia.

Golf

Cambodia is an up-and-coming golfing destination thanks to two new courses in Siem Reap (p125), one of which now hosts an annual PGA event on the Asian tour. There are also a couple of courses in Phnom Penh (p88).

Trekking

Trekking is not the first thing you associate with Cambodia due to the presence of land mines, but there are several relatively safe areas of the country, including the nascent national parks. The northeastern provinces of Mondulkiri (p298) and Ratanakiri (p291) were never mined and with their wild, natural scenery, abundant waterfalls and ethnic minority populations, they are emerging as the country's leading trekking destinations. Always take a guide, however, as there are some unexploded bombs in these areas from the American bombing campaign of the early 1970s. Elephant treks are also possible in these northeastern provinces.

Cambodia is steadily establishing a network of national parks with visitor facilities; Bokor National Park (p219), Kirirom National Park (p116) and Ream National Park (p213) all promise trekking potential.

Angkor is emerging as a good place for gentle walks between the temples – one way to experience peace and solitude as visitor numbers skyrocket.

Watersports

As the Cambodian coast takes off, there are more adrenaline buzzes available including boating, windsurfing and kite surfing off the beaches of Sihanoukville (p196).

BUSINESS HOURS

Most Cambodians get up very early and it is not unusual to see people out and about exercising at 5.30am if you are heading home – ahem, sorry, getting up – at that time. Government offices, which are open from Monday to Friday and Saturday mornings, theoretically begin the working day at 7.30am, break for a siesta from 11.30am to 2pm, and end the day at 5pm. However, it is a safe bet that few people will be around early in the morning or after 4pm, as their real income is earned elsewhere.

Banking hours vary slightly according to the bank, but most keep core hours of 8am to 3.30pm Monday to Friday, plus Saturday morning. Attractions such as museums are normally open seven days a week and these days staff have had their arms twisted to stay open through lunch.

Local restaurants are generally open from about 6.30am until 9pm and international restaurants until a little later. Local restaurants may stay open throughout, while international restaurants sometimes close between sittings. Many bars are open all day, but some open only for the night shift, especially if they don't serve food.

Local markets operate seven days a week and usually open and close with the sun, running from 6.30am to 5.30pm. Markets shut up shop for a few days during the major holidays of Chaul Chnam Khmer (Khmer New Year), P'chum Ben (Festival of the Dead) and Chaul Chnam Chen (Chinese New Year). Shops tend to open from about 8am until 6pm, sometimes later.

CHILDREN

Children can live it up in Cambodia as they are always the centre of attention and almost everybody wants to play with them. For the full picture on surviving and thriving on the road with kids, check out Lonely Planet's *Travel with Children* by Cathy Lanigan for a rundown on health precautions for kids and advice on travel during pregnancy.

Practicalities

When it comes to feeding and caring for babies, pretty much everything you'll need is available in Phnom Penh and Siem Reap, but supplies dry up quickly elsewhere. Cot beds are available in international-standard mid-range and top-end hotels, but not elsewhere. Consider investing in a sturdy hammock or two if travelling to lesser-known destinations. There are no safety seats in rented cars or taxis. Some restaurants can supply a high chair when it comes to eating.

Breastfeeding in public is very common in Cambodia, so there is no need to worry about crossing a cultural boundary. But there are few facilities for changing babies other than the usual bathrooms, so take a baby bag everywhere you go. For kiddies too young to handle chopsticks, most restaurants also have cutlery.

The main worry throughout Cambodia is keeping an eye on what strange things infants are putting in their mouths. Their natural curiosity can be a lot more costly in a country where dysentery, typhoid and hepatitis are commonplace. Keeping their hydration levels up and insisting they use sunscreen is also important.

Phnom Penh, Siem Reap and other urban areas of Cambodia are pretty straightforward these days, although be very aware of the chaotic traffic conditions in the capital – better to restrict your child's movements than have them wander into danger. Rural Cambodia is not a good travel destination for children as there are still many land mines littering the countryside. No matter how many warnings a child is given, can you be certain they won't stray from the path?

Sights & Activities

There is plenty to keep kids happy in Phnom Penh, Siem Reap and the South Coast, but in the smaller provincial towns the boredom factor might creep in. Phnom Penh has a good selection of swimming pools (p89) and even a go-cart track (p88). Boat trips on the river should be a hit, but best of all is the Phnom Tamao Wildlife Sanctuary (p115), about 45km south of the city, with tigers, sun bears and elephants.

At Angkor, the temples may be too much for younger children but will be appreciated by inquisitive older children. Younger ones might prefer crumbling ruins like Ta Prohm (p166) or Beng Mealea (p178) to the more museumlike renovated temples. *Remorque-motos* (motorbikes with a cute little hooded trailer hitched to the back) are a fun way for families to get around the Angkor area (p154). Cambodian Cultural Village (p124) may be kitsch, but it is the right tonic after the temples. Hot-air balloons and helicopter rides round off some action-packed options in Siem Reap.

The national parks don't have enough visible wildlife to deliver, but some have waterfalls, including Kirirom National Park (p116) and Bokor National Park (p219). Another area for attractive waterfalls is the northeast and the provinces of Mondulkiri and Ratanakiri, where kids can also ride elephants (p301 and p292). The air is clean, at least when cars aren't kicking up red dust, and there are wide open spaces.

Cambodia has a long coastline, and Sihanoukville (p193) is the number one beach spot. There are plenty of local children hanging out on the beach, many of them trying to make a living, and this can be an interesting bonding experience for kids. Pay close attention to any playtime in the sea, as there are some deceptively strong currents in the wet season.

CLIMATE CHARTS

Life in Cambodia is fairly steamy in the lowlands, with a classic tropical climate. It gets a little cooler up in the hills of the northeast, but even there it rarely gets cold.

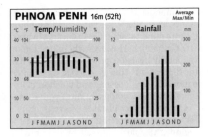

Average daily temperatures range from the high 20s in the 'cool' season of December and January, to the high 30s and beyond in the hot months of April and May. The rain kicks in around June and falls thick and fast throughout August and September, bringing the landscape back to life ready for a new harvest.

COURSES
Cooking
For the full story on cooking courses in Cambodia, see p69.

Language
The only language courses available in Cambodia at present are in Khmer and are aimed at expat residents of Phnom Penh rather than travellers. If you are going to be based in Phnom Penh for some time, however, it would be well worth learning basic Khmer. Ring the **Cambodia Development Research Institute** (☎ 023-368053; 56 St 315) for information about classes or try the Institute of Foreign Languages at the **Royal University of Phnom Penh** (Map pp74-5; ☎ 012 866826; Russian Blvd). Also check out the notice board at the Foreign Correspondents' Club (FCC; p101), where one-hour lessons are often advertised by private tutors.

CUSTOMS REGULATIONS
If Cambodia has customs allowances, it is close-lipped about them. A 'reasonable amount' of duty-free items are allowed into the country. Travellers arriving by air might bear in mind that alcohol and cigarettes are on sale at prices well below duty-free prices on the streets of Phnom Penh – a branded box of 200 cigarettes costs just US$9 and international spirits start as low as US$7 a litre.

Like any other country, Cambodia does not allow travellers to import weapons, explosives or narcotics – there are enough in the country already. It is illegal to take ancient stone sculptures from the Angkor period out of the country.

DANGERS & ANNOYANCES
As memories of war grow ever more distant, Cambodia has become a much safer country in which to travel. Remembering the golden rule – stick to the marked paths in remote areas – means you'd be very unlucky to have any problems. But it doesn't hurt to check on the latest situation before making a trip few other travellers undertake, particularly if travelling by motorcycle.

The **Cambodia Daily** (www.cambodiadaily.com) and the **Phnom Penh Post** (www.phnompenhpost .com) newspapers are both good sources for breaking news on Cambodia – check out their websites before you hit the road.

Begging
Begging is common throughout Cambodia, although much more evident in Phnom Penh and Siem Reap than elsewhere. There are many reasons for begging in a society as poor as Cambodia, some more visually evident than others, such as amputees who have lost their limbs to land mines. It is entirely up to individual visitors whether to give or not, and to decide how much to offer, but remember that it is common practice for Buddhists to give to those more needy than themselves.

Big brown eyes, runny noses and grubby hands…the sight of children begging is familiar throughout the developing world, and Cambodia is no exception. There are many child beggars around Phnom Penh and the temples of Angkor, and with their angelic faces it is often difficult to resist giving them some money. However, there are a number of issues to consider: giving to child beggars may create a cycle of dependency that can continue into adulthood; the children may not benefit directly from the money, as they are often made to beg by a 'pimp' or their family; and some child beggars, particularly around central Phnom Penh, may use the money to buy glue to feed their sniffing habit. One way to help these impoverished children is to buy them some food or drink, or give them some of your time and attention – it is amazing how quickly they will forget about begging once they are being taught something simple like a whistle, a trick or a game.

The most common beggars around the country are land-mine victims. Many of them sustained their injuries fighting, while others have had their legs blown off while working or playing innocently in the fields. You may tire of their attention after a few days in Cambodia, but try to remember that in a country with no social security network, begging is often all they can do to survive.

When giving to beggars, try to offer smaller denominations to avoid making foreigners more of a target than they already are.

Checkpoints

During the long years of civil war there were checkpoints on roads throughout the country, but these days they are a rare sight. Where there are checkpoints on major roads, spot checks may be carried out to make sure drivers have paid their road tax or are not carrying illegal guns.

If you are travelling in a taxi or pick-up truck in remote areas of Cambodia and come across a checkpoint, the driver should take care of the payment. If you are on a motorbike, you are unlikely to be stopped. However, should you ever find money being demanded of you, try to negotiate the sum to an acceptable level. Do not under any circumstances attempt to take photos of the individuals concerned as things could turn nasty in a hurry.

Scams

There are fewer scams in Cambodia than neighbouring countries, but now that tourism is really taking off this might change. Most current scams are fairly harmless, involving a bit of commission here and there for taxi or *moto* drivers, particularly in Siem Reap. More annoying are the 'cheap' buses from Bangkok to Siem Reap, deservedly nicknamed the 'The Scam Buses' for using the wrong border crossings, driving slowly and selling passengers to guesthouses (p330), but thankfully these are a dying breed.

There have been one or two reports of police set-ups in Phnom Penh, involving planted drugs. This seems to be very rare, but if you fall victim to the ploy, it will require patience and persistence to sort out, inevitably involving embassies and the like. It may be best to pay them off before more police get involved at the local station, as the price will only rise when there are more people to pay off.

Cambodia is renowned for its precious stones, particularly the rubies and sapphires that are mined around the Pailin area in western Cambodia. However, there are lots of chemically treated copies around, as much of the high-quality stuff is snapped up by international buyers. The long and the short of it is: don't buy unless you really know your stones.

On the subject of fakes, there is quite a lot of fake medication floating about the region. Safeguard yourself by only buying prescription drugs from reliable pharmacies or clinics. Similarly, there are a lot of dodgy recreational drugs around, some of which could seriously damage your health: see the boxed text Yaba Daba Do? Yaba Daba Don't! (p315) for more on this.

Security

Cambodia is a pretty safe country in which to travel these days. Once again, remember the golden rule – *stick to marked paths in remote areas.* It is now possible to travel throughout Cambodia with no more difficulty than in neighbouring Thailand or Vietnam. Politically, Cambodia has proven an unpredictable country and this makes it hard to guarantee safety of travel at any given time. Suffice to say that you are no longer a target just because you are a tourist.

Cambodia is something of a lawless society in which arms are often preferred to eloquence when settling a dispute. This 'Wild East' atmosphere rarely affects tourists, but it is worth knowing about as you can expect to hear gunshots from time to time (usually someone firing into the air when drunk). Phnom Penh (p81) is arguably one of the more dangerous places; it is here that the most guns are concentrated and the most robberies take place. This is closely followed by Sihanoukville (p196), which has sadly de-

---

PLANET OF THE FAKES

Cambodia is awash with pirated books and poor photocopies, including Lonely Planet titles. We know you wouldn't dream of buying a photocopied Lonely Planet guide, and that's very sensible given that old editions are sometimes wrapped in new covers, pages are bound in the wrong order and the type is so faded as to be almost unreadable. Be warned, if this is a photocopy, it may self-destruct in five seconds.

TRAVEL ADVISORY WEBSITES

Travel advisories on government-run websites update nationals on the latest security situation in any given country, including Cambodia. They are useful to check out for dangerous countries or dangerous times, but they tend to be pretty conservative, stressing dangers where they don't always exist…otherwise known as covering their proverbials.

Australia (www.smartraveller.gov.au)
Canada (www.voyage.gc.ca)
Germany (www.auswaertiges-amt.de)
Japan (www.anzen.mofa.go.jp)

Netherlands (www.minbuza.nl)
New Zealand (www.safetravel.govt.nz)
UK (www.fco.gov.uk/travel)
USA (www.travel.state.gov)

veloped a reputation for robbery and sneak theft. Elsewhere in the provinces you would be very unlucky to have any incident befall you, as the vast majority of Khmers are immensely hospitable, honest and helpful. More importantly, perhaps, the majority of Khmers are experiencing peace for the first time in more than 30 years and don't want it disturbed.

Trying to pinpoint any lingering areas of concern around the country is always difficult as circumstances change quickly. Pailin and large parts of Oddar Meanchey and Preah Vihear Provinces were Khmer Rouge controlled until just a few years ago, but are now considered safe. However, as the trial for surviving Khmer Rouge leaders moves forward, it could be a different story – just because the former rebels now wear baseball caps instead of Mao caps, doesn't mean they have forgotten the fight. However, since the trial began, there have been no problems in these areas.

Should anyone be unlucky enough to be robbed, it is important to note that the Cambodian police are the best that money can buy! Any help, such as a police report, is going to cost you. The going rate depends on the size of the claim, but US$5 to US$20 is a common charge. However, some tourist police will now provide this service for free.

Snakes

Visitors to Ta Prohm at Angkor and other overgrown archaeological sites should beware of snakes. They are very well camouflaged so keep your eyes peeled. For details of what to do in case of snake bite, see p349.

Theft & Street Crime

Given the number of guns in Cambodia, there is less armed theft than one might expect. Still, hold-ups and motorcycle theft are a potential danger in Phnom Penh (p81) and Sihanoukville (p196). There is no need to be paranoid, just cautious. Walking or riding alone late at night is not ideal, certainly not in rural areas.

Pickpocketing and theft by stealth is more a problem in Vietnam than in Cambodia, but it pays to be careful. The current hot spots are crowded pick-up trucks on popular tourist routes such as Siem Reap to Poipet or Phnom Penh, and the markets of Phnom Penh. Don't make it any easier for thieves by putting your passport and wads of cash in your back pocket. As a precaution, keep a 'secret' stash of cash separate from the bulk of your funds. There has been bag snatching in Phnom Penh (p78) in the last few years and the motorbike thieves don't let go, dragging passengers off *motos* and endangering lives.

Traffic Accidents

Traffic conditions in Cambodia are chaotic, although no worse than in many other underdeveloped countries. If you are riding a bike in Phnom Penh, stay very alert and take nothing for granted. Traffic moves in all directions on both sides of the road, so don't be surprised to see vehicles bearing down on you. The horn is used to alert other drivers of a vehicle's presence – get out of the way if you hear a car or truck behind you.

FESTIVAL WARNING

In the run-up to major festivals such as P'chum Ben or Chaul Chnam Khmer, there is a palpable increase in the number of robberies, particularly in Phnom Penh. Cambodians need money to buy gifts for relatives or to pay off debts, and for some individuals theft is the quick way to get this money. Be more vigilant at night at these times and don't take valuables out with you unnecessarily.

Few *moto* drivers in Cambodia use or provide safety helmets. Fortunately most of them drive at sensible speeds. If you encounter a reckless driver, ask them to slow down or pay them and find another *moto*.

Having a major traffic accident in Phnom Penh would be bad enough, but if you have one in rural Cambodia, you are in big trouble. Somehow you will have to get back to Phnom Penh for medical treatment.

The basic rule is to drive carefully – there have already been too many shattered dreams in Cambodia, and there's no need for more. See p327 for safety tips.

Undetonated Mines, Mortars & Bombs

Never touch any rockets, artillery shells, mortars, mines, bombs or other war material you may come across. A tactic of the Khmer Rouge was to lay mines along roads and in rice fields in an effort to maim and kill civilians. The only concrete results of this policy are the many limbless people you see all over Cambodia.

The most heavily mined part of the country is the Battambang and Pailin area, but mines are a problem all over Cambodia. In short: *do not stray from well-marked paths under any circumstances*. If you are planning any walks, even in safer areas such as the remote northeast, it is imperative you take a guide as there may be unexploded ordnance (UXO) from the American bombing campaign of the early 1970s.

Violence

Violence against foreigners is extremely rare and is not something you should waste much time worrying about, but it pays to take care in crowded bars or nightclubs in Phnom Penh. If you get into a stand-off with rich young Khmers in a bar or club, swallow your pride and back down. Still think you can 'ave 'em? Many carry guns: enough said.

DISCOUNT CARDS

Senior travellers and students are not eligible for discounts in Cambodia – all foreigners who are rich enough to make it to Cambodia are rich enough to pay as far as Cambodians are concerned.

EMBASSIES & CONSULATES
Cambodian Embassies & Consulates

Cambodian diplomatic representation abroad is still thin on the ground, though the situation is slowly improving. However, as e-visas are available over the internet and visas are issued on arrival at airports and at land borders, most visitors don't really need to call at a Cambodian embassy in advance.

Cambodian diplomatic missions abroad include the following:

Australia (☎ 02-6273 1259; 5 Canterbury Cres, Deakin, ACT 2600)
China (☎ 010-6532 1889; 9 Dongzhimenwai Dajie, Beijing 100600)
France (☎ 01-45 03 47 20; 4 Rue Adolphe Yvon, 75116 Paris)
Germany (☎ 030-48 63 79 01; Arnold Zweing Strasse, 1013189 Berlin)
Hong Kong (☎ 2546 0718; Unit 616, 6th fl, 3 Salisbury Rd, Tsim Sha Tsui, Kowloon)
India (☎ 011-649 5091; N-14 Panscheel Park, New Delhi 110017)
Indonesia (☎ 021-919 2895; 4th fl, Panin Bank Plaza, Jalan 52 Palmerah Utara, Jakarta 11480)
Japan (☎ 03-5412 8521; 8-6-9 Akasaka, Minato-ku, Tokyo 1070052)
Laos (☎ 21-314952; Tha Deau, Bon That Khao, Vientiane)
Malaysia (☎ 02-818 9918; 83/JKR 2809 Lingkungan, U Thant, 55000, Kuala Lumpur)
Singapore (☎ 299 3028; 152 Beach Rd, Gateway East, 189721, Singapore)
Thailand (☎ 02-254 6630; 185 Rajadamri Rd, Bangkok 10330)
UK (☎ 020-8451 7850; 64 Brondesbury Park, London, NW6 7AT)
USA (☎ 202-726 7742; 4500 16th St, NW, Washington DC 20011)
Vietnam Hanoi (☎ 04-825 3788; 71 Tran Hung Dao St); Ho Chi Minh City (☎ 08-829 2751; 41 Phung Khac Khoan St)

Embassies & Consulates in Cambodia

Quite a few countries have embassies in Phnom Penh, though some travellers will find that their nearest embassy is in Bangkok. It's important to realise what your country's embassy can and can't do to help if you get into trouble. Generally speaking, it won't be much help if the trouble you're in is remotely your own fault. Remember that you are bound by the laws of the country you are in. Your embassy won't be sympathetic if you end up in jail after committing a crime, even if such actions are legal in your own country.

In genuine emergencies you might get some assistance, but only if all other channels have been exhausted. If you have all your money and documents stolen, it might assist with getting a new passport, but a loan for onward travel is out of the question.

Those intending to visit Laos should note that Lao visas are available in Phnom Penh for US$30 to US$50, depending on nationality, and take two working days. For Vietnam, one-month single-entry visas cost US$30 to US$35 and take just one day, faster still at the Vietnamese consulate in Sihanoukville.

Embassies in Phnom Penh (023):

Australia (Map p79; ☎ 213470; 11 St 254)
Canada (Map p79; ☎ 213470; 11 St 254)
China (Map pp74-5; ☎ 720920; 256 Mao Tse Toung Blvd)
France (Map pp74-5; ☎ 430020; 1 Monivong Blvd)
Germany (Map p79; ☎ 216381; 76-78 St 214)
India (Map pp74-5; ☎ 210912; 777 Monivong Blvd)
Indonesia (Map p79; ☎ 216148; 90 Norodom Blvd)
Japan (Map pp74-5; ☎ 217161; 194 Norodom Blvd)
Laos (Map pp74-5; ☎ 982632; 15-17 Mao Tse Toung Blvd)
Malaysia (Map p79; ☎ 216177; 5 St 242)
Myanmar (Map pp74-5; ☎ 223761; 181 Norodom Blvd)
Philippines (Map p79; ☎ 222303; 33 St 294)
Singapore (Map p79; ☎ 221875; 92 Norodom Blvd)
Thailand (Map pp74-5; ☎ 726306; 196 Norodom Blvd)
UK (Map p79; ☎ 427124; 27-29 St 75)
USA (Map p79; ☎ 728000; 1 St 96)
Vietnam Phnom Penh (Map pp74-5; ☎ 362531; 436 Monivong Blvd); Sihanoukville (Map p194; ☎ 012 340495; St Ekareach)

FESTIVALS & EVENTS

For the inside story on festivals and events in Cambodia, see the Events Calendar (p19).

FOOD

Cambodian cuisine may be less well known than that of its popular neighbours Thailand and Vietnam, but it is no less tasty. See p63 for the full story on Cambodian cuisine.

GAY & LESBIAN TRAVELLERS

While Cambodian culture is tolerant of homosexuality, the gay and lesbian scene here is certainly nothing like that in Thailand. The former King Norodom Sihanouk was a keen supporter of equal rights for same-sex partners and this seems to have encouraged a more open attitude among younger Cambodians. Both Phnom Penh and Siem Reap have a few gay-friendly bars, but it is a low-key scene compared with some parts of Asia.

With the vast number of same-sex travel partners – gay or otherwise – checking into hotels across Cambodia, there is little consideration over how travelling foreigners are related. However, it is prudent not to flaunt your sexuality. As with heterosexual couples, passionate public displays of affection are considered a basic no-no.

Utopia (www.utopia-asia.com) features gay travel information and contacts, including detailed sections on the legality of homosexuality in Cambodia (it is legal but gay marriage isn't) and some local gay terminology.

HOLIDAYS
Public Holidays

During public holidays and festivals, banks, ministries and embassies close down, so plan ahead if visiting Cambodia during these times. Cambodians also roll over holidays if they fall on a weekend and take a day or two extra during major festivals (see p19). Add to this the fact that they take a holiday for international days here and there and it soon becomes apparent that Cambodia has more public holidays than any other nation on earth!

International New Year's Day 1 January
Victory over the Genocide 7 January
International Women's Day 8 March
International Workers' Day 1 May
International Children's Day 8 May
King's Birthday 13-15 May
King Mother's Birthday 18 June
Constitution Day 24 September
King Father's Birthday 31 October
Independence Day 9 November
International Human Rights Day 10 December

INSURANCE

A travel insurance policy that covers theft, property loss and medical expenses is more essential for Cambodia than for most other parts of Southeast Asia. There are a wide variety of insurance policies available, and it's wise to check with a reliable travel agent as to which is most suitable for Cambodia.

When buying your travel insurance *always* check the small print:

- Some policies specifically exclude 'dangerous activities' such as scuba diving and riding a motorcycle. If you are going to be motorbiking in Cambodia, check that you will be covered.
- Check whether the medical coverage is on a pay first, claim later basis; if this is the case, keep all documents relating to any medical treatment.

INSURANCE ALERT!

Do not visit Cambodia without medical insurance. Hospitals are extremely basic in the provinces and even in Phnom Penh the facilities are generally not up to the standards you may be accustomed to. Anyone who has a serious injury or illness while in Cambodia may require emergency evacuation to Bangkok. With an insurance policy costing no more than the equivalent of a bottle of beer a day, this evacuation is free. Without an insurance policy, it will cost between US$10,000 and US$20,000 – somewhat more than a six-pack. Don't gamble with your health in Cambodia or you may end up another statistic.

■ In the case of Cambodia, it is essential to check that medical coverage includes the cost of emergency evacuation (see above).

INTERNET ACCESS

Internet access is available in most towns throughout the country. In Phnom Penh prices just keep dropping, thankfully, and now average US$0.50 or less per hour. Siem Reap is a little more expensive at US$0.50 to US$1.50 per hour, while in other provinces it can range from US$1 an hour to as much as US$4 an hour, thanks to expensive domestic phone calls. Most internet cafés also supply headsets to allow cheap phone calls via Skype or similar programmes.

If travelling with a laptop, remember that Cambodia's power-supply voltage will vary from that at home, risking damage to your equipment. The best investment is a universal AC adapter, which enables you to plug it in anywhere without frying its innards.

Visitors carrying a laptop who are looking for a direct connection to a server have several choices. The most convenient option is usually via wi-fi networks, which are increasingly common in Phnom Penh and Siem Reap. Many cafés and restaurants offer free wi-fi for customers, while hotels often levy a small charge.

Those still working on fixed-line connections can pick up one of the prepaid internet cards offered by Online or Everyday, available from shops and some restaurants. They come in a range of values from US$10 to US$50 and can be purchased from shops, hotels and petrol stations.

Those who like contracts and paperwork can try **Online** (Map p79; ☎ 023-430000; 15 Norodom Blvd), **Camintel** (Map p79; ☎ 023-986789; 1 Sisowath Quay) or **Telesurf** (Map p79; ☎ 012 800800; 33 Sihanouk Blvd), all in Phnom Penh. Prices are high by international standards and if you are using a mobile phone from remote areas, the connection is poor.

LEGAL MATTERS

Marijuana is not legal in Cambodia and police are beginning to take a harder line on it, although usually for their own benefit rather than a desire to uphold the law. There have been several busts (and a few set-ups, too) of foreigner-owned bars and restaurants where ganja was smoked – the days of free bowls in guesthouses are now history. Marijuana is traditionally used in some Khmer food, so it will continue to be around for a long time, but if you are a smoker, be discreet. It's probably only a matter of time before the Cambodian police turn the regular busting of foreigners into a lucrative sideline.

This advice applies equally to other narcotic substances, which are also illegal. And think twice about scoring from an unfamiliar *moto* driver as it may end with you getting robbed after passing out.

MAPS

The best all-rounder for Cambodia is the Gecko *Cambodia Road Map*. At 1:750,000 scale, it has lots of detail and accurate place names. Other popular foldout maps include Nelles *Cambodia, Laos and Vietnam Map* at 1:1,500,000, although the detail is limited, and the Periplus *Cambodia Travel Map* at 1:1,000,000, with city maps of Phnom Penh and Siem Reap.

There are lots of free maps, subsidised by advertising, that are available in Phnom Penh and Siem Reap at leading hotels, guesthouses, restaurants and bars.

For serious map buffs or cartographers, Psar Thmei (Central Market) in Phnom Penh is well stocked with Vietnamese and Khmer-produced maps of towns and provinces, as well as US military maps from the 1970s at a scale of 1:50,000. Some roads have deteriorated rather than improved since the civil war, so much of the information remains accurate more than three decades on.

MONEY

Cambodia's currency is the riel, abbreviated in this guide by a lower-case 'r' written after the sum. Cambodia's second currency (some would say its first) is the US dollar, which is accepted everywhere and by everyone, though change may arrive in riel. Dollar bills with a small tear are unlikely to be accepted by Cambodians, so it's worth scrutinising the change you are given to make sure you don't have bad bills. In the west of the country, the Thai baht (B) is also commonplace. If three currencies seems a little excessive, perhaps it's because the Cambodians are making up for lost time: during the Pol Pot era, the country had *no* currency. The Khmer Rouge abolished money and blew up the National Bank building in Phnom Penh.

The Cambodian riel comes in notes of the following denominations: 50r, 100r, 200r, 500r, 1000r, 2000r, 5000r, 10,000r, 20,000r, 50,000r and 100,000r.

Throughout this book, prices are in the currency quoted to the average punter. This is usually US dollars or riel, but in the west it is often baht. While this may seem inconsistent, this is the way it's done in Cambodia and the sooner you get used to thinking comparatively in riel, dollars or baht, the easier your travels will be.

For a sprinkling of exchange rates at the time of going to print, see the Quick Reference section on the inside front cover of this book.

ATMs

There are now credit-card-compatible ATMs (Visa and MasterCard only) in most major cities including Phnom Penh, Siem Reap, Sihanoukville, Battambang and Kompong Cham. There are also ATMs at the Cham Yeam and Poipet borders if arriving from Thailand. Machines dispense US dollars. Large withdrawals of up to US$2000 are possible, providing your account can handle it. Stay alert when using them late at night. ANZ Royal Bank has the most extensive network, including ATMs at petrol stations and popular hotels, restaurants and shops, closely followed by Canadia Bank. Acleda Bank has the widest network of branches in the country, including all provincial capitals, and many have ATMs. However, these are not yet compatible with international credit cards, although rumours are that they will be upgraded soon.

Bargaining

It is important to haggle over purchases made in local markets in Phnom Penh (p109) and Siem Reap (p135), otherwise the stallholder may 'shave your head' (local vernacular for 'rip you off'). Bargaining is the rule in markets, when arranging share taxis and pick-ups and in cheaper guesthouses. The Khmers are not ruthless hagglers, so a persuasive smile and a little friendly quibbling is usually enough to get a good price. Try to remember that the aim is not to get the lowest possible price, but a price that is acceptable to both you and the seller. Remember back home, we pay astronomical sums for items, especially clothes, that have been made in poorer countries for next to nothing, and we don't even get the chance to bargain for them, just the opportunity to contribute to a corporate director's retirement fund. At least there is room for discussion in Cambodia, so try not to become

---

YABA DABA DO? YABA DABA DON'T!

Watch out for *yaba*, the 'crazy' drug from Thailand, known rather ominously in Cambodia as *yama* (the Hindu god of death). Known as ice or crystal meth back home, it's not just any old diet pill from the pharmacist, but homemade meta-amphetamines produced in labs in Cambodia and the region beyond. The pills are often laced with toxic substances, such as mercury, lithium or whatever else the maker can find. *Yama* is a dirty drug and more addictive than users would like to admit, provoking powerful hallucinations, sleep deprivation and psychosis. Steer clear of the stuff unless you plan on an indefinite extension to your trip.

Also be very careful about buying 'cocaine'. One look at the map and the distance between Colombia and Cambodia should be enough to make you dubious, but it's much worse than that. Most of what is sold as coke, particularly in Phnom Penh, is actually pure heroin and far stronger than any smack found on the streets back home. Bang this up your hooter and you are in serious trouble – several backpackers die each year in the lakeside guesthouse ghetto of Boeng Kak in Phnom Penh.

obsessed by the price. And also remember, in many cases a few hundred riel is more important to a Cambodian with a family to support than to a traveller on an extended vacation. After all, no-one bargains over a beer in a busy backpacker bar, so why bargain so hard over a cheap bottle of water?

Black Market

The black market no longer exists in Cambodia when it comes to changing money. Exchange rates on the street are the same as those offered by the banks; you just get to avoid the queues and paperwork.

Cash

The US dollar remains king in Cambodia. Armed with enough cash, you won't need to visit a bank at all because it is possible to change small amounts of dollars for riel at hotels, restaurants and markets. Hardened travellers argue that your trip ends up being slightly more expensive if you rely on US dollars rather than riel, but in reality there's very little in it. However, it never hurts to support the local currency against the greenback. It is always handy to have about US$10 worth of riel kicking around, as it is good for *motos, remorque-motos* and markets. Pay for something cheap in US dollars and the change comes in riel. In remote areas of the north and northeast, locals only deal in riel or small dollar denominations.

The only other currency that can be useful is Thai baht, mainly in the west of the country. Prices in towns such as Krong Koh Kong, Poipet and Sisophon are often quoted in baht, and even in Battambang it is as common as the dollar.

There are no banks at any of the land border crossings into Cambodia, meaning credit cards and travellers cheques are effectively useless on arrival, although there will likely be ATMs in Poipet in the near future. In the interests of making life as simple as possible, organise a supply of US dollars before arriving in Cambodia. Cash in other major currencies can be changed at banks or markets in Phnom Penh or Siem Reap. However, most banks tend to offer a miserable rate for any nondollar transaction so it can be better to use moneychangers, which are found in and around every major market.

Western Union and MoneyGram are both represented in Cambodia for fast, if more expensive, money transfers. Western Union is represented by SBC and Acleda Bank, and MoneyGram is represented by Canadia Bank.

Credit Cards

Top-end hotels, airline offices and upmarket boutiques and restaurants generally accept most major credit cards (Visa, MasterCard, JCB, sometimes American Express), but they usually pass the charges straight on to the customer, meaning an extra 3% on the bill.

Cash advances on credit cards are available in Phnom Penh, Siem Reap, Sihanoukville, Kampot, Battambang and Kompong Cham. Canadia Bank and Union Commercial Bank offer free cash advances, but most other banks advertise a minimum charge of US$5.

Several travel agents and hotels in Phnom Penh and Siem Reap arrange cash advances for about 5% commission; this can be particularly useful if you get caught short at the weekend.

Tipping

Tipping is not traditionally expected here, but in a country as poor as Cambodia, tips can go a long way. Salaries remain extremely low and service is often superb thanks to a Khmer commitment to hospitality. Hence a tip of just US$1 might be half a day's wages for some. Many of the upmarket hotels levy a 10% service charge, but this doesn't always make it to the staff. If you stay a couple of nights in the same hotel, try to remember to tip the staff that clean your room. Consider tipping drivers and guides, as the time they spend on the road means time away from home and family.

It is considered proper to make a small monetary donation at the end of a visit to a wat, especially if a monk has shown you around; most wats have contribution boxes for this purpose.

Travellers Cheques

Acleda Bank now offers travellers cheque encashment at most branches, bringing financial freedom to far-flung provinces like Ratanakiri and Mondulkiri. It is best to have cheques in US dollars, though it is also possible to change euros at Acleda Bank and most major currencies at branches of Canadia Bank. Generally, you pay about 2% commission to change travellers cheques.

PHOTOGRAPHY & VIDEO
Airport Security
The X-ray machines at Phnom Penh and Siem Reap airports are film-safe. If you are carrying 1000 ASA or higher film, store it separately and ask to have it inspected by hand.

Film & Equipment
Many internet cafés in Phnom Penh, Siem Reap, Battambang and Sihanoukville will burn CDs or DVDs from digital images using card readers or USB connections. The price is about US$2.50 if you need a CD or US$1.50 if you don't. Digital memory sticks are widely available in Cambodia and are pretty cheap. Digital cameras are a real bargain in Cambodia thanks to low tax and duty, so consider picking up a new model in Phnom Penh rather than Bangkok or Saigon.

Print film and processing is pretty cheap in Cambodia, with most labs charging about US$4 for a roll. Slide film is also available at competitive prices in Phnom Penh. Do not have slide film processed in Cambodia unless it is really urgent. Many shops claim to be able to process slide film, but you'll more than likely end up with black and white X-ray-style shots.

If you carry a video camera, make sure you have the necessary charger, plugs and transformer for Cambodia. Take care with some of the electrical wiring in guesthouses around the country, as it can be pretty amateurish. In Phnom Penh and Siem Reap, it is possible to obtain video tapes for most formats, but elsewhere around the country you are unlikely to find much of use. If you are shooting on hi-def, then pick up the tapes before arriving in Cambodia, as it's still not widely available.

Photographing People
The usual rules apply. Be polite about photographing and video taping people; don't push cameras into their faces, and have some respect for monks and people at prayer. In general, the Khmers are remarkably courteous people and if you ask nicely, they'll agree to have their photograph taken. The same goes for filming, although in rural areas you will often find children desperate to get in front of the lens and astonished at seeing themselves played back on an LCD screen. It is the closest most of them will get to being on TV.

Technical Tips
The best light conditions in Cambodia begin around 20 minutes after sunrise and last for just one to two hours, roughly corresponding to 6am to 8am. The same applies for the late afternoon light, which begins to assume a radiant warm quality around an hour before sunset. From 10am to around 4pm you can expect the light to be harsh and bleaching – there's not much you can do with it unless you have a polariser. For endless tips on better travel photography, pick up a copy of Lonely Planet's *Travel Photography*.

POST
The postal service is hit and miss from Cambodia; send anything valuable by courier or from another country. Make sure postcards and letters are franked before they vanish from your sight.

Postal rates are listed in post offices in the major towns and cities. Postcards cost 1500r to 2100r to send internationally. Letters and parcels sent further afield than Asia can take up to two or three weeks to reach their destination. Use a courier to speed things up: **DHL** (Map p79; ☎ 023-427726; www.dhl.com; 353 St 110), **FedEx** (Map pp74-5; ☎ 023-216712; www.fedex.com; 701D Monivong Blvd), **TNT** (Map p79; ☎ 023-430922; www .tnt.com; 28 Monivong Blvd) and **UPS** (Map p79; ☎ 023-427511; www.ups.com; 27 St 134). All have offices in Phnom Penh and some have branch offices in Siem Reap. A slightly cheaper courier option is **EMS** (Map p79; ☎ 023-723511; Main Post Office, St 13), with offices at every major post office in the country.

Phnom Penh's main post office (p78) has a poste restante box at the far-left end of the post counter, but long-term travellers are better off getting their stuff sent to Bangkok.

SHOPPING
There is excellent shopping to be had in Cambodia, particularly in Phnom Penh (p107) and Siem Reap (p135). As well as the inevitable range of souvenirs, there are many high-quality handicrafts made to support disadvantaged groups in Cambodia (see p108 and p136).

For tips on how to haggle, see p315.

Antiques
Cambodia has a reasonable range of antiques, although a lot disappeared or was destroyed during the war years. Popular items include

textiles, silver, swords, coins, ceramics and furniture, but when buying antiques be very careful of fakes – they are extremely common in this part of the world. If the prices seem too good to be true, then they usually are and you'll end up with a well-aged, modern copy. This is particularly the case with 'old' bronzes from 'the time of Angkor' and a lot of 'ancient' Chinese pieces. Remember that ancient sandstone carvings from the Angkorian or pre-Angkorian periods cannot legally be taken out of the country.

For those settling in Cambodia for any length of time, there are some very nice pieces of antique furniture available in markets and shops in Phnom Penh, with Chinese, French and Khmer influences all evident.

Artwork

The choice of art was, until recently, limited to the poor-quality Angkor paintings seen throughout the country. However, the selection is improving in Phnom Penh and Siem Reap. Psar Chaa (p136) in Siem Reap and the art shops on St 178 in Phnom Penh (p107) are good hunting grounds, and there are a number of upmarket galleries in the capital. Cambodia has a budding art scene and local luminaries hold regular exhibitions at hotels, restaurants and cafés.

Clothing

Many international brands are made in factories around Phnom Penh, including Colombia, Gant, Gap, Levis and Nautica; there is a lot of 'leakage', with items turning up in Psar Tuol Tom Pong (p109) in Phnom Penh at very reasonable prices.

Sculpture

The beauty and intricacy of Cambodian sculpture is evident for all to see around the temples of Angkor (p140) and in the National Museum (p84) in Phnom Penh. There are many skilled stone carvers in Cambodia today, and replica sculpture is widely available in Phnom Penh and Siem Reap. Popular items include busts of Jayavarman VII and statues of Hindu deities such as Shiva, Vishnu and Harihara. Do not attempt to buy ancient stone sculpture in Cambodia: looting is a huge problem in remote parts of the country and it would be grossly irresponsible for any visitor to add to the problem.

Silk & Textiles

Cambodia is world renowned for its exquisite silk. Much of the country's silk is still traditionally hand-woven and dyed using natural colours from plants and minerals. The best silk comes from Kompong Cham and Takeo Provinces, but not all the silk sold in Cambodia originates from here (some silk is imported from China and Vietnam). Concerted efforts are underway to reintroduce mulberry trees and locally cultivated silk across the country. There are silk farms in Siem Reap and some of the other provincial centres renowned for silk. Some of the best places to buy silk include Artisans d'Angkor (p123) in Siem Reap, which also operates branches at the international airports, at recommended shops in Phnom Penh and Siem Reap that support disabled and impoverished Cambodians, and at Psar Tuol Tom Pong (p109) in Phnom Penh. In the provinces, there are several high-quality silk operations, including Mekong Blue (p290) in Stung Treng and Weaves of Cambodia (p265) in Tbeng Meanchey.

Silver

Cambodian silver is valued overseas for the detail of hand-carving on most of the pieces. However, not all silver has that much silver content, so it is important to be careful what you buy. Cambodian silver ranges from copies with no silver, to 50% silver alloy, right up to pure silver. Reputable establishments will often tell you the purity of their silver, but market sellers might try to pull a fast one. The easiest way for novices to determine the quality is to feel the weight. Pure silver should be heavier than alloys or plate.

Woodcarving

Woodcarving is a rich tradition in Cambodia and there are many wooden items that make nice decorative pieces. Reproduction Buddhas are very popular with visitors and there is no restriction on taking Buddha images out of the country. There are also wooden copies available of most of the principal Angkorian sculptures, as well as finely carved animals. Weaving wheels are quite popular and are often elaborately decorated, making nice wall mounts. Betel nut boxes are plentiful, as are jewellery boxes inlaid with mother of pearl, lacquer or metalwork.

DOMESTIC TELEPHONE AREA CODES	
Banteay Meanchey Province	☎ 054
Battambang Province	☎ 053
Kampot Province	☎ 033
Kandal Province	☎ 024
Kep Province	☎ 036
Koh Kong Province	☎ 035
Kompong Cham Province	☎ 042
Kompong Chhnang Province	☎ 026
Kompong Speu Province	☎ 025
Kompong Thom Province	☎ 062
Kratie Province	☎ 072
Mondulkiri Province	☎ 073
Oddar Meanchey Province	☎ 065
Phnom Penh	☎ 023
Preah Vihear Province	☎ 064
Prey Veng Province	☎ 043
Pursat Province	☎ 052
Ratanakiri Province	☎ 075
Siem Reap Province	☎ 063
Sihanoukville Province	☎ 034
Stung Treng Province	☎ 074
Svay Rieng Province	☎ 044
Takeo Province	☎ 032

TELEPHONE & FAX

Cambodia's landline system was totally devastated by the long civil war, leaving the country with a poor communications infrastructure. The advent of mobile phones has allowed Cambodia to catch up with its regional neighbours by jumping headlong into the technology revolution. Mobile phones are everywhere in Cambodia, but landline access in major towns is also improving, connecting more of the country to the outside world than ever before.

Domestic Calls

Local calls are usually pretty cheap, even from hotel rooms. Calling from province to province is considerably more expensive by fixed lines. The easiest way to call in most urban areas is to head to one of the many small private booths on the kerbside, usually plastered with numbers like 012 and 016 and with prices around 300r. Operators have a selection of mobile phones and leased lines to ensure that any domestic number you want to call is cheap. Local phone calls can also be made on the MPTC and Camintel public payphones, which are sometimes still seen in places like Phnom Penh, Siem Reap and Sihanoukville. It can sometimes be difficult to get through

to numbers outside Phnom Penh, and there is no directory inquiries service. Some hotels have telephone directories for the capital if you need to track down a number. Try to find a copy of the **Yellow Pages** (www.yellowpages.com.kh), which has a pretty comprehensive coverage of businesses, services and government offices.

Fax

Sending faxes is getting cheaper as telephone charges drop. The cheapest fax services are those via the internet; these can be arranged at internet cafés for around US$1 to US$2 a page. Some of the more popular midrange hotels have reliable business centres, but be aware that faxing from Cambodia's top-end hotels is expensive, costing three times the price charged elsewhere.

International Calls

When it comes to calling overseas, there is now a whole lot more choice than in the bad old days of all calls going via Moscow. There are several telephone cards available for card phones, several prepaid calling cards for use from any telephone, private booths offering calls via mobile phones and the growing world of internet phone calls. Calling from hotels attracts a surcharge and the more expensive the hotel, the heftier the hit. As a general rule, whichever way you choose to ring, it is a little cheaper to make a call at weekends.

The cheapest way to call internationally is via internet phone. Most of the shops and cafés around the country providing internet services also offer internet calls. Calls usually cost between 200r and 2000r per minute, depending on the destination. Calling the USA and Europe is generally the cheapest, but there is a hefty surcharge for connecting to mobile numbers. While the price is undoubtedly right, the major drawback is that there is often a significant delay on the phone, making for a conversation of many 'hello?'s and 'pardon?'s. Using services such as Skype makes these calls a little clearer and slightly cheaper or you can hook up with a fellow Skype user for free. Most internet cafés also provide webcams, so you can see family and friends while catching up on the gossip.

It is straightforward to place an international call from Ministry of Post & Telecommunications (MPTC) or Camintel phone booths. Purchase a phonecard, which in larger cities can be bought at hotels,

DIRECTORY

restaurants, post offices and many shops. Phonecards come in denominations of US$5 to US$50. Before inserting the card into a public phone, always check that there is a read-out on the phone's LCD unit. If there isn't, it probably means the phone is broken or there is a power cut – inserting the card at these times can wipe the value off the card.

Camshin offers a handy tourist SIM card. This costs US$10 and can be inserted into any unlocked phone. Calls are cheap at just US$0.25 per minute and the line is usually clear. The card lasts for seven days from activation.

If dialling from a mobile or using card-phones, instead of using the original international access code of ☎ 001, try ☎ 007, which works out cheaper. The name is not Bond, but Tele2, a private operator that has recently set up shop in Cambodia.

Mobile Phones

Telephone numbers starting with ☎ 01 or ☎ 09 are mobile phone (cell phone) numbers. If you are travelling with a mobile phone on international roaming, just select a network upon arrival, dial away and await a hefty phone bill once you return home. Note: Cambodian roaming charges are extraordinarily high.

Those who are planning on spending longer in Cambodia will want to hook up with a local network. Those with their own phone need only purchase a SIM card for one of the local service providers, but if you are travelling with a locked phone linked to your network back home, then you can't switch SIM cards. Local phone shops can usually unlock your phone for a small charge. Mobile phones are very cheap in Cambodia and secondhand ones are widely available. Most of the local companies offer fixed-contract deals with monthly bills, or pay-as-you-go cards for those who want flexibility. All offer regular promotions, so it is worth shopping around.

Local companies based in Phnom Penh:
Hello (Map p79; ☎ 016 810001; www.hellogsm.com .kh; 56 Norodom Blvd)
M Fone (Map pp74-5; ☎ 023-367801; www.mfone .com.kh; 294 Mao Tse Toung Blvd)
Mobitel (Map p79; ☎ 012 801801; www.mobitel.com .kh; 33 Sihanouk Blvd)

TIME

Cambodia, like Laos, Vietnam and Thailand, is seven hours ahead of Greenwich Mean Time or Universal Time Coordinated (GMT/UTC). When it is midday in Cambodia it is 10pm the previous evening in San Francisco, 1am in New York, 5am in London, 6am in Paris and 3pm in Sydney.

TOILETS

Cambodian toilets are mostly of the sit-down variety. The occasional squat toilet turns up here and there, particularly in the most budget of budget guesthouses in the provinces. If you end up in the sticks, you will find that hygiene conditions deteriorate somewhat, but rural Cambodian bathrooms are often in a better state than those in rural China or India.

The issue of toilets and what to do with used toilet paper is a cause for concern. Generally, if there's a wastepaper basket next to the toilet, that is where the toilet paper goes, as many sewerage systems cannot handle toilet paper. Toilet paper is seldom provided in the toilets at bus and train stations or in other public buildings, so keep a stash with you at all times.

Many Western toilets also have a hose spray in the bathroom, aptly named the 'bum gun' by some. Think of this as a flexible bidet, used for cleaning and ablutions as well as hosing down the loo.

Public toilets are rare, the only ones in the country being along Phnom Penh's riverfront and some beautiful wooden structures dotted about the temples of Angkor. The charge is usually 500r for a public toilet, although they are free at Angkor. Most local restaurants have some sort of toilet; pay 500r if you are not eating or drinking anything.

Should you find nature calling in rural areas, don't let modesty drive you into the bushes: *there may be land mines not far from the road or track*. Stay on the roadside and do the deed, or grin and bear it until the next town.

TOURIST INFORMATION

Cambodia has only a handful of tourist offices, and those encountered by the independent traveller in Phnom Penh and Siem Reap are generally unhelpful unless you look like you're going to spend money. However, in the provinces it is a different story, as the staff are often shocked and excited to see visitors. They may have to drag the director out of a nearby karaoke bar, even at 10am, but once it is made clear that you are a genuine tourist, they will usually tell you everything there is to know about places of interest. More and more towns are ambitiously opening tourist offices, but they generally have little in the way of brochures or handouts. You'll find some tourist offices listed in the relevant destination sections in this book, but lower your expectations compared with regional powerhouses like Malaysia and Singapore. Generally, fellow travellers, guesthouses and hotels, and free local magazines are much more useful than tourist offices.

Cambodia has no official tourist offices abroad and it is unlikely that Cambodian embassies will be of much assistance in planning a trip, besides issuing a visa.

TRAVELLERS WITH DISABILITIES

Broken pavements (sidewalks), potholed roads and stairs as steep as ladders at Angkor ensure that for most people with mobility impairments, Cambodia is not going to be an easy country in which to travel. Few buildings in Cambodia have been designed with the disabled in mind, although new projects, such as the international airports at Phnom Penh and Siem Reap, and top-end hotels, include ramps for wheelchair access. Transport in the provinces is usually very overcrowded, but taxi hire from point to point is an affordable option.

On the positive side, the Cambodian people are usually very helpful towards all foreigners, and local labour is cheap if you need someone to accompany you at all times. Most guesthouses and small hotels have ground-floor rooms that are reasonably easy to access.

The biggest headache also happens to be the main attraction – the temples of Angkor. Causeways are uneven, obstacles common and staircases daunting, even for able-bodied people. It is likely to be some years before things improve, although some ramping is now being introduced at major temples.

Wheelchair travellers will need to undertake a lot of research before visiting Cambodia. There is now a growing network of information sources that can put you in touch with others who have wheeled through Cambodia before. Try contacting:

Mobility International USA (☎ 54-1343 1284; www .miusa.org)

Royal Association for Disability and Rehabilitation (Radar; ☎ 020-7250 3222; www.radar.org.uk)

Society for Accessible Travel & Hospitality (SATH; ☎ 212-447 7284; www.sath.org)

Lonelyplanet.com has a travel forum called the Thorn Tree, which is a good place to seek advice from other travellers.

VISAS

Most visitors to Cambodia require a one-month tourist visa (US$20), although some visitors enter on a one-month business visa (US$25). Most nationalities receive a one-month visa on arrival at Phnom Penh and Siem Reap airports, and at land borders. One passport-sized photo is required and you'll be 'fined' US$1 if you don't have one. It is also possible to arrange a visa through Cambodian embassies overseas or an online e-visa (US$25) through the **Ministry of Foreign Affairs** (http://evisa .mfaic.gov.kh). Arranging a visa ahead of time can help prevent potential overcharging at some land crossings.

Those seeking work in Cambodia should opt for the business visa as, officially, it is easily extended for long periods and, unofficially, can be extended indefinitely, including multiple entries and exits. A tourist visa can be extended only once and only for one month, and does not allow for re-entry.

Travellers are sometimes overcharged when crossing at land borders with Thailand, as immigration officials demand payment in baht and round up the figure considerably. Arranging a visa in advance avoids this potential problem. Travellers planning a day trip to Prasat Preah Vihear from Thailand do not require visas, but may be asked to leave their passport on the Thai side of the border to ensure they don't continue on into Cambodia.

Overstaying your visa currently costs a hefty US$5 a day.

Visa Extensions

Visa extensions are issued by the large immigration office located directly across the road from Phnom Penh International Airport (p111).

There are two ways of getting an extension (one official and one unofficial) and, unsurprisingly, the time and money involved differ greatly. Officially, a one-month extension costs US$35, three months US$65, six months US$125, and one year US$200; your passport will be held for 25 days and there will be more paperwork than a communist bureaucrat could dream up. This is fine for expats with an employer to make the arrangements, but

---

SHOULD WE BE VISITING ORPHANAGES?

In recent years, visiting orphanages in the developing world – and Cambodia in particular – has become a popular activity, but is it always good for the children and the country in the longer run? Tough question. 'Orphan tourism' and all the connotations that come with it could be considered a scary development that is bringing unscrupulous elements into the world of caring for Cambodian children. There have already been reports of new orphanages opening up with a business model to bring in a certain number of visitors per month. In other cases, the children are not orphans at all, but are 'borrowed' from the local school for a fee.

Many orphanages in Cambodia are doing a great job in tough circumstances. Some are world class, enjoy funding and support from wealthy benefactors and don't need visitors; others are desperate places which need all the help they can get. However, if a place is promoting orphan tourism, then proceed with caution, as the adults may not always have the best interests of the children at heart. Cambodia is a confusing and confounding place and it's not for us to play judge and jury, but we do believe travellers should be informed before they make a decision.

---

those on their own really need to go unofficial. They don't call it corruption in Cambodia but 'under the table', and you can have your passport back the next day for the inflated prices of US$45 for one month, US$80 for three months, US$165 for six months and US$265 for one year. Once you are one of the 'unofficials', it is pretty straightforward to extend the visa ad infinitum. Travel agencies and some motorbike rental shops in Phnom Penh can help with arrangements, sometimes at a discounted price.

VOLUNTEERING

There are fewer opportunities for volunteering than one might imagine in a country as impoverished as Cambodia. This is partly due to the sheer number of professional development workers based here, and development is a pretty lucrative industry these days.

Cambodia hosts a huge number of NGOs, some of whom do require volunteers from time to time. The best way to find out who is represented in the country is to drop in on the **Cooperation Committee for Cambodia** (CCC; Map p79; ☎ 023-214152; 35 St 178) in Phnom Penh. This organisation has a handy list of all NGOs, both Cambodian and international, and is extremely helpful.

Grass-roots organisations are the most appreciative of volunteers. Try the Lazy Gecko Café (p102) in Phnom Penh, which supports Jeannie's Orphanage, and the Starfish Bakery & Café (p210) in Sihanoukville, which helps to raise funds for local projects.

Other places that can readily benefit from volunteers are certain orphanages in Phnom Penh, Siem Reap and other towns in Cambodia, as some of these are in a very rundown condition.

The other avenue is professional volunteering through an organisation back home that offers one- or two-year placements in Cambodia. One of the largest organisations is **Voluntary Service Overseas** (VSO; www.vso.org.uk) in the UK, but other countries also have their own organisations, including **Australian Volunteers International** (AVI; www.australianvolunteers.com) and New Zealand's **Volunteer Service Abroad** (VSA; www.vsa.org.nz). The UN also operates its own volunteer programme; details are available at www.unv.org. Other general volunteer sites with links all over the place include www.worldvolunteerweb.com and www.volunteerabroad.com.

WOMEN TRAVELLERS

Women will generally find Cambodia a hassle-free place to travel, although some of the guys in the guesthouse industry will try their luck from time to time. Foreign women are unlikely to be targeted by local men, but at the same time it pays to be careful. As is the case anywhere in the world, walking or riding a bike alone late at night is risky, and if you're planning a trip off the beaten trail it would be best to find a travel companion.

Despite the prevalence of sex workers and women's employment as 'beer girls', dancing companions and the like, foreign women will probably find Khmer men to be courteous and polite. It's best to keep things this way by being restrained in your dress; flaunting a pierced belly button is likely to get the blood racing among Khmer males. Khmer women dress fairly conservatively, and it's best to follow suit, particularly when visiting wats. In general, long-sleeved shirts and long trousers or skirts are preferred. It is also worth having trousers for heading out at night on *motos,* as short skirts aren't too practical.

Tampons and sanitary napkins are widely available in the major cities and provincial capitals, but if you are heading into very remote areas for a few days, it is worth having your own supply.

WORK

Jobs are available throughout Cambodia, but apart from English teaching or helping out in guesthouses, bars or restaurants, most are for professionals and are arranged in advance. There is a lot of teaching work available for English-language speakers, although the salary is directly linked to experience. Anyone with an English-language teaching certificate can earn considerably more than those with no qualifications.

For information about work opportunities with NGOs call into the CCC (opposite), which has a notice board for positions vacant and may also be able to give advice on where to look. If you are thinking of applying for work with NGOs, you should bring copies of your education certificates and work references. However, most of the jobs available are likely to be on a voluntary basis, as most recruiting for specialised positions is done in home countries or through international organisations.

Other places to look for work include the classifieds sections of the *Phnom Penh Post* and the *Cambodia Daily,* and on the notice boards at guesthouses and restaurants in Phnom Penh.

Do not expect to make a lot of money working in Cambodia, but if you want to learn more about the country and help the locals improve their standard of living, it can be a very worthwhile experience.

Transport

CONTENTS

GETTING THERE & AWAY

ENTERING THE COUNTRY

Cambodia has two international gateways for arrival by air, Phnom Penh and Siem Reap, and a healthy selection of land borders with neighbouring Thailand, Vietnam and Laos. Formalities at Cambodia's international airports are traditionally smoother than at land borders, as the volume of traffic is greater. Crossing at land borders is relatively easy, but immigration officers may try to wangle some extra cash, either for your visa or via some other scam. Stand your ground. Anyone without a photo for their visa form will be charged about US$1 at the airport, and as much as 100B at land borders with Thailand.

Arrival by air is popular for those on a short holiday in Cambodia, as travelling overland to or from Cambodia puts a significant dent in your time in the country. Travellers on longer trips usually enter and exit by land, as road and river transport is very reasonable in Cambodia.

Passport

Not only is a passport essential but you also need to make sure that it's valid for at least six months beyond the *end* of your trip – Cambodian immigration will not issue a visa

---

THINGS CHANGE!

The information in this chapter is particularly vulnerable to change: prices for international travel are volatile, routes are introduced and cancelled, schedules change, special deals come and go, and rules and visa requirements are amended. You should check directly with your airline or a travel agent to make sure you understand how a fare (and ticket you may buy) works, and be aware of the security requirements for international travel.

The upshot of this is that you should get opinions, quotes and advice from as many airlines and travel agents as possible before you spend your hard-earned cash. Details given in this chapter should be regarded as pointers and are not a substitute for your own careful and up-to-date research.

---

if you have less than six months' validity left on your passport.

It's also important to make sure that there is plenty of space left in your passport. Do not set off on a six-month trek across Asia with only two blank pages left – a Cambodian visa alone takes up one page. It is sometimes possible to have extra pages added to your passport, but most people will be required to get a new passport. This is possible for most foreign nationals in Cambodia, but it can be time consuming and costly, as many embassies process new passports in Bangkok.

Losing a passport is not the end of the world, but it is a serious inconvenience. To expedite the issuing of a new passport, keep a copy of your passport details somewhere separate from your passport.

For the story on visas, see p321.

AIR
Airports & Airlines

Phnom Penh International Airport (PNH; ☎ 023-890520; www.cambodia-airports.com/phnompenh/en) is the gateway to the Cambodian capital, while **Siem Reap International Airport** (REP; ☎ 063-380283; www.cambodia-airports.com/siemreap/en) serves visitors to the temples of Angkor. Both airports have a good range of services, including restaurants, bars, shops and ATMs.

Flights to Cambodia are quite limited and most connect only as far as regional capitals. However, budget airlines have taken off in recent years and are steadily driving down prices. Bangkok offers the most connections to Cambodia, and it is usually possible to get on a flight with any of the airlines at short notice, although flying Bangkok Airways to Siem Reap can get very busy from November to March.

If you are heading to Cambodia for a short holiday and want a minimum of fuss, Thai Airways offers the easiest connections from major cities in Europe, the USA and Australia. Singapore Airlines' regional wing, Silk Air, is another good option, with at least one flight a day connecting Cambodia to Singapore. Other regional centres with flights to Cambodia are Ho Chi Minh City (Saigon), Hanoi, Vientiane, Luang Prabang, Pakse, Kuala Lumpur, Seoul, Taipei, Hong Kong, Guangzhou and Shanghai.

Airlines in Cambodia tend to open up and close down regularly. This means that those who have the choice should enter the country on an international carrier rather than a local outfit.

Some airlines offer open-jaw tickets into Phnom Penh and out of Siem Reap, which can save some time and money. The follow-ing telephone numbers are for Phnom Penh offices (☎ 023). See the Siem Reap section for airline offices there (p137).

AIRLINES FLYING TO/FROM CAMBODIA

Air Asia (AK; ☎ 356011; www.airasia.com; hub Kuala Lumpur) Daily budget flights connecting Phnom Penh and Siem Reap to Kuala Lumpur and Bangkok.

Angkor Airways (G6; ☎ 222056; www.angkorairways .com; hub Phnom Penh) Regular connections from Phnom Penh and Siem Reap to Taipei.

Asiana Airlines (OZ; ☎ 890440; www.asiana.co.kr; hub Seoul) Regular connections between Phnom Penh and Seoul.

Bangkok Airways (Map p79; PG; ☎ 722545; www .bangkokair.com; hub Bangkok) Daily connections from Phnom Penh and Siem Reap to Bangkok.

China Eastern Airlines (Map pp74–5; MU; ☎ 063-965229; www.ce-air.com; hub Shanghai) Regular flights from Siem Reap to Kunming.

China Southern Airlines (Map p79; CZ; ☎ 430877; www.cs-air.com; hub Guangzhou) Regular flights from Phnom Penh to Guangzhou.

Dragon Air (Map p79; KA; ☎ 424300; www.dragonair .com; hub Hong Kong) Daily flights between Phnom Penh and Hong Kong.

Eva Air (Map p79; BR; ☎ 219911; www.evaair.com; hub Taipei) Daily flights between Phnom Penh and Taipei.

Jetstar Asia (3K; ☎ 220909; www.jetstarasia.com; hub Singapore) Daily budget flights from Phnom Penh and Siem Reap to Singapore.

CLIMATE CHANGE & TRAVEL

Climate change is a serious threat to the ecosystems that humans rely upon, and air travel is the fastest-growing contributor to the problem. Lonely Planet regards travel, overall, as a global ben-efit, but believes we all have a responsibility to limit our personal impact on global warming.

Flying and climate change

Pretty much every form of motorised travel generates CO_2 (the main cause of human-induced climate change) but planes are far and away the worst offenders, not just because of the sheer distances they allow us to travel, but because they release greenhouse gases high into the at-mosphere. The statistics are frightening: two people taking a return flight between Europe and the US will contribute as much to climate change as an average household's gas and electricity consumption over a whole year.

Carbon offset schemes

Climatecare.org and other websites use 'carbon calculators' that allow travellers to offset the level of greenhouse gases they are responsible for with financial contributions to sustainable travel schemes that reduce global warming – including projects in India, Honduras, Kazakhstan and Uganda.

Lonely Planet, together with Rough Guides and other concerned partners in the travel industry, support the carbon offset scheme run by climatecare.org. Lonely Planet offsets all of its staff and author travel. For more information check out our website: www.lonelyplanet.com

INTERNATIONAL DEPARTURE TAX

There is a departure tax of US$25, payable by cash or credit card, on all international flights out of both Phnom Penh International Airport and Siem Reap International Airport.

Lao Airlines (Map p79; QV; ☎ 216563; www.laoairlines.com; hub Vientiane) Regular flights from Phnom Penh and Siem Reap to both Pakse and Vientiane.

Malaysia Airlines (Map p79; MY; ☎ 426688; www.malaysiaairlines.com; hub Kuala Lumpur) Daily connections from Phnom Penh and Siem Reap to Kuala Lumpur.

PMT Air (U4; ☎ 221379; www.pmtair.com; hub Phnom Penh) Regular flights from Siem Reap to Hanoi and Ho Chi Minh City.

Shanghai Airlines (FM; ☎ 723999; www.shanghai-air.com; hub Shanghai) Regular flights linking Phnom Penh with Shanghai.

Siem Reap Airways (Map p79; FT; ☎ 720022; www.siemreapairways.com; hub Phnom Penh) Regular connections from Phnom Penh and Siem Reap to Hong Kong. High season flights connect Luang Prabang and Siem Reap.

Silk Air (Map p79; MI; ☎ 426807; www.silkair.com; hub Singapore) Daily flights linking Phnom Penh and Siem Reap with Singapore.

Thai Airways (Map pp74-5; TG; ☎ 214359; www.thaiair.com; hub Bangkok) Daily flights connecting Phnom Penh and Bangkok.

Vietnam Airlines (Map p79; VN; ☎ 363396; www.vietnamair.com.vn; hub HCMC) Daily flights linking both Phnom Penh & Siem Reap with both Hanoi & Ho Chi Minh City, as well as Phnom Penh with Vientiane & Siem Reap with Luang Prabang.

Tickets

When buying airline tickets, it is always worth shopping around. Buying direct from the airline is usually more expensive, unless the airline has a special promotion. As a rule, it is better to book as early as possible, as prices only get higher as the seats fill up.

The time of year has a major impact on flight prices. Starting out from Europe, North America or Australia, figure on prices rising dramatically over Christmas and between July and August, and dropping significantly during lax periods of business like February, June and October.

Thailand is the most convenient gateway to Cambodia when travelling from outside the region. In Bangkok, the Banglamphu area, especially Khao San Rd, is a good place to buy tickets to Cambodia. Those who are travelling into Cambodia by air through Vietnam can easily pick up tickets in Ho Chi Minh City.

When buying tickets in Cambodia, the biggest agents are in Phnom Penh (p81), although many now operate branch offices in Siem Reap. Agents can normally save you a few dollars on the airline price, much more for long-haul flights or business-class seats.

To research and buy a ticket on the internet, try these services:

Cheapflights (www.cheapflights.com) No-frills website with a number of locations.

Lonely Planet (www.lonelyplanet.com) Use the Trip Planner service to book multistop trips.

OneTravel (www.onetravel.com) Another website with a number of locations.

Travel.com (www.travel.com) This website also has numerous locations.

From Australia

The best place to look for cheap fares is in the travel sections of weekend newspapers, such as the *Age* in Melbourne and the *Sydney Morning Herald*. There are good connections between major Australian cities and both Thailand and Vietnam. Elsewhere, you'll need to connect through a regional hub.

Two well-known agencies for cheap fares:

Flight Centre (☎ 133 133 using local area code; www.flightcentre.com.au) Offices throughout Australia.

STA Travel (☎ 1300 733 035 Australia-wide; www.statravel.com.au) Has offices in all major cities and on many university campuses.

From Canada

It is cheaper to fly from the west coast than it is to fly from the east. Canadian air fares tend to be higher than those sold in the USA. The *Globe & Mail*, the *Toronto Star*, the *Montreal Gazette* and the *Vancouver Sun* carry travel agency ads and are good places to look for good value fares. **Travel CUTS** (www.travelcuts.com) is Canada's national student travel agency and has offices in all major cities.

From Continental Europe

Although London is the discount-travel capital of Europe, major airlines and big travel agents usually have offers from all the major cities on the continent.

Recommended agents with branches across France:

Nouvelles Frontières (☎ 08 25 00 07 47; www
.nouvelles-frontieres.fr)
OTU Voyages (www.otu.fr) This agency specialises in
student and youth travel.
Voyageurs du Monde (☎ 01 40 15 11 15; www.vdm
.com)

Reliable agencies in Germany:
Just Travel (☎ 089-747 33 30; www.justtravel.de)
STA Travel (☎ 0180-545 64 22; www.statravel.de)

From other countries in Europe, try the fol-
lowing agencies:
Airfair (☎ 0206-20 51 21; www.airfair.nl; Netherlands)
Barcelo Viajes (☎ 902 11 62 26; www.barceloviajes
.com; Spain)
CTS Viaggi (☎ 064 62 04 31; www.cts.it; Italy)
NBBS Reizen (☎ 0900 1020 300; www.nbbs.nl;
Netherlands)
Nouvelles Frontières (☎ 902 17 09 79; www
.nouvelles-frontieres.es; Spain)
SSR Voyages (☎ 058 450 4020; www.ssr.ch; Switzerland)

From New Zealand

National newspaper the *New Zealand Herald*
(www.nzherald.co.nz) has a helpful travel section. **Flight Centre** (☎ 0800 243 544; www.flightcentre
.co.nz) has a large central office in Auckland
and many branches throughout the country.
STA Travel (☎ 0508 782 872; www.statravel.co.nz) has
offices in Auckland and other major centres
in New Zealand.

From the UK

Advertisements for many travel agencies
appear in the travel pages of the weekend
broadsheets, such as the *Independent* and
the *Sunday Times*.

Popular travel agencies in the UK include:
Flightbookers (☎ 087-0010 7000; www.ebookers.com)
North-South Travel (☎ 01245-608291; www.north
southtravel.co.uk) North-South Travel donates part of its
profit to projects in the developing world.
STA Travel (☎ 087-0160 0599; www.statravel.co.uk)
Trailfinders (☎ 084-5050 5891; www.trailfinders.co.uk)
Travel Bag (☎ 087-0890 1456; www.travelbag.co.uk)

From the USA

Ticket promotions frequently connect Asia to
San Francisco and Los Angeles, New York and
other big cities. The *New York Times,* the *Los
Angeles Times,* the *Chicago Tribune* and the
San Francisco Examiner all produce weekly
travel sections in which you will find a number
of travel agency ads and fare promos.

Useful online options in the USA:
■ www.cheaptickets.com
■ www.itn.net
■ www.lowestfare.com
■ www.sta.com
■ www.travelocity.com

LAND

For years overland travellers were restricted
to entering or exiting Cambodia at the
Bavet–Moc Bai border crossing with Vietnam.
However, lots of new land crossings between
Cambodia and its neighbours have opened,
offering overland connections with Laos,
Thailand and Vietnam. However, many of
the newly opened borders are in relatively off-
the-beaten path destinations and are aimed at
promoting trade more than serving tourists.
For the latest on Cambodian border crossings,
check out the Immigration Department website at http://cambodia-immigration.com.

Bus

It is possible to use buses to cross into
Cambodia from Thailand or Vietnam. The
most popular way to or from Vietnam is a
cheap bus via Bavet on the Cambodian side
and Moc Bai in Vietnam. From Thailand,
many travellers take the nightmare 'scam bus'
(p330) from Bangkok to Siem Reap via the
Poipet–Aranya Prathet border crossing.

Car & Motorcycle

Car drivers and motorcycle riders will need
registration papers, insurance documents and
an International Driving Licence to bring vehicles into Cambodia. It is complicated to
bring in a car, but relatively straightforward
to bring in a motorcycle, as long as you have
a *carnet de passage* (vehicle passport). This
acts as a temporary import-duty waiver and
should save a lot of hassles when dealing
with Cambodian customs. Increasing numbers of international bikers are crossing into
Cambodia, while most of the foreign cars that
tend to make it are Thai-registered.

River

There is a river border crossing between
Cambodia and Vietnam on the banks of the
Mekong. There are regular fast passenger
boats plying the route between Phnom Penh
and Chau Doc in Vietnam, via the Kaam
Samnor–Vinh Xuong border crossing. There
are also a couple of luxurious river boats

running all the way to the temples of Angkor in Cambodia. There is also a river crossing on the Mekong border with Laos, although most travellers use the road these days.

Border Crossings

Cambodia shares one border crossing with Laos, six crossings with Thailand and eight with Vietnam. Visas are now available at all the land crossings with Laos, Thailand and Vietnam.

There are now international ATMs near the Cham Yeam and Poipet borders with Thailand. However, at the rest of the borders, there are very few money-changing facilities at any of these crossings, so be sure to have some small-denomination US dollars handy or baht if crossing from Thailand. The black market is also an option for local currencies – Vietnamese dong, Lao kip and Thai baht. Remember that black marketeers have a well-deserved reputation for short-changing and outright theft.

Cambodian immigration officers at the land border-crossings have a bad reputation for petty extortion. Travellers are occasionally asked for an 'immigration fee' of some kind, particularly when entering or exiting via the Lao border. Other scams include overcharging for the visa in Thai baht (anywhere between 1000B and 1200B instead of 700B) and forcing tourists to change US dollars into riel at a poor rate. Hold your breath, stand your ground, don't start a fight and remember that not all Cambodians are as mercenary as the men in blue.

Senior government officials in Phnom Penh are trying to crack down on overcharging for visas and general petty extortion at the borders, as it gives Cambodia a bad image. In order to help bring an end to this, we suggest you ask for the name of any official demanding extra money at the border and mention you will pass it on to the Ministers of Interior and Tourism.

LAOS

Cambodia and Laos share a remote frontier that includes some of the wildest areas of both countries. There is only one border crossing open to foreigners and given the remoteness of the region, it is unlikely any more will open in the near future.

Dom Kralor–Voen Kham

The border between Cambodia and Laos is officially open from 7am to 5pm daily. It is very popular as an adventurous and cheap way to combine travel to northeastern Cambodia and southern Laos. On the Cambodian side of the border, there are confusingly two possible places to cross the border: one on the river (Koh Chheuteal Thom) and one on the old road from Stung Treng (Dom Kralor). Few travellers use the original Koh Chheuteal Thom crossing as the speedboats to Stung Treng are overpriced. More prefer to travel by minibus via the road border at Dom Kralor.

To enter Cambodia using this route, visas are available on arrival. Those exiting Cambodia for Laos should arrange a Lao visa

CAMBODIA BORDER CROSSINGS AT A GLANCE

Country	Border Crossing	Connecting
Cambodia/Laos	Dom Kralor/Voen Kham	Stung Treng/Si Phan Done
Cambodia/Thailand	Poipet/Aranya Prathet	Siem Reap/Bangkok
	Cham Yeam/Hat Lek	Koh Kong/Trat
	O Smach/Chong Jom	Samraong/Surin
	Choam/Choam Srawngam	Anlong Veng/Sangkha
	Psar Pruhm/Ban Pakard	Pailin/Chantaburi
	Kamrieng/Daun Lem	Battambang/Chantaburi
Cambodia/Vietnam	Bavet/Moc Bai	Phnom Penh/HCMC
	Kaam Samnor/Vinh Xuong	Phnom Penh/Chau Doc
	Prek Chak/Xa Xia	Kampot/Ha Tien
	Phnom Den/Tinh Bien	Takeo/Chau Doc
	O Yadaw/Le Tanh	Ratanakiri/Pleiku
	Trapaeng Thlong/Xa Mat	Kompong Cham/Tay Ninh
	Trapaeng Sre/Loc Ninh	Snuol/Loc Ninh
	Banteay Chakrey/Khanh Binh	Neak Luong/An Phu

in advance in Phnom Penh. Both sides of the border seem to charge an overtime fee for those crossing at lunch time or after dark, although the exact sum (usually US$1 to US$5) depends on gentle but persuasive bargaining.

To leave Cambodia, travel to the remote town of Stung Treng (p289). From Stung Treng there are regular minibuses (US$5 per person) heading north to the border. Longtail rocket boats (US$30 for the boat, US$5 per person, one hour) can be chartered up the Mekong and take up to six people.

The road crossing is more straightforward, as on the Mekong, Cambodian immigration is on the west bank and Lao immigration is on the east bank. Once in Voen Kham in Laos, there are outboards running up to the island of Don Khone (US$5, 20 minutes), although they drop you on the wrong side of the island, as they can't traverse the falls.

Those heading further north can take a motorcycle taxi for about US$5 to Nakasong, where it is possible to arrange a boat to Don Det or Don Khone, or arrange a *jamboh* (three-wheeled motorcycle taxi) on to Hat Xai Khun for the boat across to Don Khong.

Coming to Cambodia from Laos, the options outlined above can be run in reverse. The cheapest way is to take one of the dirt-cheap boat trips advertised on Don Khone and Don Khong, costing just a few dollars, which include the waterfalls and dolphin viewing. Once you get back to Voen Kham from viewing the dolphins, jump ship and arrange a seat in a Cambodian taxi or minibus, costing about US$5 to Stung Treng. There are also plenty of Cambodian outboards hanging around the dock at Voen Kham for the run to Stung Treng, but they seem to have fixed the price at US$10 per person, which is double what it costs to travel in the other direction.

THAILAND

Cambodia and Thailand share a lengthy border and there are now six legal international border crossings, and many more options for locals. Land borders with Thailand are open from 7am to 8pm daily. Tourist visas are available at all crossings for US$20. There are now clear signs displaying the US$20 charge, but many people are still charged 1000B. For the latest sagas on land crossings between Thailand and Cambodia, visit www.talesofasia.com.

Poipet–Aranya Prathet

The original land border crossing between Cambodia and Thailand has earned itself a bad reputation in recent years, with scams galore to help tourists part with their money. The 'scam bus' (p330) promoted on Khao San Rd in Bangkok is now legendary throughout Asia, but many travellers still succumb to the charms of cheap tickets.

There are two slow trains a day from Hualamphong train station in Bangkok to the Thai border town of Aranya Prathet (48B, six hours); take the 5.55am service unless you want to spend the night in a border town. There are also regular bus services from Bangkok's Mo Chit northern terminal to Aranya Prathet (200/160B 1st/2nd class, four to five hours). From Aranya Prathet, take a *tuk tuk* (motorised three-wheeled pedicab) for the final six kilometres to the border for about 80B.

Avoid the touts when crossing into Cambodia and don't listen to any offers of help securing a visa. Once across, try not to get roped into the 'free' tourist shuttle to the 'Tourist Lounge'. This place arranges transport to major cities, but at inflated prices: Phnom Penh (US$15, seven to eight hours); Siem Reap (US$10, five hours); Battambang (US$8, 2½ hrs). Stick solo and walk to the bus company offices for cheaper fares. Almost all buses run by all the companies depart very early in the morning (before 8am). It is also possible to negotiate taxis if you can avoid the taxi mafia. Try to pay no more than US$40 to Siem Reap or US$30 to Battambang. Finally, there is the independent option of climbing aboard a pick-up truck hanging out in front of the market near the central roundabout. It's just 50B for a spot in the back to Sisophon from where there is onward transport to Battambang or Siem Reap.

The road to Siem Reap is still unsurfaced and gets very, very ugly during the wet season. It should be the number one priority for trade and tourism, and it should finally be rebuilt during the lifetime of this book.

Leaving Cambodia, it is easy enough to get to Poipet from Siem Reap (p136), Battambang (p246) or even Phnom Penh (p110). By land there is no departure tax to leave Cambodia. From Poipet, take a *tuk tuk* to Aranya Prathet, from where there are regular buses to Bangkok between 4am and 10pm or the slow train at 1.55pm.

TRANSPORT

THE SCAM BUS

Poipet is a Wild West kind of place and has attracted a lot of unsavoury characters clinging to the coat-tails of the economic boom. Unfortunately, many of these are involved in the travel business and carry on like some sort of mafia, giving Cambodia a bad name. Welcome to the scam bus, notorious throughout Asia for ripping off foreigners. Anyone staying in Khao San Rd in Bangkok will soon notice the cheap tickets to Siem Reap and the temples of Angkor on offer. Once travellers get to the border, someone will 'help' arrange the visas and pretend the visa fee is now 1300B rather than US$20. The latest trick is to stop the buses several klicks before the border at a 'visa office' and pressure travellers into paying for an overpriced Cambodian visa.

Once inside Cambodia, a new game begins: drive as slowly as possible to Siem Reap. The road from Poipet to Siem Reap is good enough to cover in about three to four hours in the dry season, but somehow the bus driver will make sure you get there after dark, arriving at a backstreet guesthouse of their choice. Any attempt to leave this guesthouse could lead to a major bust up with the guesthouse owners, as they have already agreed to a commission with the transport company and it's nonrefundable. So the cheap bus ends up costing you time and money, deservedly earning its name the 'scam bus'. In recent years, it got worse, with Thai and Cambodian companies colluding to take travellers through the Psar Pruhm–Ban Pakard border crossing (opposite) near Pailin, a massive diversion on miserable roads. Coming this way ensures that you arrive in Siem Reap in the middle of the night, in no mood to go looking for another guesthouse.

Travelling independently is the way to go, using public buses on the Thai side and share taxis on the Cambodian side. Sure it could cost a bit more, but this way you keep your options open. Remember the phrase 'too good to be true'? That's the scam bus, through and through.

Cham Yeam–Hat Lek

The Cham Yeam–Hat Lek border crossing between Cambodia's Krong Koh Kong and Trat in Thailand is popular with travellers linking the beaches of Cambodia and Thailand.

Coming from Bangkok, take a bus to Trat (210B, five to six hours) from the city's Eastern bus station. Buses depart regularly from 6am until 11.30pm. The 11.30pm bus arrives in Trat early enough to get to Krong Koh Kong in time to catch the 8am fast boat to Sihanoukville. Another convenient option for travellers staying in the Khao San Rd area is to take one of the minibuses bound for Koh Chang, getting off at Trat.

From Trat, take a minibus straight to the Thai border at Hat Lek for 110B. The border opens at 7am so it is possible to stay the night in Trat and, with an early enough start, still make the boat to Sihanoukville – but it's tight. Alternatively, cross later in the day and stay the night in Krong Koh Kong and see the waterfalls and islands (p186) around there. Once on the Cambodian side of the border you can take a *moto* (motorcycle with driver; 50B plus 11B toll) or taxi (200B plus 44B toll) to Krong Koh Kong.

Fast boats from Krong Koh Kong to Sihanoukville (US$20 for foreigners, four hours) leave at 8am and depart Sihanoukville at 9.30am when heading in the other direction. A word of warning: the sea can be dangerously rough at times and these boats were designed for river travel, not sailing the open seas! From Sihanoukville (p211) there are cheap air-con buses to Phnom Penh (p110).

It is also possible to travel by road from Krong Koh Kong to Phnom Penh or Sihanoukville. Virak Buntham and Rith Mony run bus and minibus services to both cities (300B) every morning, or negotiate with a share taxi. It should be 400B for a seat to either destination, but it is probably worth buying two seats for comfort. The road is now surfaced with four new bridges, bringing journey times – and prices – down dramatically.

Leaving Cambodia, take either a taxi or *moto* across the bridge to the border from Krong Koh Kong. Once in Thailand, catch a minibus to Trat from where there are regular buses to Bangkok. Alternatively, stay the night in Trat and then head to Ko Chang or the surrounding islands the following day.

Other Crossings

Several more out of the way crossings are open for international traffic. The **O Smach–Chong Jom** crossing connects Cambodia's Oddar

Meanchey Province and Thailand's Surin Province with Siem Reap, but it is very remote. There are five buses per day from Surin to Chong Jom (30B, two hours). Once on the Cambodian side, you can head to Samraong (p257) on a miserable road by *moto* (250B, one hour) or private taxi (1200B, almost two hours), and arrange local transport from there on to Siem Reap. There is no public transport east to Anlong Veng or southwest to Banteay Chhmar.

The **Choam–Choam Srawngam** crossing, 16km north of Anlong Veng on unexpected paved road, puts you into a pretty remote part of Thailand and hence transport connections are, for once, harder on the Thai side. Pick-up trucks (3000/2000r inside/on the back) leave Anlong Veng early, heading to the Cambodian border town of Choam from 6am. Alternatively, charter a *moto* (10,000r) or a taxi (US$20). Once on the Thai side, there are several onward buses a day, but they are quite spaced out. Coming in the other direction from Thailand, the closest major town is Si Saket. From Si Saket there are several buses that make the journey each day to the border. Note that from Anlong Veng (p261) there is no public transport east to Prasat Preah Vihear or west to Samraong.

The border near Pailin, 102km southwest of Battambang, is open for business as well. Some foreigners are unexpectedly crossing the border at **Psar Pruhm–Ban Pakard**, courtesy of the 'scam bus' (opposite). To travel this way independently, take a bus from Bangkok to Chantaburi (160B, four hours) and then a minibus from there to Ban Pakard (150B, 1½ hours). Cross the Cambodian border into the casino area and then arrange a share taxi into Pailin (300B for the whole car, 50B per person). From Pailin it is possible to get to Battambang (200B, 2½ hours) by share taxi on a real joke of a road. Run this route in reverse to exit Cambodia; prices should be the same with a bit of bargaining here and there.

There is another remote border at **Kamrieng–Daun Lem** in Battambang Province, but it is really just an outpost with a casino catering to Thai gamblers and not very accessible from the Cambodian side.

There is also a border at **Prasat Preah Vihear** (p268), the stunning Cambodian temple perched atop the Dangkrek mountains. This is currently just a day crossing for tourists

wanting to visit the temple from the Thai side, but it may be upgraded to a full international crossing during the lifetime of this book.

VIETNAM

Cambodia and Vietnam share a long frontier with a bevy of border crossings. Foreigners are currently permitted to cross at eight places and there are new crossings opening all the time. Cambodian visas are now available at all crossings. Vietnamese visas should be arranged in advance, as they are not available on arrival. Luckily, Cambodia is the easiest place in the world to pick up Vietnamese visas. It is no longer necessary to stipulate your exact point of entry and exit on the Vietnam visa, or the exact date of arrival, making for the sort of carefree travel overlanders prefer.

Bavet–Moc Bai

The original land crossing between Vietnam and Cambodia has seen steady traffic for more than a decade. The trip by bus between Phnom Penh and Ho Chi Minh City takes about five to six hours, including the border crossing. There are now several companies offering direct services with no need to change buses. Choose from Capitol Transport, GST, Mai Linh, Mekong Express, Neak Krohorm and Phnom Penh Sorya Transport. All charge between US$9 and US$12; see p110 for contact details.

Kaam Samnor–Vinh Xuong

Cambodia and Vietnam opened their border on the Mekong back in 2000 and it is now very popular with independent travellers. It is a far more interesting trip than taking the road, as it involves a fast boat on the Mekong in Cambodia and travel along some very picturesque areas of the Mekong Delta in Vietnam. Coming from Ho Chi Minh City, it is possible to book a cheap Mekong Delta tour through to Chau Doc and then make your own way from there.

Adventurous travellers like to plot their own course. Leaving Cambodia, take a bus from Psar Thmei in Phnom Penh to Neak Luong (4500r, 1½ hours, regular departures) then jump off the bus on the west bank of the Mekong (don't take the ferry across the river!) and ask around for outboards to Kaam Samnor (one hour). They depart from a small pier about 300m south of the ferry. It costs

US$20 to charter the whole boat, but those with a little time on their hands can wait until it fills with locals and pay 16,000r (US$4) for a place. The border posts at Kaam Samnor are some way apart so hire a *moto* (US$1) to carry you from building to building to deal with the lengthy bureaucracy. There are separate offices for immigration and customs on both sides of the border, so it can end up taking as much as an hour to navigate. Luggage has to be x-rayed on the Vietnamese side of the border! Once officially in Vietnam at the village of Vinh Xuong, catch a minibus to Chau Doc (US$2, one hour). From Chau Doc, there are frequent buses to Cantho and Ho Chi Minh City. Those entering Cambodia via Vinh Xuong can just run the aforementioned route in reverse.

There are several boat companies offering direct services between Phnom Penh and Chau Doc. The more upmarket **Blue Cruiser** (☎ 016 824343; 93 Sisowath Quay; US$35) departs Chau Doc at 8.30am and Phnom Penh at 1.30pm. **Hang Chau** (☎ 012 883542; US$16) pulls out from Chau Doc at 9am and departs Phnom Penh's tourist boat dock at 12 noon. Both take about three hours or so. **Victoria Hotels** (www.victoriahotels -asia.com; US$80) also has a boat making several runs a week between Phnom Penh and its luxury Victoria Chau Doc Hotel.

Lastly, there are two companies offering luxury cruises between Ho Chi Minh City and Siem Reap via the Kaam Samnor-Vinh Xuong border crossing. International player **Pandaw Cruises** (www.pandaw.com) is an expensive option favoured by high-end tour companies. Cambodian company **Toum Teav Cruises** (www .cf-mekong.com) is smaller and is well regarded for its personal service and excellent food.

Other Crossings

It's open season when it comes to border crossings between Cambodia and Vietnam, but many are a little out of the way for the average traveller. There are rumours that a ferry may soon link Kep or Kampot with Vietnam's Phu Quoc island.

The newly opened **Prek Chak–Xa Xia** crossing has been long anticipated, connecting Kep and Kampot with the Mekong Delta town of Ha Tien. This also offers the prospect of linking the Cambodian coast with the beautiful Vietnamese island of Phu Quoc, formerly the Cambodian island of Koh Tral. As this is a fairly new crossing there is still little in the way of regular transport, but expect bus services

to start at some stage. For now, it is possible to take a *moto* from Kompong Trach (US$3), Kep (US$6) or Kampot (US$9) to the border, cross into Vietnam and take a *xe om (moto)* to Ha Tien (US$2). It is also possible to charter a taxi from Kampot (US$40), Kep (US$30) and Kompong Trach (US$20) to the border.

The **Phnom Den–Tinh Bien** crossing has been open for some time now, but is rarely used as most travellers prefer the Mekong crossing at Kaam Samnor or the new Prek Chak crossing to the south. It lies about 60km southeast of Takeo town in Cambodia and offers connections to Chau Doc. A seat in a share taxi will cost about 6000r from Takeo to the border.

There is a new border crossing in Ratanakiri province at **O'Yadaw–Le Tanh**, offering connections between Banlung and Pleiku, in Vietnam's central highlands. NH19 from Banlung to the O'Yadaw border (five hours) is still in a shameful state, so it may be some time before this border sees regular traffic. Ask around in Banlung or Pleiku about charters or try your luck with a combination of pick-ups and motos.

There are a cluster of border crossings in the east of Cambodia that connect obscure towns and are not really on the radar. The **Trapaeng Phlong–Xa Mat** and **Trapaeng Sre–Loc Ninh** crossings are both off NH7 and the Xa Mat crossing could be useful for those planning to visit the Cao Dai temple travelling to or from Ho Chi Minh City. Once the roads are all upgraded, this will probably be the favoured route for direct traffic between Siem Reap and Ho Chi Minh City. The **Banteay Chakrey–Dong Thap** crossing is really out of the way and sees almost no foreign travellers.

TOURS

In the early days of tourism in Cambodia, organised tours were a near necessity. The situation has changed dramatically and it is now much easier to organise your own trip. Budget and midrange travellers in particular can go it alone, as arrangements are cheap and easy on the ground. If you are on a tight schedule, it can pay to book a domestic flight in advance if planning to link the temples of Angkor and Siem Reap with Cambodia's capital, Phnom Penh. Once at Angkor, guides and all forms of transport under the sun are plentiful.

Shop around before booking a tour, as there is lots of competition and some companies, such as those listed here, offer more interesting itineraries than others. There are also several good companies based in Cambodia that are trying to put a little something back into the country.

Australia

Adventure World (☎ 02-8913 0755; www.adventure world.com.au) Offers adventure tours of Cambodia, as well as neighbouring Vietnam and Laos.

Intrepid Travel (☎ 1300 360 667; www.intrepidtravel .com.au) Small group tours for all budgets with an environmental, social and cultural edge.

Peregrine (☎ 02-9290 2770; www.peregrine.net.au) Small group and private tours supporting responsible tourism.

Cambodia

About Asia (☎ 855-92 121059; www.asiatravel -cambodia.com) Small bespoke travel company specialising in Siem Reap and Cambodia with a growing reputation. Profits going to build schools in Cambodia.

Cambodia Expeditions (☎ 855-12 583759; www .cambodiaexpeditions.com) Adventurous outfit promoting motorbike tours, expeditions and trekking tours.

Hanuman Tourism (☎ 855-23 218396; www .hanumantourism.com) Long-running locally-owned, locally-operated company with innovative tours like Temple Safari. Runs a charitable foundation to build bridges between tourists and worthy causes.

Journeys Within (☎ 855-63 964748; www.journeys -within.com) A boutique tourism company offering trips to Cambodia and the Mekong region. Operates a small boutique hotel in Siem Reap and has a charitable arm (see www.journeyswithinourcommunity.org for more information) helping schools and communities.

Local Adventures (☎ 855-23 990460; www .cambodia.nl) Cambodian-based company specialising in off-the-beaten path tours to the less visited regions of the country. Assists Cambodian children through the Cambodian Organisation for Learning and Training (www .colt-cambodia.org).

Pepy Ride (☎ 855-23 222804; www.pepyride.org) Specialist cycling company that runs adventurous bike rides through Cambodia to raise funds to build schools and improve education. Also offers noncycling trips.

Sam Veasna Centre (☎ 855-63 761597; www .samveasna.org) Established ecotourism operator specialising in bird-watching tours around Cambodia, including Ang Trapeang Thmor and Ttamboey. Supports conservation and education.

France

Compagnie des Indes & Orients (☎ 01-5363-3340; www.compagniesdumonde.com) Offers organised tours covering more of Cambodia than most.

Intermedes (☎ 01-4561-9090; www.intermedes.com) Offers specialised private tours.

La Route des Indes (☎ 01-4260-6090; www.laroute desindes.com) High-end tours with an academic edge.

UK

Audley Travel (☎ 01604-234855; www.audleytravel .com) Popular tailor-made specialist covering Cambodia.

Carpe Diem (☎ 0845-2262198; www.carpe-diem -travel.com) Not-for-profit travel company specialising in original adventures in Cambodia and Laos.

Cox & Kings (☎ 020-7873-5000; www.coxandkings .co.uk) Well-established high-end company, strong on cultural tours.

Explore (☎ 01252-760100; www.exploreworldwide .com) Small-group adventure travel company.

Hands Up Holidays (☎ 0776-501 3631; www.handsup holidays.com) A popular company bringing guests closer to the people of Cambodia through its responsible holidays with a spot of volunteering.

Mekong Travel (☎ 01494-674456; www.mekong -travel.com) A name to inspire confidence in the Mekong region.

Symbiosis (☎ 020-7924 5906; www.symbiosis-travel .com) Small bespoke travel company with an emphasis on cycling and diving.

Selective Asia (☎ 0845-370 3344; www.selectiveasia .com) New company that cherry-picks the best trips from leading local agents.

Wild Frontiers (☎ 020-7376 3968; www.wildfrontiers .co.uk) Adventure specialist with themed tours and innovative adventures.

USA

Asia Transpacific Journeys (☎ 800-642 2742, www .asiatranspacific.com) Group tours and tailor-made trips across the Asia-Pacific region.

Distant Horizons (☎ 800-333 1240; www.distant horizons.com) Educational tours for discerning travellers.

Geographic Expeditions (☎ 800-777 8183; www .geoex.com) Well-established high-end adventure travel company.

Global Adrenaline (☎ 800-825 1680) Luxury adventures for the experienced traveller.

GETTING AROUND

AIR
Airlines in Cambodia

Domestic flights offer a quick way to travel around the country. The problem is that the airlines themselves seem to come and go pretty quickly. There is currently only one domestic airline fully operational in Cambodia,

Siem Reap Airways (Map p79; FT; ☎ 720022; www.siem reapairways.com; hub Phnom Penh)), and that is only an offshoot of Bangkok Airways. It serves the Phnom Penh to Siem Reap route with modern ATRs from France. The government plans to relaunch a national carrier in partnership with an Indonesian business consortium.

There are up to five flights a day between Phnom Penh and Siem Reap and it is usually possible to get on a flight at short notice. However, tickets for Siem Reap Airways (US$75/115 one way/return) book out fast in peak season.

There are currently no flights to Ratanakiri, although they will likely resume at some stage. There used to be regular services to Battambang, Koh Kong, Mondulkiri and Stung Treng, but no airline has operated these routes for several years now.

The baggage allowance for domestic flights is only 10kg for each passenger, but unless you are way over the limit it is unlikely you will have to pay for excess baggage.

Helicopter

Helicopters Cambodia (p153) has offices in Phnom Penh and Siem Reap and operates reliable choppers that are available for hire. It mostly operates scenic flights around Angkor, but can be chartered for any journey. Newcomer Sokha Helicopters (p153) has also moved into this business.

BICYCLE

Cambodia is a great country for adventurous cyclists to explore. Needless to say, a mountain bike is the best bet. Basic cycling safety-equipment and authentic spare parts are also in short supply, so bring all this from home. A bell is essential – the louder the better. Many roads remain in bad condition, but there is usually a flat trail along the side. Travelling at such a gentle speed allows for much more interaction with the locals. Although bicycles are common in Cambodian villages, cycling tourists are still very much a novelty and will be wildly welcomed in most small villages. In many parts of the country there are new dirt tracks being laid down for motorcycles and bicycles, and these are a wonderful way to travel into remote parts of Cambodia.

Much of Cambodia is pancake flat or only moderately hilly. Safety, however, is a considerable concern on the newer surfaced roads, as local traffic travels at high speed. Bicycles can be transported around the country in the back of pick-ups or on the roof of minibuses.

Cycling around Angkor (p153) is an awesome experience as it really helps to get a measure of the size and scale of the temple complex. Mountain biking is likely to take off in Mondulkiri and Ratanakiri Provinces over the coming years, as there are some great trails off the beaten track. Guesthouses and hotels throughout Cambodia rent out bicycles for US$1 to US$2 per day, and a repair stall is never far away.

For the full story on cycle touring in Cambodia, see Lonely Planet's *Cycling Vietnam, Laos & Cambodia*, which has the lowdown on planning a major ride. It outlines 14 days' worth of rides in Cambodia, including a five-day ride from Phnom Penh to Ho Chi Minh City in Vietnam, travelling via Kompong Cham (p280) and Prey Veng (p278).

PEPY Ride (☎ 023-222-804; www.pepyride.org) is a bicycle and volunteer tour company offering adventures throughout Cambodia. PEPY promotes 'adventurous living, responsible giving' and uses proceeds to help build schools in rural Cambodia and fund education programmes.

BOAT

Cambodia's 1900km of navigable waterways are a key element in the country's transportation system, particularly given the state of many roads and the railways. North of Phnom Penh, the Mekong is easily navigable as far as Kratie (p285), but there are no longer regular passenger services on these routes as the roads have taken all the business. There are fast-boat services between Siem Reap and Battambang (p240), and Tonlé Sap Lake is also navigable year-round, although only by smaller boats between March and July.

Traditionally the most popular boat services with foreigners are those that run between Phnom Penh and Siem Reap (p109). The express services do the trip in as little as five hours, but the boats between Phnom

---

> **DOMESTIC DEPARTURE TAX**
>
> The airport tax for domestic flights is US$6 from Phnom Penh and Siem Reap airports, and just US$5 from regional airports.

Penh and Siem Reap are horrendously over-crowded and foreigners are charged almost twice the price of Khmers for the 'privilege' of sitting on the roof. It is not the most interesting boat journey in Cambodia, as Tonlé Sap Lake is like a vast sea, offering little scenery. It's much smarter to take a bus (p110) on the new road instead.

The small boat between Siem Reap and Battambang (p245) is more rewarding, as the river scenery is truly memorable, but it can take forever. Whichever fast-boat journey takes your fancy, you may well end up on the roof so remember to use sun block and wear a head covering.

There are now longtail rocket boats operating on northern stretches of the Mekong between Stung Treng (p291) and the Lao border. These are super fast, but are super dangerous if overcrowded or travelling after dark. Never risk departing late if it means travelling at night.

Many travellers use the fast boat between Sihanoukville and Krong Koh Kong (p330) to travel between Thailand and Cambodia.

BUS

The range of road transport is extensive in Cambodia. On sealed roads, large air-conditioned buses are the best choice. Elsewhere in the country, a pick-up truck, share taxi or minibus is the way to go.

Bus services have come on in leaps and bounds in the last few years and the situation is getting even better as more roads are upgraded. The services used most regularly by foreigners are those from Phnom Penh to Siem Reap, Battambang, Sihanoukville, Kompong Cham and Kratie, and the tourist buses from Siem Reap to Poipet.

There is a clean and comfortable bus service to towns and villages in the vicinity of Phnom Penh, such as Udong and Phnom Chisor. Operated by Phnom Penh Sorya Transport (Sorya; p110), these services are very cheap and English-speaking staff can direct you onto the right bus.

Minibuses serve most provincial routes, but are not widely used by Western visitors. They are very cheap, but often uncomfort-ably overcrowded and driven by maniacs, like the meanest of *matatus* (minibus taxis) in East Africa. Only consider them if there is no alternative.

CAR & MOTORCYCLE

Car and motorcycle rental are comparatively cheap in Cambodia and many visitors rent a car or motorcycle for greater flexibility to visit out-of-the-way places and to stop when and where they choose. Almost all car rental in Cambodia includes a driver, which is good news given the abysmal state of many roads and the prominence of the psychopathic driver gene among many Cambodian road users.

Driving Licence

A standard driving licence is not much use in Cambodia. In theory, to drive a car you need an International Driving Licence, usually issued through your automobile association back home. It is very unlikely that a driving licence will be of any use to most travellers to Cambodia, save for those coming to work with one of the many foreign organisations in Cambodia.

When it comes to renting motorcycles, it's a case of no licence required. If you can drive the bike out of the shop, you can drive it any-where, or so the logic goes.

Fuel & Spare Parts

Fuel is relatively expensive in Cambodia, at around 4000r (US$1) a litre. Fuel is readily available throughout the country, but prices rise in rural areas. Even the most isolated communities usually have someone selling petrol out of Fanta or Johnnie Walker bot-tles. Some sellers mix this fuel with kerosene to make a quick profit – use it sparingly, in emergencies only.

When it comes to spare parts, Cambodia is flooded with Japanese motorcycles, so it is easy to get parts for Hondas, Yamahas or Suzukis, but finding a part for a Harley or a Ducati is another matter. The same goes for cars – spares for Japanese cars are easy to come by, but if you are driving something obscure, bring substantial spares.

Hire
CAR

Car hire is generally only available with a driver and is only really useful for sightseeing around Phnom Penh and Angkor. Some tour-ists with a healthy budget also arrange cars or 4WDs with drivers for touring the provinces. Hiring a car with a driver is about US$25 to US$35 for a day in and around Cambodia's towns. Heading into the provinces it rises to

TRANSPORT

TRANSPORT

ROAD DISTANCES (KM)

	Ban Lung	Battambang	Kampot	Kompong Cham	Kompong Chhnang	Kompong Thom	Kratie	Phnom Penh	Poipet	Prey Veng	Pursat	Sen Monorom	Siem Reap	Sihanoukville	Sisophon	Stung Treng	Svay Rieng	Takeo
Battambang	928																	
Kampot	783	441																
Kompong Cham	515	413	263															
Kompong Chhnang	726	202	239	211														
Kompong Thom	654	322	313	139	256													
Kratie	287	641	496	228	439	367												
Phnom Penh	635	293	148	120	91	165	348											
Poipet	957	117	558	442	319	303	670	410										
Prey Veng	580	384	239	78	182	217	293	90	520									
Pursat	823	105	336	308	97	353	536	188	222	279								
Sen Monorom	155	663	518	250	461	389	215	370	692	315	558							
Siem Reap	805	171	464	290	373	151	664	317	152	407	276	540						
Sihanoukville	865	523	105	350	321	395	578	230	640	321	418	600	546					
Sisophon	908	68	509	393	270	254	621	361	49	471	173	643	103	591				
Stung Treng	165	782	637	369	580	508	141	489	811	434	677	356	659	719	762			
Svay Rieng	675	418	273	173	216	290	388	125	535	95	313	410	441	355	486	529		
Takeo	710	368	85	195	166	240	423	75	485	166	263	445	391	190	436	564	200	
Tbeng Meanchey	791	459	450	276	393	137	504	302	440	354	490	526	288	532	391	645	467	377

US$50 or more, depending on the destination, and for those staying overnight, the driver will also need looking after. Hiring 4WDs will cost around US$60 to US$120 a day, depending on the model and the distance travelled. Driving yourself is just about possible but also inadvisable due to chaotic road conditions,

WARNING

More people are now killed and injured each month in traffic accidents than by land mines. While this is partly down to land-mine awareness efforts and ongoing clearance programmes, it is also down to a huge rise in the number of vehicles on the roads and drivers travelling at dangerous speeds. Be extremely vigilant when travelling under your own steam and take care crossing the roads on the high-speed national highways. It is best not to travel on the roads at night due to a higher prevalence of accidents at this time. This especially applies to bikers, as several foreigners are killed each year in motorbike accidents.

personal liability in the case of an accident and higher charges.

MOTORCYCLE

Motorcycles are available for hire in Phnom Penh (p111) and some other popular tourist destinations. In Siem Reap and Sihanoukville, motorcycle rental is forbidden, so anyone planning any rides around Siem Reap needs to arrange a bike in Phnom Penh. In other provincial towns, it is usually possible to rent a small motorcycle after a bit of negotiation. Costs are US$3 to US$7 per day for a 100cc motorcycle and around US$10 for a 250cc dirt bike.

Drive with due care and attention, as medical facilities are less than adequate in Cambodia and traffic is erratic, particularly in Phnom Penh. If you have never ridden a motorcycle before, Cambodia is not the best place to start, but once out of the city it does get easier. If you're jumping in at the deep end, make sure you are under the supervision of someone who knows how to ride.

The advantage of motorcycle travel is that it allows for complete freedom of movement and you can stop in small villages that Westerners

---

THE MOTO BURN

Be careful not to put your leg near the exhaust pipe of a *moto* after long journeys; many travellers have received nasty burns, which can take a long time to heal in the sticky weather and often require antibiotics.

---

rarely visit. It is possible to take motorcycles upcountry for tours, but only experienced off-road bikers should take to these roads with a dirt bike. Even riders with more experience should take care if intending to ride into remote regions of Cambodia, as roads in this country are not the same as roads at home! Anyone planning a longer ride should try out the bike around Phnom Penh for a day or so first to make sure it is in good health.

For those with experience, Cambodia has some of the best roads in the world for dirt biking, particularly in the provinces of Preah Vihear (p261), Mondulkiri (p298), Ratanakiri (p291) and the Cardamom Mountains.

Hidden Cambodia (www.hiddencambodia.com) is a Siem Reap-based company specialising in motorcycle trips throughout Cambodia. It operates an annual dry-season programme that includes the remote temples of northern Cambodia and beyond.

Dancing Roads (www.dancingroads.com) offers motorbike tours around the capital and gentle tours further afield to the south coast. Based in Phnom Penh, the driver-guides are knowledgeable and fun.

The annual Extreme Rally Raid is still organised by **Angkor Dirt Bike Tours** (www.toursinthe extreme.com) each year in January. Their motto is 'no licence required' but riders will need some serious experience.

Insurance

If you are travelling in a tourist vehicle with a driver, then it is usually insured. When it comes to motorcycles, many rental bikes are not insured and you will have to sign a contract agreeing to a valuation for the bike if it is stolen. Make sure you have a strong lock and always leave it in guarded parking where available.

Do not even consider hiring a motorcycle if you are daft enough to be travelling in Cambodia without insurance. The cost of treating serious injuries is bankrupting for budget travellers.

Road Conditions & Hazards

Whether travelling or living in Cambodia, it is easy to lull yourself into a false sense of security and assume that down every rural road is yet another friendly village. However, even with the demise of the Khmer Rouge, odd incidents of banditry and robbery do occur in rural areas. When travelling in your own vehicle, and particularly by motorcycle in rural areas, make certain you check the latest security information in communities along the way.

Expatriates working in Phnom Penh may end up driving a 4WD or car, but will certainly need to drive with more care than at home. In Phnom Penh traffic is a law unto itself and in the provinces roads can resemble roller coasters. Be particularly careful about children on the road – you'll find kids hanging out in the middle of a major highway. Livestock on the road are also a menace; hit a cow on a motorcycle and you'll both be pizza.

Other general security suggestions for those travelling by motorcycle:

- Try to get hold of a helmet for long journeys or high-speed riding.
- Carry a basic repair kit, including some tyre levers, a puncture repair kit and a pump.
- Always carry a rope for towing on longer journeys in case you break down.
- In remote areas always carry several litres of water, as you never know when you will run out.
- Travel in small groups, not alone.
- When in a group, stay close together in case of any incident or accident.
- Don't be cheap with the petrol – running out of fuel in a rural area could jeopardise your health, especially if water runs out too.
- Do not smoke marijuana or drink alcohol and drive.
- Keep your eyes firmly fixed on the road; Cambodian potholes eat people for fun.

Road Rules

If there are road rules in Cambodia it is doubtful that anyone is following them. Size matters and the biggest vehicle wins by default. The best advice if you drive a car or ride a motorcycle in Cambodia is to take nothing for granted and assume that your fellow motorists are visually challenged psychopaths. Seriously though, in Cambodia traffic drives on the

TRANSPORT

TRANSPORT

right. There are few traffic lights at junctions in Phnom Penh, so most traffic turns left into the oncoming traffic, edging along the left-hand side of the road until a gap becomes apparent. For the uninitiated it looks like a disaster waiting to happen, but Cambodians are quite used to the system. Foreigners should stop at crossings and develop a habit of constant vigilance.

Phnom Penh is the one place where, amid all the chaos, traffic police take issue with Westerners breaking even the most trivial road rules (p81). Make sure you don't turn left at a 'no left turn' sign or travel with your headlights on during the day (although strangely, it doesn't seem to be illegal for Cambodians to travel without headlights at night).

HITCHING

Hitching is never entirely safe in any country, and we don't recommend it. Travellers who decide to hitch should understand that they are taking a small but potentially serious risk. People who do choose to hitch will be safer if they travel in pairs and let someone know where they are planning to go. Hitching with truck drivers is a possibility, but it is very uncomfortable and should be considered extremely unsafe for lone women. Expect to pay for the ride.

LOCAL TRANSPORT
Bus

There are currently no local bus networks in Cambodia, even in the capital Phnom Penh.

Cyclo

As in Vietnam and Laos, the *samlor* or *cyclo* (pedicab) is a cheap way to get around urban areas. In Phnom Penh *cyclo* drivers can either be flagged down on main roads or found loitering around markets and major hotels. It is necessary to bargain the fare if taking a *cyclo* from outside an expensive hotel or popular restaurant or bar. Fares range from 1000r to US$1 (about 4000r). There are few *cyclos* in the provinces and in Phnom Penh the *cyclo* is fast losing ground to the *moto*.

Lorry

No, not a big truck, but the Cambodian name for a local train made from wood and powered by a motorcycle, quite literally the motorcycle's rear wheel touching the track and propelling it along. In the Battambang area, they

> **WARNING**
>
> *Moto* drivers and *cyclo* riders with little or no English may not understand where you want them to go even though they nod vigorously. This is a particular headache in a big city like Phnom Penh – see the boxed text, p113.

are known as a *norry* or the 'bamboo train' to tourists, and they are powered by an electric motor. Great fun until you meet another train coming the other way – aaaaargh!

Moto

Motos, also known as *motodups* (meaning moto driver), are small motorcycle taxis and their drivers almost universally wear a baseball cap. They are a quick way of making short hops around towns and cities. Prices range from 1000r to US$1 or more, depending on the distance and the town; expect to pay more at night. (Inflation may also increase prices; see p15.) It used to be that prices were rarely agreed in advance, but with the increase in visitor numbers a lot of drivers have got into the habit of overcharging. It's probably best to negotiate up front, particularly in the major tourist centres, outside fancy hotels or at night.

Outboards

Outboards (pronounced 'out-boor') are the equivalent of Venice's *vaporetto,* a sort of local river-bus or taxi. Found all over the country, they are small fibreglass boats with 15hp and 40hp engines, and can carry up to six people for local or longer trips. They rarely run to schedules, but locals wait patiently for them to fill up. Those with time on their hands can join the wait, those in a hurry can charter the whole boat and take off. Another variation are the longtail rocket boats imported from Thailand that connect small towns on the upper stretches of the Mekong. Rocket is the definitive word and their safety is questionable.

Remorque-kang

The *remorque-kang* is a trailer pulled by a bicycle, effectively a kind of *cyclo* with the passenger travelling behind. The coming of the *moto* has led to a dwindling in numbers, but they are still seen in Battambang (p240) and Kampot (p215). Fares are about the same as *moto* rides.

Remorque-moto

The *remorque-moto* is a large trailer hitched to a motorcycle and pretty much operates as a low-tech local bus with oh-so-natural air-conditioning. They are used throughout rural Cambodia to transport people and goods, and are often seen on the edge of towns ready to ferry farmers back to the countryside. Fares are very cheap, at around 100r per kilometre.

Phnom Penh, Siem Reap and Sihanoukville have their very own tourist versions of the *remorque-moto,* with a cute little canopied trailer hitched to the back for two people in comfort or as many as you can pile on at night. These make a great way to explore the temples, as you get the breeze of the bike but some protection from the elements. These are often referred to as *tuk tuks* by foreigners travelling in Cambodia.

Rotei Ses

Rotei means 'cart' or 'carriage' and *ses* is 'horse', but the term is used for any cart pulled by an animal. Cambodia's original 4WD, ox carts are a common form of transport in remote parts of the country, as they are the only things that can get through thick mud in the height of the wet season. They are usually pulled by water buffalo or cows. Horse-and-carts are commonly seen in rural Cambodia, although very few tourists like the idea of being pulled along by one of these pitiful horses. Some local community tourism initiatives now include cart rides.

Taxi

Taxi hire is getting easier in Cambodia, but there are still next to no metered taxis. There are many private operators working throughout Cambodia. Guesthouses, hotels and travel agents can arrange them for sightseeing in and around towns. Even in Phnom Penh, however, it can be almost impossible to find a taxi for short hops unless you've booked a car in advance or are leaving popular nightspots late at night.

PICK-UP, SHARE TAXI & JEEP

These days the pick-up trucks are losing ground to the pumped-up Toyota Camrys that have their suspension jacked up like monster trucks. When using pick-up trucks or share taxis, it is an advantage to travel in numbers, as you can buy spare seats to make the journey more comfortable. Double the price for the front seat and quadruple it for the back row. It is important to remember that there aren't necessarily fixed prices on every route, so you have to negotiate and prices do fluctuate with the price of petrol – after all, the cost of petrol has more than doubled in the last few years.

Pick-ups and share taxis take on the bad roads that buses would break down on and some of the busier roads that buses serve. Share taxis are widely available for hire and for major destinations they can be hired individually or you can pay for a seat and wait for other passengers to turn up. Guesthouses are also very helpful when it comes to arranging share taxis – at a price, of course.

When it comes to pick-ups, passengers can sit in the cab or, if money is short and comfort an alien concept, out on the back; trucks depart when seriously full. Passengers sitting out back should carry a scarf to protect from the dust and sunscreen to protect against the sun. In the wet season a raincoat is as good as compulsory. Arranging a pick-up directly is less expensive than getting a guesthouse to organise it, but involves considerable aggravation. Haggle patiently to ensure a fair price.

In very remote areas, particularly in the wet season, when the roads are even more abysmal than usual, huge six-wheel-drive Russian military trucks serve as periodic transport. These are known as *lan damrei* (elephant trucks).

TRAIN

Cambodia's rail system is, like the old road network, one of the most notorious in Asia. There are no longer passenger services, but it may be possible to negotiate a ride on a freight train if you are feeling really masochistic. The best sections of the network are between Takeo and Kampot and from there to Sihanoukville. Trains travel at an average speed of 20km/h, bridges are not always maintained and the ride is often as bumpy as on some of the roads, as the tracks are so warped.

The railway is about to be completely overhauled to plug it into the Trans-Asian Railway which will eventually link Singapore and China, but this will take a few years. In the meantime, ardent trainspotters should be able to pay their way onto a cargo train, but bear in mind it takes more than 12 hours to Battambang, and that's if the train doesn't derail. It's more fun to take to the rails on the bamboo train (p247) around Battambang.

The rail network consists of about 645km of single-track metre-gauge lines. The 382km northwestern line, built before WWII, links Phnom Penh with Pursat (165km), Battambang (274km) and Sisophon (302km). The last stretch to Poipet was pulled up by the Khmer Rouge in the 1970s. The 263km southwestern line, which was completed in 1969, connects Phnom Penh with Takeo (75km), Kampot (166km) and the port of Sihanoukville (228km).

The civil war during much of the 1980s and 1990s led to some unique developments in the Cambodian rail system. Each train was equipped with a tin-roofed, armoured carriage sporting a huge machine gun and numerous gun ports in its sides. In addition, the first two flat-bed carriages of the train operated as mine sweepers. Travel on the first carriage was free and on the second carriage half-price and, despite the risks, these options were extremely popular with the locals.

Health Dr Trish Batchelor

CONTENTS

Your health is more of a concern in Cambodia than most other parts of Southeast Asia, due to poor sanitation and a lack of effective medical treatment facilities. Once you venture into rural areas you are very much on your own, although most towns have a reasonable clinic these days.

If you feel particularly unwell, try to see a doctor rather than visit a hospital; hospitals in rural areas are pretty primitive and diagnosis can be hit and miss. If you fall seriously ill in Cambodia you should head to major centres Phnom Penh or Siem Reap, as these are the only places in the country with decent emergency treatment. Pharmacies in the larger towns are remarkably well stocked and you don't need a prescription to get your hands on anything from antibiotics to antimalarials. Prices are also very reasonable, but do check the expiry date, as some medicine may have been on the shelves for quite a long time.

Don't let these warnings make you paranoid. Travel health depends alot on your level of predeparture preparation, your daily health care while travelling and also how you handle any medical problem that may develop. While the potential dangers can seem quite frightening, in reality few travellers experience anything more than an upset stomach.

BEFORE YOU GO

INSURANCE
Make sure that you have adequate health insurance. See p314 for details.

RECOMMENDED VACCINATIONS
Plan ahead for getting your vaccinations (see the boxed text, p342): some of them require more than one injection over a period of time, while others should not be given together. Note that some vaccinations should not be given during pregnancy or to people with allergies.

It is recommended that you seek medical advice at least six weeks before travel. Be aware that there is often a greater risk of disease during pregnancy and among children.

Record all vaccinations on an International Certificate of Vaccination, available from your doctor. It is a good idea to carry this as proof of your vaccinations when travelling in Cambodia.

FURTHER READING
If you are planning on travelling in remote areas for a long period of time, you may consider taking a more detailed health guide, such as Lonely Planet's *Healthy Travel: Asia & India,* which is a handy pocket-sized guide packed with useful information including pre-trip planning, emergency first aid, immunisation and disease information, and what to do if you get sick on the road. *Where There Is No Doctor,* by David Werner, is a very detailed guide intended for those going to work in an underdeveloped country.

Lonely Planet's *Travel with Children,* by Cathy Lanigan, includes advice on travel health for younger children.

OTHER PREPARATIONS
Make sure you're healthy before you start travelling. If you're going on a long trip, make a visit to a dentist before you depart. If you wear glasses, take a spare pair and your prescription.

HEALTH

If you require a particular medication, try to ensure that you take an adequate supply, as it may not be available locally. Take part of the packaging that shows the generic name rather than the brand only, as this will make getting replacements easier. To avoid any problems, it is also a good idea to have a legible prescription or letter from a doctor to show that you use the medication regularly.

Medical Kit Check List

Following is a list of items you should consider including in your medical kit – consult your pharmacist for brands available in your country.

- aspirin or paracetamol (acetaminophen in the USA) – for pain or fever
- antihistamine – for allergies, eg hay fever; to ease the itch from insect bites or stings; and to prevent motion sickness

---

REQUIRED & RECOMMENDED VACCINATIONS

Vaccinations you may want to consider for a trip to Cambodia are listed here, but it is imperative that you discuss your needs with your doctor. For more details about the diseases themselves, see the individual entries later in this section.

- **Diphtheria and tetanus** – vaccinations for these two diseases are usually combined. After an initial course of three injections (usually given in childhood), boosters are necessary every 10 years.

- **Hepatitis A** – this vaccine provides long-term immunity after an initial injection and a booster at six to 12 months. Alternatively, an injection of gamma globulin can provide short-term protection against hepatitis A – two to six months, depending on the dose. It is reasonably effective and, unlike the vaccine, is protective immediately but, because it is a blood product, there are current concerns about its long-term safety. The hepatitis A vaccine is also available in a combined form with the hepatitis B vaccine – three injections over a six-month period are required.

- **Hepatitis B** – travellers who should consider vaccination against hepatitis B include those on a long trip, as well as those visiting countries where there are high levels of hepatitis B infection (such as Cambodia), where blood transfusions may not be adequately screened or where sexual contact or needle sharing is a possibility. Vaccination involves three injections, with a booster at 12 months. More rapid courses are available if necessary.

- **Japanese B Encephalitis** – consider vaccination against this disease if spending a month or longer in Cambodia, when making repeated trips or if visiting during an epidemic. It involves three injections over 30 days.

- **Polio** – everyone should keep up-to-date with this vaccination, normally given in childhood. A booster every 10 years maintains immunity.

- **Rabies** – vaccination should be considered by those spending a month or longer in Cambodia, especially if they are cycling, handling animals, caving or travelling to remote areas. It's also recommended for children, as they may not report a bite. Vaccination involves having three injections over 21 to 28 days. Vaccinated people who are bitten or scratched by an animal will require two booster injections of vaccine; those not vaccinated require more.

- **Tuberculosis** – the risk of travellers contracting TB is usually very low, unless you will be living with, or closely associated with, local people. Vaccination against TB (BCG vaccine) is recommended for children and young adults who will be living in high-risk areas, including Cambodia, for three months or more.

- **Typhoid** – vaccination against typhoid may be required if you are travelling for more than a couple of weeks in Cambodia.

- **Yellow Fever** – a yellow fever vaccine is now the only vaccine that is a legal requirement for entry into Cambodia when coming from an infected area. This refers to a direct flight from an infected area, but there are no direct flights from Africa or South America, the most likely places of infection.

- cold and flu tablets, throat lozenges and nasal decongestant
- multivitamins – consider for long trips, when dietary vitamin intake may be inadequate
- antibiotics – consider including these if you're travelling well off the beaten track; see your doctor before you go, as they must be prescribed, and carry the prescription with you
- loperamide or diphenoxylate – 'blockers' for diarrhoea
- prochlorperazine or metaclopramide – for nausea and vomiting
- rehydration mixture – to prevent dehydration, which may occur, for example, during bouts of diarrhoea; rehydration mixture is particularly important when travelling with children
- insect repellent, sunscreen, lip balm and eye drops
- calamine lotion, sting relief spray or aloe vera – to ease irritation from sunburn and insect bites or stings
- antifungal cream or powder – for fungal skin infections and thrush
- antiseptic (such as povidone-iodine) – for cuts and grazes
- bandages, Band-Aids (plasters) and other wound dressings
- water purification tablets or iodine
- scissors, tweezers and a thermometer – note that mercury thermometers are prohibited by airlines
- sterile kit (sealed medical kit containing syringes and needles) – highly recommended, as Cambodia has medical hygiene problems

IN TRANSIT

DEEP VEIN THROMBOSIS (DVT)

Deep vein thrombosis (DVT) occurs when blood clots form in the legs during plane flights, chiefly because of prolonged immobility. The longer the flight, the greater the risk. Though most blood clots are reabsorbed uneventfully, some may break off and travel through the blood vessels to the lungs, where they may cause life-threatening complications.

The chief symptom of DVT is swelling or pain of the foot, ankle, or calf, usually on just one side. When a blood clot travels to the lungs, it may cause chest pain and difficulty in breathing. Travellers with any of these symptoms should immediately seek medical attention.

To prevent the development of DVT on long flights, walk about the cabin, contract the leg muscles while sitting, drink plenty of fluids, and avoid alcohol.

JET LAG & MOTION SICKNESS

Jet lag is experienced when a person travels by air across more than three time zones. It occurs because many of the functions of the human body (such as temperature, pulse rate and emptying of the bladder and bowels) are regulated by internal 24-hour cycles. When we travel long distances rapidly, our bodies take time to adjust to the 'new time' of our destination, and we may experience fatigue, disorientation, insomnia, anxiety, impaired concentration and loss of appetite. These effects will usually be gone within three days of arrival, but to minimise the impact of jet lag:

- rest for a couple of days prior to date of departure.
- try to select flight schedules that minimise sleep deprivation; arriving late in the day means you can go to sleep soon after you arrive. For very long flights, try to organise a stopover.
- avoid excessive eating (which bloats the stomach) and alcohol intake (which causes dehydration) during the flight. Instead, drink plenty of noncarbonated, nonalcoholic drinks such as fruit juice or water.
- make yourself comfortable by wearing loose-fitting clothes and perhaps bringing an eye mask and earplugs to help you sleep.
- on the flight, try to sleep at the appropriate time for the time zone to which you are travelling.

Eating lightly before and during a trip will reduce the chances of motion sickness. If you are prone to motion sickness, try to find a place that minimises movement – near the wing on aircraft, close to midships on boats, near the centre on buses. Fresh air usually helps; reading and cigarette smoke don't. Ginger (available in capsule form) and peppermint (including mint-fla-

HEALTH

HEALTH

TRADITIONAL MEDICINE IN CAMBODIA

Traditional medicine or *thnam boran* is very popular in rural Cambodia. There are *kru Khmer* or traditional medicine men in most districts of the country and some locals trust them more than modern doctors and hospitals. Working with tree barks, roots, herbs and plants, they boil up brews to supposedly cure all ills. However, when it comes to serious conditions like snake bites, their treatments can be counterproductive and infectious. Other popular traditional remedies, even in the city, include *kor kchoal*, a vigorous coin massage to take away the bad wind, and *chup kchoal*, a massage using heated vacuum cups. The first leaves red streaks on the torso like the patient has been flayed, the second large round circles like a contagious disease.

---

voured sweets) are natural preventatives of motion sickness.

IN CAMBODIA

AVAILABILITY & COST OF HEALTH CARE

Self-diagnosis and treatment of health problems can be risky, so you should always seek professional medical help. Although we do give drug dosages in this section, they are for emergency use only. Correct diagnosis is vital.

An embassy, consulate or five-star hotel can usually recommend a local doctor or clinic. Antibiotics should ideally be administered only under medical supervision. Take only the recommended dose at the prescribed intervals and use the whole course, even if the illness seems to be cured earlier. Stop immediately if there are any serious reactions and don't use the antibiotic at all if you are unsure that you have the correct one. Some people are allergic to commonly prescribed antibiotics such as penicillin or sulpha drugs; carry this information (eg on a bracelet) when travelling.

The best clinics and hospitals in Cambodia are found in Phnom Penh (p77) and Siem Reap (p122). A consultation usually costs in the region of US$20 to US$40, plus medicine. Elsewhere, facilities are more basic, although a private clinic is usually preferable to a govern-ment hospital. For serious injuries or illnesses, seek treatment in Bangkok.

INFECTIOUS DISEASES
Dengue

This viral disease is transmitted by mosquitoes and occurs mainly in tropical and subtropical areas of the world. There is only a small risk to travellers, except during epidemics, which are usually seasonal in Cambodia, during and just after the wet season.

Unlike the malaria mosquito, the *Aedes aegypti* mosquito, which transmits the dengue virus, is most active during the day and is found mainly in urban areas.

Signs and symptoms of dengue fever include a sudden onset of high fever, headache, joint and muscle pains (hence its old name, 'breakbone fever') and nausea and vomiting. A rash of small red spots appears three to four days after the onset of fever. Dengue is commonly mistaken for other infectious diseases, including influenza.

Seek medical attention if you think you may be infected. A blood test can diagnose infection, but there is no specific treatment for the disease. Aspirin should be avoided, as it increases the risk of haemorrhaging, but plenty of rest is advised. Recovery may be prolonged, with tiredness lasting for several weeks. Severe complications are rare in travellers but include dengue haemorrhagic fever (DHF), which can be fatal without prompt medical treatment. DHF is thought to be a result of secondary infection due to a different strain (there are four major strains) and usually affects residents of the country rather than travellers.

There is no vaccine against dengue fever. The best prevention is to avoid mosquito bites at all times – see Malaria, opposite, for more details.

Fungal Infections

Fungal infections occur more commonly in hot weather and are usually on the scalp, between the toes (athlete's foot) or fingers, in the groin and on the body (ringworm). Ringworm, a fungal infection, not a worm, is contracted from infected animals or other people. Moisture encourages these infections.

To prevent fungal infections wear loose, comfortable clothes, avoid artificial fibres, wash frequently and dry yourself carefully. If you do get an infection, wash the infected area at least daily with a disinfectant or medicated soap and water, and rinse and dry well. Apply an antifungal cream or powder like tolnaftate (Tinaderm). Try to expose the infected area to air or sunlight as much as possible. Wash all towels and underwear in hot water, change them often and let them dry in the sun.

Hepatitis

Hepatitis is a general term for inflammation of the liver. It is a common disease worldwide. There are several different viruses that cause hepatitis, and they differ in the way that they are transmitted. The symptoms are similar in all forms of the illness, and include fever, chills, headache, fatigue, feelings of weakness and aches and pains, followed by loss of appetite, nausea, vomiting, abdominal pain, dark urine, light-coloured faeces, jaundiced (yellow) skin and yellowing of the whites of the eyes. People who have had hepatitis should avoid alcohol for some time after the illness, as the liver needs time to recover.

Hepatitis A is transmitted by ingesting contaminated food or water. You should seek medical advice, but there is not much you can do apart from resting, drinking lots of fluids, eating lightly and avoiding fatty foods. Hepatitis E is transmitted in the same way as hepatitis A; it can be particularly serious in pregnant women.

There are almost 300 million chronic carriers of hepatitis B in the world. It is spread through contact with infected blood, blood products or body fluids; for example, through sexual contact, unsterilised needles, blood transfusions or contact with blood via small breaks in the skin. Other risk situations include shaving, tattooing or body piercing with contaminated equipment. The symptoms of hepatitis B may be more severe than type A and the disease can lead to long-term problems such as chronic liver damage, liver cancer or a long-term carrier state. Hepatitis C and D are spread in the same way as hepatitis B and can also lead to long-term complications.

There are vaccines against hepatitis A and B, but there are currently no vaccines against the other types of hepatitis. Following the basic rules about food and water (hepatitis A and E) and avoiding risk situations (hepatitis B, C and D) are important preventative measures.

HIV/AIDS

Infection with the human immunodeficiency virus (HIV) may lead to acquired immune deficiency syndrome (AIDS), which is a fatal disease. Any exposure to blood, blood products or body fluids may put the individual at risk.

The disease is often transmitted through sexual contact or dirty needles, so vaccinations, acupuncture, tattooing and body piercing can be potentially as dangerous as intravenous drug use. HIV/AIDS can also be spread through infected-blood transfusions; although the blood centre in Phnom Penh does screen blood used for transfusions, it is unlikely to be done in many of the provinces.

If you do need an injection, ask to see the syringe unwrapped in front of you, or take a needle and syringe pack with you. Fear of HIV infection should never preclude any treatment for serious medical conditions.

According to WHO figures, Cambodian rates of infection are highest among sex workers. However, due to a concerted awareness campaign, HIV/AIDS infection rates have been steadily declining in the past decade from a high of around 5% of the population in the 1990s to about 1.6% today.

Intestinal Worms

These parasites are most common in rural Cambodia. The various worms have different ways of infecting people. Some may be ingested in food such as undercooked meat (eg tapeworms) and some enter through your skin (eg hookworms). Infestations may not show up for some time, and although they are generally not serious, if left untreated they may cause severe health problems later. Consider having a stool test when you return home to check for worms to determine the appropriate treatment.

Japanese B Encephalitis

This viral infection of the brain is transmitted by mosquitoes. Most cases occur among locals living in rural areas, as the virus exists in pigs and wading birds. Symptoms include fever, headache and alteration in consciousness. Hospitalisation is needed for correct diagnosis and treatment. There is a high mortality rate among those who have symptoms; of those who survive many are intellectually disabled.

Malaria

This serious and potentially fatal disease is spread by mosquitoes. If you are travelling in endemic areas it is extremely important

HEALTH

to avoid mosquito bites and to take tablets to prevent the disease developing if you become infected. There is no malaria in Phnom Penh, Siem Reap and most other major urban areas in Cambodia, so visitors on short trips to the most popular places do not need to take medication. Malaria self-test kits are widely available in Cambodia, but are not that reliable.

Symptoms of malaria include fever, chills and sweating, headache, aching joints, diarrhoea and stomach pains, usually preceded by a vague feeling of ill health. Seek medical help immediately if malaria is suspected, as, without treatment, the disease can rapidly become more serious or even fatal.

If medical care is not available, malaria tablets can be used for treatment. You need to use a different malaria tablet to the one you were taking when you contracted the disease, as obviously the first type didn't work. If travelling widely in rural areas of Cambodia, it is worth visiting a pharmacy to purchase a treatment dose – this will save you from complications in the event of an emergency. Antimalarials are available cheaply throughout Cambodia, although buy them from a reputable clinic to be sure they are not fakes.

Travellers are advised to prevent mosquito bites at all times. The main messages:

- Wear light-coloured clothing.
- Wear long trousers and long-sleeved shirts.
- Use mosquito repellents containing the compound DEET on exposed areas (prolonged overuse of DEET may be harmful, especially to children, but its use is considered preferable to being bitten by disease-transmitting mosquitoes).
- Avoid perfumes or aftershave.
- Use a mosquito net impregnated with mosquito repellent (permethrin) – it may be worth taking your own.
- Impregnate clothes with permethrin to effectively deter mosquitoes and other insects.

MALARIA MEDICATION
Antimalarial drugs do not prevent you from being infected but they kill the malaria parasites during their developmental stage, significantly reducing the risk of becoming very ill or dying. Expert advice on medication should be sought, as there are many factors to consider, including the area to be visited, the risk of exposure to malaria-carrying mosquitoes, the side effects of medication, your medical history and whether you are a child or an adult, and whether you're pregnant. Travellers heading to isolated areas in Cambodia should carry a treatment dose of medication for use if symptoms occur. A new drug called Malarine, supplied and subsidised by the European Union (EU) and WHO, is cheaply available in pharmacies throughout Cambodia. A combination of artesunate and mefloquinine, it is undoubtedly the most effective malaria killer available in Cambodia today. See the English instructions for advice about the appropriate dosage.

Schistosomiasis
Also known as bilharzia, this disease is transmitted by minute worms. They infect certain varieties of freshwater snails found in rivers, streams, lakes and, in particular, dams. The worms multiply and are eventually discharged into the water.

The worm enters through the skin and attaches itself to the intestines or bladder. The first symptom may be feeling generally unwell, or a tingling and sometimes a light rash around the area where the worm entered. Weeks later a high fever may develop. Once the disease is established, abdominal pain and blood in the urine are other signs. The infection often causes no symptoms until the disease is well established (several months to years after exposure), when damage to internal organs is irreversible.

The main method of preventing the disease is avoiding swimming or bathing in fresh water where bilharzia is present. Even deep water can be infected. If you do get wet, dry off quickly and dry your clothes as well.

A blood test is the most reliable way to diagnose the disease, but the test will not show positive until a number of weeks after exposure.

Sexually Transmitted Infections (STIs)
Gonorrhoea, herpes and syphilis are among these infections. Sores, blisters or a rash around the genitals and discharges or pain when urinating are common symptoms. With some STIs, such as wart virus or chlamydia, symptoms may be less marked or not observed at all, especially in women. Syphilis symptoms eventually disappear

completely, but the disease continues and can cause severe problems in later years. While abstinence from sexual contact is the only 100% effective prevention, using condoms is also effective. Reliable condoms are widely available throughout urban areas of Cambodia. Different STIs each require specific antibiotics. The treatment of gonorrhoea and syphilis is with antibiotics. There is no cure for herpes or HIV/AIDS (see p345).

Typhoid

Typhoid fever is a dangerous gut infection caused by contaminated water and food. Medical help must be sought.

In its initial stages sufferers may feel they have a bad cold or flu on the way, as early symptoms are a headache, body aches and a fever that rises a little each day until it is around 40°C (104°F) or higher. The victim's pulse is often slow relative to the degree of fever present – unlike a normal fever where the pulse increases. There may also be vomiting, abdominal pain, diarrhoea or constipation.

In the second week the high fever and slow pulse continue, and a few pink spots may appear on the body; trembling, delirium, weakness, weight loss and dehydration may occur. Complications such as pneumonia, perforated bowel or meningitis may also present themselves.

TRAVELLER'S DIARRHOEA

Simple things like a change of water, food or climate can all cause a mild bout of diarrhoea, but a few rushed toilet trips with no other symptoms are not indicative of a major problem. Almost everyone gets a mild bout of the runs on a longer visit to Cambodia.

Dehydration is the main danger with diarrhoea, particularly in children or the elderly as dehydration can occur quite quickly. Under all circumstances *fluid replacement* is the most important thing to remember. Weak black tea with a little sugar, soda water, or soft drinks allowed to go flat and diluted 50% with clean water are all good. You need to drink at least the same volume of fluid that you are losing in bowel movements and vomiting. Urine is the best guide to the adequacy of replacement: if you have small amounts of concentrated urine, you need to drink more. Keep drinking small amounts often. Stick to a bland diet as you recover.

With severe diarrhoea, a rehydrating solution is preferable to replace lost minerals and salts. Commercially available oral rehydration salts are very useful; add them to boiled or bottled water. In an emergency you can make up a solution of six teaspoons of sugar and a half-teaspoon of salt to a litre of boiled or bottled water.

Gut-paralysing drugs such as Lomotil or Imodium can be used to bring relief from the symptoms of diarrhoea, although they do not actually cure the problem. Only use these drugs if you do not have access to toilets and *must* travel. For children under 12 years the use of Lomotil and Imodium is not recommended. Do not use these drugs if the person has a high fever or is severely dehydrated.

In certain situations antibiotics may be required: diarrhoea with blood or mucus (dysentery), any diarrhoea with fever, profuse watery diarrhoea, persistent diarrhoea not improving after 48 hours and severe diarrhoea. These suggest a more serious cause of diarrhoea, and gut-paralysing drugs should be avoided.

In these situations, a stool test may be necessary to diagnose what bug is causing the diarrhoea, so seek medical help urgently. Where this is not possible the recommended drugs for bacterial diarrhoea – the most likely cause of severe diarrhoea in travellers –

EVERYDAY HEALTH

Normal body temperature is up to 37°C (98.6°F); more than 2°C (4°F) higher indicates a high fever. The normal adult pulse rate is 60 to 100 beats per minute (children 80 to 100, babies 100 to 140). As a general rule, the pulse increases about 20 beats per minute for each 1°C (2°F) rise in fever.

Respiration (breathing) rate is also an indicator of illness. Count the number of breaths per minute: between 12 and 20 is normal for adults and older children (up to 30 for younger children, 40 for babies). People with a high fever or serious respiratory illness breathe more quickly than normal. More than 40 shallow breaths a minute may indicate pneumonia.

A BANANA A DAY...

If your diet is poor or limited in variety, if you're travelling hard and fast and therefore missing meals or if you simply lose your appetite, you can soon start to lose weight and place your health at risk.

Make sure your diet is well balanced. Cooked eggs, tofu, beans, lentils and nuts are all safe ways to get protein. Fruit you can peel (bananas, oranges or mandarins, for example) is usually safe and a good source of vitamins. Melons can harbour bacteria in their flesh and are best avoided. Try to eat plenty of grains (including rice) and bread. Remember that although food is generally safer if it is well cooked, overcooked food loses much of its nutritional value. If your diet isn't well balanced or if your food intake is insufficient, it's a good idea to take vitamin and iron pills.

Make sure you drink enough – don't rely on feeling thirsty to indicate when you should drink. Not needing to urinate or voiding small amounts of very dark yellow urine is a danger sign. Always carry a water bottle with you on long trips. See below for information on heat exhaustion.

are norfloxacin (400mg twice daily for three days) or ciprofloxacin (500mg twice daily for five days). These are not recommended for children or pregnant women. The drug of choice for children would be co-trimoxazole (Bactrim, Septrin or Resprim) with dosage dependent on weight. A five-day course of the drug is given. Ampicillin or amoxycillin may be given in pregnancy, but medical care is necessary.

Amoebic Dysentery & Giardiasis

Two other causes of persistent diarrhoea in travellers are amoebic dysentery and giardiasis.

Amoebic dysentery, caused by the protozoan *Entamoeba histolytica*, is characterised by a gradual onset of low-grade diarrhoea, often with blood and mucus. Cramping abdominal pain and vomiting are less likely than in other types of diarrhoea, and fever may not be present. Amoebic dysentery will persist until treated and can recur and cause other health problems.

Giardiasis is caused by a common parasite, *Giardia lamblia*. Symptoms include stomach cramps, nausea, a bloated stomach, watery, foul-smelling diarrhoea and frequent gas. Giardiasis can appear several weeks after you have been exposed to the parasite. The symptoms may disappear for a few days and then return; this can go on for several weeks.

Seek medical advice if you think you have giardiasis or amoebic dysentery, but where this is not possible, tinidazole (Fasigyn) or metronidazole (Flagyl) are the recommended drugs to take, although the side effects of Flagyl are severe. Treatment is a 2g single dose of Fasigyn or 250mg of Flagyl three times daily for five to 10 days.

ENVIRONMENTAL HAZARDS
Food

There is an old adage that says 'If you can cook it, boil it or peel it you can eat it…otherwise forget it'. This is slightly extreme, but many travellers have found it is better to be safe than sorry. Vegetables and fruit should be washed with purified water or peeled where possible. Beware of ice cream that is sold in the street or anywhere it might have been melted and refrozen. Shellfish such as mussels, oysters and clams should be avoided, as should undercooked meat, particularly in the form of mince. Steaming does not make shellfish safe for eating.

If a place looks clean and well run, and the vendor also looks clean and healthy, then the food is probably safe. In general, places that are packed with travellers or locals will be fine, while empty restaurants might be empty for a reason. The food in busy restaurants is cooked and eaten quite quickly with little standing around and is probably not reheated.

Heat Exhaustion

Dehydration and salt deficiency can cause heat exhaustion. Take time to acclimatise to high temperatures, drink sufficient liquids and do not do anything too physically demanding.

Salt deficiency is characterised by fatigue, lethargy, headaches, giddiness and muscle cramps; salt tablets may help, but adding extra salt to your food is better.

Anhidrotic heat exhaustion is a rare form of heat exhaustion that is caused by an inability to sweat. It tends to affect people who have been in a hot climate for some time, rather than newcomers. It can progress to heatstroke. Treatment involves removal to a cooler climate or immediate cold showers and wet sheets.

Heatstroke

This serious and occasionally fatal condition can occur if the body's heat-regulating mechanism breaks down, causing the body temperature to rise to dangerous levels. Long, continuous periods of exposure to high temperatures and insufficient fluids can leave you vulnerable to heatstroke.

The symptoms: feeling unwell, not sweating very much (or at all) and a high body temperature (39°C to 41°C, or 102°F to 106°F). Where sweating has ceased, the skin becomes flushed and red. Severe, throbbing headaches and lack of coordination will also occur, and the sufferer may be confused or aggressive. Eventually the victim will become delirious or convulse. Hospitalisation is essential, but in the interim get victims out of the sun, remove their clothing, cover them with a wet sheet or towel and then fan continually. Give fluids if they are conscious.

Insect Bites & Stings

Bedbugs live in various places, but particularly in dirty mattresses and bedding, and are evidenced by spots of blood on bedclothes or on the wall. Bedbugs leave itchy bites in neat rows. Calamine lotion or Stingose spray may help.

All lice cause itching and discomfort. They make themselves at home in your hair (head lice), your clothing (body lice) or in your pubic hair (crabs). You catch lice through direct contact with infected people or by sharing combs, clothing and the like. Powder or shampoo treatment will kill the lice, and infected clothing should be washed in very hot, soapy water and left to dry in the sun.

Bee and wasp stings are usually painful rather than dangerous. However, in people who are allergic to them, severe breathing difficulties may occur and urgent medical care is then required. Calamine lotion or Stingose spray will relieve itching, and ice packs will reduce the pain and swelling.

Avoid contact with jellyfish, which have stinging tentacles – seek local advice on the safest swimming waters. Dousing in vinegar will deactivate any stingers that have not 'fired'. Calamine lotion, antihistamines and analgesics may reduce the reaction and relieve the pain.

Leeches may be present in damp rainforest conditions; they attach themselves to your skin to suck your blood. Trekkers often get them on their legs or in their boots. Salt or a lighted cigarette end will make them fall off. Do not pull them off, as the bite is then more likely to become infected. Clean and apply pressure if the point of attachment is bleeding. An insect repellent may keep them away, and walkers in leech-infested areas should consider having their boots and trousers impregnated with benzyl benzoate and dibutylphthalate (available from pharmacies in Cambodia).

Always check all over your body if you have been walking through a potentially tick-infested area, as ticks can cause skin infections and other more serious diseases. If a tick is found attached, press down around the tick's head with tweezers, grab the head and gently pull upwards. Try to avoid pulling the rear of the body as this may squeeze the tick's gut contents through the attached mouth parts into the skin, increasing the risk of infection and disease. Smearing chemicals on the tick will not make it let go and this is not recommended.

To minimise your chances of being bitten by a snake, always wear boots, socks and long trousers when walking through undergrowth where snakes may be present. Don't put your hands into holes and crevices, and be careful if collecting firewood.

Snake bites in Cambodia do not cause instantaneous death, but unfortunately antivenins are not widely available in the country. Immediately wrap the victim's bitten limb tightly, as you would for a sprained ankle, and then attach a splint to immobilise the limb. Keep the victim still and seek medical attention, if possible with the dead snake for identification. However, do not attempt to catch the snake if there is any possibility of being bitten. Tourniquets and sucking out the poison are now comprehensively discredited.

Prickly Heat

Prickly heat is an itchy rash caused by excessive perspiration trapped under the skin. It usually strikes people who have just arrived in a hot climate. Keeping cool, bathing often, drying the skin and using a mild talcum or prickly heat powder, or resorting to the use of air-conditioning, may help.

HEALTH

NOT A GOOD PLACE FOR CONTACTS

People wearing contact lenses should be aware that Cambodia is an extremely dusty country and this can cause much irritation when travelling. It is generally bearable in cars, but when travelling by motorcycle or pick-up, it is most definitely not. Pack a pair of glasses.

Sunburn

You can get sunburnt surprisingly quickly, even through cloud. Use a sunscreen, a hat, and a barrier cream for your nose and lips. Calamine lotion or Stingose are good for mild sunburn. Protect your eyes with good-quality sunglasses. Sunscreen is easily available in Phnom Penh, Siem Reap and Sihanoukville, but not elsewhere.

Water

The number one rule is *be careful of the water and ice,* even though both are almost always factory-produced, a legacy of the French. If you don't know for certain that the water is safe, assume the worst. Reputable brands of bottled water or soft drinks are generally fine, but you can't safely drink tap water. Only use water from containers with a serrated seal. Tea and coffee are generally fine, as the water will have been boiled.

The simplest way of purifying water is to boil it thoroughly. Vigorous boiling should be satisfactory; however, at high altitude water boils at a lower temperature, so germs are less likely to be killed. Make sure you boil it for longer in these environments.

Consider purchasing a water filter for a long trip. Total filters take out all parasites, bacteria and viruses and make water safe to drink. They are often expensive, but can be more cost effective than buying bottled water. Simple filters (which can even be a nylon mesh bag) take out dirt and larger foreign bodies from the water so that chemical solutions work much

more effectively; if the water is dirty, chemical solutions may not work at all. Chlorine tablets (Puritabs, Steritabs or other brands) will kill many pathogens, but not some parasites like giardia and amoebic cysts. Iodine is more effective in purifying water and is available in tablet form (such as Potable Aqua).

WOMEN'S HEALTH
Gynaecological Problems

Antibiotic use, synthetic underwear, sweating and contraceptive pills can lead to fungal vaginal infections, especially when travelling in hot climates. Thrush (yeast infection or vaginal candidiasis) is characterised by a rash, itching and discharge. Nystatin, miconazole or clotrimazole pessaries or vaginal cream are the usual treatment. Maintaining good personal hygiene and wearing loose-fitting clothes and cotton underwear may help prevent these infections.

STIs are a major cause of vaginal problems. Symptoms include a smelly discharge, painful intercourse and sometimes a burning sensation when urinating. Medical attention should be sought and male sexual partners must also be treated. For more details see p346. Besides abstinence, the best thing is to practise safe sex using condoms.

Pregnancy

Most miscarriages occur during the first three months of pregnancy. Miscarriage is common and can occasionally lead to severe bleeding. The last three months of pregnancy should also be spent within reasonable distance of good medical care. A baby born as early as 24 weeks stands a chance of survival, but only in a good modern hospital such as Calmette in Phnom Penh (p77). Pregnant women should avoid all unnecessary medication, although vaccinations and malarial prophylactics should still be taken where needed. Additional care should be taken to prevent illness and particular attention should be paid to diet and nutrition.

Language

CONTENTS

The Khmer (or Cambodian) language is spoken by approximately nine million people in Cambodia, and is understood by many in bordering countries. Written Khmer is based on the ancient Brahmi script of southern India. Arguably one of the oldest languages in Southeast Asia, Khmer inscriptions have been dated back to the 7th century AD. Although separate and distinct from its Thai, Lao and Burmese neighbours, Khmer shares with them the common roots of Sanskrit and Pali – a heritage of centuries of linguistic and cultural interaction and of their shared faith in Theravada Buddhism. More recently, many French words have entered the Khmer language during the colonial period, especially medical and technical terms.

Unlike the languages of neighbouring countries, Khmer is non tonal, meaning that there are no special intonations within words that alter their meaning. This may be a relief for travellers in the region who have been frustrated in their attempts at tonal languages such as Thai, Vietnamese and Lao. However, the lack of tones is easily offset by the complexity of the Khmer pronunciation. There are 33 consonants, often paired in seemingly bizarre combinations, and some 24 vowels and diphthongs. Further complicating the language is the haphazard transliteration system left over from the days of French rule, which does not reflect accurate pronunciation of Khmer words by English speakers.

On the positive side, Khmer grammar is very simple. There are no verb conjugations or gender inflections, no endings for single or plural, masculine or feminine. Adding a few words changes sentence tense to past, present or future.

A bit of Khmer will go a long way – no matter how rough it is. The Khmers sincerely appreciate any effort to learn their language and are very supportive of visitors who give it even a halfhearted try. You'll find that as your skill and vocabulary increase, so does your social standing: people go out of their way to compliment you, *moto* fares and prices at markets drop, and you may even win a few friends.

Though English is fast becoming Cambodia's second language, the Khmer still cling to the Francophone pronunciation of the Roman alphabet and most foreign words. This is helpful to remember when spelling Western words and names aloud; thus 'ay-bee-cee' becomes 'ah-bey-sey' and so on. French speakers will definitely have an advantage when addressing the older generation, as most educated Khmers studied French at some point during their schooling. Many household items retain their French names as well, especially those which were introduced to Cambodia by the French, such as *robinet* (tap, faucet) and *ampoule* (light bulb).

Recommended reading for those interested in further study of spoken and written Khmer are *Cambodian System of Writing and Beginning Reader*, *Modern Spoken Cambodian* and any other books by Frank Huffman.

Dialects

Although the Khmer language as spoken in Phnom Penh is generally intelligible to Khmers nationwide, there are several distinct dialects in other areas of the country. Most notably, the Khmers of Takeo Province tend to modify or slur hard consonant/vowel combinations, especially those that contain 'r'; thus *bram* (five) becomes *pe-am*, *sraa* (alcohol) becomes *se-aa*, and *baraang*

(French or foreigner) becomes *be-ang*. In Siem Reap, sharp-eared travellers will notice a very Lao-sounding lilt to the local speech. Here, certain vowels are modified, such as *poan* (thousand), which becomes *peuan*, and *kh'sia* (pipe), which becomes *kh'seua*.

TRANSLITERATION

The transliteration system used in this chapter has been designed for basic communication rather than linguistic perfection. Several Khmer vowels, however, have no English equivalent, thus they can only be approximated by English spellings. Other words are written to convey the way they are pronounced and not necessarily according to the actual vowels used in the words. (Khmer place names in this book written in the Roman alphabet will follow their common or standard spellings.)

PRONUNCIATION

The pronunciation guide below covers the trickier parts of the transliteration system used in this chapter. It uses the Roman alphabet to give the closest equivalent to the sounds of the Khmer language. The best way to improve your pronunciation is to listen carefully to native speakers.

Vowels

Vowels and diphthongs with an **h** at the end should be pronounced hard and aspirated (with a puff of air).

aa	as the 'a' in 'father'
i	as in 'kit'
uh	as the 'u' in 'but'
ii	as the 'ee' in 'feet'
ei	a combination of **uh** and **ii** above, ie 'uh-ii'
eu	similar to the 'eu' in French *peuple*; try saying 'oo' while keeping the lips spread flat rather than rounded
euh	as **eu** above; pronounced short and hard
oh	as the 'o' in 'hose'; pronounced short and hard
ow	as in 'glow'
u	as the 'u' in 'flute'; pronounced short and hard
uu	as the 'oo' in 'zoo'
ua	as the 'ou' in 'tour'
uah	as **ua** above; pronounced short and hard

aa-œ	a tricky one that has no English equivalent; like a combination of **aa** and **œ**. When placed in between consonants it's often pronounced like 'ao'.
œ	as 'er' in 'her', but more open
eua	combination of **eu** and **a**
ia	as 'ee-ya'; like the 'ee' in 'beer' without the 'r'
e	as in 'they'
ai	as in 'aisle'
ay	as **ai** above, but slightly more nasal
ae	as the 'a' in 'cat'
ey	as in 'prey'
ao	as the 'ow' in 'cow'
av	no English equivalent; sounds like a very nasal **ao**. The final 'v' is not pronounced.
euv	no English equivalent; sounds like a very nasal **eu**. The final 'v' is not pronounced.
ohm	as the 'ome' in 'home'
am	as the 'um' in 'glum'
oam	a combination of 'o' and 'am'
a, ah	shorter and harder than **aa**
eah	combination of 'e' and 'ah'; pronounced short and hard
ih	as the 'ee' in 'teeth'; pronounced short and hard
eh	as the 'a' in 'date'; pronounced short and hard
awh	as the 'aw' in 'jaw'; pronounced short and hard
oah	a combination of 'o' and 'ah'; pronounced short and hard
aw	as the 'aw' in 'jaw'

Consonants

Khmer uses some consonant combinations that may sound rather bizarre to Western ears and be equally difficult for Western tongues, eg 'j-r' in *j'rook* (pig), or 'ch-ng' in *ch'ngain* (delicious). For ease of pronunciation, in this guide these types of consonants are separated with an apostrophe.

k	as the 'g' in 'go'
kh	as the 'k' in 'kind'
ng	as the 'ng' in 'sing'; a difficult sound for Westerners to emulate. Practise by repeating 'singing-nging-nging-nging' until you can say 'nging' clearly.
j	as in 'jump'
ch	as in 'cheese'

ny as in the final syllable of 'onion', ie 'nyun'

t a hard, unaspirated 't' sound with no direct equivalent in English. Similar to the 't' in 'stand'.

th as the 't' in 'two', never as the 'th' in 'thanks'

p a hard, unaspirated 'p' sound, as the final 'p' in 'puppy'

ph as the 'p' in 'pond', never as the 'ph' in 'phone'

r as in 'rum', but hard and rolling, with the tongue flapping against the palate. In rapid conversation it is often omitted entirely.

w as in 'would'. Contrary to the common transliteration system, there is no equivalent to the English 'v' sound in Khmer.

ACCOMMODATION

Where is a (cheap) hotel?
sahnthaakia/ohtail (thaok) neuv ai naa?
សណ្ឋាគារ/អូតែល(ថោក)នៅឯណា?

I've already found a hotel.
kh'nyohm mian ohtail hao-y
ខ្ញុំមានអូតែលហើយ

I'm staying at ...
kh'nyohm snahk neuv ...
ខ្ញុំស្នាក់នៅ ...

Could you write down the address, please?
sohm sawse aasayathaan ao-y kh'nyohm?
សូមសរសេរអាស័យដ្ឋានឱ្យខ្ញុំ?

I'd like a room ... *kh'nyohm sohm bantohp ...* ខ្ញុំសុំបន្ទប់ ...
  for one person
  samruh muy niak សំរាប់មួយនាក់
  for two people
  samruh pii niak សំរាប់ពីរនាក់
  with a bathroom
  dail mian bantohp tuhk ដែលមានបន្ទប់ទឹក
  with a fan
  dail mian dawnghahl ដែលមានកង្ហារ
  with a window
  dail mian bawng-uit ដែលមានបង្អួច

I'm going to stay for ...
kh'nyohm nuhng snahk tii nih ...
ខ្ញុំនឹងស្នាក់ទីនេះ ...
  one day
  muy th'ngay មួយថ្ងៃ
  one week
  muy aatuht មួយអាទិត្យ

Do you have a room?
niak mian bantohp tohmne te?
អ្នកមានបន្ទប់ទំនេទេ?

How much is it per day?
damlay muy th'ngay pohnmaan?
តំលៃមួយថ្ងៃប៉ុន្មាន?

Does the price include breakfast?
damlay bantohp khuht teang m'hohp pel pruhk reu?
តំលៃបន្ទប់គិតទាំងម្ហូបពេលព្រឹកឬ?

Can I see the room?
kh'nyohm aa-it mœl bantohp baan te?
ខ្ញុំអាចមើលបន្ទប់បានទេ?

I don't like this room.
kh'nyohm muhn johl juht bantohp nih te
ខ្ញុំមិនចូលចិត្តបន្ទប់នេះទេ

Do you have a better room?
niak mian bantohp l'aw jiang nih te?
អ្នកមានបន្ទប់ល្អជាងនេះទេ?

I'll take this room.
kh'nyohm yohk bantohp nih
ខ្ញុំយកបន្ទប់នេះ

Can I leave my things here until ...?
kh'nyohm aa-it ph'nyaa-œ tohk eiwuhn r'bawh kh'nyohm neuv tii nih dawl ... baan te?
ខ្ញុំអាចផ្ញើអីវ៉ាន់របស់ខ្ញុំនៅទីនេះដល់ ... បានទេ?
  this afternoon
  l'ngiak nih ល្ងាចនេះ
  this evening
  yohp nih យប់នេះ

CONVERSATION & ESSENTIALS
Forms of Address

The Khmer language reflects the social standing of the speaker and subject through various personal pronouns and 'politeness words'. These range from the simple *baat* for men and *jaa* for women, placed at the end of a sentence, meaning 'yes' or 'I agree', to the very formal and archaic *Reachasahp* or 'Royal language', a separate vocabulary reserved for addressing the King and very high officials. Many of the pronouns are determined on the basis of the subject's age and sex in relation to the speaker. Foreigners are not expected to know all of these forms. The easiest and most general personal pronoun is *niak* (you), which may be used in most situations, with either sex. Men of your age or older may be called *lowk* (Mister). Women of your age or older can be called *bawng srei* (older sister) or for more formal situations, *lowk srei* (Madam). *Bawng* is a good informal, neutral pronoun for men or women who are (or appear to be) older than you. For third person, male or female, singular or plural, the respectful form is *koat* and the common form is *ke*.

Hello.
  johm riab sua/sua th'dei　ជំរាបសួរ/សួស្ដី
Goodbye.
  lia suhn hao-y　លាសិនហើយ
See you later.
  juab kh'nia th'ngay krao-y　ជួបគ្នាថ្ងៃក្រោយ
Yes.
  baat　បាទ
  (used by men)
  jaa　ចាស
  (used by women)
No.
  te　ទេ
Please.
  sohm　សូម
Thank you.
  aw kohn　អរគុណ
You're welcome.
  awt ei te/sohm anjœ-in　អត់អីទេ/សូមអញ្ជើញ
Excuse me/I'm sorry.
  sohm toh　សុំទោស
Pardon? (What did you say?)
  niak niyey thaa mait?　អ្នកនិយាយថាម៉េច?
Hi. How are you?
  niak sohk sabaay te?　អ្នកសុខសប្បាយទេ?
I'm fine.
  kh'nyohm sohk sabaay　ខ្ញុំសុខសប្បាយ
Where are you going?
  niak teuv naa?　អ្នកទៅណា?

(NB This is a very common question used when meeting people, even strangers; an exact answer is not necessary.)

What's your name?
  niak ch'muah ei?　អ្នកឈ្មោះអី?
My name is ...
  kh'nyohm ch'muah ...　ខ្ញុំឈ្មោះ ...
Where are you from?
  niak mao pii prateh naa?　អ្នកមកពីប្រទេសណា?
I'm from ...
  kh'nyohm mao pii ...　ខ្ញុំមកពី ...
I'm staying at ...
  kh'nyohm snahk neuv ...　ខ្ញុំស្នាក់នៅ ...
May I take your photo?
  kh'nyohm aa-it thawt ruup niak baan te?　ខ្ញុំអាចថតរូបអ្នកបានទេ?

DIRECTIONS

How can I get to ...?
  phleuv naa teuv ..?　ផ្លូវណាទៅ ...?
Is it far?
  wia neuv ch'ngaay te?　វានៅឆ្ងាយទេ?
Is it near?
  wia neuv juht te?　វានៅជិតទេ?
Is it near here?
  wia neuv juht nih te?　វានៅជិតនេះទេ?
Go straight ahead.
  teuv trawng　ទៅត្រង់
Turn left.
  bawt ch'weng　បត់ឆ្វេង
Turn right.
  bawt s'dam　បត់ស្ដាំ
at the corner
  neuv kait j'rohng　នៅកាច់ជ្រុង
in front of
  neuv khaang mohk　នៅខាងមុខ
next to
  neuv joab　នៅជាប់
behind
  neuv khaang krao-y　នៅខាងក្រោយ
opposite
  neuv tohl mohk　នៅទល់មុខ

north
  khaang jœng　ខាងជើង
south
  khaang d'bowng　ខាងត្បូង
east
  khaang kaot　ខាងកើត
west
  khaang leit　ខាងលិច

HEALTH

Where is a ...
  ... neuv ai naa?　... នៅឯណា?
dentist
  paet th'mein　ពេទ្យធ្មេញ
doctor
  kruu paet　គ្រូពេទ្យ
hospital
  mohntrii paet　មន្ទីរពេទ្យ
pharmacy
  kuhnlaing luak th'nam/　កន្លែងលក់ថ្នាំ/
  ohsawt s'thaan　ឱសថស្ថាន

I'm ill.
  kh'nyohm cheu　ខ្ញុំឈឺ
My ... hurts.
  ... r'bawh kh'nyohm cheu　... របស់ខ្ញុំឈឺ
I feel nauseous.
  kh'nyohm jawng k'uat　ខ្ញុំចង់ក្អួត

EMERGENCIES

Help!
juay kh'nyohm phawng! ជួយខ្ញុំផង!

It's an emergency!
nih jia reuang bawntoan! នេះជារឿងបន្ទាន់!

Call a doctor!
juay hav kruu paet mao! ជួយហៅគ្រូពេទ្យមក!

Call the police!
juay hav polih mao! ជួយហៅប៉ូលីសមក!

Could you help me please?
niak aa-it juay kh'nyohm អ្នកអាចជួយខ្ញុំបានទេ?
baan te?

Could I please use the telephone?
kh'nyohm braa-œ ខ្ញុំប្រើទូរស័ព្ទបានទេ?
turasahp baan te?

I've been robbed.
kh'nyohm treuv jao plawn ខ្ញុំត្រូវចោរប្លន់.

Stop!
chohp! ឈប់!

Watch out!
prawyaht! ប្រយ័ត្ន!

Where are the toilets?
bawngkohn neuv ai naa? បង្គន់នៅឯណា?

I wish to contact my embassy/consulate.
kh'nyohm jawng hav s'thaantuut/kohngsuhl r'bawh
prawteh kh'nyohm
ខ្ញុំចង់ហៅស្ថានទូត/កុងស៊ុលរបស់ប្រទេសខ្ញុំ

I feel weak.
kh'nyohm awh kamlahng ខ្ញុំអស់កំលាំង

I keep vomiting.
kh'nyohm k'uat j'raa-œn ខ្ញុំក្អួតច្រើន

I feel dizzy.
kh'nyohm wuhl mohk ខ្ញុំវិលមុខ

I'm allergic to ...
kh'nyohm muhn treuv thiat ...
ខ្ញុំមិនត្រូវធាតុ ...

penicillin
penicillin ប៉េនីស៊ីលីន

antibiotics
awntiibiowtik អង់ទីប៊ីយោទិក

I need medicine for ...
kh'nyohm treuv ka th'nam samruhp ...
ខ្ញុំត្រូវការថ្នាំសំរាប់ ...

diarrhoea
rowk joh riak រោគចុះរាក

dysentery
rowk mual រោគមូល

fever
krohn/k'dav kh'luan គ្រុន/ក្ដៅខ្លួន

pain
cheu ឈឺ

antiseptic
th'nam samlahp me rowk ថ្នាំសំលាប់មេរោគ

aspirin
parasetamol ប៉ារ៉ាសេតាម៉ុល

codeine
codiin ខូឌីន

condoms
sraom ahnaamai ស្រោមអនាម័យ

medicine
th'nam ថ្នាំ

mosquito repellent
th'nam kaa pia ថ្នាំការពារមូស
muh

quinine
kiiniin គីនីន

razor blade
kambuht kao pohk moat កាំបិតការពុកមាត់

sanitary napkins
samlei ahnaamai សំឡីអនាម័យ

shampoo
sabuu kawk sawk សាប៊ូកក់សក់

shaving cream
kraim samruhp kao pohk ក្រែមសំរាប់ការពុកមាត់
moat

sunblock cream
kraim kaa pia pohnleu ក្រែមការពារពន្លឺថ្ងៃ
th'ngay

toilet paper
krawdah ahnaamai ក្រដាស់អនាម័យ

LANGUAGE DIFFICULTIES

Does any one here speak English?
tii nih mian niak jeh phiasaa awngle te?
ទីនេះមានអ្នកចេះភាសាអង់គ្លេសទេ?

Do you understand?
niak yuhl te/niak s'dap baan te?
អ្នកយល់ទេ/អ្នកស្ដាប់បានទេ?

I understand.
kh'nyohm yuhl/kh'nyohm s'dap baan
ខ្ញុំយល់/ខ្ញុំស្ដាប់បាន

I don't understand.
kh'nyohm muhn yuhl te/kh'nyohm s'dap muhn baan te
ខ្ញុំមិនយល់ទេ/ខ្ញុំស្ដាប់មិនបានទេ

What does this mean?
nih mian nuh-y thaa mait?
នេះមានន័យថាម៉េច?

What is this called?
nih ke hav thaa mait?
នេះគេហៅថាម៉េច?

Please speak slowly.
sohm niyay yeut yeut
សូមនិយាយយឺតៗ

Please write that word down for me.
sohm sawse piak nu ao-y kh'nyohm
សូមសរសេរពាក្យនោះឱ្យខ្ញុំ

Please translate for me.
sohm bawk brai ao-y kh'nyohm
សូមបកប្រែឱ្យខ្ញុំ

NUMBERS & AMOUNTS

Khmers count in increments of five. Thus, after reaching the number five *(bram)*, the cycle begins again with the addition of one, ie 'five-one' *(bram muy)*, 'five-two' *(bram pii)* and so on to 10, which begins a new cycle. This system is a bit awkward at first (for example, 18, which has three parts: 10, five and three) but with practice it can be mastered.

You may be confused by a colloquial form of counting that reverses the word order for numbers between 10 and 20 and separates the two words with *duhn: pii duhn dawp* for 12, *bei duhn dawp* for 13, *bram buan duhn dawp* for 19 and so on. This form is often used in markets, so listen keenly.

1	muy	មួយ
2	pii	ពីរ
3	bei	បី
4	buan	បួន
5	bram	ប្រាំ
6	bram muy	ប្រាំមួយ
7	bram pii/puhl	ប្រាំពីរ
8	bram bei	ប្រាំបី
9	bram buan	ប្រាំបួន
10	dawp	ដប់
11	dawp muy	ដប់មួយ
12	dawp pii	ដប់ពីរ
16	dawp bram muy	ដប់ប្រាំមួយ
20	m'phei	ម្ភៃ
21	m'phei muy	ម្ភៃមួយ
30	saamsuhp	សាមសិប
40	saisuhp	សែសិប
100	muy roy	មួយរយ
1000	muy poan	មួយពាន់
1,000,000	muy lian	មួយលាន

1st	tii muy	ទីមួយ
2nd	tii pii	ទីពីរ
3rd	tii bei	ទីបី
4th	tii buan	ទីបួន
10th	tii dawp	ទីដប់

SHOPPING & SERVICES

Where is a/the ...
... neuv ai naa? ... នៅឯណា?
bank
th'niakia ធនាគារ
cinema
rowng kohn រោងកុន
consulate
kohng sul កុងស៊ុល
embassy
s'thaantuut ស្ថានទូត
hospital
mohntii paet មន្ទីរពេទ្យ
market
p'saa ផ្សារ
museum
saramohntii សារមន្ទី
park
suan សួន
police station
poh polih/ ប៉ុស្តិ៍ប៉ូលីស/
s'thaanii nohkohbaal ស្ថានីយនគរបាល
post office
praisuhnii ប្រៃសណីយ
public telephone
turasahp saathiaranah ទូរស័ព្ទសាធារណៈ
public toilet
bawngkohn saathiaranah បង្គន់សាធារណៈ
temple
wawt វត្ត

How far is the ...?
... ch'ngaay pohnmaan? ... ឆ្ងាយប៉ុន្មាន?
I want to see the ...
kh'nyohm jawng teuv ខ្ញុំចង់ទៅមើល ...
mœl ...
I'm looking for the ...
kh'nyohm rohk ... ខ្ញុំរក ...
How much is it?
nih th'lay pohnmaan? នេះថ្លៃប៉ុន្មាន?
That's too much.
th'lay pek ថ្លៃពេក
I'll give you ...
kh'nyohm ao-y ... ខ្ញុំឱ្យ ...
No more than ...
muhn lœh pii ... មិនលើសពី ...
What's your best price?
niak dait pohnmaan? អ្នកដាច់ប៉ុន្មាន?

What time does it open?
wia baok maong pohnmaan?
វាបើកម៉ោងប៉ុន្មាន?

What time does it close?
wia buht maong pohnmaan?
វាបិតម៉ោងប៉ុន្មាន?

I want to change US dollars.
kh'nyohm jawng dow dolaa amerik
ខ្ញុំចង់ដូរដុល្លារអាមេរិក

What is the exchange rate for US dollars?
muy dolaa dow baan pohnmaan?
មួយដុល្លាដូរបានប៉ុន្មាន?

TIME & DAYS
What time is it?
eileuv nih maong pohnmaan?
ឥឡូវនេះម៉ោងប៉ុន្មាន?

in the morning
pel pruhk
ពេលព្រឹក

in the afternoon
pel r'sial
ពេលរសៀល

in the evening
pel l'ngiat
ពេលល្ងាច

at night
pel yohp
ពេលយប់

today
th'ngay nih
ថ្ងៃនេះ

tomorrow
th'ngay s'aik
ថ្ងៃស្អែក

yesterday
m'suhl mein
ម្សិលមិញ

Monday
th'ngay jahn
ថ្ងៃចន្ទ

Tuesday
th'ngay ahngkia
ថ្ងៃអង្គារ

Wednesday
th'ngay poht
ថ្ងៃពុធ

Thursday
th'ngay prohoah
ថ្ងៃព្រហស្បតិ៍

Friday
th'ngay sohk
ថ្ងៃសុក្រ

Saturday
th'ngay sav
ថ្ងៃសៅរ៍

Sunday
th'ngay aatuht
ថ្ងៃអាទិត្យ

TRANSPORT
Where is the ...?
... neuv ai naa?   ... នៅឯណា?
  airport
  wial yohn hawh   វាលយន្តហោះ
  bus station
  kuhnlaing laan ch'nual   កន្លែងឡានឈ្នួល
  bus stop
  jamnawt laan ch'nual   ចំណតឡានឈ្នួល
  train station
  s'thaanii roht plœng   ស្ថានីយរថភ្លើង

What time does the ... leave?
... jein maong pohnmaan?   ... ចេញម៉ោងប៉ុន្មាន?
  bus
  laan ch'nual   ឡានឈ្នួល
  train
  roht plœng   រថភ្លើង
  plane
  yohn hawh/k'pal hawh   យន្តហោះ/កប៉ាល់ហោះ

What time does the last bus leave?
laan ch'nual johng krao-y jein teuv maong pohnmaan?
ឡានឈ្នួល ចុងក្រោយចេញទៅម៉ោងប៉ុន្មាន?

I want to get off (here)!
kh'nyohm jawng joh (tii nih)!
ខ្ញុំចង់ចុះ (ទីនេះ)!

How much is it to ...?
teuv ... th'lay pohnmaan?
ទៅ ... ថ្លៃប៉ុន្មាន?

Please take me to ...
sohm juun kh' nyohm teuv ...
សូមជូនខ្ញុំទៅ ...

this address
aadreh/aasayathaan nih
អាស័យដ្ឋាននេះ

Here is fine, thank you.
chohp neuv tii nih kaw baan
ឈប់នៅទីនេះក៏បាន

Also available from Lonely Planet:
Southeast Asia Phrasebook

LANGUAGE

Glossary

apsara – heavenly nymph or angelic dancer, often represented in Khmer sculpture

Asean – Association of Southeast Asian Nations

Avalokiteshvara – the Bodhisattva of Compassion and the inspiration for Jayavarman VII's Angkor Thom

barang – foreigner

baray – reservoir

boeng – lake

CCC – Cooperation Committee for Cambodia

chunchiet – ethnic minorities

CPP – Cambodian People's Party

cyclo – pedicab; bicycle rickshaw

devaraja – cult of the god-king, established by Jayavarman II, in which the monarch has universal power

devadas – goddesses

EFEO – École Française d'Extrême Orient

essai – wise man or traditional medicine man

Funcinpec – National United Front for an Independent, Neutral, Peaceful and Cooperative Cambodia; royalist political party

garuda – mythical half-man, half-bird creature

gopura – entrance pavilion in traditional Hindu architecture

Hun Sen – Cambodia's prime minister (1998 to present)

Jayavarman II – the king (r 802–50) who established the cult of the god-king, kicking off a period of amazing architectural productivity that resulted in the extraordinary temples of Angkor

Jayavarman VII – the king (r 1181–1219) who drove the Chams out of Cambodia before embarking on an ambitious construction programme, including the walled city of Angkor Thom

Kampuchea – the name Cambodians use for their country; to non-Khmers, it is associated with the bloody rule of the Khmer Rouge, which insisted that the outside world adopt the name Democratic Kampuchea from 1975 to 1979

Khmer – a person of Cambodian descent; the language of Cambodia

Khmer Krom – ethnic Khmers living in Vietnam

Khmer Leu – Upper Khmer or ethnic minorities in northeastern Cambodia

Khmer Rouge – a revolutionary organisation that seized power in 1975 and implemented a brutal social restructuring, resulting in the suffering and death of millions of Cambodians in the following four years

kouprey – extremely rare wild ox of Southeast Asia, probably extinct

krama – checked scarf

linga – phallic symbols

Mahayana – literally, 'Great Vehicle'; a school of Buddhism (also known as the Northern School) that built upon and extended the early Buddhist teachings; see also *Theravada*

moto – small motorcycle with driver; a common form of transport in Cambodia

Mt Meru – the mythical dwelling of the Hindu god Shiva

MPTC – Cambodian Ministry of Post and Telecommunications

naga – mythical serpent, often multiheaded; a symbol used extensively in Angkorian architecture

nandi – sacred ox, vehicle of Shiva

NCDP – National Centre for Disabled Persons

NGO – nongovernmental organisation

NH – national highway

Norodom Ranariddh, Prince – son of King Sihanouk and former leader of *Funcinpec*

Norodom Sihanouk, King – former king of Cambodia, film director and a towering figure in modern-day Cambodia

Pali – ancient Indian language that, along with Sanskrit, is the root of modern *Khmer*

phlauv – street; abbreviated to Ph

phnom – mountain or hill

Pol Pot – the former leader of the Khmer Rouge who is roundly blamed for the suffering and deaths of millions of Cambodians; also known as Saloth Sar

prang – temple tower

prasat – stone or brick hall with religious or royal significance

preah – sacred

psar – market

Ramayana – an epic Sanskrit poem composed around 300 BC featuring the mythical Ramachandra, the incarnation of the god Vishnu

RCAF – Royal Cambodian Armed Forces

remorque-kang – trailer pulled by a bicycle
remorque-moto – trailer pulled by a motorcycle
rom vong – Cambodian circle dancing

Sangkum Reastr Niyum – People's Socialist Community; a national movement, led by King Sihanouk, that ruled the country during the 1950s and 1960s
Sanskrit – ancient Hindu language that, along with Pali, is the root of modern Khmer language
SNC – Supreme National Council
stung – river
Suryavarman II – the king (r 1112–52) responsible for building Angkor Wat and for expanding and unifying the Khmer empire
Theravada – a school of Buddhism (also known as the Southern School or Hinayana) found in Myanmar (Burma), Thailand, Laos and Cambodia; this school confined itself to the early Buddhist teachings; see also *Mahayana*
tonlé – large river

UNDP – UN Development Programme
Unesco – UN Educational Scientific and Cultural Organization
UNHCR – UN High Commissioner for Refugees
Untac – UN Transitional Authority in Cambodia

vihara – temple sanctuary

WHO – World Health Organization

Year Zero – 1975; the year the Khmer Rouge seized power
yoni – female fertility symbol

The Authors

NICK RAY · Coordinating Author

A Londoner of sorts, Nick comes from Watford, the sort of town that makes you want to travel. He currently lives in Phnom Penh with his wife Kulikar and young son Julian. He has written for several guidebooks including Lonely Planet's *South-East Asia on a Shoestring* and *Cycling Vietnam, Laos and Cambodia*. He also writes articles for newspapers and magazines, including *The Sunday Times* and *Wanderlust* in the UK. When not writing, he is often exploring the remote parts of Cambodia as a location scout and manager for the world of television and film, including movies *Tomb Raider* and *Two Brothers*. Motorbikes are a part-time passion (riding them a passion, maintaining them part-time).

DANIEL ROBINSON · The Environment, South Coast, Northwestern Cambodia

Daniel researched the award-winning first edition of Lonely Planet's *Cambodia* guide in 1989, when most of the country was too dangerous to visit and the ageing Soviet turboprops on the Phnom Penh–Siem Reap run had to fly over the middle of the Tonlé Sap to avoid ground fire. (The story of his misadventures in a mined Angkorian temple appears in *Lonely Planet Unpacked Again*.) An avid hiker and cyclist, Daniel especially enjoys exploring Cambodia's 'outback', including the wild Cardamoms and Preah Vihear Province. His favourite spot for chilling is the pristine west coast of Koh Kong Island. Daniel is based in Tel Aviv.

CONTRIBUTING AUTHOR

Dr Trish Batchelor wrote the Health chapter. Trish is a general practitioner and travel medicine specialist who works at the CIWEC Clinic in Kathmandu, Nepal, as well as being a Medical Advisor to the Travel Doctor New Zealand clinics. Trish teaches travel medicine through the University of Otago, and is interested in underwater and high-altitude medicine, and in the impact of tourism on host countries. She has travelled extensively through Southeast and East Asia and particularly loves high-altitude trekking in the Himalayas.

LONELY PLANET AUTHORS

Why is our travel information the best in the world? It's simple: our authors are independent, dedicated travellers. They don't research using just the internet or phone, and they don't take freebies, so you can rely on their advice being well researched and impartial. They travel widely, to all the popular spots and off the beaten track. They personally visit thousands of hotels, restaurants, cafés, bars, galleries, palaces, museums and more – and they take great pride in getting all the details right, and telling it how it is. Think you can do it? Find out how at lonelyplanet.com.

Behind the Scenes

THIS BOOK

This 6th edition of Cambodia was updated by Nick Ray and Daniel Robinson. Nick updated the previous three editions, and Daniel co-authored the original guide with Tony Wheeler back in 1992. Dr Trish Batchelor provided text for the Health chapter. This guidebook was commissioned in Lonely Planet's Melbourne office, and produced by the following:

Commissioning Editor Carolyn Boicos
Coordinating Editor Erin Richards
Coordinating Cartographer Jacqueline Nguyen
Coordinating Layout Designer Jacqueline McLeod
Managing Editor Geoff Howard
Managing Cartographer David Connolly
Managing Layout Designer Adam McCrow
Assisting Editors Gennifer Ciavarra, Simon Williamson, Susannah Farfor, Joanne Newell
Assisting Cartographer Sophie Reed
Assisting Layout Designers Wibowo Rusli, Cara Smith
Cover Designer Aimée Goggins
Colour Designer Paul Iacono
Project Managers Eoin Dunlevy, Craig Kilburn, Sarah Sloane
Language Content Coordinator Quentin Frayne

Thanks to Seda Douglas, Mark Germanchis, Nicole Hansen, Debra Herrmann, Laura Jane, Lisa Knights, Celia Wood

THANKS
NICK RAY

As always a huge and heartfelt thanks to the people of Cambodia, whose warmth and humour, stoicism and spirit make it such a happy yet humbling place to be. The biggest thanks are reserved for my lovely wife Kulikar Sotho, as without her support and encouragement the adventures would not be possible. And to our young son Julian for enlivening our lives immeasurably and bringing a new perspective to the 'For Children' sections.

Many thanks to my parents, Peter and Kate, for their support and their many visits to this part of the world. And thank you to my Cambodian family for welcoming me warmly and understanding my not so traditional lifestyle. Thanks to fellow travellers and residents, friends and contacts in Cambodia who have helped shaped my knowledge and experience in this country.

Thanks also to my co-author Daniel Robinson who put the groundwork in on this book back in 1989, when travel was a lot harder. Finally, thanks to the Lonely Planet team who have worked on this edition. The author may be the public face, but a huge amount of work goes into making this a better book behind the scenes and I thank you for your help.

THE LONELY PLANET STORY

Fresh from an epic journey across Europe, Asia and Australia in 1972, Tony and Maureen Wheeler sat at their kitchen table stapling together notes. The first Lonely Planet guidebook, *Across Asia on the Cheap*, was born.

Travellers snapped up the guides. Inspired by their success, the Wheelers began publishing books to Southeast Asia, India and beyond. Demand was prodigious, and the Wheelers expanded the business rapidly to keep up. Over the years, Lonely Planet extended its coverage to every country and into the virtual world via lonelyplanet.com and the Thorn Tree message board.

As Lonely Planet became a globally loved brand, Tony and Maureen received several offers for the company. But it wasn't until 2007 that they found a partner whom they trusted to remain true to the company's principles of travelling widely, treading lightly and giving sustainably. In October of that year, BBC Worldwide acquired a 75% share in the company, pledging to uphold Lonely Planet's commitment to independent travel, trustworthy advice and editorial independence.

Today, Lonely Planet has offices in Melbourne, London and Oakland, with over 500 staff members and 300 authors. Tony and Maureen are still actively involved with Lonely Planet. They're travelling more often than ever, and they're devoting their spare time to charitable projects. And the company is still driven by the philosophy of *Across Asia on the Cheap*: 'All you've got to do is decide to go and the hardest part is over. So go!'

BEHIND THE SCENES

DANIEL ROBINSON

In researching the South Coast chapter, I'm indebted to Sin Soeung, Jean James, Marcel Crompvoets, Dan Kreis, Stephane Arrii, my Koh Tonsay companions (Annie Kim, Suzanne Varrall and Jon Fitzmaurice), Angela Vestergaard, Cheryl Reynolds, Chey Yuthearith, Stu and Lee Verlander, Duncan Garner, Beverley Palmer, Dim Noeun, Douglas Walker, the Bob's Bar gang (Bob, Ronnie, Rick and Gypsy), Neat Oung, Jason Webb, Kong Chivin, Oran Shapira, Nhel Choun, Henri Olander and Reijo Laitinen.

In Northwestern Cambodia, I would like to thank man-of-letters Ros Saphan, John Dennis, Kan Vuthy, Heng Sopay, Moas Sy, Alban Bonnet-Casson, Jan Gracey and Chorng Lem, Lou Wallace, Patty Worboy, Anna Weekes, Kate Forrest, Merja Heitto, the dengue duo (Nisha Srinivasan and Michelle Langlois), Than Buntheth and Shin Furuno.

NGO professionals who provided me with invaluable insights include Suwanna Gauntlett and Michelle Owen of the Wildlife Alliance; Seng Bunra, Touch Nimith, Bun Kimsan and Jake Brunner of Conservation International; Stephan Bognar of MJP; ecotourism entrepreneur Anthony Simms; Yin Soriya and Sok Sophea of CC-BEN; Jocelyn Roberts and Arnaud Guidal of GERES; and Anne-Maria Makela of SNV.

And to the intrepid *moto*, *tuk tuk* and Camry driver-guides who took me around many pot-holes and puddles: Chan Than (Kep), Hang Vuthy (Sihanoukville), Chea Sarom (Kompong Thom), Ae Shhouk Rath (Prasat Preah Vihear), Sena Soun and Yearn Gueorn (Anlong Veng), Racky Thy (Battambang), Mech Nguy (Phnom Sampeau), Somphos Choun and Borey Som (Pailin) and Kimroth (Kompong Chhnang).

In the first edition of this book I wished the best to my dauntless guide, Tan Sotho, and her daughter Kulikar, then a quiet and studious high-school student. I'm happy to report that Sotho now runs a successful tourism company and Kulikar is married to my co-author, Nick Ray, whom I must thank for his willingness to go the extra mile.

Finally, I'd like to thank Rachel Safman for her support during the long months I spent in the field and glued to my computer.

OUR READERS

Many thanks to the travellers who used the last edition and wrote to us with helpful hints, useful advice and interesting anecdotes:

A Marcus Adams, Sharyn Alexander, Susan Armstrong, Claudie Audet, Jessica Avishai, **B** Mark Bailey, Louise Barker, Sam Barton, Simon Bate, William Beavitt, Michael Benenson, Ambrose Benkert,

Irene Bernhard, Ana Blanchard, Annette Bloesch, Kim Bodycombe, Kate Bohdanowicz, Clare Bolzon, Julie Booth, Arien Bosch, Kees Botschuijver, David Boyall, Titus Brand, Steve Branson, Grainne Brick, Morten Broberg, Calum Brockway, Michael Broomfield, Dave Brown, Angela Brunner, Susanne Bulten, Nellie Butler, **C** Melanie Cairns, David Cameron, Jan Camp, Vicky Cannaerts, Yolanda Benavente Carla, Michael Carson, Lindsey Cartlidge, Enrico Cazzaniga, John & Judy Charles, Cassie Childers, John Choi, Kendra Clerk, Helen Coney, Jocelyn Corniche, Shane Cowlishaw, Yvette Crafti, Carmen Cruz, **D** Stephanie Danzinger, Cherie Darnel, Harold De Haan, Andrea Dekkers, David De Rango, Jessica Derynck, Christophe Desmet, Veronique Dijkzeul, Ange Dries-Behrenbeck, Jean-Marc Dugauquier, Lliam Dunn, **E** J E Effron, Craig Eldred, John Elliott, Brad Ensminger, Stephan Erhardt, Matt & Eileen Erskine, Rv Ertyert, Manuela Essig, **F** Gawein Faes, Alan Fairclough, Gregory Fauria, Neil Ferguson, Mary Fitzhugh, James Fitzsimons, P R Fletcher, Kemmy Foo, Bryan Forbes, Gaute Skjelbred Furu, **G** Sheila Gemmell, Janelle Gibson, Susan Goodwin, Dinis Gökaydin, Dirk De Graaff, Kate Graham, James Gremo, John Grey, Kim Grimsrud, Henning Gross, **H** Anne Haden, Judith Ham, Maxie Hambrock, Sophie Hammond, Paul Hansen, Jan Harfst, Ian Harry, Fumiko Hattori, Bethan Hawkins, Seila Hierk, Britta Hillen, Agatha Hoff, Frances Hogen, Gabriella Hök, Kevin Hoschke, Beth Humphreys, Christl Hurlbut, **I** John Ireland, **J** Emily Jacobs, James James, Lian Jaspers, Rich Jenkins, John Jenks, Mohini Johnson, **K** Gerard Kamberg, Pauline Kastenberg, Margriet Katoen, Jason Keel, Joan Kenedy, Chris Kerin, Françoise Kinsella, Ilona Klein, Silvia Knaus, Robin Knowles, Michael Koelstra, Charles Kubler, Haus Kumpel,

Skyrach Kunaprathom, Thomas Kunkel, **L** Shirley Lambert, Dick Lambregts, Leng Lau, Elsbeth Lauener, David Lee, Lawrence Leong, Cheng Yeow Lim, Mandy Linsley, Malte Lippa, Andrew Long, Xingkai Loy, **M** Hilary Mackay, Maggie Mackay, Ian Mackenzie, Jane Macleod, Deon Mahoney, Erika Malitzky, Steve Matthews, Talia Mazor, Trevor Mazzucchelli, Liza Mccarthy, Ryan Mcclenaghan, Lara Mckimmie, Anthony Mcmills, Perry Mehta, Tushar Mehta, Ingun Melleberg, Carl Meyer, Jayde Mihan, Robin Mitchell, Dean Moriarty, Owen Morley, Simon Morley, Fabio Morotti, Holger Müller, Jennifer Mundy, **N** Ann Naef, Sally Nash, Augustus Nasmith Jr, Lian-Hun Ng, Anthony Nicolopoulos, Jade Noble, **O** Jade O'Brien, Graham O'Halloran, Petra O'Neill, Sean Owens, **P** Manuela Pacheco, Dior Pack, Ditte Papousek, Alison Parr, Marty Paton, Kit Peel, Jo Pennock, Joannah Petrie, Jon Pike, Alan Piper, Marianne Plourde, Mick Potter, Janet Preston, Jeffrey Prince, **R** Lauren Rachal, David Ragg, John Reinsborough, Torben Retboll, Jurrian Reurings, Gerhard & Ruth Rieder, Stefanie Röhner, Jason Rosette, Tamika Ross, Michael Royle, Rob Rushworth, Laura Russell, Noelle Ryan, **S** Leah Salomon, Simone Samuels, Aafke Sanders, Keith Sanger, Maarten Schamp, Anna-Barbara Schmidt, Simone Schneider, Christopher & Linda Scott, Guadalupe Segura, Monique Seng, Niamh Sherwin, Chris Simon, Tom De Smet, Kathryn Smith, Alisandra Snyder, Daniel Spence, Nile Sprague, Gerhard Steindl, Frank Stienhans, Ilse Straver, Bianca Symes, **T** Graham Taylor, Margaret Taylor, Jack Theuws, Margaret Thomson, Natashia Ting, Joan Tornquist, Rosemary & Neil Treyvaud, Ted Trondsen, Amy Tsui, Simon Tu, **V** Cor & Jenny Valk, Jaap Valkema, Lieven van der Borght, Wouter van Gool, Jup 'T van Veld, Caris Vanghetti, Elise Vanhoest, Peter Vennemann, Anna Verkade, Guillaume Vrignault, **W** Jeremy Wadsack, Dennis Wall, Derek Wee, Stefan Wicki, Stephane Wicky, Jo Williams, Alisa Wong, Fiona Wong, Colin Woodley, Tony Writer, Purenza Wu, **Y** Yoram Yom-Tov, Georgina Young, **Z** Rebecca Zanatta, Ombretta Zanetti, Lapurra Zara, Ignacy Zulawski.

ACKNOWLEDGMENTS

Many thanks to the following for the use of their content:

Globe on title page ©Mountain High Maps 1993 Digital Wisdom, Inc.

Internal photographs p202 (#2) p203 (#4) Suthep Kritsanavarin/OnAsia; p206 (#1), p207 (#3) Jerry Redfern/OnAsia. All other photographs by Lonely Planet Images, Daniel Boag p205 (#4); Andrew Burke p207 (#4); Frank Carter p202 (#1); Tom Cockrem p204 (#1) p205 (#3); Mick Elmore p201; Antony Giblin p206 (#2) p207 (#5); David Greedy p204 (#2).

All images are the copyright of the photographers unless otherwise indicated. Many of the images in this guide are available for licensing from Lonely Planet Images: www.lonelyplanetimages.com.

BEHIND THE SCENES

Index

INDEX

GreenDex

GOING GREEN

It's not only ecotourism that is starting to take off in Cambodia, but also community-based tourism in remote areas and a whole host of restaurants and shops dedicated to helping the disadvantaged or disabled. The following attractions, tours and accommodation choices have all been selected by Lonely Planet authors because they demonstrate an active sustainable-tourism policy. Some are involved in conservation or environmental protection, others in training and development for the disadvantaged, and some to raise funds to support social projects in healthcare or education.

We want to keep developing our sustainable-tourism content. If you think we've omitted someone who should be listed here, or if you disagree with our choices, email us at talk2us@lonelyplanet. com.au and set us straight for next time. For more information about sustainable tourism and Lonely Planet, see www.lonelyplanet.com/responsibletravel.